Lecture Notes in Computer Science

Ian Gorton George T. Heineman
Ivica Crnkovic Heinz W. Schmidt
Judith A. Stafford Clemens A. Szyperski
Kurt Wallnau (Eds.)

Component-Based Software Engineering

9th International Symposium, CBSE 2006
Västerås, Sweden, June 29 – July 1, 2006
Proceedings

Volume Editors

Ian Gorton
National ICT Australia, Eveleigh, NSW 1430, Australia
E-mail: ian.gorton@nicta.com.au

George T. Heineman
WPI, Worcester, MA 01609, USA
E-mail: heineman@cs.wpi.edu

Ivica Crnkovic
Mälardalen University, 721 23 Västerås, Sweden
E-mail: ivica.crnkovic@mdh.se

Heinz W. Schmidt
Monash University, Clayton VIC 3800 , Australia
E-mail: heinz.schmidt@csse.monash.edu.au

Judith A. Stafford
Tufts University, Medford, MA 02155, USA
E-mail: jas@cs.tufts.edu

Clemens A. Szyperski
Microsoft Corp., Redmond, WA 98053, USA
E-mail: cszypers@microsoft.com

Kurt Wallnau
Carnegie Mellon University, Pittsburgh, PA 15213-3890, USA
E-mail: kcw@sei.cmu.edu

Library of Congress Control Number: 2006927704

CR Subject Classification (1998): D.2, D.1.5, D.3, F.3.1

LNCS Sublibrary: SL 2 – Programming and Software Engineering

ISSN 0302-9743
ISBN-10 3-540-35628-2 Springer Berlin Heidelberg New York
ISBN-13 978-3-540-35628-8 Springer Berlin Heidelberg New York

Springer is a part of Springer Science+Business Media

springer.com

Printed in Germany

Typesetting: Camera-ready by author, data conversion by Scientific Publishing Services, Chennai, India
Printed on acid-free paper SPIN: 11783565 06/3142 5 4 3 2 1 0

Preface

On behalf of the Organizing Committee I am pleased to present the proceedings of the 2006 Symposium on Component-Based Software Engineering (CBSE). CBSE is concerned with the development of software-intensive systems from reusable parts (components), the development of reusable parts, and system maintenance and improvement by means of component replacement and customization. CBSE 2006 was the ninth in a series of events that promote a science and technology foundation for achieving predictable quality in software systems through the use of software component technology and its associated software engineering practices.

We were fortunate to have a dedicated Program Committee comprising 27 internationally recognized researchers and industrial practitioners. We received 77 submissions and each paper was reviewed by at least three Program Committee members (four for papers with an author on the Program Committee). The entire reviewing process was supported by Microsoft's CMT technology. In total, 22 submissions were accepted as full papers and 9 submissions were accepted as short papers.

This was the first time CBSE was not held as a co-located event at ICSE. Hence special thanks are due to Ivica Crnkovic for hosting the event. We also wish to thank the ACM Special Interest Group on Software Engineering (SIGSOFT) for their sponsorship of CBSE 2005. The proceedings you now hold were published by Springer and we are grateful for their support. Finally, we must thank the many authors who contributed the high-quality papers contained within these proceedings. As the international community of CBSE researchers and practitioners continues to prosper, we expect the CBSE Symposium series to similarly attract widespread interest and participation.

May 2006 Ian Gorton

Organization

CBSE 2006 was sponsored by the Association for Computing Machinery (ACM) Special Interest Group in Software (SIGSOFT).

Organizing Committee

Program Chair: Ian Gorton (NICTA, Australia)
Steering Committee: Ivica Crnkovic
(Mälardalen University, Sweden)
George T. Heineman
(WPI, USA)
Heinz W. Schmidt
(Monash University, Australia)
Judith A. Stafford (Tufts University, USA)
Clemens Szyperski (Microsoft Research, USA)
Kurt Wallnau
(Software Engineering Institute, USA)

Program Committee

Uwe Assmann, Dresden University of Technology, Germany
Mike Barnett, Microsoft Research, USA
Judith Bishop, University of Pretoria, South Africa
Jan Bosch, Nokia Research Center, Finland
Michel Chaudron, University of Eindhoven, The Netherlands
Shiping Chen, CSIRO, Australia
Susan Eisenbach, Imperial College, UK
Dimitra Giannakopoulou, RIACS/NASA Ames, USA
Lars Grunske, University of Queensland, Australia
Richard Hall, LSR-IMAG, France
Dick Hamlet, Portland State University, USA
George Heineman, Worcester Polytechnic Institute, USA
Tom Henzinger, EPFL, Switzerland and UC Berkeley, USA
Paola Inverardi, University of L'Aquila, Italy
Jean-Marc Jezequel, IRISA (INRIA & Univ. Rennes 1), France
Bengt Jonsson, Uppsala University, Sweden
Dean Kuo, University of Manchester, UK
Magnus Larsson, ABB, Sweden
Kung-Kiu Lau, University of Manchester, UK
Nenad Medvidovic, University of Southern California, USA
Rob van Ommering, Philips, The Netherlands
Otto Preiss, ABB Switzerland

Ralf Reussner, University of Oldenburg, Germany
Douglas Schmidt, Vanderbilt University, USA
Jean-Guy Schneider, Swinburne University of Tech., Australia
Dave Wile, Teknowledge, Corp., USA
Wolfgang Weck, Independent Software Architect, Switzerland

Previous CBSE Workshops and Symposia

8th International Symposium on CBSE, Lecture Notes in Computer Science, Vol. 3489, Heineman, G.T. et al (Eds.), Springer, St. Loius, USA (2005)

7th International Symposium on CBSE, Lecture Notes in Computer Science, Vol. 3054, Crnkovic, I.; Stafford, J.A.; Schmidt, H.W.; Wallnau, K. (Eds.), Springer, Edinburgh, UK (2004)

6th ICSE Workshop on CBSE: Automated Reasoning and Prediction
http://www.sei.cmu.edu/pacc/CBSE6. Portland, Oregon (2003)

5th ICSE Workshop on CBSE: Benchmarks for Predictable Assembly
http://www.sei.cmu.edu/pacc/CBSE5. Orlando, Florida (2002)

4th ICSE Workshop on CBSE: Component Certification and System Prediction. Software Engineering Notes, 26(10), November 2001. ACM SIGSOFT Author(s): Crnkovic, I.; Schmidt, H.; Stafford, J.; Wallnau, K. (Eds.)
http://www.sei.cmu.edu/pacc/CBSE4-Proceedings.html. Toronto, Canada, (2001)

Third ICSE Workshop on CBSE: Reflection in Practice
http://www.sei.cmu.edu/pacc/cbse2000. Limerick, Ireland (2000)

Second ICSE Workshop on CBSE: Developing a Handbook for CBSE
http://www.sei.cmu.edu/cbs/icse99. Los Angeles, California (1999)

First Workshop on CBSE
http://www.sei.cmu.edu/pacc/icse98. Tokyo, Japan (1998)

Table of Contents

Full Papers

Short Papers

Short Papers

Defining and Checking Deployment Contracts for Software Components

Kung-Kiu Lau and Vladyslav Ukis

School of Computer Science, The University of Manchester
Manchester M13 9PL, United Kingdom
{kung-kiu, vukis}@cs.man.ac.uk

Abstract. Ideally in the deployment phase, components should be composable, and their composition checked. Current component models fall short of this ideal. Most models do not allow composition in the deployment phase. Moreover, current models use only deployment descriptors as deployment contracts. These descriptors are not ideal contracts. For one thing, they are only for specific containers, rather than arbitrary execution environments. In any case, they are checked only at runtime, not deployment time. In this paper we present an approach to component deployment which not only defines better deployment contracts but also checks them in the deployment phase.

1 Introduction

Component deployment is the process of getting components ready for execution in a target system. Components are therefore in binary form at this stage. Ideally these binaries should be composable, so that an arbitrary assembly can be built to implement the target system. Furthermore, the composition of the assembly should be checked so that any conflicts between the components, and any conflicts between them and the intended execution environment for the system, can be detected and repaired before runtime. This ideal is of course the aim of CBSE, that is to assemble third-party binaries into executable systems. To realise this ideal, component models should provide composition operators at deployment time, as well as a means for defining suitable deployment contracts and checking them.

Current component models fall short of this ideal. Most models only allow composition of components in source code. Only two component models, JavaBeans [7] and the .NET component model [6, 20], support composition of binaries. Moreover, current models use only deployment descriptors as deployment contracts [1]. These descriptors are not ideal contracts. They do not express contracts for component composition. They are contracts for specific containers, rather than arbitrary execution environments. In any case, they are checked only at runtime, not deployment time.

Checking deployment contracts at deployment time is advantageous because they establish component composability, and thus avoid runtime conflicts. Moreover, they also allow the assembly to be changed if necessary before runtime. Furthermore, conflicts due to incompatibilities between components and the target execution environment of the system into which they are deployed can be discovered before runtime.

In this paper we present an approach to component deployment which not only defines better contracts but also checks them in the deployment phase. It is based on a

I. Gorton et al. (Eds.): CBSE 2006, LNCS 4063, pp. 1–16, 2006.

pool of metadata we have developed, which components can draw on to specify their runtime dependencies and behaviour.

2 Component Deployment

We begin by defining what we mean by component deployment. First, we define a 'software component' along the lines of Szyperski [24] and Heinemann and Councill [10], viz. 'a software entity with contractual interfaces and contextual dependencies, defined in a component model'.[1]

Our definition of component deployment is set in the context of the component lifecycle. This cycle consists of three phases: *design*, *deployment* and *runtime* (Fig. 1).

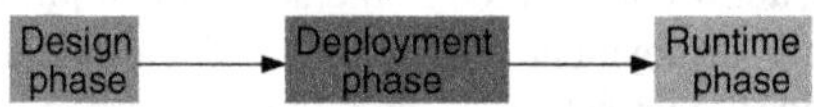

Fig. 1. Software component lifecycle

In the design phase, a component is designed and implemented in source code, by a *component developer*. For example, to develop an Enterprise JavaBean (EJB) [18] component in the design phase, the source code of the bean is created in Java, possibly using an IDE like Eclipse. A component in this phase is not intended to run in any particular system. Rather, it is meant to be reusable for many systems.

In the deployment phase, a component is a binary, ready to be deployed into an application by a *system developer*. For example, in the deployment phase, an EJB is a binary ".class" file compiled from a Java class defined for the bean in the design phase.

For deployment, a component needs to have a deployment contract which specifies how the component will interact with other components and with the target execution environment. For example, in EJB, on deployment, a deployment descriptor describing the bean has to be created and archived with the ".class" file, producing a ".jar" file, which has to be submitted to an EJB container.

An important characteristic of the deployment phase is that the system developer who deploys a component may not be the same person as the component developer.

In the runtime phase, a component instance is created from the binary component and the instantiated component runs in a system. Some component models use containers for component instantiation, e.g. EJB and CCM [19]. For example, an EJB in binary form as a ".class" file archived in a ".jar" file in the deployment phase gets instantiated and is managed by an EJB container in the runtime phase.

2.1 Current Component Models

Of the major current software component models, only two, viz. JavaBeans and the .NET component model, allow composition in the deployment phase. To show this, we first relate our definition of the phases of the component lifecycle (Fig. 1) to current component models.

[1] Note that we deal with components obeying a component model and not with COTS [2].

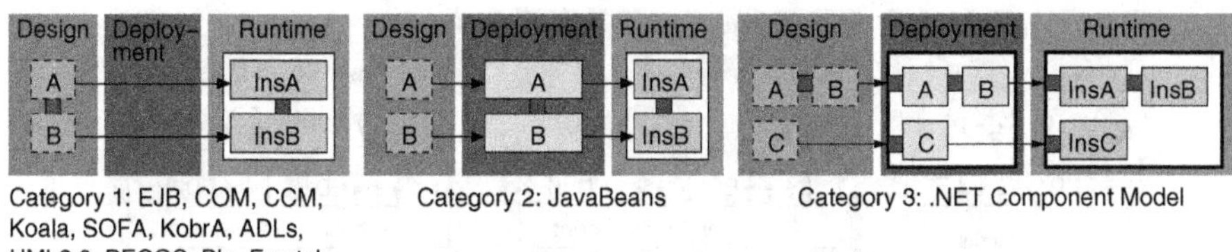

Fig. 2. Current component models

Current component models can be classified according to the phases in which component composition is possible. We can identify three categories [16] as shown in Fig. 2.

In the first category, composition (denoted by the small linking box) happens only at design time. The majority of current models, viz. EJB, COM [3], CCM,ADLs (architecture description languages) [22],[2] etc. fall into this category. For instance, in EJB, the composition is done by direct method calls between beans at design time. An assembly done at design time cannot be changed at deployment time, and gets instantiated at runtime into executable instances (denoted by InsA, InsB.)

In the second category, composition happens only at deployment time. There is only one model in this category, viz. JavaBeans. In JavaBeans, Java classes for beans are designed independently at design time. At deployment time, binary components (".class" files) are assembled by the BeanBox, which also serves as the runtime environment for the assembly. Java beans communicate by exchanging events. The assembly is done at deployment time by the BeanBox, by generating and compiling an event adapter class.

In the third category, composition can happen at both design and deployment time. The sole member of this category is the .NET component model. In this model, components can be composed as in Category 1 at design time, i.e. by direct method calls. In addition, at deployment time, components can also be composed as in Category 2. This is done by using a container class, shown as a rectanglular box with a bold border. The container class hosts the binary components (".dll" files) and can make direct method calls into them.

Finally, current component models target either the desktop or the web environment, except for the .NET component model, which is unified for both environments. Having a component model that allows components to be deployed into both desktop and web environments enhances the applicability of the component model.

2.2 Composition in the Deployment Phase

Composition in the deployment phase can potentially lead to faster system development than design time composition, since binary components are bought from component suppliers and composed using (ideally pre-existing) composition operators, which can even be done without source code development. However, composition at component deployment time poses new challenges not addressed by current component models. These stem mainly from the fact that in the design phase, component developers design

[2] In C2 [17] new components can be added to an assembly at deployment time since C2 components can broadcast events; but new events can only be defined at design time.

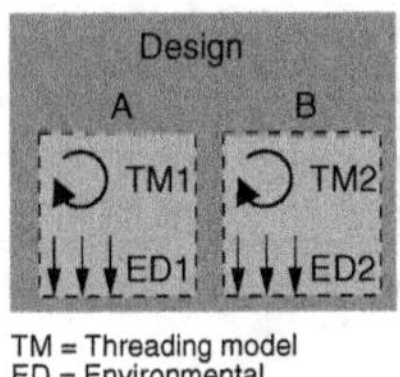

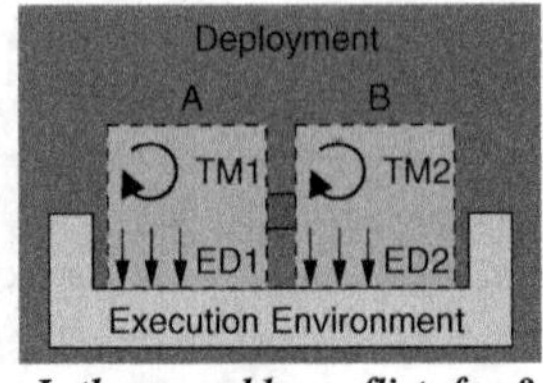

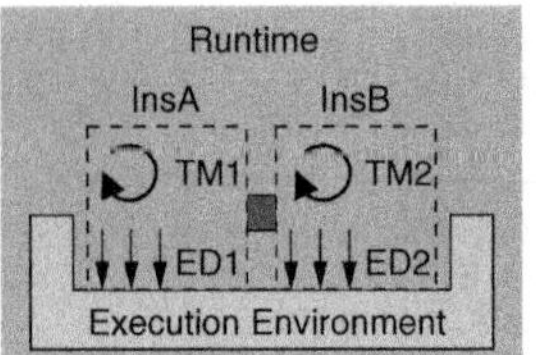

Fig. 3. Composition in deployment phase

and build components (in source code) independently. In particular, for a component, they may (i) choose any *threading model*; and (ii) define *dependencies on the execution environment*. This is illustrated by Fig. 3.

A component may create a thread inside it, use some thread synchronisation mechanisms to protect some data from concurrent access, or not use any synchronisation mechanisms on the assumption that it will not be deployed into an environment with concurrency.

Also each component supplier may use some mechanisms inside a component that require some resources from the system execution environment, thus defining the component's environmental dependencies. For instance, if a component uses socket communication, then it requires a network from the execution environment. If a component uses a file, then it requires file system access. Note that component suppliers do not know what execution environments their components will be deployed into.

In the deployment phase, the system developer knows the system he is going to build and the properties of the execution environment for the system. However, he needs to know whether any assembly he builds will be conflict-free (Fig. 3), i.e. whether (i) the threading models in the components are compatible; (ii) their environmental dependencies are compatible; (iii) their threading models and environmental dependencies are compatible with the execution environment; and (iv) their emergent assembly-specific properties are compatible with the properties of the execution environment if components are to be composed using a composition operator. The system developer needs to know all this before the runtime phase. If problems are discovered at runtime, the system developer will not be able to change the system. By contrast, if incompatibilities are found at deployment time, the assembly can still be changed by exchanging components.

By the execution environment we mean either the *desktop* or the *web* environment, and not a container (if any) for components. These two environments are the most widespread, and differ in the management of *system transient state* and *concurrency*. Since the component developer does not know whether the components will be deployed on a desktop or a web server, the system developer has to check whether the components and their assembly are suitable to run in the target execution environment.

2.3 Deployment Contracts

Deployment contracts express dependencies between components, and between them and the execution environment. As shown in [1], in most current component models a deployment contract is simply the interface of a component. In EJB and CCM,

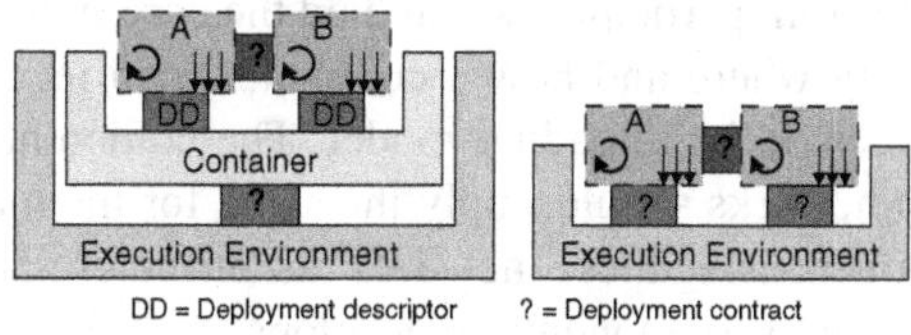

Fig. 4. Deployment contracts

deployment contracts are deployment and component descriptors respectively. As shown in Fig. 4, a deployment (or component) descriptor contractualises the management of a component by a container. However, the information about components inside the descriptors is not used to check whether components are compatible. Nor is it used to check whether a component can be deployed in an execution environment.

By contrast, our approach aims to check conflicts between components; and, in the presence of a component container, between the container and the execution environment; in the absence of a container, between components and the execution environment. This is illustrated by Fig. 4, where the question marks denote our deployment contracts, in the presence or absence of containers.

We can also check our deployment contracts, so our approach addresses the challenge of deployment time composition better than existing component models that allow deployment time composition, viz. the. NET component model and JavaBeans. In the .NET component model, *no* checking for component compatibilities is done during deployment. In JavaBeans, the BeanBox into which beans are deployed, is deployed on the desktop environment, and it checks whether beans can be composed together by checking whether events emitted by a source bean can be consumed by the target bean, by matching event source with event sink. However, this check is not adequate with regard to threading models and environment dependencies, as shown by the following example.

Example 1. Consider a Java bean that creates a thread inside itself to perform some long-running task in the background and sends an event to another bean from within that thread. The target bean may have problems. For example, if the target bean makes use of a COM component that requires a single-threaded apartment, and the bean is invoked from different threads, the component assembly is bound to fail.

This shows that the threading model of the source bean, namely sending an event from an internally created thread, and the environmental dependency of the target bean, namely the use of the COM component requiring a single-threaded apartment, are incompatible. The assembly will fail at runtime even though the BeanBox's check for component (event) compatibility is passed.

3 Defining Deployment Contracts

In this section we discuss how we define suitable deployment contracts. Our approach is based on metadata about component environmental dependencies and threading models. To determine and create suitable metadata, we studied the two most comprehensive, operating system-independent frameworks [9] for component development: J2EE [23] and .NET Framework [25]. In particular, we studied the core APIs of these two frameworks in order to identify where and how a component can incur environmental dependencies and influences on its threading model. The comprehensiveness and wide application of these frameworks should imply the same for the metada we create. We define deployment contracts using these metadata[3] as attributes that the component developer is obliged to attach to components he develops.

3.1 Environmental Dependencies

A component incurs an environmental dependency whenever it makes use of a resource offered by the operating system or the framework using which it is implemented. For each resource found this way we created an attribute expressing the semantics of the environmental dependency found. Each attribute has defined parameters and is therefore parameterisable. Moreover, each attribute has defined *attribute targets* from the set {component, method, method's parameter, method's return value, property}. An *attribute target* defines the element of a component it can be applied to.

To enable a developer to express resource usage as precisely as possible, we allow each attribute to have (a subset of) the following parameters: 1) 'UsageMode': {Create, Read, Write, Delete} to indicate the usage of the resource. Arbitrary combinations of values in this set are allowed. However, here we assume that inside a component, creation, if specified, is always done first. Also, deletion, if specified, is always done last; 2) 'Existence': {Checked, Unchecked} to indicate whether the component checks for existence of a resource or makes use of it assuming it is there; 3) 'Location': {Local, Remote} to indicate whether a resource required by component is local on the machine the component is deployed to or is remote; 4) 'UsageNecessity': {Mandatory, Optional} to indicate whether a component will fail to execute or will be able to fulfil its task if the required resource is not available.

Meaningful combinations of the values of these parameters allow an attribute to appear in different forms (120 for an attribute with all 4 parameters) which have to be analysed differently.

In addition to these four parameters, any attribute may have other parameters specific to a particular environmental dependency. For instance, consider an attribute on a component's method expressing an environmental dependency to a COM component shown in Fig. 5. (Such a component was used in Example 1.) The component has a method "Method2" that has the attribute "UsedCOMComponent" attached. The attribute has (1) shows the COM GUID used by the component; (2) says that three parameters:

```
public class B
{
  [UsedCOMComponent("DC577003-3436-470c-8161-EA9204B11EBF",     (1)
  COMAppartmentModel.Singlethreaded,                              (2)
  UsageNecessity.Mandatory)]                                      (3)
  public void Method2(...) {...}
}
```

Fig. 5. A component with an environmental dependency

[3] A full list and details can be found in [14].

Table 1. Categories of resource usage and component developer's obligations

1	*Usage of an operating-system resource.* For instance: Files, Directories, Input/Ouput Devices like Printers, Event Logs, Performance Counters, Processes, Residential Services, Communication Ports and Sockets.
2	*Usage of a resource offered by a framework.* For instance: Application and Session State storages offered by J2EE and .NET for web development, Communication Channels to communicate with remote objects.
3	*Usage of a local resource.* For instance: Databases, Message Queues and Directory Services.
4	*Usage of a remote resource.* For instance: Web Services or Web Servers, Remote Hosts, and resources from Category 3 installed remotely.
5	*Usage of a framework.* For instance: DirectX or OpenGL.
6	*Usage of a component from a component model.* For instance: a Java Bean using a COM component via EZ JCOM [8] framework.

the used COM component requires a single-threaded environment; (3) says that the usage of the COM component is mandatory. Furthermore, implicitly the attribute says that the component requires access to a file system as well as Windows Registry since COM components have to be registered there with GUID.

We have analysed the pool of attributes we have created, and as a result we can define categories of resource usage for which the component developer is obliged to attach the relevant attributes to their component's elements. The categories are shown in Table 1:

Using binary components with relevant attributes from the categories in Table 1, it is possible at deployment time to detect potential conflicts based on contentious use of resources from Table 1.

Finally, metadata about environmental dependencies can be used to check for mutual compatibility of components in an assembly. For instance, if a component from an assembly requires continuous access to a file in the file system in the write mode but another component in the assembly also writes to the same file but creates it afresh without checking whether it has existed before, the first component may lose its data and the component assembly may fail to execute.

3.2 Threading Models

A component can create a thread, register a callback, invoke a callback on a thread [4, 5], create an asynchronous method [11], make use of thread-specific storage [21] or access a resource requiring thread-affine access,[4] etc. For each of these cases, we created an attribute of the kind described in Section 3.1 expressing the semantics of the case.

For instance, consider an attribute expressing the creation of a thread by a component shown in Fig. 6. (Such a component was used in Example 1.) The component has a method "Method1" that has the attribute "SpawnThread" attached. The parameter (1) indicates the number of threads spawned. If this method is composed with another component's method requiring thread affinity, the composition is going to fail.

[4] Thread-affine access to a resource means that the resource is only allowed to be accessed from one and the same thread.

```
public class A
{
 [SpawnThread(1)]                  (1)
 public void Method1(...) {...}
}
```

Fig. 6. A component with a defined threading model

Table 2. Categories of threading issues and component developer's obligations

1	*Existence of an asynchronous method.*
2	*Registration or/and invocation of a callback method.*
3	*Existence of reentrant or/and thread-safe methods.*
4	*Existence of component elements requiring thread-affine access.*
5	*Existence of Singletons or static variables.*
6	*Spawning a thread.*
7	*Usage of Thread-specific storage.*
8	*Taking as a method parameter of returning a synchronisation primitive.*

We have analysed the pool of attributes we have created, and as a result we can define categories of threading issues for which the component developer is obliged to attach the relevant attributes to their components. These categories are shown in Table 2:

Using binary components with attributes from the categories shown in Table 2, it is possible at component deployment time to detect potential conflicts based on inappropriate usage of threads and synchronisation primitives by components in an assembly. It is also possible to point out potential deadlocks in a component assembly.

In total, for both environmental dependencies and threading models, we have created a pool of about 100 metadata attributes[5]. Now we show an example of their use.

Example 2. Consider Example 1 again.The two incompatible Java beans are shown in Fig. 7 with metadata attributes from Sections 3.1 and 3.2. Using these attributes we can detect the incompatibility of the beans at deployment time.[6]

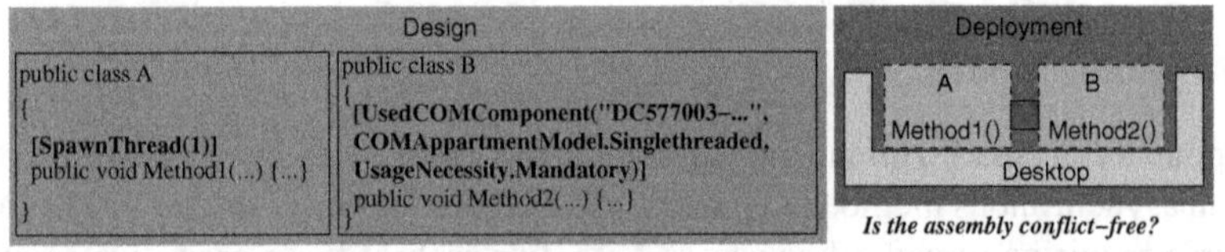

Fig. 7. Example 1 using metadata attributes

In the design phase, The two beans are the ones in Figs. 5 and 6. In the deployment phase, by performing an analysis of the metadata attributes attached to the components, we can deduce that method "A.Method1()" invokes the method "B.Method2()"

[5] In .NET Framework v2.0 there are about 200 attributes, but they are only checked at runtime.

[6] Note that this problem may also arise in other component models.

on an internally created thread. Therefore, if method "A.Method1()" is invoked several times, each time a new thread is created that makes an invocation of the method "B.Method2()". Therefore, the COM component used by method "B.Method2()" is not going to be called from one thread and its requirement for a single threaded apartment cannot be fulfiled in such composition of components A and B. Therefore, the system developer can be warned not to do such composition.

Besides this, using a COM component requires use of a file system, where the component resides, and Windows Registry, where it must be registered. The system developer can also be warned if these resources are unavailable in the system execution environment.

Moreover, in Fig. 7 the components are deployed into the desktop environment. In this environment, there is a guarantee that the main thread of the system is always the same for the lifetime of a system instance. Therefore, the system developer need not be warned that the execution environment may cause problems. Note that in the web environment there is no guarantee for the thread affinity of the main thread. If the assembly in Fig. 7 was deployed into the web environment, it would also fail since the COM component used by the component B would be accessed by different threads imposed by the web environment.

3.3 Implementing Retrievable Metadata

The attributes we have created must be retrievable at deployment time, i.e. they must be retrievable from binaries. In this section, we explain how we implement them.

Our implementation draws on .NET's facility for defining custom attributes[7]. A custom attribute in .NET is a class derived from the .NET's class System.Attribute. An example of an attribute from the attribute pool we have defined is shown below:

```
[AttributeUsage(AttributeTargets.Class|AttributeTargets.Method|
                AttributeTargets.Property, AllowMultiple=true)]
public class UsedWebService : System.Attribute {
  public UsedWebService(string url, string userName,
   string pwd, UsageNecessity usageNecessity) {...} ... }
```

The attribute above is called 'UsedWebService'. It has a constructor, which takes as parameters the url to the web service, credentials used when accessing the web service as well as whether the web service usage is mandatory for the component.

Furthermore, above the attribute declaration 'public class UsedWebService : System.Attribute', the usage of the attribute is specified by a .NET built-in attribute 'AttributeUsage' that indicates which elements of components the attribute is allowed to be applied to, as well as whether multiple attributes can be applied to the same element. Here the attribute 'UsedWebService' can be applied to either a whole class (we model components as classes) or a component's method or property. Here 'AllowMultiple=true' means that the attribute 'UsedWebService' can be applied multiple times to the same component element. That is, if a component makes use of several web services, several 'UsedWebService' attributes can be applied to indicate the component's environmental dependencies.

[7] In Java, Annotations can be used to express the metadata. However, they are somewhat less flexible than .NET Attributes.

To retrieve attributes from a binary component, we use .NET's Reflection facility from System.Reflection namespace. For instance, to retrieve attributes at component level, the following code is executed:

```
Type compType = Type.GetType(componentName);                    (i)
object[] attributes = compType.GetCustomAttributes(false);(ii)
```

(i) loads the component type from the binary component using component name in a special format, and (ii) retrieves all the attributes attached to the component. Note that no component instantiation has been done.

To retrieve attributes on component's properties, the following code is executed:

```
Type compType = Type.GetType(componentName);                    (i)
foreach(PropertyInfo prop in compType.GetProperties())         (ii)
{object[] attributes = prop.GetCustomAttributes(false);} (iii)
```

(i) loads the component type from the binary component, (ii) iterates through all the properties inside the component, and (iii) retrieves all the attributes attached to the current property.

Attributes attached to component's methods, method's parameters and return values can be retrieved in a similar but more complicated manner.

Being able to retrieve the attributes at deployment time enables us to check deployment contracts before component instantiation at run time.

4 Checking Deployment Contracts

Given an assembly of components with deployment contracts and a chosen execution environment in the deployment phase, as illustrated by Fig. 4, we can use the deployment contracts to determine whether the assembly is conflict-free. In this section we explain how we do so.[8]

The checking process first loads the binary components, and then for each binary retrieves the attributes at all levels (component, property, method, and method input and return parameters). The checking task is then divided into 2 sub-tasks: (i) Analysis of mutual compatibility of deployment contracts of components in the assembly with respect to usage of resources in the assembly's execution environment; (ii) Analysis of mutual compatibility of deployment contracts of components in the assembly with respect to their threading models in consideration of state and concurrency management of assembly's execution environment. Both sub-tasks consist of checking the deployment contracts involved. The results of the checking range over {ERROR, WARNING, HINT} with the obvious meaning.

For (i), we perform the following: For each attribute at any level we determine resource(s) required in the execution environment. If a resource is not available in the execution environment, an ERROR is issued.

Furthermore, we follow component connections in the assembly and consider how resources are used by the individual components by evaluating attached attributes'

[8] We present only an outline here.

parameters. Once an attribute representing a resource usage is found on a component, we follow the chain of components till another component with an attribute representing the usage of the same resource is found either at method or property or component level. Once such a component is found, we check the "UsageMode" parameters of the attributes on the two components for compatibility and issue ERROR, WARNING or HINT depending on the parameters' values. After that, we again follow the chain of components till the next component with an attribute representing the usage of the same resource is found and check the values of the parameter "UsageMode" on corresponding attributes of the component and the previous one in the chain. This process is repeated till all attributes representing resource usage on all components are processed.

Moreover, specific parameters of each attribute are analysed and WARNINGs and HINTs are issued if necessary. For instance, if attributes' parameters indicate that components in a component assembly use a database and not all components uniformly use either encrypted or unencrypted database connection, a WARNING is issued.

Another example is usage of cryptography files. If a cryptography file is used, it is hinted which cryptography algorithm has been used to create the certificate. This information is useful to the system developer due to the fact the different cryptography algorithms have different degrees of security and different processing times when checked. Depending on system requirements a specific cryptography algorithm may or may not be suitable.

A further example is represented by communication channels. If a communication channel is used, it is hinted which communication protocol for data transfer and which serialisation method for data serialisation is used. This information is used by the system developer, who knows system requirements, to judge whether the component is suitable for their system.

For (ii), we perform the following: We follow component connections in the assembly to determine for each component if it is stateful or stateless, and multithreaded or singlethreaded. This can be done by evaluating corresponding attributes on a component. After that we determine if the assembly is stateful or stateless, and multithreaded and singlethreaded depending on the components in the assembly. If at least one component in the assembly is stateful, the assembly is stateful. Otherwise, it is stateless. If at least one component in the assembly is multithreaded, the assembly is multithreaded. Otherwise, it is singlethreaded.

Following this, we check whether state management of the assembly's execution environment is suitable for the assembly. Furthermore, we check whether concurrency management of the assembly's execution environment is suitable for the assembly. We issue ERRORs, WARNINGs or HINTs depending on the level of incompatibility.

Apart from that, if a component can repeatedly issue a callback to another one on an internally created thread, and the callback method either requires thread-affine access; or accesses component's transient state in not read-only mode, or accesses a singleton or a static variable, and no component element enclosing it is marked as reentrant or thread-safe, an ERROR is issued pointing out a likely state corruption problem.

Moreover, if synchronisation primitives are exchanged between components, a WARNING is issued pointing out a possible cause for a deadlock.

5 Example

To illustrate the usefulness of deployment contracts we show how they can be applied to a design pattern described in [4, 5]. The design pattern is for systems including one component that loads data in the background and another one that displays the data. Furthermore, while the data is being loaded in the background, the loading component notifies the one displaying the data about the chunks of data already loaded. The component displaying data can either display the chunks of data already loaded, thus implementing so-called streaming, or just display a visualisation of it, e.g. a progress bar, which advances each time the loading component sends a notification that a chunk of data has been loaded.

Fig. 8 shows two such components. Component A has two methods "DisplayData", which displays loaded data, and "DisplayProgress", which displays a progress bar. A's developer knows that the method "DisplayProgress" may be used as a callback method by another component, which loads the data. They also know that a callback may be invoked on different threads. Since no synchronisation of multiple threads is done inside the component, state corruption will arise if it is used concurrently from multiple threads. Therefore, in the design phase, the component developer is obliged to attach the attribute "RequiredThreadAffineAccess" at component level (in the design phase) to let the system developer know that the component must not be used in multithreaded scenarios.

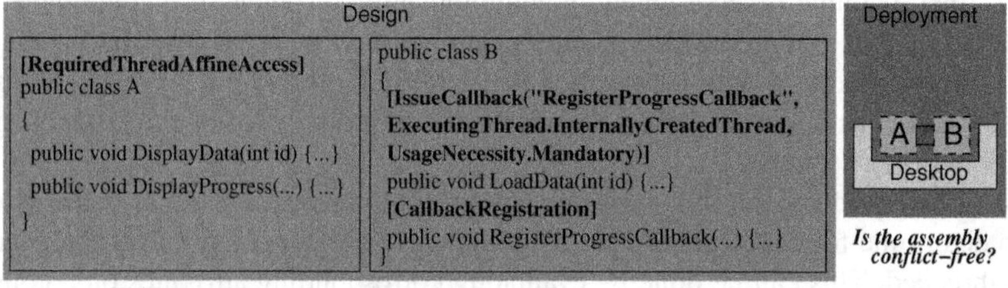

Fig. 8. Implementation of a design pattern for components with use of metadata attributes

Component B has two methods: "RegisterProgressCallback" and "LoadData". The method "RegisterProgressCallback" registers a callback of another component with the component. In this situation, the component developer is obliged to attach the attribute "CallbackRegistration" to the component's method. The method "LoadData" loads the data. Moreover, while the data is being loaded, the method invokes a callback to notify the component's user that a certain chunk of data has been loaded. In this situation, the component developer is obliged to attach and parameterise the attribute "IssueCallback". The attribute parameters show that the method will issue the callback registered with the method "RegisterProgressCallback". The thread executing the callback will be an internally created one. Furthermore, the callback is mandatory. Therefore, the component must be composed with another component in such a way that the method "RegisterProgressCallback" is called before the method "LoadData" is called.

In the deployment phase, suppose the system developer chooses the desktop as the execution environment. Furthermore, suppose the system developer decides to compose components A and B in the following way: since A displays the data and needs to know about chunks of data loaded, its method "DisplayProgress" can be registered with B to be invoked as a callback while the data is being loaded by B. Once the data has been loaded, it can be displayed using A's method "DisplayData". B offers a method "RegisterProgressCallback" with the attribute "CallbackRegistration" attached. Therefore, this method can be used to register component A's method "DisplayProgress" as a callback. After that, B's method "LoadData" can be called to initiate data loading. While the data is being loaded, the method will invoke the registered callback, which is illustrated by the attribute "IssueCallback" attached to the method.

The scenario required by the system developer seems to be fulfilled by assembling components A and B in this way. To confirm this, he can check the deployment contracts of A and B in the manner described in the previous section. We have implemented a Deployment Contracts Analyser (DCA) for automating the checking process. For this example, the result given by DCA is shown Fig. 9.

DCA finds out that component A has a component-level attribute "RequiredThreadAffineAccess" that requires all its methods to be called always from one and the same thread. The method "DisplayProgress" will be called from a thread internally created by the method "LoadData". But the method "DisplayData" will be called from the main thread. This means that methods of A will be called from different threads, which contradicts its requirement for thread-affine access. Furthermore, if data is loaded several times, the method "B.LoadData(...)" will create a new thread each time it is called thus invoking the method "A.DisplayProgress(...)" each time on a different thread. This means that A and B are incompatible.

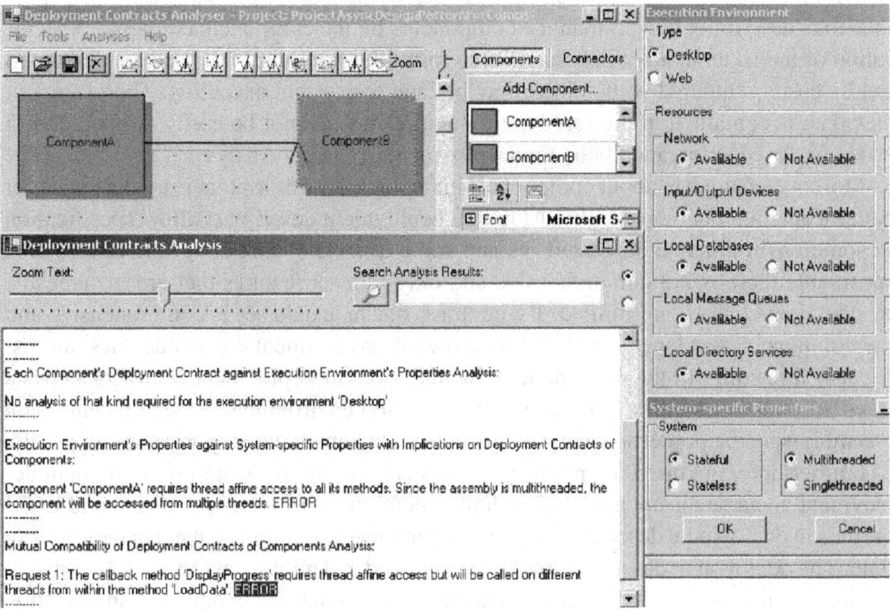

Fig. 9. Deployment Contracts Analyser

A component from the assembly AB has to be replaced by another one. Then a deployment contracts analysis has to be performed again. This process has to be repeated until an assembly of compatible components, i.e. a conflict-free assembly, is found. Once a conflict-free assembly is found, it can be executed at runtime.

6 Evaluation

The idea of deployment contracts based on a predefined pool of parameterisable attributes can be applied to any component model supporting composition of components at deployment time. We have implemented the idea in .NET, and since the .NET component model supports deployment time composition (Fig. 2), our implementation is a direct extension of the .NET component model with about 100 new attributes, together with a deployment-time analyser.

Our attributes are created by analysing the APIs of J2EE and .NET frameworks. However, the idea is general and therefore other frameworks for component development can be studied to create more attributes, thus enabling more comprehensive reasoning by extending deployment contracts analysis.

Our pool of metadata for component deployment is general-purpose since it is created by analysing general-purpose frameworks. Other pools of metadata for component deployment, see [12] for a survey, are mostly not general-purpose. For example, MetaH has a set of metadata for the domains of flight control and avionics; the CR-RIO Framework has metadata for distribution and processing policies.

Use of metadata for component deployment in current component models [12] such as EJB and CCM is restricted to component deployment descriptors that are XML specifications describing how to manage components by the component container. Specification of metadata in an easily changeable form like XML has the disadvantage that it can be easily tampered with, which may be fatal for system execution. Therefore, our metadata is contained in the real binary components, cannot be easily tampered with and is retrieved automatically by the Deployment Contracts Analyser.

Moreover, metadata about components in deployment descriptors is not analysed for component mutual compatibility. Although deployment descriptors allow specification of some environmental dependencies and some aspects of threading, the information specifiable there is not comprehensive and only reflects features that are manageable by containers, which are limited. By contrast, our metadata set is comprehensive and the component developer is obliged to show all environmental dependencies and aspects of threading for their component. In addition, our deployment contracts analysis takes account of properties of the system execution environment, as well as emergent assembly-specific properties like e.g. transient state, which other approaches do not do.

Furthermore, in current component models employing metadata for component deployment, metadata is not analysed at deployment time. For instance, in EJB and CCM the data in deployment descriptors is used by containers at runtime but not at deployment time. The deployment descriptor has to be produced at deployment time but its contents are used at runtime. In .NET, only metadata for graphical component arrangement is analysed at deployment time. By contrast, in our approach all the metadata is analysed at deployment time, which is essential when components come from different suppliers.

Currently the J2EE and .NET frameworks provide compilers for their components. However, if components are produced and compiled independently by component developers and composed later in binary form by system developers, no means for compiler-like checking of composition is provided. By contrast, our Deployment Contracts Analyser can check components for compatibility when they are in binary form and ready to be composed by a compositon operator.

Using our attributes, developers have extensive IDE support in the form of IntelliSense. Moreover, .NET developers should be familiar with the concept of attributes thus making it easy for them to employ the proposed approach using new attributes. Thanks to various parameters on each attribute, the component developer can flexibly specify how resources are used inside components and which threading aspects are available.

Furthermore, although EJB specification forbids component developers to manage threads themselves, there is nothing in current EJB implementations that would prevent the developers to do so. If enterprise beans manage threads themselves, they may interfere with the EJB container and cause the running system to fail. By contrast, our approach checks threading models of components for compatibility before runtime, thus enabling the system developer to recognise and prevent runtime conflicts before runtime.

7 Conclusion

In this paper,we have shown how to use metadata to define deployment contracts of components that express component's environmental dependencies and threading model. Such contracts bind two parties: (a) the component developer, who develops components, and (b) the system developer, who develops systems by composing pre-existing components using composition operators. The former is obliged to attach the attributes to component's elements in specified cases. The latter is guaranteed to be shown conflicts among the third-party components in assemblies they create at deployment time.

We have also shown how deployment contracts analysis can be performed to help the system developer spot these conflicts. Most importantly, incompatible components in an assembly can be replaced by other, compatible, ones to ensure conflict-freedom of the assembly, before runtime.

Besides checking deployment contracts at deployment time, we have also implemented a generic container for automated binary component composition [13] using special composition operators – exogenous connectors [15]. Our future work will combine the generic container and the Deployment Contracts Analyser, thus allowing automated component composition only if the analyser does not discover any conflicts with component assembly.

References

1. F. Bachmann, L. Bass, C. Buhman, S. Comella-Dorda, F. Long, J. Robert, R. Seacord, and K. Wallnau. Volume ii: Technical concepts of component-based software engineering, 2nd edition. Technical Report CMU/SEI-2000-TR-008, Carnegie Melon Software Engineering Institute, 2000.

2. B. Boehm and C. Abts. COTS integration: Plug and pray? *IEEE Computer*, 32(1):135–138, 1999.
3. D. Box. *Essential COM*. Addison-Wesley, 1998.
4. Schmidt D. C. *Pattern-oriented Software Architecture. Vol. 2, Patterns for Concurrent and Networked Objects*. New York John Wiley&Sons, Ltd., 2000.
5. Microsoft Corporation. Microsoft asynchronous pattern for components.
6. Microsoft Corporation. Msdn .net framework class library version 2.0, 2005.
7. R. Englander. *Developing Java Beans*. O'Reilly & Associates, 1997.
8. EZ JCom Framework web page. http://www.ezjcom.com.
9. M. Fowler, D. Box, A. Hejlsberg, A. Knight, R. High, and J. Crupi. The great j2ee vs. microsoft.net shootout. In *OOPSLA '04: Companion to the 19th annual ACM SIGPLAN conference on Object-oriented programming systems, languages, and applications*, pages 143–144, New York, NY, USA, 2004. ACM Press.
10. G.T. Heineman and W.T. Councill, editors. *Component-Based Software Engineering: Putting the Pieces Together*. Addison-Wesley, 2001.
11. A. W. Keen and R. A. Olsson. Exception handling during asynchronous method invocation. In *Parallel Processing: 8th International Euro-Par Conference Paderborn, Germany*, volume 2400 of *Lecture Notes in Computer Science*. Springer-Verlag, 2002.
12. K.-K. Lau and V. Ukis. Component metadata in component-based software development: A survey. Preprint 34, School of Computer Science, The University of Manchester, Manchester, M13 9PL, UK, October 2005.
13. K.-K. Lau and V. Ukis. A container for automatic system control flow generation using exogenous connectors. Preprint 31, School of Computer Science, The University of Manchester, Manchester, M13 9PL, UK, August 2005.
14. K.-K. Lau and V. Ukis. Deployment contracts for software components. Preprint 36, School of Computer Science, The University of Manchester, Manchester, M13 9PL, UK, February 2006. ISSN 1361 - 6161.
15. K.-K. Lau, P. Velasco Elizondo, and Z. Wang. Exogenous connectors for software components. In *Proc. 8th Int. SIGSOFT Symp. on Component-based Software Engineering, LNCS 3489*, pages 90–106, 2005.
16. K.-K. Lau and Z. Wang. A taxonomy of software component models. In *Proc. 31st Euromicro Conference*. IEEE Computer Society Press, 2005.
17. N. Medvidovic, P. Oreizy, J. E. Robbins, and R. N. Taylor. Using object-oriented typing to support architectural design in the c2 style. In *Proc. ACM SIGSOFT'96*, pages 24–32, 1996.
18. Sun Microsystems. Enterprise java beans specification, version 3.0, 2005.
19. Object Management Group (OMG). Corba components, specification, version 0.9.0, 2005.
20. D.S. Platt. *Introducing Microsoft .NET*. Microsoft Press, 3rd edition, 2003.
21. D. C. Schmidt, T. Harrison, and N. Pryce. Thread-specific storage - an object behavioral pattern for accessing per-thread state efficiently. In *The Pattern Languages of Programming Conference*, September 1997.
22. M. Shaw and D. Garlan. *Software Architecture: Perspectives on an Emerging Discipline*. Prentice Hall, 1996.
23. Sun Microsystems. *Java 2 Platform, Enterprise Edition*. `http://java.sun.com/j2ee/`.
24. C. Szyperski, D. Gruntz, and S. Murer. *Component Software: Beyond Object-Oriented Programming*. Addison-Wesley, second edition, 2002.
25. A. Wigley, M. Sutton, R. MacLeod, R. Burbidge, and S. Wheelwright. *Microsoft .NET Compact Framework(Core Reference)*. Microsoft Press, January 2003.

GLoo: A Framework for Modeling and Reasoning About Component-Oriented Language Abstractions

Markus Lumpe

Department of Computer Science
Iowa State University
Ames, IA 50011, USA
lumpe@cs.iastate.edu

Abstract. The most important contribution to the success or failure of a software project comes from the choice of the programming languages being used and their support in the target environment. The choice of a suitable implementation language is not a guarantor for success, but an unsuitable language may result in a long, error-prone, and costly implementation, often resulting in an unstable product. In this paper, we present GLoo, a framework for modeling and reasoning about *open-ended* language mechanisms for object- and component-oriented software development. At the heart of GLoo is a small *dynamic composition language* that provides abstractions to (i) define and/or import reusable software components, (ii) introduce new compositional language abstractions, and (iii) build executable and reusable component-oriented specifications. To demonstrate its flexibility and extensibility, we then present an encoding of the *traits* concept as an example of how to add support for a new and readily available language abstraction to the GLoo framework.

1 Introduction

Successful software systems have to abide by the *Laws of Software Evolution* [12], which require that software systems *must be continually adapted*, or else they become progressively less useful in a real-world environment. For this reason, software systems must be *extensible*, so that new behavior can be added without breaking the existing functionality, and *composable*, so that features can be recombined to reflect changing demands on their architecture and design.

By placing emphasis on reuse and evolution, component-oriented software technology has become the major approach to facilitate the development of modern, large-scale software systems [18,22,26]. However, component-oriented software development is in itself an inherently *dynamic* process in which we need to be able to deal with different component models, incorporate new composition techniques, and extend the means for specifying applications as compositions of reusable software components with new abstractions on demand [4]. Unfortunately, general-purpose programming languages are not suitable for this task, since they are not tailored to software composition [19]. As a consequence, when using a general-purpose programming language to specify applications as compositions of reusable software components one often has to use *awkward formulations* due to unsuitable language constructs, and *lengthy formulations* due to an unsuitable level of abstraction at which compositional abstractions can be expressed.

I. Gorton et al. (Eds.): CBSE 2006, LNCS 4063, pp. 17–32, 2006.

Consider, for example, the composition of some orthogonal behavior originating from different sources, say different base classes. We can use *multiple inheritance* for this purpose. However, while multiple inheritance appears to provide an appropriate mechanism to express the desired functionality, "there is no good way to do it" [30]. Consequently, multiple inheritance has been mostly abandoned in modern language approaches in favor of *single inheritance*, which provides a more controllable way to build classes. Unfortunately, the lack of multiple inheritance often results in unsuitably structured class hierarchies when specifying the simultaneous support for totally orthogonal behavior. In addition, such class hierarchies may be hard to maintain due to frequent occurrences of code duplications in different places.

The component-based software development approach has emerged from the object-oriented approach, which has already shown a positive influence on software evolution and reuse. These aspects do, however, not depend on object-oriented techniques [22]. Moreover, the specification of applications as compositions of reusable components requires a language paradigm different from the one being used to define the components themselves. While object-oriented programming languages are well suited for implementing components, a specially-designed *composition language* is better for building applications as compositions of reusable software components [24].

We advocate a paradigm that combines the concepts of *dynamic binding*, *explicit namespaces*, and *incremental refinements*. Dynamic binding is a key element in a software development approach that, without affecting its previous behavior, allows for new functionality to be added to an existing piece of code [5]. On the other hand, explicit namespaces [3, 14] in concert with incremental refinements provide a suitable means to directly specify the sets of both *provided* and *required* services of components [14]. From a technical point of view, explicit namespaces serve as a lookup environment with *syntactic representations* to resolve occurrences of free variables in programs. However, the values bound in these namespaces may also contain occurrences of free variables. To resolve those, we can use incremental refinements that allow for a phased recombination of mappings in a namespace to new, updated values. The notion of incremental refinement is based on $\lambda\mathcal{F}$-contexts [14]. A $\lambda\mathcal{F}$-context is a term that is evaluated with respect to a local lookup environment. For example, the $\lambda\mathcal{F}$-context `a[b]` denotes a term `a`, whose meaning depends on the values defined in `b`, if `a` contains free variables. Thus, `b` denotes the requirements posed by the free variables of `a` on its environment [17].

In this work, we present a framework for modeling and reasoning about *open-ended* language mechanisms for object- and component-oriented software development. At the center of this framework is the small *dynamic composition language* GLoo designed in the spirit of PICCOLA [13, 2], which has already demonstrated the feasibility of a high-level composition language that provides component-based, compositional interfaces to services defined in a separate host language. However, PICCOLA is far from providing the ease and flexibility required to build reliable component-based applications due to a conceptual gap between the mechanisms offered by PICCOLA and the component-based methodology that it is supposed to support.

GLoo is essentially a *pure functional* language and therefore fosters a declarative style of programming. The core elements of GLoo are *first-class namespaces*, *methods*, and *variables*, but no predefined statements like conditionals, loops, and assignment.

GLoo also provides built-in support for most operators found in Java or C#, but their semantics is *partially open*. That is, with the exception of the core integer operations addition, subtraction, multiplication, and division, for which GLoo provides a built-in implementation, all operators remain undefined and their actual semantics has to be provided by the application programmer. GLoo only specifies priority and associativity for operators, which cannot be changed.

One of the key innovations of GLoo with respect to PICCOLA is a built-in *gateway mechanism* to directly embed Java code into a GLoo specification. This mechanism is based to the $\lambda\mathcal{F}$-concept of *abstract application* [14] and allows for code abstractions defined in both GLoo and Java to coexist in one specification unit.

The rest of this paper is organized as follows: in Section 2, we briefly describe the main features and design rationale of GLoo and discuss briefly related work in Section 3. We present the design and implementation of our encoding of the traits concept in GLoo in Section 4. We conclude this paper in Section 5 with a summary of the main observations and outline future directions in this area.

2 The GLoo Language

2.1 Design Rationale

A successful component-based software development approach not only needs to provide abstractions to represent different component models and composition techniques, but it has to provide also a systematic method for constructing large software systems [4]. Unfortunately, rather then high-level *plugging*, most existing component frameworks offer, in general, only low-level *wiring* techniques to combine components. We need, however, higher-level, scalable, and domain-specific *compositional mechanisms* that reflect the characteristics and constraints of the components being composed [24,2]. The ability to define these mechanisms will provide us with more effective means to do both to reason about the properties of composition and to enhance program comprehension by reducing the exposure of the underlying wiring mechanisms to the component engineer.

The design of GLoo targets a *problem-oriented* software development approach that provides a paradigm for both *programming in-the-small* and *programming in-the-large* [6]. More precisely, GLoo aims at a higher-level and *scalable* programming approach to encapsulate domain expertise that provides support for the definition of domain-specific abstractions enabling the instantiation, coordination, extension, and composition of components. These domain-specific abstractions can be defined in GLoo, Java, or both.

2.2 The Core Language

The core of GLoo is the $\lambda\mathcal{F}$-calculus that combines the concepts of dynamic binding, explicit namespaces, and incremental refinement in one unifying framework. More precisely, the $\lambda\mathcal{F}$-calculus is a substitution-free variant of the λ-calculus in which variables are replaced by *forms* [15] and parameter passing is modeled by means of *explicit contexts* [1, 3]. Forms are first-class namespaces that provide a high-level and

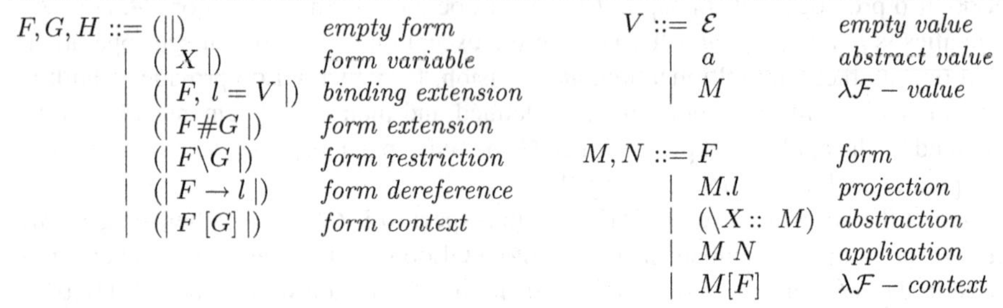

Fig. 1. GLoo-style syntax of the $\lambda\mathcal{F}$-Calculus

language-neutral abstraction to represent components, component interfaces, and their composition. Explicit contexts, on the other hand, serve as a syntactic representation that mimic λ-calculus substitutions, that is, they provide the means for a fine-grained and *keyword-based* parameter passing mechanism.

The design of the $\lambda\mathcal{F}$-calculus, like Dami's λN-calculus [5], tackles a problem that arises from the need to rely on the position and arity of parameters in mainstream programming languages. Requiring parameters to occur in a specific order, to have a specific arity, or both, imposes a specification format in which we are required to define programming abstractions that are characterized not by the parameters they effectively use, but by the parameters they *declare* [5]. However, in a framework especially designed for software composition this can hamper our ability to adapt existing software components to new requirements, because any form a parameter mismatch has to be resolved explicitly and, in general, manually.

The syntax of the $\lambda\mathcal{F}$-calculus is given in Figure 1. The $\lambda\mathcal{F}$-calculus is composed from the syntactic categories *forms*, *values*, and *terms*. Every form is derived from the empty form $(\|\|)$. A form can be extended by adding a new mapping from a label to a value using *binding extension*, or by means of *form extension* that allows for a form to be extended with a set of mappings. The difference between these two extension mechanisms lies in the way the values $\mathcal{E}$ and $(\|\|)$ are handled. If we extend a form F with a binding $l = \mathcal{E}$ using binding extension, then the resulting form F' is equivalent to a form F'' that does not contain a binding for label l. In other words, binding extension can be used to *hide* existing mappings in a form. Form extension, on the other hand, is blind for bindings involving the values $\mathcal{E}$ and $(\|\|)$. That is, if the extending form contains bindings that map to those values, then these bindings do not contribute to the extension operation. For example, $(\| \; (\| \; l = a, m = b \; \|) \; \# \; (\| \; l = d, m = \mathcal{E}, n = c \; \|) \; \|)$ yields $(\| \; l = d, m = b, n = c \; \|)$. Form restriction can be considered the inverse to form extension, which can be used to remove bindings from a form. In combination, both form extension and form restriction play a crucial role in a fundamental concept for defining adaptable and extensible software abstractions [15]. Finally, form dereference allows for a form-based interpretation of a value, whereas a form context $(\| \; F \; [G] \; \|)$ denotes a form F, whose meaning is refined by the local lookup environment G that may contain bindings for occurrences of free variables in F.

Forms and projections take the role of variables in terms. In a term, a form serves as an explicit namespace that allows for a computational model with *late binding* [14]. Abstraction and application correspond to their counterparts in the λ-calculus, whereas a $\lambda\mathcal{F}$-context is the counterpart to a form context. In contrast to λ-calculus, however, the evaluation of an abstraction allows for an incremental refinement of its body. More precisely, the evaluation of an abstraction yields a *closure* that associates the current evaluation environment with the body of that abstraction. For example, if we evaluate the abstraction $(\backslash X :: \ M)$ using the form F as an evaluation environment, then the result is a closure $(\backslash X :: \ M[F])$ in which F serves as a local lookup environment for free occurrences of variables in M. The resulting closure can be subjected to further evaluations that will allow for additional lookup environments to be added. However, to retain a *static scoping* mechanism for occurrences of free variables in the body of an abstraction, the order in which these additional lookup environments are added is significant. For example, if we reevaluate the closure $(\backslash X :: \ M[F])$ in a new evaluation environment G, then we obtain a closure $(\backslash X :: \ (M[F])[G])$ in which G serves as an incremental refinement of $M[F]$. Bindings defined in F have precedence over the ones defined in G, but bindings in G may provide values to resolve free occurrences of variables in F and therefore allow for a local refinement of the meaning of M. Parameter passing works in a similar way. If we apply a value H as argument to the closure $(\backslash X :: \ (M[F])[G])$, then we have to evaluate $(M[F])[G]$ in an evaluation environment $(| \ X = H \ |)$, that is, we have to evaluate the term $((M[F])[G])[(| \ X = H \ |)]$. In other words, parameters are passed to functions using a keyword-based mechanism. For a complete definition of the evaluation rules, the interested reader is referred to [14].

2.3 GLoo Specification Units

From a technical point of view, component-oriented software development is best supported by an approach that favors a clear separation between computational and compositional entities [24]. This requirement is captured by the maxim

"Applications = Components + Scripts." [24]

The definition of the GLoo language follows this maxim. A GLoo specification unit defines a value or *component* that can be recombined with values and/or components, which are defined in other specification units. In other words, a GLoo specification unit defines a single $\lambda\mathcal{F}$-context that can locally define new abstractions or import definitions from other $\lambda\mathcal{F}$-contexts in order to construct a new value or component.

GLoo specification units add support for basic data types, an import facility, term sequences, a *delayed evaluation* of terms, *computable* binders, and a Java gateway mechanism to the core language. These amendments solely serve to enrich the versatility of values, but do not change the underlying computational model of the $\lambda\mathcal{F}$-calculus.

As a first example, consider the specification given in Listing 1. This script defines `IntRdWrClass`, a class that is composed from the class `IntClass` and the traits `TWriteInt` and `TReadInt`. The concepts of classes and traits [23] are not native to GLoo. GLoo is not an object-oriented programming language *per se*. However, by importing the units `LanguageOfTraits.lf` and `IntClass.lf` into the scope

```
1  let
2      Services = load "System/Services.lf"
3      load "Extensions/LanguageOfTraits.lf"
4
5      IntMetaClass = load "Classes/IntClass.lf"
6      TReadInt = load "Traits/TReadInt.lf"
7      TWriteInt = load "Traits/TWriteInt.lf"
8  in
9      IntMetaClass (trait "TRdWrInt" join TWriteInt with TReadInt)
10 end
```

Listing 1. The GLoo script `IntRdWrClass.lf`

defined by `IntRdWrClass.lf`, this unit now provides support for the required object-oriented language features.

Every GLoo script defines a top-level *let-block* that contains a possibly empty set of *declarations* and a *single value*. The declarations are evaluated sequentially. Thus, the second declaration is evaluated in an environment in which the first binding is visible, and so on. There are five declarations in the script `IntRdWrClass.lf`. The integration of the core system services is defined in line 2. The unit `Services.lf` defines the basic programming abstractions for printing as well as IO, and provides also, for example, a standard implementation for conditionals. The declaration in line 3 extends the current scope with a *traits domain sublanguage* that provides support for defining, composing, and manipulating traits. The abstractions defined in the unit `LanguageOfTraits.lf` serve as *syntactic and semantic extensions* (i.e., keywords) to the GLoo language. Using this technique, we can focus on *what* an application offers (i.e., a programming approach supporting traits), without entering into the details of how it is implemented. The declarations in lines 5-7 introduce the components that we want to combine to the current scope. The reader should note that we do not acquire any explicit support for an *object model*. The object model is encapsulated in `IntClass.lf`. The details of the underlying object model of class `IntClass` do not pollute the declaration space of `IntRdWrClass.lf`. We know, however, that `IntMetaClass` is a function that may take a trait as argument.

The result of evaluating the unit `IntRdWrClass.lf` is a class `IntRdWrClass` that is composed from the class `IntClass` and the result of the composition of the traits `TWriteInt` and `TReadInt`, that is, the composite trait `TRdWrInt`. The underlying object-oriented programming abstractions guarantee the soundness of this composition. However, the details of the verification progress are encapsulated in the corresponding GLoo units and are not exposed to the current scope.

2.4 The Gateway Mechanism

The built-in gateway mechanism of GLoo provides an approach to directly incorporate Java code into the scope of a GLoo specification unit. The gateway mechanism can be used for the specification of *glue code* to adapt components to fit actual compositional requirements [24], and to extend the GLoo language either by defining supported operators, adding new value types, or incorporating new and readily available programming abstractions. Gateway code is enclosed in %{...}%, which is treated as a single

```
let
    println = %{ System.out.println( aArg.toString() ); return aArg; }%

    eval = %{ // check for lazy value
              if ( aArg instanceof LazyValue )
                // force evaluation of lazy values
                aArg = (((LazyValue)aArg).getValue()).evaluate( new EmptyForm() );

              return aArg; }%
in
    (| println = println, eval = eval |)
end
```

Listing 2. Selected abstractions provided by `Services.lf`

token by the GLoo compiler. The Java code enclosed in %{...}% is transformed into a static member function, which is emitted to a predefined runtime support class. The GLoo compiler uses *com.sun.tools.javac* to compile this runtime support class after all gateway specifications have been collected. If no errors are detected, then the generated runtime class is loaded into the GLoo system as a temporary runtime extension to support the evaluation of the top-level GLoo specification unit.

To illustrate the use of the gateway mechanism, consider Listing 2 that shows an extract of the specification unit `Services.lf`. This example illustrates how the functions `println` and `eval` can be defined in GLoo. The function `println` implements the output of the standard textual representation of each data type. It relies on the fact that all supported GLoo values have to override the `Object.toString()` method, so that a proper textual representation can be produced, if necessary. In addition, the reader should note that every gateway function takes one argument, named `aArg`, and has to return a value of a type that is a subtype of the GLoo type `Value`. For this reason, `println` returns its argument, which not only satisfies the protocol of gateway functions, but also allows applications of the function `println` to occur in positions, where its argument is required.

GLoo uses a *strict* evaluation model, that is, terms are evaluated as soon as they become bound to a variable or applied to a function. On the other hand, functions in GLoo are characterized by the arguments they use, not by the ones they define. Unfortunately, these competing aspects pose a serious conflict, because the strict evaluation model forces all arguments to a function to be evaluated before they are applied to it, even though the function may never use them. For this reason, GLoo also provides a special modifier (i.e., the symbol '$') to explicitly mark a term *lazy*. The lazy modifier is, for example, crucial to the definition of choice statements, where the individual branches must not be evaluated before a corresponding guard evaluates to the value *true* (e.g., the *if-statement*).

The evaluation of a lazy term is *delayed* until its evaluation is explicitly triggered by a corresponding program abstraction. This is the purpose of the function `eval`. The `eval` function, as shown in Listing 2, taps directly into the GLoo evaluation machinery. More precisely, this function checks, whether its argument `aArg` needs to be evaluated or not by checking if it is an instance of type *LazyValue*. In such a case, `eval` forces the evaluation of `aArg` by calling its `evaluate` method using an empty evaluation

```
let
    if = %{ /* Java code defining the ternary procedure if-then-else */ }%
in
    (|
        if_1 = (\Bool:: if (| condition = Bool,
                              then = (\Arg:: eval Arg),
                              else = (\Arg:: (||)) |) ),
        if_2 = (\Bool:: if (| condition = Bool,
                              then = (\Then:: (\Else:: eval Then)),
                              else = (\Then:: (\Else:: eval Else)) |) )
    |)
end
```

Listing 3. Definition of conditionals in `Services.lf`

environment (i.e., an empty form). This approach allows programmers to switch to a *lazy evaluation* model for selected arguments, and to determine when such arguments should be evaluated, if at all.

2.5 Support for the Definition of Language Abstractions

The specification shown in Listing 3 illustrates how conditionals can be defined in GLoo. In this example, we define an *if-statement* for both a single-armed and a two-armed version. The underlying semantics of the if-statement is implemented in the ternary gateway function `if`, whose visibility is restricted to the scope of the specification unit `Services.lf`. The functions `if_1` and `if_2` both define a wrapper for the local `if` function in order to implement the desired corresponding behavior of a single-armed and two-armed if-statement, respectively. More precisely, `if_1` and `if_2` both define appropriate *continuations* to consume the remaining arguments to a given if-statement. In the case of `if_1`, the continuations either force the evaluation of the next argument (i.e., the value `Bool` denotes *true*) or simply discard it (i.e., the value `Bool` denotes *false*). On the other hand, the continuations defined by `if_2` have to consume two arguments in turn, but evaluate only the one that corresponds to the truth value denoted by `Bool`. The reader should note that all arguments except `Bool` have to be marked lazy in order to prevent their premature evaluation, which could interfere with the commonly accepted conceptual model underlying the if-statement.

3 Related Work

Python [16], Perl [29], Ruby [27], Tcl [31], CLOS [25], Smalltalk [10], Self [28], or Scheme [7] are examples of programming languages in which programs can change their structure as they run. These languages are commonly known as *dynamic programming languages* and *scripting languages* [21], respectively. However, the degree of dynamism varies between languages. For example, Smalltalk and Scheme are languages that permit simultaneously *syntactic* and *semantic extensions*, that is, everything is available for modification without stopping to recompile and restart. Python, Perl, JavaScript, and Self, on the other hand, support only semantic extensions either by *dynamic (re-)loading* of runtime modules, *runtime program construction*, or *copying and modifying prototypes*. However, program extensions defined in this way can only be expressed in either the language itself, C/C++, or a corresponding API. Extensions written in other languages may not be integrated as easily.

Since Smalltalk and Scheme both provide support for syntactic extensions, these languages are also examples of so-called *open-ended* programming languages. Open-ended languages allow for extending the language with new programming abstractions on demand. However, in the case of Smalltalk and Scheme, these extensions can only be defined in the very same language as the host language. An extreme example of an *open-ended* language is CDL [11], which is a programming language with an empty kernel. More precisely, CDL admits only one type, the *word*, which can be interpreted in the language only by means of *macros*. No other predefined concrete algorithms, types, or objects exist in the language. CDL provides, however, construction mechanisms for algorithms. Types and objects, on the other hand, cannot directly be expressed in the language. These have to be supplied by means of CDL's extensions mechanisms, which enable one to *borrow* new language constructs from outside the language. Language extensions are defined in *macro libraries* that serve as *semantic extensions* (CDL does not support *syntactic extensions*). In practice, these macro libraries are organized as standard API's capturing a specific application domain. As a result, programming in CDL is not much more cumbersome than programming in a mainstream and general-purpose programming language like C, Java, or C#.

4 A Model for Traits

In this section, we present a model of traits [23] as an example of how to add support for a new language abstraction to the GLoo framework.

Traits offer a simple compositional model for factoring out common behavior and for integrating it into classes in a manner consistent with inheritance-based class models [23]. Traits are essentially sets of related methods that serve as (i) a building block to construct classes, and (ii) a primary unit of code reuse. Reuse is a primary tenant in a component-oriented software development approach and it is, therefore, natural that we seek to explore the means for providing support for traits in the GLoo framework.

Unfortunately, to view a trait simply as set of methods is rather misleading, as traits require a rich supporting infrastructure in order to unfold their expressive power. Schärli et al. [23] characterize the properties of traits as follows:

- A trait exposes its behavior by a set of *provided* methods.
- A trait declares its dependencies by a set of *required* methods that serve as arguments to the provided behavior.
- Traits are stateless. A trait does not define any state variables, and its provided behavior never refers to state variables directly.
- Classes and traits can be composed to construct other classes or traits. Trait composition is commutative, but conflicts have to be resolved explicitly and manually.
- Trait composition does not affect the semantics of both classes and traits. Adding a trait to a class or trait is the same as defining the methods obtained from the trait directly in the class or trait.

```
let
    read = (\()::  Services.print "Input number: ";
                   Services.stringToInt (Services.readString (||)))

    TReadIntProvides =
        (|
            readInt = (\():: (self (||)).setIntField (| aIntField = read (||) |))
        |)

    TReadIntRequires =
        (|
            readInt = (| setIntField = "Int -> Unit" |)
        |)
in
    trait "TReadInt" provides TReadIntProvides requires TReadIntRequires
end
```

Listing 4. Definition of trait `TReadInt`

In addition, to facilitate conflict resolution, Schärli et al. [23] propose two auxiliary operations: *method aliasing*, and *method exclusion*. These operations together with a suitable *flattening mechanism* for trait composition are required in a comprehensive approach that provides support for the traits concept in a class-based programming model.

The first two trait properties can easily be mapped to the concept of explicit namespaces. Unfortunately, trait composition, method aliasing, and method exclusion require an additional compile-time support that is not part of the GLoo framework by default. However, as we have shown in earlier work [20], object- and component-oriented abstractions can most easily be modeled if they are represented as *first-class entities*. We can use this approach to define a *meta-level* architecture that provides the means to differentiate the compositional aspects from the programming aspects of the traits concept.

4.1 Specifying Traits in GLoo

Programmatically, we define a trait as illustrated in Listing 4. The specification shown in Listing 4 defines a trait, called `TReadInt`, that defines one provided method `readInt`, and declares the method `setIntField` with the signature `Int -> Unit` as a required method of `readInt`. The focus of this work is on a suitable representation of traits, not on a type system for traits. It is, however, highly desirable to provide additional information regarding their compositional constraints for required methods of a trait. For this reason, we utilize the type syntax proposed by Fisher and Reppy [8] for a statically typed calculus of traits, classes, and objects, but the type annotations are for documentation purposes only. A future model of traits in GLoo may also define a type verification process that takes these annotations to perform additional checks.

The general format of a trait specification follows the structure used to define the trait `TReadInt`. Within the local scope of a trait, we define the sets of provided and required methods. The set of provided methods is a form that maps the provided methods to their corresponding implementations. In method bodies, the term `(self (||))` yields the current instance, and allows for *dynamic binding* of methods. Provided methods may

```
let
    MetaTraits = load "Extensions/Traits.lf"
in
    (|
        trait = (\Name:: (\Cont:: Cont (| traitName = Name |))),
        provides = (\Args:: (\P:: (\Cont:: Cont (| Args, provides = P |)))),
        requires = (\Args:: (\R:: MetaTraits.newTrait (| Args, requires = R |)))
        join = (\Args:: (\L:: (\Cont:: Cont (| Args, left = L |)))),
        with = (\Args:: (\R:: MetaTraits.composeTraits (| Args, right = R |)))
    |)
end
```

Listing 5. Selected abstractions provided by `LanguageOfTraits.lf`

also rely on some private behavior not exposed to clients. For example, the method `readInt` calls the private method `read` to fetch an integer value from the console.

The set of required methods is also represented by a form. However, each binding in that form maps to another form that records all methods, including their signatures, a given provided method depends on. This format is more verbose than the original specification of Schärli et al. [23], but it addresses a problem that can occur when defining the *exclusion of a method* in a trait. In such a case, we need to add the excluded method potentially to the set of required methods. In order to decide this question, we need to explore all remaining provided methods. Without the additional structure in our model, we have to extend the search to the source code of the provided methods, which may not be accessible anymore at the time of the search.

The required core abstractions to define traits are shown in Listing 5. The bindings defined in the unit `LanguageOfTraits.lf` serve as language extensions to an importing scope. The associated functions are defined in *continuation-passing style* (CPS) that mimics the parsing process of the corresponding syntactic categories. For example, `trait` is a function that takes a name of a trait and returns a function that consumes a continuation to construct a new trait. The continuation can be either the function `provides` to build a new trait or the function `join` to compose a trait with another trait. Both `provides` and `join` yield a function that takes a final continuation to actually perform the desired operation. In case of `provides`, we need to use the function `requires` that passes its arguments to meta level function `newTrait` to register a new trait with the meta level trait infrastructure. The function `join`, on the other hand, requires the function `with` that passes its arguments to `composeTraits`, a meta level function to construct a composite trait.

4.2 Operational Support for Traits

In order to add support for the traits concept to the GLoo framework, we represent traits at both a meta level and a programming level. The meta level defines the abstractions to (i) compose traits, (ii) alias methods, (iii) exclude methods, and (iv) encode metadata associated with traits. The programming level, on the other hand, provides a set of high-level abstractions to define and use traits. The programming level completely encapsulates the meta level and therefore shields the application programmer from the underlying complexity of the traits concept. Moreover, both the meta level and the programming level constitute a narrow-focused *domain-specific sublanguage* that enables

```
composeTraits =
(\Arg::
    let
        left = getTraitInfo Arg->left
        right = getTraitInfo Arg->right
    in
        Services.if_2
            (is_trait_composition_sound
                (| common = Services.intersection (| left = left->provides,
                                                     right = right->provides |),
                   left_origins = left->origins,
                   right_origins = right->origins |))
            ($ let
                provides = (| (| left->provides |) # (| right->provides |) |)
                requires =
                    filter_required
              (| required = (| (| left->requires |) # (| right->requires |) |),
                        provided = provides    |)
                origins = (| (| left->origins |) # (| right->origins |) |)
            in
                registerTrait (| traitName = Arg.traitName, provides = provides,
                                 requires = requires, origins = origins |)
            end)
            ($ (Services.error "Conflicting trait methods encountered!"))
    end)
```

Listing 6. Definition of method `composeTraits` in `Traits.lf`

us not only to use traits in GLoo specifications, but also to reason about the features and constraints of the traits concept.

The meta level support for traits is defined in the unit `Traits.lf` that defines an internal representation of traits called `MetaTrait`. A `MetaTrait` encodes the metadata associated with every trait. It records (i) the trait name, (ii) the set of provided methods, (iii) the set of required methods, and (iv) the *origins* of all provided methods. The latter is used for conflict resolution and enables us to check whether conflicting methods originate from the same trait in which case the conflict is resolved immediately.

The meta level also defines the functions `registerTrait`, `filterRequired`, and `is_trait_composition_sound` to name a few. These functions[1] are used to define the function `composeTraits` (cf., Listing 6), which takes two traits and builds their union, if possible. The purpose of `is_trait_composition_sound` is to check that the provided methods of the two traits being composed are pairwise distinct. In order to verify this condition, we also pass the origins of both traits to `is_trait_composition_sound`. We acquire the origins of both traits by calling the function `getTraitInfo`, which returns the metadata associated with the corresponding trait. If the soundness test succeeds, then we are actually composing both traits by building (i.e., *flattening*) the new sets of provided and required methods, and the new joined origins. We pass these data together with the corresponding trait name to the meta-function `registerTrait`, which (i) registers the newly composed trait with the meta-level infrastructure, and (ii) returns the programming representation of it.

The unit `Traits.lf` also defines functions for method exclusion and method aliasing. These functions take a trait and a list of method names to either be excluded or

[1] A detailed presentation of these functions has been omitted due to a lack of space.

aliased. The structure of these functions resembles the one of `composeTraits`. However, a detailed presentation of them has been omitted due to lack of space.

4.3 Using Traits

In the previous section, we have presented the core abstractions for trait construction and composition. In this section, we illustrate briefly how to composes classes and traits.

Trait composition is commutative, that is, the composition order is irrelevant. Conflicts must be explicitly resolved. However, Schärli et al. [23] define two additional criteria that must be also satisfied in the case of the composition of classes and traits:

1) *"Class methods take precedence over trait methods."*
2) *"Trait methods take precedence over superclass methods."'*

In order words, the provided methods of a trait have to be *inserted* into a class between its inherited behavior and the behavior defined by that class. This is a logical consequence of the *flattening property* that requires that methods obtained from a trait must behave as if they were defined in the class directly [23].

To illustrate the composition of classes and traits, consider the GLoo specification unit shown in Listing 7. This unit defines a *meta-class* of the class `IntClass` that defines two public methods `getIntField` and `setIntField`, and a private instance variable `fIntField`. The general structure of a class definition is given by three abstractions: (i) a incremental modification, (ii) a generator, and (iii) a class wrapper [15]. In the case of class `IntClass`, these abstractions are `deltaIntClass`, `IntClassG`, and `IntClassW`, respectively. These abstractions not only define the required behavior of class `IntClass`, but also the underlying object model[2], which, in the case of `IntClass`, adheres to Java semantics.

We use the abstractions `deltaIntClass`, `IntClassG`, and `IntClassW` to construct a meta-class of class `IntClass`. This meta-class is actually a function that may take a trait as argument. To instantiate a class, we have to call this function using either a trait or an empty form as argument. The latter will simply instantiate the corresponding class, since we have applied an empty extension. If we, however, apply a proper trait, then the behavior defined by this trait is composed with the behavior defined by the class in accordance with the criteria for the composition of classes and traits. First, we verify that the composition is closed, that is, all required trait methods are implemented by the class. Secondly, we merge the methods of both the trait and the class. By using form extension class methods are given precedence over trait methods. The result denotes a new incremental modification of the class that is obtained from the composition of the original incremental modification and the trait methods. The class generator finally merges any present inherited behavior with the new incremental behavior[3] to create instances of the extended class.

---

[2] These two aspects should be specified in different scopes in order to separate the concerns and to raise the level of abstraction. We have proposed a solution for this problem in [15].

[3] The class `IntClass` does not inherit any behavior, hence this step is the identity function.

```
let
    fix = load "System/fix.lf"
in
    (\Trait::
        let
            IntClassBehavior =
            (|
             getIntField = (\():: State.fIntField ),
             setIntField = (\Args:: self (| State, fIntField = Args.aIntField |) )
             |)
            deltaIntClass =
                let
                    pureTrait = Traits.pureTrait Trait
                in
                    (Services.if_1
                      (Services.not_empty pureTrait)
                      ($ let
                       allRequired =
                       Traits.buildAllRequired(Traits.getTraitInfo Trait)->requires
                          inU:\BPO\Lncs\4063\Editing\40630017\40630017.tex
                              (Services.if_1
                                  (Services.not_empty
                                    (| (| allRequired |) \ (| IntClassBehavior |) |))
                                  ($ (Services.error "Composition incomplete!")))
                          end));
                      (| pureTrait # IntClassBehavior |)
                end
            IntClassState = (| fIntField = 0 |)
            deltaClass = (\State:: deltaIntClass)
            IntClassG =
                (\OArgs:: deltaClass
                    (| OArgs # (|IntClassState\(|fIntField=OArgs.fIntField |) |)|))
            IntClassW = (\OArgs:: (fix (| f=(\self:: IntClassG) |)) OArgs)
        in
            (| W=IntClassW, G=IntClassG |)
        end)
end
```

Listing 7. Definition of the (meta-)class `IntClass`

5 Conclusion and Future Work

In this paper, we have presented GLoo, a framework for modeling and reasoning about component-oriented language abstractions. At the center of this framework is a small dynamic composition language that is based on the $\lambda\mathcal{F}$-calculus [14]. The main tenants of the GLoo programming paradigm are dynamic binding, explicit namespaces [3], and incremental refinement. These concepts together with a built-in gateway mechanism to incorporate Java code directly into the scope of GLoo specification units provides us with the means for a problem-oriented software development approach.

To demonstrate how a domain-specific sublanguage can be defined, we have implemented the traits concept [23] in GLoo. The *language of traits* is defined as a readily available language abstraction that can be loaded on demand. The specific added value of this abstraction is a clear separation between compositional and programming aspects of traits, which facilitates both the construction and the composition of traits.

We have studied the encoding of classes, traits, and objects in GLoo. We need, however, also support for the integration of external software artifacts into the GLoo framework. We plan, therefore, to further explore the gateway concept in order to incorporate existing Java classes and components. Like the language of traits, we envision a narrow-focused domain sublanguage of classes and components that will allow application programmers to use existing Java abstraction as they were defined in GLoo directly.

Acknowledgements

We are deeply grateful to Andrew Cain for suggesting the name GLoo and Jean-Guy Schneider and the anonymous reviewers for their valuable comments and discussions.

References

1. Martín Abadi, Luca Cardelli, Pierre-Louis Curien, and Jean-Jacques Lèvy. Explicit Substitutions. In *Proceedings of the 17th Annual ACM Symposium on Principles of Programming Languages (FSE '90)*, pages 31–46, San Francisco, California, 1990. ACM.
2. Franz Achermann. *Forms, Agents and Channels: Defining Composition Abstraction with Style*. PhD thesis, University of Bern, Institute of Computer Science and Applied Mathematics, January 2002.
3. Franz Achermann and Oscar Nierstrasz. Explicit Namespaces. In Jürg Gutknecht and Wolfgang Weck, editors, *Modular Programming Languages*, LNCS 1897, pages 77–89. Springer, September 2000.
4. Uwe Aßmann. *Invasive Software Composition*. Springer, 2003.
5. Laurent Dami. A Lambda-Calculus for Dynamic Binding. *Theoretical Computer Science*, 192:201–231, February 1998.
6. Frank DeRemer and Hans H. Kron. Programming in the Large versus Programming in the Small. *IEEE Transactions on Software Engineering*, SE–2(2):80–86, June 1976.
7. Kent Dybvig. *The Scheme Programming Language*. MIT Press, third edition, October 2003.
8. Kathleen Fisher and John Reppy. Statically typed traits. Technical Report TR-2003-13, University of Chicago, December 2003.
9. GLoo. http://www.cs.iastate.edu/~lumpe/GLoo.
10. Adele Goldberg and David Robson. *Smalltalk-80: The Language*. Addison-Wesley, September 1989.
11. Cornelis H.A. Koster and H.-M. Stahl. *Implementing Portable and Efficient Software in an Open-Ended Language*. Informatics Department, Nijmegen University, Nijmegen, The Netherlands, 1990.
12. M. M. Lehman, D. E. Perry, J. C. F. Ramil, W. M. Turski, and P. Wernik. Metrics and Laws of Software Evolution – The Nineties View. In *Proceedings of Fourth International Symposium on Software Metrics, Metrics 97*, pages 20–32, Albuquerque, New Mexico, November 1997. Also as chapter 17 in Eman, K. El, Madhavji, N. M. (Eds.), Elements of Software Process Assessment and Improvement, IEEE CS Press, Los Alamitos, CA, 1999.
13. Markus Lumpe. *A π-Calculus Based Approach to Software Composition*. PhD thesis, University of Bern, Institute of Computer Science and Applied Mathematics, January 1999.
14. Markus Lumpe. A Lambda Calculus With Forms. In Thomas Gschwind, Uwe Aßmann, and Oscar Nierstrasz, editors, *Proceedings of the Fourth International Workshop on Software Composition*, LNCS 3628, pages 83–98, Edinburgh, Scotland, April 2005. Springer.
15. Markus Lumpe and Jean-Guy Schneider. A Form-based Metamodel for Software Composition. *Science of Computer Programming*, 56:59–78, April 2005.

16. Mark Lutz. *Programming Python.* O'Reilly & Associates, October 1996.
17. Oscar Nierstrasz and Franz Achermann. A Calculus for Modeling Software Components. In Frank S. de Boer, Marcello M. Bonsangue, Susanne Graf, and Willem P. de Roever, editors, *Proceedings of First International Symposium on Formal Methods for Components and Objects (FMCO 2002)*, LNCS 2852, pages 339–360, Leiden, The Netherlands, 2003. Springer.
18. Oscar Nierstrasz and Laurent Dami. Component-Oriented Software Technology. In Oscar Nierstrasz and Dennis Tsichritzis, editors, *Object-Oriented Software Composition*, pages 3–28. Prentice Hall, 1995.
19. Oscar Nierstrasz and Theo Dirk Meijler. Requirements for a Composition Language. In Paolo Ciancarini, Oscar Nierstrasz, and Akinori Yonezawa, editors, *Object-Based Models and Languages for Concurrent Systems*, LNCS 924, pages 147–161. Springer, 1995.
20. Oscar Nierstrasz, Jean-Guy Schneider, and Markus Lumpe. Formalizing Composable Software Systems – A Research Agenda. In *Proceedings the 1st IFIP Workshop on Formal Methods for Open Object-based Distributed Systems*, pages 271–282. Chapmann & Hall, 1996.
21. John K. Ousterhout. Scripting: Higher Level Programming for the 21st Century. *IEEE Computer*, 31(3):23–30, March 1998.
22. Johannes Sametinger. *Software Engineering with Reusable Components*. Springer, 1997.
23. Nathanael Schärli, Stéphane Ducasse, Oscar Nierstrasz, and Andrew Black. Traits: Composable Units of Behavior. In Luca Cardelli, editor, *Proceedings ECOOP 2003*, LNCS 2743, pages 248–274. Springer, July 2003.
24. Jean-Guy Schneider. *Components, Scripts, and Glue: A conceptual framework for software composition.* PhD thesis, University of Bern, Institute of Computer Science and Applied Mathematics, October 1999.
25. Guy L. Steele. *Common Lisp the Language.* Digital Press, Thinking Machines, Inc., 2nd edition, 1990.
26. Clemens Szyperski. *Component Software: Beyond Object-Oriented Programming*. Addison-Wesley / ACM Press, Second edition, 2002.
27. Dave Thomas. *Programming Ruby – The Pragmatic Programmers' Guide.* The Pragmatic Bookshelf, LLC, second edition, 2005.
28. David Ungar and Randall B. Smith. SELF: The Power of Simplicity. In *Proceedings OOPSLA '87*, volume 22 of *ACM SIGPLAN Notices*, pages 227–242, December 1987.
29. Larry Wall, Tom Christiansen, and Jon Orwant. *Programming Perl.* O'Reilly & Associates, Third edition, July 2000.
30. Peter Wegner. OOPSLA'87 Panel P2: Varieties of Inheritance. *SIGPLAN Not.*, 23(5):35–40, May 1988.
31. Brent B. Welch. *Practical Programming in Tcl and Tk.* Prentice Hall PTR, second edition, 1997.

Behavioral Compatibility Without State Explosion: Design and Verification of a Component-Based Elevator Control System*

Paul C. Attie[1], David H. Lorenz[2], Aleksandra Portnova[3], and Hana Chockler[4]

[1] American University of Beirut, Beirut, Lebanon
paul.attie@aub.edu.lb
[2] University of Virginia, Charlottesville, VA 22904, USA
lorenz@cs.virginia.edu
[3] Northeastern University, Boston, MA 02115, USA
portnova@ccs.neu.edu
[4] WPI, Worcester, MA 01609, USA
hanac@theory.csail.mit.edu

Abstract. Most methods for designing component-based systems and verifying their compatibility address only the syntactic compatibility of components; no analysis of run-time behavior is made. Those methods that do address run-time behavior suffer from *state-explosion*: the exponential increase of the number of global states, and hence the complexity of the analysis, with the number of components. We present a method for designing component-based systems and verifying their behavioral compatibility and temporal behavior that is not susceptible to state explosion. Our method is mostly automatic, with little manual deduction required, and does not analyze a large system of connected components at once, but instead analyzes components two-at-a-time. This pair-wise approach enables the automatic verification of temporal behavior, using model-checking, in time polynomial in the number and size of all components. Our method checks that behavior of a pair of interacting components conforms to given properties, specified in temporal logic. Interaction of the components is captured in a product of their behavioral automata, which are provided as a part of each component's interface. We demonstrate the effectiveness of our method by applying it to the design and verification of a component-based elevator control algorithm.

1 Introduction

Monolithic software systems are fragile and unreliable. *Component-based software engineering* (CBSE) [34, 38, 19] alleviates this inherent software problem. Third-party composition of software systems, comprising reliable components from trustworthy third-party providers, reduces the system's overall fragility. In

* This work was supported in part by NSF's Science of Design program under Grants Number CCF-0438971 and CCF-0609612.

I. Gorton et al. (Eds.): CBSE 2006, LNCS 4063, pp. 33–49, 2006.

practice, however, part of the fragility is merely shifted from the component artifacts to the connectors and the composition process [28]. When the composition is unreliable, component systems are just as fragile and unreliable as monolithic software. Improving the theoretical and practical foundation of third-party composition techniques is thus essential to improving overall component software reliability.

In this paper, we lay a foundation for a new component model which supports behavioral interoperability and is based on the use of temporal logic and automata to specify and reason about concurrent component systems. Unlike other temporal logic and automata-based methods for software components, our work avoids using exhaustive state-space enumeration, which quickly runs up against the *state-explosion problem*: the number of global states of a system is exponential in the number of its components. We present formal analysis and synthesis techniques that addresses issues of behavioral compatibility among components, and enables reasoning about global behavior (including temporal behavior, i.e., safety and liveness) of an assembly of components.

We illustrate the model concretely by means of an example design for an elevator system, which can scale up in size (number of floor and button components) and still be model-checked. Designing a component-based elevator system that can be scaled up is a canonical Software Engineering problem since it runs up against state-explosion. Our methodology, however, permits model-checking in time polynomial in the number and size of components.

2 Problem and Approach in a Nutshell

For two components, which were independently developed, to be deployed and work together, third-party composition must allow the flexibility of assembling even dissimilar, heterogeneous, precompiled components. In achieving this flexibility, a delicate balance is preserved between prohibiting the connecting of incompatible components (avoiding false positives), while permitting the connecting of "almost compatible" components through adaptation (avoiding false negatives). This is achieved during assembly through introspection, compatibility checks, and adaptability.

CBSE builder environments typically apply two mechanisms to support third-party composition. First, to check for *interface compatibility*, builders use *introspection*. Introspection is a means of discovering the component interface. Second, builders support *adaptability* by generating adapters to overcome differences in the interface. Adapters are a means of fixing small mismatches when the interfaces are not syntactically identical.

The goal in *behavioral compatibility* for components is to develop support in CBSE for *behavioral introspection* and *behavioral adaptability* that can be scaled up for constructing large complex component systems. While there is progress in addressing behavioral introspection and adaptability [40, 35, 39, 36, 37] there is little progress in dealing with the *state explosion problem*.

2.1 The State Explosion Problem

Many current mechanical methods for reasoning about behavior (of finite state systems) generally rely on some form of exhaustive state-space search to generate all the possible behaviors. These methods are thus susceptible to state explosion: the number of global states of a concurrent system consisting of n components, each with $O(l)$ local states, is in $O(l^n)$. Approaches to dealing with state explosion include compositional verification [29, 18, 13, 9, 8, 25] (and the strongly related assume-guarantee reasoning [1, 20]), abstraction [30, 12, 23, 24], and symmetry reduction [15, 16, 11, 10].

Current methods typically rely on defining finite-state "behavioral" automata that express state changes. The automata-theoretic product of the behavioral automata of two components will then describe the resulting behavior when these two components are connected. Thus, the two components can be checked for compatibility by model checking this product. When a third component is subsequently connected to the first two, one then needs to generate the product of all three behavioral automata. Thus, this fails to provide a practical method for checking large systems, since taking the product of n automata incurs state explosion.

2.2 Avoiding State-Explosion by Pair-Wise Composition

To overcome state-explosion, we eschew the computation of the product of all n behavioral automata. Instead, we compute the products of *pairs* of behavioral automata, corresponding to the pairs of components that interact directly.[1] In the worst case, where all components interact (where the largest component has $O(l)$ local states), this has complexity $O(n^2l^2)$. This low polynomial complexity means that our method scales up to large systems. We verify temporal behavior "pair-properties" of these "pair-products." These give us properties of the interactions of all component-pairs, when considered in isolation. We then combine such "pair-properties" to deduce global properties of the entire system by means of temporal logic deductive systems [17]. Since the pair-properties embody the complexity of the component interaction, this deductive part of the verification is quite short.

Our approach involves abstraction in going from a component to its behavioral automaton. It applies even when all components are functionally different, and so is not a form of symmetry reduction. Our approach combines pair-properties verified of each pair-product to deduce the required global properties. Each pair-product represents two components *interacting in isolation*. Our approach therefore does not involve the usual "assume-guarantee" proof rule typical of compositional approaches, where each component is verified correct using the assumption that the other components are correct, with due care taken to avoid cyclic reasoning.

[1] For clarity, we assume all connectors involve exactly two components. The methodology can be easily generalized to verify connectors between multiple components.

The main insight of this paper is that components can be designed to enable this pair-wise verification, thus supporting behavioral compatibility checks that scale up to large complex systems [7].

3 Technical Preliminaries

I/O automata We augment the standard definition of I/O automata [31] to accommodate propositional labelings of states. An *augmented input/output (I/O) automaton* A is a tuple

$$\langle states(A), start(A), sig(A), steps(A), prop(A), label(A)\rangle$$

as follows. $states(A)$ is a set of states; $start(A) \subseteq states(A)$ is a nonempty set of start states; $sig(A) = (in(A), out(A), int(A))$ is an action signature, where $in(A)$, $out(A)$ and $int(A)$ are pair-wise disjoint sets of input, output, and internal actions, respectively, (let $acts(A) = in(A) \cup out(A) \cup int(A)$); $steps(A) \subseteq states(A) \times acts(A) \times states(A)$ is a transition relation; $prop(A)$ is a set of atomic propositions; and $label(A) : states(A) \mapsto 2^{prop(A)}$ is a labeling function. If $states(A)$, $acts(A)$ and $prop(A)$ are all finite, then A is a *finite-state* I/O automaton. $label(A)(s)$ gives the atomic propositions that are true in state s.

Let $s, s', u, u', \ldots$ range over states and $a, b, \ldots$ range over actions. Write $s \xrightarrow{a}_A s'$ iff $(s, a, s') \in steps(A)$. We say that a is *enabled* in s. Otherwise a is *disabled* in s. I/O automata are required to be *input enabled*: every input action is enabled in every state. An *execution fragment* α of automaton A is an alternating sequence of states and actions $s_0 a_1 s_1 a_2 s_2 \ldots$ such that $(s_i, a_{i+1}, s_{i+1}) \in steps(A)$ for all $i \geq 0$, i.e., α conforms to the transition relation of A. Furthermore, if α is finite then it ends in a state. An *execution* of A is an execution fragment that begins with a state in $start(A)$. $execs(A)$ is the set of all executions of A. A state of A is *reachable* iff it occurs in some execution of A. Two I/O automata are *compatible* iff they have no output actions and no atomic propositions in common, and no internal action of one is an action of the other. A set of I/O automata is compatible iff every pair of automata in the set is compatible.

Definition 1 (Parallel Composition of I/O automata). *Let $A_1, \ldots, A_n$, be compatible I/O Automata. Then $A = A_1 \parallel \cdots \parallel A_n$ is the I/O automaton[2] defined as follows. $states(A) = states(A_1) \times \cdots \times states(A_n)$; $start(A) = start(A_1) \times \cdots \times start(A_n)$; $sig(A) = (in(A), out(A), int(A))$ where $out(A) = \bigcup_{1 \leq i \leq n} out(A_i)$, $in(A) = \bigcup_{1 \leq i \leq n} in(A_i) - out(A)$, $int(A) = \bigcup_{1 \leq i \leq n} int(A_i)$; $steps(A) \subseteq states(A) \times acts(A) \times states(A)$ consists of all the triples $(\langle s_1, \ldots, s_n\rangle, a, \langle t_1, \ldots, t_n\rangle)$ such that $\forall i \in \{1, \ldots, n\}$: if $a \in acts(A_i)$, then $(s_i, a, t_i) \in steps(A_i)$, otherwise $s_i = t_i$; $prop(A) = \bigcup_{1 \leq i \leq n} prop(A_i)$; and $label(A)(\langle s_1, \ldots, s_n\rangle) = \bigcup_{1 \leq i \leq n} label(A_i)(s_i)$.*

[2] Formally, A is a state-machine. It is easy to show, though, that A is in fact an I/O automaton.

Let $A = A_1 \| \cdots \| A_n$ be a parallel composition of n I/O automata. Let s be a state of A. Then $s \lceil A_i$ denotes the i'th component of s, i.e., the component of s that gives the local state of A_i, $i \in \{1, \ldots, n\}$. Let $\varphi = \{i_1, \ldots, i_m\} \subseteq \{1, \ldots, n\}$. Then $s \lceil A_\varphi$ denotes the tuple $\langle s_j \lceil A_{i_1}, \ldots s_j \lceil A_{i_m} \rangle$. A *s*ubsystem of A is a parallel composition $A_{i_1} \| \cdots \| A_{i_m}$, where $\{i_1, \ldots, i_m\} \subseteq \{1, \ldots, n\}$. We define the projection of an execution of A onto a subsystem of A in the usual way: the state components for all automata other than $A_{i_1}, \ldots, A_{i_m}$ are removed, and so are all actions in which none of the $A_{i_1}, \ldots, A_{i_m}$ participate:

Definition 2 (Execution projection). *Let $A = A_1 \| \cdots \| A_n$ be an I/O automaton. Let $\alpha = s_0 a_1 s_1 a_2 s_2 \ldots s_{j-1} a_j s_j \ldots$ be an execution of A. Let $\varphi = \{i_1, \ldots, i_m\} \subseteq \{1, \ldots, n\}$, and let $A_\varphi = A_{i_1} \| \cdots \| A_{i_m}$. We define $\alpha \lceil A_\varphi$ as the sequence resulting from removing all $a_j s_j$ such that $a_j \notin acts(A_\varphi)$ and replacing each s_j by $s_j \lceil A_\varphi$.*

Proposition 1 (Execution projection). *Let $A = A_1 \| \cdots \| A_n$ be an I/O automaton. Let $\alpha \in execs(A)$. Let $\varphi = \{i_1, \ldots, i_m\} \subseteq \{1, \ldots, n\}$, and let $A_\varphi = A_{i_1} \| \cdots \| A_{i_m}$. Then $\alpha \lceil A_\varphi \in execs(A_\varphi)$.*

Proof. Immediate from the standard execution projection result for I/O automata [31], when considering the subsystem A_φ as a single I/O automaton.

4 Formal Methods for Composition Correctness

Attie and Emerson [4, 5] present a temporal logic synthesis method for shared memory programs that avoids exhaustive state-space search. Rather than deal with the behavior of the program as a whole, the method instead generates the interactions between processes *one pair at a time*. Thus, for every pair of processes that interact, a *pair-machine* is constructed that gives their interaction. Since the pair-machines are small ($O(l^2)$), they can be built using exhaustive methods. A *pair-program* can then be extracted from the pair-machine. The final program is generated by a syntactic composition of all the pair-programs.

Here, we extend this method to the I/O automaton [31] model, which is *event-based*. Unlike [4, 5], which imposed syntactic restrictions (variables must be shared pairwise), the method presented here can be applied to any component-based system expressed in the I/O automaton notation. It is straightforward to extend the results presented here to any event-based formalism with a well-defined notion of composition.

The method of [4] is *synthetic*: for each interacting pair, the problem specification gives a formula that specifies their interaction, and that is used to synthesize the corresponding pair-machine. We also consider the *analytic* use of the pair-wise method: if a program is given, e.g., by manual design, then generate the pair-machine by taking the concurrent composition of the components one pair at a time. The pair-machines can then be model-checked for the required conformance to the specification. If the pair-machines behave as required, then we can deduce that the overall program is correct.

In our method, the desired safety and liveness properties are automatically verified (e.g., by model checking) in pair systems and the correctness of the whole system deduced from the correctness of these pair systems. We start with formally proving the propagation of safety and liveness properties from pair systems to the large system. We use propositional linear-time temporal logic [33, 17] without the nexttime modality (LTL-X), and with weak action fairness, to specify properties. LTL-X formulae are built up from atomic propositions, boolean connectives, and the temporal modality U (strong until). LTL-X semantics is given by the $\models$ relation, which is defined by induction on LTL-X formula structure. Let $\alpha = s_0 a_1 s_1 a_2 s_2 \ldots$ be an infinite execution fragment of A, $\alpha^i = s_i a_{i+1} s_{i+1} a_{i+2} s_{i+2} \ldots$, a suffix of α, and p be an atomic proposition. Then $A, \alpha \models p$ iff $p \in \mathit{label}(A)(s_0)$, and $A, \alpha \models f \mathsf{U} g$ iff $\exists i \geq 0 : A, \alpha^i \models g$ and $\forall j \in \{0, \ldots, i-1\} : A, \alpha^j \models f$. We define the abbreviations $\mathsf{F} f = \mathbf{true} \mathsf{U} f$ ("eventually"), $\mathsf{G} f = \neg \mathsf{F} \neg f$ ("always"), $f \mathsf{U_w} g = (f \mathsf{U} g) \vee \mathsf{G} f$ ("weak until"), and $\overset{\infty}{\mathsf{F}} f = \mathsf{GF} f$ ("infinitely often").

Fairness constraints allow us to filter away irrelevant executions. We use weak action fairness: an execution fragment α of A is fair iff it is infinite and every action of A is either infinitely often executed along α or infinitely often disabled along α. Define $A, s \models_\Phi f$ iff f holds along all fair execution fragments of A starting in s, and $A \models f$ iff f holds along all fair executions of A.

Let $A = A_1 \parallel \cdots \parallel A_n$ be the large system, and let $A_{ij} = A_i \parallel A_j$ be a pair-system of A, where $i, j \in \{1, \ldots, n\}, i \neq j$. Then, if $A_{ij} \models_\Phi f_{ij}$ for some LTL-X formula f_{ij} whose atomic propositions are all drawn from $\mathit{prop}(A_{ij})$, we would like to also conclude $A \models_\Phi f_{ij}$. For safety properties, this follows from execution projection. For liveness properties, we need something more, since the projection of an infinite execution of A onto A_{ij} could be a finite execution of A_{ij}, and so the liveness property in question may not be satisfied along this finite projection, while it is satisfied along all the infinite extensions. We therefore require that along an infinite global execution α, for every pair-system A_{ij}, an action involving A_{ij} occurs infinitely often along α. Write $A, \alpha \models \overset{\infty}{\mathsf{F}} ex(A_{ij})$ iff α contains infinitely many actions in which A_i or A_j or both participate in (this implies that α is infinite). Write $A, s \models_\Phi \overset{\infty}{\mathsf{F}} ex(A_{ij})$ iff for every infinite fair execution α starting in s: $A, \alpha \models \overset{\infty}{\mathsf{F}} ex(A_{ij})$. If $s = \langle s_1, \ldots, s_n \rangle$ is a state of A, then define $s{\restriction}ij = \langle s_i, s_j \rangle$, i.e., $s{\restriction}ij$ is the projection of s onto the pair-system A_{ij}.

Theorem 1. *Let $A = A_1 \parallel \cdots \parallel A_n$ be an I/O automaton. Let $i, j \in \{1, \ldots, n\}$, $i \neq j$, and let $A_{ij} = A_i \parallel A_j$. Assume that $A, u \models \overset{\infty}{\mathsf{F}} ex(A_{ij})$ for every start state u of A. Let s be a reachable state of A, and let f_{ij} be an LTL-X formula over $\mathit{prop}(A_{ij})$. Then*

$$A_{ij}, s{\restriction}ij \models_\Phi f_{ij} \ \textit{ implies } \ A, s \models_\Phi f_{ij}.$$

The proof of Theorem 1 is available in the full version of the paper.[3] By applying the above result to all pair-programs, we obtain:

$$\bigwedge_{ij}(A_{ij} \models_\Phi f_{ij}) \text{ implies } A \models_\Phi \bigwedge_{ij} f_{ij}.$$

We then show that the conjunction $\bigwedge_{ij} f_{ij}$ of all the pair-properties implies the required global correctness property f, i.e., $(\bigwedge_{ij} f_{ij}) \Rightarrow f$. This leads to the following rule of inference:

$$\frac{\bigwedge_{ij}(A_{ij} \models_\Phi f_{ij}) \qquad (\bigwedge_{ij} f_{ij}) \Rightarrow f}{A \models_\Phi f}.$$

4.1 Characterizing the Global Properties That Can Be Verified

A natural question that arises is: how much verification power do we give up by the restriction to pairs? Are there interesting global properties that cannot be verified using our approach?

Let e_i $(i \geq 1)$ denote an event, i.e., the execution of an action. Let $part(e_i)$ denote the components that participate in e_i. With respect to safety, we consider event ordering, i.e., $e_1 < e_n$, meaning that if e_1 and e_n both occur, then e_1 occurs before e_n. This can be verified by finding events $e_2, \ldots, e_{n_1}$ such that, for all $i = 1, \ldots, n-1$, $e_i < e_{i+1}$ can be verified in some pair. That is, there exist components $A \in part(e_i)$, $A' \in part(e_{i+1})$, and $A \parallel A'$ is a pair system that satisfies $e_i < e_{i+1}$. With respect to liveness, we consider leads-to properties, i.e., $e_1 \leadsto e_n$, meaning that if e_1 occurs, then e_n subsequently occurs. This can be verified by a similar strategy as outlined above for $e_1 < e_n$. Event ordering is sufficiently powerful to express many safety properties of interest, including mutual exclusion, FIFO, and priority. Leads-to is sufficiently powerful to express many liveness properties of interest, including absence of starvation and response to requests for service.

More generally, any global property that can be expressed by an LTL formula f which is deducible from pair-formulae f_{ij} can be verified. A topic of future work is to characterize this class of LTL formulae exactly.

4.2 Behavioral Automaton of a Component

A behavioral automaton of a component expresses some aspects of that components run-time (i.e., temporal) behavior. Depending on how much information about temporal behavior is included in the automaton, there is a spectrum of state information ranging from a "maximal" behavioral automaton for the component (which includes every transition the component makes, even internal ones), to a trivial automaton consisting of a single state. Thus, any behavioral automaton for a component can be regarded as a homomorphic image of the maximal automaton. This spectrum refines the traditional white-box/black-box

[3] `http://www.cs.virginia.edu/~lorenz/papers/cbse06/`

Table 1. The interoperability space for components

Compatibility:	Interface	Automaton	Behavioral
Export	interface	interface + automaton	complete code
Reuse	black box	adjustable	white box
Encapsulation	highest	adjustable	lowest
Interoperability	unsafe	adjustable	safe
Time complexity	linear	polynomial for finite state	undecidable
Assembly properties	none	provable from pair properties	complete but impractical
Assembly behavior	none	synthesizable from pair-wise behavior	complete but impractical

spectrum of component reuse, ranging from exporting the complete source code (maximal automaton) of the component—white-box, to exporting just the interface (trivial automaton)—black box. Table 1 displays this spectrum.

The behavioral automaton can be provided by the component designer and verified by the compiler (just like typed interfaces are) using techniques such as abstraction mappings and model-checking. Verification is necessary to ensure the correctness of the behavioral automaton, i.e., that it is truly a homomorphic image of the maximal automaton. Alternatively, the component compiler can generate a behavioral automaton from the code, using, for example, abstract interpretation or machine learning [32]. In this case, the behavioral automaton will be correct by construction. We assume the behavioral automaton for third party components is provided by the component designer.

4.3 Behavioral Properties of a Pair-Program

In general, we are interested in behavioral properties that are expressed over many components at once. We infer such properties from the verified pair-properties. Such inference can be carried out, for example, in a suitable deductive system for temporal logic. The third-party assembler would have to specify the pair-properties and the pairs of interacting components and then carry out the deduction.

It is usually the case that the pairs of interacting processes are easily identifiable just based on the nature of process interactions in a distributed system. For example, in mutual exclusion, a pair-program is two arbitrary processes; in the elevator example the pair-program involves a floor component and an elevator controller component. Sometimes pair-properties to be verified are the same as the global specification, just projected onto a pair. For example, in mutual exclusion, the global property is just the quantification over all pairs of the pair-property given for some arbitrary processes i and j, i.e., $\bigwedge_{ij} \mathsf{G}\neg(C_i \wedge C_j)$, where C_i is a state of a process P_i corresponding to this process being in the critical section.

However, sometimes pair-properties are not straightforward projections of the required global properties. These pair-properties have to be derived manually.

Then we have to prove that the conjunction of these pair-properties implies the global specification by the means of temporal logic deductive systems [17]. These proofs are usually quite small (e.g., 27 lines for the elevator example) and straightforward.

4.4 Verification of Behavioral Properties of the Large Program

At the verification stage the component assembler would have to choose a model-checker which he plans to do verification in, then provide to the model-checker a description of a behavioral automaton of the pair-program and the pair-properties in a suitable format. If verification is successful then the pair-properties hold in the global program and, as proven during the assembly phase, conjunction of these pair-properties implies the global property of the program. If verification is not successful then the third party assembler would have to either swap in a different component and repeat verification process or change the global property to be verified.

5 Implementation: Pair-Wise Component Builder

We now describe the working of a pairwise verification methodology in a *pair-wise component builder* tool. This tool allows for interactive component design and pair-wise verification. The pair-wise builder is based on Sun's Bean Development Kit (BDK) and the ContextBox [27, 26] software. Verification is done using the Spin model-checker [21] that uses LTL as a specification language and Promela as a modeling language. The goal is to provide the user with a list of design recommendations that should be considered when developing components in order to be able to use the tool for the subsequent component composition and verification.

A builder is used for creating a compound component out of subcomponents. The builder hence has two main functions:

- governing the connecting activity and dealing with problems of *interoperability*; and
- *encapsulating* the assembled components into the compound component.

Traditionally, builders focus on interoperability in the restricted sense of only considering interface compatibility, and support for system behavior prediction [14] is not available. In our framework, behavioral compatibility can also be checked. Hence, within our framework we implement a stronger notion of a builder, which, in addition to interface compatibility, can also deal with:

- *temporal behavior of connectors*, since we accommodate a stronger notion of interoperability, which encompasses both the interface between components and the temporal behavior of their connection (i.e., pair-properties), and
- *global temporal behavior*, that is, the temporal behavior of the assembled system. The deductive proofs that infer such properties of this global behavior from the known pair-properties are carried out within the builder.

For a component to be pair-wise composable in our builder, one takes the following steps. The component interface must be a collection of separate interfaces, each interface addressing a related connector. This corresponds to a JavaBeans component implementing several event listener interfaces, but does not need to be necessarily fine grained. This interface separation enables capturing only interface information relevant to a pair-system, which is model-checked during third-party assembly.

The inputs to our builder tool are components that have separate interfaces per connector. In the BDK this corresponds to a component's BeanInfo having a list of named operations that can be invoked by events. These functions are grouped and labeled according to components whose events this component subscribes to. Pair-wise composable components, as part of their BeanInfo, also have a high level description in Promela of their behavioral automata. The components are connected in the builder. As a result, relevant changes are made to their state machines to reflect components subscribing to each others events (i.e., Promela code of a pair-program is generated based on the interfaces and the behavioral automata of the pair).

Depending on component assembly, the user specifies properties of the model (as LTL formulae) that she wishes to verify. Properties can be over a single component or over a pair of components that were connected. The builder communicates the LTL specification and the generated Promela description of the pair-program to the Spin interface. Then Spin model-checks the LTL formulae. Since model checking is over pair-systems, it is efficient. If violation of a property is detected, the user can modify either (1) the component, or (2) the component system design or (3) the properties, and then repeat the process.

6 Case Study: Elevator System

We now present a case study of a component-based algorithm that was pair-wise verified using our pair-wise component builder. This component-based elevator algorithm was implemented with a collection of interfaces to enable pair-wise verification. The elevator model consists of four types of components: *floor components* (numbered 1 to N), *panel button components*, the *user component*, and the *controller component*. The controller component (*controller*) represents the elevator, and hence implements the elevator's movement. Each floor component (*floor(f)*) represents a specific floor and maintains information about the floor and requests for this floor. Each panel button component (*panelbutton(f)*) represents a specific panel button inside an elevator. The events that floor components and controller component listen to (up requests and down requests for each floor) are generated by the user component (*user*) and by the buttons on the panel from inside the elevator.

6.1 Informal Description

When moving upwards, the elevator controller satisfies requests in the upwards direction up to where it perceives the uppermost currently outstanding request

to be, where this can be a panel request or a floor request in either direction. The elevator then reverses its direction and proceeds to satisfy the requests in the downwards direction until reaching what it perceives to be the lowermost currently outstanding request, then reverses again, etc. As the elevator passes floor f, it checks in with the *floor(f)* controller to determine if it needs to stop floor f due to an outstanding request in the direction of its movement, and stops if *floor(f)* so indicates. The *controller* maintains the following information.
Controller (elevator cabin):

`int g`—current elevator location
`int top`—the uppermost requested floor, set to 0 when this floor is reached
`int bottom`—the lowermost requested floor, set to 0 when this floor is reached
`boolean up`—true if the direction of the elevator movement is up, false if down
`boolean stop`—true if the elevator is not moving

Upon reaching the uppermost (lowermost) requested floor, the controller sets `top` (`bottom`) to 0, which is an invalid floor number. This indicates that the uppermost (lowermost) request currently known to the controller has been satisfied.

When a request for floor f is issued, an event is sent to the *floor(f)* component, where records the request, and also to the controller, which updates its `top` and `bottom` variables if necessary.

There are N floor components. Each floor component's state captures whether floor f is requested in either direction.
Floor(f), ($f = 1, \ldots, N$):

`bool up(f)`—true if the floor is requested for a stop in the upwards direction
`bool down(f)`—true if the floor is requested for a stop in the downwards direction

There are three types of event generators (button up at the floor, button down at the floor, floor number button on the panel), but only two event types (requests) are generated.

down button pushed at a floor$f$ generates a `downwards(f)` request.
up button pushed at a floor f generates an `upwards(f)` request.
floor f pushed on the panel inside an elevator, generates either a `upwards(f)` or `downwards(f)` request based on the elevator position.

The `upwards(f)` and `downwards(f)` events are randomly generated by a user component and N separate panel-button components that implement the panel buttons. The correctness of the algorithm obviously depends on correct maintenance of the `top` and `bottom` variables so that none of the requests are lost. It is important to update these variables not only when the new requests are issued but also to make sure they get reset after being reached, so that no subsequent requests are lost. Our update algorithm guarantees that all the requests are taken into account (only once).

6.2 Specification

There are two requirements that the elevator model must satisfy. (1) Safety: an elevator does not attempt to change direction without stopping first, since this would damage the motor, and (2) Liveness: every request for service is eventually satisfied

When connecting the controller component to the floor component, the builder would typically generate a CommandListener adapter, which subscribes to request events, so when an upwards request event is received from the floor, it invokes the up method of the controller. Now, the motor, due to physical constraints, cannot be switched from going up to going down without stopping first. Builders in current systems would not detect if the request sequence violated this constraint, and consequently the motor could be damaged at runtime. The safety property that we verified is the following:

If the elevator is moving up (down) then it continues doing so until it stops. The LTL formula for this is:

$$\mathsf{G}(\texttt{up} \Rightarrow \texttt{up}\mathsf{U}_\mathsf{w}\texttt{stop}) \;\wedge\; \mathsf{G}(\neg\texttt{up} \Rightarrow (\neg\texttt{up})\mathsf{U}_\mathsf{w}\texttt{stop}) \tag{1}$$

Where `boolean up` indicates direction of elevator movement and `boolean stop` indicates whether the elevator is moving or not. Recall that G is the "always" modality: $\mathsf{G}p$ means that p holds in all states from the current one onwards. U_w is "weak until": either p holds from now on, or q eventually holds, and p holds until then. This property can be verified by checking the controller alone, and so is not challenging, since the controller by itself has only a small number of states.

The interesting property that we verified is liveness: if a request is issued, it is eventually satisfied. The LTL formulae for this are:

$$\mathsf{G}(\texttt{up(f)} \Rightarrow \mathsf{F}(\texttt{g} = \texttt{f} \wedge \texttt{stop} \wedge \texttt{up})) \tag{2}$$

$$\mathsf{G}(\texttt{down(f)} \Rightarrow \mathsf{F}(\texttt{g} = \texttt{f} \wedge \texttt{stop} \wedge \neg\texttt{up})) \tag{3}$$

Where `g` is the elevator location variable and `f` is the number of the requested floor; `up(f)` and `down(f)` indicate request for floor f in a certain direction. $\mathsf{F}p$ means that p eventually holds.

6.3 Model-Checking

Our interconnection scheme enables the separation of the state spaces of the various components. Instead of constructing the global product automaton of N *floor components*, the *user component*, N *panel buttons*, and the *controller component* in the elevator system, we only construct N different *pair-machines*, and model-check each pair-machine separately. A *pair-machine* consists of a *controller component* and a single *floor component*, for each floor. We can then verify behavioral properties of each of these pair-machines in isolation, and then combine these properties deductively to obtain properties of the overall system.

Safety. Safety is a property local to the *controller component*, hence, it can be verified within the component. Since the *controller component* was model-checked in isolation, we needed to ensure that we are model-checking it in a correct environment (i.e., random request sequences). This is done through *input-enabledness* of the behavioral automaton. This ensures that if there is a transition that depends on the input from some other component we replace this transition by a set of transitions that embody all the possible input values from the other component (i.e., one transition per input value). The *controller component* non-deterministically chooses one of these transitions. During model-checking such input-enabledness creates an environment that produces the same execution traces as the product behavioral automaton of the two components. However, we avoid the extra states that would have been contributed by the second component that are unnecessary for this verification confined only to this component.

Liveness. We verified that liveness holds in our model by checking the model against the LTL formula (2). We verified liveness in the model with various number of floors N. This amounted to model-checking a system with N *floor(f)*, N *panelbutton(f)*, 1 *controller*, and 1 *user.*

To achieve pair-wise verification we needed to decompose the liveness property into pair-properties. Our pair consisted of a controller component and a floor component, where our pair-model was input-enabled for the input coming from other components. The pair-properties were manually derived for this pair-program. The global liveness property (the LTL formulae (2, 3)) of a system as a whole was deduced from the conjunction of the following pair-properties. These pair-properties were checked for each of N pairs *controller* $\|$ *floor(f)*. Define $p \leadsto q = \mathsf{G}(p \Rightarrow \mathsf{F}q)$.

When request is issued, it gets processed by the controller:
(p 1.1) $up(f) \leadsto top \geq f \bigwedge up(f) \bigwedge bottom \leq f$
(p 1.2) $down(f) \leadsto top \geq f \bigwedge down(f) \bigwedge bottom \leq f$

The *controller* actually moves up or down without changing its direction:
(p 2.1) $(g = g_0 < f \bigwedge up(f) \bigwedge up \bigwedge bottom \leq f \leq top) \leadsto$
$(g = g_0 + 1 \leq f \bigwedge up(f) \bigwedge up \bigwedge bottom \leq f \leq top)$
(p 2.2) $(g = g_0 \geq f \bigwedge up(f) \bigwedge \neg up \bigwedge bottom \leq f \leq top) \leadsto$
$(g = g_0 - 1 \leq f \bigwedge up(f) \bigwedge \neg up \bigwedge bottom \leq f \leq top)$
(p 2.3) $(g = g_0 < f \bigwedge down(f) \bigwedge up \bigwedge bottom \leq f \leq top) \leadsto$
$(g = g_0 + 1 \leq f \bigwedge down(f) \bigwedge up \bigwedge bottom \leq f \leq top)$
(p 2.4) $(g = g_0 \geq f \bigwedge down(f) \bigwedge \neg up \bigwedge bottom \leq f \leq top) \leadsto$
$(g = g_0 - 1 \leq f \bigwedge down(f) \bigwedge \neg up \bigwedge bottom \leq f \leq top)$

The *controller* stops once reaching the requested floor:
(p 3.1) $(up(f) \bigwedge up \bigwedge g = f) \leadsto (stop \bigwedge g = f \bigwedge \neg up(f))$
(p 3.2) $(down(f) \bigwedge \neg up \bigwedge g = f) \leadsto (stop \bigwedge g = f \bigwedge \neg down(f))$

The *controller* reverses direction at the top and the bottom:

(p 4.1) $(g = bottom \bigwedge up(f) \bigwedge \neg up \bigwedge bottom \leq f < top) \leadsto$
$(g = bottom \bigwedge up(f) \bigwedge up \bigwedge bottom \leq f \leq top)$

(p 4.2) $(g = top \bigwedge up(f) \bigwedge up \bigwedge bottom \leq f \leq top) \leadsto$
$(g = top \bigwedge up(f) \bigwedge \neg up \bigwedge bottom \leq f \leq top)$

(p 4.3) $(g = bottom \bigwedge down(f) \bigwedge \neg up \bigwedge bottom \leq f \leq top) \leadsto$
$(g = bottom \bigwedge down(f) \bigwedge up \bigwedge bottom \leq f \leq top)$

(p 4.4) $(g = top \bigwedge down(f) \bigwedge up \bigwedge bottom \leq f \leq top) \leadsto$
$(g = top \bigwedge down(f) \bigwedge \neg up \bigwedge bottom \leq f \leq top)$

Boundary (efficiency) condition

(p 5) $\mathsf{G}(bottom \leq g \leq top)$

6.4 Verification Results

We constructed models with $N = 3, 5, 7, 9, 10, 12, 30, 100$, where N is the number of floors. The systems were model-checked as a whole system and pair-wise.[4] The number of states in a whole system grew too large for Spin to model-check above $N = 10$. On the other hand, model-checking pair-wise was achieved up to $N = 100$ without experiencing exponential blow up. In the verification results (Table 2), "number of transitions" is the number of transitions explored in the search. This is indicative of the amount of work performed in model-checking the given properties, for the given value of N. Pair-wise model checking first suffers from some overhead due to the Spin model representation for $N \leq 10$, and then shows a polynomial increase in N, as expected from the theoretical analysis.

Table 2. Spin model-checking performace for an elevator system

Number of Floors (N)	Whole system		Pair-wise	
	# Transitions	Run Time	# Transitions	Run Time
3	3.6×10^8	45	4.6×10^3	1
5	5.6×10^8	74	5.1×10^4	1
7	7.6×10^8	121	2.4×10^5	1
9	9.4×10^8	169	7.7×10^5	1
10	8.9×10^8	170	1.2×10^6	1
12	N/A	N/A	2.9×10^6	1
30	N/A	N/A	1.9×10^8	8
100	N/A	N/A	1.9×10^9	109

7 Conclusion and Related Work

Component-based systems are widely acknowledged as a promising approach to constructing large-scale complex software systems. A key requirement of a

[4] 1.7 GHz with 8Gb of RAM.

successful methodology for assembling such systems is to ensure the behavioral compatibility of the components with each other. This paper presented a first step towards a *practical* method for achieving this.

We have presented a methodology for designing components so that they can be composed in a pair-wise manner, and their temporal behavior properties verified without state-explosion. Components are only required to have interface separation per connector to enable disentanglement of intercomponent communication and specification of the externally visible behavior of each component as a behavioral automaton.

Vanderperren and Wydaeghe [40, 35, 39, 36, 37] have developed a component composition tool (PascoWire) for JavaBeans that employs automata-theoretic techniques to verify behavioral automata. They acknowledge that the practicality of their method is limited by state-explosion. Incorporating our technique with their system is an avenue for future work.

DeAlfaro and Henzinger [2] have defined a notion of interface automaton, and have developed a method for mechanically verify temporal behavior properties of component-based systems expressed in their formalism. Unfortunately, their method computes the automata-theoretic product of all of the interface automata in the system, and is thus subject to state-explosion.

Our approach is a promising direction in overcoming state-explosion. In addition to the elevator problem, the pairwise approach has been applied successfully to the two-phase commit problem [5], the dining and drinking philosophers problems [4], an eventually serializable data service [6] and a fault-tolerant distributed shared memory [3]. Release of the pair-wise component builder will contribute to the ease of the exploitation of our methodology and its subsequent application.

References

[1] Abadi, M., Lamport, L.: Composing specifications. ACM Transactions on Programming Languages and Systems **15**(1) (1993) 73–132

[2] de Alfaro, L., Henzinger, T.A.: Interface automata. (2001) In *Proceedings of the 9th Annual Symposium on Foundations of Software Engineering (FSE)*, pages 109–120. ACM.

[3] Attie, P.C., Chockler, H.: Automatic verification of fault-tolerant register emulations. In: Proceedings of the Infinity 2005 workshop. (2005)

[4] Attie, P.C., Emerson, E.A.: Synthesis of concurrent systems with many similar processes. ACM Transactions on Programming Languages and Systems **20**(1) (1998) 51–115

[5] Attie, P.C.: Synthesis of large concurrent programs via pairwise composition. In: CONCUR'99: 10th International Conference on Concurrency Theory. Number 1664 in Lecture Notes in Computer Science, Springer-Verlag (1999)

[6] Attie, P.C.: Synthesis of large dynamic concurrent programs from dynamic specifications. Technical report, American University of Beirut (2005) Available at `http://www.cs.aub.edu.lb/pa07/files/pubs.html`.

[7] Attie, P.C., Lorenz, D.H.: Correctness of model-based component composition without state explosion. In: ECOOP 2003 Workshop on Correctness of Model-based Software Composition. (2003)

[8] Cheung, S., Giannakopoulou, D., Kramer, J.: Verification of liveness properties in compositional reachability analysis. In: 5th ACM SIGSOFT Symposium on the Foundations of Software Engineering / 6th European Software Engineering Conference (FSE / ESEC '97), Zurich (1997)

[9] Cheung, S., Kramer, J.: Checking subsystem safety properties in compositional reachability analysis. In: Proceedings of the 18th International Conference on Software Engineering, Berlin, Germany, ICSE 1996, IEEE Computer Society (1996)

[10] Clarke, E., Enders, R., Filkorn, T., Jha, S.: Exploiting symmetry in temporal logic model checking. Formal Methods in System Design **9**(2) (1996)

[11] Clarke, E.M., Filkorn, T., Jha, S.: Exploiting symmetry in temporal logic model checking. In: Proceedings of the 5th International Conference on Computer Aided Verification. Number 697 in LNCS, Berlin, Springer-Verlag (1993) 450–462

[12] Clarke, E., Grumberg, O., Long, D.: Model checking and abstraction. ACM Transactions on Programming Languages and Systems **16**(5) (1994) 1512–1542

[13] Clarke, E.M., Long, D., McMillan, K.L.: Compositional model checking. In: Proceedings of the 4th IEEE Symposium on Logic in Computer Science, New York, IEEE (1989)

[14] Crnkovic, I., Schmidt, H., Stafford, J., Wallnau, K., eds.: Proceedings of the 4th ICSE Workshop on Component-Based Software Engineering: Component Certification and System Prediction, Toronto, Canada, IEEE Computer Society (2001)

[15] Emerson, E.A., Sistla, A.P.: Symmetry and model checking. In: Proceedings of the 5th International Conference on Computer Aided Verification. Number 697 in Lecture Notes in Computer Science, Berlin, Springer-Verlag (1993) 463–477

[16] Emerson, E.A., Sistla, A.P.: Symmetry and model checking. Formal Methods in System Design: An International Journal **9**(1/2) (1996) 105–131

[17] Emerson, E.A.: Temporal and modal logic. In Leeuwen, J.V., ed.: Handbook of Theoretical Computer Science. Volume B, *Formal Models and Semantics.* The MIT Press/Elsevier, Cambridge, Mass. (1990)

[18] Grumberg, O., Long, D.: Model checking and modular verification. ACM Transactions on Programming Languages and Systems **16**(3) (1994) 843–871

[19] Heineman, G.T., Councill, W.T., eds.: Component-Based Software Engineering: Putting the Pieces Together. Addison-Wesley (2001)

[20] Henzinger, T.A., Qadeer, S., Rajamani, S.K.: You assume, we guarantee: Methodology and case studies. In: Proceedings of the 10th International Conference on Computer-Aided Verification (CAV). (1998)

[21] Holzmann, G.J.: The SPIN Model Checker. Addison Wesley, San Francisco, California, USA (2003)

[22] Proceedings of the 23rd International Conference on Software Engineering, Toronto, Canada, ICSE 2001, IEEE Computer Society (2001)

[23] Kesten, Y., Pnueli, A.: Verification by augmented finitary abstraction. Information and Computation **163**(1) (2000) 203–243

[24] Kesten, Y., Pnueli, A., Vardi, M.Y.: Verification by augmented abstraction: The automata-theoretic view. Journal of Computer and System Sciences **62**(4) (2001) 668–690

[25] Lamport, L.: Composition: A way to make proofs harder. In de Roever, W.P., Langmaack, H., Pnueli, A., eds.: Compositionality: The Significant Difference (Proceedings of the COMPOS'97 Symposium). Number 1536 in Lecture Notes in Computer Science, Bad Malente, Germany, Springer Verlag (1998) 402–423

[26] Lorenz, D.H., Petkovic, P.: ContextBox: A visual builder for context beans (extended abstract). In: Proceedings of the 15th Annual Conference on Object-Oriented Programming Systems, Languages, and Applications, Minneapolis, Minnesota, OOPSLA'00, ACM SIGPLAN Notices (2000) 75–76

[27] Lorenz, D.H., Petkovic, P.: Design-time assembly of runtime containment components. In Li, Q., Firesmith, D., Riehle, R., Pour, G., Meyer, B., eds.: Proceedings of the 34th International Conference on Technology of Object-Oriented Languages and Systems, Santa Barbara, CA, IEEE Computer Society (2000) 195–204

[28] Lorenz, D.H., Vlissides, J.: Designing components versus objects: A transformational approach. In: ICSE 2001 [22] 253–262

[29] Lynch, N., Tuttle, M.: An introduction to input/output automata. CWI-Quarterly **2**(3) Centrum voor Wiskunde en Informatica, Amsterdam, The Netherlands (1989) 219–246

[30] Lynch, N., Vaandrager, F.: Forward and backward simulations — part I: Untimed systems. Information and Computation **121**(2) (1995) 214–233

[31] Lynch, N.A.: Distributed Algorithms. Morgan-Kaufmann, San Francisco, California, USA (1996)

[32] Mäkinen, E., Systä, T.: MAS - an interactive synthesizer to support behavioral modeling in UML. In: ICSE 2001 [22] 15–24

[33] Pnueli, A.: The temporal logic of programs. In: IEEE Symposium on Foundations of Computer Science, IEEE Press (1977) 46–57

[34] Szyperski, C.: Component Software, Beyond Object-Oriented Programming. Addison-Wesley (1997)

[35] Vanderperren, W., Wydaeghe, B.: Towards a new component composition process. In: Proceedings of the 8th International Conference on the Engineering of Computer Based Systems, ECBS'01, IEEE Computer Society (2001) 322–331

[36] Vanderperren, W., Wydaeghe, B.: Separating concerns in a high-level component-based context. In EasyComp Workshop at ETAPS 2002 (2002)

[37] Vanderperren, W.: A pattern based approach to separate tangled concerns in component based development. In: Proceedings of the 1st AOSD Workshop on Aspects, Components, and Patterns for Infrastructure Software, ACP4IS'02, Enschede, The Netherlands (2002) 71–75

[38] Wallnau, K.C., Hissam, S., Seacord, R.: Building Systems from Commercial Components. Software Engineering. Addison-Wesley (2001)

[39] Wydaeghe, B., Vanderperren, W.: Visual component composition using composition patterns. In: Proceedings of the 39th International Conference on Technology of Object-Oriented Languages and Systems, Santa Barbara, CA, TOOLS 39 USA Conference, IEEE Computer Society (2001) 120–129

[40] Wydaeghe, B.: PACOSUITE: Component composition based on composition patterns and usage scenarios. PhD thesis (2001)

Verification of Component-Based Software Application Families*

Fei Xie[1] and James C. Browne[2]

[1] Dept. of Computer Science, Portland State Univ., Portland, OR 97207
xie@cs.pdx.edu
[2] Dept. of Computer Sciences, Univ. of Texas at Austin, Austin, TX 78712
browne@cs.utexas.edu

Abstract. We present a novel approach which facilitates formal verification of component-based software application families using model checking. This approach enables effective compositional reasoning by facilitating formulation of component properties and their environment assumptions. This approach integrates bottom-up component verification and top-down system verification based on the concept of application family architectures (AFA). The core elements of an AFA are architectural styles and reusable components. Reusable components of a family are defined in the context of its architectural styles and their correctness properties are verified in bottom-up component compositions. Top-down system verification utilizes architectural styles to guide decomposition of properties of a system into properties of its components and formulation of assumptions for the component properties. The component properties are reused if already verified; otherwise, they are verified top-down recursively. Architectural style guided property decomposition facilitates reuse of verified component properties. Preliminary case studies have shown that our approach achieves order-of-magnitude reduction on verification complexities and realizes major verification reuse.

1 Introduction

Model checking [1] has great potential in formal verification of software systems. The massive effort required for model checking whole systems "from scratch" has, however, hindered application of model checking to software. The observations that many software systems are members of families of related systems which share common architectural styles and common components and that compositional reasoning [2, 3] is one of the most effective methods for reducing model checking complexities suggest component-based software verification, where verification of whole systems is based on compositional reasoning and on reuse of verified component properties.

A key challenge in component-based verification is formulation of component properties and their environment assumptions, i.e., what properties to verify on a component and what are the assumptions under which the properties should be verified. This challenge is largely due to lack of knowledge about possible environments of components. In the state of the art, property and assumption formulation is often ad-hoc and system-specific. There has been recent research [4, 5] on automatic generation of assumptions

* This research was partially supported by NSF grants IIS-0438967 and CNS-0509354.

I. Gorton et al. (Eds.): CBSE 2006, LNCS 4063, pp. 50–66, 2006.

for safety properties of components. However, formulation of component properties and formulation of assumptions for liveness properties still needs to be addressed.

This paper presents and illustrates a novel approach which facilitates formal verification of component-based software application families using model checking. This approach contributes to addressing the component property and assumption formulation challenge through extending the concept of software architectures to the concept of application family architectures (AFA). An AFA of an application family consists of the computation model, component model, architectural styles, and reusable components of the family. Intuitively, the AFA concept addresses lack of knowledge about possible environments of components by capturing common usage patterns and compositions of components and provides a hierarchy of reusable components with verified properties.

In this approach, *bottom-up component verification* and *top-down system verification* are integrated based on assume-guarantee compositional reasoning [2, 3] and the AFA concept. The integration works as follows. Basic reusable components of a family are derived from its architectural styles and are developed bottom-up as the family is initialized. Properties of these components are derived from the architectural styles and verified in the environments defined by these styles. The properties then serve as abstractions of the components in bottom-up verification of larger composite components. Top-down verification of a member system utilizes architectural styles to guide decomposition of properties of the system into properties of its components and formulation of environment assumptions of the component properties. The component properties are reused, if already verified; otherwise, they are verified top-down recursively. Architectural style driven property decomposition addresses formulation of component properties and their assumptions, and facilitates reuse of verified properties of reusable components. Additional reusable components may be introduced as the family evolves.

Preliminary case studies on web service based systems have shown that our approach is very effective in scaling verification: It achieved order-of-magnitude verification complexity reductions for non-trivial component-based systems and realized major verification reuse. The cost of our approach lies in configuring and evolving the AFA of a family and is amortized among member systems of the family. Further case studies are under way to evaluate if benefits obtained in verification and reuse justify the cost.

The rest of this paper is organized as follows. In Section 2, we introduce the concept of AFA and present an AFA for the domain of university information systems (UIS) based on web services. In Section 3, we discuss integrated bottom-up and top-down verification for an application family, which is illustrated with its application to the UIS domain in Section 5. In Section 6, we analyze the effectiveness and cost of integrated verification. We discuss related work in Section 7 and conclude in Section 8.

2 Application Family Architectures (AFAs)

AFAs extend the concept of software architectures [6, 7] and target model checking of component-based application families. An AFA for an application family is derived via domain analysis of this family. It captures common architectural styles of the systems in this family, which suggest properties that need to be verified on these systems and provide knowledge about possible composition environments for reusable components.

It also catalogs reusable components and their verified properties. An AFA is a 4-tuple, (computation model, component model, architectural style library, component library):

- The *computation model* defines the basic elements of a system: (1) the basic functional entities, (2) the interaction mechanism of these entities, and (3) the units of execution, and specifies the execution semantics in terms of these basic elements.
- The *component model* defines the concept of component, specifying the elements of a component: executable representation, interfaces (including functional interfaces and component properties), etc. It also defines the component composition rule.
- The *architectural style library* contains the common architectural styles that appear in systems of this family. An architectural style specifies the types of components that can be used in this style, the component interactions under this style, and a set of properties required by this style on these components and on their composition.
- The *component library* contains the reusable components that have been constructed for developing systems in this family. These components are reused in development of new systems. This library is expanded when new components are introduced.

2.1 AFA for University Information System

To illustrate this concept, we present an AFA for the domain of university information systems (UIS). A modern university is supported by many information systems such as the registration system, the library system, and the event ticketing system. Their central functionality is to process various electronic transactions. These systems are required to *correctly* process these transactions following the designated protocols.

Computation Model. An emerging trend is to develop information systems using web service technologies. Components of such systems are web services, implemented in program languages such as Java and C# or design-level executable languages such as Business Process Execution Language for Web Services (BPEL4WS) [8]. We formalize (with simplifications) the semantics of web service based systems as an Asynchronous Interleaving Message-passing (AIM) computation model. In this model, a system is a finite set of interacting processes. The processes interact via asynchronous message-passing. A system execution is an interleaving of the state transitions of these processes. In our previous work [9], we have developed the ObjectCheck toolkit which supports model checking of systems that follow the AIM semantics. We employ ObjectCheck as the model checker for verifying components and systems of the UIS family.

Component Model. Web services, the components in web service based systems, can be *primitive* (directly implemented) or *composite* (composed from simpler web services). Their interfaces are specified in XML-based interface specification languages, Web Service Definition Language (WSDL) [10] and Web Service Choreography Interface (WSCI) [11]. WSDL defines the message types supported by a web service. WSCI defines how the message types are interrelated in a choreographed interaction with the web service.

Component – A component C is a pair $(E, \{S\})$. E is the executable specification of C. Conceptually, E is a set of interacting AIM processes. (A primitive component may contain multiple AIM processes.) Practically, E can be implemented in Java, C#, or BPEL4WS. $\{S\}$ is a set of services and each service S is a pair $(M,\ F)$ as follows.

- M is the messaging interface through which C provides the service S and requests the services necessary for providing S. M contains input and output message types and is specified in WSDL.
- F is the functional specification of the service S and is a pair *(provides, requires)*. The *provides* is a pair $(P(pro),\ A(pro))$ where $P(pro)$ is the temporal properties that define the service S and $A(pro)$ specifies the assumptions of $P(pro)$ on the components that request S. To provide S, C often requires other services. The *requires* is a set and each entry of the set is a pair $(P(req),\ A(req))$. $A(req)$ specifies the assumptions on a service S' required by C. $P(req)$ specifies the properties of C necessary for *enabling* the assumptions in $A(req)$, i.e., when C requests the service S', it must behave as $P(req)$ specifies. The properties and assumptions are formulated on the message types in M and are specified in WSCI.

This component definition facilitates assume-guarantee compositional reasoning by specifying properties with their assumptions and guides verification reuse by grouping properties and assumptions into the *provides* and *requires* format.

Component Composition – Composition of a set of components, $C_0, \ldots, C_{m-1}$, creates a composite component, $C = (E,\ \{S\})$, which provides services that aggregate the services provided by $C_0, \ldots, C_{m-1}$. Suppose the services $(M_0,\ F_0), \ldots, (M_{n-1},\ F_{n-1})$ of $C_0, \ldots, C_{m-1}$ are used to compose the service $(M,\ F)$ of C. (n can be bigger than m since multiple services of a component may be involved.)

- E is constructed from $E_0, \ldots, E_{m-1}$ by establishing mappings between incoming message types in M_i and outgoing message types in M_j, $0 \leq i, j < n$, in order to fully or partially satisfy the *requires* of F_i with the *provides* of F_j.
- M includes all message types in $M_0, \ldots, M_{n-1}$ that are needed for C to interact with its environment. F is defined on M. The *provides* of F is derived from the *provides* of one or several F_i's. The *requires* of F is derived from all entries in the *requires* of $F_0, \ldots, F_{n-1}$ that are not satisfied inside the composition.

F is verified on an abstraction of $C_0, \ldots, C_{m-1}$ constructed from $F_0, \ldots, F_{n-1}$. The abstraction includes all properties in the *provides* and *requires* of $F_0, \ldots, F_{n-1}$ whose assumptions are satisfied by the composition or the assumptions in the *provides* and *requires* of F. F is verified by checking the properties in the *provides* and *requires* of F on the abstraction. (See [12] for details of abstraction construction.)

Architectural Style Library. An architectural style is a triple, (component templates, service invocation graph, properties). The *component templates* are specified by component service interfaces which can be complete or partially defined, i.e., with partially defined messaging interfaces and *(provides, requires)* pairs. A component matches a component template if its interfaces match the interfaces of the component template. The *service invocation graph* is a directed graph that defines how the *requires* of the component templates are satisfied by the *provides* of other component templates. In a composite component following this style, the *provides* and *requires* of the subcomponents corresponding to the component templates must conform to the satisfaction relationships. The *properties* are required to hold on a composite component following this style. They are formally defined on the interfaces of the component templates if the interfaces provide sufficient semantic information; otherwise, they are informally specified. A component is reusable if it matches a component template and its functionality is common across multiple composite components following this style.

The UIS architectural style library includes (but not limited to) the following styles:

- *Three-tier architecture.* (1) Component templates: The application logic, the business logic, and the database engine. The database engine is reusable. (2) Service invocation graph: This style features layered service invocation. The user logic invokes the business logic which, in turn, invokes the database engine. (3) Properties: The three components interact properly to ensure that their composition correctly processes each transaction received. The properties are informally specified due to insufficient semantic information about the transactions.
- *Agent-dispatcher.* (1) Component templates: A pool of agents and a dispatcher managing the agents. The dispatcher is a reusable component while the agents are different for different transactions, however, the agents conform to a partial interface whose *provides* is partially determined by the *requires* of the dispatcher. (2) Service invocation graph: The environment of a composite component following this style invokes the services of the dispatcher and agents. The dispatcher invokes the service of the agents. An agent provides services to the environment of the composite component and the dispatcher via the same messaging interface. (3) Properties: Upon a request from the environment if a free agent exists it must be dispatched. A dispatched agent is eventually freed. The properties are formally defined on the interfaces of the dispatcher template and the agent template.

Systems in the UIS family are transaction-oriented and circular service invocation is not permitted. The service invocation graphs are directed and acyclic. Dependencies between a service requester and its provider are captured in their *requires* and *provides*. Such dependencies do not cause circular reasoning due to the sequencing relationships among the messages of two interacting sub-components in executing a transaction.

Component Library. Basic reusable components of the UIS family, such as the database engine, are derived from its architectural styles. The desired properties of the database engine assert that it correctly handles each query. The properties have assumptions that databases are locked before and unlocked after they are queried and if multiple databases are accessed, they must be locked in a proper order to avoid deadlocks. The properties and their assumptions are parameterized by how many and what databases are accessed simultaneously. An instantiation of the properties for accessing a single database is shown in Figure 1. Space limitation prohibits showing the WSCI representations of the properties and assumptions. Instead, in Figure 1, the properties and assumptions are concisely specified in an ω-automaton based property specification language [9]. Each assertion is instantiated from a property template and is corresponding to an ω-automaton. Properties in this language are intuitive, for instance, the first assertion in Figure 1 asserts that after receiving a *lock* message, the database engine will eventually reply with a *locked* message. These specifications are translated from the WSCI specifications when the properties are verified using the ObjectCheck toolkit.

Provides:
P(pro):
After(Lock) **Eventually**(Locked); **Never**(Locked) **UnlessAfter**(Lock);
After(Locked) **Never**(Locked) **UnlessAfter**(Lock);
After(Unlock) **Eventually**(Unlocked); **Never**(Unlocked) **UnlessAfter**(Unlock);
After(Unlocked) **Never**(Unlocked) **UnlessAfter**(Unlock);
A(pro):
After(Lock) **Never**(Lock) **UnlessAfter**(Unlocked);
After(Locked) **Eventually**(Unlock); **Never**(Unlock) **UnlessAfter**(Locked);
After(Unlock) **Never**(Unlock)**UnlessAfter**(Locked);

Fig. 1. Properties of Database Engine

(For simplicity, only properties that are related to locking/unlocking are shown and the transaction identifiers are omitted from the messages.) The properties in *P(pro)* define the desired behaviors of the database engine. The assumptions in *A(pro)* specify the required behaviors of other components requesting the service. The database engine requires no other services. Besides the database engine, the agent-dispatcher style suggests the dispatcher service. These components are the initial components in the library.

2.2 Relationships of AFA to Verification

AFA extends the concept of software architectures to enable operational support for bottom-up component verification, top-down system verification, and their integration. The inclusion of a computation model and a component model in an AFA relates software architectures to component implementations and compositions, thus making the concept of software architectures operational for verification. The computation model guides the selection of model checkers. The component model provides compositional structures necessary for compositional reasoning. The architectural styles suggest component properties and how these properties are decomposed if needed.

3 Integrating Bottom-Up and Top-Down Verification

In this section, we present how the AFA concept facilitates bottom-up component verification, top-down system verification, and their integration. Our approach utilizes architecture styles captured by the AFA to guide property formulation and decomposition, and reduces complexities of verifying member systems based on compositional reasoning and on reuse of verified properties of reusable components available in the AFA.

3.1 Bottom-Up Component Verification in Family Initialization

As an application family is initialized, its basic reusable components are derived from its architectural styles. The properties of the components are formulated according to these styles. The assumptions of the component properties are also formulated according to how the components interact under the architectural styles. Derivation of reusable components and formulation of properties and assumptions requires manual efforts. Verification of the component properties follows the bottom-up approach developed in our previous work [12]. The properties of a primitive component, which is developed from scratch, are directly model-checked. The properties of a composite component, instead of being checked on the component directly, are checked on its abstractions that are constructed from the verified properties of its sub-components. If the properties of the composite component cannot be verified on the abstractions, the abstractions are refined by introducing and verifying additional properties of the sub-components.

3.2 Top-Down System Verification in Member System Development

Development of a member system of an application family is top-down. The system is partitioned into its components which are reused from the component library, directly implemented, or partitioned recursively. A system is a composite component. Therefore, we discuss how a composite component is verified as it is developed top-down.

For a composite component following an architectural style, we integrate verification into its top-down development and utilize the architecture style to guide the decomposition of its properties into the properties of its sub-components.[1] We assume that the component interface has been designed. The properties of the composite component are formulated in the *(provides, requires)* format based on the interface and according to the architectural style. For architecture styles with informally specified properties, for instance, the 3-tier architecture, the property formulation requires manual efforts. The composite component is developed and verified using a top-down process as follows:

1. *Composite component layout.* The component is partitioned into its sub-components according to the architectural style. The sub-component interfaces are defined and the sub-component interactions are specified. This step requires manual efforts of the designers. The representation for sub-component interactions, for instance, High-level Message Sequence Charts (HMSC) [13] for the UIS family, are selected in conformance to the computation model and the component model of the family.
2. *Architectural style driven property decomposition.* The properties of the composite component are decomposed into the properties of its sub-components. The decomposition is guided by the architectural style and based on the sub-component interactions. How architectural styles guide property decomposition is discussed in detail in Section 4. The validity of the decomposition is established by ensuring that the properties of the sub-components imply the properties of the composite component and there exists no circular reasoning among sub-component properties. For a well-studied application domain, this step can be largely automated.
3. *Reuse or recursive development of sub-components.* The architectural style suggests whether a sub-component is reusable. There may be a set of components in the library which are reusable in a given sub-component role even though they are different in their interfaces or properties. A component is selected from the set based on their interfaces and properties. If no qualified component is found for a sub-component or it is suggested to be application-specific by the architectural style, it needs to be developed. If the sub-component is primitive, it is implemented, and its properties are verified through direct model checking of its implementation. If the

[1] A composite component may or may not follow an architecture style. A composite component following no style can be verified through compositional reasoning based on user-guided decomposition of properties of the composite component into properties of its sub-components.

sub-component is composite, it is developed and verified top-down. If it follows an architectural style, the top-down process discussed herein is applied recursively.

4. *Composition.* After all the sub-components are selected from the library or recursively developed, they are composed to construct the composite component by using the composition rule in Section 2.1 following the architectural style.

In each step of this process, failure to achieve the goal of the step will lead to revisions and re-executions of the previous steps or abortion of this process.

3.3 Bottom-Up Component Verification in Component Library Expansion

In the top-down development and verification of a member system, new components may be introduced. Some of these components are application-specific while the others are reusable. The properties of the reusable components have been established when the system is verified. These newly introduced reusable components may be further composed among themselves or with the existing reusable components to build larger reusable components bottom-up. Such a composite component is identified in the development of the member system and its sub-components together achieve a reusable functionality. The interface of the composite component is derived from the interfaces of its sub-components. The properties of the composite component are verified on its abstractions constructed from the properties of its sub-components. The sub-component properties are available from either verification of the member system or the component library. All these reusable components are then included into the component library.

3.4 Interactions of Bottom-Up and Top-Down Verification

Bottom-up and top-down verification are synergistic in their integration into the development lifecycle of an application family. Bottom-up component verification in family initialization provides the basis for verification reuse. Top-down member system development and verification expands the component library by introducing new reusable components and by enabling bottom-up construction and verification of larger reusable components. Component library expansion raises the level of component reuse and reduces the number of decompositions needed in top-down verification of a new system.

4 Architectural Style Driven Decomposition

The central step of top-down system verification is the architectural style driven property decomposition. In this step, the properties of a composite component (a system is a composite component) are decomposed into the properties of its sub-components based on the architectural style guiding the composition and on the sub-component interactions. For a well-studied domain, the decomposition procedure can be largely automated. How the decomposition procedure operates also depends on the representations of architectural styles, component interfaces, component interactions, and properties.

We present a decomposition procedure for the UIS family. (With slight modifications, this procedure can be generalized to many other transaction processing centric families.) Given a composite component C and a service (M, F) that C is expected to provide, the procedure decomposes the properties and assumptions in the *provides* and *requires* of F into the properties and assumptions of the sub-components of C following the architectural style of C. Properties and assumptions of a sub-component are grouped to define the services provided and required by the sub-component.

Under the UIS architectural styles, component interactions are transaction-oriented. To provide the service S, the sub-components $C_0, \ldots, C_{n-1}$ of C interact following a transaction: a sequence of message communications through the messaging interfaces of $C_0, \ldots, C_{n-1}$. Component interfaces are service-oriented: a component provides a service and to provide the service, it requires services from other components.

We assume as C is designed, the interactions among $C_0, \ldots, C_{n-1}$ are specified as a High-level Message Sequence Chart (HMSC) [13]. A HMSC allows branching upon different messages, repetitions of sub-sequences, and skips of sub-sequences. We also extend HMSCs by grouping the messages interactions among the sub-components according to service invocations. The message interactions for invoking a service are explicitly annotated. The external component that requires the service of C (denoted by *P-ENV*) and the set of the external components that provide the services required by C (denoted by *R-ENV*) are also represented in the HMSC. The message communications with *P-ENV* and *R-ENV* are derived from the *provides* and *requires* of F. Specifying HMSCs adds little extra costs to the design process of message-passing based systems.

The decomposition procedure for compositions whose service invocation graphs have tree structures is given as pseudo code in Figure 2. (Space limitation prohibits

```
procedure Decompose (style, comp-set, hmsc, current, parent)
begin
 if (current == P-ENV) then
   {children} = Find-Children (style, comp-set, hmsc, current);
   foreach child ∈ {children} do
     Decompose (style, comp-set, hmsc, child, current);
   endfor;
 elseif (current ∉ R-ENV) then
   provides = Derive-Provides-from-HMSC (hmsc, current, parent));
   {children} = Find-Children (style, comp-set, hmsc, current);
   foreach child ∈ {children} do
     req = Derive-Requires-from-HMSC (hmsc, current, child);
     requires = requires ∪ {req};
     Decompose (style, comp-set, hmsc, child, current);
   endfor;
   Attach-Service-to-Component (current, (provides, requires));
 endif;
end;
```

Fig. 2. The decomposition procedure

presenting the more complex decomposition procedure for compositions with directed acyclic service invocation graphs, which follows the same basic idea.) It inputs the architectural style guiding the composition, the set of sub-components represented by their messaging interfaces, the HMSC, the *current* sub-component whose service is to be derived, and the *parent* sub-component that requires the service of the *current* sub-component. The parent-children relationships among the sub-components are determined by the service invocation relationships among the sub-components defined in the architectural style and the service annotations in HMSC. A component may appear in the children set of another components multiple times if it provides multiple services to its parent. The procedure is invoked with *P-ENV* as the *current* and NULL as the *parent* since *P-ENV* is the root of the transaction, and invokes itself recursively.

1. If *current* is *P-ENV*, the procedure locates all sub-components providing services to *P-ENV* and invokes itself recursively on each of these sub-components.
2. If *current* is not *P-ENV* and also not in *R-ENV*, the procedure first derives the *provides* of *current* from its interactions with its parent (the sub-component to which it provides the service). The procedure then finds all children of *current* (the sub-components that provide services to *current*), derives each entry of the *requires* of *current* from the interaction with each child, and invokes itself recursive on each child. The service, *(provides, requires)*, is then associated with *current.*
3. If *current* is in *R-ENV*, then nothing need be done.

Deriving the *provides* and *requires* of *current* from the HMSC is essentially projecting the HMSC onto *current* and the sub-components that interact with *current.* To derive the *provides*, the interactions of *current* with its parent are projected. To derive an entry of the *requires*, the interactions of *current* with one of its children are projected. The properties and assumptions in the *provides* and the *requires* are specified as WSCI processes. A WSCI process is a simple state machine that captures the behaviors of a sub-component as specified in the HMSC: receiving incoming messages and responding with outgoing messages. The derivation algorithm is straightforward. Receiving and sending messages in the HMSC is captured as atomic messaging activities in the WSCI process. Sequencing relationships among messages in the HMSC are captured by sequence activities in the WSCI process. Branchings according to different messages received in the HMSC are captured by choice activities in the WSCI process.

Space limitation precludes presentation of a detailed correctness proof of the decomposition procedure. The intuition is as follows. The procedure always terminates since it goes through each component following an order determined by the architectural style. The procedure ensures that the composition of the derived services of the sub-components implies the service of the composite component. The *requires* of *P-ENV* is satisfied by the *provides* of its children sub-components whose *requires* are satisfied by their children recursively. The *requires* of the sub-components that interact with *R-ENV* are satisfied by the *provides* of *R-ENV*. Therefore, the composite provides the *requires* of *P-ENV* if *R-ENV* provides the *requires* of the composite. In addition, the acyclic service invocations among the sub-components and the sequencing relationships among the messages of two interacting sub-components prevent circular reasoning.

5 Integrated Bottom-Up and Top-Down Verification of UIS

5.1 Bottom-Up Component Verification in Family Initialization

As the UIS family is initialized, its architectural styles suggest two reusable components: the database engine and the dispatcher. Verification of database engines is out of the scope of this paper. We assume that the properties of the database engine hold. The

Provides:
P(pro): After(Login) **Eventually**(TryLater + Dispatch); **Never**(TryLater + Dispatch) **UnlessAfter**(Login);
After(TryLater + Dispatch) **Never**(TryLater + Dispatch) **UnlessAfter**(Login);
A(pro): (Empty)
Requires:
A(req): After(Dispatch) **Eventually**(Free); **Never**(Free) **UnlessAfter**(Dispatch);
After(Free) **Never**(Free) **UnlessAfter**(Dispatch);
P(req): After(Dispatch) **Never**(Dispatch) **UnlessAfter**(Free);

Fig. 3. Properties of Dispatcher

dispatcher is a primitive component. Its properties and their assumptions are shown in Figure 3. The properties in *P(pro)* and *P(req)* are checked on the dispatcher under a non-deterministic environment whose interface complements the interface of the dispatcher and which is constrained by the assumptions in *A(pro)* and *A(req)*. The properties were verified in 0.9 seconds and 0.16 megabytes which are order-of-magnitude lower than the time and memory usages for verifying a system utilizing the dispatcher service (see Section 6). No composite reusable components are introduced in family initialization.

5.2 Top-Down System Verification in Member System Development

We illustrate top-down system verification through verifying the registration system from the UIS family. The registration system is structured following the 3-tier architecture. It consists of three components: the application logic, the business logic, and the database engine. The interactions among these components and the environment of the registration system are captured by a HMSC. Upon a login request, the system execution may take three branches: (1) log the user in; (2) reject the user; (3) ask the user to try later. For illustration purposes, the first two branches are shown in Figure 4 as two

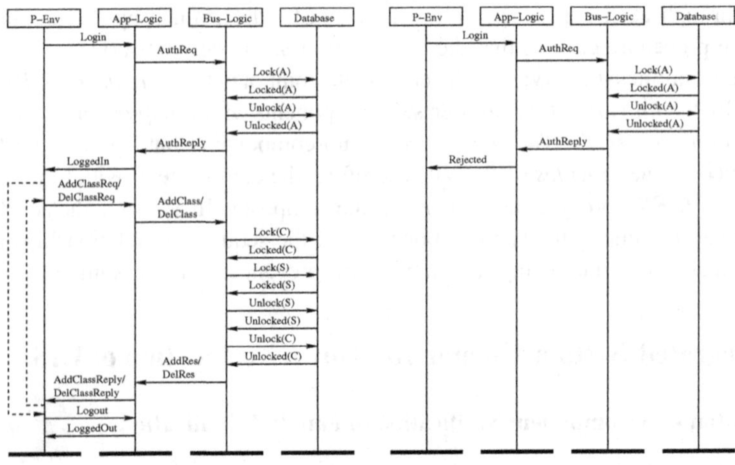

Fig. 4. A flattened view of the HMSC for component interactions under the 3-tier architecture

MSCs with the following extensions: The forward dashed arrow denotes the skip of a sub-sequence and the backward dashed arrow denotes the repetition of a sub-sequence. For instance, after a user logs in, she may or may not add or delete classes, and she may add or delete multiple classes. In Figure 4, service annotations that group messages into service invocations are not shown for simplicity. The message interactions between the application logic and the business logic are grouped into two service invocations: one for authentication and the other for adding or deleting classes. Similarly, the message interactions between the business logic and the database engine are grouped into two service invocations: one for access to the authentication database and the other for simultaneous access to the class database and the student database.

The 3-tier architecture requires verifying that the registration system follows the designated message sequences for a registration transaction when interacting with a well-behaved user. Essentially, we verify that the system interacts with such a user following the message sequences between *P-ENV* and the application logic in Figure 4.

The properties of the registration system can be automatically derived from the HMSC as follows. A WSCI process is created from the HMSC and captures the messages from *P-ENV* to the system, the response messages of the system, and the sequencing relationships among the messages observed by the system. Essentially, the WSCI process is obtained from the HMSC by projecting the interactions between the system and *P-ENV* onto the system. Space limitation prohibits showing the WSCI process. Instead, its formal translation is shown in Figure 5. The temporal predicates in *P(pro)* encode the WSCI process, i.e., capturing the temporal relationships among the messages, for instance, the first three predicates in *P(pro)* capture the temporal relationships between *Login* and *LoggedIn*, *Rejected*, and *TryLater*. *A(pro)* is derived from the HMSC by projecting the interactions of *P-ENV* and the system onto *P-ENV*. For instance, the first predicate in *A(pro)* specifies an assumption on *P-ENV* that it never sends an *AddClassReq*, *DelClassReq*, or *Logout* message unless after it receives a *LoggedIn* message. The properties in *P(pro)* and the assumptions in *A(pro)* are inter-dependent and together they capture the message interactions between *P-ENV* and the system. Since the registration system requires no other services, its *requires* is empty.

Provides:
P(pro):
After(Login) **Eventually**(LoggedIn+Rejected+TryLater);
Never(LoggedIn+Rejected+TryLater) **UnlessAfter**(Login);
After (LoggedIn+Rejected+TryLater) **Never** (LoggedIn+Rejected+TryLater) **UnlessAfter**(Login);
After(AddClassReq) **Eventually**(AddClassReply); **Never**(AddClassReply) **UnlessAfter**(AddClassReq);
After(AddClassReply) **Never**(AddClassReply) **UnlessAfter**(AddClassReq);
After(DelClassReq) **Eventually**(DelClassReply); **Never**(DelClassReply) **UnlessAfter**(DelClassReq);
After(DelClassReply) **Never**(DelClassReply) **UnlessAfter**(DelClassReq);
After(Logout) **Eventually**(LoggedOut); **Never**(LoggedOut) **UnlessAfter**(Logout);
After(LoggedOut) **Never**(LoggedOut) **UnlessAfter**(Logout);
A(pro):
Never(AddClassReq+DelClassReq+Logout) **UnlessAfter**(LoggedIn);
After(AddClassReq) **Never** (AddClassReq+DelClassReq+Logout) **UnlessAfter**(AddClassReply);
After(DelClassReq) **Never** (AddClassReq+DelClassReq+Logout) **UnlessAfter**(DelClassReply);
After(LoggedIn) **Eventually** (Logout); **After**(Logout) **Never**(AddClassReq+DelClassReq+Logout);

Fig. 5. Properties of Registration System

The properties of the registration system are decomposed into the properties of its sub-components by the decomposition procedure in Section 4. The procedure starts with *P-ENV* and invokes itself recursively on the three sub-components of the system following the service invocation graph of the 3-tier architecture. The first component whose properties are derived is the application logic. The derived properties and assumptions of the application logic are shown in Figure 6. The application logic

Provides: (same as the *provides* in Figure 5.)
Requires 1:
A(req):
After(AuthReq) **Eventually**(AuthReply); **Never**(AuthReply) **UnlessAfter**(AuthReq);
After(AuthReply) **Never**(AuthReply) **UnlessAfter**(AuthReq);
P(req): After(AuthReq) **Never**(AuthReq) **UnlessAfter**(AuthReply);
Requires 2:
A(req):
After(AddClass) **Eventually**(AddRes); **Never**(AddRes) **UnlessAfter**(AddClass);
After(AddRes) **Never**(AddRes) **UnlessAfter**(AddClass);
After(DelClass) **Eventually**(DelRes); **Never**(DelRes) **UnlessAfter**(DelClass);
After(DelRes) **Never**(DelRes) **UnlessAfter**(DelClass);
P(req):
After(AddClass) **Never**(AddClass+DelClass) **UnlessAfter**(AddRes);
After(DelClass) **Never**(AddClass+DelClass) **UnlessAfter**(DelRes);

Fig. 6. Properties of Application Logic

provides the registration service to *P-ENV*. The procedure derives the *provides* interface of the application logic from its message interactions with *P-ENV*. The *provides* interface is derived by projecting the message interactions between *P-ENV* and the application logic and it is essentially the same as the *provides* interface of the registration system. The procedure determines from the HMSC that to provide the registration service, the application logic requires two services from the business logic: one for authentication and the other for adding or deleting classes. The corresponding *requires* entry for each of the two services is derived from the message interactions with the business logic. The *A(req)* is derived by projecting the message interactions onto the business logic while *P(req)* is derived by projecting the message interactions onto the application logic.

Following the service invocation relation between the application logic and the business logic, the decomposition procedure is invoked to derive the properties of the business logic. Based on the HMSC service annotations, the procedure is invoked for each service that the business logic provides. The properties are shown in Figure 7, capturing the services provided to the application logic and required from the database engine.

The database engine processes two types of service invocations: access to the authentication database and simultaneous access to the student and class databases. The properties and assumptions in the *provides* of the database engine are the same as the assumptions and properties in the *requires* of the business logic. The database engine has no *requires*. The properties and assumptions of the two service invocations differ since they are instantiated differently. The database engine introduced in the family initialization is selected for reuse since it has a matching messaging interface and its properties (or assumptions), instantiated by how many and what databases are accessed, imply (or are implied by) the properties (or assumptions) derived in the top-down decomposition.

/* Service 1 */
Provides:
P(pro) (or **A(pro)**, respectively) is the same as *A(req)* (or *P(req)*) of *Requires 1* of Application Logic.
Requires:
A(req) (or **P(req)**, respectively) is same as *P(pro)* (or *A(pro)*) of *Provides* of the DB engine in Figure 1.
/* Service 2 */
Provides:
P(pro) (or **A(pro)**) is same as *A(req)* (or *P(req)*) of *Requires 2* of Application Logic.)
Require:
A(req):
After(Lock(C)) **Eventually**(Locked(C)); **Never**(Locked(C)) **UnlessAfter**(Lock(C));
After(Locked(C)) **Never**(Locked(C)) **UnlessAfter**(Lock(C));
After(Lock(S)) **Eventually**(Locked(S)); **Never**(Locked(S)) **UnlessAfter**(Lock(S));
After(Locked(S)) **Never**(Locked(S)) **UnlessAfter**(Lock(S));
After(Unlock(S)) **Eventually**(Unlocked(S)); **Never**(Unlocked(S)) **UnlessAfter**(Unlock(S));
After(Unlocked(S)) **Never**(Unlocked(S)) **UnlessAfter**(Unlock(S));
After(Unlock(C)) **Eventually**(Unlocked(C)); **Never**(Unlocked(C)) **UnlessAfter**(Unlock(C));
After(Unlocked(C) **Never**(Unlocked(C)) **UnlessAfter**(Unlock(C));
P(req):
After(Lock(C)) **Never**(Lock(C)) **UnlessAfter**(Unlocked(C));
After(Locked(C)) **Eventually**(Lock(S)); **Never**(Lock(S)) **UnlessAfter**(Locked(C));
After(Lock(S)) **Never**(Lock(S)) **UnlessAfter**(Locked(C));
After(Locked(S)) **Eventually**(Unlock(S)); **Never**(Unlock(S)) Unless**After**(Locked(S));
After(Unlock(S)) **Never**(Unlock(S)) **UnlessAfter**(Locked(S));
After(Unlocked(S)) **Eventually**(Unlock(C)); **Never**(Unlock(C)) **UnlessAfter**(Unlocked(S));
After(Unlock(C)) **Never**(Unlock(C)) **UnlessAfter**(Unlocked(S))

Fig. 7. Properties of Business Logic

The structure of the application logic follows the agent-dispatcher style. For each user request, the dispatcher dispatches an agent to serve the user if there exists a free agent; otherwise, it asks the user to try later. The properties of the application logic are decomposed into the properties of the dispatcher and the agents. Based on the derived properties for the dispatcher, the dispatcher that has been introduced and verified when the UIS family is initialized is selected for reuse. The *provides* and *requires* of the agents are largely the same as those of the application logic except the properties and assumptions that are related to agent dispatching, which are shown in Figure 8.

Provides:
P(pro):
After(Dispatch) **Eventually**(LoggedIn+Rejected); **Never**(LoggedIn+Rejected) **UnlessAfter**(Dispatch);
After(LoggedIn+Rejected) **Never**(LoggedIn+Rejected) **UnlessAfter**(Dispatch);
After(Dispatch) **Eventually**(Free); **Never**(Free) **UnlessAfter**(Dispatch);
After(Free) **Never**(Free) **UnlessAfter**(Dispatch);
A(pro): After(Dispatch) **Never**(Dispatch) **UnlessAfter**(Free);

Fig. 8. Properties and Assumptions of Agents Related to Dispatching

The business logic is partitioned into the authentication processor and the registration processor. Each implements a service of the business logic shown in Figure 7.

5.3 Bottom-Up Component Verification in Component Library Expansion

As the registration system is developed, the authentication processor is introduced in the business logic layer and it interacts with the database engine to provide the user authentication. The two components is composed bottom-up to build an authentication service that processes authentication requests and replies to these requests. The desired properties of the authentication service is shown in Figure 9. The properties, instead

Provides:
A(req):
After(AuthReq) **Eventually**(AuthReply); **Never**(AuthReply) **UnlessAfter**(AuthReq);
After(AuthReply) **Never**(AuthReply) **UnlessAfter**(AuthReq);
P(req): After(AuthReq) **Never**(AuthReq) **UnlessAfter**(AuthReply);

Fig. 9. Properties of Authentication Service

of being checked directly on the authentication service, is checked on its abstraction. The abstraction is constructed from the verified properties of the authentication processor and the database engine. The properties of the authentication processor have been established in the top-down system verification while the properties of the database engine have been established in the family initialization. The introduction of the authentication service suggests the introduction of a new architectural style: 3-tier architecture with authentication, as shown in Figure 10. In development of new systems such as the

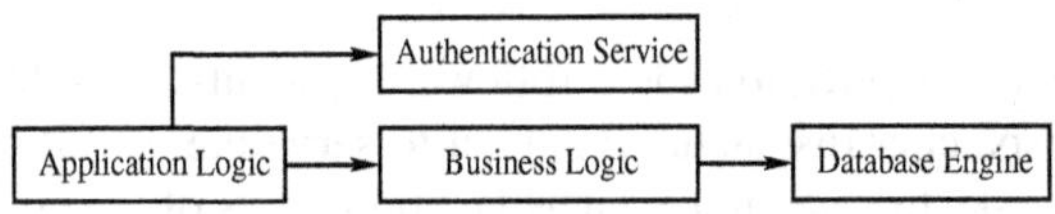

Fig. 10. 3-tier architecture with authentication

library system and the ticket sale system, the new style can be selected to structure these systems and, therefore, facilitate reuse of the authentication service and its properties.

6 Effectiveness and Cost of Integrated Verification

Our integrated approach has major potential for improving reliability of a component-based application family. It enables effective verification of member systems of the family by greatly reducing verification complexities of the systems and facilitating verification reuse. Direct verification of the properties of the registration system with a configuration of 3 concurrent users and 2 agents takes 7034.27 seconds and 502.31 megabytes and it does not scale to large configurations. In verifying the same system with our approach, only the properties of the agent, the authentication processor, and the registration processor must be verified and the properties of other components are reused. The time and memory usages for verifying these components are shown in Table 1. It can be observed that our approach achieves order-of-magnitude reduction in verification time and memory usages. Our approach scales to member systems of large configuration via systematic partition of a system into components of manageable size.

Table 1. Verification time and message usage

	Agent	Authentication Processor	Registration Processor
Time (Seconds)	0.75	0.1	4.09
Memory (MBytes)	0.29	0.31	0.31

The cost of our approach lies in initializing, maintaining, and evolving the AFA: identifying and capturing architectural styles, bootstrapping the component library, and expanding the library. The cost, however, is amortized across the member systems of an application family. Architectural style driven property decomposition procedures are often reused across multiple application families, for instance, the decomposition procedure in Section 4 can be reused across many transaction processing centric families. We are currently conducting further case studies on families of web service based systems and embedded systems to evaluate whether the cost of applying our approach can be justified by the benefits obtained in system verification and verification use.

7 Related Work

The concept of AFAs extends the concept of software architectures [6, 7] and targets verification of families of component-based systems. Space limitation prohibits full coverage of related work on software product families. The Product Line Initiative [14] at SEI focuses on design and implementation issues for software product families. Our work differentiates by focusing systematic verification of software application families.

Pattern reuse is often conducted at two levels: design level and architectural level. Design patterns [15] are concerned with reuse of programming structures at the algorithmic or data structure level. Architectural styles (a.k.a., architectural patterns) [6, 7] are concerned with reusable structural patterns of software systems with respect to their components. Architectural styles have been applied in system design, documentation, validation, etc. Our research utilizes architectural styles of a component-based application family to facilitate component property formulation and decomposition.

A major challenge to assume-guarantee compositional reasoning is formulation of component properties and their environment assumptions. There are approaches [4, 5] to automatic generation of assumptions for safety properties of components. Our approach addresses this challenge via architectural style guided property formulation in bottom-up component verification and via architectural style driven property decomposition in top-down system verification. It handles both safety and liveness properties and complements automatic assumption generation for safety properties of components.

8 Conclusions and Future Work

We have presented a novel approach to formal verification of software application families. This approach synergistically integrates bottom-up component verification and top-down system verification into the development lifecycle of software application families. Its application to the UIS family has shown that it enables verification of non-trivial systems and reuse of major verification efforts. Currently, we are conducting further case studies to evaluate whether the benefits obtained by our approach in system verification and verification reuse can justify the cost of our approach.

References

1. Clarke, E.M., Grumberg, O., Peled, D.: Model checking. MIT Press (1999)
2. Chandy, K.M., Misra, J.: Proofs of networks of processes. IEEE TSE **7**(4) (1981)
3. Jones, C.B.: Development methods for computer programs including a notion of interference. PhD thesis, Oxford University (1981)
4. Gannakopoulou, D., Pasareanu, C., Barringer, H.: Assumption generation for software component verification. In: ASE. (2002)
5. Alur, R., Madhusudan, P., Nam, W.: Symbolic compositional reasoning by learning assumptions. In: CAV. (2005)
6. Perry, D., Wolf, A.L.: Foundations for the study of software architecture. SIGSOFT SEN **17**(2) (1992)
7. Shaw, M., Garlan, D.: Software Architecture: Perspective on An Emerging Discipline. Prentice Hall (1996)
8. IBM: Business Process Execution Language for Web Services (BPEL4WS), Ver. 1.1. (2003)
9. Xie, F., Levin, V., Kurshan, R.P., Browne, J.C.: Translating software designs for model checking. In: FASE. (2004)
10. W3C: Web Services Description Language (WSDL), Ver. 1.1. (2001)
11. W3C: Web Service Choreography Interface (WSCI), Ver. 1.0. (2002)
12. Xie, F., Browne, J.C.: Verified systems by composition from verified components. In: ESEC/SIGSOFT FSE. (2003)
13. ITU: Rec. Z.120, Message Sequence Chart. (1999)
14. Clements, P.C., Northrop, L.M.: Software Product Lines: Practices and Patterns. Addison-Wesley (2002)
15. Gamma, E., Helm, R., Johnson, R., Vlissides, J.: Design Patterns: Elements of Object-Oriented Software. Addison-Wesley (1994)

Multi Criteria Selection of Components Using the Analytic Hierarchy Process

João W. Cangussu, Kendra C. Cooper, and Eric W. Wong

University of Texas at Dallas,
Department of Computer Science,
Richardson TX 75083, USA
{cangussu, kcooper, ewong}@utdallas.edu

Abstract. The Analytic Hierarchy Process (AHP) has been successfully used in the past for the selection of components, as presented in case studies in the literature. In this paper, an empirical study using AHP to rank components is presented. The components used in the study are for data compression; each implements one of the Arithmetic Encoding (AREC), Huffman coding (HUFF), Burrows-Wheeler Transform (BWT), Fractal Image Encoding (FRAC), and Embedded Zero-Tree Wavelet Encoder (EZW) algorithms. The ranking is a semi-automated approach that is based on using rigorously collected data for the components' behavior; selection criteria include maximum memory usage, total response time, and security properties (e.g., data integrity). The results provide a clear indication that AHP is appropriate for the task of selecting components when several criteria must be considered. Though the study is limited to select components based on multiple non-functional criteria, the approach can be expanded to include multiple functional criteria.

1 Introduction

The selection of components is recognized as a challenging problem in component based software engineering [1, 2, 3], as there are complex technical, legal, and business considerations that need to be simultaneously and iteratively addressed as development proceeds. When selecting a component, the number of criteria can be large. Established metaheuristic search techniques [4] from the artificial intelligence community have been proposed to search for software components including genetic algorithms [5, 6] and evolutionary algorithms [7]. Alternative approaches using multi-criteria decision making (MCDM) techniques have also been employed as a solution to this problem [2, 8, 9, 10, 11, 12]. One well known MCDM technique is the Analytic Hierarchy Process (AHP).

Case studies are available in the literature that report the successful use of the AHP approach [9, 10, 11]. The data supporting the description of the components in these studies appears to be obtained from vendor specifications, etc. Here, we rigorously collect data about the components as the foundation for their selection. We note that other sources [1, 13] have provided arguments against the use of the AHP approach for the selection of components; this is discussed in Section 4.

I. Gorton et al. (Eds.): CBSE 2006, LNCS 4063, pp. 67–81, 2006.

In this paper we present an empirical study for the ranking, using AHP, of components based on non-functional criteria. To the best of our knowledge, no such work is currently available. A relatively small number of empirical studies in component based software engineering have become available over the years, which include the representation and selection of UNIX tool components [14], support for regression testing of component based software [15], design of a knowledge base used for business components [16], variations in COTS-based software development processes used in industry [17], and the use of fuzzy logic to specify and select components based on a single selection criterion [18]. Due to the very limited number of empirical studies available in the area of component based software engineering, this study makes a substantial contribution to the literature.

The results of this study provide a clear indication of the suitability of AHP for this task. In addition, the approach can be extended to incorporate functional requirements and the possible integration of components when no suitable alternative implements all required functionality.

The remainder of this paper is organized as follows. A general description of AHP is presented in Section 2. An empirical study for the selection of components for non-functional requirements using AHP is the subject of Section 3. Section 4 presents relevant related work. Conclusions and extensions of the work described in this paper are addressed in Section 5.

2 Analytic Hierarchy Process (AHP)

The problem of selecting the best alternative from a set of options that are characterized by criteria that may be qualitative, quantified with different units of measure, and conflict with each other has been under investigation for centuries [19]. The decision making approaches proposed to address this problem are called multi-criteria decision making (MCDM) methods. There are numerous MCDM methods available including the Weighted Sum Method, Weighted Product Method and Analytic Hierarchy Process (AHP) [20, 21].

The AHP method has three main steps [22] (refer to Figure 1). The first step is to structure the decision making problem as a hierarchical decomposition, in which the objective or goal is at the top level, criteria used in the evaluation are in the middle levels, and the alternatives are at the lowest level. The simplest form used to structure a decision problem consists of three levels: the goal at the top level, criteria used for evaluation at the second level, and the alternatives at the third level. We use this form to present the second and third steps in the AHP.

The second step is to create decision tables at each level of the hierarchical decomposition. The matrices capture a series of pairwise comparisons (PC matrices) using relative data. The comparison can be made using a nine point scale or real data if available. The nine point scale includes: $[9, 8, 7, \ldots, 1/7, 1/8, 1/9]$, where 9 means extreme preference, 7 means very strong preference, 5 means strong preference, and continues down to 1, which means no preference. The

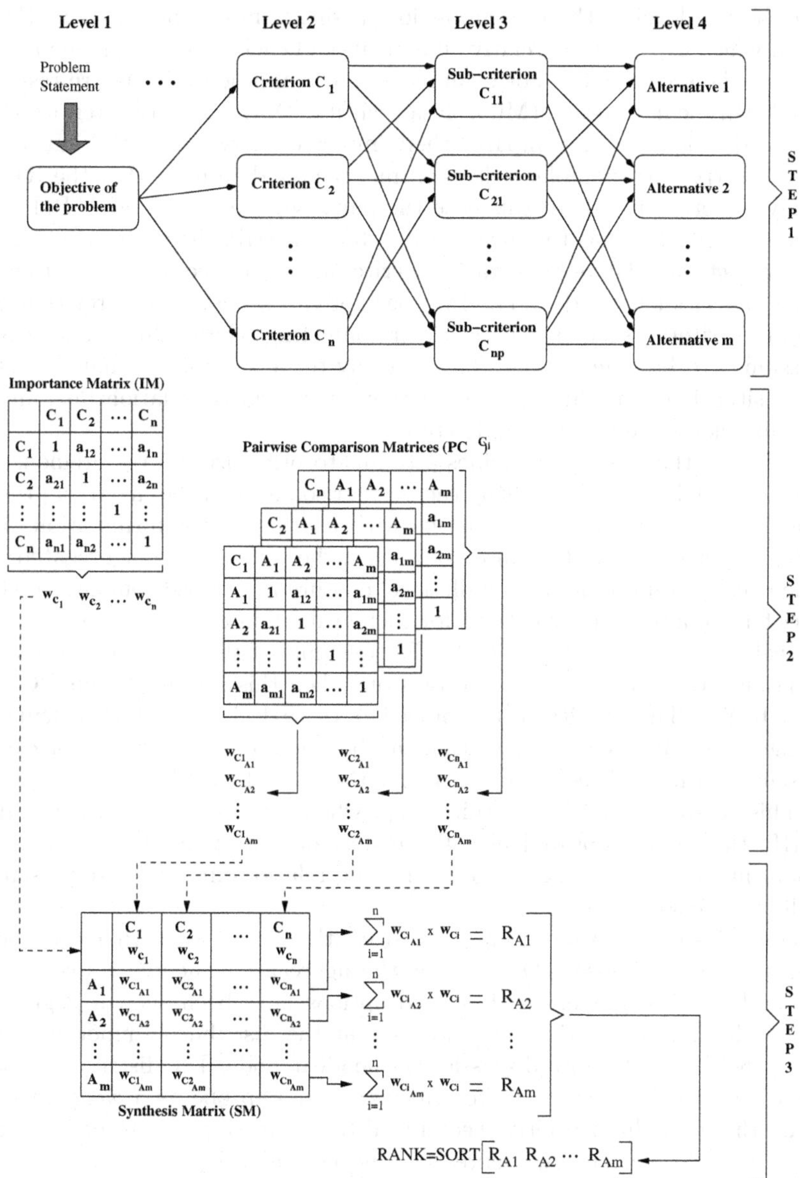

Fig. 1. General structure of the AHP approach

reciprocals of the above levels are also available. For example, if a comparison between "a" and "b" is evaluated as 7, then the comparison between "b" and "a" is 1/7.

For the top level of the decomposition, a single importance matrix (IM) is defined, which captures the relative importance of each criterion; these are considered in the second level. For example, if the evaluation criteria are response time (RTP), memory usage (MU), data security (DS), and data integrity (DI), then the decision maker compares their importance, two at a time in a four by four matrix. For example, a decision maker may determine that the RTP is strongly preferred to DI. In this case the pairwise comparison of RTP/DI has the value 5; DI/RTP has the inverse value 1/5. In AHP, the values captured in the IM reflect the relative importance of criteria, i.e., the requirements, from the decision maker's perspective. The IM does not capture additional relationships among the criteria, such as synergistic or conflicting relationships. The criteria are assumed to be independent. This is likely to be the case in many decision making situations, in which the conflicting or synergistic relationships among the requirements are not well understood.

The IM for the top level provides a means to prioritize the requirements for the decision making process. Using the comparison data in the matrix a priority vector can be calculated, for example, with an eigenvector formulation. This priority vector is used in the third step, when the priorities are aggregated.

The decision tables for the middle level capture a pairwise comparison (PC) matrix for the alternative solutions for each evaluation criterion. Consequently, each evaluation criterion has a PC^{C_i}. For example, if there are four evaluation criteria and five alternatives to choose from, then this results in four PC that are five by five. The priority vector for each of these decision tables is calculated. Here again, an eigenvector calculation can be used. The priority vector can be represented in normalized form, such that the sum of the elements is equal to one. This vector is used in the third step, when the priorities are aggregated. In AHP, the values captured in a PC matrix do not explicitly capture other relationships such as synergistic or conflicting relationships that are present in the alternative solutions.

The third step aggregates, or synthesizes, the priorities so that the "best" alternative can be chosen. Options for the aggregation include a distributive mode and an ideal mode. As these two options have been shown to give the same result 92% of the time [23], we present the distributive mode here and refer the reader to [23] for a discussion of the ideal mode. The distributive mode calculation uses the priority vector calculated in step one as a weight vector, W, and the normalized priority vectors calculated in step two to define a new matrix A. Each element A_{ij} represents the normalized priority calculated in step two for alternative i and evaluation criteria j. To calculate an alternative's overall priority, each row in the matrix is multiplied by the weight vector and the multiplied elements are added together:

$$Alternative\ priority\ i = \sum_{j=1}^{4}(w_j * A_{ij}) \tag{1}$$

The alternative with the largest value represents the best alternative.

3 Empirical Study

An empirical study of how to select components based on non-functional criteria is addressed in this Section. First, a set of available components is described in Section 3.1. This is followed by Section 3.2, which presents all the steps to rank these components according to two distinct scenarios.

3.1 Compression Components

Though there exist a large number of compression techniques, the subset used in this section has been reduced to five compression components: Arithmetic Encoding (AREC), Huffman coding (HUFF), Burrows-Wheeler Transform (BWT), Fractal Image Encoding (FRAC), and Embedded Zero-Tree Wavelet Encoder (EZW). It is our understanding that they provide a broad spectrum in terms of the features of interest (e.g., response time, compression ratio, quality, etc). Source code for these components is available over the Internet. As a first step, the credibility of the source code for both compression and decompression has been assured based on available reviews and references given by various web sites, a thorough code walk through, and testing the components. In some cases the source code has been modified so that it could compile in the lab environment using the g++ compiler (with default settings) on Sun Solaris. A brief description of the components/techniques used in the case study follows.

- Huffman Coding: this is a lossless approach based on statistical features of the file to be compressed. The more frequently the occurrence of a symbol, the smaller the bit code used to represent it.
- Arithmetic Coding: differently from Huffman Coding, this approach assigns a floating point output number to a sequence of input symbols. The number of bits in the output number is directly proportional to the size and complexity of the sequence to be compressed. It is also a lossless method.
- Burrows-Wheeler Transform: this method is based on sorting the input sequence in a certain way to improve the efficiency of compression algorithms. As the previous two methods, it is also a lossless approach.
- Embedded Zero-Tree Wavelet Encoder: this approach is based on the use of wavelet transforms to compress images (2D-signals). Extensions to other signal dimensions is also possible. Images are compressed using a progressive encoding with increasing accuracy. The better the accuracy, the better the quality of the image. Therefore, this is not a lossless approach.
- Fractal Image Encoding: this method is based on the representation of an image as an iterated function system (IFS). Blocks of the image that are similar are then equally represented. This is also a loss data approach.

Based on the characteristics of compression algorithms, four attributes are analyzed here: total execution time (TET), compression ratio (CR), maximum memory usage (MU), and root mean-square error (RMSE), where total execution time is the combination of compression plus decompression time and RMSE is a quality measure. Other features can be easily included according to users' needs. A set of 271 images were collect to evaluate the components. To capture the performance for small, medium, and large images, their size were uniformly distributed in the range from 10KB to 10MB. Also, different types of images were used (e.g., raw, pgm, jpg, and png). To compute the averages and standard deviations in Table 1, each component was executed 10 times for all the images.

Table 1. Average and standard deviation results for the five compression components and each feature of interest

	TET (in s)		MU (in KB)		CR		RMSE	
	avg	std	avg	std	avg	std	avg	std
HUFF	111.3	132.4	2135270	21.63	1.167	0.379	0	0
AREC	180.3	237.3	2135103	3.37	1.248	0.555	0	0
BWT	473.3	371.1	2137885	603.5	3.334	13.277	0	0
FRAC	89.5	73.3	2138986	2155.99	58.427	104.68	50.55	32.43
EZW	380.4	485.4	2142957	4732	4.226	0.837	39.35	27.91

3.2 AHP Steps

The three steps defined in Section 2 and seen in Figure 1 are presented next in the context of the selection of components for image compression.

AHP Step 1. At this point the structure of the problem has already been defined as a three level hierarchical decomposition. The problem is the selection of image compression components; the four criteria of interest have been defined. The data for each of the available alternatives have also been collected, providing 2710 data points for each alternative.

AHP Step 2. The first step after defining the features to be considered in the computation of the rank of the five components is to decide their relative importance. Using Saaty's scale [22], the user defines the relative importance of each feature compare to each other. Since four features are under consideration here, a 4×4 matrix, as seen in Table 2 results. For example, if the user defines that TET is two times more important than CR then $IM_{1,2} = 2$; consequently, $IM_{1,2} = 1/2$ in Table 2. If quality (represented by RMSE) is three times more important than MU then $IM_{3,4} = 3$ and $IM_{4,3} = 1/3$, as seen in Table 2.

Table 2. Importance Matrix (IM) for the four features of interest for scenario 1

	TET	CR	RMSE	MU
TET	1	2	1/3	5
CR	1/2	1	4	3
RMSE	3	1/4	1	2
MU	1/5	1/3	1/2	1

The goal of creating the IM is to facilitate the computation of the weights of each feature. It is, in general, difficult for the user to directly compute the weights. Using the AHP approach, the user decides the relative importance of just two features, which greatly eases the task. The weights can now be computed by finding the eigenvector associated with the largest eigenvalue of IM. In this case, the eigenvector is

$$x^{IM} = [\ 0.5373\ 0.6616\ 0.5035\ 0.1417\ ]^T \tag{2}$$

In order to avoid scale issues, the values in x^{IM} are normalized to 1 using to Eq. 3. The measurements under consideration here are all in a ratio scale which is closed for arithmetic operations. Therefore, the normalized results obtained from Eq. 3 maintain the same scale properties as the original data.

$$x_i^{IM^N} = \frac{x_i^{IM}}{\sum_{j=1}^{4} x_j^{IM}} \tag{3}$$

The new normalized weights x^{IM^N} for the features are now:

$$\begin{aligned} x^{IM^N} &= [\ w_{TET}\ w_{CR}\ w_{RMSE}\ w_{MU}\ ]^T \\ &= [\ 0.2914\ 0.3588\ 0.2730\ 0.0768\ ]^T \end{aligned} \tag{4}$$

As can be verified from Eq. 4, the sum of the weights is 1. Also, it is clear that compression ratio (the weight of CR is represented by the second value in the vector) plays a more important role in the users selection while memory usage (the weight of MU is represented by the fourth value in the vector) has almost no influence. The other two features have similar importance.

The next step on the AHP approach is to compute pair-wise comparison matrices (PC matrices) for each feature. Using the average values of TET from Table 1 we can compute the entries for PC^{TET}. Each entry is computed using Eq. 5 below.

$$PC_{i,j}^{TET} = \frac{TET_j}{TET_i} \tag{5}$$

where TET_k, for $k = \{1(AREC), 2(HUFF), 3(BWT), 4(EZW), 5(FRAC)\}$ is the average total execution time (extracted from Table 1) for each of the alternatives. For example, $TET_{AREC} = 180$ and $TET_{HUFF} = 111$ resulting in $PC_{2,1}^{TET} = 1.62$. It should be noticed that execution time has an inverse effect, that is, the lower the execution time the better. Therefore, the numerator and denominator in Eq. 5 are inverted. The same is true for RMSE and MU. Table 3 presents the results of the pair-wise comparison for PC^{TET}. As before, to find the rank/weight for execution time for each alternative, we compute the normalized (to avoid scale issues when comparing, for example, execution time with RMSE) eigenvector associated with the largest eigenvalue for PC^{TET}. This results in the values in Eq. 6

$$x^{TET^N} = [\ 0.1819\ 0.2947\ 0.0693\ 0.0862\ 0.3679\ ]^T \tag{6}$$

Table 3. Pair-wise comparison (PC^{TET}) matrix for total execution time (TET) for the five available components

TET	AREC	HUFF	BWT	EZW	FRAC
AREC	1.0000	0.6172	2.6252	2.1101	0.4945
HUFF	1.6203	1.0000	4.2536	3.4189	0.8012
BWT	0.3809	0.2351	1.0000	0.8038	0.1883
EZW	0.4739	0.2925	1.2441	1.0000	0.2343
FRAC	2.0224	1.2482	5.3093	4.2675	1.0000

Based solely on execution time and Eq. 6, the rank for the components would be: 1st-FRAC, 2nd-HUFF, 3rd-AREC, 4th-EZW, and 5th-BWT. Sorting the execution time column of Table 1 leads to the exactly same order which is a good indication of the accuracy of the approach. Therefore, one could argue against the computation of eigenvalues and eigenvectors when it is much easier to simply sort the average execution time. This could be true when only one criterion is being considered, but does not apply for multi-criteria problems as the one described here. Therefore, we need to consider the computation of weights for the remaining features.

Table 4. Pair-wise comparison (PC^{MU}) matrix for memory usage (MU) for the five available components

MU	AREC	HUFF	BWT	EZW	FRAC
AREC	1.0000	1.0001	1.0013	1.0037	1.0018
HUFF	0.9999	1.0000	1.0012	1.0036	1.0017
BWT	0.9987	0.9988	1.0000	1.0024	1.0005
EZW	0.9963	0.9964	0.9976	1.0000	0.9981
FRAC	0.9982	0.9983	0.9995	1.0019	1.0000

Table 5. Pair-wise comparison (PC^{RMSE}) matrix for root mean square error (RMSE) for the five available components

RMSE	AREC	HUFF	BWT	EZW	FRAC
AREC	1.0000	1.0000	1.0000	40.3588	51.5568
HUFF	1.0000	1.0000	1.0000	40.3588	51.5568
BWT	1.0000	1.0000	1.0000	40.3588	51.5568
EZW	0.0248	0.0248	0.0248	1.0000	1.2775
FRAC	0.0194	0.0194	0.0194	0.7828	1.0000

The pair-wise comparison matrices PC^{MU} for memory usage and PC^{RMSE} for root mean square error are computed similarly to what has been done to PC^{TET}. They are shown, respectively, in Tables 4 and 5. To avoid division by zero problems, a value 1 has been added to each entry, related to RMSE, in Table 1. Now, following exactly the same steps used in the computation of

x^{TET^N}, the eigenvectors x^{MU^N} and x^{RMSE^N} are computed and the results are shown in Eqs. 7 and 8.

$$x^{MU^N} = [\ 0.2003\ 0.2003\ 0.2000\ 0.1995\ 0.1999\ ]^T \quad (7)$$

$$x^{RMSE^N} = [\ 0.3285\ 0.3285\ 0.3285\ 0.0081\ 0.0064\ ]^T \quad (8)$$

As expected, due to only small variations on the amount of memory used by each approach, there is little difference in the weights in x^{MU^N}. Also, as can be seen in Eq. 8, the weights for AREC, HUFF, and BWT are the same and are much larger than the weights for EZW and FRAC. This behavior is expected since the first three are lossless approaches.

The computation of the weights for Compression Ratio (CR) presents a small distinction when compare to the previous features. The computation of the weights for TET, MU, and RMSE are based on an inverted gain, i.e., the smaller the value, the better. This is captured in Eq. 5 by switching the numerator and denominator. In the case of CR (the larger the ratio the better), such inversion is not necessary which leads to the use Eq. 9.

$$PC_{i,j}^{CR} = \frac{CR_i}{CR_j} \quad (9)$$

Table 6. Pair-wise comparison (PC^{CR}) matrix for compression ratio (CR) for the five available components

CR	AREC	HUFF	BWT	EZW	FRAC
AREC	1.0000	1.0691	0.3743	0.2953	0.0214
HUFF	0.9354	1.0000	0.3501	0.2762	0.0200
BWT	2.6717	2.8563	1.0000	0.7890	0.0571
EZW	3.3861	3.6201	1.2674	1.0000	0.0723
FRAC	46.8079	50.0414	17.5198	13.8234	1.0000

Using the values from Table 1 and Eq. 9 leads to matrix PC^{CR} presented in Table 6. The computation of the normalized eigenvector x^{CR^N} is done as before resulting in the values presented in Eq. 10

$$x^{CR^N} = [\ 0.0182\ 0.0171\ 0.0488\ 0.0618\ 0.8541\ ]^T \quad (10)$$

AHP Step 3. The final step in the computation of the rank for the five components is to combine the weights for each feature $[\ w_{TET}\ w_{CR}\ w_{RMSE}\ w_{MU}\ ]$ (line 1 in Table 7) with the weights computed for all the pair-wise comparison matrices. Each column in Table 7 correspond respectively to x^{TET^N}, x^{CR^N}, x^{RMSE^N}, and x^{MU^N}. Now, using Eq. 1 from Section 2 leads us to the results in Table 8. All the values used up to this point are referred to as Scenario 1 in Table 8.

Table 7. Synthesis Matrix (SM) for the ranking of the five compression components

	TET $w_{TET} = 0.2914$	CR $w_{CR} = 0.3588$	RMSE $w_{RMSE} = 0.2730$	MU $w_{MU} = 0.0768$
AREC	0.1819	0.0182	0.3285	0.2003
HUFF	0.2947	0.0171	0.3285	0.2003
BWT	0.0693	0.0488	0.3285	0.2000
EZW	0.0862	0.0618	0.0081	0.1995
FRAC	0.3679	0.8541	0.0064	0.1999

Table 8.

Alternative	Scenario 1 - Rank		Scenario 2 - Rank	
Components	Value	Position	Value	Position
AREC	0.164627	(3)	0.236828	(2)
HUFF	0.197080	(2)	0.263210	(1)
BWT	0.142737	(4)	0.214710	(4)
EZW	0.064837	(5)	0.052667	(5)
FRAC	0.430719	(1)	0.232586	(3)

FRAC has the first position in the rank, as seen in Table 8. This is clearly the best choice as FRAC has the best response time (TET) and by far the best compression ratio (CR). These two features have the two highest weights, as seen in Eq. 4. The difference of these two features for FRAC is so large that it compensates the poor quality of the compressed images (due to a high RMSE). The second and third positions in the rank, respectively HUFF and AREC, present average execution time and reasonably compression ratio when compare to the two approaches in the bottom of the rank. In addition, they are lossless approaches justifying their rank placement. EZW is clearly the last place in the rank; it has poor response time, the compression ratio is not outstanding, and RMSE is high. We can conclude that, for this scenario, the rank computed using AHP has been able to capture the user's preference in an adequate manner.

Now let us assume a different scenario, refer hereafter as Scenario 2. To compute the rank of the components for a new scenario, only the importance matrix needs to be changed. That is, what is changing are the user's preferences (captured now by a new IM in Table 9) and not the comparative behavior of the components (still captured by PC^{TET}, PC^{CR}, PC^{RMSE}, and PC^{MU}). As can be seen in Table 9, quality (RMSE) has now a much higher importance than in the previous scenario.

The new normalized weights x^{IM^N} for scenario 2 are presented in Eq. 11.

$$x^{IM^N} = [\ 0.2353\ 0.1445\ 0.5240\ 0.0961\ ]^T \tag{11}$$

Replacing the values from Eq. 11 in Table 7 leads to the results of Scenario 2 in Table 8. As can be seen, the increase of the importance for quality (RMSE)

Table 9. Importance Matrix for the four features of interest for scenario 2

	TET	CR	RMSE	MU
TET	1	2	1/5	5
CR	1/2	1	1/4	3
RMSE	5	4	1	2
MU	1/5	1/3	1/2	1

results in two lossless components (HUFF and AREC) overtaking FRAC in the rank. Again, AHP has been able to properly select the best alternatives under a given scenario. Additional scenarios were also used in this study. In all cases, the AHP approach has been able to rank the components and identify the best alternative.

As we can see from the two scenarios described above, changes in IM lead to changes in the selection of components. Therefore it is important to know how sensitivity is IM to these changes. Initial experiments indicate that the sensitivity depends not only on the values of IM but also on the values for SM. That is, if the values in one column of SM are close, a small change in IM may change the rank of the components. However, if the values are far apart, changes in IM need to be more significant in order to affect the rank.

4 Related Work

Diverse approaches to component selection have been proposed such as processes that use MCDM [2, 8, 9, 10, 11, 12], keyword matching combined with knowledge based approaches [24, 25], analogy based approaches (including case based reasoning) [26, 27, 28], and fuzzy logic [18, 29].

The AHP, an established MCDM approach, has been adopted in component selection approaches that have reported successful case studies [9, 10, 11]. OTSO, for example, is one of the earliest component selection approaches that uses AHP [9]. The OTSO process is composed of subprocesses to search, screen, and evaluate component alternatives; there is an additional subprocess to rigorously define the evaluation criteria. The evaluation definition subprocess refines the requirements for the components into a hierarchical decomposition. The evaluation criteria include functional, quality (non-functional), business concerns, and relevant software architecture. The AHP was selected in OTSO for the component evaluation because it provided a systematic, validated MCDM approach. The OTSO approach has been applied in two case studies with Hughes corporation in a program that develops systems to integrate and make available Earth environment data from satellites [9]. One study has involved the selection of a hypertext browser tool. Initially, the search resulted in over 48 tools; the screening process reduced this to four tools which were evaluated with respect to evaluation criteria refined from the initial requirements. The evaluation required 322 pairwise comparisons by the evaluators. This was deemed feasible because AHP tool support was used. The results of the case study indicated that the AHP approach produced relevant information for component selection and the information was perceived as more reliable by decision makers. ArchDesigner [30, 31] is another example of a component selection approach based on AHP. Their results are also a indication of AHP's applicability for the component selection problem.

The strengths and limitations of using AHP have been discussed within the context of component selection [1, 13]. The strengths presented include that it only requires a pairwise comparisons of alternatives and a pairwise weighting of selection criteria, which reduces the burden on experts and it enables consistency analysis of the comparisons and weights, which allows the quality of the information on the criteria and alternatives to be assessed. In addition, the AHP allows the use of a relative ratio scale [1..9] or real data for the comparisons [23] and has been successfully used in component selection approaches, as reported in case studies.

The limitations presented include the assumption of independence among the evaluation criteria, the difficulty in scaling the approach to problems with a large number of comparisons, which would burden the experts in a manual approach, and determining if the AHP is the best approach among the many MCDM alternatives available. Stating these limitations, the approach has been questioned by some for its usefulness in component based software engineering.

Given the arguments that support and question the use of AHP in component selection, we believe a more extensive empirical study investigating the effectiveness of using the AHP approach for component selection in a semi-automated approach is needed.

5 Conclusions and Future Work

An empirical study is presented in this work to investigate using the AHP approach to select components using non-functional criteria. The application of AHP has been constrained to non-functional attributes of functionally equivalent components. The approach is semi-automated, to provide scalability. The importance matrix, which reflects the required behavior of the component, is created manually. Data about the non-functional behavior of a set of compression components are collected including memory usage, response time, root mean square error, and compression ratio; the data are used to automatically create the pairwise comparison decision tables for the criteria. The data collected about the behavior of the components (e.g., criteria such as memory and response time) reflect the intrinsic synergistic and conflicting relationships among the criteria in the components. Once the importance matrix and the pairwise comparison tables are available, the data are synthesized and a ranking is automatically calculated. The results of the study indicate the AHP is an effective ranking approach. This approach can be applied to the selection of components using other non-functional criteria, however, designing the data collection for the components' behavior may be non-trivial.

The limitations of the study include that a comparison on the use of AHP and alternative MCDM techniques is not considered. This study needs to be conducted in the future work. In addition, the limitation of using the AHP with respect to the assumption of independence is not addressed in this study. In the future, the composition of multiple components that will integrate together and provide a set of functional capabilities with minimal overlap will be investigated. The extension can be considered as follows. First, non-functional requirements can be used to rank the components as done in this paper, let us refer to this rank as R_{nf}. Now, let us assume that a set of K functionalities is desired $F = \{f_1, f_2, \ldots, f_K\}$. An IM matrix comparing the relative importance of each functionality f_i can be used to define their weights. PC matrices can then be constructed to verify which alternative implements each of the functionalities. The availability of these matrices allows for the computation of a new rank R_f accounting for the functional requirements. Ranks R_{nf} and R_f can now be combined to compute the final rank of the available components. Let us assume a component C_j is the first choice in that rank.

It is likely that the selected component C_j does not implement all the desired functions. In this case, the process above can be repeated for the remaining components but now focusing only on the functionality that is not implemented by C_j. This process can be repeated until all functional requirements have been satisfied. Clearly, there are compositional issues that still need to be addressed. However, the goal of this section is to present a potential expansion of the use of AHP and not to validate it.

References

1. C. Alves and A. Finkelstein, "Challenges in cots decision-making: a goal-driven requirements engineering perspective," in *Proceedings of the 14th international conference on Software engineering and knowledge Engineering*, (Ischia, Italy), pp. 789–794, 2002.
2. "Commercial-off-the-shelf (cots) evaluation, selection, and qualification process." Systems Engineering Process Office - Space and Naval Warfare Systems Center, October 2002.
3. F. Navarrete, P. Botella, and X. Franch, "How agile cots selection methods are (and can be)?," in *31st EUROMICRO Conference on Software Engineering and Advanced Applications*, pp. 160–167, 30 Aug.-3 Sept. 2005.
4. C. Blum and A. Roli, "Metaheuristics in combinatorial optimization: Overview and conceptual comparison," *ACM Computing Surveys*, vol. 35, no. 3, pp. 268–308, 2003.
5. S. Wadekar and S. Gokhale, "Exploring cost and reliability tradeoffs in architectural alternatives using a genetic algorithm," in *Proceeding of 10th International Symposium on Software Reliability Engineering*, pp. 104–113, November 1999.
6. T. Tseng, W. Liang, C. Huang, and T. Chian, "Applying genetic algorithm for the development of the components-based embedded system," *Computer Standards & Interfaces*, vol. 27, no. 6, pp. 621–635, 2005.

7. W. Chang, C. Wu, and C. Chang, "Optimizing dynamic web service component composition by using evolutionary algorithms," in *Proceeding of 2005 IEEE/WIC/ACM International Conference on Web Intelligence*, pp. 708–711, September 2005.
8. B. C. Phillips and S. M.Polen, "Add decision analysis to your cots selection process," *CrossTalk the journal of defense software engineering*, April 2002. available at: http://www.stsc.hill.af.mil/crosstalk/2002/04/index.html.
9. J. Kontio, "A cots selection method and experiences of its use," in *Proceedings of the 20th Annual Software Engineering Workshop*, (Maryland), November 1995.
10. C. Ncube and N. Maiden, "Guiding parallel requirements acquisition and cots software selection," in *Proceedings of the IEEE International Symposium on Requirements Engineering*, pp. 133–140, 1999.
11. A. Lozano-Tello and A. Gomez-Perez, "Baremo: how to choose the appropriate software component using the analytic hierarchy process," in *Proceedings of the 14th international conference on Software engineering and knowledge engineering*, (Ischia, Italy), pp. 781 – 788, 2002.
12. C. Ncube and N. Maiden, "Selecting cots anti-virus software for an international bank: Some lessons learned," in *Proceedings 1st MPEC Workshop*, 2004.
13. L. C. Briand, "Cots evaluation and selection," in *Proceedings of the International Conference on Software Maintenance*, pp. 222–223, 1998.
14. W. Frakes and T. Pole, "An empirical study of representation methods for reusable software components," *IEEE Transactions on Software Engineering*, vol. 20, pp. 617–630, August 1994.
15. A. Orso, M. J. Harrold, D. Rosenblum, G. Rothermel, M. L. Soffa, and H. Do, "Using component metacontents to support the regression testing of component-based software," in *Proceedings of the IEEE International Conference on Software Maintenance (ICSM)*, November 2001.
16. P. Vitharana, F. M. Zahedi, and H. Jain, "Knowledge-based repository scheme for storing and retrieving business components: A theoretical design and an empirical analysis," *IEEE Transactions on Software Engineering*, vol. 29, pp. 649–664, July 2003.
17. J. Li, F. O. Bjoernson, R. Conradi, and V. B. Kampenes, "An empirical study of variations in cots-based software development processes in norwegian it industry," in *Proceedings. 10th International Symposium on Software Metrics*, pp. 72 – 83, 2004.
18. K. Cooper, J. W. Cangussu, R. Lin, G. Sankaranarayanan, R. Soundararadjane, and E. Wong, "An empirical study on the specification and selection of components using fuzzy logic," in *Lecture Notes in Computer Science*, vol. 3489, pp. 155–170, Springer-Verlag, April 2005. Eighth International SIGSOFT Symposium on Component-based Software Engineering (CBSE 2005), Co-Located with ICSE-2005, St. Louis, Missouri, May 15-21, 2005.
19. K. R. Hammond, J.S. and H. Raiffa, *Smart Choices A Practical Guide to Making Better Decisions.* Harvard Business School Press, 1999.
20. M. Mollaghasemi and J. Pet-Edwards, *Making Multiple-Objective Decisions.* IEEE Computer Society Press, 1997.
21. E. Triantaphyllou, *Multi-criteria decision making methods: a comparative study.* Kluwer Academic Publishers, 2000.
22. T. Saaty and L. Vargas, *Methods, Concepts & Applications of the Analytic Hierarchy Process.* Kluwer Academic Publishers, 2001.
23. T. Saaty, *Fundamentals of Decision Making and Priority Theory.* RWS Publications, 1994.

24. R. Seacord, D. Mundie, and S. Boonsiri, "K-bacee: Knowledge-based automated component ensemble evaluation," in *Proceedings of the 2001 Workshop on Component-Based Software Engineering*, 2001.
25. L. Chung and K. Cooper, "A cots-aware requirements engineering process: a goal-and agent oriented approach," in *Proceedings of the International Council on Systems Engineering Symposium*, (Las Vegas, Nevada), 2002.
26. B. H. C. Cheng and J.-J. Jeng, "Reusing analogous components," *IEEE Transactions on Knowledge and Data Engineering*, vol. 9, pp. 341–349, March-April 1997.
27. P. Gonzalex, "Applying knowledge modelling and case-based reasoning to software reuse," *IEE Proceedings Software*, vol. 147, pp. 169–177, October 2000.
28. M. Gu, A. Aamodt, and X. Tong, "Component retrieval using conversational case-based reasoning," in *Proceedings of the ICIIP, International Conference on Intelligent Information Systems*, (Beijing, China), October 21-23 2004.
29. T. Zhang, L. Benini, and G. D. Micheli, "Component selection and matching for ip-based design," in *Proc. of Conference and Exhibition on Design, Automation and Test in Europe.*
30. A.Liu and I. Gorton, "Accelerating cots middleware technology acquisition: the i-mate process," *IEEE Software*, vol. 20, pp. 72–79, March/April 2003.
31. T.Al-Naeem, I.Gorton, M. A. Babar, F.Rahbi, and B. Boualem, "A quality-driven systematic approach for architecting distributed software applications," in *International Conference on Software Engineering (ICSE).*

From Specification to Experimentation: A Software Component Search Engine Architecture

Vinicius Cardoso Garcia[1], Daniel Lucrédio[2], Frederico Araujo Durão[1], Eduardo Cruz Reis Santos[1], Eduardo Santana de Almeida[1], Renata Pontin de Mattos Fortes[2], and Silvio Romero de Lemos Meira[1]

[1] Informatics Center – Federal University of Pernambuco & C.E.S.A.R. – Recife Center for Advanced Studies and Systems
{vinicius.garcia, frederico.durao, eduado.cruz, eduardo.almeida, silvio}@cesar.org.br

[2] Institute of Mathematical and Computing Sciences – São Paulo University
{lucredio, renata}@icmc.usp.br

Abstract. This paper presents a software component search engine, from the early specification and design steps to two experiments performed to evaluate its performance. After the experience gained from the use of this first version, several improvements were introduced. The current version of the engine combines *text mining* and *facet-based* search. The experiments indicated, so far, that using these two techniques together is better than using them separately. From the experience obtained in these experiments and in industrial tests, we point out possible improvements and future research directions, which are presented and discussed at the end of the paper.

1 Introduction

In a software development process, reuse is characterized by the use of software products in a situation that is different from when and where they were originally constructed. This idea, which is not new [1], brings crucial benefits to organizations, such as reduction in costs and time-to-market, and quality improvement.

Component repositories are among the factors that promote the success in reuse programs [2, 3]. However, the simple acquisition of a component repository does not lead to the expected benefits, since other factors must also be considered, such as management, planning, reuse processes, among others [4, 5].

Current component managers and repositories are, mostly, products that work only with *black-box* components [6], i.e., components that are packaged without the source code, inhibiting tasks such as adaptation and evolution. Moreover, the adoption of this kind of repository often implicates in reengineering the software factories, since making components available for reuse repositories (documentation, packaging) have to follow some predetermined criteria [4]. Additionally, these repositories represent isolated solutions, not associated to commonly used development tools such as Eclipse [7]. This increases the barrier for their adoption and utilization.

I. Gorton et al. (Eds.): CBSE 2006, LNCS 4063, pp. 82–97, 2006.

Thereby, an initial way of stimulating the reuse culture in organizations, and obtaining its initial benefits [8], must concentrate in offering subsidies and tools for the reuse of *white-box* components - where the source code is available - and already existent source code, whether from the organization itself, from previous projects, or from repositories available on the Internet.

In this context, this paper presents the specification, design and implementation of an architecture for a component search engine, to help promoting reuse during software development, and solving the mentioned problem. In previous work [9] we introduced the search engine and described our initial experience in its specification and construction. This paper makes two novel contributions:

- Some refinements on the search engine;
- An experiment that evaluates the feasibility of Maracatu search engine use in industrial contexts, aiding in the software development process with reuse of components or source code parts.

2 Basic Component Search Requirements

Current research in component search and retrieval has focused in key aspects and requirements for the component market, seeking to promote large scale reuse [9].

Lucrédio et al. [9] present a set of requirements for an efficient component search and retrieval engine, standing out:

a. High precision and recall. High precision means that most components that are retrieved are relevant. High recall means that few relevant components are left behind without being retrieved.

b. Security. In a global component market, security must be considered a primordial characteristic, since there is a higher possibility that unauthorized individuals try to access the repository.

c. Query formulation. There is a natural loss of information when users formulate queries. According to [10], there is a conceptual gap between the *problem* and the *solution*. Components are often described in terms of their functionalities, or the solution (*"how"*), and the queries are formulated in terms of the problem (*"what"*). Thus, a search engine must provide means to help the user in formulating the queries, in an attempt to reduce this gap.

d. Component description. The search engine is responsible for identifying the components that are relevant to the user, according to the query that is formulated and compared with the components descriptions.

e. Repository familiarity. Reuse occurs more frequently with well-known components [11]. However, a search engine must help the user in exploring the repository and gaining knowledge about other components that are similar to the initial target, facilitating future reuse and stimulating component vendors competition [12].

f. Interoperability. In a scenario involving distributed repositories, it is inevitable not to think about interoperability. In this sense, a search engine that functions in such scenario must be based on technologies that facilitate its future expansion and integration with other systems and repositories.

g. Performance. Performance is usually measured in terms of response time. In centralized systems, this involves variables related to the processing power and the search algorithms. In distributed systems, other variables must be considered, such as, for example, network traffic control, geographic distance and, of course, the number of available components.

These requirements, however, are related to a component market that is based on *black-box* reuse. To a search engine that also retrieves *white-box* components and reusable source code, different requirements must be considered, as presented next.

2.1 Features and Technical Requirements

A search engine based on *white-box* reuse should consider the evolving and dynamic environment that surrounds most development organizations. Differently from *black-box* reuse, where there is usually more time to encapsulate the components and to provide well-structured documentation that facilitates searching, most development repositories contain work artifacts, such as development libraries and constantly evolving components. Documentation is usually minimal, and mostly not structured.

In this sense, such engine should support two basic processes: **i)** to locate all reusable software artifacts that are stored in project repositories, and to maintain an index of these artifacts. The indexing process should be automatic, and should consider non-structured (free text) documentation; and **ii)** to allow the user to search and retrieve these artifacts, taking advantage of the index created in process **i)**.

Since in this scenario the artifacts are constantly changing, the first process must be automatically performed on the background, maintaining the indexes always updated and optimized according to a prescribed way. On the other hand, the developer is responsible for starting the second, requesting possible reusable artifacts that suits his/her problem. For the execution of these two basic processes, some macro requirements should be fulfilled:

i. Artifacts filtering. Although ideally all kinds of artifacts should be considered for reuse, an automatic mechanism depends on a certain level of quality that the artifact must have. For example, a keyword-based search requires that the artifacts contain a considerable amount of free text describing it, otherwise the engine cannot perform the keywords match. In this sense, a qualitative analysis of the artifacts must be performed, in order to eliminate low-quality artifacts that could prejudice the efficiency of the search.
ii. Repositories selection. The developer must be able to manually include the list of the repositories where to search for reusable artifacts. It must be possible, at any moment, to perform a search on these repositories in order to find newer versions of the artifacts already found, or new artifacts.
iii. Local storage. All artifacts that were found must be locally stored in a *cache*, in order to improve performance (reusable components repository centralization).

iv. Index update. Periodically, the repositories that are registered must be accessed to verify the existence of new artifacts, or newer versions of already indexed artifacts. In this case, the index must be rebuilt to include the changes.
v. Optimization. Performance is a critical issue, specially in scenarios where thousands of artifacts are stored into several repositories. Thus, optimization techniques should be adopted. A simple and practical example is to avoid to analyze and index software artifacts that were already indexed by the mechanism.
vi. Keyword search. The search can be performed through keywords usage, like most web search engines, in order to avoid the learning of a new method. Thus, the search must accept a *string* as the input, and must interpret logical operators such as *"AND"* and *"OR"*.
vii. Search results presentation. The search result must be presented in the developer's environment, so he/she can more easily reuse the artifacts into the project he is currently working on.

3 Design of the First Maracatu Search Engine

Maracatu architecture was designed to be extensible to different kinds of reusable artifacts, providing the ability to add new characteristics to the indexing, ranking, search and retrieval processes. This was achieved through the partitioning of the system into smaller elements, with well-defined responsibilities, low coupling and encapsulation of implementation details.

However, as in any software project, some design decisions had to be made, restricting the scope and the generality of the search engine. Next we discuss these decisions, and the rationale behind them:

Type of the artifacts. Although theoretically all kinds of artifacts could be indexed by the search engine, a practical implementation had to be limited to some specific kinds of artifact. This version of Maracatu is restricted to Java source code components, mainly because it is the most common kind of artifacts found, specially in open source repositories and in software factories.
CVS Repositories. Maracatu was designed to access CVS repositories, because it is the most used version control system, and also to take advantage of an already existent API to access CVS, the *Javacvs* API [13].
Keyword indexing and component ranking. To perform indexing and ranking of the artifacts, the Lucene search engine [14] was adopted. Lucene is a web search engine, used to index web pages, and it allows queries to be performed through keywords. It is open-source, fast, and easy to adapt, and this is the reason why it was chosen to become part of Maracatu architecture.
Artifacts filtering. As a strategy for filtering the *"quality"* artifacts (with high reuse potential), the *JavaNCSS* [15] was used, to perform source code analysis in search for JavaDoc density. Only components, with more than 70% of its code documented, are considered. This simple strategy is enough to guarantee that Lucene is able to index the components, and also requires little effort to implement.

User environment. Maracatu User Interface, where the developer can formulate the queries and view the results, was integrated to Eclipse platform, as a *plug-in*, so that the user does not need to use a different tool to search the repositories.

Maracatu architecture is based on the client-server model, and uses *Web Services* technology [16] for message exchange between the subsystems. This implementation strategy allows Maracatu Service to be available anywhere on the Internet, or even on corporative Intranet, in scenarios where the components are proprietary.

Maracatu is composed of two subsystems:

Maracatu Service: This subsystem is a Web Service, responsible for indexing the components, in background, and responding to user's queries. It is composed of the following modules: the **CVS** module, which accesses the repositories in the search for reusable components; the **Analyzer**, responsible for analyzing the code in order to determine if it is suitable for indexing; the **Indexer**, responsible for indexing the Java files that passed through the Analyzer, also rebuilding the indexes when components are modified or inserted; the **Download** module, which helps the download (check-out) process, when the source code is transferred to the developer machine, after a request; and the **Search** module, which receives the parameters of a query, interprets it (for example, *"AND"* and *"OR"* operators), searches the index, and returns a set of index entries.

Eclipse *plug-in*: This subsystem is the visual interface the developer sees. It acts as a Web Service client to access Maracatu Service.

The first version of Maracatu can be seen in Figure 1, which shows Maracatu plug-in[1] being used in Eclipse development environment **(1)**.

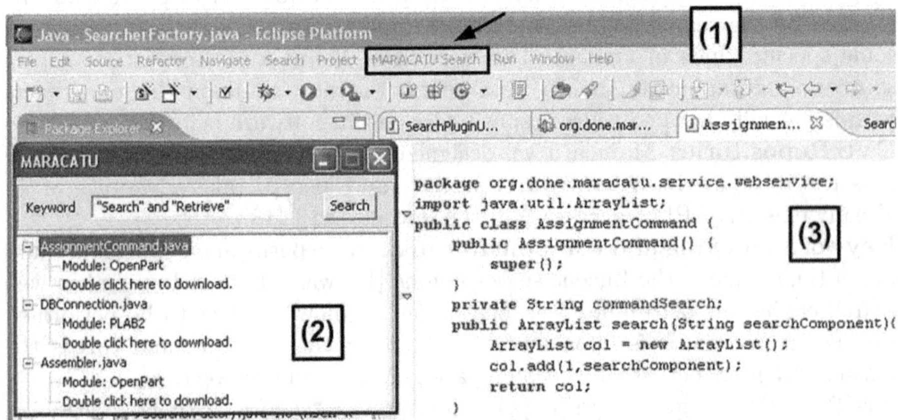

Fig. 1. Maracatu running on Eclipse environment

[1] The version 1.0 of the plug-in may be obtained on the project site `http://done.dev.java.net`

The Figure shows a screen of the plug-in **(2)**, where the developer may type a string to retrieve the components. In the example, a search was performed with the string *"Search" & "Retrieve"*, obtaining as a result the following components: *AssignmentCommand*, *DBConnection*, *Assembler*, among others. From this result, it is possible to identify which project (repository) this component belongs to (represented in *"Module"*), and download the component to the local machine. Next, the developer may import the component into his/her Eclipse project **(3)**. In the example of the Figure, the developer has chosen the *AssignmentCommand.*

The first version of Maracatu plug-in implementation contained 32 classes, divided into 17 packages, with 955 lines of code (not counting comments).

4 Maracatu Search Engine: Current Stage

After the first release of Maracatu, and its initial utilization in the industry, several enhancements started to be suggested by its users. Some of these were added, giving origin to the current version of the tool. Maracatu's first version was used to aid in the second version development. It helped the team to understand how to use some API, consulting the open source code as example of its use and to reduce the time to release the second prototype.

Next sections describe the new features that were included. The improvements took place both in the client (plug-in) and in the server side (Maracatu Service).

4.1 Usability Issues

As expected, the first problems detected by the users were related to the User Interface. In this sense, improvements were introduced into Maracatu's Eclipse *plug-in*:

i) Component pre-visualization: Before actually downloading a component, it is interesting to have a glimpse on its content, so that the user may determine if it is worth to retrieve that component or not. This saves considerable time, since the *check-out* procedure, needed to download a component from CVS, requires some processing. In this sense, two options were implemented, as shows Figure 2. The user may choose, in a pop-up menu **(1)**, either to see a text **(2)** or UML **(3)** version of the component, which he/she can then analyze before actually downloading the component. The UML was obtained by a parser which analyze the Java code and perform a transformation to write the UML.
ii) Drag and Drop functionality: With this new feature, components listed in the tree view can be directly dragged to the user workspace project, been automatically added to the project.
iii) Server Configuration: In the first version of Maracatu, the repositories addresses were not dynamically configurable. The user could not, for example, add new repositories without manually editing the server's configuration files. In order to solve this inconvenience, a menu item was added, to show a window where the user can configure which repositories are to be considered in the search.

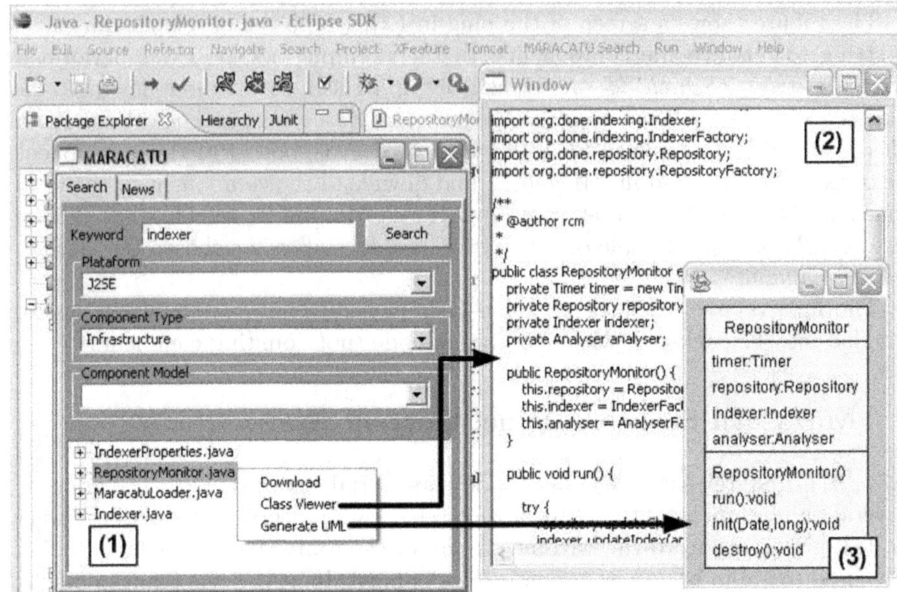

Fig. 2. Class Viewer and UML Generator

4.2 Facet-Based Search

The current version of Maracatu supports Facet-Based classification and search [17] of the components. Components now can be browsed by platform, component type and component model. It is also possible to combine facet-based search with text-based search. By choosing only the desired facets, the search universe is reduced, improving the search performance.

A new module, called Classifier, was introduced in the server-side of Maracatu's architecture. This module is responsible for:

i) Reading the components from Maracatu's repository, identifying the facets to be extracted and inserted in the new search method. The extractor looks for pre-defined facets, defined in a configuration file, together with rules for their identification. Currently the rules consist of a combination of correlated terms that must appear inside a component's code in order to determine if it is classified within the facet. New facets can be inserted by modifying this configuration file. **ii)** After the identification and extraction of the facets, components are classified according to them. The extraction and classification works together.

In the client side (Eclipse *plug-in*), modifications were made on the interface, with a *"selector"* for each facet, allowing the developer to select the desirable values for each one. The field for typing the regular text-based query was maintained, so the user may combine facet-based search with text-based search. The search is now preceded by a filtering, which excludes components that do not satisfy the constraints (facets). The keyword-based search is then performed over the filtered result.

Currently, Maracatu is capable of classifying components according to three facets (F), with the following values:

F1: Platform - **Values:** J2EE, J2ME or J2SE;
F2: Component Type - **Values:** Web Services, GUI, Networking, Infrastructure, Arithmetic, Security, Java 3D or Data Source; and
F3: Component Model - **Values:** EJB, CORBA or JavaBeans.

The user may choose combinations of these facets and values, performing queries such as: retrieve all Infrastructure or Networking components that are developed for J2EE Platform in the EJB Component Model.

5 Practical Usage in the Industry

Currently, the second version of Maracatu is being used in the industrial context, at C.E.S.A.R.[2], a Brazilian company. It is initially being used in two projects, developed by RiSE[3] group. These projects involve the development of a component manager and a shared component library for Brazilian companies. The two projects are supported by the Brazilian Government, under a budget of around $1.5 millions. The team that uses Maracatu in these projects is composed by 13 members, divided as follows: project manager (1), software quality engineer (1), software configuration manager (1), team leader (1), technical leader (1) and software engineers (8). The experience gained in this usage is important to identify opportunities for new features and improvements.

These projects' repository contains 5 sub-projects, involving around 4200 artifacts created and shared by the development team. These artifacts may be reused in different ways, offering different kinds of contribution to new projects: source code can be directly reused, but they can also serve as examples of some particular implementation or structural design.

The second version of Maracatu plug-in implementation contained 106 classes, divided into 55 packages, with 3844 lines of code (not counting comments).

6 Experiments

Two experiments were performed in order to analyze and compare the mechanisms of keyword matching and facet searching. The goal was to verify if the second version became more useful than the first one, since the facet mechanism was included.

For each experiment, four metrics were considered: the *recall*, the *precision* and the *f-measure*. Recall is the number of relevant components retrieved over the number of relevant components in the database [18]. The precision is the number of relevant components retrieved over the total number of components retrieved. Recall and precision are the classic measures of the effectiveness of

[2] Currently, this company has about 700 employees and is preparing to obtain CMMi level 3.

[3] `http://www.cin.ufpe.br/~rise`

an information retrieval system. Ideally, a search mechanism should have good precision and good recall. To assess this, mechanisms can be evaluated through the *f-measure*, which is the harmonic mean of precision and recall [19]. The closer the *f-measure* is to 1.0, the better the mechanism is. But this will only occur if both precision and recall are high. If some mechanism have excellent precision, but low recall, or excellent recall, but low precision, the *f-measure* will be closer to zero, indicating that this mechanism does not perform well in one of these criteria.

6.1 Context

According to Prieto-Díaz [17] the facet approach provides higher accuracy and flexibility in classification. The facet searching is based on the controlled vocabulary and relies on a predefined set of keywords used as indexing terms. These keywords are defined by experts and are designed to best describe or represent concepts that are relevant to the domain question.

From these experiments, we expect to obtain similar results, i.e., the facet approach should have better accuracy in classifying the components, and therefore the recall should be higher. On the other hand, free text search should have higher precision, since it only retrieves components that has terms provided in the query. If our results are correct, the combination of text and facet-based search should provide the best results, resulting in higher *f-measure* than the isolated approaches. These results would indicate that Maracatu's mechanisms were consistently implemented, and that the theory behind it is well-founded.

We considered that values close to 50 % for recall and values close to 20 % for precision are satisfactory, since they come close to measurements made by other authors [20, 11]. However, these values are only considered as a reference, and these results were not included in the hypotheses of the experiments.

The dependent variables for the experiments are recall, precision, search time, and *f-measure*. The independent variable is the searching method with three approaches: keyword, facet, and keyword + facet. Differences in subjects' skills were also considered, to explain the results.

The null hypotheses, i.e., the hypotheses that the experimenter wants to reject, are:

- H_{0a}: facet-based search has lower recall than keyword search
- H_{0b}: keyword-based search has lower precision than facet-based search
- H_{0c}: the combination of facet-based and keyword-based search does not have a greater *f-measure* than the isolated approaches

By rejecting these hypotheses, we expect to favor the following alternative hypotheses:

- H_1: facet-based search has higher recall than keyword search
- H_2: keyword-based search has higher precision than facet-based search
- H_3: the combination of facet-based and keyword-based search have a greater *f-measure* than the isolated approaches

If null hypotheses H_{0a} and H_{0b} are rejected, the results would indicate the theory that facet-based search retrieves more relevant components, and that keyword-based search is more precise. But the main result to be expected comes from null hypothesis H_{0c}. If rejected, the results would indicate that the combination of facet-based and keyword-based search takes advantage of the best of each approach, producing a better overall result. By following this rationale, the new version of Maracatu is more useful than the first one.

6.2 Preparation of the Experiments

In the first experimental environment, a repository was divided into 14 index files for 4017 source code components distributed in 8 different projects from Java.net (`http://java.net/`) and SourceForge (`http://www.sourceforge.com`) developers site, and two RiSE projects. The second experimental environment had a repository divided into 14 index files for 3819 source code components distributed in 7 different projects, from the same developers site.

One particularly challenging task is to obtain a precise measure of the recall, since the experimenter needs to know exactly how many relevant components exist in the repository for each query. To overcome this problem, both experiments adopted the same strategy: one of the projects inserted into the repository, called **known project**, (with about 200 components), was from a very specific domain, and was very well known by an expert. In this way, he could provide a number of relevant components for each query with some assurance, since he has a good knowledge of that project. Each experiment had a different known project.

The experiments were conducted in a single machine, a Compaq Presario with 2,4 GHz, 512 MB RAM and Windows XP SP1. The subjects in this study were 4 researches of the RiSE Group and C.E.S.A.R, primarily software engineers and analysts. Each subject was given a set of ten queries for each searching method (keywords, facets and keywords + facets), and was asked to find all items in the repository relevant to the query. The expert for each known project should be consulted in this activity.

The queries were elaborated with the help of the expert for each known project, and were specific to its domain, so that the number of relevant components outside the known project - which would be unknown to the expert - would be minimum.

6.3 Analysis of Experimental Results

Recall. Table 1 shows the recall results for both experiments. For each approach, the table shows the mean of the recall for the ten queries, the standard deviance and the variance.

In experiment 2, if we consider the worst case of the standard deviance, the null hypothesis H_{0a} - facet-based search has lower recall than keyword search- fails to be rejected, since there is a possibility that keyword-based approach has greater recall than facet-based. However, in experiment 1, even considering

Table 1. Recall for both experiments

Approach	Experiment 1			Experiment 2		
	Recall	Std.Dev.	Variance	Recall	Std.Dev.	Variance
Keyword	0,4356	0,1434	0,0206	0,4867	0,2813	0,0791
Facet	0,8046	0,1562	0,0244	0,6936	0,2749	0,0756
Kw./Facet	0,4584	0,1646	0,0271	0,3158	0,2665	0,0710

the worst case of the standard deviance, the null hypothesis H_{0a} is rejected. This favors alternative hypothesis H_1: facet-based search has higher recall than keyword search.

Precision. Table 2 shows the precision results for both experiments. For each approach, the table shows the mean of the precision for the ten queries, the standard deviance and the variance.

Table 2. Precision for both experiments

Approach	Experiment 1			Experiment 2		
	Precision	Std.Dev.	Variance	Precision	Std.Dev.	Variance
Keyword	0,2084	0,2745	0,0753	0,1556	0,2655	0,0705
Facet	0,0071	0,0102	0,0001	0,0155	0,0238	0,0006
Kw./Facet	0,2616	0,2786	0,0776	0,2530	0,4658	0,2169

In both experiments, if looking only at the mean values, one may tend to think that null hypothesis H_{0b} - keyword-based search has lower precision than facet-based search - was rejected. However, although this is probably true, it is not guaranteed by statistical results, since the standard deviance was too high, which may indicate that the mean could drastically change. However, in practice, due to the high difference in the mean values in both experiments, we can favor the alternative hypothesis H_2: keyword-based search has higher precision than facet-based search.

f-measure. Table 3 shows the *f-measure* results for both experiments. For each approach, the table shows the mean of the *f-measure* for the ten queries, the standard deviance and the variance.

By looking at these results, we may immediately discard the facet-based approach, since it has a very low *f-measure* for both experiments. However, null hypothesis H_{0c} - the combination of facet-based and keyword-based search does not have a greater *f-measure* than the isolated approaches - cannot be statistically rejected by these results. If we look at both experiments, and if we consider the worst case of the standard deviance, the mean could change drastically, and the *f-measure* for the keyword approach could be higher than the keyword + facet approach.

Table 3. *F-measure* for both experiments

Approach	Experiment 1			Experiment 2		
	F-meas.	Std.Dev.	Variance	F-meas.	Std.Dev.	Variance
Keyword	0,2544	0,2584	0,0668	0,2109	0,3181	0,1012
Facet	0,0136	0,0189	0,0004	0,0294	0,0443	0,0020
Kw./Facet	0,3127	0,2592	0,0672	0,2361	0,2559	0,0655

However, in practice, considering just the mean values, both experiments tend to reject Null hypothesis H_{0c}, since in both cases the combination of facets and keywords had a greater *f-measure*. Thus, if we had to make a decision, we would favor alternative hypothesis H_3: the combination of facet-based and keyword-based search have a greater *f-measure* than the isolated approaches. However, more experiments are needed in order to provide a more solid confirmation of this hypothesis.

6.4 Discussion

Subject preferences for the searching methods was obtained by asking the subjects to answer which approach was preferred. Keyword + facet was ranked higher, followed by keyword and only then the facets.

The three null hypotheses were practically rejected, although not statistically. This favors the alternative hypotheses, and specially H_3, which states that the new version of Maracatu, combining facet-based search with keyword-based search, is more useful than the first one, which only had keyword-based search.

As expected, the recall and precision rates, in the best cases, were very close to the values obtained by other authors [20] [11] (50% recall and 20% for precision). We can not say which mechanism is better, nor that these mechanisms are similar, since several other factors could influence the result. The same set of components and queries should be replicated to all mechanisms in order to obtain a more meaningful comparison result. However, this indicates that the research on Maracatu is on the right direction.

7 Related Work

The Agora [21] is a prototype developed by the SEI/CMU[4]. The objective of the Agora system is to create a database (repository), automatically generated, indexed and available on the Internet, of software products assorted by component type (e.g. *JavaBeans* or *ActiveX* controls). The Agora combines introspection techniques with Web search mechanisms in order to reduce the costs of locating and retrieving software components from a component market.

The Koders [22] connects directly with version control systems (like CVS and Subversion) in order to identify the source code, being able to recognize

[4] Software Engineering Institute at Carnegie Mellon University.

30 different programming languages and 20 software licenses. Differently from Maracatu, which can be used in an Intranet, Koders can be only used via its Web Site, which makes it unattractive for companies that want to promote in-house reuse only, without making their repositories public.

In [23], Holmes and Murphy present *Strathcona*, an Eclipse plug-in that locates samples of source code in order to help developers in the codification process. The samples are extracted from repositories through six different heuristics. The *Strathcona*, differently from Maracatu, is not a Web Service client, and thus it is not as scalable as Maracatu. Besides, Maracatu can access different remotely distributed repositories, while the *Strathcona* can access only local repositories.

Another important research work is the *CodeBroker* [11], a mechanism for locating components in an active way, according to the developer's knowledge and environment. Empirical evaluations have shown that this kind of strategy is effective in promoting reuse. From the functional view, Maracatu follows the same approach as *CodeBroker*, except for being passive instead of active.

8 Maracatu's Agenda for Research and Development

As a result of the research and tests made with the tool, the team responsible for the project identified the necessity for the development of new features and new directions for research. A formal schedule of these requirements is being defined by C.E.S.A.R. and RiSE group, and will address the following issues.

8.1 Non-functional Requirements

Usability. Macaratu's usability might be enhanced with features such as giving the user the possibility to graphically view the assets and its interdependencies. This would help the user to keep track of assets cohesion and to learn more about the assets relationships and dependencies. Another usability feature could be to highlight the searched text. And finally, it would be interesting for the user to select the repositories he/she wants to search, as an additional filter.
Scalability. On the server side, there are not features for load balancing. This will be an important feature in the future, as the tool starts to be used with a larger number of developers simultaneously searching for assets on the Intranet or even on the Internet.
Security. A common problem that a company may face when promoting reuse is the unauthorized access to restricted code. The idea is to improve software reuse, but there are cases where not every user can access every artifact. User authentication and authorization need to be implemented in order to solve these questions.

8.2 Functional Requirements

Improved facet search. The facet search might be enhanced, by using more complex, flexible and dynamic rules. Currently, facet rules are specific for Java source code, and use a very simple structure. A rule engine should be used to improve it. This would bring the necessary flexibility for the administrator or the developer to define specific semantic-aware rules to associate pre-defined facets. Besides, a more flexible facet extractor would be easier to adapt to organizational structures, facilitating the adoption of the search engine.

Semantic Search. Semantic search might be added to improve recall, since it would retrieve not only the specific assets the user searched for, but also others that are semantically related. Current facet search is a form of semantic search, since the facets are semantically defined to represent and group some information on the repository. However, new semantic engines could provide more benefits.

Specialized Algorithm. On its second prototype, Maracatu uses the Lucene Search system to index and retrieve source code. This algorithm is not optimized or specialized for source code search. A feature that might be added is to count the source code dependencies when indexing and ranking it. So a developer could choose to retrieve the assets with less dependencies, for example. One example of such work can be seen on Component Rank [24].

Metrics. The use of more complex metrics than JavaNCSS might be interesting. Currently the only metric information used is the amount of Javadoc documentation. We can evaluate other code quality features in order to improve the filter process.

Query by reformulation. There is a natural information loss when the reuser is formulating a query. As pointed out by [10], there is also the conceptual gap between the problem and the solution, since usually components are described in terms of functionality (*"how"*), and queries are formulated in terms of the problem (*"what"*). In [11], the authors state that retrieval by reformulation *"is the process that allows users to incrementally improve their query after they have familiarized themselves with the information space by evaluating previous retrieval results."*.

Information Delivery. Most tools expect user's initiative to start searching for reusable assets. Unfortunately, this creates a search gap, because the user will only search for components he/she knows or believes to exist in the repository [11]. On the other hand, using context-aware features, the tool can automatically search for relevant information without being requested, bringing components that the user would not even start looking for, increasing the chance of reuse.

We are aware that this is not a definitive set of improvements. However, these are proved solutions that could increase Maracatu's performance and usefulness.

9 Concluding Remarks

Since 1968 [1], when McIlroy proposed the initial idea of a software component industry, the matter has been the subject of research. Over from decades [9], the component search and retrieval area evolved, with mechanisms that, initially, facilitated the reuse of mathematical routines, up to robust mechanisms, which help in the selection and retrieval of *black-box* components, either in-house or in a global market.

In this paper, we presented Maracatu, a search engine for retrieving source code components from development repositories. The tool is structured in a client-sever architecture: the client side is a *plug-in* for Eclipse IDE, while the server side is represented by a web application responsible for accessing the repositories in the Internet or Intranets. Two versions of the engine were developed so far, with new features being added as it is used in industrial practise. We also presented two experiments, comparing the text matching mechanism (first version) with the facet mechanism implemented in the last version. The experiment showed that the facet-based mechanism alone does not have good performance but, when combined with text-based search, is a better overall solution.

Additionally, we discussed Maracatu's agenda for future research and development, listing it features still to be implemented. Issues concerned with usability, scalability and security gain importance in future releases, as pointed out by the experiments and pactical usage. Particularly, the facet searching mechanism could benefit from more sophisticated, flexible and dynamic rules. Semantic search would be another important approach to be studied, as well as more specialized algorithms for component ranking.

In the view of the RiSE framework for software reuse [25], Maracatu is a search tool to incorporate the first principles and benefits of reuse into an organization. However, reusability will not occur by itself, and it is an illusion to think that the adoption of tools could do it either. There must be a strong organizational commitment to reuse program; adherence to a reuse process; an effective management structure to operate a reusability program with the resources and authority required to provide the overall culture to foster reuse. Maracatu facilitates the task of reusing software artifacts, but we hope that the first benefit it brings can encourage project managers and CIOs to pay attention to the software reuse as a viable and mandatory investment in their software development agenda.

References

1. McIlroy, M.D.: Software Engineering: Report on a conference sponsored by the NATO Science Committee. In: NATO Software Engineering Conference, NATO Scientific Affairs Division (1968) 138–155
2. Frakes, W.B., Isoda, S.: Success Factors of Systematic Software Reuse. IEEE Software **11**(01) (1994) 14–19
3. Rine, D.: Success factors for software reuse that are applicable across Domains and businesses. In: ACM Symposium on Applied Computing, San Jose, California, USA, ACM Press (1997) 182–186
4. Morisio, M., Ezran, M., Tully, C.: Success and Failure Factors in Software Reuse. IEEE Transactions on Software Engineering **28**(04) (2002) 340–357
5. Ravichandran, T., Rothenberger, M.A.: Software Reuse Strategies and Component Markets. Communications of the ACM **46**(8) (2003) 109–114
6. Szyperski, C., Gruntz, D., Murer, S.: Component Software: Beyond Object-Oriented Programming. Addison Wesley (2002)
7. Gallardo, D., Burnette, E., McGovern, R.: Eclipse in Action. A Guide for Java Developers. In Action Series. Manning Publications Co., Greenwich, CT (2003)

8. Griss, M.: Making Software Reuse Work at Hewlett-Packard. IEEE Software **12**(01) (1995) 105–107
9. Lucrédio, D., Almeida, E.S., Prado, A.F.: A Survey on Software Components Search and Retrieval. In Steinmetz, R., Mauthe, A., eds.: 30th IEEE EUROMICRO Conference, Component-Based Software Engineering Track, Rennes - France, IEEE/CS Press (2004) 152–159
10. Henninger, S.: Using Iterative Refinement to Find Reusable Software. IEEE Software **11**(5) (1994) 48–59
11. Ye, Y., Fischer, G.: Supporting Reuse By Delivering Task-Relevant and Personalized Information. In: ICSE 2002 - 24th International Conference on Software Engineering, Orlando, Florida, USA (2002) 513–523
12. Banker, R.D., Kauffman, R.J., Zweig, D.: Repository Evaluation of Software Reuse. IEEE Transactions on Software Engineering **19**(4) (1993) 379–389
13. NetBeans: Javacvs project (2005)
14. Hatcher, E., Gospodnetic, O.: Lucene in Action. In Action series. Manning Publications Co., Greenwich, CT (2004)
15. Lee, C.: JavaNCSS - A Source Measurement Suite for Java (2005)
16. Stal, M.: Web services: beyond component-based computing. Communications of ACM **45**(10) (2002) 71–76
17. Prieto-Díaz, R.: Implementing faceted classification for software reuse. Communications of the ACM **34**(5) (1991) 88–97
18. Grossman, D.A., Frieder, O.: Information Retrieval. Algoritms and Heuristics. Second edn. Springer, Dordrecht, Netherlands (2004)
19. Robin, J., Ramalho, F.: Can Ontologies Improve Web Search Engine Effectiveness Before the Advent of the Semantic Web? In Laender, A.H.F., ed.: XVIII Brazilian Symposium on Databases, Manaus, Amazonas, Brazil, UFAM (2003) 157–169
20. Frakes, W.B., Pole, T.P.: An Empirical Study of Representation Methods for Reusable Software Components. IEEE Transactions on Software Engineering **20**(8) (1994)
21. Seacord, R.C., Hissam, S.A., Wallnau, K.C.: Agora: A Search Engine for Software Components. Technical Report CMU/SEI–98–TR–011, ESC–TR–98–011, CMU/SEI - Carnegie Mellon University/Software Engineering Institute (1998) CMU/SEI - Carnegie Mellon University/Software Engineering Institute.
22. Koders: Koders - Source Code Search Engine, URL: http://www.koders.com (2006)
23. Holmes, R., Murphy, G.C.: Using structural context to recommend source code examples. In: 27th International Conference in Software Engineering, St. Louis, MO, USA, ACM Press (2005) 117–125
24. Inoue, K., Yokomori, R., Fujiwara, H., Yamamoto, T., Matsushita, M., Kusumoto, S.: Component Rank: Relative Significance Rank for Software Component Search. In: 25th International Conference on Software Engineering (ICSE2003). (2003) 14–24
25. Almeida, E.S., Alvaro, A., Lucrédio, D., Garcia, V.C., Meira, S.R.L.: RiSE Project: Towards a Robust Framework for Software Reuse. In: IEEE International Conference on Information Reuse and Integration (IRI), Las Vegas, USA, IEEE/CMS (2004) 48–53

Architectural Building Blocks for Plug-and-Play System Design

Shangzhu Wang, George S. Avrunin, and Lori A. Clarke

Department of Computer Science
University of Massachusetts, Amherst, MA 01003, USA
{shangzhu, avrunin, clarke}@cs.umass.edu

Abstract. One of the distinguishing features of distributed systems is the importance of the interaction mechanisms that are used to define how the sequential components interact with each other. Given the complexity of the behavior that is being described and the large design space of various alternatives, choosing appropriate interaction mechanisms is difficult. In this paper, we propose a component-based specification approach that allows designers to experiment with alternative interaction semantics. Our approach is also integrated with design-time verification to provide feedback about the correctness of the overall system design. In this approach, connectors representing specific interaction semantics are composed from reusable building blocks. Standard communication interfaces for components are defined to reduce the impact of changing interactions on components' computations. The increased reusability of both components and connectors also allows savings at model-construction time for finite-state verification.

1 Introduction

One of the distinguishing features of distributed systems is the importance of the interaction mechanisms that are used to define how the sequential components interact with each other. Consequently, software architecture description languages typically separate the computational *components* of the system from the *connectors*, which describe the interactions among those components (e.g., [1, 2, 3, 4]). Interaction mechanisms represent some of the most complex aspects of a system. It is the interaction mechanisms that primarily capture the non-determinism, interleavings, synchronization, and interprocess communication among components. These are all issues that can be particularly difficult to fully comprehend in terms of their impact on the overall system behavior.

As a result, it is often very difficult to design a distributed system with the desired component interactions. The large design space from which developers must select the appropriate interaction mechanisms adds to the difficulty. Choices range from shared-memory mechanisms, such as monitors and mutual exclusion locks, to distributed-memory mechanisms, such as message passing and event-based notification. Even for a single interaction mechanism type, there are usually many variations on how it could be structured.

I. Gorton et al. (Eds.): CBSE 2006, LNCS 4063, pp. 98–113, 2006.

Because of this complexity, design-time verification of distributed systems is particularly important. One would like to be able to propose a design, use verification to determine which important behavioral properties are not satisfied, and then modify and reevaluate the system design repeatedly until a satisfactory design is found. With component-based design, existing components are often used and glued together with connectors. In this mode of design, one would expect that the interaction mechanisms represented by the connectors would need to be reconsidered and fine-tuned several times during this design and design-time verification process, whereas the high-level design of the components would remain more stable. If using a finite-state verifier, such as SPIN [5], SMV [6], LTSA [7], or FLAVERS [8], a model of each component and each connector could be created separately and then the composite system model could be formed and used as the basis for finite-state verification.

A major obstacle to the realization of this vision of component-based design is that the semantics of the interactions are often deeply intertwined with the semantics of the components' computations. Changes to the interactions usually require nontrivial changes to the components. As a result, it is often difficult and costly to modify the interactions without looking into and modifying the details of the components. Consequently, there is little model reuse during design-time finite-state verification.

In this paper, we propose a component-based approach that allows designers to experiment with alternative interaction semantics in a "plug-and-play" manner, using design-time verification to provide feedback about the correctness of the overall system design. The main contributions of our approach include:

- Defining a small set of *standard interfaces* by which components can communicate with each other through different connectors: These standard interfaces allow designers to change the semantics of interactions without having to make significant changes to the components.
- Separating connectors into *ports and channels* to represent different aspects of the semantics of connectors: This decomposition of connectors allows us to support a library of parameterizable and reusable *building blocks* that can be used to describe a variety of interaction mechanisms.
- Combining the use of standard component interfaces with reusable building blocks for connectors: This separation allows designers to explore the design space and experiment with alternative interaction semantics more easily.
- Facilitating design-time verification: With the increased reusability of components and connectors, one can expect savings in model-construction time during finite-state verification.

This paper presents the basic concepts and some preliminary results from an evaluation of our approach. Section 2 illustrates the problem we are trying to address through an example. Section 3 shows how the general approach can be applied to the message passing mechanism. In section 4, we demonstrate through examples how designers may experiment with alternative interaction semantics using our approach. Section 5 describes the related work, followed by conclusions and discussions of future work in Section 6.

2 An Illustrative Example

As an example, consider a bridge that is only wide enough to let through a single lane of traffic at a time [7]. For this example, we assume that traffic control is provided by two controllers, one at each end of the bridge. Communication between controllers as well as between cars and controllers may be necessary to allow appropriate traffic control. To make the discussion easier to follow, we refer to cars entering the bridge from one end as the blue cars and that end's controller as the blue controller; similarly the cars and controller on the other end are referred to as the red cars and the red controller, respectively. We start with a simple "exactly-N-cars-per-turn" version of this example, where the controllers take turns allowing some fixed number of cars from their side to enter the bridge. Note that since each controller counts the fixed number of cars entering and exiting the bridge, no communication is needed between the two controllers.

For an architectural design of this simple version of the system, one needs to identify the components and the appropriate interactions among the components. It is natural to propose a system composed of a *BlueController* component, a *RedController* component, and one or more *BlueCar* components and *RedCar* components. In such a distributed system, message passing seems to be a natural choice for the component interactions. Four connectors then need to be included to handle message passing among the components as indicated in Figure 1: a *BlueEnter* connector between the *BlueCar* components and the *BlueController* component, a *BlueExit* connector between the *BlueCar* components and the *RedController* component, and similarly a *RedEnter* connector and a *RedExit* connector.

As described in Figure 1(a), a car sends an *enter_request* message to the controller at the end of the bridge it wants to enter and then proceeds onto the bridge. When it exits the bridge, it notifies the controller at the exit end by sending an *exit_request* message. Controllers receive *enter_request* and *exit_request* messages, update their counters, and decide when to switch turns. Since there may be multiple cars that communicate with each controller, messages are buffered in the connectors between car components and controller components.

Astute readers will notice that according to the description in Figure 1(a), cars from different directions can be on the bridge at the same time, which could cause a crash. This is due to an erroneous design in the component interactions. With this design, a car sends an *enter_request* message and immediately goes onto the bridge without confirming that its request has been accepted by the controller. This controller, however, may still be waiting for exit requests from cars from the other direction, and the enter request message from this car may still be in the buffer, waiting to be retrieved and handled. Therefore, a car may enter the bridge while there are still cars traveling in the opposite direction. Obviously, what is needed here is synchronous communication between a car and its controller rather than asynchronous communication.

One way to fix this problem is to have the controller send a *go_ahead* message after receiving each enter request to authorize that car to enter the bridge. After

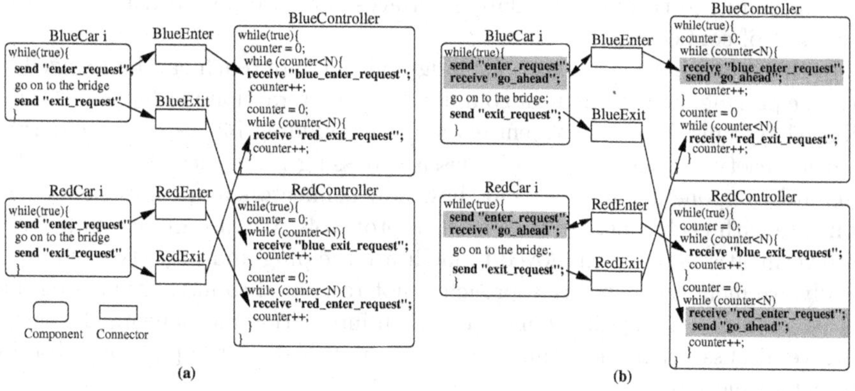

Fig. 1. Architecture design and illustration of component interactions for the single-lane bridge example

sending the enter request, the car would wait for this acknowledgement before entering the bridge, as shown in Figure 1(b) (the highlighted areas indicate the changes). These changes, involving both the car components and the controller components, effectively make the communication between them synchronous and solve the problem caused by the asynchronous communication.

This example shows the typical design practice in which the semantics of the interactions are not specified independently, but instead are spread among the connectors and the components. This is a trivial example, but it is easy to envision how the intertwined semantics of the connectors and components increases the challenge of discovering and correcting errors in the design of more complex systems. Therefore, we prefer an approach that allows us to modify connectors and components more independently of each other.

3 Plug and Play with Message Passing

As illustrated in the example above, changing from asynchronous message passing to synchronous message passing requires changes in the components, not just in the connectors. In practice, designers must consider a wide range of alternative semantics when selecting the appropriate interaction mechanism for a connector. If it is subsequently discovered, perhaps through verification, that the selected interaction mechanism is wrong, then it is likely that, not only the connector, but the associated components will need to be modified and then reevaluated. Therefore, the impact of changes in connectors on components will not only make it more challenging for designers to find a suitable design, but will also affect the maintainability and reusability of the system components. Our approach tries to address these problems by decomposing connectors into ports and channels, by representing the semantic variations for both ports and channels as building blocks that can be assembled to provide the desired interaction mechanism, and by designing these building blocks so that components can communicate through standard interfaces that are designed to work with any kinds of connectors.

In this section, we show how our plug-and-play approach can be realized for message passing, one of the most commonly used interaction mechanisms for distributed systems. We first present examples of building blocks that are derived from a variety of commonly used message passing semantics. We then define standard component interfaces and show how connectors and components communicate with each other through a set of protocols. We also discuss how finite-state verification can be employed to facilitate the plug-and-play style of design. Finally, we mention that this approach is not restricted to message passing, but can be applied to many of the most common interaction mechanisms. In particular, we discuss briefly how this can be accomplished for the publish/subscribe interaction mechanism.

3.1 Message Passing Variations and Building Blocks

Many languages such as CSP [9] and Linda [10] incorporate message passing facilities. There are also message passing libraries such as MPI [11]. Although the fundamentals of message passing interactions are sending and receiving messages, there are a surprising number of semantic variations for these two operations, as well as variations in the communication media used to store and deliver messages.

For example, a synchronous send operation will block the sender until the message is delivered to the recipient, while other variations would allow the sender to continue execution immediately or as soon as the message is stored in the buffer. Similarly, a receiver component may be blocked or may return immediately when a desired message cannot be retrieved from the buffer at the moment. A receive may also allow messages to be selectively retrieved from the buffer based on a matching criteria. Other variations of message passing semantics involve the message buffers, such as the size of the buffer and the ordering of messages been stored and delivered.

With such variations, determining a particular kind of message passing interaction for a system essentially means selecting a combination of these semantics. As we have demonstrated in the previous sections, this large design space may make it difficult for designers to choose the correct and desirable semantics. Our approach helps designers with such choices by creating building blocks that capture the different combinations of the variations for each aspect of the message passing semantics, and therefore allowing designers to experiment with the variations by plugging and playing with these building blocks. Our building blocks include different kinds of send ports, receive ports, and channels that together cover a number of variations for the most commonly used message passing semantics. A small sample of the message passing building blocks, selected to include those used in our examples, is given in Figure 2.

Figure 3(a) shows an example of how one may specify an asynchronous message passing communication between a pair of sender and receiver components. The connector is composed of an asynchronous blocking send port, a blocking receive port, and a channel that buffers one message. Through this connector,

Send Port	**Asynchronous Nonblocking**	Waits for a message from the sender and sends a confirmation back immediately the message may or may not be accepted and handled by the channel.
	Asynchronous Blocking	Waits for a message from the sender and sends a confirmation back AFTER the message has been accepted by the channel.
	Asynchronous Checking	Waits for a message from the sender and forwards it to the channel. If the message cannot be accepted by the channel, it returns and sends a notification to the sender; Otherwise it blocks until the message is accepted and sends a confirmation back to the sender.
	Synchronous Blocking	Waits for a message from the sender and sends a confirmation back AFTER it is notified by the channel that the message has been received by the receiver.
	Synchronous Checking	Similar to "asynchronos checking send" except that when the message can be accepted by the channel, it blocks until the message is received by the receiver and then sends a confirmation back to the sender.
Receive Port	**Blocking**	Waits for a "receive request" from the receiver and forwards it to the channel. It blocks until a desired message is retrieved from the channel and sends a confirmation to the receiver.
	Nonblocking	Similar to "blocking receive" except that it returns immediately if no desired message can be retrieved currently. It then sends a notification along with an empty message to the receiver.
Channel	**1-slot buffer**	A buffer of size 1.
	FIFO queue	A FIFO queue of size N.
	Priority queue	A priority queue of size N.

Fig. 2. A set of message passing building blocks

the sender component sends a message without waiting for an acknowledgement from the receiver but blocks until the message is stored in the channel. The receiver component blocks until a message can be received. By replacing the asynchronous send port with a synchronous one from the library, the new connector in Figure 3(b) allows the sender to block not only until the message is stored in the channel but also until it has been delivered to the receiver. Similarly, channels can also be easily replaced. For example, the single-slot buffer can be replaced by a FIFO queue channel that holds up to 5 messages, when messages need to be buffered (as shown in Figure 3(c)). Moreover, the replacement of channels can be done independently of the replacement of ports. This kind of "plug-and-play" development facilitates experimentation with alternative interaction semantics. We have also found that our approach helps reduce the effort needed for repeated model construction when designers use design-time finite-state verification to check their design choices.

3.2 Component Interfaces and Protocols Among Building Blocks

In this section , we describe the standard component interfaces for sending and receiving messages and the protocols used between these interfaces and different kinds of connectors. The component interfaces are used as follows: A sender component first issues a send command and then waits to receive a *SendStatus* message from the connector; similarly, a receiver component first sends a receive request to the port, waits for a *RecvStatus* message, followed by another message from the connector that may contain the requested data. These interfaces are designed to work with connectors having different send and receive semantics. For example, in the case of asynchronous message passing, the connector returns the *SendStatus* message to the sending component immediately, while for synchronous message passing, the connector returns the *SendStatus* until after the sender's message has been delivered. The *RecvStatus* message indicates whether the requested message has been successfully retrieved, that is, whether the subsequent message contains the real data. Different connectors may send these

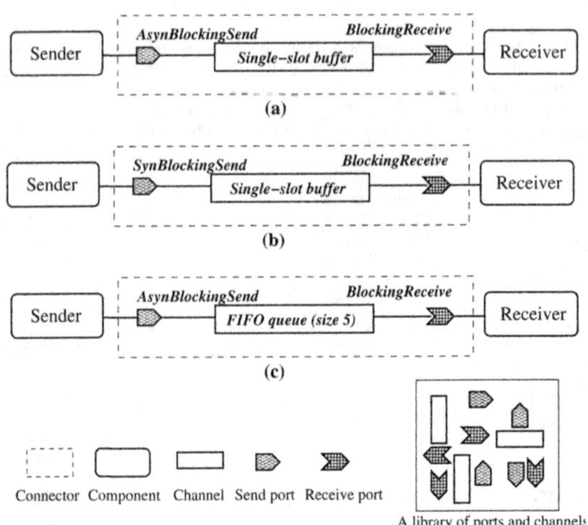

Fig. 3. Constructing message passing connectors

messages at different stages of retrieving a message. Moreover, always sending a message after the *RecvStatus* allows this interface to work with nonblocking receives that allow failure of retrieving messages.

To see how different connectors may interact with these interfaces, one has to first understand the important role of ports in supporting the kind of plug-and-play design we propose. In our approach, connectors are decomposed into channels that represent the communication media (in this case the message buffers), and ports that capture the synchronization semantics of the communication. This separation frees components from being tied to any specific synchronization semantics and therefore allows easy manipulation of all aspects of interaction semantics. It is the ports that handle the interleavings of communications between components and channels and deciding when a specific status or data message should be forwarded, hiding all the details from both components and channels.

Using a notation similar to Message Sequence Charts, Figure 4 and 5 show the typical protocols used between components, ports and channels for sending and receiving messages. In Figure 4,we see that for both asynchronous send and synchronous send, the same set of protocols are used between the sender component and the send port, and between the send port and the channel. It is the send port that controls the relaying and interleaving of the internal events, and thus whether the message passing is synchronous or asynchronous. In Figure 4(a), the asynchronous send port returns the *sendOk* message to the sending component without waiting for the channel to deliver the message and simply discards the *receiveOk* message from the channel when it arrives. The synchronous send port in Figure 4(b) waits to receive the *receiveOk* message from the channel before sending *sendOk* to the sending component, which is therefore blocked until after the message m is received. Neither the sending component nor the channel needs to know whether the connector is implementing synchronous or

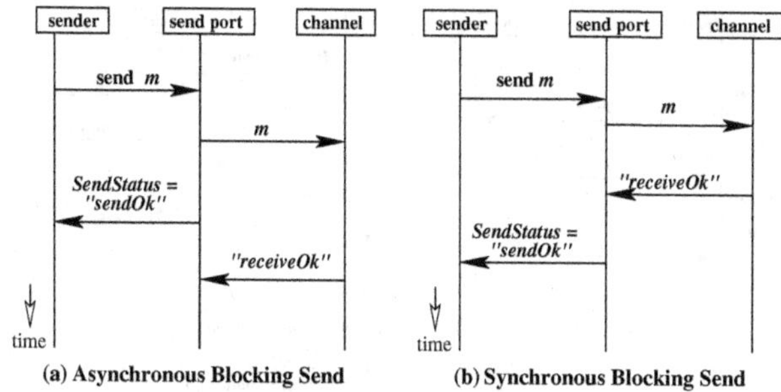

Fig. 4. Example scenarios of message passing interactions (using send ports)

asynchronous message passing; the designer can swap one send port for another to switch the semantics of the connector.

Similarly, Figure 5 shows that same protocols can be used for both blocking receive and nonblocking receive. In Figure 5(a), after forwarding the *ReceiveRequest* from the receiver to the channel, the port blocks until an *outOk* message is received from the channel indicating that the desired message is available. A *recvSucc* confirmation is then sent to the receiver following the retrieved message. To implement the semantics of nonblocking receive (Figure 5(b)), a receive port may immediately return when the desired message is not available (*outFail*) by sending a *recvFail* message followed by an empty message to the receiving component. In a fashion similar to that illustrated above, we are able to support the plug-and-play of a number of different send and receive ports as well as channels defined in Figure 2.

3.3 Design-Time Verification

In addition to providing a convenient and efficient way of specifying and experimenting with various interaction semantics, we also support design-time verification for checking specification properties of the system. For finite-state verification techniques such as model checking, formal models of the system need to be constructed before verification can be applied. For the purpose of our approach, predefined and reusable formal models can be created for each building block in our library. Formal models of the selected building blocks are then composed at verification time with formal models of the components to form a system model that is then checked against the properties specified. Note that the designer is responsible for providing the models of the components and specifying the properties.

Through verification, designers may find unexpected behaviors or errors in their system design. If the problems are caused by the interaction mechanisms, changes can be made by simply adjusting the building blocks of the connectors, perhaps without having to modify the components. When this occurs, there is no need to recreate the component models. Moreover, predefined models for the building blocks can be used in most cases to represent the modified interaction mechanisms, also reducing the cost of model construction.

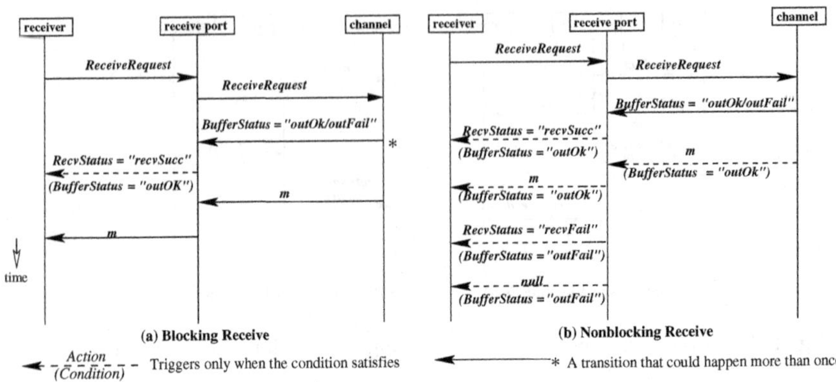

Fig. 5. Example scenarios of message passing interactions (using receive ports)

To evaluate our approach, we have used SPIN [5] to verify a series of designs using our building blocks. In our evaluation, the formal models of components and building blocks are described in Promela, the input language of SPIN. We use the default message passing operations ("?" and "!") in Promela to implement the communications among components, ports and channels. Each port is a Promela *proctype* that takes two Promela native channels as parameters for communications with the component and the channel that are connected to this port. For the purpose of the evaluation, we have coded models in a way that reflects our goal of reusable and parameterizable building blocks. For a particular choice of interaction mechanisms, it might well be possible to implement connectors more directly using features of the Promela language. The full description of the Promela models for the building blocks is given in [12].

Notice that by using SPIN and Promela to support design-time verification, we are showing only one possible way to combine our design approach and verification. Our approach is not tied to particular formalisms or verification techniques. In fact, we have defined the same set of building blocks in the process algebra FSP and used LTSA [7] to verify the system designs. It is reasonable to expect, however, that when using different formalisms and verification techniques, specialized optimizations will need to be developed.

3.4 Other Interaction Mechanisms

Although here we have described this approach for message passing interactions, we believe that the overall approach can be applied to most commonly used interaction mechanisms. To validate this claim, we have also applied this approach to publish/subscribe interactions, another commonly used interaction mechanism. In publish/subscribe systems, the fundamental communications between components and connectors are the announcement of events by components, the delivery of events to components, and the subscription or unsubscription by which components indicate their interest in particular events. It is straightforward to map these communications to sending and receiving messages; therefore they

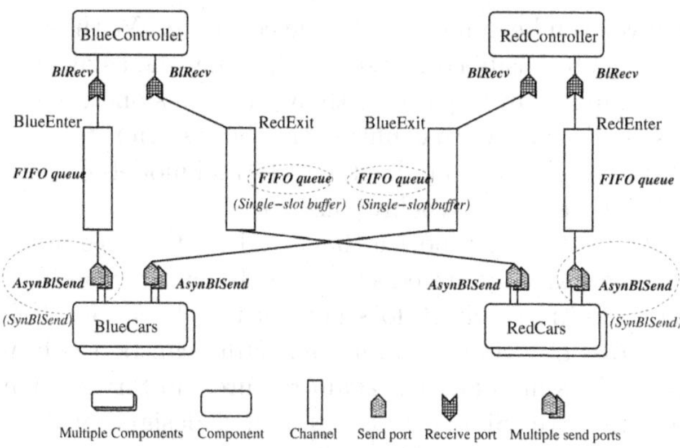

Fig. 6. An initial design of the "exactly-N-cars-per-turn" single-lane bridge

can be described using available message passing building blocks. In message passing, it is almost always the case that the sender initiates the communication by pushing messages to the connector and the receiver pulls messages from the connector. Unlike message passing, however, most publish/subscribe systems support one or more combinations of *push/pull* on both the publisher side and the subscriber side. To describe these semantics, new kinds of send and receive ports that capture such *push/pull* semantics are defined. A more detailed discussion about the building blocks for publish/subscribe can be found in in [12].

4 The Single-Lane Bridge Example Revisited

We now return to the single-lane bridge example introduced in Section 2 to illustrate how the techniques described above facilitates iterative exploration and verification of designs. Figure 6 shows an architecture design of the exactly-N-cars-per-turn version of the system. All the cars from the same direction (indicated as having the same color) communicate with the controller at each side through a single connector. For the initial design, asynchronous message passing is chosen for both the communication between a car and the controller on its entering side and the communication between the car and the controller on the other side. FIFO queues are selected for buffering messages.

One important property of the system that we want to check is that cars traveling in opposite directions can never be on the bridge at the same time. By composing the Promela models of the components provided by the designer and the prebuilt models of the building blocks from the library, we can use SPIN to determine whether the system satisfies the property. In this case, of course, SPIN produces a counterexample in which a blue car sends an *enter_request* message and enters the bridge, followed by a red car sending an *enter_request* message and entering the bridge. As noted above, the problem is obviously the result of the careless design of the asynchronous communication between cars and the controller handling enter requests, which allows cars to enter the bridge before their enter requests have even been received by the controller. With our approach, the erroneous design can be easily corrected by replacing the asynchronous blocking send ports for sending enter requests with synchronous ones, and no changes in the components are necessary. To confirm that the system now satisfies the property, the verification can be repeated with the formal models of the asynchronous ports replaced by those of the synchronous ones.

In fact, astute readers may notice that the FIFO queues used for buffering *exit_request* messages are not necessary since the exact ordering in which the *exit_request* messages are received does not matter. Therefore, the FIFO queue channels used in *BlueExit* and *RedExit* connectors can be safely replaced with single-slot buffers. This modification again requires no further changes in other parts of the architecture. Similarly, the modified design can be re-verified as before to make sure the system still satisfies the property.

Of course, not all modifications to a system require only simple changes in the interaction mechanisms. Suppose that, in order to improve traffic flow, the designer wishes to modify the bridge system so that when there are fewer than N cars crossing the bridge from one side, the turn can be yielded without waiting for N cars to cross, allowing cars from the other side to enter the bridge. To change the previous design of the single-lane bridge into this "at-most-N-cars-if-waiting" version, additional communication between the controllers needs to be added. Although this functional change of the system unavoidably requires changes in the controller components, we can see that with our approach, we can reduce the impact of these changes on both the design and the verification.

Figure 7 shows a possible architecture for the modified system, with two new connectors between the controllers to allow the communication of the current traffic status at each end. The interactions between two controllers are represented in a synchronous message passing connector composed of a synchronous blocking send port, a nonblocking receive port, and a reliable single-slot buffer. Since the controllers now have to actively poll enter request messages from cars to check if there is any car waiting to enter the bridge, we also need to change the blocking receive ports used by the controllers in the previous design into nonblocking ones. To verify that this new system still prevents crashes on the bridge, the component models need to be modified to reflect the new communications. Models of the new connectors, however, can be constructed from models of the building blocks in the library.

A third and more realistic variation of the single-lane bridge example might involve traffic control of emergency vehicles. Although this again cannot avoid functional changes in the components, the necessary changes in the interaction mechanisms would not affect the components and can be made easily. For example, the FIFO queues used for buffering enter request messages may be replaced with priority queues to handle emergency requests. The new design can be verified again in the same manner as described above. The detailed design and formal models of the three versions of the example are described in [12].

Through this example, we illustrate how our plug-and-play approach, integrated with design-time verification, may assist the designer exploring a series

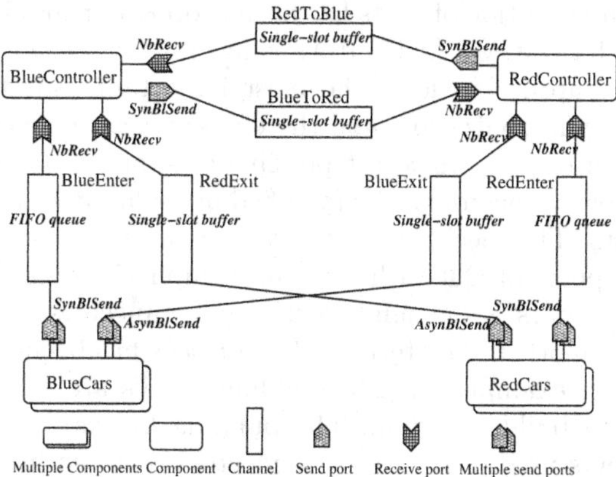

Fig. 7. The architecture design of the "at-most-N-cars-if-waiting" single-lane bridge

of system designs. With our approach, the impact of each change can be kept relatively local, in that components only need to be modified when they must handle new functionality. Changes in a connector can be made relatively easily by selecting alternative building blocks to define that connector.

5 Related Work

The limitations and frustrations of component-based development are well known (e.g., [13, 14]). Previous work, such as [15, 1, 2, 3, 4, 16], has proposed treating connectors as first-class entities in component-based development, although [16] in particular, has put the focus at a lower level of abstraction (programming level) than what we are interested in.

The idea of specifying complex connectors and modeling them for verification is, of course, not new. The Wright architecture description language [1], for example, uses the CSP process algebra to describe arbitrary connectors. The Architectural Interaction Diagrams (AIDs) of Ray and Cleaveland [17] use process algebra methods to construct connectors hierarchically. Constraint automata based approaches have also been proposed to specify and analyze the semantics of connectors composed from a set of primitive channels [18, 19]. In approaches like these, the burden is on the designer to construct connectors with the right semantics from powerful, but low-level, primitives. Our approach is aimed more at providing a library of building blocks from which connectors representing widely used interaction mechanisms can be easily constructed, offering "ready-to-use" pieces that hide from the user most of the details of how these pieces are actually constructed and modeled. The interaction mechanisms we describe are at a lower level of abstraction than the communication patterns described in [20]. Our approach defines finer-grained patterns that express specific semantics of interactions, and provide a mechanism that allows the designer to work with the detailed semantics.

Although a similar notion of ports has been proposed in architectural description languages such as ACME [21] and ArchJava [22], in our approach, ports are used to explicitly capture some of the most important aspects of interaction semantics such as synchronization, and therefore are treated as parts of connectors. Our definition of ports makes it possible to support standard component interfaces that allow connectors to be modified or replaced with minimal impact on the components. The mechanism we use to realize this is closely related to the connector wrappers of [23], although their emphasis is on adapting existing connectors whereas ours is on building up new connectors that can be easily exchanged for one another. The term *building blocks* has been often used in different contexts. For example, in [24], building blocks are referred to as parts of software used to build a system. The building blocks in our approach are design-level elements used to construct connectors representing interactions.

Our work on the semantics of interaction mechanisms is related to the work on categorizing connectors (e.g. [25,26]). In particular, our analysis of the variations of message passing semantics is similar in spirit to the analysis of publish/subscribe systems in [27]. There has been extensive work on applying verification to systems employing a single type of interaction mechanism (e.g. [28,29,30]). Our approach is intended to support many kinds of mechanisms, rather than being restricted to a single type.

A number of middleware frameworks support component-based development, although each typically allows a somewhat limited range of interaction mechanisms and provides no direct support for verification. Some work, such as the Cadena system [31], has been directed at providing verification support for systems built on standard middleware. There is also work on the verification of middleware-based software architecture [32]. A number of tools and approaches have also been proposed for assembling existing components into applications, including mediators [33], Piccola [34], and various techniques for wrapping components. Our interest here is more in the choice of interaction mechanisms between components and less on the adaptation of existing components to interact with each other. Our approach also differs from previous work on architectural evolution (e.g., [35,36]) in our focus on supporting the exploration of different interaction mechanisms at the design stage and our emphasis on modeling and verification.

6 Conclusion and Future Work

In this paper, we propose a compositional specification approach that helps designers more easily experiment with different interaction mechanisms between components. By decomposing the connectors into ports and channels, and using ports as mediators between components and channels, we are able to keep the interface of the components simple and standardized so that changes to the interaction mechanisms can be made with little or no modification to the components. The decomposition also allows us to build a library of ports and channels as reusable building blocks to construct connectors with different semantics. Our approach is also integrated with finite-state verification techniques, facilitating design-time verification and the early detection of design errors. Using our approach, designers may experiment with their choice of design for a variety of interaction semantics by simply plugging in, or replacing, building blocks and then using verification to check their design choices. Since this design process may be repeated to reflect system changes, our approach allows considerable reuse of the models of components and connectors. Consequently, we also save on model-construction time while doing the finite-state verification.

We are currently implementing our approach by developing plugins to the architecture design environment AcmeStudio[1] developed at CMU. Our prototype tool will allow designers to define and use building blocks to specify component interactions. It will also allow the specification of component models and the use of a model checker to verify the design. We are also carrying more case studies to demonstrate and further evaluate our approach.

We intend to explore other commonly used interaction mechanisms and, when necessary, to construct additional building blocks to express their semantics. There are a number of interesting issues related to design-time verification. For instance, optimizations could be developed to reduce the system models that are composed from the building blocks and models of the components; these depend, of course, on the particular modeling formalism and verification tools being applied. We need to explore these optimizations and learn when they can be profitably applied.

Acknowledgements

This material is based upon work supported by the National Science Foundation under awards CCF-0427071 and CCR-0205575 and by the U.S. Department of Defense/Army Research Office under award DAA-D19-01-1-0564 and award DAAD19-03-1-0133. Any opinions, findings, and conclusions or recommendations expressed in this publication are those of the authors and do not necessarily reflect the views of the National Science Foundation or the U. S. Department of Defense/Army Research Office. We are grateful to Prashant Shenoy for helpful conversations about this work.

References

1. Allen, R., Garlan, D.: A formal basis for architectural connection. ACM Trans. on Softw. Eng. and Methodol. (1997) 140–165
2. Shaw, M., Garlan, D.: Softw. Architecture:Perspectives on an Emerging Discipline. Prentice-Hall (1996)
3. Magee, J., Dulay, N., Eisenbach, S., Kramer, J.: Specifying distributed software architectures. In: Proc. 5th European Softw. Eng. Conf., Sitges, Spain (1995) 137–153

[1] Available at `http://www.cs.cmu.edu/~acme/AcmeStudio/AcmeStudio.html`

4. Perry, D.E., Wolf, A.L.: Foundations for the study of software architecture. SIGSOFT Softw. Eng. Notes **17**(4) (1992) 40–52
5. Holzmann, G.J.: The SPIN Model Checker. Addison-Wesley, Boston (2004)
6. K.L.McMillan: Symbolic Model Checking: An approach to the State Explosion Problem. Kluwer Academic (1993)
7. Magee, J., Kramer, J.: Concurrency State Models and Java Programs. John Wiley and Sons (1999)
8. Dwyer, M.B., Clarke, L.A., Cobleigh, J.M., Naumovich, G.: Flow analysis for verifying properties of concurrent software systems. ACM Trans. on Softw. Eng. and Methodol. **13**(4) (2004) 359–430
9. Hoare, C.A.R.: Communicating Sequential Processes. Englewood Cliffs, NJ:Prentice-Hall Intl. (1985)
10. Carriero, N., Gelernter, D.: Linda in context. Comm. ACM **32**(4) (1989) 444–58
11. Snir, M., Otto, S., Huss-Lederman, S., Walker, D., Dongarra, J.: MPI: The Complete Reference. MIT Press (1996)
12. Wang, S., Avrunin, G.S., Clarke, L.A.: Architectural building blocks for plug-and-play system design. Technical Report UM-CS-2005-16, Dept. of Comp. Sci., Univ. of Massachusetts Amherst (2005)
13. Garlan, D., Allen, R., Ockerbloom, J.: Architectural mismatch, or, why it's hard to build systems out of existing parts. In: Proc. 17th Intl. Conf. on Softw. Eng., Seattle, Washington (1995) 179–185
14. Inverardi, P., Wolf, A.L.: Uncovering architectural mismatch in component behavior. Science of Computer Programming **33**(2) (1999) 101–131
15. Bálek, D., Plášil, F.: Software connectors and their role in component deployment. In: Proc. Third Intl. Working Conf. on New Developments in Distributed Applications and Interoperable Systems, Deventer, The Netherlands (2001) 69–84
16. Gensler, T., Lowe, W.: Correct composition of distributed systems. In: Tech. of Object-Oriented Languages and Systems. (1999)
17. Ray, A., Cleaveland, R.: Architectural interaction diagrams: AIDs for system modeling. In: Proc. 25th Intl. Conf. on Softw. Eng. (2003) 396–406
18. Arbab, F., Baier, C., Rutten, J.J.M.M., Sirjani, M.: Modeling component connectors in reo by constraint automata: (extended abstract). Electr. Notes Theor. Comput. Sci. **97** (2004) 25–46
19. Mehta, N.R., Medvidovic, N., Sirjani, M., Arbab, F.: Modeling behavior in compositions of software architectural primitives. In: 19th IEEE Intl. Conf. on Automated Softw. Eng. (2004) 371–374
20. Buschmann, F., Meunier, R., Rohnert, H., Sommerlad, P., Stal, M.: Pattern-oriented software architecture: a system of patterns. John Wiley & Sons, Inc., New York, NY, USA (1996)
21. Garlan, D., Monroe, R.T., Wile, D.: Acme: Architectural description of component-based systems. In Leavens, G.T., Sitaraman, M., eds.: Foundations of Component-Based Systems. Cambridge University Press (2000) 47–68
22. Aldrich, J., Chambers, C., Notkin, D.: Archjava: Connecting software architecture to implementation. In: Proc. 26th Intl. Conf. on Softw. Eng., Orlando, FL, USA, ACM (2002)
23. Spitznagel, B., Garlan, D.: A compositional formalization of connector wrappers. In: Proc. 2003 Intl. Conf. on Softw. Eng., Portland, Oregon (2003)
24. van der Linden, F.J., Mller, J.K.: Creating architectures with building blocks. IEEE Softw. **12**(6) (1995) 51–60

25. Hirsch, D., Uchitel, S., Yankelevich, D.: Towards a periodic table of connectors. In: Proc. Third Intl. Conf. on Coordination Languages and Models, London, UK (1999) 418
26. Mehta, N.R., Medvidovic, N., Phadke, S.: Towards a taxonomy of software connectors. In: Proc. 22nd Intl. Conf. on Softw. Eng., Limerick, Ireland (2000) 178–187
27. Garlan, D., Khersonsky, S., Kim, J.S.: Model checking publish-subscribe systems. In: Proc. 10th Intl. SPIN Workshop on Model Checking of Softw., Portland, Oregon (2003)
28. Bradbury, J.S., Dingel, J.: Evaluating and improving the automatic analysis of implicit invocation systems. In: Proc. 11th ACM Symp. on Found. of Softw. Eng., Finland (2003)
29. Zanolin, L., Ghezzi, C., Baresi, L.: An approach to model and validate publish/subscribe architectures. In: Proc. Specification and Verification of Component-Based Systems, Helsinki, Finland (2003) 35–41
30. Giannakopoulou, D., Magee, J.: Fluent model checking for event-based systems. In: Proc. 9th European Softw. Eng. Conf. / 11th ACM SIGSOFT Intl. Symp. on Found. of Softw. Eng., Helsinki, Finland (2003) 257–266
31. Childs, A., Greenwald, J., Ranganath, V.P., Deng, X., Dwyer, M.B., Hatcliff, J., Jung, G., Shanti, P., Singh, G.: Cadena: An integrated development environment for analysis, synthesis, and verification of component-based systems. In: Proc. of Fund. Approaches to Softw. Eng., 7th Intl. Conf. (2004) 160–164
32. Caporuscio, M., Inverardi, P., Pelliccione, P.: Compositional verification of middleware-based software architecture descriptions. In: Proc. 26th Intl. Conf. on Softw. Eng., Washington, DC, USA, IEEE Computer Society (2004) 221–230
33. Sullivan, K.J., Notkin, D.: Reconciling environment integration and software evolution. ACM Trans. Softw. Eng. Methodol. **1**(3) (1992) 229–268
34. Achermann, F., Lumpe, M., Schneider, J.G., Nierstrasz, O.: Piccola – a small composition language. In Bowman, H., Derrick, J., eds.: Formal Methods for Distributed Processing – A Survey of Object-Oriented Approaches. Cambridge University Press (2001) 403–426
35. Medvidovic, N., Rosenblum, D.S., Taylor, R.N.: A language and environment for architecture-based software development and evolution. In: Proc. 21st Intl. Conf. on Soft. Eng., Los Angeles (1999) 44–53
36. van der Hoek, A., Mikic-Rakic, M., Roshandel, R., Medvidovic, N.: Taming architectural evolution. In Inverardi, P., ed.: Proc. 8th European Softw. Eng. Conf./9th Symp. on the Found. of Softw. Eng., Vienna (2001) 1–10

A Symmetric and Unified Approach Towards Combining Aspect-Oriented and Component-Based Software Development

Davy Suvée, Bruno De Fraine, and Wim Vanderperren

System and Software Engineering Lab (SSEL)
Vrije Universiteit Brussel
Pleinlaan 2
1050 Brussels, Belgium
{dsuvee, bdefrain, wvdperre}@vub.ac.be

Abstract. In this paper, we propose a novel approach towards integrating the ideas behind Aspect-Oriented and Component-Based Software Development. Our approach aims at achieving a symmetric, unified component architecture that treats aspects and components as uniform entities. To this end, a novel component model is introduced that does not employ specialized aspect constructs for modularizing crosscutting concerns. Instead, an expressive configuration language is provided that allows to describe both regular and aspect-oriented interactions amongst components. This paper presents the ongoing FuseJ research, a first experiment for realizing this symmetric and unified aspect/component architecture.

1 Introduction

Aspect-Oriented Software Development (AOSD) [11] is a recent software engineering paradigm that aims at improving the separation of concerns offered by present-day software engineering methodologies. A proper separation of concerns is crucial for implementing comprehensible, reusable and maintainable software applications [15]. AOSD research argues that by employing classic software engineering approaches, including Component-Based Software Development (CBSD) [5], the implementation of certain concerns, such as logging, security and caching, cannot be confined into a single logical module. These concerns are called *crosscutting* as their implementation virtually crosscuts the traditional decomposition of an software application. AOSD provides a solution for modularizing these crosscutting concerns by introducing a new modularization entity, called an *aspect*.

Currently, a wealth of technologies are available that all aim at integrating the ideas of both AOSD and CBSD. Examples of such technologies include JAC [16], JAsCo [20], Caesar [14], CAM/DAOP [18], JBoss/AOP [4], AspectWerkz [3] and Spring/AOP [8]. Some AOSD technologies introduce an *asymmetric*, AspectJ-like [10] approach, where crosscutting concerns are implemented through means

I. Gorton et al. (Eds.): CBSE 2006, LNCS 4063, pp. 114–122, 2006.

of a dedicated aspect language. Other, framework-based AOSD technologies implement aspects through the base programming language. Although framework-based approaches allow for a more straightforward integration of aspects within the standard software development process, they still enforce aspects to implement a set of so-called *aspect* interfaces. Hence, similar to asymmetric AOSD approaches, aspects are still considered, treated and implemented as different kinds of entities within the application. This explicit distinction between aspects and components however induces several disadvantages. Inherently, the behavior provided by aspects is not that different from regular component behavior. Both implement some functionality required within the application and it is only the way in which they interact with the rest of the software system that differs. The crosscutting composition mechanism of current aspect modules however, resides itself tangled with the behavior of the concern, explicitly ruling out other ways of integrating its behavior within the application. In addition, the reusability and applicability of existing software components is constrained. Nowadays, several mature, feature-rich components are available that for instance allow managing the security issues within an application. At the moment however, there is no elegant and straightforward solution available for integrating the behavior of existing components in an aspect-oriented fashion.

The research presented in this paper aims at exploring the possibilities and advantages of introducing a symmetric, unified approach towards combining the ideas and concepts of AOSD and CBSD. Instead of introducing and considering aspects as specialized entities, we propose to apply aspect-oriented composition mechanisms upon the existing component constructs. On the one hand, this allows aspects to straightforwardly adopt the same characteristics of components, namely being reusable and independently deployable while at the same time exposing and adhering to a contractually specified interface [21]. On the other hand, the decision whether components should be integrated in a regular or an aspect-oriented manner can be postponed until component composition time and can easily be changed afterwards.

The remainder of this paper presents the ongoing FuseJ research [19], a first experiment for achieving a symmetric and unified aspect/component architecture. The next section introduces the FuseJ component model and its configuration language by presenting a small case study situated in a *Peer-To-Peer* (P2P) file sharing environment. Section 3 discusses related work. Finally, we present our conclusions and future work.

2 The FuseJ Approach

In order to achieve a seamless unification between aspects and components, FuseJ mingles ideas from the AOSD and CBSD world in a simple, expressive component model and introduces a novel configuration language for describing the aspect/component composition. As a small case study, we employ a simplified and partial implementation of a P2P file sharing application. The *download controller subsystem* is responsible for managing the retrieval of shared file

```
interface TransferI {
   byte[] getFileFragment(String aFileName)
   FileFragementInfo findFileFragment(String aFileName);
}

interface NetworkI {
   void send(String host, String info);
   byte[] get();
}

service TransferS {
   provides TransferI;
   expects NetworkI;
}
```

Listing 1. The TransferS service specification

fragments from remote hosts. It features four components, namely `Transfer`, `Network`, `Optimizer` and `Logger`. The `Transfer` component retrieves file fragments and employs the functionalities offered by the `Network` component to communicate with remote hosts. The `Optimizer` component is responsible for optimizing the file fragment transfer strategy depending on several user criteria: one user could be interested in first downloading file fragments that are not very well spread, while other users could be interested in first downloading file fragments from hosts that have a broadband connection. Instead of hard-coding and tangling the logic of these various transfer strategies within the implementation of the `Transfer` component itself, one can better opt for modularizing these strategies as aspects. The next subsections illustrate how FuseJ implements both regular and crosscutting concerns as components and elucidates how the FuseJ configuration language helps at integrating and composing them in the P2P download controller subsystem.

2.1 FuseJ Component Model

FuseJ employs a simple, straightforward Java-based component model, built upon the well-known concept of *provided-expected* interfaces. Its main objective is to keep coupling amongst components as low as possible, hence achieving maximum reusability. To this end, FuseJ proposes the concept of a *service specification*. A service specification defines the set of operations implementing components should *provide* to and can *expect* to be offered by the environment in which they are eventually deployed. The *provided* and *expected* operations of a service specification are described in terms of regular Java interfaces.

Listing 1 illustrates the `TransferS` service specification. Components that implement this service specification are required to provide an implementation for operations that are part of the `TransferI` interface, while at the same time they can employ operations that are part of the `NetworkI` interface within their internal implementation. Hence, the set of provided interfaces make up the publicly accessible interface of the component, while the expected interfaces describe the set of interaction points with operations offered by other components.

Listing 2 illustrates the simplified implementation of the `TransferC` component that implements the `TransferS` service specification. This component

```
class TransferC implements TransferS {

   public byte[] getFileFragment(String aFileName) {
      FileFragementInfo info = findFileFragment(aFileName);
      send(info.host(), "get|" + aFileName + "|" + info.filefragement());
      return get(); }

   public FileFragementInfo findFileFragment(String aFileName) {
      /* Code for sequential retrieval of file fragments */ }

}
```

Listing 2. The TransferC component implementation

is required to provide an implementation for all operations defined within the `TransferI` interface. Whenever the `TransferC` component is ordered to retrieve a shared file fragment, it employs the `findFileFragment` operation. The default implementation of the `findFileFragment` operation employs a non-optimized download strategy, namely a sequential retrieval of file fragments. When a specific file fragment to download is found, the *expected* operations `send` and `get` are employed in order to retrieve the file fragment from a remote host. All operations that are part of the expected interfaces of a component (e.g. the `send/get` methods) can be transparently invoked from within the component implementation. Hence, the entire implementation of a concrete component is implemented in terms of its own service specification, this way minimizing coupling with other concrete service specifications and components.

The FuseJ component model does not support the language level specification of non-functional properties typically encountered in CBSD systems, such as quality of service, security and life-cycle management. As these kind of non-functional properties have already been identified as being crosscutting [7], FuseJ provides and models these properties as regular components, which are later on composed with specific application concerns in an aspect-oriented fashion. The next section describes how components are composed/integrated into a single application by making use of the FuseJ configuration language.

2.2 FuseJ Configuration Language

For describing the component composition process, the FuseJ configuration language makes use of an explicit *configuration* construct, a concept borrowed from architecture systems [6]. A configuration acts as a kind of mediator, which prescribes how two or more components should interact by linking *provided/expected* operations. Listing 3 illustrates the structure of a FuseJ configuration entity. Each configuration configures two or more components and the resulting composition again complies with a particular service specification. Each configuration is built up out of one or more *linklets*. Each linklet *links* the operations defined in one or more components and is generally built up out of four individual parts:

- A **target role** that enumerates the set of operations to execute (line 3).
- A **source role** that enumerates the set of operations that act as trigger (line 4).

```
1 configuration <name> configures (<comp>|<serv>)+ as <serv> {
2     (linklet <linkname> {
3         execute|expose : (<compop>|<servop>)+
4         for|before|after|around|as : (<compop>|<servop>)+
5         (where: (<parameter_mapping>)+)?
6         (when: (<compop>|<servop>)+)?
7     })+
8 }
```

Listing 3. General structure of a FuseJ configuration entity

- An optional **property mapping** that enumerates the set of property mappings, described in terms of source, target or external operations (line 5).
- An optional **condition specification** that enumerates the set of preconditions, described in terms of source, target or external operations (line 6).

As FuseJ implements both regular and crosscutting concerns as basic components in order to achieve unification, the distinction between both, namely the way in which their interaction takes place, emerges at the configuration level. In its most basic form, a linklet links up two operations, either defined at the component or the service level.

```
configuration TransferNetC configures
   TransferC, NetworkC as TransferNetS {

   linklet send {
      execute:
        NetworkC.sendData(Ip ip, String st);
      for:
        TransferC.send(String ho, String st);
      where:
        ip = IpConvertC.convert(ho);
   }

   linklet get { ... }
}
```

Fig. 1. A component-based interaction between the TransferC - NetworkC components

Figure 1 illustrates a configuration that specifies two regular, component-based interactions. It *configures* the `TransferC` and `NetworkC` components as the new `TransferNetC` component that complies with the `TransferNetS` service specification. Two separate *linklets* are employed. The `send` linklet interconnects the `send` and `sendData` operations of respectively the `TransferC` and `NetworkC` components. Hence, whenever the `TransferC` component employs the *expected* `send` operation, the *provided* `sendData` operation of the `NetworkC` component is executed. A linklet also prescribes how operation properties (i.e. input and output parameter) are matched. Properties employed within the source and target roles of a linklet are specified through a unique identifier. When these specified identifiers match in both a source and target role (e.g. the `st` parameter), they are automatically reified. When this is not possible (because of distinct parameter types), the *where*-clause declares how the mapping takes place (e.g. the `ho` String parameter that gets converted to a parameter of type `Ip`).

In order to comply with the `TransferNetS` service specification, the configuration implicitly exposes the `getFileFragment` and `findFileFragment` operations of the `TransferC` component, although a separate *expose-as* linklet can be employed if required. The newly configured `TransferNetC` component can be employed within other configurations, hence supporting the hierarchical construction of applications.

```
configuration LoggedTransferNetC configures
   TransferNetC, LoggerC as TransferNetS {

   linklet log {
      execute:
        Logger.log(String st);
      before:
        TransferNetC.*(..);
      where:
        st = Source.getMethodSignature();
   }

}
```

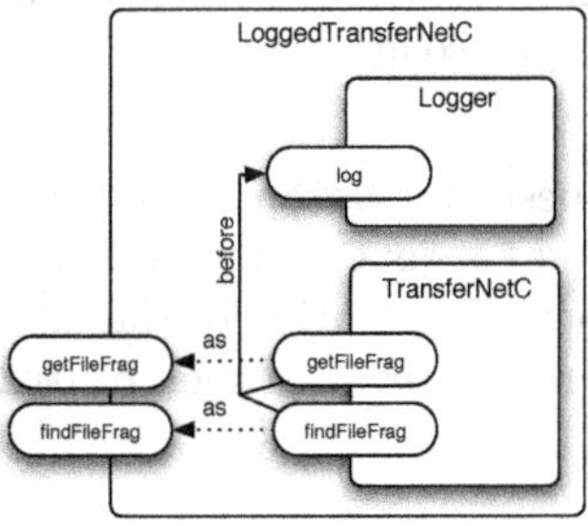

Fig. 2. An aspect-oriented before interaction between the TransferNetC - LoggerC components

Next to regular, component-based interactions, a configuration can also describe aspect-oriented interactions, this by declaring the source role as being advised. At the moment, three kinds of crosscutting interactions are supported, namely *before*, *after* and *around*. The *before* and *after* interactions trigger the behavior of additional operations, which act as *advice*, before or after an advised operation. The configuration illustrated in Figure 2 for instance, makes sure that each execution of an operation that is part of the `TransferNetC` component is logged for future reference. For this, *quantification* is employed in order to select the appropriate methods that should be advised by the `Log` operation of the `Logger` component. The *where* clause inits the *st* parameter with the method signature of the triggering operation. For this, it accesses the `Source` object, a component that is the run-time reification of the operation that triggered the interaction (i.e. *join point*). In a similar fashion, `Target` allows to access the run-time reification of the operation that is executed by the interaction.

An *around* interaction wraps and possibly replaces the original behavior of an operation. FuseJ models the continuation of an around advice, which corresponds with the *proceed* concept in asymmetric AOSD approaches, through means of an explicit proceed operation, specified as an *expected* operation. Figure 3 illustrates a configuration that specifies a crosscutting around interaction through its *optimize* linklet. It recuperates the `LoggedTransferNetC` component and wraps the behavior of its `findFileFragement` operation with the `optimize` operation declared by the `OptimizerC` component. Depending on whether the

```
configuration OptimizedLoggedTransferC configures
   LoggedTransferNetC, OptimizerC as TransferNetS {

   linklet optimize {
      execute:
        OptimizerC.optimize(String f);
      around:
        TransferNetC.findFileFragment(String f);
   }

   linklet optimizeproceed { }
}
```

Fig. 3. An aspect-oriented around interaction between the LoggedTransferNetC - OptimizerC components

request can be optimized, the original file fragment retrieval behavior of the `TransferNetC` component is either executed or not. For this, the `subjectedop` expected operation of the `OptimizerC` component is back-linked to the advised operation through the `optimizeproceed` linklet.

3 Related Work

Several aspect-oriented technologies have been introduced that also aim at avoiding a specialized aspect module. Multi-Dimensional Separation Of Concerns is one of the first approaches that promotes the simultaneous modularization of multiple concerns, without one dominating the other [13]. HyperJ, its practical realization, captures concerns in so called *hyperslices*. *Hypermodules* are used to compose a set of hyperslices in order to build up the application. One of the main differences between HyperJ and FuseJ however, is that FuseJ concentrates on describing interactions between components, while HyperJ focuses on describing mappings. In many cases, the HyperJ approach requires components to share common method names and arguments, which easily gives raise to problems when combining independently specified third-party components.

Invasive Software Composition is a component-based approach that unifies several software engineering techniques, such as architecture systems and generic and aspect-oriented programming [2]. Invasive Software Composition aims at improving the reusability of software components. To this end, software components are equipped with both explicit and implicit hooks. These hooks are composed using a separate composition mechanism. Hooks are similar to the *provided/expected* operations of FuseJ components. FuseJ component operations however, only expose the component's public interface, while hooks can be attached at any programming construct. Hence, hooks support a finer level of granularity and the resulting composition has more expressive power. The downside however is that, as the internals of a component are not contractually specified, the composition could easily break later on when the component implementation evolves.

More recently, two approaches, namely FAC [17] and DyMac [12], have emerged that, similar to FuseJ, specifically aim at eliminating the dissimilarities between aspects and components. When FAC and DyMac are employed, software applications are decomposed into regular components and *aspect components*, where an aspect component is a regular component that modularizes the behavior of a crosscutting concern. Similar to FuseJ, dedicated binding constructs are introduced that specify the (crosscutting) interactions amongst individual components. In contrast with FuseJ however, FAC and DyMac do not strive for a full unification between aspect and components. Component methods that are employed as advices still need to comply to a particular set of requirements (for instance method names and argument types), which obstructs a full symmetric model for aspects and components.

4 Conclusions and Future Work

In this paper we present the ongoing FuseJ research, a symmetric and unified approach towards combining the ideas and concepts of aspects and components. To this end, the FuseJ research introduces a novel component model that does not employ specialized aspect constructs for modularizing crosscutting concerns. Instead, aspect-oriented composition mechanisms are provided through means of an expressive component configuration language that allows to describe both regular and aspect-oriented interactions amongst components. Next to the features described in this paper, the FuseJ configuration language also provides support for more advanced aspect-oriented mechanisms including more involved *pointcut* designators such as *cflow*, *dynamic triggering conditions* and *aspectual polymorphism*. A first prototype implementation of the FuseJ component architecture is available.

Although the FuseJ unified aspect/component architecture yields several advantages, some aspect-oriented encapsulation and composition techniques still need to be integrated in order to achieve full AOSD expressiveness. For instance, the integration of *aspect precedence/combinations* still needs to be examined. In addition, experiments will be conducted that investigate the applicability of aspects at the architectural level itself.

References

1. M. Akşit, editor. *Proc. 2nd Int' Conf. on Aspect-Oriented Software Development (AOSD-2003)*. ACM Press, Mar. 2003.
2. U. Aßmann. *Invasive Software Composition*. Springer, 1st edition, 2003.
3. J. Bonér and A. Vasseur. AspectWerkz: simple, high-performant, dynamic, lightweight and powerful AOP for Java. Home page at `http://aspectwerkz.codehaus.org/`, 2004.
4. B. Burke et al. JBoss Aspect-Oriented Programming. Home page at `http://www.jboss.org/products/aop`, 2004.
5. F. Duclos, J. Estublier, and P. Morat. Describing and using non functional aspects in component based applications. In Kiczales [9], pages 65–75.

6. D. Garlan and M. Shaw. An introduction to software architecture. *Advances in Software Engineering and Knowledge Engineering*, 1:1–40, 1994.
7. S. Göbel, C. Pohl, S. Röttger, and S. Zschaler. The COMQUAD component model: enabling dynamic selection of implementations by weaving non-functional aspects. In K. Lieberherr, editor, *Proc. 3rd Int' Conf. on Aspect-Oriented Software Development (AOSD-2004)*, pages 74–82. ACM Press, Mar. 2004.
8. R. Johnson et al. *Spring Java/J2EE Application Framework, Reference Documentation*, 2004. Available at http://www.springframework.org/docs/spring-reference.pdf.
9. G. Kiczales, editor. *Proc. 1st Int' Conf. on Aspect-Oriented Software Development (AOSD-2002)*. ACM Press, Apr. 2002.
10. G. Kiczales, E. Hilsdale, J. Hugunin, M. Kersten, J. Palm, and W. G. Griswold. An overview of AspectJ. In J. L. Knudsen, editor, *Proc. ECOOP 2001, LNCS 2072*, pages 327–353, Berlin, June 2001. Springer-Verlag.
11. G. Kiczales, J. Lamping, A. Mendhekar, C. Maeda, C. Lopes, J.-M. Loingtier, and J. Irwin. Aspect-oriented programming. In M. Akşit and S. Matsuoka, editors, *11th Europeen Conf. Object-Oriented Programming*, volume 1241 of *LNCS*, pages 220–242. Springer Verlag, 1997.
12. B. Lagaisse and W. Joosen. Component-based open middleware supporting aspect-oriented software composition. In *Proceedings of CBSE 2005*, pages 139–254, St. Louis, USA, May 2005.
13. H. Ossher and P. Tarr. Multi-dimensional separation of concerns and the hyperspace approach. In Kluwer, editor, *Proceedings of the Symposium on Software Architectures and Component Technology: The State of the Art in Software Development*, 2000.
14. K. Ostermann and M. Mezini. Conquering aspects with Caesar. In Akşit [1], pages 90–99.
15. D. L. Parnas. On the criteria to be used in decomposing systems into modules. *Comm. ACM*, 15(12):1053–1058, Dec. 1972.
16. R. Pawlak, L. Seinturier, L. Duchien, L. Martelli, F. Legond-Aubry, and G. Florin. Aspect-oriented software development with Java Aspect Components. In R. E. Filman, T. Elrad, S. Clarke, and M. Akşit, editors, *Aspect-Oriented Software Development*, pages 343–369. Addison-Wesley, Boston, 2005.
17. N. Pessemier, L. Seinturier, T. Coupaye, and L. Duchien. A model for developing component-based and aspect-oriented systems. In *Proceedings of the 5th International Symposium on Software Composition*, Vienna, Austria, 2006.
18. M. Pinto, L. Fuentes, M. Fayad, and J. M. Troya. Separation of coordination in a dynamic aspect oriented framework. In Kiczales [9], pages 134–140.
19. D. Suvée, B. De Fraine, and W. Vanderperren. FuseJ: An architectural description language for unifying aspects and components. In L. Bergmans, K. Gybels, P. Tarr, and E. Ernst, editors, *Software Engineering Properties of Languages and Aspect Technologies*, Mar. 2005.
20. D. Suvée and W. Vanderperren. JAsCo: An aspect-oriented approach tailored for component based software development. In Akşit [1], pages 21–29.
21. C. Szyperski. *Component Software: Beyond Object-Oriented Programming*. 1st edition, 1998.

Designing Software Architectures with an Aspect-Oriented Architecture Description Language

Jennifer Pérez, Nour Ali, Jose A. Carsí, and Isidro Ramos

Department of Information Systems and Computation
Polytechnic University of Valencia
Camino de Vera s/n
E-46022 Valencia, Spain
{jeperez, nourali, pcarsi, iramos}@dsic.upv.es

Abstract. A great deal of languages have emerged and have demonstrated the advantages that Aspect-Oriented Programming offers. For this reason, the aspect-oriented approach is being introduced into the early phases (analysis and design) of the software life cycle. In this work, we present an Aspect-Oriented Architecture Description Language (AOADL) to specify software architectures of complex, dynamic and distributed software systems. This AOADL follows the PRISMA approach, which integrates the advantages of Component-Based Software Development (CBSD) and Aspect-Oriented Software Development (AOSD). The PRISMA AOADL combines components and aspects in an elegant and novel way achieving a better management of crosscutting-concerns. In addition, it is independent of the technology, and it has great expressive power in order to facilitate the automatic code generation from its specifications. In this work, we demonstrate how PRISMA AOADL improves the management, maintainability and reusability of software architectures introducing the notion of aspect in its ADL.

1 Introduction

Nowadays, software systems are becoming more and more difficult to develop due to their complex structures, non-functional requirements and distributed and dynamic nature. Two approaches of software development have emerged to overcome these needs: Component-Based Software Development (CBSD) [7, [27] and Aspect-Oriented Software Development (AOSD) [2].

On the one hand, CBSD reduces the complexity of software development and improves its maintenance by increasing software reuse. CBSD decomposes the system into reusable entities called components. By extension, this advantage is provided by software architectures [8] due to the fact that architectural models are constructed using components. As a result, software architectures have emerged as a solution for the development process of complex software systems.

On the other hand, AOSD allows the separation of concerns by modularizing crosscutting concerns into a separate entity, the aspect. The encapsulation of the aspect permits the reusability of the same aspect in different objects, and the evolution of an aspect without affecting the other objects and aspects. The main emphasis in this approach has been made at the implementation level, by introducing the Aspect

I. Gorton et al. (Eds.): CBSE 2006, LNCS 4063, pp. 123 – 138, 2006.

Oriented Programming (AOP) as a new paradigm of software development. A great number of aspect-oriented programming languages have been proposed and have demonstrated that AOP improves the structure and reusability of the code [10].

PRISMA is an approach to develop complex software systems that has been designed taking into account different solutions of interest: CBSD and AOSD. This approach provides a model and an Aspect-Oriented Architecture Description Language (AOADL). The model defines software architectures by integrating aspect-oriented software development (AOSD) and component-based software development (CBSD). This integration is directly reflected in its AOADL. In this work, we specially focus on the demonstration of the improvement of the reusability, the development, and the maintainability of architectures using the PRISMA AOADL.

PRISMA AOADL defines the semantics of the architectural models in a formal way in order to validate and verify PRISMA architectural models and to automatically generate source code from the PRISMA AOADL. It is important to keep in mind that the PRISMA language is independent of the technology and it has great expressive power. These properties allow us to generate code from its specifications and to choose among different technologies at the time of generating the code. For this reason, we can compile the same PRISMA architectural model into different programming languages and technologies, thereby reducing the development time and preserving the traceability between an architectural model and its application code.

The structure of the paper is the following: Section 2 presents a brief summary of related work. Section 3 gives an overview of the PRISMA approach and presents in detail the PRISMA AOADL by demonstrating its main advantages. Conclusions and further work are presented in the last section.

2 Related Work

A wide variety of models based on the separation of concerns have been proposed [21], [28], etc. However, the most widely used is the Aspect-Oriented Paradigm (AOP). Aspect-Oriented models can be classified into two different categories: static models and dynamic models. The static models are not able to change aspects and their weaving at run-time, whereas the dynamic ones offer this advantage. Examples of dynamic models are the Mask Model [22] and the Dynamic Aspect-Oriented Platform (DAOP) [18].

A well-accepted aspect-oriented programming language is AspectJ [10], which is an extension of Java, where the code is separated into aspect and non-aspect code (objects). However, based on experiments implementing different aspects such as persistence and distribution [25], this model has many drawbacks (static, limited reusability). Therefore, in [19], work has been done to provide dynamic weaving using the Java Virtual Machine Debugger Interface (JVMDI).

AOP is being transferred to other platforms such as .NET by means of extensions. However, the existing .NET approaches for supporting AOP are still in an early phase and only Rapier-Loom.Net [23] supports mechanisms for adding or removing aspects dynamically. However, it defines the weavings inside the aspects thereby losing their reusability. EOS [20] is another dynamic approach that is able to attach aspects at the instance level by means of events. However, none of these approaches takes into account the emerging relations that result from the aggregation of various aspects at the same point of the base code (joinpoint). The JAsCo [26] approach is presented as a solution of this lack. It provides an expressive language that permits the definition of relations among aspects. JAsCo integrates AOSD and CBSD at the implementation level by extending the JavaBeans and introducing connectors to perform dynamic aspect weaving by preserving the aspect reuse. The inconvenience of this approach is that the dynamic weaving of aspects to the base code is referential but not inclusive. As a result, base code and the aspects are not inside the same entity when they are instantiated and the code mobility is limited. As mobility is an essential feature of software components, PRISMA AOADL provides all these needed properties at the same time. These properties are the following: dynamic weaving (run-time evolution), the join of the base code and the aspects inside the same entity (mobility support), and the reuse of aspects (reusability). Finally, an important difference between these AOP approaches and PRISMA AOADL is the technological independence; all these properties are going to be integrated at the architectural level of the software development process, instead of integrating them at the implementation level.

A wide variety of ADLs have been proposed at the architectural level, an interesting comparison between these languages has been made in the work by [11]. Some proposals for the integration of the software architecture and the AOSD have emerged in order to take advantage of both approaches [5]. Each one introduces aspects in their Architecture Description Languages (ADLs) in a different way: as a component [13], as a connector among components [18], as a view of the architecture [9], etc. However, PRISMA introduces the aspect in its ADL as a new concept without simulating it with any other architectural term (components, connectors, views, etc).

Our approach does not only introduce aspects as new requirements [13], it takes advantage of the notion of aspect from the beginning of the system definition. Also, the complete view of the software architecture is not lost by the use of aspects as [9]. Moreover, at the configuration level, when the architectural elements are instantiated, we do not lose the structural and architectural view of the system due to the fact that our components are connected by means of connectors instead of aspects [18]. As Shaw presents in her work [24], the specification of software systems with complex coordination protocols is too difficult without the connector architectural element. This is because the connector provides the separation of the component interaction achieving a higher level of abstraction, modularity and architectural view of the system. TranSAT [3] is another approach that incorporates aspects that refine the original component specification and generates another one that includes them without losing the black box view of the component. However, this approach is only focused on technical aspects.

In [4], the main requirements for developing aspect-oriented software architectures are presented. They are the linguistic support for weaving aspects, dynamic adaptability, and reusability. PRISMA AOADL is presented as a good solution to specify aspect-oriented software architectures because it satisfies these requirements.

3 PRISMA: An Aspect-Oriented Architecture Description Language (AOADL)

The PRISMA approach allows the definition of software architectures of complex software systems by integrating AOSD and CBSD. PRISMA uses AOSD to separate the crosscutting concerns (distribution, security, context-aware, coordination, etc.) of the architecture in aspects. In this way, the PRISMA architectural elements are defined by using aspects to define their behaviour.

A PRISMA architectural element can be analyzed from two different views, internal and external. The internal view (see Figure 1) shows an architectural element as a prism with each side of the prism being an aspect that is imported by this architectural element. This represents that an architectural element of PRISMA is formed by a set of aspects and weavings relationships among aspects. Whereas, the external view (see Figure 2) is an architectural element that encapsulates its functionality as a black box, and by means of its ports publishes and receives a set of services to and from the rest of the architectural elements.

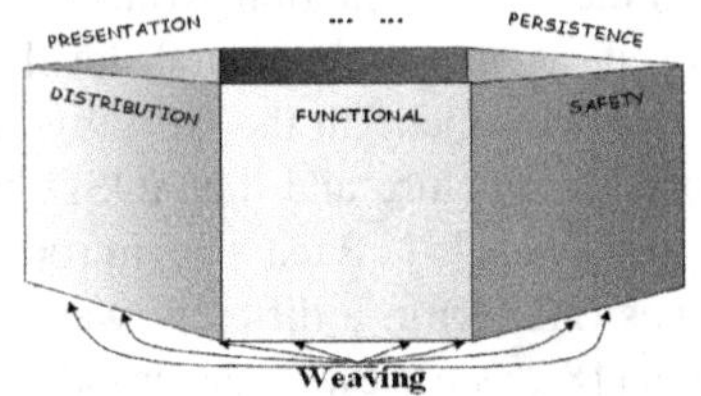

Fig. 1. Internal View of an Architectural Element

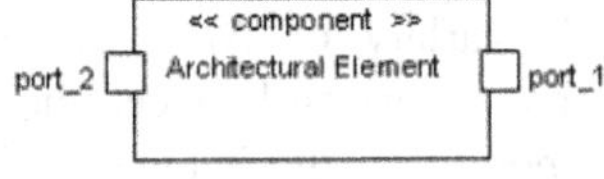

Fig. 2. External View of an Architectural Element

The PRISMA AOADL defines the architectural elements at different levels of abstraction: the type definition level and the configuration level. The type definition level defines architectural types with a high abstraction level. Its main advantages are software reuse and complexity reduction by integrating components and aspects. The PRISMA types defined at this level are stored in a PRISMA repository so that they can be reused by other types or specific architectures.

The configuration level designs the architecture of software systems by creating and interconnecting instances of the defined architectural elements in the type definition level. In other words, we specify the topology of a specific software system at this level.

In the following sections, a very simple banking system example is going to be used to illustrate the PRISMA AOADL. An information system that contains a client-server architecture between two components is defined. By this simple banking system, we present the specification of different aspects (coordination, distribution and functional aspects) and architectural types.

There are two components that are involved in the banking system and are connected with each other: an *ATM* and an *Account.* The ATM is the client component that requires *withdrawal* and *balance* services from the *Account.* The *Account* is the server component that offers the required services to the *ATM.* The

ATM stores an ATM number that identifies it (*numberId*), the amount of money available in the ATM (*money*) and where the ATM is located (*address*). The *Account* stores an account number that identifies it (*numberId*), the amount of money (*money*), and the postal address of its owner (*address*). The system has a connector *ATMAccount* that controls the communication process between the two components. In order to simplify the example we do not take the persistence aspect into account and we assume that the information is stored in the main memory.

3.1 The Type Definition Level

The type definition level of PRISMA defines architectural patterns (complex components) and the first-class citizens of the language: interfaces, aspects, components, and connectors. They are stored in the PRISMA repository in order to be reused.

3.1.1 Interfaces

An *interface* publishes a set of services. It describes the signature of the services that can be invoked or requested through that interface. The arguments that define a service can be *input* or *output*. *Input* arguments are necessary to perform the execution of a service, and *output* arguments will store the result of the service execution. Interfaces publish services without taking into account the ports and aspects that are going to use them. In the following, we present some interfaces of the banking system.

```
Interface ICreditCardTransactions
    withdrawal(input Quantity: currency, output MyMoney: currency);
    balance(output MoneyBalance:currency);
    changeAddress(input NewAdd: string);
End_Interface ICreditCardTransactions;


Interface IMobility
    move(input NewLoc:loc);
End_Interface IMobility;
```

3.1.2 Aspects

An *aspect* defines the structure and the behaviour of a specific *concern* of the software system. Examples of concerns are functionality, coordination, safety, distribution, among others. A common syntax of aspects has been defined. This common syntax is going to be presented using the functional aspect.

- **Functional Aspect**

The head of an aspect specifies its name and the kind of concern it defines: *functional, distribution, coordination,* etc. Moreover, interfaces whose semantics is defined by the aspect are detailed next to the reserved word *using*. We are going to define a functional aspect which specifies the semantics of the *ICreditCardTransaction* interface (see Figure 3, nº 1).

Attributes are specified inside an aspect. These attributes are necessary to store information about the characteristics of the aspect. Attributes are preceded by the *Attributes* reserved word and they have a name and a type (see Figure 3, nº 2). This type defines the kind of values that the attribute can store. There are three kinds of attributes:

- *Constant:* Their stored values cannot change
- V*ariable:* The stored values can be modified
- *Derived:* The value is calculated on demand applying its derivation rule.

An aspect defines the semantics of services. The set of services specified in an aspect must contain the *begin* service, the *end* service, and the interface services that this aspect uses (see Figure 3, nº 3). *Begin* and *end* services do not mean that it is possible to instantiate an aspect by itself; they make a reference to the creation and destruction services of the architectural element that the aspect will belong to, and where it will be instantiated. The semantics of services is defined by means of preconditions and valuations. *Preconditions* establish the condition that must be satisfied to execute a specific service (see Figure 3, nº 5). *Valuations* specify the changes in the value of attributes and parameters by the execution of services (see Figure 3, nº 4).

With regard to services, it is important to take into account that the same service can have two different behaviors: client and server. The client behavior is when a service is invoked by an aspect. The server behavior is when a service is offered and processed by an aspect. Sometimes, it is necessary to distinguish between these two behaviors. The syntactical difference between client or server service is the reserved word *in, out* and *in/out.*

The aspect example shown in Figure 3 has a precondition to indicate when the service *withdrawal* can be executed and the valuation of the *withdrawal* indicates how the *money* attribute is updated when this service is executed. The precondition ensures that there is enough money to be able to withdraw the required quantity, and the valuation of the withdrawal updates the quantity of the available money. Services, preconditions and valuations are preceded by the reserved words *Services, Preconditions*, and *Valuations,* respectively.

It is necessary to specify the protocol to describe the order and the state in which a service could be executed (see Figure 3, nº7). The protocol is a textual specification of a transition state machine.

An aspect also defines the set of roles that can be played taking into account the semantics of the services. They are called *played_roles* (see Fig 3, nº6). A played_role is a projection of the protocol that defines the partial behaviour belonging to a specific role. This role must be compliant with the signature and the process of the protocol. As a result, the played_role is performed inside the global behaviour of the protocol, and its calculations are a subset of the calculations of the protocol.

Every service that composes a played_role belongs to the same interface. This is specified at the beginning of the played_role specification with the *for* keyword and the name of the interface. A played_role is a partial view of the protocol that has its own meaning, a specific behaviour that can be later associated to a port. This association allows us to define the behaviour of ports.The formal language that we used to describe the *Played_Roles* and *Protocols* is the poliadic π-calculus [12]. The main advantage of this language is the fact that it allows us to describe processes and services that can be executed concurrently in a simple way.

```
1 Functional Aspect BankInteraction using
   ICreditCardTransaction
2   Attributes
        numberId: number;
        name: string;
        address: string
        money: currency;
3   Services
        begin;
        in/out withdrawal(input Quantity: currency, output
                         MyMoney:currency);
4                 Valuations
                         [in withdrawal(Quantity, MyMoney)]
                           money := money - Quantity;
                            MyMoney := Quantity;
        in/out balance(output MoneyBalance:currency);
4                  Valuations
                         [in balance(MoneyBalance)]
                           MoneyBalance := money;

        in/out changeAddress(input NewAdd: string);
4                  Valuations
                       [in changeAddress(NewAdd)]
                         address := NewAdd;
        end;
5   Preconditions
        in withdrawal(Quantity)
             if Quantity <= money;
6   Played_Roles
        BANK for ICreditCardTransaction ::=
                     (withdrawal ?(Quantity, MyMoney)
                      → withdrawal !(Quantity, MyMoney))
                      +
                      (balance ?(Quantity, MyMoney)
                       → balance !(Quantity, MyMoney))
                      +
                      (changeAdress ?(Newadd)
                      → changeAdress !(Newadd));
        CUSTOMER for ICreditCardTransaction:: =
                     ( withdrawal !(Quantity, MyMoney)
                      → withdrawal ?(Quantity, MyMoney))
                      +
                      (balance !(Quantity, MyMoney)
                       → balance ?(Quantity, MyMoney)
                      +
                      (changeAdress !(Newadd)
                      → changeAdress ?(Newadd));
7   Protocol
        BANKINTERACTION ::= begin → TRANSACTION;
        TRANSACTION = (BANK || CUSTOMER) → TRANSACTION + end;
End_Aspect BankInteraction;
```

Fig. 3. *BankInteracation* Functional Aspect

- **Distribution Aspect**

This aspect has the same sections of a functional aspect with some predefined attributes and services. The distribution aspect [1] specifies the locations of the instances. However, if the location is specified in the distribution aspect, the same distribution aspect cannot be reused in different architectural elements if instances are distributed in different locations. This problem is solved using the PRISMA AOADL due to the fact that it is separated into the Type Definition Language and the Configuration Language. Thus, the Type Definition Language specifies that a type has a location without assigning it a value. The value of the location is assigned when architectural elements are instantiated in the Configuration Language.

```
Distribution Aspect ExtMbile using IMobility
   Attributes
      id: nat;
      location: LOC NOT NULL;
   Services
     in move(input NewLoc:LOC);
        Valuations
           [in move(NewLoc)] location:= NewLoc;
  Played_Roles
     MOVEMYSELF::= IMobility.move ? (NewLoc);
  Protocols
        EXTMBILE ≡ begin → MOVEMENT;
        MOVEMENT ≡ MOVEMYSELF  → MOVEMENT +
                   end;
End_Distribution Aspect ExtMbile;
```

Fig. 4. *ExtMbile* distribution aspect

The distribution aspect presented in Figure 4 specifies the behaviour of a mobile architectural element enabling the change of the location attribute by the *move* service *valuation*. The attribute *location* has an abstract data type called *LOC*. This data type hides the different mechanisms of locations of an architectural element at a physical level, e.g. it can be a URL, an IP, etc. The *location* attribute should have a value when an architectural element is instantiated; this is indicated by the *NOT NULL*.

- **Coordination Aspect**

This aspect presents the same sections as a functional one. The difference between both aspects is their purpose, functionality is for computation and coordination is for synchronization of architectural elements. Figure 5, shows the coordination aspect which allows the synchronization of two architectural elements whose port type is the *ICreditCardTransaction* interface.

In Figure 5 the *BankCoordination* coordination aspect does not have attributes because it does not perform computations, it only synchronizes. However, a coordination aspect can have attributes to take coordination decisions in complex protocols. Figure 5 also shows that the coordination played roles are the opposite processes of the functional played_roles (see Figure 3). This is due to the fact that the coordinator units have the opposite process view of the computational units, i.e., an output action for a computation unit is an input action for a coordinator unit and vice versa.

```
Coordination Aspect BankCoordination using ICreditCardTransaction
    Services
       begin;
        in/out withdrawal(input Quantity: currency, output
                         MyMoney:currency);
        in/out balance(output MoneyBalance: currency);
        int/out changeAddress(input NewAdd: string);
        end;
   Played_Roles
       CUSTOMER for ICreditCardTransaction ::=
                  (withdrawal ?(Quantity, MyMoney)
                  → withdrawal !(Quantity, MyMoney))
                  +
                  (balance ?(Quantity, MyMoney)
                   → balance !(Quantity, MyMoney))
                  +
                  (changeAdress ?(Newadd)
                  → changeAdress !(Newadd));
       BANK for ICreditCardTransaction:: =
                  ( withdrawal !(Quantity, MyMoney)
                  → withdrawal ?(Quantity, MyMoney))
                  +
                  (balance !(Quantity, MyMoney)
                   → balance ?(Quantity, MyMoney)
                  +
                  (changeAdress !(Newadd)
                  → changeAdress ?(Newadd));
7   Protocol
      BANKCOORDINATION ::= begin → STNCHRONIZE;
      SYNCHRONIZE ::=
        (CUSTOMER.withdrawal ?(Quantity, MyMoney)
         → BANK.withdrawal!(Quantity, MyMoney))→ SYNCHRONIZE
        +
        (CUSTOMER.balance ?(Quantity, MyMoney)
        → BANK.balance!(Quantity, MyMoney)) → SYNCHRONIZE
        +
        (CUSTOMER.changeAdress ?(Newadd))
        →(BANK.changeAdress !(Newadd)) → SYNCHRONIZE
        +
        (BANK.withdrawal ?(Quantity, MyMoney)
        → CUSTOMER.withdrawal!(Quantity, MyMoney))→SYNCHRONIZE
        +
        (BANK.balance ?(Quantity, MyMoney)
        → CUSTOMER.balance !(Quantity, MyMoney)) → SYNCHRONIZE
        +
        (BANK.changeAdress ?(Newadd))
        →(CUSTOMER.changeAdress !(Newadd)) → SYNCHRONIZE
        + end;
   End_Coordination Aspect BankCoordination;
```

Fig. 5. *BankCoordination* Coordination Aspect

3.1.3 Components and Connectors

A simple architectural element is specified with the set of ports, the aspects it is formed of, and the aspect weavings. It can be noticed from the aspects specification in section 3.1.2, that an aspect definition does not include the points where an aspect needs to coordinate with the rest of other aspects (aspect weavings). In this way, aspects are completely maintainable and reusable. Therefore, when architectural elements are defined they import the aspect types from the PRISMA repository and define their weavings. An aspect weaving is specified by determining the aspects that participate in the weaving, the services of the aspects where they are weaved, and the weaving methods. A weaving that relates service s1 of aspect A1 and service s2 of aspect A2 can be specified using the following operators:

- A2.s2 **after** A1.s1: A2.s2 is executed after A1.s1
- A2.s2 **before** A1.s1: A2.s2 is executed before A1.s1
- A2.s2 **instead** A1.s1: A2.s2 is executed in place of A1.s1

```
Component Account

  Functional Aspect Import BankInteraction;
  Distribution Aspect Import ExtMbile;

  Weavings
    BankInteraction.changeAddress(NewAdd: string)
    before
    ExtMbile.move(NewAdd: string);
  End_Weaving;

  Ports
    AccountCnct: ICreditCardTransactions
                 Played_Roles BankInteraction.CUSTOMER;
    AccountSys: ICreditCardTransactions
                 Played_Roles BankInteraction.CUSTOMER;
  End_Ports;
End_Component Account;

Component ATM

  Functional Aspect Import BankInteraction;
  Distribution Aspect Import ExtMbile;

  Ports
    ATMCnct: ICreditCardTransactions
             Played_Roles BankInteraction.BANK;
  End_Ports;
End_Component ATM;
```

Fig. 6. Definition of Components

Simple architectural elements in PRISMA are components and connectors. A component is an architectural element that captures the functionality of the information system and does not act as a coordinator between other architectural elements; whereas, a connector is an architectural element that acts as a coordinator between other architectural elements. In order to better understand how to specify components and connectors, we show their syntax by means of the specification of the *ATM* and *Account* components and the connector that connects them.

The specified aspects in section 3.1.2 are going to be reused to define the architectural elements of the example. The same *ExtMbile* distribution aspect (see Figure 4) specifies the *Account* and *ATM* components (see Figure 6), and the

ATMAccount connector (see Figure 7). The *BankInteraction* functional aspect (see Figure 3) is reused in the *Account* and *ATM* components (see Figure 6). The *BankCoordination* coordination aspect (see Figure 5) is used to define the connector *ATMAccount* (see Figure 7). However, it is important to note that these aspects could be reused to create other architectural elements. We present the synchronization between aspects in the *Account* component; for example, when the customer address changes (*ChangeAddress*), the account of this customer must be moved to another place nearer to his/her new address (see weaving section in the *Account* component in Figure 6).

```
Connector ATMAccount

   Coordination Aspect Import BankCoordination;
   Distribution Aspect Import ExtMbile;

   Port
      ATM: ICreditCard_Transactions
            Played_Roles BankCoordination.BANK;
      Account: ICreditCard_Transactions
            Played_Roles BankCoordination.CUSTOMER;
   End_Port;
End_Connector ATMAccount;
```

Fig. 7. Definition of Connectors

3.1.4 Systems, Attachments and Bindings

PRISMA components can be simple or complex. The complex ones are called systems. A PRISMA system is a component that includes a set of connectors, components, and other systems that are correctly linked.

A system is specified as a pattern so that it can be reused in any software architecture that could be necessary. The difference between a system and a simple component is that it needs attachments and bindings:

-Attachments: They are connection relationships that establish the connection among ports of components and connectors.

- Bindings: They are connection relationships that establish the connection among the system (complex component) and the architectural elements it contains. The bindings allow the system to define its exterior behaviour (ports) by means of the architectural elements it contains.

Figure 8 shows the definition of the *SimpleBank* type. The set of architectural elements, that are necessary to define the system, are imported, and the number of instances that can be specified at configuration time are constrained. In the specification of the *SimpleBank* system (see Figure 8), this number is not specified and the default value (min=1, max=n) is applied to each type. In addition, the connections among the different types of architectural elements are specified in order to define the architectural pattern. The *SimpleBank* type has two types of attachments. They establish the connections among ports of components (*ATM, Account*) and ports of connectors (*ATMAccount*). Each type constrains the cardinality of the attachment at configuration time. The *SimpleBank* bindings establish the connection among the systems ports (*SimpleBank*) and the connectors or/and components ports (*Account*) that the system is composed of (see bindings section). Each type constrains the cardinality of the binding at configuration time. The cardinality constrains of the system allow us to define a specific pattern of communication that must be satisfied at the configuration time.

```
System  SimpleBank
   Ports
      Banksystem: ICreditCardTransactions;
   End_Port;

   Import Architectural Elements ATM, Account, ATMAccount;

   Attachments
      Account.AccountCnct (1..n) ←→ (1..1) ATMAccount.Account;
      ATM.ATMCnct (1..n) ←→ (1..1) ATMAccount.ATM;
   End_Attachments;

   Bindings
      SimpleBank.Banksystem (1..1) ←→ (1..n) Account.AccountSys;
   End_Bindings;
                              End System SimpleBank;
```

Fig. 8. *SimpleBank* system specification

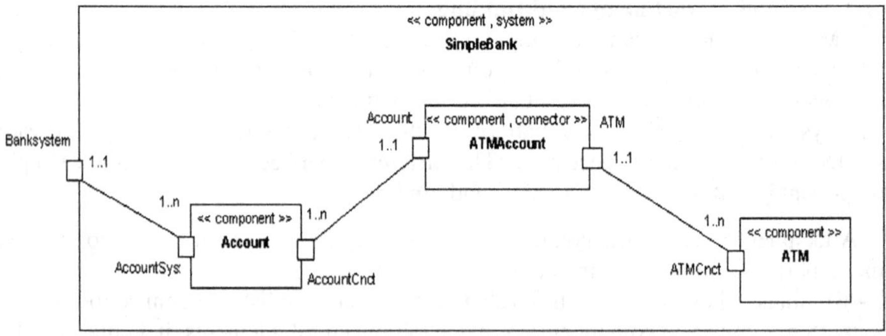

Fig. 9. *SimpleBank* system graphical representation[1]

Figure 9 illustrates the graphical view of the architecture that has been specified in Figure 8.

3.2 The Configuration Level

The configuration level is used to define a specific architectural model for a software system. In order to do this all required connectors, components and systems types should be instantiated, and attachment and binding instances should be added among them. At this moment, constraints that have been defined in systems are validated in order to ensure the pattern satisfaction. An example of a configuration is to define a

[1] The figure has been designed using the Poseidon Tool, http://www.gentleware.com

specific architectural model for a bank by reusing the system type that we have defined in the previous section (see Figure 10).

```
Architectural Model
  MySimpleBank = new SimpleBank(){
     MyFirstCustomer = new Account (0000001, Jose, Main Street 20,
                                   100, mainhost);
     MainATM = new ATM{ATM1, MainBranchATM, London Road, 1000000,
                      localhost);
     BankController = new ATMAccount()
    Attachments
     MyFirstCustomer.AccountCnct <-> BankController.Account;
     MainATM.ATMCnct <-> BankController.ATM;
    End_Attachments;
    Bindings
     MySimpleBank.Banksystem <-> MyFirsCustormer.AccountSys;
    End_Bindings;
  };
End_Architectural Model;
```

Fig. 10. Architectural Model of the *MySimpleBank* Bank System

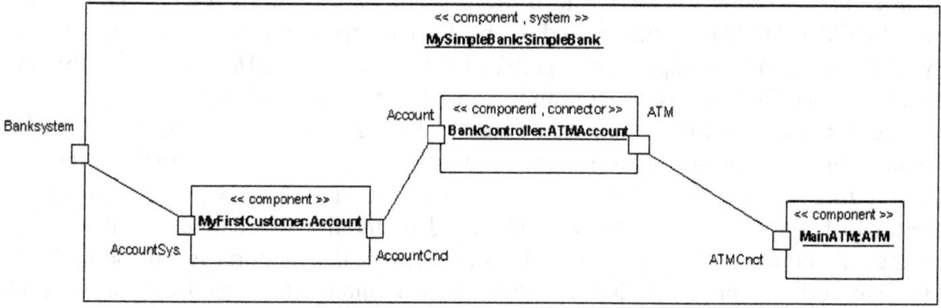

Fig. 11. Graphical representation of the *MySimpleBank* Architectural model[1]

Properties	Style	To Do Items	Source code
Name	MySimpleBank		
Namespace	BankSoftwareArchitecture		
Type	SimpleBank		
Modifiers	☑ active		

Properties	Style	To Do Items	Source code
Name	MyFirsCustomer		
Namespace	BankSoftwareArchitecture		
Type	Account		
Modifiers	☐ active		

Fig. 12. Information related to the instantiation from the types of PRISMA library[1]

Figure 11, shows the graphical representation of the *MySimpleBank* system instance defined in Figure 10. Underlined names indicate that they are instances of a type (see Figure 12).

4 Conclusions and Further Work

In this paper, an AOADL to specify complex, dynamic and distributed information systems has been presented in detail. This language allows us to define PRISMA architectural models. The structure, design and maintainability of architectures specified in the PRISMA AOADL are improved by reusing entities at different levels of granularity (interfaces, aspects, components, connectors and systems). This reusability is achieved by means of the division of the language into two levels of abstraction and the integration of AOSD and CBSD into the language. The stored types defined at the type definition level can be reused by the configuration level to define a specific software architecture. In addition, the fact that interfaces and aspects are first-class citizens of the language increases the reusability because an interface can be used by several aspects and an aspect can be used by several architectural elements. The example of the paper has demonstrated this high level of reusability by reusing an interface to define two aspects, a distribution aspect to define two components and one connector, and other functional aspect to define two components.

We have used a simple example to present the language in order to facilitate the understanding of the language capabilities to the reader instead of using a complex one. However, it is important to keep in mind that PRISMA does not specify simple architectural systems for academic projects such as: pipelines, filters, blackboards, etc. PRISMA AOADL is being used to specify industrial projects where the software systems are complex, open, and active such as the *TeachMover* robot [16] and EFTCoR [17]. EFTCoR is a robot family that cleans the hulls of ships.

The PRISMA AOADL provides a better management of evolution and maintenance of crosscutting-concerns and software architectures. The maintenance of crosscutting-concerns is improved due to the fact that if we want to change the features of a specific concern, we only need to modify or change the aspect that defines the concern, and every architectural element that imports it will be updated. However, other approaches that use non-aspect-oriented ADLs need to look for each statement that is related to the concern in the tangled code of every architectural element of the system. The maintenance of software architecture is improved because the PRISMA approach supports evolution by means of a meta-level which provides a set of evolution services to evolve software architectures at run-time [16].

The PRISMA AOADL has a graphical notation that is based on a UML profile. As a result, PRISMA reduces the complexity in software development by providing a graphical notation and a modelling tool to support more intuitive and friendly software architecture modelling [14].

It is important to take into account that most ADLs only allow us to specify the skeleton of architectures and the services that are interchanged among their different architectural elements. However the PRISMA AOADL has a great expressive power to specify more features and requirements related with the software system by means of aspects in order to facilitate the code generation. We are currently developing the model compiler using DSL tools [6]. This is going to permit the compilation of the same PRISMA architectural model into different programming languages and technologies, thereby reducing the development time and preserving the traceability between an architectural model and its application code. We are improving the graphical modelling tool using DSL tools and we are starting to generate C# code and

PRISMA specifications from graphical PRISMA architectural models. Despite the fact that .NET framework does not provide support for the Aspect-Oriented approach, we are able to execute the C# code generated using our model compiler by developing a .NET middleware for our PRISMA approach called PRISMANET [15]. PRISMANET extends the .NET technology by the execution of aspects on the .NET platform, the reconfiguration of software architectures (local and distributed) and the addition and removal of aspects from components at run-time.

As future work, we are going to introduce validation and verification techniques in our modelling tool. Currently, we support cardinality constrains to define architectural patterns (systems). We are going to extend the language to support other kinds of constrains. In addition, we want to measure the benefits of the language with several case studies.

Acknowledgements

This work has been funded by the Department of Science and Technology (Spain) under the National Program for Research, Development and Innovation, DYNAMICA project TIC2003-7804-C05-01.

References

1. Ali, N., Ramos, I., Carsí, J.A.: A Conceptual Model for Distributed Aspect-Oriented Software Architectures. International Conference on Information Technology Coding and Computing (ITCC), IEEE Computer Society, Las Vegas, NV, USA. (2005)
2. AOSD. Aspect-Oriented Software Development, http://aosd.net (2005)
3. Barais, O., Cariou, E., Duchien, L., Pessemier, N., Seinturier L.: "Transat: A framework for the specification of software architecture evolution". *In* ECOOP First *International Workshop on Coordination and Adaptation Techniques for Software Entities (WCAT04)*, Oslo, June. http://wcat04.unex.es/. bib. (2004)
4. Constantinides, C.A., Elrad, T.: On the Requirements for Concurrent Software Architectures to Support Advanced Separation of Concerns. In proceedings of OOPSLA Workshop on Advanced Separation of Concerns in Object-Oriented Systems. Available at: http://trese.cs.utwente.nl/Workshops/OOPSLA2000/papers/constantinides.pdf. (2000)
5. Cuesta C.E., Romay M.P., De la Fuente P., Barrio-Solórzano M., Architectural Aspects of Architectural Aspects, Second European Workshop on Software Architecture (EWSA), Springer LNCS 3527, Pisa, June (2005)
6. Domain-Specific Language (DSL) Tools, http://lab.msdn.microsoft.com/ teamsystem/ workshop/dsltools/default.aspx
7. D'Souza, D., Wills, A. : "Objects, Components and Frameworks with UML: The Catalysis approach"; Addison-Wesley. (1999)
8. Garlan D., Perry D.: Introduction to the Special Issue on Software Architecture, IEEE Transactions on Software Engineering, 21(4), April (1995)
9. Katara, M., Katz, S.: Architectural Views of Aspects. International Conference on Aspect-Oriented Software Development (AOSD), ACM Press, March, (2003)
10. Kiczales, G., Hilsdale, E., Huguin, J., Kersten, M., Palm, J., Griswold, W.G.: An Overview of AspectJ. In proceedings of the European Conference on Object-Oriented Programming, Springer-Verlag. (2001)

11. Medvidovic, N., Taylor, R. N.: A classification and Comparison Framework for Software Architecture Description Languages. IEEE Transactions of SW Engineering, Vol. 26, nº 1, January. (2000)
12. Milner, R.: π- Cálculo Poliadico: A tutorial. (1991)
13. Navasa, A., Perez, M.A., Murilllo J.M.: .Aspect Modelling at Architecture Desing. 2nd European Workshop in Software Architectures, Pisa, Italy, June, LNCS 3527, Springer Verlang. (2005)
14. Pérez, J., Navarro, E., Letelier, P., Ramos, I.: Graphical Modelling for Aspect Oriented SA, Proceedings on the 21st Annual ACM Symposium on Applied Computing (SAC), ACM ,Dijon, France, April 23 -27, 2006. (short paper)(accepted, to appear)
15. Pérez, J., Ali, N., Costa, C., Carsí, J. A., Ramos, I.: Executing Aspect-Oriented Component-Based Software Architectures on .NET Technology. 3rd International Conference on .NET Technologies, Plzen, Pilsen, Czech Republic, 30 May-1 June. (2005)
16. Pérez, J. Ali, N., Carsí, J.A., Ramos, I.: Dynamic Evolution in Aspect-Oriented Architectural Models. 2nd European Workshop in Software Architectures, Pisa, Italy, June, LNCS 3527, Springer Verlang. (2005)
17. Pérez, J., Ali, N., Ramos, I., Pastor, J.A., Sánchez, P., Álvarez, B. : Tele-operated Systems Development using the PRISMA approach. VIII conference on Software Engineering and Databases, Alicante, Spain. (2003) (in spanish).
18. Pinto, M., Fuentes, L., Troya, J. M.: DAOP-ADL: An Architecture Description Language for Dynamic Component and Aspect-Based Development. Generative Programming and Component Engineering: Second International Conference, GPCE 2003, Erfurt, Germany, September 22-25, Springer Verlag Computer Science, ISSN: 0302-9743. (2003)
19. Popovici, A., Gross, T., Alonso, G.: Dynamic Weaving for Aspect-Oriented Programming. In proceedings of the 1st international conference on Aspect-oriented software development, Enschede, The Netherlands, April. (2002)
20. Rajan, H., Sullivan, K., Eos: Instance-Level Aspects for Integrated System Design. In the proceedings of the 2003 Joint European Software Engineering Conference and ACM SIGSOFT Symposium on the Foundations of Software Engineering (ESEC/FSE), Helsinki, Finland, September. (2003).
21. Rashid, A.: A Hybrid Approach to Separation of Concerns: The Story of SADESK. Proc. Reflection conf., Springer-Verlang, LNCS, 2192, pp. 231-249. (2001)
22. Sánchez, F.: Mask Model: Towards adaptability of synchronization restrictions in LCOO. PhD. dissertation, Extremadura University, Spain. (1999)
23. Schult, W. , Polze, A.: Aspect-Oriented Programming with C# and .NET. In 5th IEEE International Symposium on Object-Oriented Real-time Distributed Computing, (Washington, DC), IEEE Computer Society Press, pp.241-248. (2002)
24. Shaw M.: Procedure Calls Are the Assembly Language of Software Interconection: Connectors Deserve First-Class Status. Proceedings of Workshop on Studies of Software Design, January. (1994)
25. Soares, S., Laureano, E., Borba, P.: Implementing Distribution and Persistence Aspects with AspectJ. In proceedings of the 17th ACM Conference on Object-Oriented programming systems, languages, and applications, *OOPSLA'02*, Seattle, WA, USA, 174-190. (2002)
26. Suvee, D., Vanderperren, W., Jonckers, V.: JasCo: an Aspect-Oriented approach tailored for Component Based Software Development. In proceedings of the 2nd international conference on Aspect-oriented software development. Boston Massachusetts, March. (2003)
27. Szyperski C.: Component software: beyond object-oriented programming, ACM Press and Addison Wesley, New York, USA. (1998)
28. Tarr, P., Ossher, H., Harrison, W.H., Sutton, S. M.: "N Degrees pf Separation: Multi-Dimensional Separation of Concerns". Internacional Conference on Software Engineering (ICSE), ACM, pp. 1907-119. (1999)

A Component Model Engineered with Components and Aspects

Lionel Seinturier[1], Nicolas Pessemier[1], Laurence Duchien[1], and Thierry Coupaye[2]

[1] INRIA Futurs - LIFL, Projet Jacquard/GOAL
Bâtiment M3, 59655 Villeneuve d'Ascq, France
{seinturi, pessemie, duchien}@lifl.fr
[2] France Telecom R&D
28 chemin du Vieux Chêne, BP98
38243 Meylan, France
Thierry.Coupaye@francetelecom.fr

Abstract. This paper presents AOKell, a framework for engineering component-based systems. This framework implements the Fractal model, a hierarchical and dynamic component model. The novelty of this paper lies in the presentation of AOKell, an implementation of the Fractal model with aspects. Two dimensions can be isolated with Fractal: the functional dimension, which is concerned with the definition of application components, and the control dimension, which is concerned with the technical services (e.g. lifecycle, binding, persistence, etc.) that manage components. The originality of AOKell is, first, to provide an aspect-oriented approach to integrate these two dimensions, and second, to apply a component-based approach for engineering the control dimension. Hence, AOKell is a reflective component framework where application components are managed by other, so-called, control components and where aspects glue together application components and control components.

1 Introduction

Software components are more and more used in various application domains. This trend is supported by the fact that many component models are available, coming either from the industry such as Sun EJB [1], Microsoft .NET/COM+, OMG CCM [2], OSGi [3], or from research teams (e.g. ArchJava [4], Fractal [5], FuseJ [6], K-Component [7], OpenCOM [8]).

In our opinion, the domain of component-based software engineering is characterized by two main requirements: the need for components goes beyond the boundaries of programming languages, and components need to be used in various execution contexts, such as embedded applications with strong constraints in terms of memory footprint and execution costs, information systems hosted on application servers, or grid computing. In this paper, we argue that the challenge for component models is to be able to handle these requirements. So far, existing component frameworks are mostly seen as closed, black box entities

I. Gorton et al. (Eds.): CBSE 2006, LNCS 4063, pp. 139–153, 2006.

which provide artefacts to design and program applications with components. The components are handled by the framework, which provides a set of services to manage these application components. Yet, this set of services is most of the time closed. This is the case for example, with the EJB [1] component model, where new services cannot be added to the container.

In this paper we propose AOKell, which is an open implementation in Java of the Fractal component model. By implementation, we mean a software infrastructure for defining and executing components. The implementation is open in the sense that the services provided by the AOKell framework are fully accessible and programmable. By giving programmers a way to engineer these services, AOKell eases the task of adapting component-based applications to different execution contexts. This approach also fosters the development of various forms of control for components such as the ones needed to program self healing components, self-testing components, or components that carry their proofs or their specifications. Two main software techniques are used to engineer these services: components and aspects. Both the applications and the services provided to the applications are designed and implemented with components. Aspects glue together these two dimensions. This paper presents the design and the implementation of AOKell in Java with the AspectJ [9] aspect-oriented language. Although we do not report on it in this paper, AOKell has also been ported to the .NET platform [10].

The paper is organized as follows. Section 2.1 presents the background of this work: the Fractal component model and aspect-oriented programming. Section 3 is the core of the paper and presents the design of the AOKell framework. We show how aspects are used in AOKell (section 3.1) and we present the model for customizing the control dimension (section 3.2). Section 4 reports some performance measurements. Section 5 compares AOKell to similar existing projects. Section 6 concludes this paper and presents our future work directions.

2 Background

2.1 The Fractal Component Model

The Fractal component model [5] is a general model for developing component-based systems. The model is sufficiently open to accommodate the needs of various application domains. For example, the model has been used to implement applications for grid computing [11], operating systems [12], the GoTM transaction monitor [13], a version of the JORAM [14] JMS [15] server and the Speedo [16] JDO [17] persistence framework.

AOKell, the framework presented in this paper, is an implementation of the Fractal component model for the Java programming language. Implementations exist in other programming languages: FracTalk in Smalltalk, Plasma in C++, Think [12] in C, FractNet [10] for the .NET platform. Two additional implementations in Java exist: Julia, which is the reference implementation, and ProActive, which is an implementation for grid computing. Information about these implementations can be found on the Fractal web site[1]. As this will be explained in section 3, the added value of AOKell compared to these implementations is to be based on some concepts of aspect-oriented programming and to introduce the notion of a control component.

Fractal is a hierarchical and dynamic component model. The model is hierarchical in the sense that a component can be composite or primitive. A composite component contains other primitive or composite components. A primitive component is the smallest unit of code packaged as a component. The model is dynamic in the sense that the software architecture of a Fractal application can be manipulated at runtime: components can be created, containment hierarchies can be modified, and bindings (which are communication paths between components) can be set and unset. Components can be shared which means that a component can be included in several non nested composite components. This feature allows designing as components shared resources such as pools (for threads, network sockets, etc.).

Two dimensions can be isolated in the Fractal component model: the functional dimension and the control dimension.

Functional Dimension. The functional dimension is concerned with programming the core functionalities of the application. Besides the notion of a component, which can be primitive or composite, two main artefacts are provided to engineer the functional dimension: interface and binding.

An interface is an access point to a component and supports a finite set of operations. An interface can be of two kinds: server and client. Server interfaces correspond to the services provided by the components, whereas client interfaces correspond to the ones required by the components.

A binding is a communication path between two components, more precisely between a client interface and a server interface. Bindings can be dynamically set and unset to adapt, at runtime, the architecture of the application. The default semantics for the communication in a binding is that of a local method call. However, Fractal components can accommodate various other communication modes such as remote method call, asynchronous message passing, publish/subscribe.

Several other artefacts are provided such as the notion of a template. A template is an existing component assembly that can be cloned. Templates are a powerful means of instantiating, in just one step, complex software architectures containing several components and bindings.

The Fractal component model is associated with an API. The implementations of the model may conform to one of the levels defined in the Fractal Specifications [18], i.e. implementing the whole API is not mandatory. One of the tools worth noticing is Fractal ADL which is an architecture description language (ADL). Assemblies of components can be defined with this XML-based language, which is a front-end for the Fractal API. All architecture descriptions written with Fractal ADL are translated, either statically or dynamically, into series of calls to the API. These calls install the assemblies described with Fractal ADL.

[1] `http://fractal.objectweb.org`

The next piece of XML code illustrates the syntax of Fractal ADL. This sample defines one composite component (`HelloWorld`) and two primitive ones: `client` (line 3) and `server` (line 8). `HelloWorld` provides the `run` interface (line 2). This interface is bound (line 12) to the `run` interface provided by `client`. The `server` component provides a `s` interface (line 9), which is bound (line 13) to the `s` interface requested (line 5) by `client`.

```
 1 <definition name="HelloWorld">
 2   <interface name="run" signature="Runnable" role="server"/>
 3   <component name="client">
 4     <interface name="run" signature="Runnable" role="server"/>
 5     <interface name="s" signature="IService" role="client"/>
 6     <content desc="ClientImpl"/>
 7   </component>
 8   <component name="server">
 9     <interface name="s" signature="IService" role="server"/>
10     <content desc="ServerImpl"/>
11   </component>
12   <binding client="this.run" server="client.run"/>
13   <binding client="client.s" server="server.s"/>
14 </definition>
```

Control Dimension. The control dimension of the Fractal component model is concerned with the supervision and the management of functional components. This dimension provides the services to handle components. The range of services incorporated into the control dimension can vary from basic services such as managing component names, to lifecycle services, or to more complex services such as persistence or transaction services. The control dimension plays a role rather similar to the one played by containers in component models such as EJB [1], except that this control dimension is open and fully programmable with Fractal. Two main artefacts are provided to engineer the control dimension: *membrane* and *controller*.

Each functional component is associated with a membrane. A membrane is composed of a set of smaller units, called controllers. A controller implements a particular control function and is associated to an interface. Controllers may either provide new functionalities to components, such as the ability to set or unset binding, or control existing functionalities, such as intercepting requests or blocking calls on a stopped component.

The Fractal Specifications [18] defines seven control interfaces. However this set is not closed and programmers can still develop their own control interfaces. Furthermore, although the signatures of these interfaces are defined in the specifications, their semantics is only weakly specified. The idea is to accommodate various implementations tailored to developers needs.

Among the seven predefined Fractal control interfaces, three are defined for managing component attributes, component bindings (with methods for setting, unsetting, retrieving and listing bindings), and component lifecycles (starting and stopping a component). Two additional control interfaces are available for managing containment hierarchies: the content control interface manages (adding, removing, listing) sub-components contained in a composite, and the super control interface manages the super components attached to a component. The factory control interface is available for cloning a template. Finally, the component control interface is available for retrieving the basic information about a component such as the list of interfaces. This interface is similar to the `IUnknown` interface of the COM component model.

2.2 Aspect-Oriented Programming

Aspect-Oriented Programming (AOP) [19] is a software engineering technique for modularizing applications with many concerns. The general idea of AOP is that, whatever the domain, applications tend to be decomposed according to a dominant concern. The concerns which do not fit into this decomposition cannot be cleanly modularized.

This issue is illustrated with the well-known example of the Tomcat servlet server where some concerns such as XML parsing are cleanly modularized, whereas others, such as user session management, are implemented in many different classes. This leads to code that is said to be scattered (the implementation of a concern is scattered around several different locations), and tangled (a same piece of code mixes different concerns). AOP aims at providing solutions for untangling and unscattering applications. The notion of an aspect is available to modularize such concerns, which are said to be crosscutting. Several languages and frameworks such as AspectJ [9], JBoss AOP [20], AspectWerkz [21], JAC [22] or JAsCo [23] are available for programming aspect-oriented applications.

The AspectJ language has been chosen to develop the aspects needed by AOKell. This choice has been motivated by the fact that AspectJ is a stable and mature project, well integrated with widely used IDEs such as Eclipse. Also the fact that AspectJ currently provides features for compile-time and load-time weaving, allows covering a wide range of needs.

3 The AOKell Framework

AOKell is our implementation of the Fractal component model for the Java language. The functional dimension of a component-based application with AOKell strictly conforms to the Fractal model. By this way, AOKell can execute any Fractal system. AOKell differs from other existing implementations of the Fractal model by relying on aspects and components for engineering the control dimension, i.e. the services provided to functional components. By providing these two advanced software engineering techniques, we hope to promote flexibility and to allow adapting component-based applications to execution contexts with various and changing constraints.

Section 3.1 describe the structure of a component with AOKell and explain the role devoted to aspects. Next, section 3.2 presents the concepts which have been set up for "componentizing" the membranes.

3.1 Integrating the Control Dimension with Aspects

This section describes how aspects are used in AOKell to integrate control services into components. Section 3.2 will elaborate on the way these control functions are designed and implemented.

Component models such as EJB or CCM provide an architecture where components are hosted by containers that provide technical services. For example, the EJB specifications [24] define services for managing security, transaction, persistence and lifecycle. Most of the time, this set of services is closed and hard-coded in the container. One exception is the JBoss J2EE application server [25] where services can be wrapped and accessed with aspects defined with the JBoss AOP framework [20].

The general idea illustrated with the case of the JBoss server is that aspects, while providing a way for modularizing crosscutting concerns, allow smoothly integrating a concern into applications. This leads to a common practise of AOP: the aspect modularizes a given concern, and either implements it directly, or delegates it to an external module. The separation of concern is almost optimal in the sense that the aspect is only concerned with the logic for integrating the concern into the application.

This pattern is used with AOKell to integrate the control logic into components. More precisely, each control function (a so-called controller in Fractal terms) is associated with an aspect which is responsible for integrating this logic into components. This solution is illustrated in figure 1.

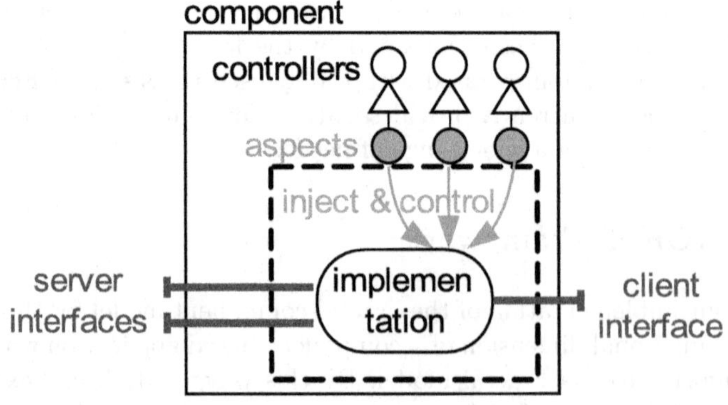

Fig. 1. Structure of a component with AOKell

The integration performed by aspects relies on two mechanisms: feature injection and behavior extension. The first mechanism is known, in AspectJ, under the term inter-type declaration (ITD). With ITD, aspects can declare members (methods and/or fields) to be injected into the classes, in our case into component implementations. All existing control interfaces are injected with this ITD mechanism.

The second mechanism is known, in AspectJ, under the term code advising. Aspects define so-called pointcuts and advice code. Pointcuts pick out a set of join points, which corresponds to the points of the program execution where the aspect needs to be executed. The advice code is a piece of code which will be executed at these points. Code advising is used in AOKell to intercept operation calls and executions. For example, when controlling a component, the lifecycle controller may reject operation executions while the component has not been started. This feature is implemented by defining, in the aspect associated to the lifecycle controller, pointcuts and pieces of advice code.

3.2 Componentized Membranes

The previous section showed how aspects are used with AOKell to integrate the control logic into components. This section elaborates on the way this control logic is designed and implemented.

We have seen that the control logic is defined in the Fractal component model with a membrane composed of controllers, each one being specialized with a particular control mechanism (binding management, lifecycle, etc.). Far from being autonomous, these controllers need to collaborate to achieve the global control function assigned to the membrane. For example, when starting a composite component, the content of this composite needs to be traversed to recursively start sub-components[2]. This implies that the lifecycle controller depends on the content controller. Several other similar dependencies exist between controllers. For clarity sake, we omit details for all these dependencies, which come from the semantics assigned to controllers. Readers can find them in [26].

However, the fact that these dependencies between controllers are hidden and not clearly expressed prevent developers from reusing controllers independantly. Our idea is to apply to the design of the control layer the same principles which were applied to the application layer: engineer the control with components. By "contractually specifying the interfaces" [27] of these control components, we hope to foster their reuse, to clarify the architecture of the membrane, and to ease the development of new ones. By supplying a component-based approach for engineering the control layer, we also hope to obtain gains in terms of flexibility: it will be easier to develop new control layers and thus to adapt applications to execution contexts with different characteristics in term of resource management (memory, threads, etc.).

As a consequence, AOKell is a framework where the concepts of a component, of an interface and of a binding are used to engineer the functional dimension and the control dimension as well. A control membrane with AOKell is a composite component providing the control interfaces associated to that membrane. This composite contains sub-components. Each sub-component implements the control functionality associated to a controller. As explained in the previous section, this component is associated to an aspect that integrates this control logic into application level components. Furthermore, these sub-components are

[2] Note that this is not a formal obligation. One may design a control function where the starting is not recursive.

bound together according to their dependencies. Figure 2 summarizes these elements. For clarity sake, the control membrane for the third component has been omitted.

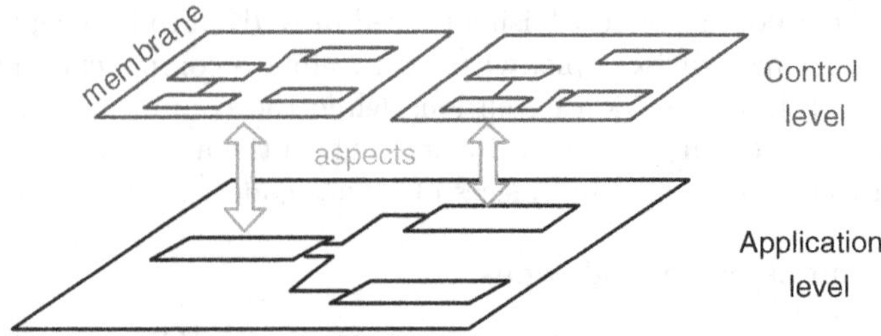

Fig. 2. AOKell component layers

The most widely used control membrane in Fractal applications is the one associated with primitive components. The architecture of this membrane is illustrated in figure 3. This membrane provides five controllers, for managing the lifecycle (`LC`), the bindings (`BC`), the component name (`NC`), the super components (`SC`) and a controller (`Comp`) implementing the general `Component` interface, which is available for all Fractal components. As a matter of convention, provided interfaces are drawn on the left side of the components, and required interfaces are on their right side. Bindings represent communication paths between the controllers.

The architecture presented in figure 3 illustrates that the control function for primitive components is not simply realized by five isolated controllers, but is the result of the collaboration of these five controllers. Compared to a purely object-oriented approach, a component-based solution for the implementation of control

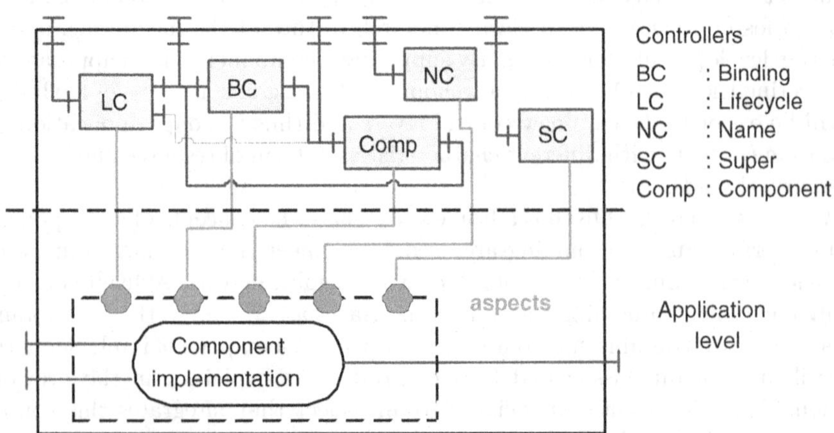

Fig. 3. Primitive membrane: control level for primitive components

membranes allows describing explicitly the dependencies between controllers. New control membranes can be developed by extending existing ones, or simply by developing a whole new architecture.

The benefits of engineering the control dimension with components have been experimented by implementing the Dream framework [28]. Dream is a framework for developing middleware platforms with Fractal. The purpose is to ease the development of middleware by providing a library of component with advanced control functionalities. For example, Dream provides a membrane to define active components, i.e. components with threads or pools of threads to handle their requests. Based on these membranes, a version of the JORAM [14] JMS [15] server has been developed with Dream. Basically, implementing the Dream framework with AOKell consists in implementing a component-based version of the controllers and of defining the architecture of the membranes.

4 Performance Evaluation

This section evaluates the cost of running a component based application with AOKell. We are mainly interested in measuring the cost induced by the component framework and the componentization of membranes. To do so, we compare an application developed with AOKell with the same one developed with a pure object-oriented approach.

AOKell is written in Java and uses AspectJ 1.2.1. The AOKell source code size is 12,604 lines with 104 classes and 13 aspects[3]. Other technical details can be found in [26]. AOKell has also been ported to the .NET platform [10]. For this porting, AspectJ has been replaced by AspectDNG [29].

The tests are conducted with a simple application containing two components: a client component and a server component. The server component provides an interface with eight methods. Each method owns a different signature, either without parameters, or with primitive parameters, or with object references parameters, and/or with return types.

The measures are done on a 2Ghz Pentium 4 PC running Windows XP Pro and Sun JDK 1.5.0. A warm-up phase is performed before taking measures to avoid bootstrapping and class loading costs induced by the JVM. The test consists of series of calls emitted from the client component to the server component. In table 1, the figures correspond to the times taken by 8,000,000 calls (1,000,000 per method defined in the interface provided by the server component). The given figures correspond to the average value of 4 runs.

Table 1 presents the result obtained for this microbenchmark with five different techniques.

- Fractal/Julia: this is a component-based Fractal implementation of the microbenchmark. This version is linked with the Julia (version 2.1.1) reference implementation of the Fractal Specifications.

[3] AOKell can be downloaded from `http://fractal.objectweb.org`

Table 1. Cost of invoking and executing an operation (x 8,000,000)

	Operation execution time	
	without interception	with interception
Pure Java 1.5.0	178ms	
AspectJ 1.2.1		209ms
Fractal/Julia 2.1.1	237ms	515ms
Fractal/AOKell 1.1	215ms	559ms
JBoss AOP 1.1.1		1046ms

- Fractal/AOKell: this Fractal version of the microbenchmark is linked with the AOKell implementation presented in this paper. These two last versions allow comparing a purely object-oriented implementation of the control dimension (Fractal/Julia) with an implementation where the control dimension is componentized (Fractal/AOKell).
- Java: this is a pure object-oriented Java implementation. No components are involved. The client and the server are Java objects. This implementation gives a reference to evaluate the cost of running a componentized application.
- AspectJ: this version is implemented with AspectJ version 1.2.1. No components are involved. The client and the server are Java objects. The server object is advised by an empty around advice. This version gives a clue on the cost of intercepting a method with AspectJ.
- JBoss AOP: this version is implemented with the JBoss AOP [20] (version 1.1.1) framework for dynamic AOP. No components are involved. The client and the server are Java objects. The server object is advised by an empty around advice. This version gives a clue on the cost of intercepting a method with JBoss AOP.

We saw in section 3.1 that controllers may, via aspects, either inject new features or modify the behavior of components by intercepting existing features. The microbenchmark reported in table 1 provides a measure of the interception cost of both Fractal versions.

Control without interception. When compared to the Java implementation, the AOKell version is 21% costlier. The main reason is that the binding between the client and the server component is dynamic: before each call, the reference to the target server component must be resolved. This ensures that at any time the architecture is modified, the communication path between components will be updated accordingly. We believe that this penalty is acceptable compared to the benefits of having a component architecture dynamically updatable.

The figures given in table 1 show that AOKell performs better than Julia. We believe that this is due to the way controllers are implemented in Julia: a mixin mechanism is provided to modularize the different concerns addressed by each controller. When mixed together, these different pieces of code are assembled in a class which contains more indirections than the AOKell version where controllers have been implemented directly. Compared to Julia controllers, AOKell controllers are then less modular in terms of separation of concerns, but they are implemented as components (Julia controllers are objects) and they perform slightly better.

Control with interception. The interception costs reported in the second column of table 1 is due to the Fractal lifecycle controller. The purpose of this controller is to ensure that a call cannot be issued on a stopped component. This mechanism is implemented in Julia by engineering the bytecode of components with the ASM library [30], and in AOKell with AspectJ. When the interception mechanism is activated, the figures in table 1 shows that, compared to Julia, the overhead of running AOKell is 8.5%. This is mainly due to the use of AspectJ compared to that of ASM. In our opinion, this penalty is acceptable compared to the benefits of a high level language such as AspectJ compared to a bytecode engineering library such as ASM.

5 Related Work

This section compares AOKell to related projects.

OpenCOM. v1 [8] and v2 [31] is a component model with support for runtime dynamic reconfiguration. OpenCOM supports different kinds of deployment environments (e.g. operating systems, PDAs, embedded devices, network processors) and allows the particularities of those environments to be selectively hidden from or made visible to the OpenCOM programmer. At the application level, OpenCOM components provide interfaces and receptacles (required interfaces). Interceptor components can be associated with interfaces. The architecture of an OpenCOM application is introspectable and can be dynamically modified. Since v2, OpenCOM provides the four following notions: capsule, caplet, loader, and binder. A capsule is a unit of scope that contains and manages the application components. A caplet is a sub-scope within a capsule that contains a subset of the application components. Binders and loaders are first-class entities that provide various ways of binding and loading components. Caplets, loaders and binders are implemented as components, and several implementations may be provided.

Compared to Fractal, capsules and caplets are similar to composite components. Binders and loaders are similar to Fractal controllers. By customizing the implementation of caplets, loaders and binders, programmers have the ability to adapt applications to different deployment environments. The approach is similar in AOKell where controllers are programmed as components. However, we can put forth three differences with OpenCOM. First, AOKell controllers are not restricted to a particular set of functionalities and can implement any kind of services. Second, controllers are components too, but we have gone a step further by introducing the notion of a component architecture at the control level. Finally, the integration of the control dimension and of the functional dimension is achieved with aspects.

Asbaco. [32], like AOKell, is a proposal for extending the membrane of the Fractal components. The authors introduce the term microcomponent to designate a component that implements a control functionality. Like AOKell, Asbaco microcomponents are associated with the same notions as regular components: they may own client and server interfaces, and bindings can be created between components. However, the API for manipulating bindings between microcomponents is different from the one available for regular components. With AOKell, this API is the same at both levels which leads to a model which is more symmetric. With Asbaco, integrating controllers and regular components is performed with a load-time mixin technique based on the ASM bytecode engineering library [30]. With AOKell, this integration is performed with AspectJ [9]. We believe that the use of AspectJ leads to programs that are easier to write, understand and debug. Although we are currently using the compile-time weaving facility provided by AOKell, we plan to investigate the use of both the compile-time and the load-time features to make the weaving of the control dimension more dynamic.

FuseJ. [6], and JAsCo [23], which is the previous project by the same team, is an architectural description language (ADL) that aims at unifying aspects and components. The FuseJ ADL introduces the notions of a gate and of a connector. A gate, much like an interface in Fractal, is a component communication point. Output and input gates may be defined. Gates are bound to methods provided or required by components. Connectors are responsible for declaratively specifying the architecture of the application. Two kinds of interactions may be specified by connectors: component-based and aspect-oriented. The former case is similar to a binding in Fractal and binds a required gate with a provided one. The latter allows defining an around advice.

Fractal/AOKell and FuseJ differ in the way aspects are used: with AOKell, aspects are only used as a technique for integrating the control and functional dimensions of the component model. The goal of FuseJ is to make aspects first class entities in the component-based programming model. In that sense, FuseJ is similar to another of our project, called FAC [33], which has been build on top of AOKell.

6 Conclusion

This paper presented AOKell, which is a framework for developing component-based applications. AOKell is an implementation of the Fractal Specifications [18] [5]. AOKell is implemented in Java with the AspectJ [9] aspect-oriented language. AOKell has been ported to the .NET platform [10].

Fractal/AOKell provides a component model with two dimensions: the functional and the control dimension. The functional dimension is concerned with the development of application-level functionalities, while the control dimension is concerned with the supervision and the technical services required by the application. While this dichotomy can be found in other component models, e.g. EJB [1] with the notion of a component and of a container, the originality of AOKell is to open the control dimension and to make it programmable. Furthermore, AOKell provides the same concepts for engineering both dimensions. The notions of a component, of a provided or required interface, and of a binding, are used both to engineer the functional dimension and the control dimension.

AOKell is reflective in the sense that the notion of a component is used both at the functional level and at the control level which can be seen as a kind of meta-level. With AOKell, components are controlled by other, so-called control components. One of the benefits of this approach is to provide a highly dynamic model. By modifying the components assemblies at the control level, programmers can modify the control of their application components. AOKell also enables the precise engineering of the control level. This allows adapting components to execution environments with various needs in term of control, and to foster the development of various forms of control such as the ones needed to program self healing components, self-testing components, or components carrying their proofs or their specifications.

With AOKell, application-level components are controlled by so-called membranes, which are assemblies of control components. Each control component provides a particular control function and may require the services provided by other control components. By componentizing membranes, we foster the reuse, the evolvability and the maintenance of control policies. We then facilitate the development of various control policies, and we obtain a general component model, which can be adapted to application domains with various needs in terms of resources (memory, thread, etc.) and of technical services.

The second originality of AOKell is to use an aspect-oriented approach [19] to integrate the control and the functional dimension of our component model. Each control component is associated with an AspectJ [9] aspect, which is responsible for introducing and supervising the functional component in order to meet the requirement of the control component. In terms of software engineering, this aspect orientation gives a highly expressive solution that facilitates the development and the debugging of the control logic.

As a matter of perspective, we plan to investigate the dynamicity of the relation between a component-based application and its componentized membrane. So far, we have been using the compile-time weaving facility of AspectJ for integration. A load-time weaving mode is also available with AspectJ. Furthermore, other dynamic frameworks are available such as AspectWerkz [21], JAC [22] or JAsCo [23] for runtime weaving. By investigating these solutions, we will be able to provide a fully dynamic model where any modification in the assembly of control components, including features related to interception, will be dynamically applied to the application components without recompilation.

Acknowledgments

This work is partially funded by France Telecom under the external research contract #46131097.

We thank Romain Rouvoy for many discussions about AOKell and for numerous bug reports, Philippe Merle and Renaud Pawlak for their valuable comments about this article.

References

1. Bodoff, S., Armstrong, E., Ball, J., Carson, D.: The J2EE Tutorial. Addison-Wesley (2004) 2nd edition. `java.sun.com/j2ee/1.4/docs/tutorial/doc/index.html`.
2. Siegel, J.: CORBA 3 Fundamentals and Programming. 2nd edn. Wiley (2000)
3. OSGi Alliance: OSGi Technical Whitepaper. (2004) Revision 3.0. `www.osgi.org`.
4. Aldrich, J., Chambers, C., Notkin, D.: ArchJava: Connecting software architecture to implementation. In: Proceedings of the 24th International Conference on Software Engineering (ICSE'02), ACM Press (2002) 187–197
5. Bruneton, E., Coupaye, T., Leclercq, M., Quema, V., Stefani, J.B.: An open component model and its support in Java. In: Proceedings of the 7th International Symposium on Component-Based Software Engineering (CBSE-7). Volume 3054 of Lecture Notes in Computer Science., Springer (2004) 7–22
6. Suvée, D., Vanderperren, W., Jonckers, V.: FuseJ: An architectural description language for unifying aspects and components. In: Workshop Software-engineering Properties of Languages and Aspect Technologies (SPLAT) at AOSD'05. (2005) `ssel.vub.ac.be/Members/dsuvee/papers/splatsuvee2.pdf`.
7. Dowling, J., Cahill, V.: The K-Component architecture meta-model for self-adaptative software. In: Proceedings of Reflection'01. Volume 2192 of Lecture Notes in Computer Science., Springer-Verlag (2001) 81–88
8. Clarke, M., Blair, G., Coulson, G., Parlavantzas, N.: An efficient component model for the construction of adaptive middleware. In: Proceedings of Middleware'01. (2001)
9. Kiczales, G., Hilsdale, E., Hugunin, J., Kersten, M., Palm, J., Griswold, W.: Getting started with AspectJ. Communications of the ACM **44**(10) (2001) 59–65
10. Escoffier, C., Donsez, D.: FractNet: An implementation of the Fractal component model for .NET. In: 2ème Journée Francophone sur Développement de Logiciels par Aspects (JFDLPA'05). (2005) `www-adele.imag.fr/fractnet/`.
11. Baude, F., Caromel, D., Morel, M.: From distributed objects to hierarchical grid components. In: Proceedings of the International Symposium on Distributed Objects and Applications (DOA'03). (2003)
12. Fassino, J.P., Stefani, J.B., Lawall, J., Muller, G.: Think: A software framework for component-based operating system kernels. In: Proceedings of the USENIX Annual Technical Conference. (2002) 73–86
13. Rouvoy, R., Merle, P.: Abstraction of transaction demarcation in component-oriented platforms. In: Proceedings of the 4th ACM/IFIP/USENIX International Conference on Distributed Systems Platforms and Open Distributed Processing (Middleware'03). Volume 2672 of Lecture Notes in Computer Science., Springer-Verlag (2003) 305–323
14. ObjectWeb: JORAM: Java open reliable asynchronous messaging. `joram.objectweb.org` (2002)
15. Sun Microsystems: Java Message Service Specification Final Release 1.1. (2002) `java.sun.com/jms`.
16. Alia, M., Chassande-Barrioz, S., Déchamboux, P., Hamon, C., Lefebvre, A.: A middleware framework for the persistence and querying of java objects. In: Proceedings of the 18th European Conference on Object-Oriented Programming (ECOOP'04). Volume 3086 of Lecture Notes in Computer Science., Springer-Verlag (2004) 292–316

17. Sun Microsystems: Java Data Objects. (2002) java.sun.com/products/jdo/.
18. Bruneton, E., Coupaye, T., Stefani, J.B.: The Fractal Component Model. ObjectWeb. (2004) Version 2.0.3. fractal.objectweb.org/specification/index.html.
19. Kiczales, G., Lamping, J., Mendhekar, A., Maeda, C., Lopes, C., Loingtier, J.M., Irwin, J.: Aspect-oriented programming. In: Proceedings of the 11th European Conference on Object-Oriented Programming (ECOOP'97). Volume 1241 of Lecture Notes in Computer Science., Springer (1997) 220–242
20. Burke, B.: It's the aspects. Java's Developer's Journal (2003) www.sys-con.com/story/?storyid=38104&DE=1.
21. Bonér, J., Dahlstedt, J., Vasseur, A.: AspectWerkz 2: An extensible aspect container. TheServerSide.com (2004) www.theserverside.com/articles/article.tss?l=AspectWerkzP1.
22. Pawlak, R., Seinturier, L., Duchien, L., Florin, G., Legond-Aubry, F., Martelli, L.: JAC: An aspect-based distributed dynamic framework. Software Practice and Experiences (SPE) **34**(12) (2004) 1119–1148
23. Suvée, D., Vanderperren, W., Jonckers, V.: JAsCo: An aspect-oriented approach tailored for component based software development. In: Proceedings of the 2nd International Conference on Aspect-Oriented Software Development (AOSD'03), ACM Press (2003) 21–29
24. Sun Microsystems: Enterprise Java Beans. (1997) www.javasoft.com/products/ejb.
25. Fleury, M., Reverbel, F.: The JBoss extensible server. In: Proceedings of the 4th ACM/IFIP/USENIX International Conference on Distributed Systems Platforms and Open Distributed Processing (Middleware'03). Volume 2672 of Lecture Notes in Computer Science., Springer-Verlag (2003) 344–373
26. Seinturier, L., Pessemier, N., Coupaye, T.: AOKell: An aspect-oriented implementation of the Fractal specifications. Objectweb Fractal Workshop, Grenoble, France (2005)
27. Szyperski, C.: Component Software - Beyond Object-Oriented Programming. 2nd edn. Addison-Wesley (2002)
28. Leclercq, M., Quema, V., Stefani, J.B.: DREAM: a component framework for the construction of resource-aware, configurable middleware. IEEE Distributed Systems Online **6**(9) (2005)
29. Gil, T., Evain, J.B.: AspectDNG. DotNetGuru. (2005) www.dotnetguru.biz/aspectdng/.
30. Bruneton, E., Lenglet, R., Coupaye, T.: ASM: A code manipulation tool to implement adaptable systems. In: Journées Composants 2002 (JC'02). (2002) asm.objectweb.org/current/asm-eng.pdf.
31. Coulson, G., Blair, G., Grace, P., Joolia, A., Lee, K., Uyema, J.: A component model for building systems software. In: Proceedings of the IASTED Software Engineering and Applications (SEA'04). (2004)
32. Mencl, V., Bures, T.: Microcomponent-based component controllers: A foundation for component aspects. In: Proceedings of the 12th Asia-Pacific Software Engineering Conference (APSEC'05). (2005)
33. Pessemier, N., Seinturier, L., Duchien, L., Coupaye, T.: A model for developing component-based and aspect-oriented systems. In: Proceedings of the 5th International Symposium on Software Composition (SC'06). Lecture Notes in Computer Science, Springer (2006)

CBSE in Small and Medium-Sized Enterprise: Experience Report

Reda Kadri[1], François Merciol[2], and Salah Sadou[2]

[1] Alkante Company, RENNES , France
[2] Valoria Lab,Yves Coppens Research Center
University of South Brittany, France
r.kadri@alkante.com,
{Francois.Merciol, Salah.Sadou}@univ-ubs.fr

Abstract. Although the CBSE has a great success in software engineering, only large scale companies use it through their research and development department. Small and medium size enterprises still have some hesitations that deprives them of the various advantages offered by CBSE. This is mainly due to the economic constraints that large companies don't have. How can we make them benefit from this technology? Do they have to develop their own models? Should they obtain a modified version of this technology? What will happen to the code that already exists? What are the costs of such migration? How to proceed? In this paper we present an experiment carried out in using CBSE within the framework of a partnership[1] between a small and medium-sized enterprise and an academic research team. We present the results and the way in which this migration has been performed, by hoping that this would be an answer to the above questions.

1 Introduction

In spite of the enormous evolution which software engineering using CBSE has made, and of the advantages offered by it, most of the small and medium-sized enterprises (SMEs) hesitate to migrate towards this technology. Considering their structures and their constraints, SMEs should be the first concerned by CBSE's advantages: i) these types of companies generally have a restricted number of developers; ii) they do not easily take into account new types of different requirements due to their use of classical architectures; iii) Their developer turnover[2] is very high; iv) They are the first concerned by the decomposition of the application delivery phenomenon. This phenomenon corresponds to the decomposition of an application according to various criteria. One of the most important criteria is the adaptation to the customers planning and to their constraints (training, budget, ...).

[1] This work is the result of the cooperation between "Software Evolution" team, Valoria and Alkante. Alkante is a company specialized in the design of various types of information systems (in particular Geographic Information System).

[2] In US financial terminology, turnover refers to the rate at which an employer gains and loses staff.

I. Gorton et al. (Eds.): CBSE 2006, LNCS 4063, pp. 154–165, 2006.

Their hesitation to migrate to CBSE may be due to the fear of an unknown costs. It also may be due to the lack of information and lack of experience in CBSE. But the main reason behind this hesitation is related to the importance of the already existing code. They don't want to neglect years of developing.

Usually, an SME don't has enough budget to create its own research and development department (R&D). Our solution is to cooperate with a research laboratory in order to acquire the R part of R&D. Our aim is to ensure and plan a controlled evolution of our development methodology. So, we have defined a strategy for a smooth migration to CBSE. This strategy is based on a transitional architecture in order to preserve our existing code. In this transitional architecture, existing code is embedded in pseudo components with provided and required interfaces. To validate our solution we compared the development costs for traditional architecture with those for transitional one.

In the remaining part of this paper we describe the limits of the traditional development organisation (section 2). Then we describe and explain our transitional architecture (section 3). In section 4, we describe the migration of a component, from transitional architecture to an implemented component model. Finally, we conclude with some results from our experience.

2 Limits of Traditional Development Process

Most of SMEs use traditional development process where an application is taken as a monolithic element. In this case, the reuse of packages implies systematically an adaptation. During the first years of our company, we were only concerned by the development costs, since the applications were new, the code adaptation problems appeared later. In this section we will discuss the costs related to code adaptation.

2.1 Problem Statement

After a few development years, we acquired a significant number of packages corresponding to reusable entities. Even if we develop applications from the same family (ex: GIS), they use more and more different technologies: database, directories and devices (PDA, mobile phone, ...). This leads to a various adaptation of our packages. We quickly noticed that these adaptations generate an important costs.

As our packages are not interdependent, often the adaptation of one creates modification on another. This often create additional costs that are not anticipated.

Another problem, which is more specific to SMEs, concerns the decomposition of applications delivery. To become competitive, SMEs cut out their applications in several parts according to needs of their client. The different parts are delivered according to a predefined schedule.

If companies invoice the integration costs, often called main application update costs, the application would reach a very high costs.

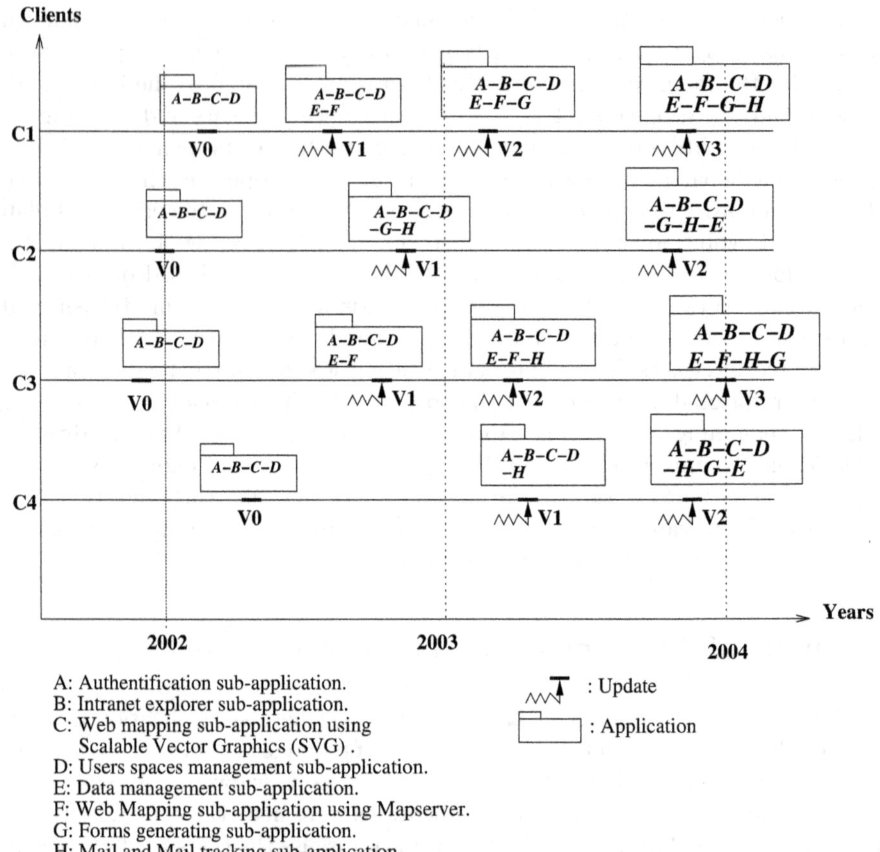

Fig. 1. Sub-applications delivery schedule

Figure 1 shows the deliveries for four clients (C1, C2, C3 and C4) over two years. Each client's application was assembled from different sub-applications. Some of them already exist, whereas the others were developed during this period. In the first delivery all applications were based on the same set of sub-applications (A, B, C and D).

Each sub-application was designed with the same architectural base and the same development process like the main application. So, sub-applications may encapsulate other entities. For example, the authentication sub-application (A) encapsulates an NT Lan Manager (NTLM) authentication and a Single Sign-On (SSO) using Central Authentication Service (CAS). This sub-application may be enriched by adding other authentication mechanisms.

2.2 Development Costs

In this paper we illustrate only the first level of composition. In this case, each additional sub-application corresponds to an update of the main application.

Table 1 shows costs of each version of the application. Each version corresponds to a client's delivery.

Table 1. Different versions costs

	V0	V1	V2	V3	TOTAL
C1	63	1496	168	336	2081
C2	58	495	932		1485
C3	1910	38	327	183	2458
C4	49	321	1150		1520

The important costs occur during the first development of a sub-application (C3xV0, C1xV1, etc). When we use an existed sub-application, for a new application (ex: C3xV1), the costs are indeed low, but not null. In fact, the reuse of a sub-application for a new delivery generate two kinds of costs (adaptation and integration) as shown below. We call these costs, "assembly costs".

The measurements carried out in the company enabled us to do a precise calculation of the first sub-applications development costs, as shown in table 2.

Table 2. Sub-applications' costs

Sub-applications	A	B	C	D	E	F	G	H
Costs(hours)	90	140	750	930	900	540	115	300

So, we use the elements of table 1 and table 2 to extract the assembly costs. Table 3 illustrates these assembly costs for each version and for each customer.

Table 3. Assembly costs

	V1	V2	V3	Total
C1	56	31	36	123
C2	40	32		72
C3	38	27	28	93
C4	21	95		116
TOTAL (Hours)	155	185	64	404

We note that the costs increase as the number of added sub-application increases. For instance:

- C1xV1 sub-applications E and F were added and costed 56 hours of development, whereas sub-application G costed 32 hours in C1xV2.
- C4xV1 sub-application H was added and costed 21 hours of development, whereas sub-applications G and E costed 95 hours in C4xV2.

2.3 Discussion

In this study of costs, we did not illustrate those depending on maintenance. We will study them in another work, devoted to the software evolution.

We focus our study on the assembly costs as they appear in figure 1 and table 1: the clients C1 and C3 have the same application (V3), but assembled in a different order. Finally, the difference is (2458-2081=) 377 hours. These additional costs are generated by transitional versions.

Some companies with experience, tend to reduce their assembly costs by using sub-application deliveries always in the same order. But any modification of planning or assembly order need a new design which creates expensive costs.

In our study, the assembly costs are equivalent to those of one sub-application development. At this stage, the traditional architecture can not help us to minimize those costs. According to Ommering's [2] and Shilaghi's [9] case studies, CBSE allows to efficiently create a variety of complicated products with a short lead time.

Examples of companies using CBSE are Nokia and Philips Corporation, Nokia maintains a large library of software components that they use to build their family of cell phones [11], Koala [5] model of Philips is also a good example of such assembly costs minimization.

3 Transitional Architecture

Before the migration to CBSE, several reasons led us to make a transitional architecture:

- The absence of well defined methods for CBSE migration.
- The presence of a great number of codes.
- The hesitation of developers to switch toward new technologies (training aspects).
- The need of more time and sufficient maturation to choose a CBSE implemented model (FRACTAL [10], EJB [4], ...).

Our decision was based on the following assumption: *"with a slowly developing maturity of software components comes a slow liberation from overly traditional objects, much can be learned from object technology, and some of it can be generalized or transformed to serve components"* [1]. So, we defined a transitory architecture as near as possible to component models. Our new development process is designed in an organization that separates the developers in two teams: the first one relates to the module developers, called Components Development Team (CDT); the second one relates to the application developers, called Application Development Team (ADT). Figure 2 illustrates our organization which corresponds with a real development platform.

The platform contains developers workspaces, a concurrent version system for team work and management of different file versions (all the source code is stored in it). It contains a dedicated application for pseudo components deployment and

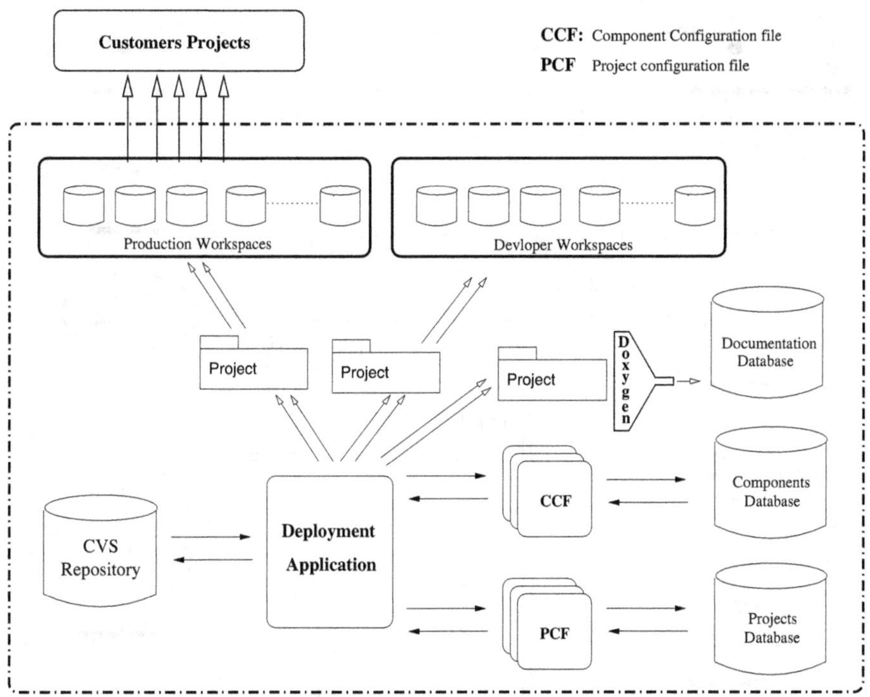

Fig. 2. Development platform

assembly. It also includes a source code documentation and reverse engineering tool. Another workspace is intended for updating the customers applications and updating one or several of their pseudo components. Each pseudo component is described by a Configuration Component File (CCF) written in XML and stored in Components Database (Component repository). We describe in CCFs required, provided and control pseudo components interfaces. Each component encapsulates its documentation which describes it and also its interfaces.

For clarification, the components documentation is not represented in the figure 2, but a the code and the project design documentations are stored in a repository. Pseudo components are the base elements of applications. Each application is described by its Project Configuration File (PCF) and stored in Project Database (Project repository).

The CFF and PCF are high level representation and handling tools, they are not dependent on a particular technology. We should respect an independence between our high level representation and software functionalities. For more flexibility, the CFF do not contain a code but refer to the pieces of software present in CVS repository. In this way the CFF is seen as a wrapper of components. It is possible for us to assemble several components to obtain high level components. Those components correspond to sub-applications as those shown in figure 1. So, a sub-application is represented by a CCF.

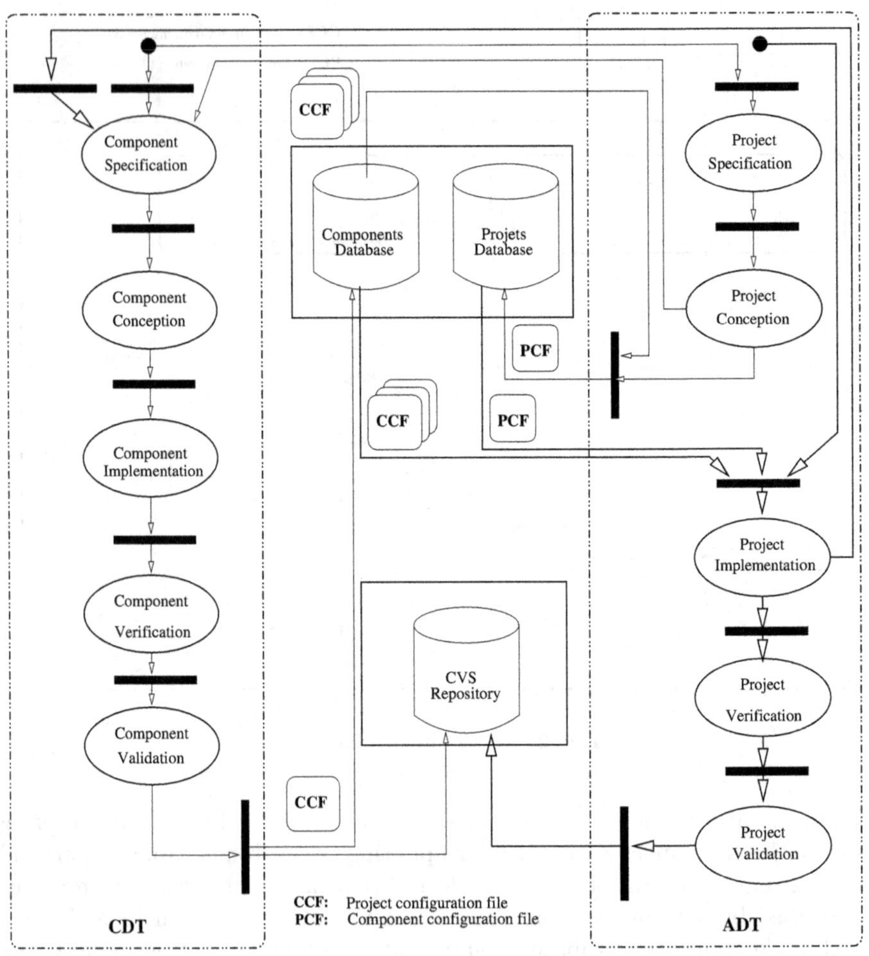

Fig. 3. Development process

The usability of this platform is made easy by its deployment and assembly components application. On one hand, it allows the CDT developers to access the list of the components and allows the addition of new components. On the other hand, it allows ADT developers to create new projects and to choose an adequate components for them. For ADT developers this common platform is regarded as a read only access On The Shelves (OTS) components.

ADT developers work is personalization and respect of the project specifications. CDT developers work is implementation and respect of the component specifications.

3.1 Development Process

The Development organization and the platform merge for an effective development process. We will describe it with the following process:

- After the specification validation, a project manager is chosen.
- The project manager is in charge of the two developer teams (CDT and ADT).
- using the last deployment application he creates the project.
- He selects the necessary components and writes the specifications for the new ones.
- He notifies the creation of the project to the developers.
- The mission of CDT is to develop the new components and their integration in components repository.
- The mission of ADT is to deploy the project and satisfy the application specifications.
- If necessary, the ADT team may initiate a new components specification.

Each development team respects the same progression steps, from specifications to validations. The interaction between the two teams is materialized by three repositories as shown in figure 3 : i) CVS repository; ii) components repository; iii) project repository. It is filled progressively with components satisfying new requirements. These are not the components that we find OTS, but their wrappers. Each wrapper represents a piece of software in the CVS repository. Wrappers are written in different languages and correspond to the functionalities required from a component.

The assembly tools use those wrapped components to produce an application. An application is materialized by a PCF file. In figure 3, we illustrate in a synthetic way the following three roles:

- CDT team, who is responsible for the development of components OTS.
- ADT team, who is responsible for the application development.
- The platform composed of assembly tools which coordinates the activities of the two previous teams.

The distribution of these roles enabled us to have more flexibility in our development and enabled us to capitalize standard components.

So, how to check the benefits of this transitional component approach. The simplest way would be to reiterate the same development process for same clients with the same development teams. But this solution is not economically acceptable for a company and is more unacceptable for SMEs. So, the solution we choose is to evaluate the costs of the platform setup and the new assembly costs. For the assembly costs evaluation we repeat the same study with two new clients C5 and C6 as shown in figure 4 and table 5.

The same method of measurements gave us the composition costs of old sub-applications, shown in table 4, and gave us the platform costs which correspond to 1260 hours.

Table 4. Composition costs of the old sub-applications

Sub-applications	A	B	C	D	E	F	G	H
Costs(hours)	12	40	68	69	54	46	23	16

This composition concerns only the eights sub-applications and not what they encapsulate. We just defined a membrane around these sub-application and we made them interdependent. To access component service, we must use its provided and required interfaces. Its control interfaces are used during the adaptation process.

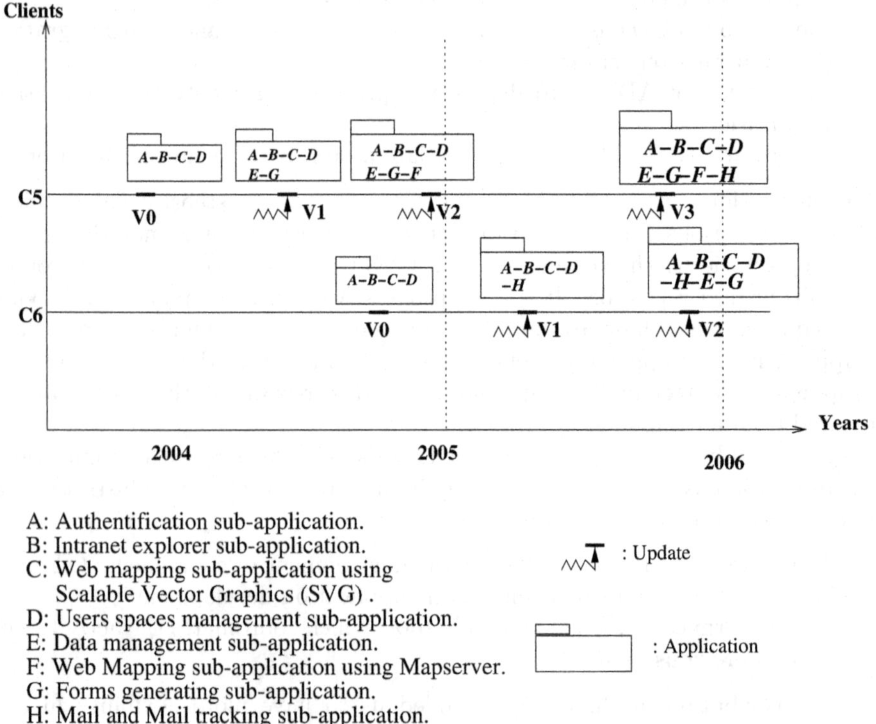

Fig. 4. Sub-applications delivery schedule after transition

Table 5. Assembly costs

	V1	V2	V3	Total
C5	16	11	14	41
C6	14	18		32
TOTAL (Hours)				73

After having attested and certified the significant costs minimization of the transitional architecture, we become aware about the benefits we will get by using CBSE. We notice that our developers became familiarized with CBSE concepts just by using the transitional architecture. Now its time to start the completion of CBSE migration.

4 Example of CBSE Component Resulting from Our Transitional Architecture

To migrate towards a concrete component technology, we choose Fractal [10] and its implementation platform Julia [10] for the following reasons:

- We have a component technology using specification written in XML.
- We should automate the migration towards such technology.
- We already have several Fractal tools developed by our research laboratory partner.

One of our best sale is a cartographic application based on (Scalable Vector Graphics) SVG. It uses different data translators. Those data translators are available in several plugins format added to other applications. The regular evolution of these applications involves several updates of the plugins. We decided to compose those translators and make them independent from other applications. After having composed each of them we encapsulated them in a single component called Geoconv.

In figure 5 Geoconv encapsulates two translation components. Each one was implemented by a part which was extracted from the plugins applications, and another part which was extracted from application using those plugins. In this example, the component "ShapeToSvg" is used to convert Shape Files Format (Shp) using two encapsulated components ("ReadShape", "ReadDbf") to obtain coordinates, styles and data flows. The component "MapInfoToSvg" is used to

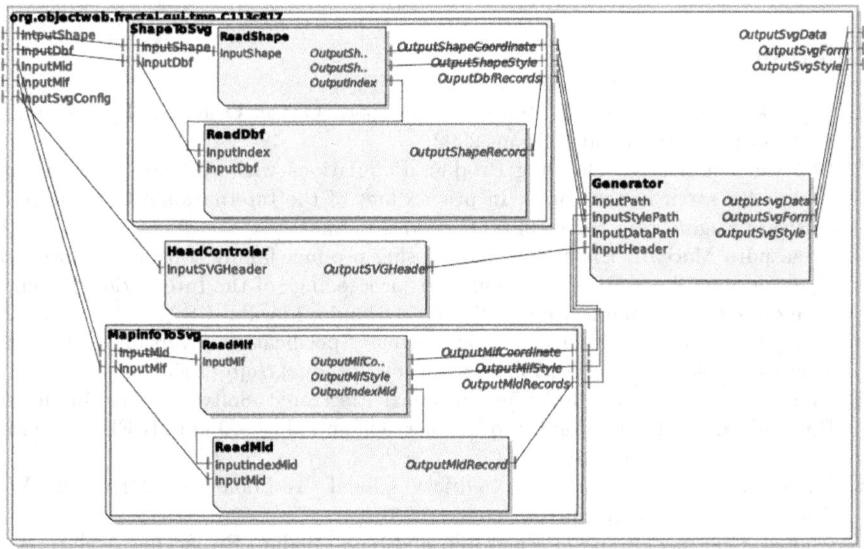

Fig. 5. Geoconv component

convert Mid and Mif format using two encapsulated components ("ReadMif", "ReadMid") to obtain coordinates, styles and data flows. Because of different interpretation of SVG headers by different web browsers, "Headcontroler" is a component used for generating and updating this Header if it is changed. "Generator" component is used to generate SVG file from those flows and the header. When a new format of data is added to translate, we have to just add a new component in GeoConv. This last component should have three provided interfaces to bind them with "Generator" required interfaces.

5 Conclusion

This study is an important experience for our SME, it improved our development process. This process allows development with a low cost and delivers several products in a short time. It makes us more competitive from other SMEs by quick response to client offers. It also allows us a smooth transition to CBSE. This transition permits our developers to acquire CBSE concepts since they are easily able to find composable parts of our existing code. Our developers sometimes develop with existing libraries and packages, they also develop applications which integrates with other client applications, it's not easy for us because those client applications are not based on component technologies. We noticed that the component industry is not mature because it does not sell components adapted for all technologies that we are using. We continue collaboration with our research laboratory partners to minimize the evolution and maintenance costs of components. We test and validate tools developed for this purpose in our enterprise.

References

1. Syperski, C.: Component Software: Beyond Object-Oriented Programming. Addison-Wersley Second Edition, 2002
2. Rob van Ommering.: Building Product Populations with Software Components. Philips Research Laboratories. In proceedings of the International Conference on Software Engineering (ICSE'02), Orlando, Florida, USA.
3. Alessandro Maccari. Experience in assessing product family software architecture for evolution. Nokia Research Center. In proceedings of the International Conference on Software Engineering (ICSE'02), Orlando, Florida, USA.
4. Sun-Microsystems: Enterprise JavaBeans Specification, version 2.1. Sun-Microsystems Web Site: http://java.sun.com/products/ejb (2003)
5. The Koala Component Model for Consumer Electronics Software. Van Ommering, Rob and van der Liden, Frank and Kramer, Jeff and Magee, Jeff In IEEE Computer, vol. 33, num. 3 (2000) 78-85
6. Microsoft: COM: Component Object Model Technologies. Microsoft Web Site:http://www.microsoft.com/com/(2005)
7. Chouki Tibermacine, Regis Fleurquin and Salah Sadou. Preserving Architectural Choices throughout the Component-based Software Development Process. In proceedings of the 5th Working IEEE/IFIP Conference On Software Architecture (WICSA'05), Pittsburgh, Pennsylvania, USA November 2005.

8. Konstantin Beznosov. Experience Report: Design and Implementation of a Component-Based Protection Architecture for ASP.NET Web Services. In proceedings of the International Symposium on Component-Based Software engineering (CBSE'05).
9. Raul Silaghi and Alfred Strohmeier. Integration CBSE, SoC, MDA, and AOP in a software Development Method. In proceeding of the seventh International Enterprise Distributed Object Computing Conference. (EDOC'03).
10. Bruneton, Eric and Coupaye, Thierry and Leclerq, Matthieu and Quema, Vivien and Stefani, Jean-Bernard: An Open Component Model and its Support in Java. In Proceedings of the International Symposium on Component-Based Software Engineering (CBSE'04). Held in conjuction with ICSE'04. Edinburgh, Scotland (2004)
11. Jan Bosch, Software Product Families in Nokia. In Proceedings of Software Product Lines, 9th International Conference (SPLC'05), Rennes, France, September 26-29, (2005)

Supervising Distributed Black Boxes

Philippe Mauran[1], Gérard Padiou[1], and Xuan Loc Pham Thi[2]

[1] Institut de Recherche en Informatique de Toulouse, UMR CNRS 5505, ENSEEIHT, 2 rue Camichel, BP 7122, 31071 Toulouse cedex 7, France
{mauran, padiou}@enseeiht.fr

[2] College of Information Technology, Can Tho University
1, Ly Tu Trong Street, Can Tho City, Vietnam
ptxloc@cit.ctu.edu.vn

Abstract. Software components bring in an interesting alternative to the traditional, centralized, approach to software development. The core idea is indeed to enable the (end) user to build and customize his own application, by assembling pre-existing ("off the shelf") components. However, picking predefined, off-the-shelf components raises the question of the suitability of these components to a peculiar use. In this setting, the ability to supervise and adapt components appears to be crucial, in order to make the component-oriented approach to software design really effective.

The fact that a component is and must remain a black box for its clients makes a significant difference as regards instrumentation, and thus supervision of components. This paper introduces a supervision service fitted for software components. The main features of this service are that:

- it proposes an instrumentation protocol that keeps the opacity of components, with respect to their implementation, whilst it allows to instrument components independently from their design.
- it facilitates the supervision of components by providing a simple coupling between the component's internal control, and the control provided by the user of the component, based on user-specified criteria.

This paper motivates the interest of such a supervision service, outlines its implementation, and illustrates its use.

1 Introduction

The implementation of distributed services raises several design issues that require the development of new software technologies. These technologies rely on the notion of middleware for remote interactions, and are based on the software component paradigm to ensure modularity, portability, and versatility in the deployment and maintenance of such distributed architectures. In this paper, we focus more particularly on building and using distributed, open, and dynamic services by assembling and reusing software components.

Software reuse comes up against a recurring problem: there usually, and a priori, is a semantic gap between the design of a component and its context of use. Thus *reuse* requires *adaptation*. In concrete terms, this involves, on the one

I. Gorton et al. (Eds.): CBSE 2006, LNCS 4063, pp. 166–181, 2006.

hand, a correct specification of the context of use, and, on the other hand, an adaptation of the component to this context.

Adaptation can be carried out statically, e.g. when components are connected, and/or when they are deployed. In this paper, we consider a more dynamic adaptation, inasmuch as it is centered on the requirements of the clients of the server component. Such an approach seems better fitted to a highly dynamic and open environment, such as Web Services. However, this approach requires to supervise the component, for monitoring its state and its behavior, in order to adapt the component, should it come to stray from its users expectations. Thus, use-centered dynamic adaptation necessitates to implement an appropriate support for component supervision. We shall relate, more particularly, these supervision mechanisms to debugging, insofar as they show certain similarities. In a (highly) dynamic setting, *adaptation* thus requires *supervision.*

Lastly, *supervision* calls for *instrumentation.* In fact, supervision involves gathering data about the state and the behavior of the component. We take a declarative approach to this instrumentation, which consists, on the one hand, in exporting component attributes, under the component designer's control, and on the other hand, in monitoring state predicates, connected to adaptation reactions, both specified by the component user (independently from the designer of the component).

Hence, our approach rests on defining a component supervision service (CSS) fitted to software components, prompted by reuse, and based on a safe instrumentation of distributed components.

2 Bringing the Supervision Service to the User, as a Key to Software Reuse

In the spirit of component-oriented design, the use of the CSS invites to consider (at least) two roles in the design of a service: the designer of (reusable) components, and the application architect.

The designer of components defines and provides elementary services/components. To facilitate components reuse, the component designer has to complement the interface(s) which specify the service provided by the component, by several pieces of information, which relate to the implementation of the component, while keeping this implementation hidden:

- required interfaces/services, to enable composition, without having to inspect/access the implementation of the component ;
- technical constraints (such as target runtime environments), to support deployment ;
- configurable properties, to allow a (limited) customization of some aspects of the component

Our proposal represents a step further in this direction, by providing the designer of components with the ability to delegate the handling of specific situations, that result from the runtime context or from the context of use. To this end, the designer of the component simply has to specify the properties and/or the methods of the component that can be referred to by the conditions evaluated by the CSS. This sharing out of roles appears to follow closely two design principles stated by Butler Lampson in the setting of the design of Operating Systems [Lam83], which are archetypal complex software systems[1]:

- *do one thing at a time, and do it well*: here, the programmer focuses on the implementation (efficient) of the base case;
- *leave it to the client*: this is literally the purpose of the CSS.

In light of this, the CSS can be seen as a relevant tool in the setting of the component-oriented approach to the design of complex systems.

The application architect assembles components to build an architecture of components which implements the service required by the (end) user. Besides, the CSS allows this designer to express and to automate the preferences and the strategies of use, in a way closely fitted to (the circumstances of) each use. For example, in the framework of the development of a virtual travel agency, the base components may allow to lookup and book:

- trips, with various means of transportation
- accommodations
- visits
- events ...

Out of these components, an application can be designed, which allows to build journeys, from:

- constraints or preferences given by the user, about the service itself: means of transportation, stopovers, requirements in terms of comfort ...
- strategies to use whenever some constraints cannot be satisfied: lookup for equivalent or different services, search for alternate routes, drop all or part of the services ...
- constraints on the runtime context, or on the QoS, in the case of interactive sessions, for example.

Such a variety of uses can hardly be anticipated during the design of components. These constraints, preferences, and strategies can themselves be reusable, i.e. be considered as components. From this point of view the conditions defined by the user can be seen as a new kind of connector, which the CSS allows to implement.

[1] Moreover it does not seem to infringe another of these principles : keep (implementation) secrets, as the programmer controls the observability of properties and methods w.r.t. condition evaluation.

3 Software Component Supervision

Our purpose is to design a service for software component supervision. More precisely, we aim at enabling the user to *control* (in every sense of the word) the dynamics of a component while he uses it, that is:

- to track, to *observe* the changes of the component;
- to *check* the consistency of these changes w.r.t. the use of the component;
- *direct* these changes, according to the intended use of the component.

From a functional point of view, this situation appears to be very close to the situation of a programmer when he is debugging a program: his aim is then to check, at runtime, the accordance of the actual behavior of the program with its expected behavior. In the setting of program debugging, the expected behavior is not (fully) explicitly stated, and the nature and the extent of the conformity check is left to the programmer, who can be assisted in this task by fine-grained supervision tools, namely debuggers. We rest on this similarity of situation to work out the main features for the supervision of software components:

- *monitoring* and *editing* the state (and more widely the runtime context) of supervised components
- *synchronizing* component execution and interventions related to component monitoring. In a debugging tool, this synchronization is specified as stopping conditions that are defined with respect to the control flow (step by step execution, breakpoints...) or with respect to the program state (watchpoints).

While component supervision and program debugging look similar in terms of functionalities, their expression appears to be quite different, due to the separation between the designer, and the user of a component, and due to the opaqueness of components to their users. Actually, whereas the programmer can access the program code, and knows the expected semantics for the program (though this semantics may not be explicitly stated), the very notion of component involves that the actual (operational) semantics of a component remains hidden to its users. Furthermore, and also as a key concept to the notion of component, the documentation of the component is the only means of communication between the designer of a component and the users of the component. A fortiori, we cannot expect the user (or the designer) to carry out by himself the checking of the correspondence between the actual and the expected (w.r.t. a given use) semantics of the component. Thus, our problem is to define a protocol

- that allows to implement supervision of components at the user level;
- that accounts for the gap between designers of components, and users of components;
- where supervision can be specified regardless of the internal control flow or code of components.

The lack of reference to components' code or control flow leads to a declarative expression of the coordination between a component's (internal) actions and the (possible) actions superposed by its users. This expression is based on the observable *state* (or runtime context) of the component and/or on the *interaction* (method calls) between the component and its client(s). More precisely, we propose a protocol that allows the user to specify observable conditions, and to provide their corresponding reactions (handlers). An observable condition is either a state predicate, binding component's properties, or a scheduling constraint on the component's use, such as a path expression.

The elements of protocol we have introduced take into account the separation between the designer, and the user of a component, from the user's point of view: they aim at allowing a declarative, large-grained (i. e. independent from the code), supervision of components, by the users of components. In other words, the user of a component is given tools that enable him to control the runtime behavior of the component, in accordance with the semantics he expects from the component, and these tools are suited to using components as black boxes. Conversely, it is interesting to consider the separation between the designer, and the user of a component, *from the designer's point of view*, that is to enable the designer to control how a component can be instrumented. Our approach has to allow the designer of a component to specify what can be observed in the component. In this way, the designer contributes to instrumentation, while he retains the ability to control it by setting a model of the part(s) of the component that can be instrumented. This model limits the uses and the operations that the designer deems compatible with the "internal" semantics of the component. To this end, the designer can specify which aspects of the component can be supervised, by defining the observable state space of the component (e.g. as a list of properties), and (possibly) the coupling between the users' points of observations and the (internal) control flow of the component[2]. This approach appears to fit the essence of the notion of software component: in the same vein, the specification of required interfaces allows to connect components as black boxes, regardless of their implementation.

4 Component Supervision Service (CSS)

This section outlines our design of the supervision service. The implementation of the supervision service we present here was performed in the setting of a Java ORB implementation of CORBA (and of an IDL to Java object mapping). However, the design, the architecture, and the corresponding protocol are based on general principles, independent from the peculiarities of the CORBA model or the Java platform. The transposition to other component-oriented environments and middlewares should be rather straightforward, as long as the target platform provides a basic form of reflection. For example, we already have developed an implementation of the supervision service for the Java 2 platform as a package where interactions are based on RMI [PTMP05]. This section presents the design principles of the supervision service, and then illustrates the use of this service.

[2] The notion of *pointcut* introduced in Aspect Oriented Programming [KHH+01] gives a way to specify this coupling, without unveiling the control flow of a component.

The Component Supervision Service superposes a supervision service to the base(functional) service provided by a component, so as to turn this "standard" component into a "supervisable" (instrumented) component. This superposition is carried out by inserting an interceptor between the original component and its client(s). The interceptor encapsulates the base component: it accepts client calls through the base component's interface, handles these calls with respect to supervision, and then delegates them to the base component; in the same way, the interceptor filters and interprets the base component's results before passing them back to the caller.

Besides the base component's interface, intended to allow a transparent supervision of the base component, the interceptor provides an interface that enables to supervise the base component. This interface adapts the basic supervision operations (monitoring, editing, synchronization) to the features of software component design and use: separation between user and designer, component implementation hiding, concurrent use of components. On these grounds,

- *the designer of a component defines a set of observable properties of the component.* These properties are implemented as private attributes, that can be accessed through read-only (public) accessors. Observable properties represent the part of the state space (and/or of the runtime context, and/or of the execution trace of the component) that the designer of the component allows to be used for supervision. The designer of the component manages (and controls) the update of observable properties. We present further on a general framework for implementing these updates, in the prospect of automating (or assisting) the generation of this code.
- *the user of the component can specify and submit, through the supervision interface, a set of conditions on observable properties* (defined by the designer of the component). A reaction (handler) is provided by the user, for each of these conditions. When such a condition becomes invalid, the instrumented component has to call back the corresponding reaction. The evaluation of conditions is performed by the instrumented component.

Using an instrumented (supervisable) component. By way of illustration, we consider an elementary example using the Component Supervision Service (CSS) that we have implemented on the CORBA/Java platform. In this example, a client uses a bounded buffer of integers, specified by the following CORBA IDL module:

```
module example {
   exception BufferIsFullException{} ;
   exception BufferIsEmptyException{} ;
   interface SimpleBuffer {  /* base object */
     readonly attribute short NbUsed ;
     readonly attribute short Size ;
     void Insert (in short i)  raises (BufferIsFullException);
     short Remove() raises (BufferIsEmptyException) ;
   } ;
}
```

In the context of the CORBA to Java mapping, this service is defined by the SimpleBufferOperations interface, which provides (in particular) two accessors, NbUsed() and Size() that correspond to observable (read-only) properties NbUsed and Size. This interface is implemented by the SimpleBufferServant class, which is the actual "functional" part of the buffer, and (indirectly[3]) by an interceptor, SimpleBufferPOATie, which (in substance) performs the CORBA handling of requests on the server side, and then delegates these requests to the applicative ("functional") servant. Our approach, in the context of the CORBA/Java platform, was to transform this interceptor, by weaving supervision handling and CORBA handling of requests.

The programmer, on the client side, wants to be sure that the buffer he uses is never occupied above one half of its capacity. To this end, he defines a proper condition (the HalfLoadCondition class below), along with its corresponding handler (the handleCondition method of the ClientServant class below), that will be called by SimpleBufferPOATie, when the threshold defined by HalfLoadCondition is reached. The HalfLoadCondition condition is described by the following Java class:

```
public class HalfLoadCondition implements Condition {
  private SimpleBufferPOATie   obsv;
  private ConditionObserver    obsrvr;
  private String               rfr;
  private String[]             opds = {"NbUsed","Size"};

  public void initialize(String ref, Object tgt, ConditionObserver oc) {
      rfr  = ref;  obsrvr = oc;  obsv = (SimpleBufferPOATie) tgt;
  }
  public Object target() { return obsv;}
  public ConditionObserver observer() { return obsrvr; }
  public String[] operands() { return opds;}
  public String reference() { return rfr;}
  public boolean evaluate() { return (2*obsv.NbUsed()<obsv.Size()); }
}
```

HalfLoadCondition is defined in accordance with a pattern stated by the supervision protocol. It provides read-only accessors to attributes that store a reference to the supervised component, (which is an instance of SimpleBufferPOATie), a reference to its client (which is an instance of ConditionObserver), the identifiers of the observable properties bound by the condition, and the URL of the code of HalfLoadCondition (in order to allow its dynamic loading by SimpleBufferPOATie). The initialize(...) method is used to instantiate HalfLoadCondition. The evaluate() method is the evaluation code for the condition.

The handler corresponding to a condition is described by the handleCondition method, in a class that must implement the interfaces ConditionObserver (instrumentation aspect) and ClientOperations (CORBA remote access aspect).

[3] Actually: SimpleBufferPOATie extends SimpleBufferPOA, which implements SimpleBufferOperations.

```
public class ClientServant implementsConditionObserver,ClientOperations {
  public SimpleBuffer ti = nil;  // target object
  public ClientServant (SimpleBuffer b){ ti = b; }
  // user-defined handler -> rC: condition class URL
  public void handleCondition (String rC) {
    System.out.println("threshold: " + ti.getNbUsed());
    try {
      ti.Remove(); ti.Remove();
    } catch (Exception e) {
      System.out.println("handleCondition: "+e);
    }
    System.out.println("new NbUsed: " + ti.getNbUsed());
  }
} // ClientServant
```

The client application creates a remotely accessible Client object. This object is implemented by ClientServant, that provides the user-defined handler:

```
class Application {
 public static void main(String[] args){
  // CORBA initializations: naming context (nc), ORB, POA, ...
  // connect the client to the remote SimpleBuffer object
  org.omg.CORBA.Object obj = nc.resolve_str("SimpleBuffer");
  SimpleBuffer          ti = SimpleBufferHelper.narrow(obj);
  ClientServant client = new ClientServant(nc);
  ClientPOA theClient  = new ClientPOATie(client,rootPOA);
  rootPOA.activate_object(theClient);
  Client proxyClient = theClient._this();
  try {
    SupervisableComponentSupport spv =
       SupervisableComponentSupportHelper.narrow(nc.resolve_str("CSS"));
    spv.activate(
       new java.io.File("HalfLoadCondition.class").toURL().toString(),
       proxyClient, ti
       );
    for (int k=1;k<100;k++) {
         ti.Insert(2*k); ti.Insert(k); ti.Remove();
    }
  } catch (Exception e) { System.out.println("main: "+e); }
 }
}
```

Conditions Evaluation. A supervision class, which is integrated with the supervised component, manages conditions, and the corresponding synchronization with the clients of the supervised component. In the general case, a cyclic activity, a monitor, can be associated to the supervised component. This monitor tracks the evolution of the observable properties, (re)evaluates the conditions that may have become invalid, due to this evolution, and, if the case arises, calls back the corresponding handlers. As a matter of fact, the designer of a component indirectly controls the evaluation of conditions, inasmuch as he controls the evolution of the observable properties.

The protocol we have defined aims at making explicit this coupling between the control of the changes in the observable properties, on the one hand, and the synchronization with users' supervision, on the other hand. To this end, the protocol requires the component designer to notify to the users the changes he deems relevant, Therefore, the designer of the component is responsible for managing the changes of observable properties, whereas the evaluation of the conditions is managed by the supervision class, which is integrated with the supervised component.

Although the designer of a component can define his own protocol to manage and notify the evolution of the observable properties, we propose a generic framework for notifying observable properties changes, in the (rather common) case where observable properties relate to functional aspects, i.e. the state of the supervised component. Then,

- observable properties changes result from the execution of methods called by the clients of the component;
- insofar as the implementation of a component must remain hidden to its user(s), we consider that any interaction or synchronization between a component and its client should be avoided, while a call is being processed. Thus, we choose to postpone the evaluation of the conditions (which can result in such a synchronization) until the end of the processing of a call.

In this perspective, the protocol we present

- defines a write accessor for each observable property of the supervised component. This accessor is private to the component[4]. It must be called for any update of an observable property. It systematically notifies the updates to a supervision support class, which is integrated with the supervised component.
- ends each public method of the component by calling the condition evaluation method.

This framework enables to deal routinely (and therefore, automatically, in the long run) with the handling of the updates of observable properties, along with the evaluation of the supervision conditions.

On the other hand, the diversity, and the versatility, of non-functional aspects (i.e. aspects that are related to the execution context of the supervised component), do not seem very propitious to the development of simple and generic coupling patterns. Therefore, for now, we only consider cyclic activities, which periodically check the observable properties for updates, and (possibly) notify the supervision support class, which evaluates the corresponding conditions. This pattern looks appropriate when different users work on different instances of a component. It can be replaced by ad-hoc monitoring activities, for aspects that

[4] This accessor is thus out of the users' scope: the reason for its definition is to facilitate the implementation of the supervision class.

do not compose well with supervision, e.g. when concurrent calls to the same component need to be synchronized, which can affect the instants of observations granted to the concurrent users. In the latter case, the designer of the component has to manage the updates of the observable properties, and the evaluation of the conditions, depending on the aspect to be implemented. While the composition of supervision with non functional aspects is an important and open matter, that must be dealt with, it is , for now, outside the scope of this study.

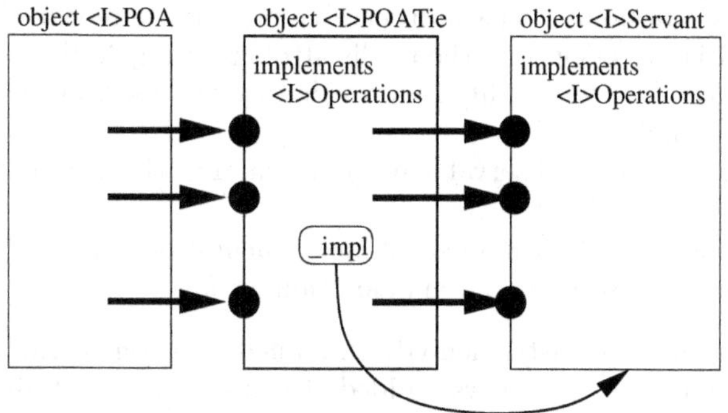

Fig. 1. Interception pattern

Instrumented Component Implementation. To complement the previous example, we present the server-side implementation of the supervision service, in the setting of a Corba to Java mapping. In this context, each interface $<I>$ defined in an IDL module is compiled (mapped) into a set of Java source files. Amongst these files, $<I>$POATie.java implements an interceptor for the method calls to the object that implements $<I>$, as shown in figure 1. We use this interceptor as a basis for the instrumentation of the Corba object. To this end, the interceptor's code is supplemented by:

- the declaration of a monitoring object, which is an instance of the SupervisableComponentSupport class. This object, which implements the supervision service. is defined as a (private) attribute of the interceptor, following a pattern similar to the implementation of Java Beans properties. This class provides, in particular:
  - the user supervision operations, introduced in the beginning of this section: submit a new condition (method activate), remove a formerly submitted condition (method desactivate), list the observable properties (method listObservableAttributes).
  - The (des)activateObservableAttribute method(s), which enable the designer of the component to dynamically control the set of observable properties, i.e. properties that can appear in a condition submitted by a user. Initially, every property is observable. These methods take a parameter, which is the identifier of the observable property.

  - The evaluateConditions method, which performs the evalutation of the conditions that are submitted by the user, and calls the corresponding reactions, if needed. This method is systematically called at the end of each method of the component's (functional) interface, but it can also be called by the component's internal activities that monitor non functional aspects.
  - the attributeChangeNotify method, which takes the identfier of the updated property as a parameter. This method is called after each write access to an observable property. To this end, the setXxx(...) accessor which corresponds to each observable property is redefined: it first calls the initial accessor, and then calls attributeChangeNotify.
- the evaluation of the conditions provided by the user, at the end of each (public) method ;
- the registration of the observable properties and methods with the supervisor module ;
- the methods needed to implement instrumentation (observable properties activation, desactivation, and enumeration ...).

In our example, the instrumented (simplified) version of the SimpleBuffer-POATie interceptor is as follows (added declarations and statements are in italics):

```
public class SimpleBufferPOATie extends SimpleBufferPOA {
  // supervision management object
  private SupervisableComponentSupport spvr =
                 new SupervisableComponentSupport(this);
  private example.SimpleBufferOperations _impl;
  private org.omg.PortableServer.POA      _poa;
  // Constructors
  public SimpleBufferPOATie (example.SimpleBufferOperations delegate){
      this._impl = delegate;
      spvr.activateObservableAttribute(''NbUsed'');
      spvr.activateObservableAttribute(''Size'');
      ...
  }
  public example.SimpleBufferOperations _delegate() { return this._impl; }
  public void _delegate (example.SimpleBufferOperations delegate){
      this._impl = delegate;
  }
  ...
  /* base object */
  public short NbUsed() { return _impl.NbUsed(); }
  public short Size() { return _impl.Size(); }
  protected void setNbUsed(int value) {
    _impl.setNbUsed(value); spvr.attributeChangeNotify("NbUsed");
  }
  public void Insert (short i) throws example.BufferIsFullException {
    _impl.Insert(i); spvr.evaluateConditions();
  } // Insert
```

```
public short Remove () throws exemple.BufferIsEmptyException {
    short image = _impl.Remove(); spvr.evaluateConditions() ;
    return image ;
} // Remove

// instrumentation methods
Vector listObservableAttributes() {
      return spvr.listObservableAttributes();
}
Vector listObservableMethods() {
      return spvr.listObservableMethods();
}
void activate(String refCondition, ConditionObserver oc)
    throws UnknownConditionException, NonActiveOperandsException {
    spvr.activate(refCondition,oc);
}
void desactivate(String refCondition, ConditionObserver oc)
    throws UnknownConditionException {
    spvr.desactivate(refCondition,oc);  // refCondition = condition URL
}
} // class SimpleBufferPOATie
```

5 Related Work and Extensions to the CSS

Supervision protocol setting. Our proposal can be seen as a generalization of "callbacks"[5], and also of "active interfaces" [Hei98], insofar as the user of a component is given the ability to superpose handlers he defines to the regular component behaviour. It is a generalization, as the coupling between the handlers and the component is also defined by the user, and as this coupling is not limited to a closed set of events (given by the designer of the component), as with callbacks, active interfaces, or publish/subscribe protocols defined for the Java Beans or for the CORBA Event Service [OMG01].

In this respect, the protocol we propose can be seen as an extension of the Java Beans. In fact, the Java Beans introduce the notion of observable property, together with a related publish/subscribe protocol for updates, and therefore allow the user of a Bean to control the value and updates of these properties. This basic instrumentation pattern is extended by JMX[6], which allows to define "operations", that correspond to the observable methods of our protocol. From this standpoint, the coupling by means of conditions that we propose appears to be the matching part, in terms of control, of the notion of property: it aims at enabling the user of a component to define a *customizable control flow*, since the execution of the component can be controlled by the user, and synchronized with a computation provided by the user, according to user-defined criteria. The

[5] Which itself appears as a generalization of the notion of exception.

[6] JMX [Sun02] is a J2EE component, dedicated to the low-level supervision of distributed (J2EE) components. We sketch the main features of JMX in the following.

latter point shows the difference between our proposal and the Java Beans (or their JMX extension): whereas the latter focuses on the control of properties, and limits the support for coordination to a set of events related to properties updates or defined by the *designer* of the component, *we lay the stress on expressing a user-defined coordination*, based on properties. Supervised components can thus be viewed as "instrumented" Java Beans. Similarly to the Java Beans, the supervision service is implemented as a class, which is an attribute of the supervised component.

Evaluation of the CSS. A direct comparison between our approach and existing supervision tools would not be very relevant, since different goals are pursued: the latter aims at efficiency, while the former strives for versatility and adaptability.

Whereas the implementation of the CSS can be optimized, it is intrinsically costly (when compared to the running time of the supervised components), since it consists in an on-the-fly check of the soundness of the behaviour of components with respect to specifications provided by the users. Therefore, our supervision service is mainly intended for dynamic, open systems, where the needs for supervision or adaptation are important, and where available components are black boxes, that cannot be easily modified, and that have loose or unfitting semantics with respect to user requirements. This sort of setting can be found notably in critical systems [7], where compliance with requirements is essential, and also in distributed systems and services, where supervision is an active research area, for such purposes as management [DL02], tracking, debugging [GSZ01], QoS or correctness assessment [CSDS03]. In particular, Web Services [SG04] currently are a prominent applicative field for works in the latter research domain. As for us, in the broader perspective of distributed Informations Systems development, we rely on the CSS for implementing a *Safety of Service service (SSS)* [PTMP03a], which allows to check and enforce the compliance of the overall use of a service (i.e. not only a single component), with specifications stated by the user through *use profiles* [PTMP03b].

Extensions to the CSS. To be actually usable, supervision by means of the CSS should be as simple as possible, from the designer's point of view, as well as from the user's standpoint. From the designer's point of view, the protocol we present sets rules for a systematic implementation of the supervision service. Although

[7] While it may sound paradoxical at first sight (critical systems are supposed to be (thoroughly) verified *before* their deployment), the use of a supervision service may prove quite interesting, as

- it provides a complementary means to verify the correctness of a system ;
- it enables to check properties that cannot be checked statically ;
- it can be used to check at runtime the assumptions made, during the design stage, on the system environment and behaviour, thus allowing to ascertain the soundness of the underlying system model ;
- critical systems are a setting where implementing a supervision service may appear to be worth its extra cost.

these rules are uninvolved, their implementation by designers of components remains rather tedious, and, above all, error-prone. Therefore, it seems interesting to supplement this level of specification, which is needed for a fine-grained control of observable properties, by a "compiler" for supervisable components, which, given initial components and observable properties, would generate supervised components, in the same way as IDL/stub compilers use Interface Definitions to generate the code for handling remote interactions[8]. This "supervisable component compiler" can be implemented directly, or it can be built upon the features offered by:

- aspect programming languages and environments, such as AspectJ [KHH+01], since supervision can be considered as a specific aspect, which must be woven with the code of the component to be supervised ;
- reflexion-based component platforms and models, such as Fractal [BCL+04], which enables to program interceptors ("controllers", in the Fractal terminology) bound to components, thus allowing a dynamic weaving of non-functional aspects;
- the JMX distributed supervision architecture [Sun02]. JMX defines a framework for low-level monitoring and management of distributed components, in the setting of the J2EE platform. JMX facilitates more particularly open, distributed and dynamic systems supervision by
  - supporting the adaptation of existing supervision and management protocols (e.g. SNMP ...);
  - allowing to reconfigure observable properties or methods at runtime;
  - integrating base distributed services (naming, security...) with supervision.

  In this respect, and in the prospect of a broader use of the CSS ,JMX can provide a basis for implementing a higher-level supervision service, such as ours, in a distributed environment.

On the user side, we are currently working on the ease of use of the supervision protocol, by allowing to enable/disable dynamically the CSS with respect to a component.

6 Conclusion

The CSS aims at allowing to superpose a supervision service to existing components, for standard maintenance, debugging, tracking, or adaptation purposes. Due to the very nature of components, this service has the distinctive feature of allowing to define supervision from a specification of the properties that the user expects from the component, independently from the component implementation and control flow. This supervision service therefore allows to check that a component conforms to its user's needs, nay to adapt this component to its

[8] Such supervisable components can be generated *independently from* the conditions to be monitored.

user's needs, without having to consider the semantics or the implementation of the component.

By stating observable methods and properties, the designer specifies and controls the possible instrumentation of the component that he provides. From that point, the CSS provides the user of the component with a generic and non intrusive supervision protocol, that enables the user to perform the adaptations that he deems relevant, independently from the designer of the component.

For example, if the purpose of adaptation is to maintain at runtime the consistency of the component's behavior with respect to a given model, as is the case with Self-Healing Systems [GS02, WE04], then the CSS provides a basis for instrumentation, and allows to take into account a variety of system models[9].

Self-adaptation is just an example, as the CSS potentially provides a basis for any external adaptation of supervisable components. This leads to the difficult question of controlling the bounds of adaptation. Indeed, the protocol that we present does not prevent users from completely altering the functionality of a component, by superposing a completely unrelated behavior. In fact, we do not tackle this matter directly, as our choice, and aim, is to provide the user with a supervision *mechanism*, and let him be the judge of the relevance of his own adaptations. This is a proven strategy [Lam83], in spite of its weaknesses, which are those of the user.

Acknowledgements

We would like to thank the anonymous referees for their constructive and insightful comments, which helped us to improve this paper significantly.

References

[BCL+04] Eric Bruneton, Thierry Coupaye, Matthieu Leclercq, Vivien Quema, and Jean-Bernard Stefani. An open component model and its support in java. In *Component-Based Software Engineering: 7th International Symposium (CBSE 2004)*, pages 7 – 22, May 2004.

[CSDS03] F. Casati, E. Shan, U. Dayal, and M.-C. Shan. Business-oriented management of web services. *Communications of the ACM*, 46(10):55 – 60, October 2003.

[DL02] P.-C. David and T. Ledoux. An Infrastructure for Adaptable Middleware. In *DOA'02*, October 2002.

[GS02] David Garlan and Bradley Schmerl. Model-based adaptation for self-healing systems. In *WOSS '02: Proceedings of the first workshop on Self-healing systems*, pages 27–32, New York, NY, USA, 2002. ACM Press.

[GSZ01] J. Gao, S. Shim, and E. Zhul. Tracking software components. *Journal of Object-Oriented Programming*, October 2001.

[9] This example is somewhat particular insofar as adaptive maintenance may require meta-level actions, which may appear to come amiss the modularity principle on which the CSS is based.

[Hei98] G. T. Heineman. A model for designing adaptable software components. In *22nd Annual International Computer Science and Application Conference (COMPSAC-98)*, pages 121–127, August 1998.

[KHH+01] Gregor Kiczales, Erik Hilsdale, Jim Hugunin, Mik Kersten, Jeffrey Palm, and William G. Griswold. An overview of aspectj. In *15th European Conference on Object-Oriented Programming*, pages 327–353, June 2001.

[Lam83] Butler W. Lampson. Hints for computer system design. In *SOSP '83: Proceedings of the ninth ACM symposium on Operating systems principles*, pages 33–48, New York, NY, USA, 1983. ACM Press.

[OMG01] OMG. Event service specification. Technical Report http://www.w3.org/TR/2004/NOTE-ws-arch-20040211/, OMG, March 2001.

[PTMP03a] Xuan Loc Pham Thi, Philippe Mauran, and Grard Padiou. Sret de service des composants logiciels. In Marc Bui, editor, *First International Conference RIVF'03, Hanoi*, pages 159–162, February 2003.

[PTMP03b] Xuan Loc Pham Thi, Philippe Mauran, and Grard Padiou. Try and patch : an approach to improve the trust in software components. In Olivier Camp, Joaquim Filipe, Slimane Hammoudi, and Mario Piattini, editors, *Fifth International Conference on Enterprise Information Systems, Angers*, pages 505–508, April 2003.

[PTMP05] Xuan Loc Pham Thi, Philippe Mauran, and Grard Padiou. Instrumenter pour superviser, superviser pour adapter, adapter pour rutiliser. In Patrick Bellot, Duong Vu, and Marc Bui, editors, *RIVF'05 3rd International Conference*, February 2005.

[SG04] J. P. Sousa and D. Garlan. Web services architecture. W3C Working Group Note http://www.w3.org/TR/2004/NOTE-ws-arch-20040211/, W3C, February 2004.

[Sun02] Sun. Javatm management extensions instrumentation and agent specification, v1.2. Technical Report http://java.sun.com/products/JavaManagement, Sun Microsystems Inc., October 2002.

[WE04] David S. Wile and Alexander Egyed. An externalized infrastructure for self-healing systems. In *Fourth Working IEEE/IFIP Conference on Software Architecture (WICSA'04)*, pages 285–288, 2004.

Generic Component Lookup

Till G. Bay[1], Patrick Eugster[2], and Manuel Oriol[1]

[1] Chair of Software Engineering, Swiss Federal Institute of Technology in Zürich CH-8092 Zürich, Switzerland

[2] Purdue University, Dept. of Computer Science, West Lafayette, IN 47907, USA

Abstract. The possibilities currently offered to conduct business at an electronic level are immense. Service providers offer access to their attendances through components placed on the Internet; such components can be combined to build applications, which can themselves be used as components by further business units. The final leg of the way to this paradigm has been paved by the advent of service-oriented architectures in general, and Web Services in particular.

With protocols existing for any parties to communicate, the most critical ingredient to the success of a business idea remains the task of choosing one's business partners. At a technical level, this translates to the issue of identifying *which* components represent the most adequate services to build a final application.

While each middleware technology and system proposed in the past has been described with its scheme for "looking up" components, this paper chooses the more difficult approach of trying to distill the fundamentals of component lookup. We propose a generic model of component lookup — applicable to settings as diverse as tagged sets, classic white pages, or even method dispatch — and its implementation. We illustrate our model through various examples of existing lookup schemes. It turns out that in our generic context the common distinction between name-based and type-based lookup becomes rather artificial.

1 Introduction

The evolution from the Internet to the World Wide Web, more recently boosted by the advent of the semantic web and Web Services, has marked the gradual transformation of a communication infrastructure consisting of bare metal into a mighty platform fostering interaction of business parties.

The possibilities currently offered to conduct business at an electronic level are amazingly vast. Service providers offer access to their attendances through components placed on the Internet; such components can be combined to build applications, which can themselves be used as components by further business units. Web Service technologies typically provide the glue between individual components by proposing safe, efficient, and flexible communication protocols.

The most critical ingredient to the success of a business idea remains the task of setting up interactions, that is, choosing one's business partners. The success – or failure – of an entire business plan can depend on a single participant. At a technical level, the selection of appropriate business partners translates to the issue of identifying *which* components represent the most adequate services to build a final application. In particular, application designers have to face the challenge of specifying their own components, and choosing foreign components according to potentially several specifications.

I. Gorton et al. (Eds.): CBSE 2006, LNCS 4063, pp. 182–197, 2006.

Coding algorithms to perform such selections is an onerous task, and the outcome is usually an ad-hoc solution of limited application scope.

Each middleware technology and system proposed in the past has typically been described with its own scheme for "looking up" components, i.e., seeking, selecting, and connecting to components. In fact, the high number of non-redundant systems for looking up components advocates for a tighter integration or a composition model for such systems. In this paper, we try to distill the fundamentals of component lookup. We propose a generic model of multiple specifications component lookup based on mathematical formulae, called $\mathcal{COLOS}$ (generic COmponent LOokup based on Specification matching). By differentiating between *explicit* and *implicit* component specifications, as well as between *internal* and *external* ones, our model becomes applicable to settings as diverse as tagged sets, name-based schemes, or even method dispatch. What we propose is thus a framework intended to provide programmers with an infrastructure to use and freely encode specifications and add them to associated components. By offering the possibility of combining specifications by the means of mathematical operators, our system is able to sort the components that match with a *group of specifications* and put first the components that match *best* according to user-defined criteria.

Our way of combining specifications and their matching is robust to distribution as results can be collected in a peer-to-peer manner. Our implementation is itself based on collections of components that can be combined, and includes the foundations for building secure matching as it can also be used for locking.

We illustrate our model through various examples of existing lookup schemes. Quite interestingly, it turns out that in the generic context we consider, the traditional differentiation made in the past between value-based ("white pages") and type-based ("yellow pages") is artificial.

Roadmap. Section 2 presents preliminary material, including our model of components and their specifications, and related approaches. Section 3 elaborates on our generic model of component matching. Section 4 illustrates that model through various matching schemes. Section 5 discusses the deployment and the use of our implementation based on $\mathcal{COLOS}$. Section 6 draws final conclusions.

2 Preliminaries

Various systems and models have been described in the past for coordinating components in distributed settings. This section starts by presenting a simple abstract model of lookup, and then relating that model to a set of predating approaches.

2.1 Lookup Model

Components are described towards the outside world by respective *specifications* (see Figure 1). Lookup services basically provide components, on one hand, a means to construct and advertise such specifications, and on the other hand, a mechanism to query components based on (specification) *templates*. The composition and nature of these specifications and templates, as well as the *matching* between them, vary between approaches.

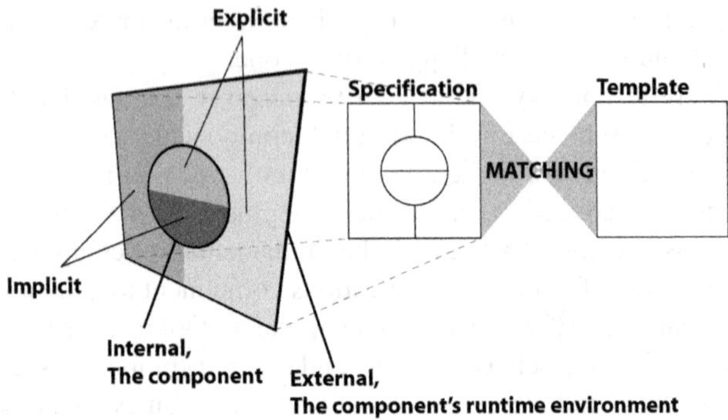

Fig. 1. Component and lookup model

Internal vs. external specification. When viewing specifications as being based on different properties, one can in a first step distinguish between *internal* and *external* properties. Internal properties are based on the nature of components themselves, i.e., they reflect properties of a given component. External criteria reflect properties which pertain to the surroundings of the component, such as its context or (runtime) environment.

Implicit vs. explicit specification. In a second step, one can distinguish between *implicit* and *explicit* properties. The former kind of criteria reflect intrinsic properties *of the services provided* by a given component; they are not influenced by the nature and set of targeted clients for that component, or the means by which the component is made available to such consumers. Explicit criteria in contrast, manifest in the way the component's very design is influenced by the perspective of making it ultimately available to the outside world.

Static vs. dynamic evaluation. Furthermore, the evaluation of the matching can be *static*, i.e., based on attributes of component specifications which are evaluated once and for all when the component is loaded, or *dynamic*, in which case the matching becomes a continuous process (see Section 5.1).

2.2 Examples

We illustrate the above model through a set of well-known lookup services, and overviewing derivatives for each. Results are summarized in Table 1 (due to the sparse occurrence of dynamic criteria in common lookup services the distinction static/dynamic is however omitted).

Domain Name System (DNS). DNS is very likely to be the most frequently used, static, name-based lookup system. Components are IP addresses, the specifications are (internal) host names, the templates are host names as well, and the matching tries to find the component that registers with a given host name (explicitly) and returns it's IP if possible.

Network Information Service (NIS). NIS is one of the oldest type-based, static lookup systems. Components are the entries of the maps (external), the specifications are map names (implicit), the templates are either map names or nicknames (e.g., $passwd$ for $passwd.byname$), and the matching is the result of the `ypcat` command.

CORBA. The Common Object Request Broker Architecture (CORBA) [1] defines both a Naming Service and Trading Object Service for name-based and type-based lookup of objects respectively. The Naming Service represents the original means of looking up objects based on a *hierarchical* naming scheme, where an object is registered (explicit) and made available by attaching it (external) a unique name $N_1. \cdots .N_n$ of which each component N_i is a name/kind-pair. In this case, specifications and templates are both defined as sets of such pairs. Names for the Java RMI registry, or regular expressions, are similar in that sense, with $n = 1$.

The Trading Object Service offers rich combinations of means of defining the service type of a component. The most preferred way of attaching a type specification to a component consists in attaching it a name/value-pair. This definition of a component is external and explicit as well: the "type" describes actual properties of the component itself, but is not implicit like the actual classification of a component according to the type system of the considered language/environment.

Note that the OMG has more recently specified the Interoperable Name Service, defining URL-format object references that can be typed into a program to reach services at a remote location, including the Naming Service.

RM-ODP. The Reference Model for Open Distributed Processing (RM-ODP) [2] defines, similarly to CORBA, both a "white pages" (name-based) and "yellow pages" (type-based) lookup service (both explicit and external), going by the names of relocator and trader respectively. The latter service describes two roles which interacting components may take: *exporters* of services, and *importers*. A *service description* is an interface (type) and a set of properties attached to it, and a *service offer* binds a service description to a concrete component, which can be a CORBA object or another object. Properties are thus used to describe specifications and templates, the latter ones being more precisely combinations of properties; rules are expressed based on properties and operators (these are called matching criteria).

A novelty of the trader specification is the description of delegation and collaboration among individual trader units, which however does not seem to impact the model ultimately perceived by an application programmer, as, expressed in our terminology, specifications are simply cascaded.

UDDI. The *universal description, discovery and integration* (UDDI) [3] specification defines a lookup service for Web Services. Such a *registry* is centered around a *public cloud*, a set of replica nodes storing white pages (abstract services by "name"), yellow pages (by "type"), and green pages (by "description" and "location"). Targeting at Web Services, UDDI encompasses a set of XML messages for SOAP-based interaction with registries. Each party is described through a *business entity*, several of which can be linked through *publisher assertions*. A *business service* is a particular Web Service offered by a business entity. Such a service is described by one or more *binding templates*, which optionally contain textual service descriptions, and URLs for the respective services. Finally, *binding templates* refer to one or more *tModel*s, which contain the pointers to actual descriptions of the services offered, and delineate the interaction protocols with the respective services. All the above-mentioned entities describe a refined pattern for specifications in the sense of our model introduced before-hand. The enforcing of authentication is covered in our model by external explicit criteria (see Section 4.5). The load distribution among nodes forming the public cloud is achieved in our implementation in an efficient manner by distributing the matching, greatly transparently, over a peer-to-peer overlay network (see Section 5.1).

Note that UDDI is a rare example of dynamic lookup, where components can be notified of changes in specifications of other components. Further examples are given by load balancing, or reuse frequency [4].

Service Groups. Sadou et al. [5] introduce a notion of *service group* to mediate between client and server components. These are motivated by the desire for type evolution, e.g., the possibility of adding parameters to methods. Just like in RM-OPD, the approach introduces both a notion of *type* which reflects provided services (i.e., the server side) in the terminology introduced by the authors, and a notion of *role* which represents the needs of customers (i.e., the client side).

At a first glance, one could hence be brought to viewing the types of [5] as specifications in our case, roles as templates, and service groups as defining the matching, respectively. However, the emphasis of [5] consists in making services of a given type available to clients expecting a slightly different type. Service groups are thus a form of glue aiming at expressing *how to pass from a given type to a given role*. They consist in stubs for respective server objects, which transform invocations based on a given role (the expected type) such as to fit the effective type. In our model, this represents explicit, internal component registration, and the specifications are made up of the stubs.

In a sense, HydroJ [6] and LuckyJ [7], can be seen as similar approaches to service groups, as these are also based on some notion of type. Borrow/Lend [8], a derivative of the Type-based Publish/Subscribe (TPS) abstraction [9], as suggested by the name of the latter paradigm, in contrast, is primarily based on type-based matching of inherent Java object types (implicit, internal). The types are augmented by (dynamic) predicate evaluation, and with keys (explicit, external).

Coordination Spaces. The Borrow/Lend abstraction can in fact be seen as a variant of the Linda Tuple Space [10] with callback functionalities. The original Tuple Space is a means of exchanging information among distributed components, based on tuples of place holders (types) and values, i.e., a mixture of value-based and type-based matching, where values can also be character strings. This demonstrates how thin the border between types and values is.

Just like Borrow/Lend, Tagged Sets [11] are a variant of Tuple Spaces, where tuple items can also be predicates (leading to a dynamic evaluation), or keys (symmetric or asymmetric). Similarly, SecOS [12], supports the use of keys, with a partial matching. Clearly, any such criterion is explicit and external.

Table 1. Coarse classification of lookup services

Criteria	Explicit	Implicit
External	UDDI, CORBA Naming, Trading, Java RMI, Linda, Regular Expressions, Tagged Sets, Borrow/Lend, SecOS	Reuse Frequency, Load Balancing, NIS
Internal	HydroJ, LuckyJ, Service Groups, DNS	Method Dispatch, Borrow/Lend

2.3 A Note on Values and Types

A distinction that is often made when discussing component lookup is the one between *values* and *types*. This is nicely illustrated by the metaphors of "white pages" and "yellow pages" respectively.

However, component lookup in a distributed heterogeneous environment is basically untyped. Matching components for their "type" boils down to matching such components for the *name of their type*, an internal property of these components. The possibility of registering several objects under a same given name, as supported by many systems, illustrates this seamless transition; by doing so, such a name becomes more a type description than a unique identifier. The issue of matching in such a setting becomes essentially a question of *depth*, in a way similar to the issue of object copying/cloning [13]. Any categorical distinction between values and types at this level seems unnatural. This is captured by our abstract notions of specifications and templates, which will become clearer through the matching model presented in Section 3, and illustrations thereof in Section 4.

3 Matching Model

The matching model presented in this section has resulted from the desire of capturing all the different lookup criteria outlined in the previous section.

In our model, the matching of components against requirements builds on the two basic notions introduced in the previous section, namely *specifications* and *templates*. The former roughly represent actual component descriptions (i.e., server-side views of components, see Figure 1), and the latter represent requirement descriptions (i.e., client-side views of components). In our matching model, specifications and templates are related by *matching modules*. Our goal is to be able to combine several specifications and templates into a compact notation and to design a lookup mechanism that sorts the retrieved components in a list.

Our solution relies on mathematical formulae containing templates. As an example the formula $t_0 + 3.0 - t_1 * t_2$ combines the three templates t_0, t_1 and t_2. Such a formula will be evaluated for each component C that has specifications s_0, s_1 and s_2 respectively corresponding to each template. The evaluation replaces each template with a value (the matching value) that is calculated by applying a matching function ($?_i$) between the specifications of the component and the templates. As an example evaluating the formula with given specifications will return the evaluation of:

$$(?_0(s_0, t_0) + 3.0 - ?_1(s_1, t_1) * ?_2(s_2, t_2))$$

For each component, this formula yields its matching value. When a client looks a component up, it is given a list of components sorted by their matching values in descending order. Components for which the matching value is 0 or below are omitted from the list. In the remainder of the section we define the theoretical framework to formalize this intuition using denotational semantics.

3.1 Matching Modules

A *matching module* is a triplet encompassing a set of specifications $\mathfrak{S}$, a set of templates $\mathfrak{T}$ and a matching relation ?.

$$mm ::= (\mathfrak{S}, \mathfrak{T}, ?) \quad where\ ? : \mathfrak{S} \times \mathfrak{T} \rightarrow \mathbb{N}$$

3.2 Specifications

A specification $\mathfrak{S}$ is itself a set of *specification terms* s_i. Informally, a specification term is the specification for a component according to a given formalism. A template $\mathfrak{T}$ is itself a set of *templates terms* t_i. Informally, a template term delineates a set of components according to a given formalism. The matching relation ? is a function that takes a specification term and a template term as arguments and returns a natural number.

In short, we define here what we need for providing ways of matching specifications and templates. Our goal being to integrate several of these modules into a multi-module specification, we do not enter into details but rather give examples of this in Section 4.

3.3 Qualified Specifications

A *qualified specification term* qs is a specification term annotated with a *qualifier*.

$$\begin{aligned} s &\in \mathfrak{S}_i \\ val &::= n \in \mathbb{N} \\ comp &::= \ < \mid > \mid \neq \mid \leq \mid \geq \mid = \\ qualifier &::= \ \textbf{required}\ comp\ val \mid \varnothing \\ qs &::= \ s\ qualifier \end{aligned}$$

Qualifiers on specification terms are used as a way for the component provider to order differences in the treatment of the matching. We specify two different types of qualifiers: ∅ that means that we do not modify the basic mechanism (that we always omit in practice as a notation abuse) and **required** that allows us to filter and impose a condition on the matching for specific specification terms. This latter qualifier allows us, in particular to envision security-constrained matching as shown in Section 4.5. Even if, for now, we only consider the qualifiers **required** and ∅ we could imagine other qualifiers that modify the infrastructure's behavior accordingly.

A *component specification* CS consists of a set of qualified specification terms that appear at most once in the set of specifications of a given matching module.

$$CS ::= \{qs_1, ..., qs_n\} \quad such\ that\ \forall\ i,\ j \in\ [1, n]\ \ s_i \in s_0\ s_j \in s_0\ \Rightarrow\ i = j$$

A component specification is the way a component provider can describe its components.

3.4 Templates

A *template* $T \in \mathfrak{T}$ consists of a mathematical formula using mathematical operators and *template terms*.

$$\begin{aligned} t &\in \mathfrak{T}_i \\ op &::= \; + \mid - \mid * \mid / \\ T &::= \; n \in \mathbb{N} \mid t \mid T \; op \; T \end{aligned}$$

The idea is, that unlike qualified specification terms that are composed in a list to make the component specification, we compose template terms to a mathematical formula in order to allow component seekers to allocate more weight to some specification. It also allows to exclude components that answer to a specification by using subtractions and divisions to lower their matching values and possibly rule them out of the returned list.

3.5 Matching

The *valued matching* of a component specification CS with a template T consists in matching on the specification and calculating its value according to the template definition. It is defined as follows:

$$valuedMatch \quad ::= CS?_v T$$

$$\begin{aligned} &\mathcal{V}[\![\cdot]\!] : valuedMatch \rightarrow \mathbb{Q} \cup \{\infty\} \\ &\mathcal{V}[\![CS?_v n]\!] &&= n \\ &\mathcal{V}[\![CS?_v t]\!] &&= 0 \; if \; \nexists \, qs = s_0 \, q_0 \in CS \\ & && \quad such \; as \; \exists \, mm_0 = (\mathfrak{S}_0, \mathfrak{T}_0, ?_0) \mid t \in \mathfrak{T}_0, \; s_0 \in \mathfrak{S}_0 \\ & && \quad ?(s, \; t) \; otherwise \\ &\mathcal{V}[\![CS?_v T_1 \; op \; T_2]\!] &&= \mathcal{V}[\![CS?_v T_1]\!] \; op \; \mathcal{V}[\![CS?_v T_2]\!] \end{aligned}$$

The intuition behind the matching we describe is the following: each template term within the mathematical formula of the template is replaced by the result of the application of the matching relation between the template term and the specification term of the component specification.

The *matching compliance* of a component specification CS with a template T describes the specification terms matched. It is defined as follows:

$$compliesToMatch \quad ::= CS?_c T$$

$$\begin{aligned} &\mathcal{C}[\![\cdot]\!] : compliesToMatch \rightarrow \mathbb{B} \\ &\mathcal{C}[\![\{s \; \textbf{required} \; compo_0 \; n_0\}?_c T]\!] &&= \text{TRUE} \; if \; \exists \, t \; in \; T \; s.a. \; \mathcal{V}[\![s?_v t]\!] \; compo_0 \; n_0 \\ & && \quad \text{FALSE} \; otherwise \\ &\mathcal{C}[\![\{s\varnothing\}?_c T]\!] &&= \text{TRUE} \\ &\mathcal{C}[\![\{qs_1, \; ..., \; qs_n\}?_c T]\!] &&= \mathcal{C}[\![\{qs_1\}?_c T]\!] \wedge ... \wedge \mathcal{C}[\![\{qs_n\}?_c T]\!] \end{aligned}$$

As a simple explanation, a template complies with a specification if all the required conditions on the specifications are fulfilled by any of the basic templates.

3.6 Component Selection

Finally, we can define the *selection* mechanism built on top of the valued matching and the matching compliance. A component C declares its interface in its component specification CS. The component repository $\mathfrak{C}$ consists in a set of components stored with their specifications. These can be selected using the selection operator $\downarrow$ that returns a list of components for which we show the semantics $\mathcal{E}$.

$$\begin{array}{ll} \mathfrak{C} & ::= \{(CS_1, C_1), ..., (CS_n, C_n)\} \\ lookup & ::= \mathfrak{C} \downarrow T \end{array}$$

$$\begin{array}{rcl} \mathcal{E}[\![\cdot]\!] : lookup \rightarrow list\ of\ (CS_i, C_i) & & \\ \mathcal{E}[\![\mathfrak{C} \downarrow T]\!] & = & \{(CS'_1, C'_1), ..., (CS'_m, C'_m)\} \subseteq \mathfrak{C} \\ & & such\ that \\ & & \forall i \in [1, m], \mathcal{C}[\![CS'_i ?_c T]\!]\ and\ \mathcal{V}[\![CS'_i ?_v T]\!] > 0 \\ & & and\ \forall i, j \in [1, m],\ i < j \Leftrightarrow \mathcal{V}[\![CS'_i ?_v T]\!] \geq \mathcal{V}[\![CS'_j ?_v T]\!] \end{array}$$

Intuitively, the final result of a component selection on a repository is a list containing elements from the repository ordered by decreasing matching values. That way, we can obtain the component that is best adapted regarding to the templates we defined. In the next section we show examples of such matching modules and how they can be used.

4 Illustration

This section illustrates our generic model of component lookup through a small set of existing lookup schemes. More examples can be found in a longer version of this paper [14] (e.g. examples based on nominal and structural subtyping or on reuse frequency [4]).

4.1 Unique Identifiers

As a first simple example, we consider the selection mechanism based on a unique component identifier. In that case the matching module can be described by the following triplet:

$$\begin{array}{rcl} mm_{\mathfrak{uid}} ::= (\mathbb{N}, \mathbb{N}, ?_{\mathfrak{uid}}) & & \\ where\ ?_{\mathfrak{uid}} : & & \mathbb{N} \times \mathbb{N} \mapsto \{\,0,\,1\,\} \\ ?_{\mathfrak{uid}}(x, y) & = & 1\ if x = y \\ & & 0\ otherwise \end{array}$$

As a first example of use, we can imagine a collection of software components that have unique identifiers:

$$\mathfrak{C} = \{(\{1_{\mathfrak{uid}}\}, C_1), ..., (\{1337_{\mathfrak{uid}}\}, C_{1337}), ..., (\{n_{\mathfrak{uid}}\}, C_n)\}$$

Looking up component identified by number 1337 can be made as follows:

$$\mathfrak{C} \downarrow 1337_{\mathfrak{uid}} = \{(\{1337_{\mathfrak{uid}}\}, C_{1337})\}$$

Note that a variation of this module can be used to describe the DNS.

4.2 Regular Expressions

Among the most widespread and popular descriptions of components are component APIs, and component documentation. One can imagine selecting components based on criteria expressed on their textual description, in addition to other specifications. An example is selecting components according to their author(s), as appearing in the documentation. This constitutes the case of matching regular expressions (note that we use the original regular expressions as defined in Kleene algebra):

$$
\begin{array}{ll}
char & ::= a \mid ... \\
string & ::= char \mid string\ string \\
expr & ::= \varnothing \mid char \mid (expr\ expr) \mid (expr + expr) \mid expr* \\
mm_{\mathfrak{regexp}} & ::= (string, expr, ?_{\mathfrak{regexp}}) \\
 & \quad where\ ?_{\mathfrak{regexp}} : string \times expr \mapsto \mathbb{N} \\
 & \quad ?_{\mathfrak{regexp}}(s, e) = number\ of\ occurrences\ of\ s\ in\ e
\end{array}
$$

Now imagine that a user wants to obtain a component for which John Doe is indicated as the main author of that component in the accompanying documentation and preferably take the component with the unique identifier 1337. A collection including such a component could then be:

$$
\begin{array}{l}
\mathfrak{C} = \{ (\{1_{\mathfrak{uid}}, \text{“...}author : John\ Doe\text{...”}_{\mathfrak{regexp}}\}, C_1), ... \\
\quad (\{1337_{\mathfrak{uid}}, \text{“...}author : John\ Doe\text{...”}_{\mathfrak{regexp}}\}, C_{1337}), ... \\
\quad (\{n_{\mathfrak{uid}}\}, C_n)\}
\end{array}
$$

Looking up a component fulfilling at least one of these characteristics would then produce:

$$
\begin{array}{l}
\mathfrak{C} \downarrow (1337_{\mathfrak{uid}} + \text{“} * author : John\ Doe * \text{”}_{\mathfrak{regexp}}) = \\
\{ (\{1337_{\mathfrak{uid}}, \text{“...}author : John\ Doe\text{...”}_{\mathfrak{regexp}}\}, C_{1337}), \\
\quad (\{1_{\mathfrak{uid}}, \text{“...}author : John\ Doe\text{...”}_{\mathfrak{regexp}}\}, C_1)\}
\end{array}
$$

Looking up a component fullfilling both criteria can be made as follows:

$$
\begin{array}{l}
\mathfrak{C} \downarrow (1337_{\mathfrak{uid}} * \text{“} * author : John\ Doe * \text{”}_{\mathfrak{regexp}}) = \\
\{ (\{1337_{\mathfrak{uid}}, \text{“...}author : John\ Doe\text{...”}_{\mathfrak{regexp}}\}, C_{1337})\}
\end{array}
$$

4.3 Load Balancing

Another criterion of component linking, is its current load.

$$
\begin{array}{ll}
mm_{\mathfrak{load}} & ::= (\mathbb{N},\ \varnothing,\ ?_{\mathfrak{load}}) \\
 & \quad where\ ?_{\mathfrak{load}} : \mathbb{N} \times \varnothing \mapsto \mathbb{N}^+ \\
 & \quad ?_{\mathfrak{load}}(n) = number\ of\ components\ currently\ using\ component\ n
\end{array}
$$

Imagine that a user wants to obtain the component which is currently experiencing the smallest load written by John Doe. Suppose also that some components support only up to 10 clients at the time. A collection containing such components could then be specified as follows:

$$\mathfrak{C} = \{(\{1_{\mathfrak{UJD}}, \text{"...}author : John\ Doe\text{..."}_{\mathfrak{regexp}}, C_1), ...$$
$$(\{1337_{\mathfrak{UJD}}, \text{"...}author : John\ Doe\text{..."}_{\mathfrak{regexp}}, \textbf{required}\ 1337_{\mathfrak{load}} < 10.0\}, C_{1337}), ...$$
$$(\{n_{\mathfrak{UJD}}, n_{\mathfrak{load}}\}, C_n)\}$$

A programmer wishing to get such a component should perform the following lookup (note that the result is dependant of the number of clients currently connected to both components):

$$\mathfrak{C} \downarrow (\text{"}* author : John\ Doe *\text{"}_{\mathfrak{regexp}}/(1.0+_{\mathfrak{load}})) =$$
$$\{ (\{1_{\mathfrak{UJD}}, \text{"...}author : John\ Doe\text{..."}_{\mathfrak{regexp}}, C_1),$$
$$(\{1337_{\mathfrak{UJD}}, \text{"...}author : John\ Doe\text{..."}_{\mathfrak{regexp}}\}, C_{1337})\}$$

4.4 Compliance to an Interface

It very often happens that programmers want to obtain components that comply to a given interface. Informally, compliance to an interface is expressed in terms of a structural subtyping relationship. Suppose that I_1 is compliant to I_2 if and only if I_1 has at least the same procedures as I_2.

$$\begin{array}{lll} p & & procedure\ names \\ t & & types\ names \\ procedure & ::= & (p, \{t_0, ..., t_n\}) \\ I & ::= & \{procedure_1, ..., procedure_n\} \\ mm_{\mathfrak{compl}\mathfrak{y}} & ::= & (Interfaces,\ Interfaces,\ ?_{\mathfrak{compl}\mathfrak{y}}) \\ & & where\ ?_{\mathfrak{compl}\mathfrak{y}} : Interfaces \times Interfaces \mapsto \{0,\ 1\} \\ & & ?_{\mathfrak{compl}\mathfrak{y}}(I_1, I_2) = 1\ iff\ I_2 \subseteq I_1,\ 0\ otherwise \end{array}$$

Supposing that some components offer procedures to set and get their internal attributes, the collection of components could be:

$$\mathfrak{C}=\{(\{1_{\mathfrak{UJD}}, \{set\_a\ \{Void,\ string\}, get\_a\ \{string\}, decrement\ \{\}\}_{\mathfrak{compl}\mathfrak{y}}, C_1), ...$$
$$(\{1337_{\mathfrak{UJD}}, \text{"...}author : John\ Doe\text{..."}_{\mathfrak{regexp}}\}, C_{1337}), ...$$
$$(\{n_{\mathfrak{UJD}}, n_{\mathfrak{load}}, \{set\_a\ \{Void,\ string\}, get\_a\ \{string\}\}\}_{\mathfrak{compl}\mathfrak{y}}, C_n)\}$$

Then a program seeking for components that comply to an interface containing *set_a* and *get_a* could make the following lookup:

$$\mathfrak{C} \downarrow \{set\_a\ \{Void,\ string\}, get\_a\ \{string\}\}_{\mathfrak{compl}\mathfrak{y}} =$$
$$\{ (\{1_{\mathfrak{UJD}}, \{set\_a\ \{Void,\ string\}, get\_a\ \{string\}, decrement\ \{\}\}_{\mathfrak{compl}\mathfrak{y}}, C_1),$$
$$(\{n_{\mathfrak{UJD}}, n_{\mathfrak{load}}, \{set_a\ \{Void,\ string\}, get_a\ \{string\}\}\}_{\mathfrak{compl}\mathfrak{y}}, C_n)\}$$

Variants of this example are countless as we could return the number of procedures in common, or the number of lacking procedures etc. However this is the simplest variant and it corresponds to the approach of service groups [5].

4.5 Secure Linking

By specifying a **required** clause, a component *provider* can enforce the matching of a specification as a necessary precondition for handing out any reference to its component. Our current example is presenting encrypted matching and can be considered as a subset of tagged sets [11] or any other matching mechanisms driven or restricted by encryption [12, 8].

We call $E(K, value)$ the encryption and $D(K, value)$ the decryption, for which we give the semantics $\mathcal{S}[\![\cdot]\!]$ that we detail below.

$$
\begin{array}{ll}
SKey & SymetricKeys \\
\overline{AKey} & Asymmetric\ Keys\ (private) \\
AKey & Asymmetric\ Keys\ (public) \\
value & ::= basic_v alue \mid value_{\overline{AKey}} \mid value_{SKey} \\
e & ::= value \mid E(SKey, e) \mid E(\overline{AKey}, e) \mid D(SKey, e) \mid D(AKey, e)
\end{array}
$$

$$
\begin{array}{l}
\mathcal{S}[\![\cdot]\!] : e \mapsto value \\
\mathcal{S}[\![value]\!] = value \\
\mathcal{S}[\![value]\!] = value \\
\mathcal{S}[\![E(SKey, e)]\!] = \mathcal{S}[\![e]\!]_{SKey} \\
\mathcal{S}[\![E(\overline{AKey}, e)]\!] = \mathcal{S}[\![e]\!]_{\overline{AKey}} \\
\mathcal{S}[\![D(SKey, e_{SKey})]\!] = \mathcal{S}[\![e]\!] \\
\mathcal{S}[\![D(AKey, e_{\overline{AKey}})]\!] = e
\end{array}
$$

The associated matching module is then:

$$
\begin{array}{l}
mm_{\mathfrak{crypt}} ::= (Keys,\ Keys,\ ?_{\mathfrak{crypt}}) \\
\qquad where\ ?_{\mathfrak{crypt}} : Keys \times Keys \mapsto \{0,1\} \\
\qquad\qquad ?_{\mathfrak{crypt}}(K_1,K_2)=1\ if\ \mathcal{S}[\![D(K_2, E(K_1, value))]\!]=value \\
\qquad\qquad\qquad 0\ otherwise
\end{array}
$$

A collection containing components being locked by an asymmetric key $AKey$ could then be :

$$
\begin{array}{l}
\mathfrak{C} = \{(\{1_{\mathfrak{uid}}, \text{"...}author : John\ Doe\text{..."}_{\mathfrak{regexp}}, C_1), \ldots \\
(\{1337_{\mathfrak{uid}}, \text{"...}author : John\ Doe\text{..."}_{\mathfrak{regexp}}, \mathbf{required}AKey_{\mathfrak{crypt}}{=}1.0\}, C_{1337}), \ldots \\
(\{n_{\mathfrak{uid}}, n_{\mathfrak{load}}, AKey_{\mathfrak{crypt}}\}, C_n)\}
\end{array}
$$

A programmer wishing to know all the components locked with $AKey$ should then make the following lookup:

$$
\begin{array}{l}
\mathfrak{C} \downarrow \overline{AKey}_{\mathfrak{crypt}} = \\
\{(\{1337_{\mathfrak{uid}}, \text{"...}author : John\ Doe\text{..."}_{\mathfrak{regexp}}, \mathbf{required}AKey_{\mathfrak{crypt}} = 1.0\}, C_{1337}) \\
(\{n_{\mathfrak{uid}}, n_{\mathfrak{load}}, AKey_{\mathfrak{crypt}}\}, C_n)\}
\end{array}
$$

Implementation-wise, locking a component with a cryptographic key means that the access to the component should be made on the platform where the component is located. Similarly to tagged sets [11], the keys do not need to transit through the network.

5 *COLOS* Implementation

This section first presents our Eiffel implementation of the model described in Section 3. Thereafter, we show how to use the implementation of *COLOS* in practice.

5.1 Implementation

The implementation of the $\mathcal{COLOS}$ model consists mainly in the specifications, templates and the surrounding component infrastructure. Currently the framework consists of 21 classes with 1700 lines of code altogether. We are extending it to more component models and plan on making it available as open source.

Specifications. *LL_SPECIFICATION* is a list of *LL_SPECIFICATION_TERM*s. The deferred (abstract) class *LL_SPECIFICATION_TERM* should be subclassed by a programmer who wants to define his own matching module. The only mandatory feature to be implemented returns a *STRING* representing the name of the corresponding matching module. The infrastructure already implements the features to look through the specifications given that the *LL_SPECIFICATION_TERM*s return the correct matching module name. This enables an implementation based on hashtables. Just like for templates, which are described in following Section, we use the possibility to define our own infix operators for setting constraints on the specifications that describe a component. The Eiffel programming language makes it easy to define these operators and together with automatic conversion functions they allow writing easily readable code.

Templates. To implement our prototype, we relied on two features of the Eiffel language, namely (1) user-defined infix operators and (2) user-defined automatic type conversion. Infix operators allow us to compose templates using the infix operators as defined by the natural mathematical intuition while automatic conversion lets us have valid types for general mathematical operations. According to the latest definition of Eiffel and the priority of the operators, the usual priorities apply. The infix operators are coded into *LL_TEMPLATE* and are thus inherited by all templates. The automatic conversion from **DOUBLE** to *LL_TEMPLATE* ensures that we can compose doubles and templates in a same expression containing infix operators. In short, the Eiffel compiler (ISE Eiffel 5.7) converts mathematical formulae containing templates by transforming the doubles that they contain into *TEMPLATES*. As an example, the formula

$$template := 2.0 * template0 - 1.0/(template1 - template2)$$

is automatically transformed by the compiler into:

$$\begin{aligned} &template := \\ &\quad ((\textbf{create}\ \{LL\_TEMPLATE\}.make\_from\_double(2.0)) * template0) - \\ &\quad ((\textbf{create}\ \{LL\_TEMPLATE\}.make\_from\_double(1.0))/(template1 - template2)) \end{aligned}$$

The deferred class *LL_TEMPLATE_TERM*, inherits from the class *LL_TEMPLATE*. A programmer wishing to implement a matching module should subclass it and implement the feature *match* that takes an *LL_SPECIFICATION_TERM* as an argument and he should also provide a feature returning the name of the matching module as mentioned previously. Note that in our infrastructure the only *LL_SPECIFICATION_TERM*s that can be passed as parameter to the *match* feature are the ones actually belonging to the same matching module.

Decentralized lookup. The current matching prototype infrastructure performs centralized component lookup. We are currently in the process of augmenting our implementation for efficient component lookup in peer-to-peer (P2P) settings, which will make our infrastructure available as a service within a peer group of JXTA networks [15].

In order to complete such a decentralized lookup efficiently, it is very useful to be able to "decompose" the matching. The idea can be viewed as a generalization of the problem of content-based event routing in P2P networks, where event contents are viewed as consisting in several properties which are each matched against values, and an overlay network can be built which regroups participants with common interests and whose nodes many perform matching of only subsets of the properties (e.g. [16]).

In order to be able to decompose the matching in the lookup problem, a little help is however required from the programmer. Both specifications and templates have to provide access to a tree-based representation of themselves, akin to abstract syntax trees. The individual tree nodes represent elementary matching operations, and can be performed in a decentralized, yet minimally redundant, manner.

The logical regrouping of several *tModel*s to a *bindingTemplate*, several *bindingTemplate*s to a *businessEntity*, and several instances of latter kind to a *businessService* in UDDI (see Section 2.2), is but an illustration of such a decomposition.

5.2 Using the Implementation

In the current state of the implementation of $\mathcal{COLOS}$, a programmer wishing to use the component lookup mechanism can simply instantiate the class *LL_COMPONENT_-COLLECTION* and the components along with their specifications. By subclassing the two deferred (abstract) classes *LL_SPECIFICATION_TERM* and *LL_TEMPLATE_-TERM*, the programmer can implement a matching module. It implies setting two variables and redefining the feature *match*. Note that keeping a reference to the object encapsulating a component with its specification allows revoking parts of the specification dynamically.

In the following example (see Figures 2 and 3) we show how one describes a component and then uses our lookup mechanism to match requirements against the entire component repository. We see how the specification terms are first declared and enriched with the corresponding information. Then they are added to the component's specification. Note how the *less* operator is used to impose a constraint on the specification about the component's load. In the second listing (see Figure 3) of the example it is shown how to prepare a component lookup. Instead of specifications we are now preparing templates that are put together to match against the component repository. The ^-operator is used to initiate the matching. In the resulting list the components are ordered according to rating of the matching in respect to the template formula. In this case we are only interested in the component with the highest rating and we are therefore only obtaining the first component of the resulting list.

```
uid_specification_term : LL_UID_SPECIFICATION_TERM
regexp_specification_term : LL_REGEXP_SPECIFICATION
load_specification_term : LL_LOAD_SPECIFICATION ... create
uid_specification_term .make ("1337") create
regexp_specification_term .make ("This component ...
                    author: John Doe")
create load_specification_term .make (Current.component)

Current. add_specification_term_to_spec ( uid_specification_term )
Current. add_specification_term_to_spec ( regexp_specification_term )
Current. add_specification_term_to_spec ( load_specification_term <10.0)
...
```

Fig. 2. Specification declaration

```
uid_template : LL_UID_TEMPLATE regexp_tempalte: LL_REGEXP_TEMPLATE
load_template : LL_LOAD_TEMPLATE component: LL_COMPONENT
components: LL_COMPONENT_COLLECTION ... create uid_template.makr
("1337") create regexp_tempalte .make ("*author: John Doe*") create
load_template .make component:=
(components^(( uid_template + regexp_tempalte ) /(1.0+ load_template ))) . get_first_component
...
```

Fig. 3. Using the lookup infrastructure

6 Conclusions

Lookup mechanisms are an essential part of the very foundations of distributed component interaction. Various systems and specifications have been proposed in the literature, each targeting at a specific setting.

We have presented $\mathcal{COLOS}$, a generic model of component lookup, which can be used to express most predating lookup schemes. $\mathcal{COLOS}$ matches component specifications against templates using mathematical formulae. We have described this matching through denotational semantics, illustrated it through various examples, and presented an implementation of $\mathcal{COLOS}$ in Eiffel. The implementation reflects exactly the theory and uses automatic transformations as well as infix operators to obtain extremely compact and intuitive code. We envision the definition of further "common" matching modules, and intend to implement our framework on top of a fully decentralized peer-to-peer overlay network. Furthermore, we plan to port it to a wider range of programming languages and platforms in order to obtain interoperability.

References

1. Group, O.M.: The Common Object Request Broker Architecture: Core Specification, Version 3.0.3. OMG (2004)
2. Blair, G., Stefani, J.B.: Open Distributed Processing and Multimedia. Addison-Wesley (1997)

3. ShaikhAli, A., Rana, O., Al-Ali, R., Walker, D.: Uddie: An extended registry for web services. In: SAINT-W '03: Proceedings of the 2003 Symposium on Applications and the Internet Workshops (SAINT'03 Workshops). (2003) 85
4. Pauls, K., Bay, T.: Reuse Frequency as Metric for Dependency Resolver Selection. In: Component Deployment: Third International Working Conference, CD 2005. Volume 3798. (2005) 164–176
5. Sadou, S., Koscielny, G., Mili, H.: Abstracting Services in a Heterogeneous Environment. In: IFIP/ACM International Conference on Distributed Systems Platforms (Middleware 2001). (2001) 141–159
6. Lee, K., LaMarca, A., Chambers, C.: Hydroj: object-oriented pattern matching for evolvable distributed systems. In: OOPSLA '03: Proceedings of the 18th annual ACM Conference on Object-Oriented Programing, Systems, Languages, and Applications. (2003) 205–223
7. Oriol, M., Di Marzo Serugendo, G.: A disconnected service architecture for unanticipated run-time evolution of code. IEE Proceedings-Software, Special Issue on Unanticipated Software Evolution **151**(2) (2004) 95–107
8. Eugster, P., Baehni, S.: Abstracting Remote Object Interaction in a Peer-to-Peer Environment. Concurrency & Computation: Practice and Experience **17**(7-8) (2005)
9. Eugster, P., Guerraoui, R.: Distributed Programming with Typed Events. IEEE Software **2**(21) (2004) 56–64
10. Carriero, N., Gelernter, D.: Applications experience with Linda. ACM Sympos. on Parallel Programming (1985)
11. Oriol, M., Hicks, M.: Tagged Sets: A Secure and Transparent Coordination Medium. In: 7th Int. Conf. on Coordination Models and Languages. (2005)
12. Bryce, C., Oriol, M., Vitek, J.: A Coordination Model for Agents Based on Secure Spaces. In: 3rd Int. Conf. on Coordination Models and Languages. (1999) 4–20
13. Gregono, P., Sakkinen, M.: Copying and Comparing: Problems and Solutions. In: 14th European Conference on Object-Oriented Programming (ECOOP 2000). (2000) 226–250
14. Bay, T., Eugster, P., Oriol, M.: A First Order Model of Component Lookup. Technical report, Swiss Federal Institute of Technology in Zurich (ETHZ) (2006)
15. Oaks, S., Gong, L.: Jxta in a Nutshell. O'Reilly & Associates, Inc. (2002)
16. Eugster, P., Guerraoui, R.: Probabilistic Multicast. In: 3rd IEEE International Conference on Dependable Systems and Networks (DSN 2002). (2002) 313–323

Using a Lightweight Workflow Engine in a Plugin-Based Product Line Architecture

Humberto Cervantes and Sonia Charleston-Villalobos

Universidad Autonoma Metropolitana-Iztapalapa (UAM-I),
San Rafael Atlixco N° 186, Col. Vicentina, C.P. 09340, Iztapalapa. D.F., Mexico
{hcm, schv}@xanum.uam.mx

Abstract. This paper presents a software product line architecture where applications are assembled by installing a set of plugins on a common software base. In this architecture, the software base embeds a lightweight workflow engine that guides the main flow of control and data of the application. This architecture eliminates the problem of scattered flow of data and control and facilitates plugin substitution. This architecture is currently being used to build a biomedical engineering research application on top of the Eclipse platform.

1 Introduction

In recent years, computer users have witnessed the emergence of a wave of successful applications whose functionalities can be extended via the addition of *plugins*. Plugins are binary extension units for an application whose architecture allows functionalities to be introduced by end-users at well-defined places once the application has been installed. Plugins are software entities that are closely related to components. Component-based development, however, does not usually consider that components can be added to applications after the applications have been installed. Components are rather used to facilitate the construction of the applications themselves (extensible or not) [9].

Building an application as a plugin-based system makes sense both from a technical and an economical point of view. Technically it makes sense because the approach promotes a high level of modularity and decoupling between the *base* (or main) application and the plugins which can be developed independently, helping reduce delivery periods. Economically, the approach also makes sense, since a developer can concentrate on the development of the base application or the development of its extensions. Furthermore, since development lifecycles are independent, plugins can be deployed separately from the base application. Plugin deployment activities, which are usually performed by end users, include install, update and removal of the plugins.

A field where the plugin-based approach can be particularly useful is the construction of software product lines. Software product lines represent sets of applications (typically from a common application domain) that share features and are developed by reusing certain elements, such as an architectural foundation [1]. If this architectural foundation is built following a plugin-based approach, the construction of the different applications can be achieved by installing different sets of plugins on

I. Gorton et al. (Eds.): CBSE 2006, LNCS 4063, pp. 198–205, 2006.

top of the foundation. One difficulty with this approach resides, however, in the fact that applications must typically execute workflows associated with their particular domain. In the case where an application is built as a set of plugins installed on a common foundation, the control and data flow of the application is usually scattered among the foundation and the set of plugins that compose the application. This situation limits the possibility of plugin update or substitution, since it is difficult for replacement plugins to guarantee that they implement the correct part in the control and data flow.

This paper proposes a solution to this problem that introduces concepts from workflow-based applications into a plugin-based architecture. Workflow-based applications support the definition and execution of business processes. In such applications, the definition and execution of the appropriate control and data flow, and the invocation of the application logic blocks are externalized. As a consequence, changes to the process can be done without impacting the application logic blocks which become independent from the main data and control flow and as a consequence can be replaced more easily [5]. The work presented in this paper is currently being applied in the construction of a biomedical engineering research application on top of the Eclipse platform.

The remainder of the paper is structured as follows: section 2 discusses plugin-based application development using Eclipse and discusses the scattered flow of control problem, section 3 describes the proposed architecture, section 4 presents current and future work respectively, section 5 presents related work and finally, section 6 concludes the paper.

2 Plugin-Based Application Development

This section discusses plugin-based application development and the problem of scattered flow of control. Due to space restrictions, discussion around plugins focuses mainly on the Eclipse platform, which is used to implement the ideas described in this paper.

2.1 Plugin-Based Applications and Eclipse

Today, a wide variety of plugin-based applications exist; these applications include web browsers, image editing tools and integrated development environments (IDEs). All of these tools are characterized by the fact that they are built as standalone applications that provide an initial degree of functionality when installed. This functionality is available even when no plugins are present; for example, when a web browser is installed, it allows pages to be read but multimedia content cannot usually be displayed.

Among plugin-based applications, the Eclipse platform [4] has some particular characteristics. This platform was originally conceived as a foundation to facilitate the construction of IDEs. As such it provided, in addition to standard elements such as a text editor, development facilities that included team development support. A specific development environment could be built by adding a set of tools, for example a compiler for a particular language, to the base platform. The different tools were delivered as plugins. Today, the Eclipse platform has evolved from being an IDE-oriented foundation to become a generic plugin-based application foundation. Development specific elements have been moved out of the base platform which is now called the Rich Client Platform [6]. The Rich Client Platform (RCP) provides the minimal functionality required to allow all-purpose plugin-based client-side applications to be built on top of it.

Eclipse's plugin model allows plugins to interact directly with other plugins and not only with the base application. As a result, plugins can be composed in a similar way to components. Eclipse's plugins provide *extensions* when they contain new functionalities to be introduced into the base application or into another plugin. Plugins can also declare *extension points* which are locations where other plugins can introduce their own extensions and enrich the original plugin's functionality. Furthermore, extension points are always optional, meaning that any provider of an extension point must be capable of functioning even if no provider of extensions for that extension point are present. Finally, the vision behind the Eclipse's architecture is that everything is built out of plugins, including the base RCP itself, which currently consists of around 11 different plugins whose presence is mandatory. The plugins that form the RCP manage plugin deployment activities and declare a series of extension points which allow other plugins to introduce new functionalities such as toolbars, menu entries and views. Today, the RCP is gaining much momentum as the Eclipse IDE itself facilitates enormously the task of constructing plugin-based applications on top of the RCP through its Plugin Development Environment (PDE).

2.2 The Structure of an Application Developed on Top of Eclipse

In a certain way the Eclipse's plugin approach is a hybrid between "traditional" plugin approaches and component-based development. In Eclipse, a customized (or extended) base platform is assembled by selecting a set of plugins that will provide functionalities that are added to the basic ones already provided by the RCP. Once assembled, this extended base platform is delivered to end users as a standalone application. The plugins that form this application may not be removed afterwards. However, after this application is installed, end users can continue extending the functionality of the application by installing additional plugins into it. The architecture of a typical application built on top of the RCP is depicted in figure 1. This figure also shows that plugins can interact directly among each other without extending the base platform.

2.3 The Problem of Scattered Flow of Control

Eclipse plugins typically provide user interface elements that allow the user to interact with the application. These user interface elements, such as buttons on a toolbar, for example, are associated with handlers that can invoke methods declared on an interface provided by a different plugin's extension. In such a situation the logic that guides the flow of control and data of the application ends up being scattered among the plugin set and the base platform. This situation can limit the substitutability of the plugins used to build the application. For instance, when a plugin is substituted by another plugin, either by a newer version or by a different plugin that provides the

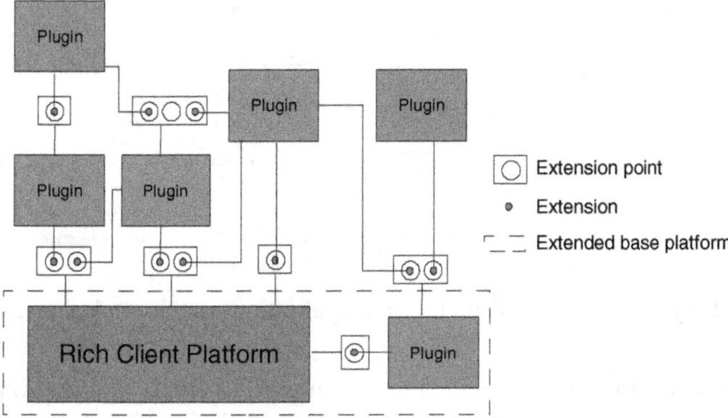

Fig. 1. Architecture of an application built on top of the Eclipse Rich Client Platform

same extension, the replacing plugin must correctly implement its predecessor's part of the flow of control and data that is necessary for the application to function correctly.

In today's applications these problems are addressed by limiting substitutability and by constraining the places where plugins can extend the base application. This solution is, however, undesirable for the context of plugin-based product line architectures, where it is necessary to allow a large number of plugins to be substituted by completely different sets.

3 A Workflow-Based Product Line Architecture

This section introduces the concepts workflow-based applications and discusses how these concepts are used to solve the problem exposed in the previous section.

3.1 Workflow-Based Applications

Workflow-based applications support the definition and execution of business processes (composed of activities associated to a particular domain). In such applications, the definition and execution of the appropriate control and data flow, and the invocation of the application logic blocks are externalized. This allows the workflow to be changed without impacting the application logic blocks [5]. In workflow-based applications, logic blocks become flow-independent in the sense that they do not contain application logic associated with the execution of the business process. This facilitates the replacement of logic blocks.

3.2 Using Workflows in a Plugin-Based Product Line Architecture

To limit the problem of scattered flow of data and control and to facilitate plugin substitutability and reusability, the concepts of workflow-based applications can be introduced in a plugin-based product line architecture. The fundamental idea is to limit the degree of direct interaction among plugins and to introduce a third party (a mediator) responsible for controlling the application's main flow of control and data.

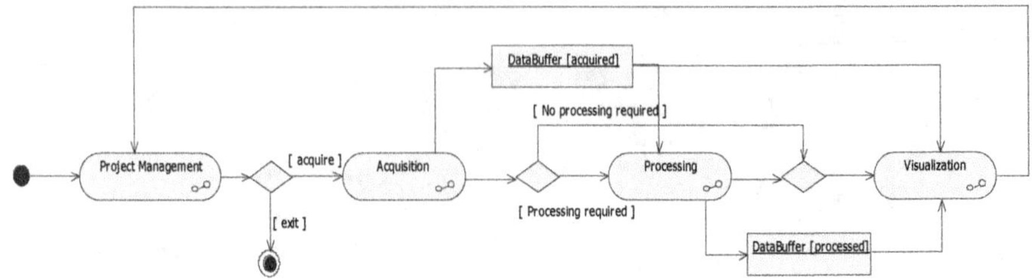

Fig. 2. Typical workflow found in DSP applications for biomedical research

In the context of this work, this idea has been used to create a plugin-based product line architecture oriented towards the construction of digital signal processing (DSP) applications for biomedical engineering research. In this field, these applications are generally guided by the workflow depicted in figure 2. This main workflow contains four different activities: project management, data acquisition, processing and visualization. The activity diagram shows that data that is acquired can be visualized immediately or be processed by applying different algorithms before visualization. Each of the activities of the main workflow is itself guided by a specific sub-workflow. Figure 3 shows the sub-workflow associated to the acquisition activity in the main workflow. This sub-workflow allows users to test the acquisition device before performing the actual data acquisition and storing the corresponding data.

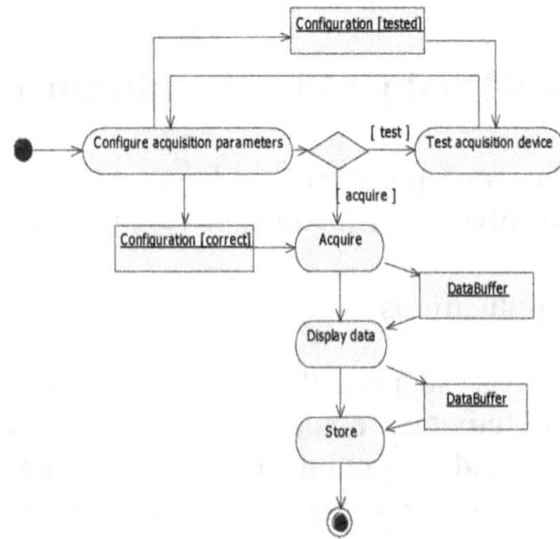

Fig. 3. Detail of the sub-workflow associated to the acquisition activity

To achieve a workflow based approach in plugin-based product line architecture, the different workflow definitions are contained and executed by the product-line architecture. Figure 4 illustrates how this is achieved: the product-line architecture, which is the common element to specific applications, is constructed as an extended Eclipse base platform that contains a lightweight workflow engine. Plugins are associated with particular activities, such as data acquisition or visualization. Every plugin's extension interface provides methods that fall into three different categories. The first category of methods allow the workflow engine to control the execution of

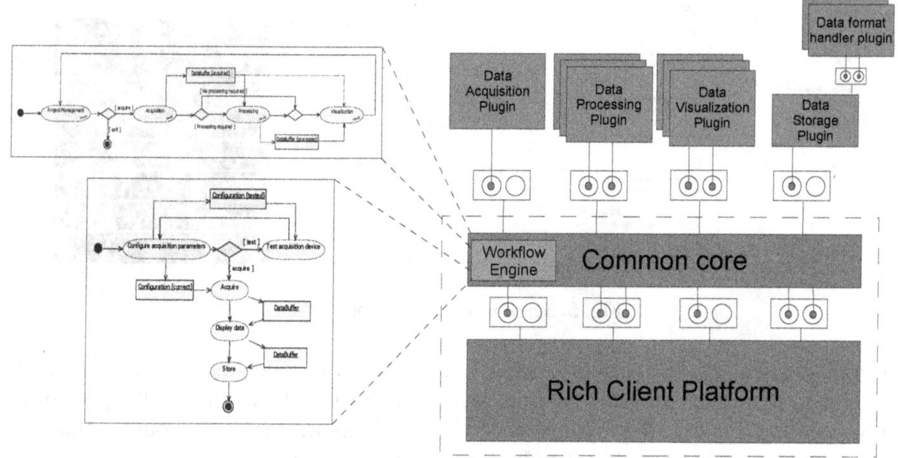

Fig. 4. Architecture with the lightweight workflow engine

an activity. The second category allows the workflow engine to register itself as an observer of activity events. The events produced by the plugins include activity termination and cancellation. The third category of methods allow the workflow engine to perform data transfer. As a result, workflows are executed as the engine initiates activities and receives notifications from the plugins.

Finally, even tough the approach described here requires that plugins associated with different activities to not interact directly, it does not limit plugins associated to a particular activity from providing extension points that allow other plugins to extend their functionality. An example of this occurs in the plugin associated with the data storage activity in figure 4, this plugin can be extended by specialized plugins that allow the data to be stored in different formats. The fact that the data storage plugin is extended by other plugins is, however, irrelevant to the application's workflow.

4 Current Results and Future Work

The work presented in this paper is part of an ongoing project that is realized at the Universidad Autónoma Metropolitana Iztapalapa in Mexico City. This project received an Eclipse innovation grant from IBM in 2005. The goal of this project is to build an application to acquire data obtained from respiratory sounds. This application will be deployed in a hospital environment where it will allow both physicians to better diagnose certain respiratory conditions and biomedical researchers to gather data on the field. This project is realized following the Unified Process development-methodology and is currently in the construction phase. A screen capture of an executable prototype for the project is depicted in figure 5. This prototype is built on top of the base architecture described in the previous section.

Future work includes the construction of a different but related application on top of the same product-line architecture with a set of different plugins. Other areas of interest include the use of a language to describe the workflows (currently this is done

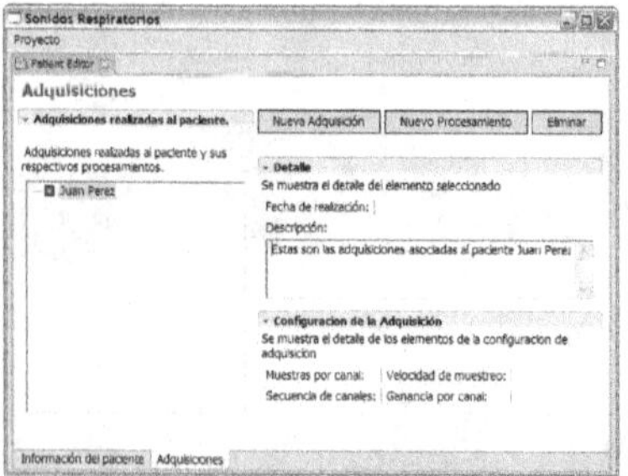

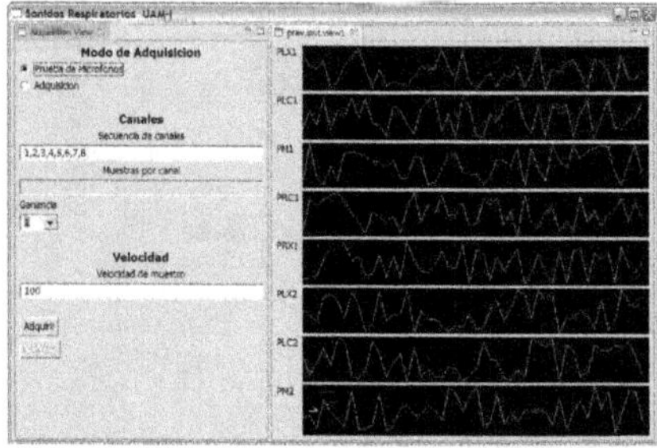

Fig. 5. Screenshots of the application

programmatically). Furthermore, workflow description could itself be delivered via plugins to facilitate extension. A final area of interest to the authors is the possibility of supporting dynamic deployment activities in the application, this would include the install, update and removal of the plugins during execution.

5 Related Work

The work presented in this paper is related to three main research areas which include component-based software development, product line architectures and workflow-based applications.

5.1 Component-Based Software Development

As mentioned before, components and plugins have similar features. Examples of existing component models are JavaBeans [8] and the CORBA Component Model [7]. Such models are successfully used today in the construction of applications both on the client and on the server side. However, component models are not really oriented towards supporting plugin-oriented features such as end-user managed evolution or the interaction with an extensible application core. It is possible to implement a plugin-based architecture over a standard component model, but this is not straightforward.

5.2 Software Product Line Architectures

Among the core assets of a software product line, the software architecture plays the most central role [1]. One of the most successful plugin-based product line architectures is the original Eclipse platform, which allowed different IDEs to be built. A framework that supports the construction of plugin-based product line architectures is described in [2]. The approach proposed, however, does not deal with the issue of scattered flow of control.

5.3 Workflow-Based Applications

The concepts of workflow-based applications are particularly popular in the area of service oriented architectures (SOA). The Business Process Execution Language

(BPEL) supports the execution of processes that interact with web services [3]. There are some similarities between SOA and plugin-based architectures: the plugin-based application core is similar to a service requester that searches the plugin registry to discover available services (provided by registered plugins). Once the core finds them, it interacts with these service providers. In service orientation, there are no guarantees that a service requester may find a particular service; this is the same for a plugin-based application since there is no guarantee that a particular plugin will be present. There are, however, some differences with SOA, since in SOA, service providers and requesters may arrive or depart constantly, and such a high level of dynamism is not currently present in plugin-based architectures.

6 Conclusions

This paper has presented a plugin-based software product line architecture where the architecture embodies a lightweight workflow engine to facilitate plugin substitutability and specific product development. This architecture is currently being applied in the construction of a biomedical engineering research tool. It must be noted that the ideas presented in this paper are not specific to plugin-based applications; they can also be beneficial to the construction of standard component-based applications.

Acknowledgments. The authors wish to acknowledge IBM for its financial support, and the students who are participating in the project and who make it possible.

References

1. Bass, L. and Clements, P. and Kazman, R., "*Software Architecture in Practice (2d Edition),*" Addison Wesley, 2003
2. Caporuscio, M. and Muccini, H. and Pelliccione, P. and Di Nisio, E. "*Towards a Plugin-based Implementation of Product Line Architectures,*" unpublished paper found online at http://se2c.uni.lu/tiki/se2c-bib_abstract.php?id=1948. Visited 01/06
3. Curbera, F. and Al., "Business Process Execution Language (BPEL) for Web Services, Version 1.1," Online document at http://www-128.ibm.com/developerworks/library/specification/ws-bpel/, last visited 01/06
4. The Eclipse Foundation, Official Eclipse Homepage at http://www.eclipse.org, last visited 01/2006.
5. Leymann, F. and Roller, D., "*Workflow-based applications,*" IBM Systems Journal, Vol. 36, No. 1, (pp. 102), 1997.
6. McAffer, J. and Lemieux, J-M., "*Eclipse Rich Client Platform,*" Eclipse Series, Addison Wesley, 2006
7. Object Management Group (OMG), "*CORBA Component Model, Version 3.0,*" Online document available at http://www.omg.org/technology/documents/formal/components.htm, June 2002
8. Sun Microsystems, "*Java Beans Specification, Version 1.01*", Available online at http://java.sun.com/products/javabeans/, July 1997.
9. Clemens Szyperski, "*Component Software: beyond object-oriented programming,*" 2d Edition, Addison-Wesley Professional, 2002.

A Formal Component Framework for Distributed Embedded Systems

Christo Angelov, Krzysztof Sierszecki, Nicolae Marian, and Jinpeng Ma

Mads Clausen Institute for Product Innovation, University of Southern Denmark, Grundtvigs Alle 150, 6400 Soenderborg, Denmark
{angelov, ksi, nicolae, jinpeng}@mci.sdu.dk

Abstract. The widespread use of embedded systems mandates the development of industrial software design methods based on formal models (frameworks) and prefabricated components. This paper presents a formal specification of the *COMDES* framework, focusing on the main architectural issues and the specific line of reasoning that was followed while developing a hierarchy of executable models describing relevant aspects of system structure and behaviour. The above framework has been used to systematically define a hierarchy of reusable and reconfigurable components - simple and composite function blocks, reconfigurable state machines and function units - implementing the executable models presented in the paper.

1 Introduction

The widespread use of embedded systems mandates the development of industrial software design methods, i.e. computer-aided design and engineering of embedded applications using formal models (frameworks) and repositories of prefabricated components, following practices already established in mature areas of engineering, such as mechanical engineering and electronics.

A framework is defined hereafter as a set of executable models that are used to specify relevant aspects of system structure and behaviour. Furthermore, executable models are implemented as reusable and reconfigurable components that can be stored in permanent memory in binary format and used as building blocks for embedded applications. With this approach, model-based configuration is substituted for model-based program generation, whereby the configuration specification is stored in data structures containing relevant information such as component parameters, input/output links, sequence of execution, etc. Hence, it is possible to reconfigure applications by updating data structures rather than reprogramming the application and reloading the newly generated code.

The main problem that has to be addressed in this context is to develop a *comprehensive*, yet *intuitive* and *open* framework for embedded systems. There are currently a considerable number of frameworks and component models, which have been developed by various research groups and organizations. Most of them have their origins in the traditional Software Engineering domain, e.g. components with operational interfaces and various types of port-based objects [1, 2, 8, 16-18]. However, it can be argued that the proper way of developing such frameworks is to use decomposition

I. Gorton et al. (Eds.): CBSE 2006, LNCS 4063, pp. 206 – 221, 2006.

criteria that are derived from the areas of control engineering and systems science, taking into account that modern embedded systems are predominantly control and monitoring systems [5]. This approach has been used for some time with industrial control systems, whose software is built from component objects *(function blocks)* that implement standard application functions and interact by exchanging signals. Accordingly, function blocks are 'softwired' into function block diagrams that are mapped onto real-time control tasks, e.g. standards *IEC 61131-3* [6] and *IEC 61499* [7].

However, this is a relatively low-level solution, which is inadequate for modern embedded systems. The latter vary from simple applications to highly complex, time-critical and distributed systems featuring autonomous subsystems *(function units)* that have to interact with one another within various types of distributed transactions. The above standards do not provide modeling techniques and component definitions at this level, subsystem and task interaction is not specified either, and distributed systems are implemented in a non-transparent fashion using so-called service interface function blocks [7].

Therefore, the basic control engineering approach has to be extended into a *systems engineering approach,* in order to take into account the complexity of real-world applications. The framework must support compositionality and scalability through a well-defined hierarchy of reusable and reconfigurable components. On the other hand, it has to adequately specify system behaviour for a broad range of sequential, continuous and hybrid applications. Last but not least, the modeling techniques and notations used must be intuitive and easy to understand by application experts.

These guidelines have been used to develop the *COMDES* framework *(Component-based Design of Software for Distributed Embedded Systems),* which has been informally presented elsewhere [8-10]. This paper presents a formal specification of the framework, focusing on the main architectural issues and the specific line of reasoning that was followed in order to systematically develop executable models describing various aspects of system structure and behaviour. These have been implemented as a hierarchy of executable components such as function units, function unit activities and function blocks. Furthermore, the models have been used to systematically derive tabular data structures that can be used to represent system configurations in a computer-aided software development environment.

The rest of the paper is organized as follows: Section 2 presents a top-down specification of system structure in terms of subsystems *(function units)* and their interactions, as well as the internal structure of function units. The latter are modeled as software integrated circuits encapsulating autonomous threads of control – *activities,* which are built from *function blocks.* Section 3 presents a specification of system behaviour, which combines the reactive and transformational aspects of activity behaviour into a hierarchical executable model *(hybrid state machine),* which is implemented as a function block of class State Machine. The discussion is illustrated with a real example – a DC Motor Speed and Direction Control System, which has been implemented as a time-driven distributed control system operating in a Controller Area Network. Related research is discussed in Section 4. A summary of the proposed software design method and its implications is given in the concluding section of the paper.

2 Specification of System Structure

2.1 Embedded Control System Specification

The embedded control system is conceived as a composition of software components (function units) that may be viewed as the software equivalent of subsystems such as sensor, controller, actuator, etc., which have to be *softwired* with one another in order to configure particular applications. Accordingly, function units interact by exchanging *signals,* i.e. labeled messages (pressure, temperature, etc.), within various types of distributed transactions such as producer-consumer and client-server. Producer-consumer communication, and in particular - *state message communication* - is considered better suited for real-time applications because of its non-blocking nature and inherent support for broadcast/multicast interaction [14]. Therefore, this type of interaction will be assumed in the following discussion.

Under this assumption, the control system configuration can be described by a function unit diagram, i.e. a data flow graph (DFG) specifying function units and their interactions. The latter can be formally specified as:

$$DFG = \langle \boldsymbol{U}, \boldsymbol{S}, \boldsymbol{M} \rangle, \tag{1}$$

where $\boldsymbol{U}$ is the set of function units; $\boldsymbol{S}$ is the set of communication variables (signals) generated by various function units, where each signal $s_i \in \boldsymbol{S}$, is defined in terms of constituent variables: $s_i = \{ v_1^i, v_2^i, \ldots, v_k^i \}$.

It is obvious that:

$$\boldsymbol{S} = \bigcup_{(\boldsymbol{U})} \boldsymbol{Y}_i, \tag{2}$$

where $\boldsymbol{Y}_i$ is the subset of signals generated by the function unit $u_i \in \boldsymbol{U}$.

Accordingly, $\boldsymbol{M}$ is a set of mappings:

$$\boldsymbol{M} = \{ M_{u1}, M_{u2}, \ldots, M_{un} \}, \tag{3}$$

where M_{ui}: $u_i \rightarrow \boldsymbol{U}$ is a mapping specifying the subset of function units receiving signals from the function unit $u_i \in \boldsymbol{U}$. Furthermore, it is possible to represent M_{ui} as:

$$M_{ui} = \bigcup_{(Y_i)} M(s_j / s_j \in \boldsymbol{Y}_i), \tag{4}$$

where $M(s_j)$ is a subset of function units receiving signal $s_j \in \boldsymbol{Y}_i$ generated by the function unit $u_i \in \boldsymbol{U}$.

By defining the above mappings for each function unit and signal generated, it is possible to derive the subset of input signals $\boldsymbol{X}_i$ for each function unit $u_i \in \boldsymbol{U}$, resulting in the construction of a data flow graph whose arcs are labeled with the signals exchanged between various function units. It can be explicitly specified using a graphical notation – a function unit diagram, e.g. Fig. 1. Alternatively, the data flow graph can be specified implicitly by defining the subsets $\boldsymbol{X}_i$ and $\boldsymbol{Y}_i$, i.e. the signals received and sent out, for each one of the constituent function units $u_i \in \boldsymbol{U}$ (see also Tables 1 and 2).

The function unit diagram represents the static aspect of subsystem interaction. The dynamic aspects are to be treated in the context of system reactions to specific events that are executed as distributed transactions. However, complex potentially distributed reactions can be viewed as a sequence of local reactions executed by function unit activities in response to various types of events, i.e. timing, external and message arrival events (see next section). Activities are mapped onto real-time tasks, e.g. *Sensor (S), Controller (C) and Actuator (A)*, which are executed in a timed multitasking environment (see Fig. 2).

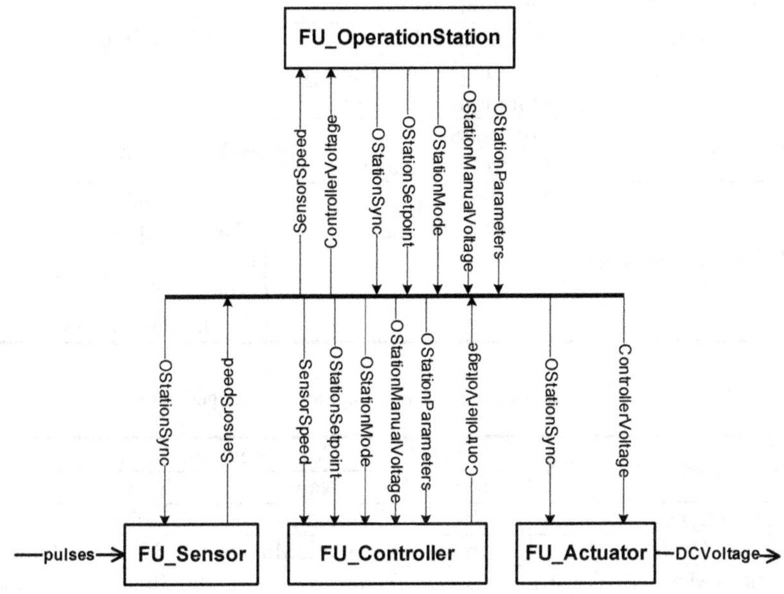

Fig. 1. Control system specification: DC motor control system - function units and signals

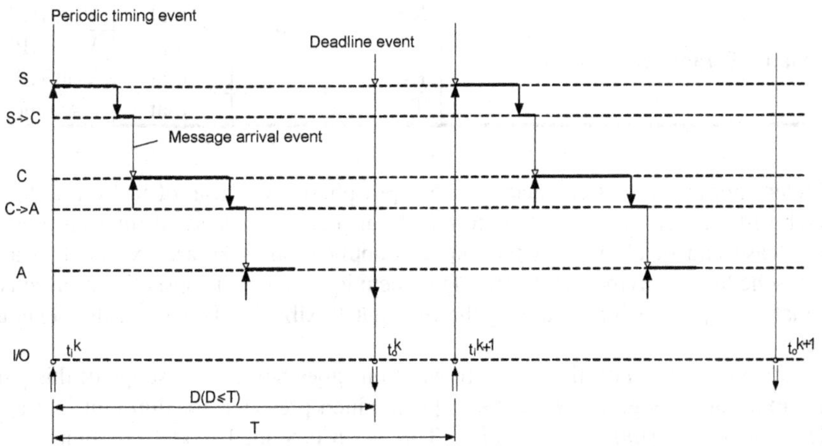

Fig. 2. Function unit interaction in a distributed timed multitasking environment

Table 1. DC motor control system: function units and their interactions

Function unit – u_i	Signals received – X_i	Signals sent – Y_i
FU_Sensor	**pulses** (physical input)	SensorSpeed
	OstationSync	
FU_Controller	SensorSpeed	ControllerVoltage
	OStationSetpoint	
	OstationMode	
	OStationManualVoltage	
	OStationParameters	
FU_Actuator	OstationSync	**DCVoltage** (physical output)
	ControllerVoltage	
FU_OperationStation	SensorSpeed	OStationSync
	ControllerVoltage	OStationSetpoint
		OStationMode
		OStationManualVoltage
		OStationParameters

Table 2. DC motor control system: messages (signals) exchanged between function units

External signals – $s_i \in \boldsymbol{S}$	Message priority	Constituent variables – $v_j^i \in s_i$		
		Name	Type	Unit
OstationSync	7	timeStamp	ULONG	tick
OStationMode	6	automaticManual	UBYTE	boolean
OStationManualVoltage	5	i_volt	float	Volt
SensorSpeed	4	realRPM	float	RPM
ControllerVoltage	3	o_volt	float	Volt
OStationSetpoint	2	setRPM	float	RPM
OStationParameters	1	Kp	float	Volt/RPM
		Ki	float	Volt/RPM
		Kd	float	Volt/RPM
		Ts	float	second

Timed multitasking is characterized by split-phase execution of tasks and drivers, whereby I/O drivers are executed atomically at precisely specified time instants, i.e. task release and deadline instants, whereas application tasks are executed in a dynamic scheduling environment [16]. This technique makes it possible to effectively eliminate I/O jitter, while retaining the inherent flexibility of dynamically scheduled systems.

Detailed discussion of distributed transactions goes beyond the scope of this paper; more information is given in the paper [10], which presents function unit interaction under *Distributed Timed Multitasking.* This is an extended model combining timed multitasking and transparent signal-based communication in the context of the *COMDES* framework, which is supported by the timed-multitasking version of the *HARTEX* kernel. Subsequent discussion will focus on the specification of function units and function unit activities, as well as their composition from executable components such as function blocks.

2.2 Function Unit Specification

The function unit (FU) is an active object encapsulating one or more threads of control (activities) that generate application-specific reactions in response to certain timing and/or external events.

Formally, a function unit can be defined as:

$$FU = \langle \boldsymbol{X}, \boldsymbol{Y}, \boldsymbol{E}, \boldsymbol{A} \rangle , \tag{5}$$

where $\boldsymbol{X}$ and $\boldsymbol{Y}$ are the sets of input and output signals, respectively; $\boldsymbol{E}$ is the set of activating events; $\boldsymbol{A}$ is the set of activities, triggered by events $e \in \boldsymbol{E}$.

In the general case, the set of input signals can be presented as:

$$\boldsymbol{X} = \boldsymbol{X}_L \bigcup \boldsymbol{X}_R , \tag{6}$$

where $\boldsymbol{X}_L$ is the set of local (physical) input signals that might be analog, discrete or binary-coded, depending on the application; $\boldsymbol{X}_R$ is the subset of remote input signals, i.e. signal messages that are generated by remote devices and communicated over the network; $\boldsymbol{X}_R \subset \boldsymbol{S}$.

Likewise, $\boldsymbol{Y} = \boldsymbol{Y}_L \bigcup \boldsymbol{Y}_R$, where $\boldsymbol{Y}_L$ is the subset of locally generated (physical) output signals and $\boldsymbol{Y}_R$ is the subset of remote output signals, i.e. signals that are sent to remote devices via the communication network; $\boldsymbol{Y}_R \subset \boldsymbol{S}$.

This aspect of the specification is illustrated by Table 1, e.g. function unit *FU_Controller*, where $\boldsymbol{X}_R$ = { *SensorSpeed, OStationSetpoint, OStationMode, OStationManualVoltage, OStationParameters* }, and $\boldsymbol{Y}_R$ = { *ControllerVoltage* }.

The above definition has also structural implications: input and output signals are associated with internal components – signal drivers that are used to communicate with other function units and the environment. These may be triggered at precisely specified time instants within various types of distributed transactions [10]. In particular, input drivers are executed when the activity task is released, whereas output drivers are executed when its deadline arrives or when the task comes to an end (if no deadline has been specified).

An incoming signal is received by an input signal driver (ISD), which converts the signal $x_i \in \boldsymbol{X}$ into a subset of internal variables $v_1^i, v_2^i, \dots , v_k^i$ depending on the composition of the message, e.g. *OStationParameters* = { K_P, K_I, K_D, T_S }.

The union of these subsets defines the set of internal function unit variables $\boldsymbol{V}$:

$$\boldsymbol{V} = \bigcup_{(X)} V_i , \tag{7}$$

where V_i = { $v_1^i, v_2^i, \dots , v_k^i$ } is the subset of internal signals constituting the input signal $x_i \in \boldsymbol{X}$.

Internal input variables are processed by FU activities whereby each activity A_j is associated with a subset of relevant variables V_j, such that:

$$\boldsymbol{V} = \bigcup_{(A)} V_j . \tag{8}$$

Likewise, each output signal is associated with an output signal driver (OSD), which converts a subset of internal variables, e.g. w_1^i, w_2^i, ... , w_k^i into the corresponding output signal $y_i \in \boldsymbol{Y}$.

The union of these subsets defines the set of internal output variables:

$$\boldsymbol{W} = \bigcup_{(Y)} W_i \,, \tag{9}$$

where $W_i = \{ w_1^i, w_2^i, \dots, w_k^i \}$ is the subset of internal signals constituting the output signal $y_i \in \boldsymbol{Y}$.

Internal output variables are generated by FU activities, whereby each activity A_j is associated with a subset of relevant variables W_j, such that

$$\boldsymbol{W} = \bigcup_{(A)} W_j \,. \tag{10}$$

The above discussion can be illustrated with the specification of function unit *FU_Controller* (see Fig. 3 and Tables 3, 4 and 5).

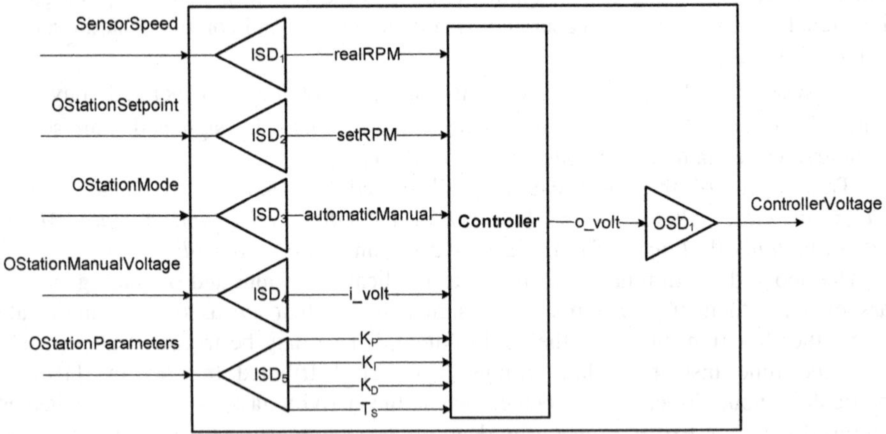

Fig. 3. Function unit specification: *FU_Controller*

Table 3. Function unit *FU_Controller*: input signal drivers, input signals and internal signals produced

ISD	Input signals – $x_i \in \boldsymbol{X}$	Internal signals produced – $v_j^i \in x_i$
ISD_1	SensorSpeed	realRPM
ISD_2	OStationSetpoint	setRPM
ISD_3	OStationMode	automaticManual
ISD_4	OStationManualVoltage	i_volt
ISD_5	OStationParameters	K_P
		K_I
		K_D
		T_S

Table 4. Function unit *FU_Controller*: activities and internal signals consumed and produced

Activities – A_i	Internal signals consumed – V_i	Internal signals produced – W_i
Controller	realRPM	o_volt
	setRPM	
	automaticManual	
	i_volt	
	K_P	
	K_I	
	K_D	
	T_S	

Table 5. Function unit *FU_Controller*: output signal drivers, internal signals consumed and output signals produced

OSD	Internal signals consumed – $w_j^i \in y_i$	Output signals – $y_i \in \boldsymbol{Y}$
OSD_1	o_volt	ControllerVoltage

Finally, the set of activating events $\boldsymbol{E}$ can be specified as:

$$\boldsymbol{E} = \boldsymbol{E}_t \bigcup \boldsymbol{E}_e \bigcup \boldsymbol{E}_m \ . \tag{11}$$

Here, $\boldsymbol{E}_t$ is the set of timing events, $\boldsymbol{E}_t = \{ \uparrow (kT_i) \}$; $\boldsymbol{E}_e$ is the set of external events, $\boldsymbol{E}_e = \{ \uparrow x_j \}$; $\boldsymbol{E}_m$ is the set of message arrival events, $\boldsymbol{E}_m = \{ \uparrow m_j \}$. Events are processed by function unit activities that generate output signals in response to specific events (see next section).

3 Specification of System Behaviour

System behaviour can be specified in terms of *global* and *local* reactions that are generated in response to certain events taking place in the environment. A global reaction corresponds to a distributed transaction involving a subset of communicating function units/activities (e.g. Fig. 2), whereas a local reaction corresponds to a transaction phase executed by a function unit activity.

Avoiding excessive detail involving the internal representation of system signals, it can be seen that every activity $A \in \boldsymbol{A}$ is essentially associated with subsets of activating events $E \in \boldsymbol{E}$, input signals $X \in \boldsymbol{X}$ and output signals $Y \in \boldsymbol{Y}$. The occurrence of the event $e(t) \in E$ triggers the activity A, resulting in a sequence of computations implementing some input-to-output signal transformation, which ends up with the generation of one or more output signals, e.g. $y_k \in Y$. The latter can be described by a function, defined on a subset of input signals $x \in X$, such that $y_k(t) = f_k(x(t))$ and $y_k(t)$ can be viewed as a reaction to the occurrence of event $e(t)$:

$$r_j:\ e(t) \rightarrow y_k(t),\ y_k \in Y \ . \tag{12}$$

Consequently, the behavior of the activity A, as a whole, can be specified in terms of the corresponding subsets of reactions and signal transformation functions.

The above discussion highlights two basic and interrelated aspects of system behavior, i.e. the reactive and transformational (signal processing) aspects. Currently used models emphasize one of these two aspects depending on the application context. For example, discrete-event control systems usually emphasize the reactive aspect of system behavior, in the context of event-driven operation and control flow models, e.g. state machines. Conversely, continuous control systems emphasize the transformational aspect in the context of continuous data flow models such as function block diagrams. This has resulted in widely differing design methods and languages for continuous and sequential control systems.

Such a differentiation of system models is largely artificial, and it clearly comes into conflict with the nature of real plants, which are more or less hybrid, even if they are treated as predominantly discrete or continuous. This is even more obvious in complex hybrid control systems, e.g. modal control systems.

The above problem can be solved via an augmented process (activity) model, which takes into account both the reactive and the transformational aspects of system behaviour. Such a model can be specified in terms of activating events, input and output signals, as follows:

$$A = \langle X, Y, E, R, F \rangle \ , \tag{13}$$

where: X is the set of input signals processed by A, $X \subseteq \mathbf{X}$; Y is the set of output signals generated by A, $Y \subseteq \mathbf{Y}$; E is the set of events activating A, $E \subseteq \mathbf{E}$; R is a function specifying system reactions, i.e. output signals that have to be generated by the activity in response to certain events in E, and F is a set of functions that specify the computation of output signals during the execution of system reactions.

3.1 Specification of Reactive Behaviour

System reactions can be determined via the function R, specifying which output signal(s) have to be generated in response to certain activating events. This function can be derived given certain assumptions about the type of system, e.g. continuous, sequential or hybrid control system.

In the general case, activity behaviour can be modeled with a state machine, whereby the generation of a control signal $y(t)$ at time t is dependent on the current state $q(t)$; $q \in Q$, where Q is the set of states. The transition to the current state is defined in terms of a previous state $q(t\text{-})$, an activating event $e(t)$, and eventually the value of some guard $g(t)$, $g \in G$, where G is a set of guards (predicates) defined in the set of input signals X.

Accordingly, the reaction function can be defined as a partial function:

$$R: Q \times E \times G \rightarrow Y \ . \tag{14}$$

Furthermore, it can be shown to be a composition of a state transition function ς and an output function σ, such that $R = \sigma \circ \varsigma$. Here, the state transition function is defined as a partial function:

$$\varsigma: Q \times E \times G \rightarrow Q \ , \tag{15}$$

and the output function is:

$$\sigma : Q \rightarrow Y . \tag{16}$$

Consequently, for each $q_m \in Q$, and for a subset of events and the corresponding subset of guards enabling transitions out of that state, it is possible to define a subset of successor states $Nq_m = \{ q_{n1}, q_{n2}, ..., q_{nr} \}$, to be further denoted as the *next-state mapping* of q_m. Accordingly, each state q_{nj} is associated with one or more output signals $y_i \in Y$ that constitute the reaction to the event triggering the transition to that state.

Applying that technique to all states results in the construction of the state transition graph (STG) of the activity:

$$STG(A) = \langle Q, X, Y, E, G, N, O \rangle , \tag{17}$$

where N is the set of next-state mappings: $N = \{ Nq_i \}$, Nq_i: $q_i \longrightarrow Q$, and O is the set of output mappings: $O = \{ Oq_i \}$, Oq_i: $q_i \longrightarrow Y$. It is assumed that the STG satisfies completeness and consistency requirements [13].

This discussion is illustrated with the hierarchical state transition graph shown in Fig. 4. It specifies the reactive behaviour of the *Controller* activity, which is triggered by a periodically arriving timing event $\uparrow(kT)$. The first-level state machine of that model is also presented in tabular form (see Table 6).

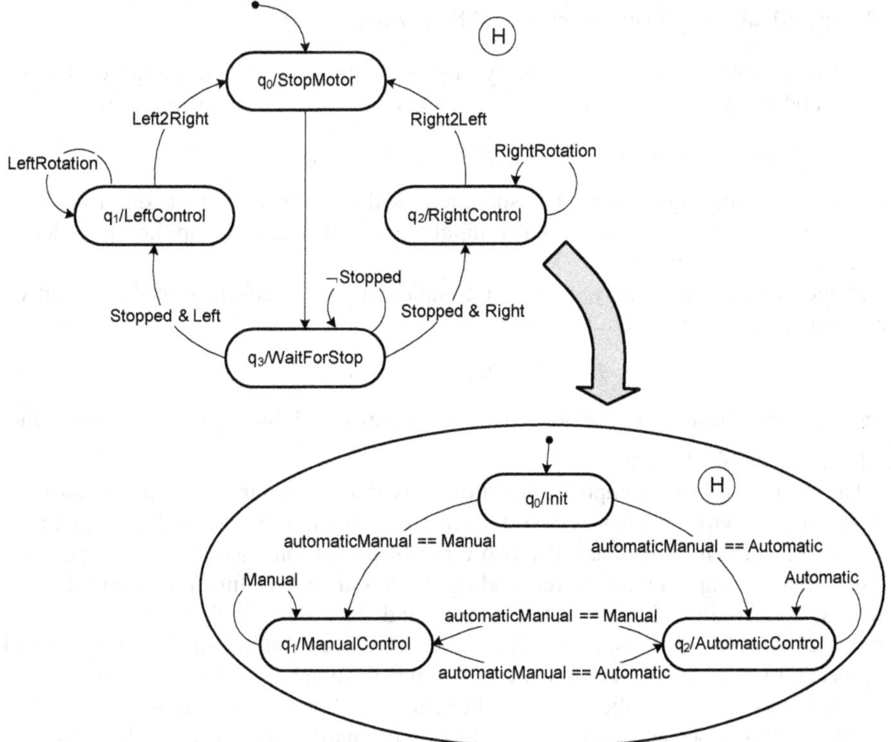

Fig. 4. Specification of reactive behaviour: *Controller* state machine (first and second level)

Table 6. *Controller* state machine (first level)

Next state mapping $Nq(t\text{-})$	Event $e(t)$	Guard $g(x(t))$	Next state $q(t)$	Action $y(t) \leftrightarrow q(t)$
Nq_0	↑(kT)	1	q_3	WaitForStop
Nq_1	↑(kT)	Left2Right	q_0	StopMotor
	↑(kT)	LeftRotation	q_1	LeftControl
Nq_2	↑(kT)	Right2Left	q_0	StopMotor
	↑(kT)	RightRotation	q_2	RightControl
Nq_3	↑(kT)	Stopped & Left	q_1	LeftControl
	↑(kT)	Stopped & Right	q_2	RightControl
	↑(kT)	¬Stopped	q_3	WaitForStop

The above definition has obviously the semantics of a Moore machine. However, it has been further extended, so as to cover the behavior of various types of control system, i.e. continuous, discontinuous as well as hybrid controllers. To that end, system reactions are co-defined by the corresponding signal transformation functions, whose arguments can be any type of input signal – on/off (Boolean), binary-coded (integer) or analog (real), depending on the application context.

3.2 Specification of Transformational Behaviour

Signal transformation functions specify how the output signals are generated for the corresponding system reactions and the associated activity states. Specifically:

$$\forall y_i \in Y, \exists f_i \in F\colon y_i(t) = f_i\,(x_1^{\,i}(t), x_2^{\,i}(t), \ldots, x_m^{\,i}(t)),\ x_j^{\,i} \in X\ , \tag{18}$$

i.e. each output signal can be specified with a function that describes the transformation, involving one or more input signals, that must be applied in order to generate the output signal.

In the general case f_i may specify a complex signal transformation that might be represented as a composite function:

$$f_i = \varphi_l^i \circ \varphi_{l-1}^i \circ \ldots \circ \varphi_1^i\ , \tag{19}$$

where φ_j^i are basic application functions encapsulated into reusable components called function blocks (FBs).

The introduction of composite functions has thus important implication not only for system behavior but also – for system structure that has to be modeled at the lower (activity) level. There are basically two types of model that can be used to specify a sequence of computations corresponding to a composite function: control flow models, e.g. computation sequence graphs, and data flow models, which are also known as *function block diagrams*. The latter have been traditionally used by control engineers to specify the computation of control signals for both continuous and discontinuous control applications [6]. Function block diagrams may also be used to specify computations needed for the evaluation of guard variables (e.g. a Boolean flag indicating that a process variable value is higher than its Hi-limit).

A function block diagram is a data flow graph that can be defined in terms of function blocks and their connections. A function block is defined as:

$$FB = \langle I, J, Z, \Phi \rangle \,, \tag{20}$$

where: I is a set of input signals; J is a set of output signals; Z is a set of internal (persistent) variables, and Φ is a set of functions relating output signals to input signals, parameters and persistent variables. Accordingly, the function block diagram can be formally specified as a data flow graph, using notations similar to those already introduced in the context of higher-level function unit diagrams (see section 2.1).

In our example, the second level state machine executes the control action *AutomaticControl* within state q_2 (see Fig. 4). This control action is specified with a function block diagram composed of function blocks *PID* and *MUX*, implementing the desired control signal transformation (see Fig. 5). That diagram is also presented in tabular form in Table 7, where the positioning of function blocks implies their execution sequence, in accordance with the flow of signals in the diagram.

A function block diagram can be ultimately encapsulated into a higher-level component, i.e. a *composite function block (CFB).* The latter is externally indistinguishable from a basic function block; the only difference is that its function is a composite one but this is transparent to the external observer.

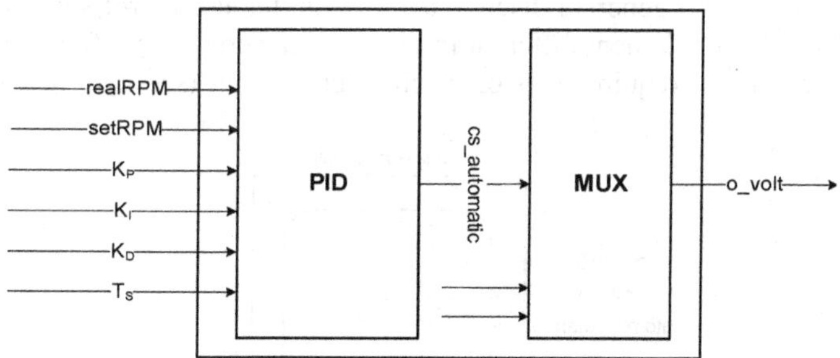

Fig. 5. Specification of transformational behaviour: function block diagram of control action *AutomaticControl* (state q_2 of the second level of *Controller* state machine)

Table 7. Control action *AutomaticControl*: function block diagram

<table>
<tr><th>FB type[instance]</th><th>Function $\varphi_i \in \Phi$</th><th>Input: internal signal – $v_i \in I$</th><th>Output: internal signal $w_i \in J$</th></tr>
<tr><td rowspan="6">PID[1]</td><td rowspan="6">pid</td><td>Param_K_P: K_P</td><td rowspan="6">Control signal: cs_automatic</td></tr>
<tr><td>Param_K_I: K_I</td></tr>
<tr><td>Param_K_D: K_D</td></tr>
<tr><td>Param_T_S: T_S</td></tr>
<tr><td>ProcesVariable: realRPM</td></tr>
<tr><td>Setpoint: setRPM</td></tr>
<tr><td rowspan="3">MUX[1]</td><td rowspan="3">channel1</td><td>Input1: cs_automatic</td><td rowspan="3">MUXOutput: o_volt</td></tr>
<tr><td>Input2: cs_manual</td></tr>
<tr><td>Input3: cs_stop</td></tr>
</table>

3.3 Combining the Reactive and Transformational Aspects of Activity Behavior

The same principle of encapsulation can be used to ultimately represent the mechanism of generating reaction signal y_i using a composite function of even higher order:

$$y_i = \psi_i(x)\,, \tag{21}$$

where:

$$\psi_i = f_i \circ R\,. \tag{22}$$

However, this is a hierarchical type of composition, whereby $\forall\,(e_i, y_j), \exists\,\psi_i : (R(e_i) = y_j) \rightarrow (y_j = f_j(x))$.

Composite functions ψ_j constitute the set Ψ, which can be used to redefine a function unit activity:

$$A = \langle X, Y, E, \Psi \rangle\,, \tag{23}$$

where Ψ represents an integral body of computation, which is always executed in response to events $e_i \in E$. This computation can be encapsulated into a reconfigurable function block of class *State Machine* [9, 11]. This is essentially a *hybrid* state machine in the sense that it can process discrete and/or analog input signals, and likewise – generate discrete and/or continuous control signals. It can be configured so as to implement different instances of the constituent functions R and f_i, in accordance with the requirements of specific applications (see e.g. Fig. 6).

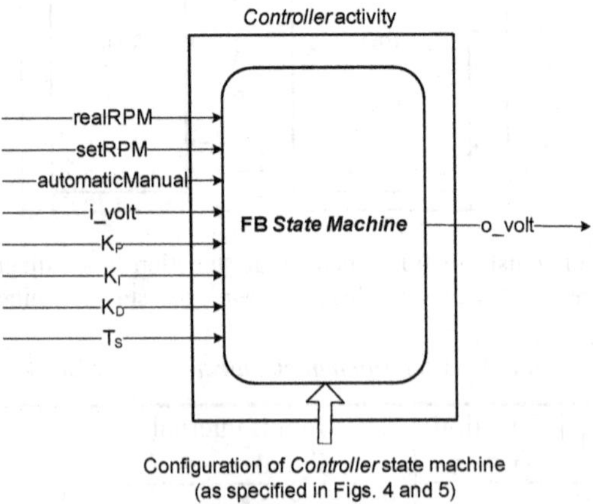

Fig. 6. *Controller* activity implemented with an instance of function block *State Machine*

The above formulation can be further simplified assuming time-driven execution, whereby the activity is triggered by periodically arriving timing events $\{\uparrow(kT)\}$. Hence,

$$A = \langle X, Y, \Psi \rangle\,, \tag{24}$$

where Ψ represents the body of computation executed with every timing event.

The generalized model of activity behavior has important implications. In particular, this model makes it possible to uniformly specify activity structure and behavior in terms of function blocks belonging to the *COMDES* component hierarchy [9]. In simple terms, this means that an activity is always specified and implemented with function blocks. These may be simple and/or composite function blocks – with continuous control systems, and function blocks of class *State Machine* – with sequential or hybrid control systems. In the latter case complex behavior is transparent, i.e. it is hidden in the corresponding instance of the function block.

4 Related Research

Component frameworks developed in the Software Engineering domain use most often some kind of port-based objects (PBOs). Port-based objects provide for loose coupling between components, which facilitates system reconfiguration. However, there are different PBO types, ranging from passive objects [12] to active single-threaded objects used in frameworks such as *Port-Based Objects, Giotto and Timed Multitasking* [16-18], as well as multi-threaded and composite port-based objects, e.g. *ROOM* [3]. Port-based objects can be combined with different models of computation resulting in widely differing frameworks – from very simple ones to heterogeneous and hierarchical frameworks, featuring sophisticated interaction protocols and complex component interfaces, e.g. 'polymorphic' interfaces used in *Ptolemy II* [4] or parameterized port objects [12].

The use of port-based objects results in relatively complex models featuring multiple ports and port connections (diagram clutter), e.g. replicated and relay ports used in composite port-based objects [3]. This problem is avoided in frameworks developed in the Control Engineering domain by adopting domain-specific modelling and interaction techniques, i.e. function block diagrams and signal-based communication [6, 7]. However, these are essentially flat models that are nor quite adequate for complex hierarchical and distributed systems. That observation has motivated the development of the *COMDES* framework, which has been specifically designed to address the above issues. This has been achieved through a well-defined hierarchy of components featuring transparent signal-based communication between components and subsystems (function units).

Another limitation of industrial standards is the use of function blocks having only stateless (transformational) behaviour, e.g. basic and composite function blocks that implement specific signal transformations such as *filter, PID*, etc. This limitation has been relaxed in the newer standard *IEC 61499*, where function blocks incorporate a simple modal state machine [7]. However, that state machine is 'hardwired' in the function block, i.e. it uses a predefined set of inputs and outputs and its configuration cannot be changed without reprogramming. This problem has been addressed in *COMDES* by developing a function block of class *State Machine*, featuring a fully reconfigurable execution control state machine [11].

Furthermore, it is possible to invoke continuous signal-processing function blocks within the states of the execution control state machine. This feature is usually not supported in hierarchical state machine models but it is present in hybrid models, such as mode automata implemented in *LUSTRE* [15] and heterogeneous models combining the state-machine and data-flow domains in *Ptolemy II* [4]. However, these are not implemented as reusable and reconfigurable components.

Finally, is should be noted that instances of function block *State Machine* can be hierarchically nested. Thus, it is possible to implement complex behaviours similar to those that can be specified by *Statecharts* and other hierarchical/concurrent state machine models. However, in our case the model is executable - it can be implemented using prefabricated components, i.e. function blocks, following the principle *"what you specify is what you verify, execute and test"*.

5 Conclusion

The paper has presented *COMDES* - a domain-specific framework for hard real-time distributed control systems.

Under this framework, distributed applications are specified in terms of autonomous subsystems (function units), such as sensor, actuator, control unit, operator station, etc., that have to be suitably configured and softwired with one another. Accordingly, function units are conceived as software integrated circuits encapsulating one or more dynamically scheduled activities, as well signal drivers that are used to communicate with the outside world and other function units. Activities are configured from prefabricated components - function blocks, whereby activity structure is described with a function block diagram. Activity behaviour is specified in terms of hybrid state machines – a hierarchical executable model that takes into account both the reactive and the transformational aspects of system behaviour. Hence, it can be potentially used to specify a broad range of embedded applications such as discrete, continuous and hybrid control systems.

The presented framework has been used to systematically develop design patterns for reusable components - simple and composite function blocks and reconfigurable state machines, implementing the executable models presented in the paper. These have been validated in a number of real-time control experiments, e.g. a distributed control system of an industrial plant specified in the Production Cell Case Study. A prototype version of a system configuration toolset is now under development.

Signal-based communication is an outstanding feature of the *COMDES* framework. Software components, and specifically - function units, interact by exchanging signals, i.e. labeled messages with state message semantics, rather than using I/O ports or operational interfaces. This feature facilitates system reconfiguration and provides for transparent communication between function units, resulting in flexible and truly open distributed systems.

Signal-based communication is also used for internal interactions involving activities belonging to one and the same function unit, as well as function blocks constituting an activity. Consequently, activities do not need shared data structures and never block during execution. Hence, the application is configured entirely from non-blocking components that communicate by exchanging signals with state message semantics. This has obvious implications for system safety and predictability.

The above model of communication has been further elaborated using the concept of Distributed Timed Multitasking. This technique can be used to eliminate I/O jitter and thus engineer highly predictable distributed systems while retaining the flexibility and ease of reconfiguration that are inherent to dynamically scheduled systems.

References

1. ARTIST Project IST-2001-34820: Selected Topics in Embedded Systems Design: Roadmaps for Research. Project report (2004)
2. European Research Consortium for Informatics and Mathematics: ERCIM News, N 52, (2003) Special Issue on Embedded Systems
3. Selic B., Gullegson G., and Ward P.T.: Real-Time Object-Oriented Modeling. John Wiley & Sons (1994)
4. Lee, E.A, Xiong, Y.: System-Level Types for Component-Based Design. Proc. of the First Workshop on Embedded Software EMSOFT'2001, Lake Tahoe USA (2001)
5. Software Technologies, Embedded systems and Distributed systems in FP6. Workshop on Software Technologies, Embedded Systems and Distributed Systems in the 6th Framework Programme for EU Research, Brussels, Belgium (2002)
6. John, K.H., Tiegelkamp, M.: IEC 61131-3: Programming Industrial Automation Systems. Springer (2001)
7. Lewis, R.: Modeling Control Systems Using IEC 61499. Institution of Electrical Engineers (2001)
8. Angelov, C., Sierszecki, K., and Marian, N.: Component-Based Design of Embedded Software: an Analysis of Design Issues, in N. Guelfi et al. (Eds.): FIDJI 2004, LNCS 3409, (2005) 1-11
9. Angelov, C., Sierszecki, K.: A Software Framework for Component-Based Embedded Applications. Proc. of the Asia-Pacific Software Engineering Conference APSEC'2004, Busan Korea (2004)
10. Angelov, C., Berthing, J., Sierszecki, K., and Marian, N.: Function Unit Specification in a Timed Multitasking Environment. Proc. of the 17th International Conference on Software and Systems Engineering and Their Applications ICSSEA'04, Paris France (2004)
11. Angelov C., Sierszecki K. and Marian N.: Design Models for Reusable and Reconfigurable State Machines, in L.T. Yang et al. (Eds): Embedded and Ubiquitous Computing EUC 2005, LNCS 3824, (2005) 152-163
12. Wang S., Shin K.G.: Constructing Reconfigurable Software for Machine Control Systems. IEEE Trans. on Robotics and Automation, 18 (4), (2002) 475-486
13. Heimdahl, M. P. E., Leveson, N.G.: Completeness and Consistency Analysis of State-Based Requirements. IEEE Transactions on Software Engineering, TSE 22(6), (1996) 363-377
14. Kopetz, H.: Real-Time Systems, Design Principles for Distributed Embedded Applications, Kluwer Academic Publishers (1997)
15. Maraninchi, F., Remond, Y.: Applying Formal Methods to Industrial Cases: the Language Approach (The Production-Cell and Mode-Automata). Proc. of the 5th International Workshop on Formal Methods for Industrial Critical Systems, Berlin (2000)
16. Liu J., and Lee E.A.: Timed Multitasking for Real-Time Embedded Software. *IEEE Control Systems Magazine: Advances in Software Enabled Control*, (2003) 65-75
17. Stewart D.B., Volpe R.A., and Khosla P.K.: Design of Dynamically Reconfigurable Real-Time Software Using Port-Based Objects. IEEE Trans. on Soft. Eng., TSE 23(12), (1997) 759-776
18. Isovic D., Norström C.: Components in Real-Time Systems. Proc. of the 8th Int. Conf. on Real-Time Comp. Systems and Applications RTCSA'2002, Tokyo Japan (2002)

A Prototype Tool for Software Component Services in Embedded Real-Time Systems

Frank Lüders[1], Daniel Flemström[1], Anders Wall[2], and Ivica Crnkovic[1]

[1] Dept. of Computer Science and Electronics, Mälardalen University
Box 883, SE-721 23 Västerås, Sweden
{frank.luders, daniel.flemstrom, ivica.crnkovic}@mdh.se
[2] ABB Corporate Research, Forskargränd 8, SE-721 78 Västerås, Sweden
anders.wall@se.abb.co

Abstract. The use of software component models has become popular during the last decade, in particular in the development of software for desktop applications and distributed information systems. However, such models have not been widely used in the domain of embedded real-time systems. There is a considerable amount of research on component models for embedded real-time systems, or even narrower application domains, which focuses on source code components and statically configured systems. This paper explores an alternative approach by laying the groundwork for a component model based on binary components and targeting the broader domain of embedded real-time systems. The work is inspired by component models for the desktop and information systems domains in the sense that a basic component model is extended with a set of services for the targeted application domain. A prototype tool for supporting these services is presented and its use illustrated by a control application.

1 Introduction

The use of software component models has become increasingly popular during the last decade, especially in the development of software for desktop applications and distributed information systems. Popular component models include *JavaBeans* [5] and *ActiveX* [4] for desktop applications and *Enterprise JavaBeans* (EJB) [11] and *COM+* [15] for distributed information systems. In addition to basic standards for naming, interfacing, binding, etc., these models also define standardized sets of run-time services oriented towards the application domains they target. Unlike for these domains, there has been no widespread use of software component models in the domain of real-time and embedded systems, presumably due to the special requirements such systems have to meet with respect to timing predictability and limited use of resources. Much research has therefore been directed towards defining new component models for real-time and embedded systems. Typically, such models are based on static configurations of source code components and target relatively narrow application domains. Examples include the *Koala* component model for consumer electronics [22], *PECOS* for industrial field devices [6], and *SaveCCM* for vehicle control systems [7].

I. Gorton et al. (Eds.): CBSE 2006, LNCS 4063, pp. 222–237, 2006.

An alternative approach is to strive for a component model based on binary components and targeting a broader domain of applications, similar to the domain targeted by a typical real-time operating system. The approach pursued in this paper is to provide a combination of restrictions and extensions of an existing component model to adapt it to our target domain. Adapting an existing component model has several advantages: It may be possible to use existing (integrated) development environments; existing components can be re-used or adapted for the real-time domain; integration with application from other domains becomes significantly simpler, and so on.

Our previous work has demonstrated that the key concepts of the *Component Object Model* (COM) [3] can be used with advantage in the development of an embedded real-time system [10]. A study of COM and its extension *Distributed COM* (DCOM) [17] shows that these models are not inherently incompatible with real-time requirements, although some restrictions on how the models are used may be necessary to ensure predictability [9]. Some reasons that COM is an attractive starting point are that the model is relatively simple, commercial COM implementations are already available for a few real-time operating systems, and COM is already well-known and accepted in industry. The goal of this paper is to lay the groundwork for a software component model for embedded real-time systems by using the basic concepts of COM as the starting point and extending the basic model with standardized services of general use for this application domain, much like COM+ extends COM with services for distributed information systems.

The remainder of the paper is organized as follows. In Section 2 we clarify what we mean by software component services and identify some useful services for embedded real-time systems. Section 3 is an overview of a prototype tool we are developing to support such services, including an example control application to demonstrate the use of the tool. Related work is reviewed in Section 4 and conclusions and some ideas for further work are presented in Section 5.

2 Component Services

In this paper we define component services as solutions to common problems that can be added to components without modifying them and with little or no adaptation of application code. This is similar to the concept of component services in EJB and COM+, where examples of services include transaction control, data persistence, and security. Our focus is on services that address common challenges in embedded real-time systems, including logging, synchronization, and timing control. Traditionally, such functions have to be hand coded and off line deduced using complex theories, which can be very time consuming and sometimes impossible in complex industrial systems. If third party components are used, it may also be impossible to implement functions by modifying the components. In the following subsections we describe some of the services we have identified in more depth and outline how they may be implemented. In general, we propose that services are implemented through the use of proxy

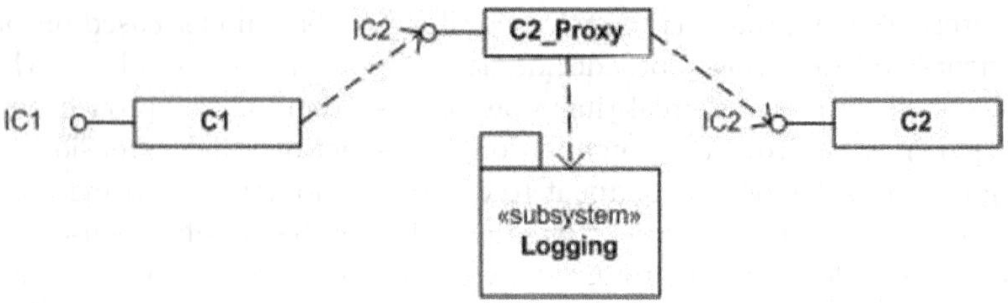

Fig. 1. Implementing a logging service through a proxy object

objects, which are automatically generated from configuration files written in an XML based format.

2.1 Logging

A logging service allows the sequence of interactions between components to be traced. Our suggested solution for achieving this is to use a proxy object as illustrated in the UML class diagram in Fig. 1. In the diagram, the object C2 implements an interface IC2 for which we wish to apply a logging service. A proxy object that also implements IC2 is placed between C2 and a client that uses the operations exposed through IC2. The operations implemented by the proxy forward all invocations to the corresponding operations in C2 in addition to writing information about parameter values, return codes, and invocation and return times to some logging medium. To add logging of all operation invocations through an interface, we simply add an entry in the configuration file:

```
<application>
  ...
<component name="myProject.C2">
  <interface name="IC2">
    <service type ="Logging"/>
  </interface>
</component>
  ...
</application>
```

No programming is required in the client C1 or the component C2. To add logging only for a particular operation, the entry is modified as follows:

```
  <interface name="IC2">
    <operation name="DoSomething">
      <service type ="Logging"/>
    </operation>
  </interface>
```

2.2 Execution Time Measurement

This service allows operation invocations to be monitored and information about execution times accumulated. Different measurements, such as worst-case, best-case, and average execution time may be collected. A possible use of the information is to dynamically adapt an on-line scheduling strategy. The suggested solution is to use a forwarding proxy that measures the time elapsed from each operation call till it returns and collects the desired timing information. As with the logging service, the time measurement service is specified in the configuration file:

```
<interface name="IC2">
  <service type="Timing">
    <measurement type="Mean" />
    <measurement type="Worst"/>
  </service>
</interface>
```

Again, no programming is required.

2.3 Synchronization

A synchronization service allows components that are not inherently thread-safe to be used in multi-threaded applications. The suggested solution is to use forwarding proxies that use the basic mechanisms of the underlying operating system to implement the desired synchronization policies. A synchronization policy may be applied to a single operation or to a group of operations, e.g. all operations of an interface or a component. Several different policies may be useful and will be described further in this section. Most synchronization policies rely on blocking and it may be useful to combine such policies with timeouts to limit blocking time. If the blocking time for an operation call reaches the timeout limit, the proxy return an error without forwarding the call. A more advanced timeout policy is one where the proxy tries to determine if a call can be satisfied without violating the timeout limit a priori and, if not, returns an error immediately.

The simplest synchronization policy is *mutual exclusion*, which blocks all operation calls except one. After the non-blocked call completes, the waiting calls are dispatched one by one according to the priority policy. This policy may be applied merely by adding an entry in the configuration file but, if timeouts are used, the client should be able to handle the additional error codes that may arise. Another class of synchronization policies is different *reader/writer* policies. These differs from the previously described policy in that any number of calls to read operations may execute concurrently, while each call to write operations has exclusive execution. Thus, the operations subjected to a reader/writer policy must be classified as either writer or reader operations, depending on whether they may modify state or not. Concurrent read calls are scheduled according to their priorities.

Using this policy requires that it be specified for each operation whether it is a read or write type of operation. This can be done in the component specification (e.g. a COM IDL file) or in the configuration file. If this is left unspecified for an operation, the proxy must assume it may write data. No programming is required, except possibly to handle error codes resulting from timeouts. For all synchronization policies, we may select if the priority of the dispatching thread should be the same as the calling thread, or explicitly specified in the configuration file. A specification of a reader/writer policy may look as follows:

```
<interface name="IC2">
  <service type="Synchronization" policy="RWPolicyX"/>
  <operation name="DoSomething" type="Write"/>
  <operation name="WriteData"   type="Write"/>
  <operation name="ReadData"    type="Read" />
</interface>
```

2.4 Execution Timeout

This service can be used to ensure that a call to a component´s operation always terminate within a specified deadline, possibly signaling a failure if the operation could not be completed within that time. The solution is to use a proxy that that use a separate thread to forward each operation call and then wait until either that thread terminates or the deadline expires. In the latter case the proxy signals the failure by returns an error code. Also, it is possible to specify different options for what should be done with the thread of the forwarded call if the deadline expires. The simplest option is to forcefully terminate the thread, but this may not always be safe since it may leave the component in an undefined and possibly inconsistent state. Another option is to let the operation call run to completion and disregard its output. Obviously, using this service requires that the client is able to handle timeouts. Again, the service is specified in the configuration file:

```
<interface name="IC2">
  <service type="Timeout" deadline="10ms" fail="Terminate"/>
</interface>
```

2.5 Vertical Services

In addition to the type of services discussed above, which we believe are generally useful for embedded real-time systems, one can imagine many services aimed at more specific application domains, often called *vertical services* [8]. Among the services we have considered are cyclic execution, which are much used in process control loops [1], and support for redundancy mechanisms such as N-version components, which are useful in fault-tolerant systems [2]. The prototype tool presented in the next section includes an implementation of a cyclic execution service.

3 Prototype Tool

This section outlines a prototype tool we are developing that adds services to COM components on *Microsoft Windows CE*. The tool generates source code for proxy objects implementing services by intercepting method calls to the COM

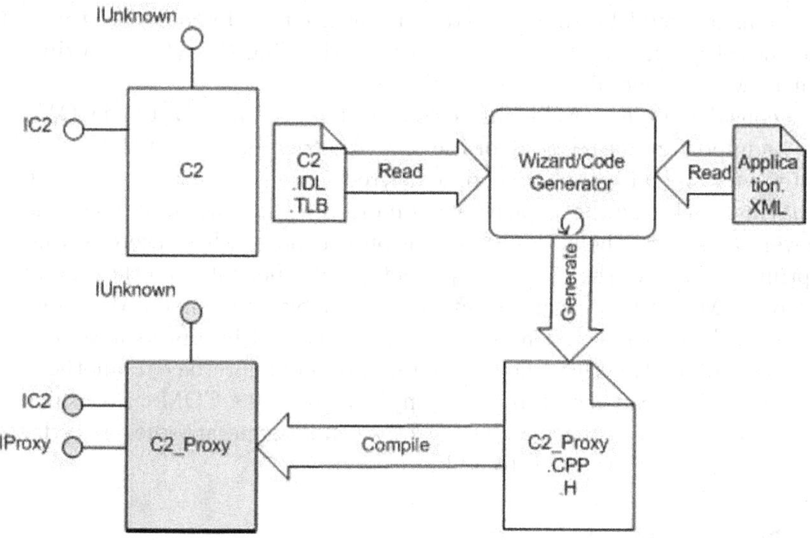

Fig. 2. Generating a proxy object for a component service

objects. The tool takes as inputs component specifications along with a specification of the desired services for each component. Component specifications may be in the form of Interface Definition Language (IDL) files or their binary equivalent Type Library (TLB) files. Desired services are either specified in a separate file using an XML-based format or in the tool´s graphical user interface, described further below. Note that access to component source code is not required. Based on these inputs, the tool generates a complete set of files that can be used with *Microsoft eMbedded Visual C++* (sic) to build a COM component implementing the proxy objects (i.e., the proxies are themselves COM objects). This process is depicted in Fig. 2.

3.1 Design Consideration

The use of proxy objects for interception is heavily inspired by COM+. However, rather than to generate proxies at run-time, we suggest that these are generated and compiled on a host computer (typically a PC) and downloaded to the embedded system along with the application components. There, the proxy COM classes must be registered in the COM registry in such a way that proxy objects are placed between interacting application components. This process may occur when the software is initially downloaded to the system or as part of dynamic reconfiguration of a system that supports this. In the latter case, one can imagine updating or adding proxies without updating or adding any application components. The current version of the tool only generates proxy code and does not address the registration and run-time instantiation of components. This means that the client code must instantiate each proxy along with the affected COM object and set up the necessary connection between them. A desirable improvement would be to automate this task, either by generating code that performs setup for each proxy object or by extending the COM run-time environment with a general solution.

We consider staying as close as possible to the original COM and COM+ concepts an important design goal for the tool. Another goal is that the programmer or integrator should be able to choose desired services for each component without having to change the implementation or doing any programming. There are however cases, e.g. when adding invocation timeouts, where there is a need for adapting the code of the client component to fully benefit from the service. Specific to COM is that a component is realized by a set of COM classes that, in turn, each implements a number of interfaces. All interfaces have a method called *QueryInterface* that allows changing from one interface to another on the same COM class. Since each proxy is implemented by a COM class, which must satisfy the definition of QueryInterface, we must generate one proxy for each COM class to which we wish to add any services.

3.2 Supported Services

Fig. 3 shows the graphical user interface of the tool. After a TLB or IDL file has been loaded all COM classes defined in the file are listed. Checking the box to the left of a COM class causes a proxy for that class to be generated when the button at the bottom of the tool is pressed. Under each COM class, the interfaces implemented by the class is listed and, under each interface, the operations implemented by the interface. In addition, the available services are listed with their names set in brackets. Checking the box to the left of a service causes code to be generated that provides the service for the element under which the service is listed. In the current version of the tool, a service for cyclic execution may only be specified for the IPassiveController interface (see example below), while all other services may only be specified for individual operations. Checking the box to the left of an interface or operation is simply a quick way of checking all boxes further down in the hierarchy.

If the cyclic execution service is checked, the proxy will implement an interface called IActiveController instead of IPassiveController (see example below). Checking the logging service results in a proxy that logs each invocation of the affected operation. The timing service causes the proxy to measure the execution time of the process and write it to the log at each invocation (if timing is checked but not logging, execution times will be measured but not saved). The synchronization service means that each invocation of the operation will be synchronized with all other invocations of all other operations on the proxy object for which the synchronization service is checked. The only synchronization policy currently supported is mutual exclusion. The timeout service has a numeric parameter. When this service is selected (by clicking the name rather than the box) as in Fig. 3, an input field marked Milliseconds is visible near the bottom of the tool. Checking the service results in a proxy where invocations of the operation always terminate within the specified number of milliseconds. In the case that the object behind the proxy does not complete the execution

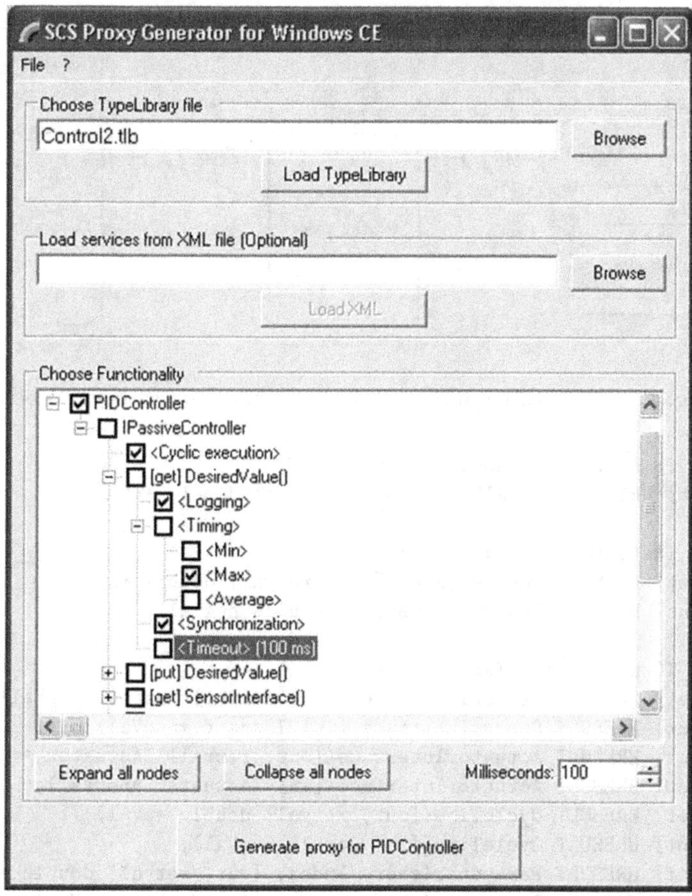

Fig. 3. The graphical user interface of the prototype tool

of the operation within this time, the proxy forcefully terminates the execution and returns en error code.

3.3 Example Application

To illustrate the use of the tool we have implemented a component that encapsulates a digital Proportional-Integral-Differential (PID) controller [1]. For the purpose of comparison, we first implemented a component that does not rely on any services provided by the tool. Fig. 4 shows the configuration of a an application that uses this component. PIDController is a COM class that implements an interface IActiveController and relies on the two interfaces ISensor and IActuator to read and write data from/to the controlled process. For the purpose of this example, these interfaces are implemented by the simple COM class DummyProcess that does nothing except returning a constant value to the controller. The interfaces are defined as follows:

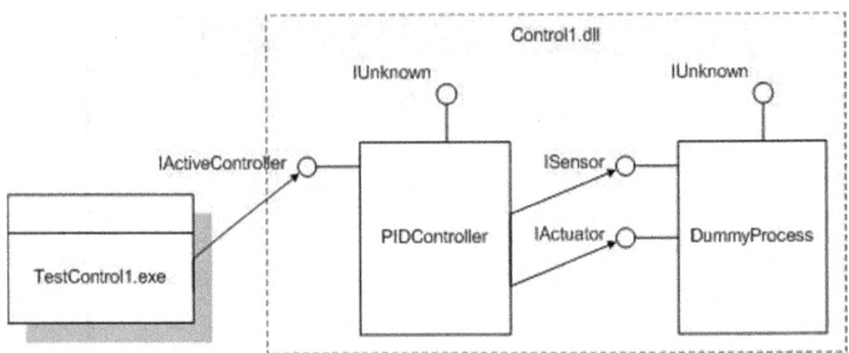

Fig. 4. An application using a controller component without services

```
interface ISensor : IUnknown  {
  [propget] HRESULT ActualValue([out, retval] double *pVal);
};
interface IActuator : IUnknown  {
   [propget] HRESULT DesiredValue([out, retval] double *pVal);
   [propput] HRESULT DesiredValue([in] double newVal);
};
interface IController : IActuator {
   [propget] HRESULT SensorInterface([out, retval] ISensor **pVal);
   [propput] HRESULT SensorInterface([in] ISensor *newVal);
   [propget] HRESULT ActuatorInterface([out, retval] IActuator **pVal);
   [propput] HRESULT ActuatorInterface([in] IActuator *newVal);
   [propget] HRESULT CycleTime([out, retval] double *pVal);
   [propput] HRESULT CycleTime([in] double newVal);
   [propget] HRESULT Parameter(short Index, [out, retval] double *pVal);
   [propput] HRESULT Parameter(short Index, [in] double newVal);
};
interface IActiveController : IController  {
   [propget] HRESULT Priority([out, retval] short *pVal);
   [propput] HRESULT Priority([in] short newVal);
   HRESULT Start();
   HRESULT Stop();
};
```

IController is a generic interface for a single-variable controller with configurable cycle time and an arbitrary number of control parameters. PIDController uses three parameters for the proportional, integral, and differential gain. IActiveController extends this interface to allow control of the controller´s execution in a separate thread. The reason for splitting the interface definitions like this is that we wish to reuse IController for a controller that uses our cyclic execution service rather than maintaining its own thread. Note that IController inherits the DesiredValue property from IActuator. This definition is chosen to allow the interface to be used for cascaded control loops where the output of one controller forms the input to another.

The test application TestControl1.exe creates one instance of PIDController and one instance of DummyController. It then connects the two objects by setting the SensorInterfaca and ActuatorInterface properties of the PIDController object. After this it sets the cycle time and the control parameters before invoking the Start operation. This causes the PIDController object to create a new thread that executes a control loop. A simple timing mechanism is used to control the execution of the loop in accordance with the cycle time property. At each iteration the loop reads a value from the sensor interface, which it uses in conjunction with the desired value, the control parameters, and an internal state based on previous inputs to compute and write a new value to the actuator interface. To minimize jitter (input-output delay as well as sampling variability), this part of the loop uses internal copies of all variables, eliminating the need for any synchronization.

Next, the control loop updates its internal variables for subsequent iterations. Since the desired value and the control parameters may be changed by the application while the controller is running, this part of the loop uses a mutual exclusion mechanism for synchronization. In addition to performing its control task the loop timestamps and writes the sensor and actuator data to a log. The control loop is illustrated by the following pseudo code:

```
while (Run) {
   WaitForTimer();
   ReadSensorInput();
   ComputeAndWriteActuatorOutput();
   WriteDataToLog();
   WaitForMutex();
   UpdateInternalState();
   ReleaseMutex();
}
```

Note that, due to the simple timing mechanism, the control loop will halt unless all iterations complete within the cycle time.

Next, we implemented a component intended to perform the same function, but relying on services provided by generated proxies. A test application using this component and generated proxies is shown if Fig. 5. In this application, PIDController is a COM class that implements the IPassiveController interface. Note that, although this COM class has the same human readable name as in the application described above, it has a distinct identity to the COM run-time environment. To avoid confusion we use the notation Control2.PIDController when appropriate. IPassiveController extends IController as follows:

```
interface IPassiveController : IController {
   HRESULT UpdateOutput();
   HRESULT UpdateState();
};
```

These operations are used by the PIDController_Proxy object to implement a control loop that performs the same control task as in the previous example.

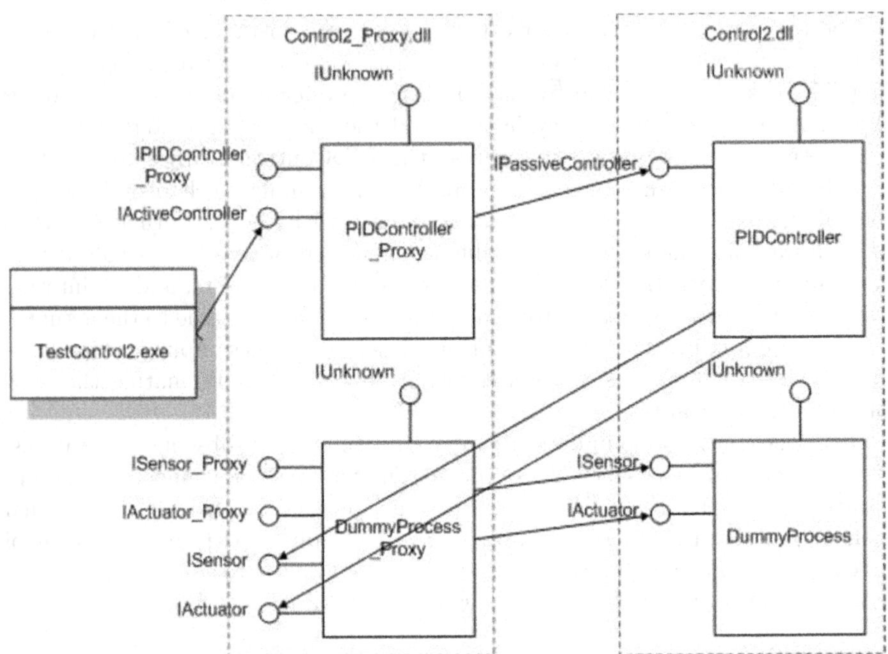

Fig. 5. An application using a controller component with services

PIDController_Proxy was generated with the use of the tool by checking the cyclic execution service under the Control2.PIDController´s IPassiveController interface and the synchronization service under the UpdateState operation as well as the operations for accessing the desired value and the control parameters. The DummyProcess_Proxy provides the interface pointers for the controller´s SensorInterface and ActuatorInterface properties. Behind this proxy is a DummyProxecess object with the same functionality as in the previous example. DummyProcess_Proxy was generated by the tool with the logging service checked. As a result, all data read and written via the sensor and actuator interfaces are logged. The interfaces ISensor_Proxy, IActuator_Proxy and IPIDController_Proxy are only used to set up the connections between proxies and other objects. They are defined as follows:

```
interface ISensor_Proxy : IUnknown {
   HRESULT Attach([in] ISensor *pTarget);
};
interface IActuator_Proxy : IUnknown {
   HRESULT Attach([in] IActuator *pTarget);
};
interface IPIDController_Proxy : IUnknown {
   HRESULT Attach([in] IPassiveController *pTarget);
};
```

In order to evaluate to two test applications we built and executed them on the Windows CE 4.0 Emulator. Since the timing accuracy on the emulator is 10 milliseconds, it was not possible to measure any timing differences between the two applications. In both cases the controller worked satisfactory for cycle times of 20 milliseconds or more (the measured input-output delay as well as sampling variability was zero—from which we can only conclude that the actual times are closer to zero than 10 milliseconds). For shorter cycle times, both controllers ultimately halted since the limited timer accuracy caused the control loop to fail to complete its execution before the start of the next cycle. Also, we were not able to see any systematic difference in memory usage for the two applications. Clearly, further evaluation of the effects of the services on timing and memory usage is desirable.

To estimate the difference in programming effort and code size for the two applications we compared the amounts of source code and sizes of compiled files. These size metrics for the various components are presented in Table 1. The middle column shows the number of non-empty lines of source code. For the first three components, the number only include the source code of the C++ classes implementing the COM objects, i.e. the automatically generated code included in all COM components is not included. Taking these numbers as (admittedly primitive) measurements of programming effort, we see that using the tool to generate service proxies has resulted in a saving of 127 lines or 42 per cent. On the other hand, we see that the effort required for the client program is substantially greater in the case where the proxies are used. This is due to the need for the program to set up the connections between the proxies and the other objects. We conclude that the usefulness of our approach would greatly benefit from automation of this task.

As for the code size, there is only a small difference between the three COM components, leading to an overhead of roughly 100 per cent from using the proxies. This is largely due to the fact that the implemented COM objects are relatively small, leading to the obligatory house-keeping code of all COM components taking up a large percentage of the code size. For larger COM objects, the relative code sizes approaches the relative sizes of the source code. The small size of the COM objects is also the main reason that the component implementing the proxy objects is the largest of all the components. In addition, the generated code is designed to be robust in the sense that all the operations of the proxy objects verify that the interface pointers have been set before forwarding operation

Table 1. Size metrics for components

Component	Lines of source code	File size in KB
Controller1.dll	300	56.5
Controller2.dll	173	53.5
Controller2_Proxy.dll	351	60.5
TestControl1.exe	81	12.5
TestControl2.exe	157	14.0

calls. An obvious trade-off would be to sacrifice this robustness for less overhead in execution time as well as space. From the file size of the two test programs we find that the code overhead for setting up the connections between the proxies and the other objects is a little more than 10 per cent. This overhead, unlike the overhead on programming effort, cannot be eliminated by automating the setup task.

4 Related Work

The services discussed in this paper have already been adopted by some current and emerging technologies. As a base for our discussions, we have selected a few of the most common solutions for these. In addition, this section briefly reviews some existing research on binary components for real-time systems.

Microsoft´s component model COM [3] originally targets the desktop software domain. Thus, it has good support for specifying and maintaining functional aspects of components while disregarding temporal behavior and resource utilization. Often this can only be overcome with a substantial amount of component specific programming. There is no built in support to automatically measure and record execution times for methods in components. This is typically done by third party applications that instrument the code in run-time. These applications are typically not well suited for executing on embedded resource constrained systems. The desktop version of COM, as well as the DCOM package available for Windows CE, has some support for synchronizing calls to components that are not inherently thread safe. This is achieved through the use of so-called *apartments*, which can be used to ensure that only one thread can execute code in the apartment at a time. Since this technique origins from the desktop version of COM, there is no built in support for time determinism and the resource overhead is larger than desired for many embedded systems.

COM+ [15] is Microsoft's extension of their own COM model with services for distributed information systems. These services provide functionality such as transaction handling and persistent data management, which is common for applications in this domain and which is often time consuming and error prone to implement for each component. Builders of COM+ application declare which services are required for each component and the run-time system provides the services by intercepting calls between components. COM+ is a major source of inspiration for our work in two different ways. Firstly, we use the same criteria for selecting which services our component model should standardize, namely that they should provide non-trivial functionality that is commonly required in the application domain. Since our component model targets a different domain than COM+, the services we have selected are different from those of COM+ as weöö. Secondly, we are inspired by the technique of providing services by interception. This mechanism is also used in other technologies and is sometimes called *interceptors* rather than proxies, e.g. in the *Common Object Request Broker Architecture* (CORBA) [14] and the *MEAD* framework for fault-tolerant real-time CORBA applications [13].

The approach presented in this paper is similar to the concept of aspects and weaving. In [21], A real-time component model called *RTCOM* is presented which have support for weaving of functionality into components as aspects while maintaining real-time policies, e.g. execution times. However, RTCOM is a proprietary source code component model. Moreover, functionality is weaved in at the level of source code in RTCOM whereas in our approach, services are introduced at the system composition level.

Another aspect-oriented approach is presented in [18], which describes a method using C# attributes to generate a proxy that handles component replication for fault tolerance. Our work is primarily targeting COM and C++, which does not support attributes as used in that paper. An obstacle to the use of C# for the type of systems we are interested in is the lack of real-time predictability in the underlying *.NET Framework* [16]. The possibility of adding real-time capabilities to the .NET framework are described in [23].

A model for monitoring of components in order to gain more realistic WCET estimations is described in [20]. In this model the WCET is guessed at development time and the component is then continuously monitored at runtime and measurements of execution times are accumulated. This technique is very similar to our execution time measurement service.

Another effort to support binary software components for embedded real-time systems is the *ROBOCUP* project [12], which builds on the aforementioned Koala model and primarily targets the consumer electronics domain. This work is similar to ours in that the component model defined as part of this project is largely based on the basic concepts of COM. Furthermore, the sequel of the project, called *Space4U* [19], also seems to use a mechanism similar to proxy objects, e.g. to support fault-tolerance.

5 Conclusion and Future Work

The aim of this work has been to lay the groundwork for component services for embedded real-time systems using COM as a base technology. A major benefit of this approach is that industrial programmers can leverage their knowledge of existing technologies. Also, extending COM with real-time services probably requires less effort than inventing a new component technology from the ground.

The initial experiences with the prototype shows that it is possible to create a tool that more or less invisibly add real-time services to a standard component model. The example application demonstrates that the use of generated proxies to implement services may substantially reduce the complexity of software components. Another conclusion to be drawn from the example is that our approach would benefit from also automating the configuration of applications with proxies.

We have been able to identify some component services which we believe are useful for embedded real-time systems. As part of our future work, we plan to evaluate the usefulness of the services as well as to extend the set of services. We hope to do this with the help of input from organizations developing products in such domains as industrial automation, telecommunication, and vehicle control systems.

We realize that the proposed solutions imposes some time and memory overhead, and we believe that this is an acceptable price for many embedded real-time systems if using the model reduces the software development effort. It is, however, necessary that this overhead can be kept within known limits. So far, our prototype implementation has been tested with the Windows CE emulator, where we have found no noticeable run-time overheads. In our future work, we plan to evaluate the solution experimentally on a system running Windows CE. Measurements will be made to determine the effect on timing predictability as well as time and memory overhead.

We furthermore aim to empirically evaluate our approach with respect to its effect on development effort and such quality attributes as reliability and reusability. Our hypothesis concerning reliability is that it may improve as a result of reduced complexity of application components, provided off course that the generated proxies are reliable. We also believe reusability may be affected positively, as e.g. the use of synchronization services could make it easier to reuse components across applications that share some functionality but rely on different synchronization policies. The primary evaluating technique will be to conduct replicated student projects where software is developed both with and without the prototype tool. A possible complementary technique is industrial case studies, which implies a lower level of control and replication but may allow more realistic development efforts to be investigated.

References

1. K. J. Åström and B. Wittenmark. *Computer Controlled Systems — Theory and Design.* Prentice Hall, 2nd edition, 1990.
2. A. Avizienis. The methodology of N-version programming. In M. R. Lyu, editor, *Fault Tolerance.* Wiley, 1995.
3. D. Box. *Essential COM.* Addison-Wesley, 1997.
4. D. Chappell. *Understanding ActiveX and OLE.* Microsoft Press, 1996.
5. R. Englander. *Developing Java Beans.* O'Reilly, 1997.
6. T. Genßler, C. Stich, A. Christoph, M. Winter, O. Nierstrasz, S. Ducasse, R. Wuyts, G. Arévalo, B. Schönhage, and P. Müller. Components for embedded software — The PECOS approach. In *Proceedings of the 2002 International Conference on Compilers, Architectures and Synthesis for Embedded Systems*, 2002.
7. H. Hansson, M. Åkerholm, I. Crnkovic, and M. Törngren. SaveCCM — A component model for safety-critical real-time systems. In *Proceedings of the 30th EROMICRO Conference*, 2004.
8. G. T. Heineman and W. T. Council. *Component-Based Software Engineering — Putting the Pieces Together.* Addison-Wesley, 2001.
9. F. Lüders. Adopting a software component model in real-time systems development. In *Proceedings of the 28th Annual IEEE/NASA Software Engineering Workshop*, 2004.

10. F. Lüders, I. Crnkovic, and P. Runeson. Adopting a component-based software architecture for an industrial control system — A case study. In C. Atkinson, C. Bunse, H.-G. Gross, and C. Peper, editors, *Component-Based Software Development for Embedded Systems.* Springer, 2005.
11. R. Monson-Haefel, B. Burke, and S. Labourey. *Enterprise JavaBeans.* O'Reilly, 4th edition, 2004.
12. J. Muskens, M. R. V. Chaudron, and J. J. Lukkien. A component framework for consumer electronics middleware. In C. Atkinson, C. Bunse, H.-G. Gross, and C. Peper, editors, *Component-Based Software Development for Embedded Systems.* Springer, 2005.
13. P. Narasimhan, T. A. Dumitras, A. M. Paulos, S. M. Pertet, C. F. Reverte, J. G. Slember, and D. Srivastava. MEAD: Support for real-time fault-tolerant CORBA. *Concurrency and Computation: Practice and Experience*, 17(12):1527–1545, February 2005.
14. Object Management Group. Common object request broker architecture: Core specification, March 2004. OMG formal/04-03-12.
15. D. S. Platt. *Understanding COM+.* Microsoft Press, 1999.
16. D. S. Platt. *Introducing Microsoft .NET.* Microsoft Press, 3rd edition, 2003.
17. F. E. Redmond III. *DCOM — Microsoft Distributed Component Object Model.* Hungry Minds, 1997.
18. W. Schult and A. Polze. Aspect-oriented programming with C# and .NET. In *Proceedings of the Fifth IEEE International Symposium on Object-Oriented Real-Time Distributed Computing*, 2002.
19. Space4U Project. Space4U public hompage, January 2006. http://www.hitech-projects.com/euprojects/space4u/, Accessed on 28 April 2006.
20. D. Sundmark, A. Möller, and M. Nolin. Monitored software components — A novel software engineering approach. In *Proceedings of the 11th Asia-Pacific Software Engineering Conference, Workshop on Software Architectures and Component Technologies*, 2004.
21. A. Tešanović, D. Nyström, J. Hansson, and C. Norström. Aspects and components in real-time system development: Towards reconfigurable and reusable software. *Journal of Embedded Computing*, 1(1), February 2004.
22. R. van Ommering, F. van der Linden, J. Kramer, and J. Magee. The Koala component model for consumer electronics software. *Computer*, 33(3):78–85, 2000.
23. A. Zerzelidis and A. J. Wellings. Requirements for a real-time .NET framework. *ACM SIGPLAN Notices*, 40(2):41–50, 2005.

Service Policy Enhancements for the OSGi Service Platform

Nico Goeminne, Gregory De Jans, Filip De Turck,
Bart Dhoedt, and Frank Gielen

Ghent University, Gaston Crommenlaan 8, bus 201,
B-9050 Gent, Belgium
{Nico.Goeminne, Gregory.DeJans, Filip.DeTurck, Bart.Dhoedt,
Frank.Gielen}@intec.ugent.be
http://www.ibcn.intec.ugent.be/

Abstract. New content and service providers emerge every day. Each player offers new software components or services to support their technology. In these multi-vendor environments there is a genuine need for integration and interoperability. Integration and interoperability is a first step, once this is achieved components can seamlessly use services from different providers, and that is when service policies come into play. A policy mechanism allows fine grained control over the service usage. The OSGi Service Platform allows seamless integration of components and services but lacks a well defined mechanism for dynamic service policy management. Two approaches are presented for enhancing the OSGi Service Platform with policies. The first approach extends the platform while the second one adapts the plug-in components. Finally they are compared and evaluated against multiple requirements; usability, performance, transparency and backward compatibility.

1 Introduction

Today, content/service providers and hardware manufacturers have their own set of technologies and software components. Integration and interoperability are the most important factors to make this multi-vendor environment successful. New design philosophies and concepts are built around these values such as the Service Oriented Architecture (SOA). Within the service oriented architecture a service is an entity that performs some functionality and which can be shared among multiple components.

Whenever services are exposed or shared, there is a need for service policy management. The top level of that mechanism is the policy decision logic, which is the place where rules are imposed on service use. The rules can be defined in various formats, languages and libraries such as JRules[1], Jena[2] and others. Defining the rules and knowing when they should be applied is not sufficient, they need to be enforced within the lower layer. This paper presents the components needed in OSGi Service Platform[3][4] to support the lower layer of the policy mechanism.

I. Gorton et al. (Eds.): CBSE 2006, LNCS 4063, pp. 238–253, 2006.

The OSGi Service Platform technology allows integration of components and services from different vendors or service providers. The unit of deployment is a component called a bundle. A bundle is a Java archive(jar) file, and the code inside can be activated by the framework through the bundle's activator class. A bundle may contain multiple OSGi services, which are plain old java objects that are registered within the platform's service registry. Each of those services can be used by other bundles, thus creating some kind of dependency among each other.

Service dependency management tries to offer an answer to the question *'What should a bundle do when a service becomes (un)available?'* There are several approaches to help the bundle developer manage those dependencies. For example use the ServiceTracker, Service Binder[5][6][7], or Declarative Services[8][9] to reduce the impact of service dependencies. Releasing a service and in particular a java object may prove to be more difficult then one would think as pointed out by [10], but solutions are in development[11].

So, in contrast to service dependency management there is service policy management which offers an answer to the question *'How can one manage which bundle is allowed to use a service, taking into account the service's usage by other bundles?'* This work will focus on that question.

Section 2 outlines two use cases which show the need for service policy management and introduces two models, the Framework Extensions model and the Bundle Adaptation model that could be used to support service policies within the OSGi Service Platform. The Framework Extensions model adds interfaces and behaviour definitions to the OSGi R3 specifications. The Bundle Adaptation model implements the same behaviour outside the OSGi core framework. It requires some modifications to bundles who wish to participate. Sections 3 and 4 describe the models in detail. Section 5 describes how to build a policy enforcement component using the models. Their performance is analyzed in section 6 and the remaining conclusions are in section 7.

2 Service Policy Management

The following use cases clearly show the need for some kind of service policy management.

Use Case 1: Appliance Control. When both a power saving service and a home surveillance service use a lighting service to toggle the lights on-off status, some rules should be in place to govern the priorities. We do not want the power saving service turning off the lights when the home surveillance service detects some suspicious activities and tries to turn the lights on.

Use Case 2: Content Management. When there are two digital photograph albums, each image, from a common set of images, should be displayed in only one album at a time. The digital photograph albums are OSGi bundles, and the images are OSGi services. One of the two albums is a master album, each image shown in this album, should not be shown in the other album, the slave.

The current OSGi Specifications are not sufficient to support the use cases. They do not allow fine grained service management and only support a flat view on the Service Registry also pointed out by [12]. A service exported by a bundle can be used by all bundles. The Permissions Admin Specification (R3) and the Conditional Permission Admin Specification (R4), provide means of managing access to a service, but do not define a model of behaviour. What should happen when the usage of a service is prohibited for a specific bundle? Furthermore their management capabilities do not correspond with the dynamic nature of the Service Platform. In order to support fine grained service management two models are proposed and implemented.

Model 1: Framework Extensions. In this model bundles are unaffected, yet the OSGi framework is slightly extended. Great care should be taken to make the extensions as 'natural' as possible, meaning the extensions follow the design philosophy of the service platform.

Model 2: Bundle Adaptations. In this model the OSGi Service Platform is not affected, allowing the model to be implemented as a set of bundles that are backward compatible with any OSGi R3 platform. Yet in this model the bundles that wish to support policies are adapted.

There are a number of important criteria to evaluate; backward compatibility with legacy OSGi Service Platforms or bundles, performance, usability, footprint, transparency. The complete set of criteria is listed in Table 1 and will be explained int the remaining sections of the paper.

Table 1. Comparison of two approaches to support service policies: the framework extensions model allows backward compatibility with existing OSGi bundles while the bundle adaptation model can be plugged into legacy OSGi service platforms

	Model 1: Framework Extensions	**Model 2: Bundle Adaptations**
Legacy bundles	supported	supported but at a price: use of AOP or conversion tool
System Services	supported	not supported
Legacy OSGi frameworks	not supported	supported
Footprint size	minimal	minimal increase with number of bundles
Performance issues	minimal	minimal when using a conversion tool or considerable when using dynamic AOP
Programming model	transparent	developers aware of policies or transparent when using a conversion tool or AOP
Extra benefits	rule logic and language independent; subcomponents useful for: monitoring service behaviour, profiling; could be used for other means than policy handling, such as configuring and debugging	

3 Model 1: Framework Extensions

The model as shown in Fig. 1 contains three separate components, their roles, implications and implementations are discussed below.

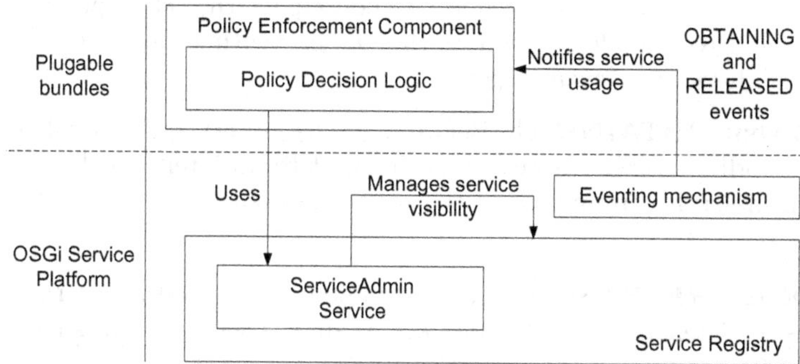

Fig. 1. Global decomposition and operation of model 1: Framework extensions. The Eventing mechanism, the Service Admin and the Policy Enforcement Component work together extending the OSGi Service Platform with service policy capabilities.

Eventing Mechanism. The subsystem gives notifications when a service is being obtained or released. The subsystem can only be implemented as a direct hook into the OSGi framework.

ServiceAdmin Service. The ServiceAdmin service is a system service that offers an interface to manage the visibility of a service toward a bundle. The service can only be implemented as a direct hook into the OSGi framework.

Policy Enforcement Component. The PEC processes the information provided by the eventing mechanism and makes decisions based on that information to adjust the service's visibility towards the bundles. The PEC is a standalone bundle and does not need framework modification, it just uses the newly provided capabilities and is common for both models as described in section 5.

3.1 Service Event Extensions

The OSGi specification (R3-R4), currently offers three kinds of service events. A bundle may wish to register a ServiceListener and act on those events.

ServiceEvent.REGISTERED. When a bundle offers a service to the platform, it registers the service in the platform's service registry. A registered service event is issued.

ServiceEvent.MODIFIED. When the properties of the service are changed by the owning bundle, a modified service event is sent.

ServiceEvent.UNREGISTERING. An unregistering service event is generated when a service is about to be removed from the service registry.

Yet two other major service related 'actions', the obtaining and the releasing of a service, have no corresponding event, although they are indicated by the getService and the ungetService API method calls. When investigating the service usage one must always use the request response pattern (active polling) instead of the event driven model. Therefore the OSGi eventing mechanism should be extended with two new event types:

ServiceEvent.OBTAINING. Before a service object is delivered to the requesting bundle, a service event should be sent to all interested listeners, indicating which service (by means of the service reference) is requested by which bundle.

ServiceEvent.RELEASED. After a bundle released a certain service object, all interested listeners should be notified. Again the service event should denote which bundle is releasing the service.

It should be noted that the OSGi spec had foreseen future additions to the service event types. The class org.osgi.framework.ServiceEvent was adjusted to handle the two new event types.

```
public class ServiceEvent extends EventObject {

  public final static int REGISTERED = 0x00000001;
  public final static int MODIFIED = 0x00000002;
  public final static int UNREGISTERING = 0x00000004;
  public final static int OBTAINING = 0x00000008;              *
  public final static int RELEASED = 0x00000010;               *

  private transient ServiceReference reference;
  private transient int type;
  private transient Bundle bundle;                             *

  public ServiceEvent(int type, ServiceReference reference) {
    this(type, reference, reference.getBundle());              *
  }
  public ServiceEvent(int type, ServiceReference reference,    *
                      Bundle bundle) {                         *
    super(reference);
    this.reference = reference;
    this.type = type;
    this.bundle = bundle;                                      *
  }
  public ServiceReference getServiceReference() {
    return (reference);
  }
  public Bundle getBundle() {                                  *
    return (bundle);                                           *
  }                                                            *
  public int getType() {
    return (type);
  }
}
```

The changes are reflected by an asterix (*) and are fairly straightforward. The only real interface change is the extra getBundle method. It gets the bundle responsible for causing the event; the bundle that is registering, modifying, unregistering, obtaining or releasing the service. Thus the role of the bundle depends on the event type, it is the bundle owning the service in case of a registering, modifying or unregistering event and it is the bundle using the service in case of an obtaining or releasing event.

An obvious choice for listening to these new service events would be the existing ServiceListener interface. That approach has three disadvantages. First, there is no control over which listener will be notified first. In some cases one may wish to create some kind of manager that reacts upon an obtaining request. They would prefer to get notified before other bundles are notified.

As a second disadvantage, each time a service is requested or released all listeners are notified. This means a big performance loss, since services are obtained and released a lot, (as shown in Table 2) especially at peak moments during bootstrap or shutdown and to a lesser extent at bundle deployment time. Besides those moments the service platform is rather stable. The performance impact of having many listeners is analysed in section 6.

Table 2. The number of events that were processed by the framework when a bootstrap is immediately followed by a shutdown. The different configurations use the Knopflerfish[13] http service, desktop and tray icons (windows configuration).

Configuration	**init**	**http**	**desktop**	**windows**	**desktop-http**
Number of bundles	3	9	10	12	15
Event type			**Counts**		
REGISTERED	2	5	16	17	20
MODIFIED	0	0	0	0	0
OBTAINING	3	6	67	72	83
RELEASED	3	6	67	72	83
UNREGISTERING	2	5	16	17	20

The third disadvantage: bundles that erroneously rely on the fact that there are only three service event types are broken.

```
public class WrongListener implements ServiceListener {

  public void serviceChanged(ServiceEvent event) {
    if (event.getType() == ServiceEvent.REGISTERED ||
        event.getType() == ServiceEvent.UNREGISTERING){
      // Do something
    }
    else {
      // Make the wrong assumption that the event type is MODIFIED
    }
  }
}
```

To avoid such mistakes one should always use the switch statement, unfortunately not all bundle developers do.

To solve all three disadvantages a new interface that extends ServiceListener was defined. The SynchronousServiceListener (cf. SynchronousBundleListener) interface outline:

```
public abstract interface ServiceListener extends EventListener {
    public abstract void serviceChanged(ServiceEvent event);
}

public abstract interface SynchronousServiceListener extends ServiceListener {
}
```

All notifications are handled by the inherited serviceChanged method. The service platform delivers both the existing as the newly added event types to the SynchronousServiceListener, whereas ServiceListeners only receive the old service events. This solves the performance and the legacy listener problem in one effort. Furthermore all events are delivered to the SynchronousServiceListeners before they are delivered to the ServiceListeners. Now, the three disadvantages are resolved.

Using the new service event types one can observe and profile the service usage of a bundle or of a service, making it easier to debug. For example one could build a debug tool, where authorized service usage (per bundle) is logged and unauthorized or unpredicted usage is reported. Furthermore one could build watches on services. To illustrate the capabilities of these extra advantages a simple logging example is shown below.

```
public class SynchronousServiceListenerImpl implements SynchronousServiceListener {
  public void serviceChanged(ServiceEvent event) {
    System.out.print("[SSL](" + event.getServiceReference()
        + ")(" + event.getBundle() +")(");
    switch(event.getType()){
      case ServiceEvent.REGISTERED:
        System.out.print("REGISTERED");
        break;
      case ServiceEvent.MODIFIED:
        System.out.print("MODIFIED");
        break;
      case ServiceEvent.OBTAINING:
        System.out.print("OBTAINING");
        break;
      case ServiceEvent.RELEASED:
        System.out.print("RELEASED");
        break;
      case ServiceEvent.UNREGISTERING:
        System.out.print("UNREGISTERING");
        break;
    }
    System.out.println(")");
  }
}
```

The main difference between a plain old listener and the SynchronousServiceListener is that the old service listener will never receive OBTAINING or RELEASED events. In fact, legacy listeners omit the two cases. The difference in operation is shown in Fig. 2. Both listeners can be added to the framework the same way using the bundle context; no new API method is required and the same filter rules can be applied to both synchronous and non-synchronous service listeners.

```
bc.addServiceListener(new ServiceListenerImpl());
bc.addServiceListener(new SynchronousServiceListenerImpl());
```

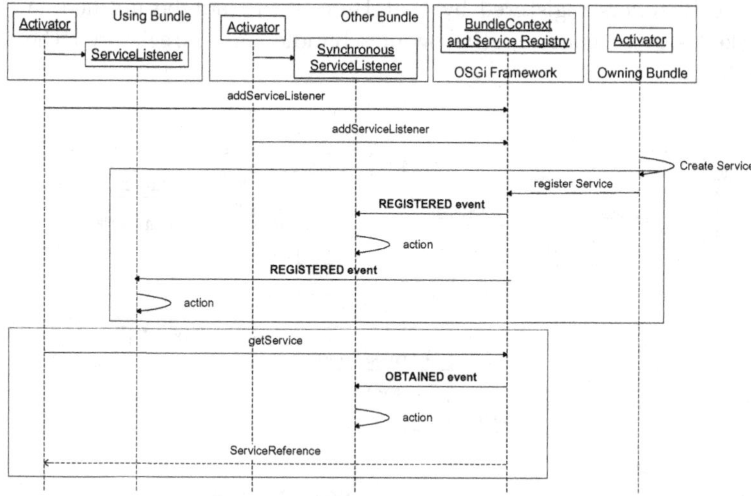

Fig. 2. Sequence diagram showing the actions following registration or obtaining a service. Note that the SynchronizedServiceListener is notified first and the plain old service listener is not notified in case of the obtaining event. Consider the start method of the bundle's activator class as the 'main' method of a normal Java program.

3.2 Service Registry Extensions

In order to support service policies, we need more control over which bundle may use which service. The security facilities within the OSGi platform offer some control, but are rather static. In fact once a service usage is granted it is hard to return on that decision, because security checks are only done when the service is first requested. Denying access afterwards comes only in effect when the service is released and requested a second time. The model clearly lacks essential functionality if one wishes to revoke a service from a using bundle.

In this proposal, a bundle gets a filtered view on the service registry. A management interface called the ServiceAdmin service is available for fine-tuning that view and is listed below.

```
public interface ServiceAdmin {

  public void setServiceVisibility(ServiceReference serviceReference,
    Bundle bundle, boolean visible);

  public ServiceReference [] getInVisibleServices (Bundle bundle);

  public boolean isVisible(ServiceReference serviceReference, Bundle bundle);
}
```

A service can be made invisible for a bundle by using the setServiceVisibility method. The service visibility status towards a bundle can be analyzed by the two other methods. Bundles that are blocked from seeing certain services will not see them when invoking a getServiceReference on the BundleContext, and ServiceListeners registered by that Bundle will not be notified. As far as the blocked service concerns the owning bundle has unregistered the service (cf. Fig. 3).

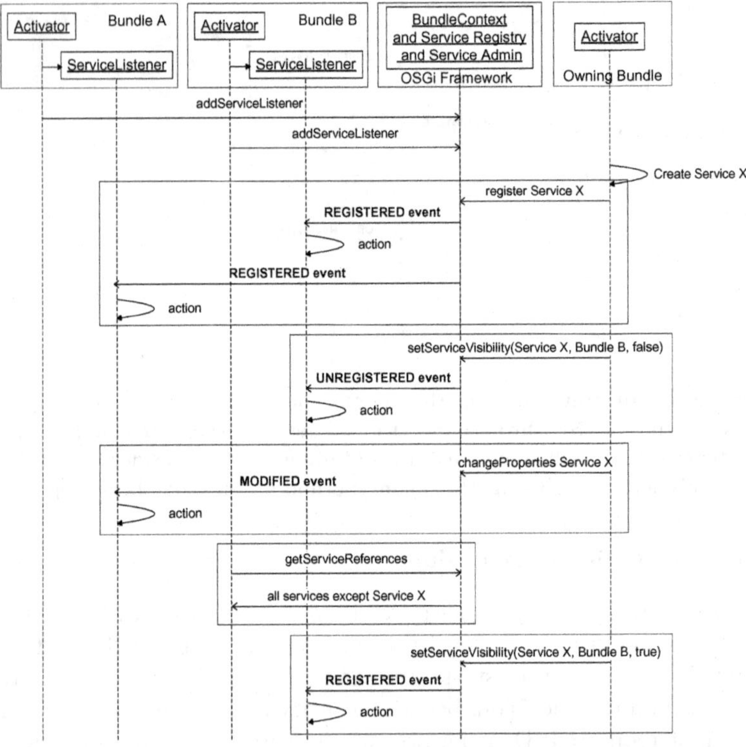

Fig. 3. Sequence diagram showing the actions and consequences when using the ServiceAdmin service

The concept of filtering has already been used in the OSGi platform R3, when a bundle does not have the right permission. Or in release R4, where due to the support of multiple packages, service requests by interface name or LDAP filter may cause returning a non class compatible service, which is thus filtered out. Where the standard OSGi frameworks just do filtering, our adaptation sends events, notifying bundles that the service they are using has been unregistered. That event is only delivered to the one blocked bundle. In fact that bundle thinks the service is no longer available, and thus releases the service, while other bundles do not receive the unregistered event, and are still using the service. When the service gets unblocked for our blocked bundle, a registered event is sent towards the blocked bundle, which thinks the service is newly available and can start using it. As mentioned before while being in blocked state, the bundle does not receive any event notification of the service (As far as the blocked bundle is concerned the service does not exist).

4 Model 2: Bundle Adaptations

The functional requirements for this model are exactly the same as for model 1. Interested bundles should still be notified of the service usage behaviours, as well as they should be able to manage the service visibility. Therefore the three main components, the Eventing mechanism, the Service Admin service and the Policy Enforcement Component stay exactly the same. Two non functional requirements are added, first the model should not require any OSGi framework extensions (should run on every OSGi framework) and secondly, the model should support legacy bundles (bundles and their developers are unaware of the policy management component). The model is shown in Fig. 4.

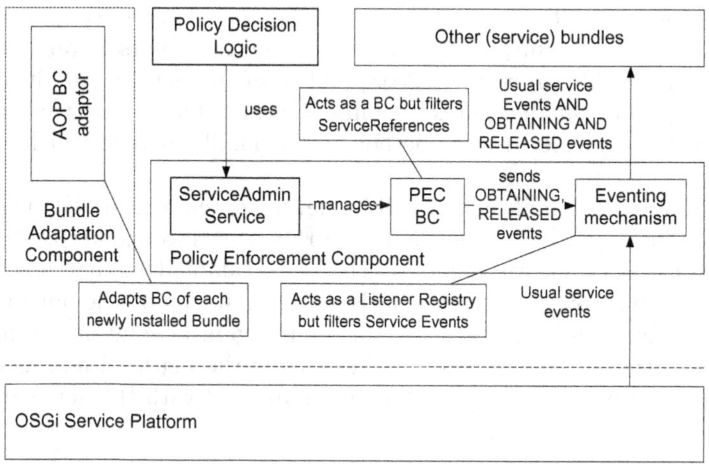

Fig. 4. Global decomposition and operation of model 2: bundle adaptations. All components that were placed inside the OSGi Service Platform are now placed in separate bundles.

4.1 Removing the Framework Extensions

When shifting these components out of the OSGi framework some problems arise.

Eventing Mechanism. Two problems are manifested, first how can this subcomponent discover the exact time a service is obtained or released? And secondly, how can it filter out events for invisible services?

ServiceAdmin Service. Again there are two problems to deal with. How can it send the unregistered event for a service towards a bundle and thus making the service invisible for that bundle? And how can it filter out invisible services when a bundle issues the getServiceReferences method on the bundle context?

Policy Enforcement Component. The PEC is already a standalone bundle and is common for both models as described in section 5.

A solution to all of those problems can be found by wrapping the bundle context and providing the bundle with a special bundle context. The bundle context is the bundle's interface towards the framework. When a bundle requests or releases a service it will invoke the getService or ungetService on the bundle context. The wrapping bundle context intercepts those calls and this solves the first problem.

Service listeners are registered with the OSGi framework by invoking the registerServiceListener method on the bundle context. At that time the wrapping bundle context can choose to add the listener to the eventing mechanism instead of adding it to the framework. The eventing mechanism now has full control over all service listeners, which solves the second problem. It listens to the framework and filters out service events before delivering the events to the service listeners. As a surplus it can send specialized events towards a certain service listener, which solves the first problem of the Service Admin. Furthermore the wrapping bundle context can filter out invisible services when a bundle invokes the getServiceReferences method on the bundle context, which solves the last problem.

By wrapping the bundle context all framework extensions are eliminated, but at a price. The policy enforcement framework now has to manage and maintain all service listeners and the bundles need to be adapted so they are provided with the wrapping bundle context. In the long run wrapping the bundle context has another small disadvantage. It is not robust against evolutionary changes in the OSGi platform. That is, if future versions of the platform add methods to the bundle context the wrapper needs to be updated with the new methods as well.

4.2 Bundle Adaptations

Supplying a bundle with a wrapping bundle context can be done using AOP or possibly by Java 5 annotations. Depending on the AOP implementation used it may introduce new package dependencies on the AOP library, and the host JVM should support AOP. Since the OSGi platform is targeted at J2ME CDC Foundation Profile and upward, Java 5 is not always a possible option. For that reason the AOP and Java 5 annotations are not feasible.

An alternative approach uses a bundle conversion tool. The tool adds a new bundle activator and adapts the bundle manifest so that the framework will call the new activator. The new bundle activator creates a wrapping bundle context and then calls the old activator with the wrapping bundle context. This approach does not tweak or touch the original code. The tool itself is also a bundle and can be applied automatically whenever a new bundle is installed, using the *'double install'* technique as shown in Fig. 5.

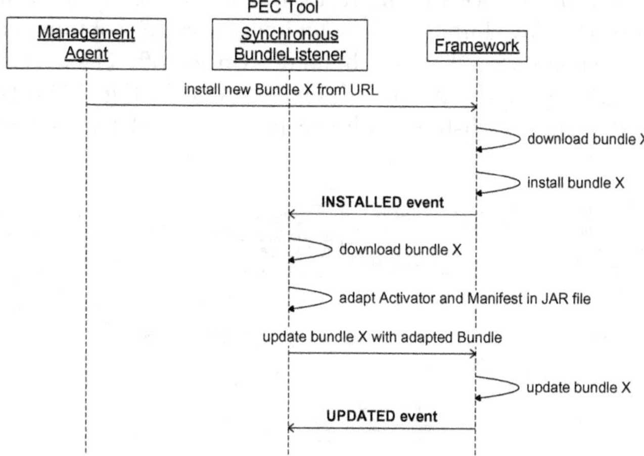

Fig. 5. This figure shows the 'double install' mechanism, the tool bundle acts upon install events, downloads the jar a second time, makes adaptations and updates the bundle.(In R4 it is possible to get the jar entries)

5 A Policy Enforcement Component

The policy enforcement component is a separate bundle and is common for both models. The proposed models provide a sufficient toolset to implement any kind of service policy management component. In fact, the PEC's decision logic could be provided and implemented by third parties using different technologies, e.g. hard coded rules, XML configuration, rule based, etc.

A simple PEC implementation for use case 2 could look like the code below.

```
public class SynchronousServiceListenerImpl implements SynchronousServiceListener {

  private Bundle master, slave;
  private ServiceAdmin admin;

  public SynchronousServiceListenerImpl(Bundle master, Bundle slave, ServiceAdmin admin) {
    this.master = master;
    this.master = slave;
    this.admin = admin;
  }
  public void serviceChanged(ServiceEvent event) {
    ServiceReference ref = event.getServiceReference();
    switch(event.getType()){
      case ServiceEvent.OBTAINING:
        if (master.getBundleId() == event.getBundle().getBundleId()){
            admin.setServiceVisibility(ref,slave,false);
        } break;
      case ServiceEvent.RELEASED:
        if (master.getBundleId() == event.getBundle().getBundleId()){
            admin.setServiceVisibility(ref,slave,true);
        } break;
    }
  }
}
```

The listener uses the ServiceAdmin service to control the visibility of the image services towards the slave bundle. When an image service is obtained by the master bundle the visibility for the slave bundle is turned off. The overall operation is shown in Fig. 6 and the outcome is demonstrated in Fig. 7. Furthermore an OSGi filter makes sure the listener only receives events related to image services.

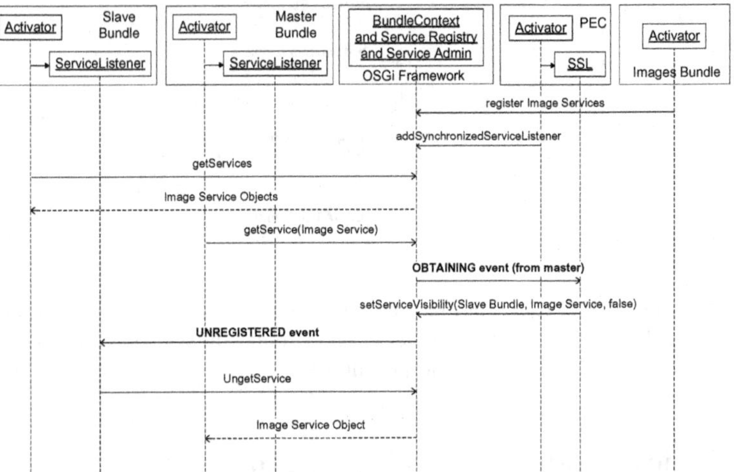

Fig. 6. Sequence diagram showing how the policy enforcement reacts when the master bundle is requesting a managed service

master album obtaining the image services

slave album forced to release the image services

Fig. 7. Demonstration of the complete policy enforcement framework. The system can be used for configuring the Knopflerfish desktop. Each graphical desktop component can be made invisible since each component is a service. The proof of concept implementation does not make the visibility rules persistent across a framework restart, but this could be done easily by saving the persistent service IDs and bundle IDs.

6 Performance

In section 3 the SynchronousServiceListener was introduced as a way to reduce the performance impact of the models. Having obtaining and released delivered to more listeners would result in a reduced overall performance as shown in the Fig. 8, so delivering to a reduced set of specialized listeners performs better.

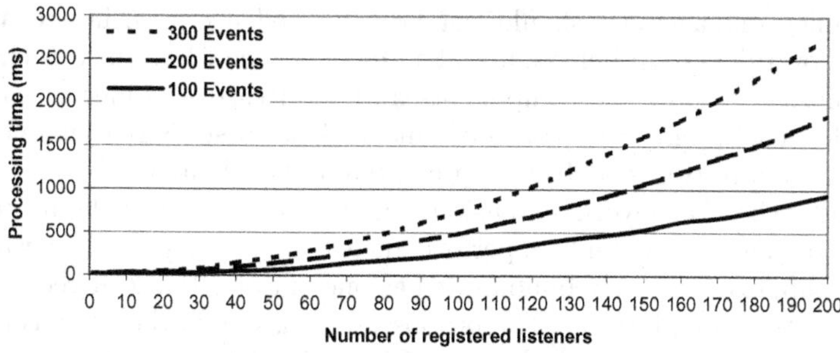

Fig. 8. Measured times needed for the delivery of 100, 200 and 300 obtaining and released events. The actual event handling is not included. The information from table 2 shows that the delivery of 100 events is a realistic amount of events during a peak moment. Furthermore delivery to all listeners is not very scalable.

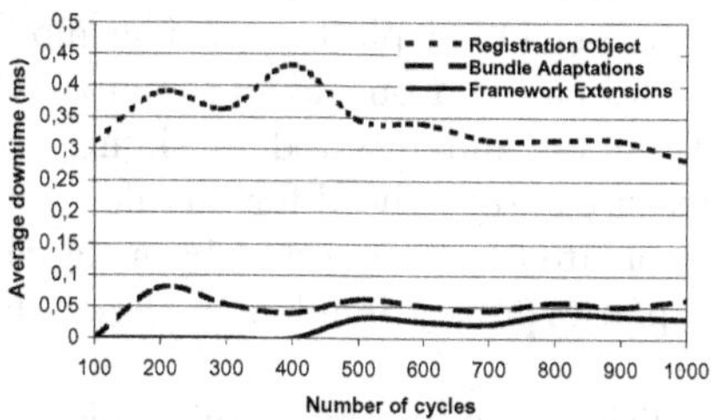

Fig. 9. Average downtime

Fig. 10. Absolute downtime

A second series of test (cf. Fig. 9, Fig. 10) were performed to analyze the impact of changing the visibility of a service. In the test setup a bundle is measuring the downtime of a service. (The time in ms it cannot use the service). A service is brought down and up by changing the visibility using the ServiceAdmin service (a cycle). The two models are compared against each other. Furthermore they are compared against the situation where the bundle owning the service, unregisters and reregisters the service by using the ServiceRegistration object and the bundle context.

As expected the standard third method, which does not allow service policies, performs worst. When the service was brought down and up a 1000 times, the absolute downtime is more then 250 ms. The average downtime for the standard method is about 0.3 ms. The same test for the bundle adaptations model results in an absolute downtime of 62 ms and an average downtime of 0.05 ms. And finally the best results were obtained using the framework extension model where an absolute downtime of 32 ms and an average downtime of 0.03 ms.

7 Conclusions

This paper indicated the need for component and service integration frameworks in a multi-vendor environment. Furthermore, as shown in use cases 1 and 2, service policy management should not be neglected if one wishes to avoid inconsistent overall system behaviour. The OSGi Service Platform was chosen for its capabilities to integrate components and services from different providers. The platform was analyzed and found insufficient to support dynamic service policies. Therefore two models were presented and evaluated.

Although the framework extensions model is more feasible in terms of architectural design, capabilities, performance, transparency and backward compatibility support for legacy bundles, it has one major setback; it requires modifications to the core platform. The proposed extensions to the platform are still within the design philosophy of the OSGi Service Platform and great care is being taken to avoid changes in the OSGi programming model. This approach results in extensions that do not have any impact on the development of bundles. In fact these extensions are completely transparent to both the providing and the using bundles.

The key requirement that needed to be fulfilled in the bundle adaptations model was backward compatibility with existing OSGi platforms. The model was defined as a pluggable set of bundles and can run on any R3 compatible platform. Achieving this goal created a trade-off and resulted in slightly reduced performance, a more complex architecture and the need for bundles to be adapted. Luckily the adaptation can be automated by a tool and by using the double install mechanism plugged into the platform as a bundle. In short, this approach is ready to go.

Both models offer a complete set of capabilities to implement a policy management component as demonstrated in section 5. Finally we propose to incorporate the framework extensions within a future release of the OSGi Service Platform.

Acknowledgements

This research has been partly funded by the IBBT-TCASE project [14] which focuses on service delivery to the end-user environment, service and business logic execution and common service capabilities.

References

1. ILOG JRules,
   http://www.ilog.com/products/jrules/
2. Jena A Semantic Web Framework for Java,
   http://jena.sourceforge.net/
3. The Open Services Gateway Initiative, OSGi Service Platform Release 3, IOS Press, Amsterdam, The Netherlands, March 2003. http://www.osgi.org/
4. The OSGi Alliance, OSGi Service Platform Core Specification Release 4, October 2005. http://www.osgi.org/
5. Oscar - An OSGi framework implementation http://oscar.objectweb.org/
6. Apache Felix Project http://incubator.apache.org/felix/
7. Humberto Cervantes, Richard S. Hall, Service Binder,
   http://gravity.sourceforge.net/servicebinder

8. The OSGi Alliance, OSGi Service Platform Service Compendium Release 4, October 2005. http://www.osgi.org/
9. Humberto. Cervantes and Richard .S. Hall. Automating Service Dependency Management in a Service-Oriented Component Model, Proceedings of the Sixth Component-Based Software Engineering Workshop, May 2003, pp. 91-96.
10. Almut Herzog, Nahid Shahmehri, Problems Running Untrusted Services as Java Threads, In Certification and Security in Inter-Organizational E-Services. E. Nardelli, M. Talamo (eds). Pages: 19-32. Springer Verlag. 2005.
11. The Java Community Process,
JSR 121: Application Isolation API Specification,
JSR 278: Resource Management API for Java ME,
JSR 284: Resource Consumption Management API,
http://www.jcp.org/
12. Richard .S. Hall and Humberto. Cervantes. An OSGi Implementation and Experience Report, Proceedings of the IEEE Consumer Communications and Networking Conference, January 2004.
13. The Knopflerfish Project,
http://www.knopflerfish.org/
14. IBBT, The Interdisciplinary institute for BroadBand Technology,
http://www.ibbt.be/

A Process for Resolving Performance Trade-Offs in Component-Based Architectures

Egor Bondarev[1], Michel Chaudron[1], and Peter de With[2]

[1] Eindhoven University of Technology, System Architectures and Networking group
5600 MB, Eindhoven, The Netherlands
[2] LogicaCMG, 5605 JB, Eindhoven, The Netherlands
e.bondarev@tue.nl

Abstract. Designing architectures requires the balancing of multiple system quality objectives. In this paper, we present techniques that support the exploration of the quality properties of component-based architectures deployed on multiprocessor platforms. Special attention is paid to real-time properties and efficiency of resource use. The main steps of the process are (1) a simple way of modelling properties of software and hardware components, (2) from the component properties, a model of an execution architecture is composed and analyzed for system-level quality attributes, (3) for the composed system, selected execution scenarios are evaluated, (4) Pareto curves are used for making design trade-offs explicit. The process has been applied to several industrial systems. A Car Radio Navigation system is used to illustrate the method. For this system, we consider architectural alternatives, show their specification, and present their trade-off with respect to cost, performance and robustness.

1 Introduction

A major challenge in system development is finding the best balance between different quality requirements that a system has to meet. Time-to market constraints require that design decisions be taken as early as possible. To address this challenge, the architect should be able to solve a number of orthogonal issues: a) construct the component architecture satisfying the functional requirements, b) evaluate (predict) the extra-functional quality properties of the composed architecture, and c) identify several architecture alternatives that satisfy both types of requirements. Essentially, he needs a means to efficiently explore this architectural design space against multidimensional quality attribute scale.

A concurrent trend is the assembly of systems out of existing components (which can be both software and hardware), as this reduces development time and cost. Within this component-based approach, the challenge of early architecture assessment shifts to the evaluation of global system properties based on the properties of the constituent components. For this reason, the component-oriented society needs to develop techniques for modelling component properties such that these can be composed into a system model. Each model type usually addresses one attribute (performance, behaviour or cost). Upon component

I. Gorton et al. (Eds.): CBSE 2006, LNCS 4063, pp. 254–269, 2006.

integration, models of the same type are composed into a system model of the corresponding system attribute. There has been a broad range of approaches towards this problem, known as *predictable assembly* ([1], [2] and [3]). The CB-SPE approach [4] provides a solid technique for evaluating the performance of component-based software systems. A prediction method based on formal specification of component non-functional properties is presented in [5]. Currently, these approaches focus on prediction of a single quality attribute (QA). To motivate various design trade-offs, assessment of multiple QAs is needed. The process, described in this paper, allows prediction of performance, robustness and cost QAs, and enables design space exploration with respect to these attributes.

The following methods feature multi-objective trade-off analysis. The method presented in [9] uses Petri nets with parameterized interfaces to assess performance and safety. For large system this method becomes computation expensive. Less calculation expensive PISA framework for design space exploration featuring QA prediction have been proposed in [10] for network processor architectures. It uses Real-Time Calculus that abstracts from the state space and has low calculation complexity. Recently proposed SESAME framework [11] uses simulation, application and architecture models to predict performance properties and explore design choices. The SPIE2 framework [12] adds the possibility to optimize the architecture using genetic algorithms. However, none of the last three methods supports designing a system out of conventional component with provides and requires interfaces. Instead, they define a component as an active entity (task or process). In [16] the authors propose compile-time framework that explores and optimizes performance properties of systems built out of active conventional components.

Contribution. In this paper we present the design space exploration (DSE) process that supports both active and passive COTS components. It allows software and hardware composition and mapping the components on the hardware nodes. The process enables accurate prediction of system performance attributes by composition of performance models of individual components. The component performance models are easy to construct and use, which speeds up the architecture assessment time. The supporting RTIE tool, developed by us, helps to construct multiple architecture alternatives and find the optimal solutions against multiple criteria. We illustrate the process by a case study on finding the optimal architecture for the Car Radio Navigation (CRN) system.

The paper is structured as follows. Section 2 explains the requirements of the CRN system to be designed. Section 3 describes our multidimensional DSE process in detail. Section 4 shows how we used the process to design and assess the architectures for CRN system, besides, it reveals the experimental results of the case study. Section 5 concludes the paper.

2 Car Radio Navigation System

We illustrate our process for resolving performance design trade-offs in CBA by designing a Car Radio Navigation system. This CRN system had to be built according to the component-based paradigm on a cost-limited (yet not predefined) hardware platform. However, the major challenge was to find at an early design stage an optimal system architecture in terms of the vital QAs like real-timeliness, robustness and cost. Technically speaking, the goal was the following: *given* a set of functional and extra-functional requirements, as well as a set of software and hardware components, to *determine* a set of architecture solutions, that are optimal with respect to the above-mentioned quality attributes.

Requirements. We divided the requirements into two categories: functional (Fn) and extra-functional (RTn). The main ones are summarized below:
F1: The system shall be able to gradually (scale = 32 grads) change the sound volume.
RT1: The response time of the operation F1 is less than 200 ms (per grade).
F2: The system shall be able to find and retrieve an address specified by the user.
RT2: The response time of the operation F2 is less than 200 ms.
F3: The system should be able to receive and handle Traffic-Message-Channel (TMC) messages.
RT3: The response time of the operation F3 for one message is less than 350 ms.

Functional Decomposition. Requirement analysis led us to a conceptual software view depicted in Fig. 1.

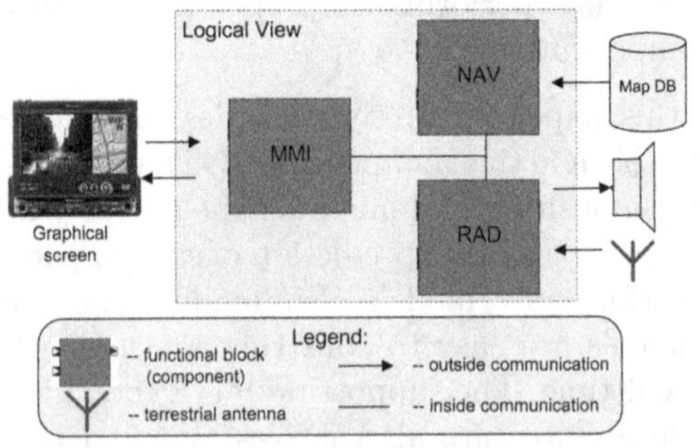

Fig. 1. Overview of the CRN system functionality

The CRN logical view has three major functional blocks:

- The man-machine interface (MMI), that takes care of all interactions with the end-user, such as handling key inputs and graphical display output.
- The navigation functionality (NAV) is responsible for destination entry, route planning and turn-by-turn route guidance giving the driver visual advices. The navigation functionality relies on the availability of a map database and positioning information.
- The radio functionality (RAD) is responsible for tuner and volume control as well as handling of TMC traffic information services.

In the next section, we illustrate our DSE process that enables architecture comparison and supports resolving design trade-offs with respect to multiple performance attributes and cost.

3 Multidimensional Design Space Exploration Process

Fig. 2 depicts our DSE process that uses a component-based architecture as the skeletal structure, onto which the composition of QAs can be performed out of models of individual components. We developed an RTIE (Real-Time Integration Environment) toolset that supports all the steps in the DSE flow. A distinguishing feature of our process is that the analysis is based on the evaluation of a number of key execution *scenarios*. The use of scenarios enables efficient analysis while also enabling the architect to trade modelling effort (modelling multiple scenario's improves the 'coverage' of the behaviour of the system) against confidence in the results. The other cornerstones of the approach are:

- *modelling* of software components, processing nodes, memories and bus links,
- *composition* of system QAs out of these models,
- *prediction of a system timing behaviour and resource usage*, required for real-time system design,
- *pareto curves* for identification of optimal architecture alternatives.

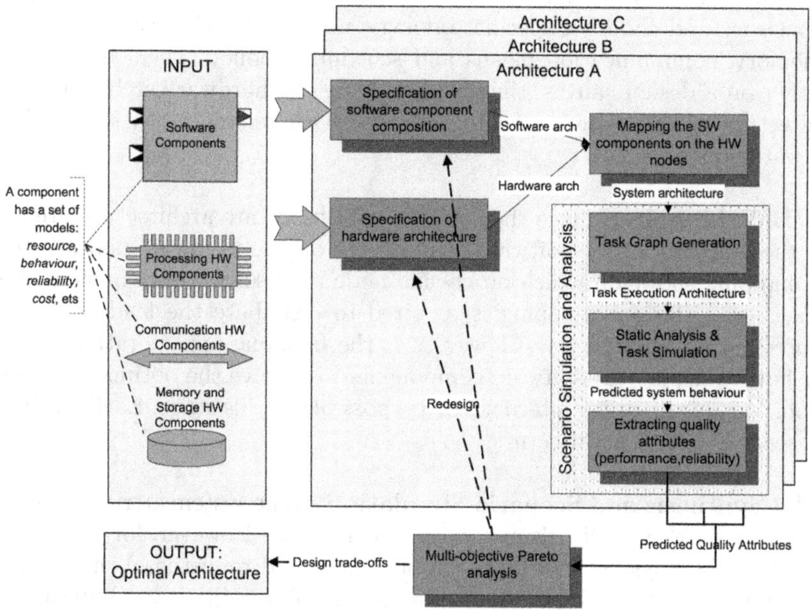

Fig. 2. Multidimensional design space exploration process

Let us outline the process phases. As input for an architecture, the system designer has various third-party hardware and software components (in a repository). Each component should be supplied with a set of models addressing important component attributes, like timeliness, cost, resource use. Relevant types of models for a software (SW) component are: functional, resource and behaviour models. Our example shows that these models can be made with comparatively little effort. Typical models for hardware (HW) components are: memory, communication and processing models.

The following steps are to be done for each architectural alternative (see Fig. 2). Considering more alternative solutions leads to more complete coverage of the design space.

Software Architecture Composition. The designer selects from the (RTIE) repository the software components that together satisfy the defined functional requirements and *may* satisfy extra-functional requirements. The component selection is done by checking the functional models of available components with respect to the functional requirements. The process assumes that the selected components are supplied along with corresponding set of models. By means of the RTIE graphical tool, the designer specifies component composition by instantiating and connecting components. The resulting composition is converted into XML-file with links to the individual component models stored in the repository.

Hardware Architecture Specification. The hardware architecture specification can be done in parallel. In most of the cases, a hardware platform is prespecified. If not, the designer can select available hardware components from a repository and choose a specific topology, number of processing nodes, types of memory, communication means and scheduling policy. Then, he puts these together on a design canvas, thereby specifying the hardware architecture. The architecture is also represented in XML-file with references to the models of hardware nodes.

SW/HW Mapping. Once the software and hardware architecture are specified, the mapping of the software components on the hardware nodes is made. The mapping shows on which processing node each software component should be executed. Efficient mapping is required to distribute the load of hardware resources in an optimal way. However, at the first mapping iteration, it is not clear how to deploy the software components to achieve the optimal load distribution. Various mapping alternatives are possible at this stage. Each alternative represents a system architecture.

Model Synthesis and Scenario Simulation. Some system attributes like *cost* can be found analytically given a static architecture. However, for prediction of other important system attributes (performance and robustness) the behaviour of a system needs to be found. In our process, we obtain these attributes through the *scenario simulation method* [6]. This method synthesize a model of the *task* *execution architecture* by composing *resource* and *behaviour* models of individual software components, *performance* models of hardware nodes and *scenario* model of the constructed software composition. All these models enable parameter-dependent specification. For the details of parameter-dependent modeling the reader is referred to [15]. The following two paragraphs specify models in more detail.

The *resource model* contains parameter-dependent processing and memory requirements of each operation implemented by the component. The resource requirements can be obtained by profiling of each individual component on a reference processor. The reference processor is also specified in the model in order to scale the operation resource requirements to any other processor. The *behaviour model* specifies for each implemented operation a parameter-dependent sequence of external calls to operations offered by other interfaces. The external call is a (synchronous or asynchronous) invocation of other interface's operation made inside the implemented operation. The data for the behaviour model can be obtained by the source-code analysis. The *performance model* of a hardware block specifies its capabilities. A performance model for a processing core defines its instruction type (RISC, CISC or VLIW) and execution frequency. A model for a memory IP block describes a memory type (SRAM, SDRAM, etc), a memory size in MBytes and addressing type. A bus performance model specifies the scheduling protocol (TDMA, CDMA, fare use, etc) and bandwidth size. The data for performance models can be obtained by measurements or from supplier data sheets.

For software composition architecture, the designer defines a set of resource-critical scenarios and for each of them specifies an application *scenario model.* Critical scenarios are the application execution configurations that may introduce processor, memory or bus overload. In the scenario, the designer may specify environmental stimuli (events or thread triggers) that influence the system behaviour. For a stimulus, the designer may define the burst rate, minimal inter-arrival time, period, deadline, offset, jitter, task priority, and so on. By defining the stimuli, the designer specifies autonomous behaviour of the system, or emulates an environmental influence (interrupts, network calls) to the system.

The scenario, resource, behaviour and performance models are synthesized by the RTIE tool. The objective of the synthesis is to reconstruct (generate) the tasks running in the application. Prior to the synthesis, the task-related data is spread over different types of models. For instance, the *task periodicity* may be specified in an application scenario model, whereas the information about the *operation call sequence* comprising the task is spread over corresponding component behaviour models. The compiler combines these two types of data in the task information containing period, jitter, offset, deadline and operation sequence call graph. The synthesis results in the *task execution architecture* that contains parameter-dependent data on the tasks running in the designed system and data on the allocation of these tasks on the software and hardware architectures. An example of this allocation is given in Fig. 3. Here, the system executes three tasks using two processors and five deployed service instances. The

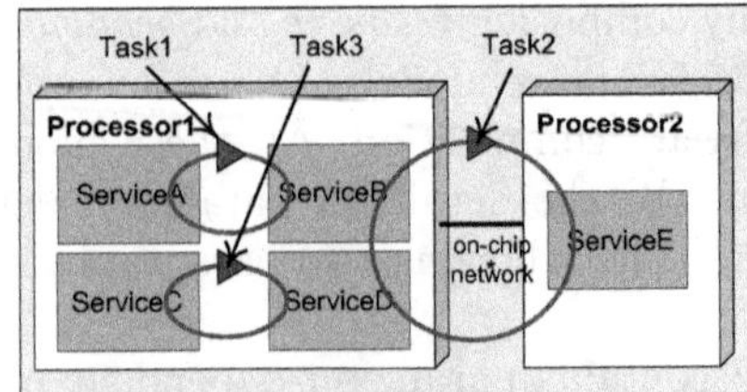

Fig. 3. Task allocation on the component and hardware architecture

Task1 executes on Processor1 and consists of operations offered by ServiceA and ServiceB. The Task3 execution is spread over both processors and includes a communication via the on-chip network. The task executes operations offered by three service instances: ServiceB, ServiceD and ServiceE.

The obtained task execution architecture is a subject for virtual scheduling (simulation). A simulation-based analysis employs virtual schedulers that simulate the execution of the tasks specified in the system model for some period of time. The selection of a scheduling algorithm is dictated by the types of communication lines and operating system used for the designed system. The RTIE tool provides the following virtual schedulers: rate monotonic (RM), deadline monotonic (DM), earliest deadline first (EDF), constant bandwidth server (CBS), time division multiple access (TDMA) and fare-use algorithms. The simulation techniques feature both processing and communication resources scheduling. An example of the simulation results is given in Fig. 4.

The diagram shows the execution timelines of the three processors and the bus-load timeline. For each processor timeline, the tasks executing the operations of the services that are mapped on the processor are shown. For each task instance, its initiation and completion times are given. Beside this, the diagram reflects the time slots when a task instance misses its deadline. The bus-load timeline represents the timed bus utilization done by the communicating operations in these three tasks. The statistics, generated from the simulation timelines, gives the overall data on the predicted task properties and load of the resources.

Quality Attribute Extraction. The *throughput*, *latency* and *resource consumption* QAs are extracted in a straightforward way from the generated task simulation timeline. For other attributes, like *robustness* additional computation is needed. Robustness can be calculated as performance sensitivity to stimuli rate increase. For this, the designer changes the stimuli rate in each of the scenario system models and redo the simulations. Comparison of the new task latencies or resource use with the old values answers the question on how sensitive is the architecture against the input event rate changes.

Multi-objective Pareto Analysis. At this stage, having defined a number of alternative architectures and predicted multiple QAs for each of them, we look for an optimal design alternative. Pareto analysis is a powerful means for resolving conflicting objectives [7]. The multi-objective optimization problem

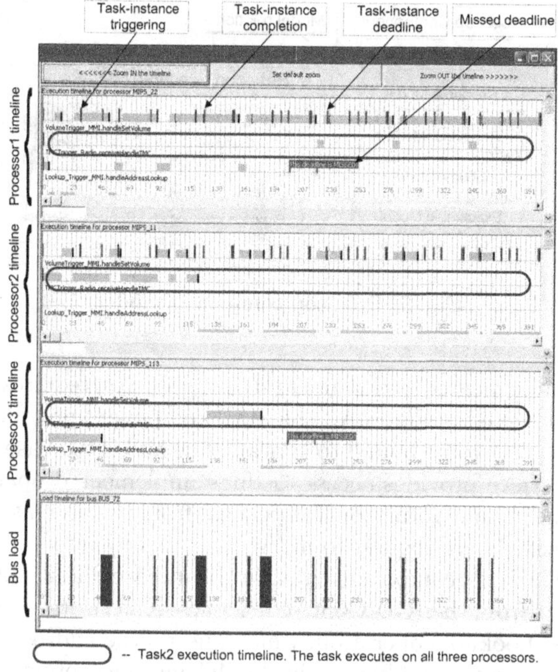

Fig. 4. Execution timelines for tasks on three processors obtained by RMA simulation

does not yield a unique solution, but a set of solutions that are Pareto-optimal. An example of the Pareto analysis is shown in Section 4.4.

4 The Quest for an Optimal CRN Architecture

For this case study, we implemented and packaged three Robocop software components: RAD, MMI and NAV, which correspond to above-mentioned CRN functional blocks. The Robocop component model [8] supports modelling and composition of a wide spectrum of component attributes and is targeted to embedded systems domain. The Robocop component is an open set of models (see Fig. 5).

For example, the functional model specifies the component functionality, while resource model (see Fig. 6.B) specifies resource utilization of the component operations. The executable entity (.dll file) is also considered as a special type of model. A Robocop component can be downloaded from a common repository as a black-box and used for third-party binding. A component developer is responsible for specification of the models. The executable component may include a number of executable entities called services. A service may have provides and requires interfaces. The provides interfaces specify and give access to operations implemented by the service.

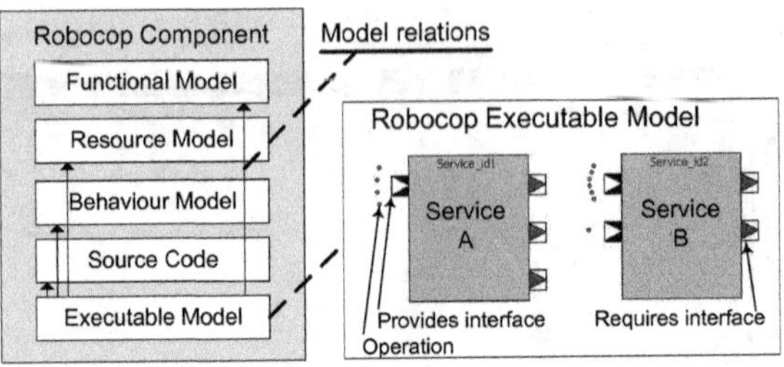

Fig. 5. Robocop component model

The three implemented components, their provides/requires interfaces and operations are depicted in Fig. 6.A. The MMI component provides IGUIControl interface and requires to be bound to IParameters and IDatabase interfaces. The GUIControl interface provides access to three implemented operations: setVolume (handles the volume rotary button request from the user), setAddress (handles the address keyboard request from the user) and updateScreen (updates the GUI display). The NAV component provides IDatabase, ITMC interfaces and requires operations from the IGUIControl interface. The IDatabase interface gives access to addressLookup() operation, which queries the address in the database and finds a path to this address. The ITMC interface provides an access to decodeTMC() operation. The RAD component provides IParameters, IReceiver interfaces and requires ITMC interface. The two operations implemented by this component are adjustVolume() and receiveTMC().

Each component is accompanied by *resource*, *behaviour* (see Fig. 6.B), and *cost* models. The resource model specifies resource requirements per individual operation. The behaviour model describes the operation's underlying calls to operations of other interfaces. Besides, the model may specify a periodic thread triggers (like Posix thread with a periodic timer), if they are implemented inside the component. Both resource and behaviour models are composable, i.e. from a number of behaviour models of constituent components one can generate a system behaviour model. The composition principles are explained in detail in [6]. The resource requirements (CPU claim) has been obtained by profiling of each individual component on a reference RISC processor. The operation behaviour data has been generated from the component source code. For example, the RAD behaviour model describes that the operation adjustVolume() synchronously calls once the IGUIControl. updateScreen() operation. This model also shows the bus usage of the adjustVolume() operation: 4 bytes. That means the operation sends outside (as an argument of updateScreen()) 4 bytes of data.

4.1 Defining Architecture Alternatives

Following the process, we composed a component assembly (see Fig. 7.A) from the available components. We were able to design only one software architecture alternative due to a limited number of available software components. These

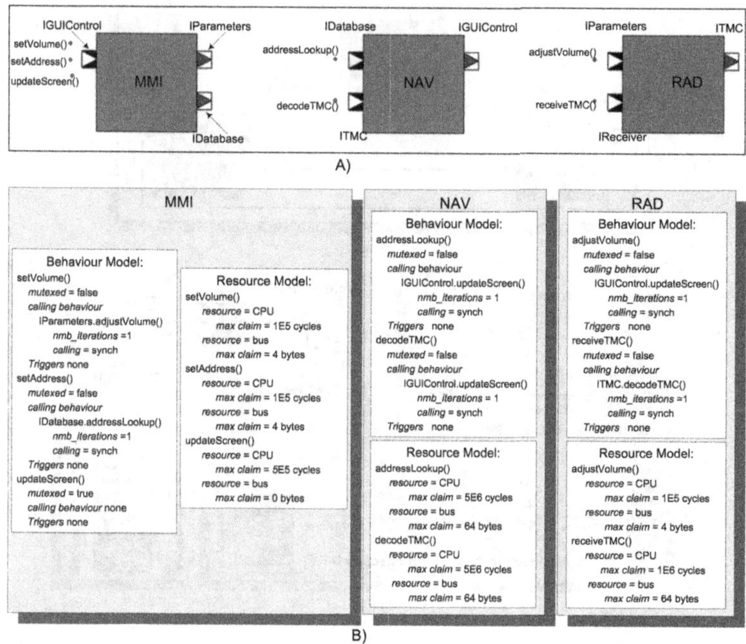

Fig. 6. (A) Components used for the case study; (B) Behaviour and resource models of the selected components

three components were instantiated and bound together via pairs of their provides/requires interfaces. This assembly satisfies the three defined functional requirements: F1, F2 and F3.

The next phase is to define a set of hardware architectures and map the software components onto hardware. We reused five feasible alternative hardware architectures with different mapping schemas proposed in [13] (see Fig. 7.B). For instance, in Architecture A there are three processing nodes connected with a single bus of 72 kbps bandwidth. The MMI_Inst component is executed (mapped) on a 22-MIPS processor, the NAV_Inst component is mapped on a 113-MIPS processor, and RAD_Inst component executes on a 11-MIPS processor. The capacity of the processing nodes and communication infrastructure was taken from the datasheets of several commercially available automotive CPUs. The multi-objective DSE process has been performed for these five solutions.

4.2 Scenarios and Task Generation

For our case study, we selected three distinctive execution scenarios to assess the architecture against the six defined requirements. These scenarios should impose the highest possible load on the hardware resources for accurate evaluation of the real-time requirements RT1, RT2 and RT3.

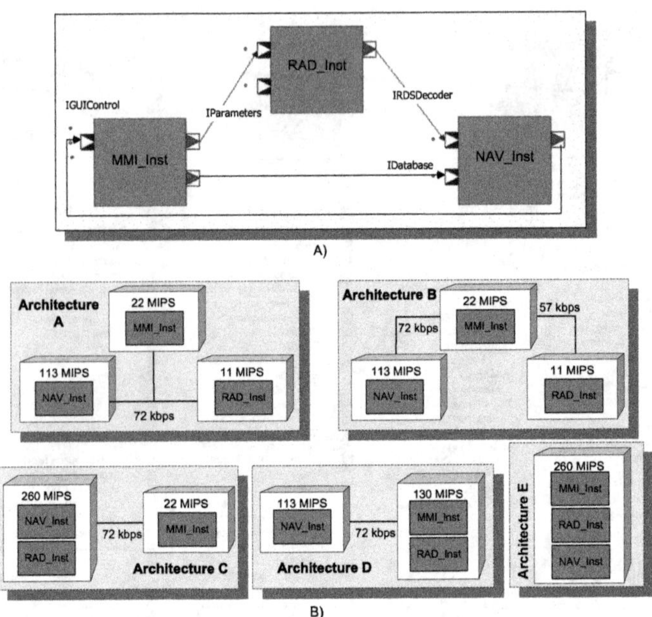

Fig. 7. (A) Software component assembly of the CRN system. (B) Five alternative system architectures to explore.

"Change Volume" Scenario. The user turns the rotary button and expects instantaneous audible and visual feedback from the system. The maximum rotation speed of the button is 1 sec from lowest to highest position. For emulating this user activity, we introduced a VolumeStimulus task trigger, which initiates execution of the IGUIControl.setVolume() operation. The trigger parameters are defined in the following way: the event period is set to 1/32 sec, as the volume button scale contains 32 grades. The task deadline is set to 200 ms, according to R1. The trigger and component assembly resemble a scenario model.

For this scenario, the RTIE tool generated (from the behaviour models of participating components) the message sequence chart (MSC) of operation calls involved in the task execution. The scenario model and obtained MSC are shown in Fig. 8.A. The task is executed periodically (31 ms) and passes through MMI_Inst and RAD_Inst.

"Address Lookup" Scenario. Destination entry is supported by a smart typewriter style interface. The display shows the alphabet and the user selects the first letter of a street. By turning a knob the user can move from letter to letter; by pressing it the user selects the currently highlighted letter. The map database is searched for each letter that is selected and so on. We assume that the worst-case rate of the letter selection is 1 time per second. This user activity was emulated with a LookupStimulus trigger, which initiates execution of the IGUIControl.setAddress() operation. The trigger period was set to 1000 ms. The deadline for the address lookup task is 200 ms, according to RT2.

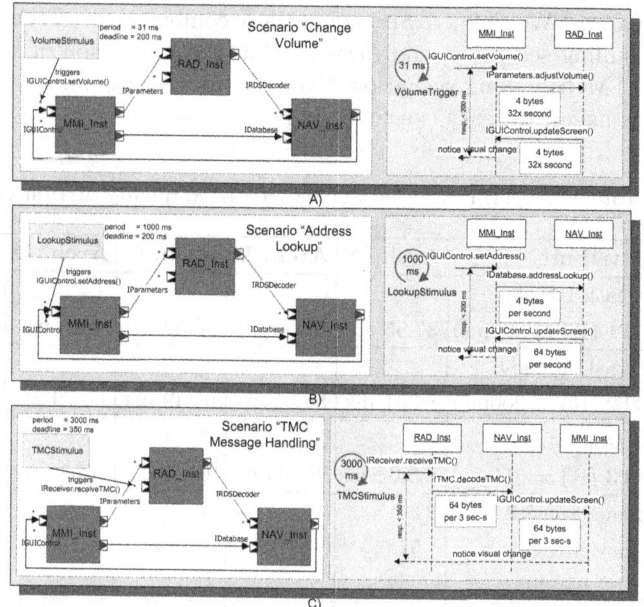

Fig. 8. Model and message sequence chart for scenarios: (A) Change Volume; (B) Address Lookup, and (C) TMC Message Handling

The task-generation procedure outputs the task MSC for this scenario. The obtained scenario model and MSC are shown in Fig. 8.B. The task is executed periodically (1000 ms) and passes the MMI_Inst and NAV_Inst components.

"TMC Message Handling" Scenario. RDS TMC is a digital traffic information that enables automatic replanning of the route in case of traffic jam. Traffic messages are received by the RAD component (in the worst case 1 time per 3 seconds). We introduced a TMCStimulus trigger emulating these TMC messages. The trigger initiates execution of the IReceiver.receiveTMC() operation. The period is set to 3000 ms. The deadline for the TMC handling task is set to 350 ms, according to RT3.

The task-generation procedure resulted in the task MSC for this scenario. The obtained scenario model and task are represented in Fig. 8.C. The task is executed periodically (3000 ms) and passes through three component instances: RAD_Inst, MMI_Inst and NAV_Inst. The fully decoded messages are forwarded to the user.

4.3 Simulation and Attribute Extraction

The scenarios sketched above have an interesting property: they can occur in parallel. TMC messages must be processed while the user changes the volume or enters a destination address at the same time. Therefore, we combined these three scenarios into two in order to get worst-case load on the system resources during simulation. We defined *ScenarioA* as a combination of the SetVolume and TMCHandling scenarios, and *ScenarioB* as a combination of the Address-Lookup and TMCHandling scenarios. From the processing point of view, both new scenarios have two tasks executing in parallel.

Table 1. Experimental data of the predicted quality attributes

Attribute	Arch. A	Arch. B	Arch. C	Arch. D	Arch. E
Max. task latency against RT1 (RT1=200ms)	37.55 ms	37.55 ms	30.52 ms	9.18 ms	3.58 ms
Max. task latency against RT2 (RT2=200ms)	86.51 ms	86.51 ms	61.49 ms	63.79 ms	21.05 ms
Max. task latency against RT3 (RT3=350ms)	325.05 ms	395.05 ms	101.71 ms	114.12 ms	46.02 ms
Performance sensitivity (latency increase for TMC handling)	57.6%	51.1%	3.2%	3.1%	0.0%
Cost, euro	290	305	380	335	340

Following our DSE process, we simulated the execution of these two scenarios for each of the five system architectures. Before simulation, the following pre-processing of the computation and communication time data is performed. For each of the processing nodes, the execution times of all operations to be executed on the node are calculated from the *component resource* and *node performance* models (execution_time = *CPU_claim*_value * processor_speed). The communication time of the operation calls made through the processor boundaries is calculated by dividing the *bus claim* value of an operation on a bus bandwidth value, defined in a bus performance model.

The scenario simulation by preemptive RM algorithm (other policies can also be used) resulted in (a) predicted system timing behaviour description and (b) resource consumption of a system for each scenario and task worst-case latencies. First, we analyzed the predicted *task latencies* against the real-time requirements RT1, RT2 and RT3 for each of the five architectures (see Table 1).

Analyzing the table data, we concluded that except for Architecture B, the rest of the four architectures satisfy the given real-time requirements. The Architecture B does not satisfy the requirement RT3, because it has TMCHandling task latency higher than 350 ms. Architecture A can be considered fast enough; architecture E is the fastest solution. Then, we analyzed the architecture robustness as a performance *sensitivity* to the changes in the input event rates (arrival period of the three stimuli). We increased the data rate of the three stimuli by 5% (i.e. VolumeStimulus to 33.6 events/s, LookupStimulus to 1.05 events/s and TMCStimulus to 0.35 events/s). Afterwards, we re-simulated the adjusted scenarios and obtained new task latencies. The fourth row in Table 1 describes the increase of the latency of the TMC handling task as percentage of the normal latency per architecture. For instance, the end-to-end delay of the TMC message handling task for architecture A increased by 57.6%! This happened due to a high overload of the 22-MIPS processor in this scenario.

The system cost attribute was calculated as a cumulative *cost* of the system hardware and software components. The software component cost has been defined with correlation to the component source code complexity (in reality, the cost of a third-party component is defined by the component producer). The cost of the hardware components was calculated from the available market prices. The total calculated cost for each architecture is given in Table 1. The most expensive architecture was number C due to the costly high-performance processing nodes.

4.4 Analysis of Architecture Alternatives

The performance, robustness and cost attributes were selected as main objectives for our design space exploration. Using the RTIE Pareto analysis tool, we obtained several two-dimensional Pareto graphs. Two of them, *robustness vs. cost* and *performance vs. cost* are depicted in Fig. 9.

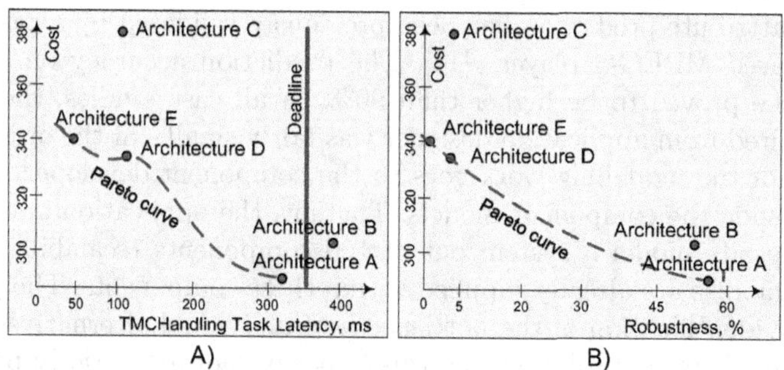

Fig. 9. Pareto exploration graphs based on A) performance vs. cost, B) robustness vs. cost quality attributes

The graphs can be evaluated as follows. The Pareto curve is drawn by connecting the alternatives that are closest to the origin. This curve defines a set of optimal alternatives. With respect to the cost-robustness trade-off (see Fig. 9.B), the optimal architectures are E, D and A, because they create the curve closest to the null-coordinate point. The alternatives C and B are non-optimal. The choice from the three alternative architectures depends on a weighting function (priority) for the cost and robustness attributes. If cost has higher priority then Architecture A should be selected. If performance sensitivity is a critical factor, then the Architecture A is not the best candidate. Moreover, looking at the cost-performance trade-off (see Fig. 9.A), we can observe that TMC task latency for Architecture A is close to its deadline. Thereby, low robustness (57.6%) of Architecture A cannot be tolerated.

With respect to the cost-performance trade-off, again the optimal alternatives are E, D and A, though C is not positioned on the hypothetical ideal Pareto curve. The Architecture B gets out of competition because its TMC task latency is higher than task deadline. Despite of its low cost, the Architecture A with low performance and insufficient robustness can be also omitted.

Concluding, the Architectures E and D can be considered as optimal alternatives. If the cost weighting function is higher than performance or robustness weighting function, the architecture E can be adopted for further development and *vice versa.* In addition, we may also re-iterate the DSE process to achieve acceptable performance for less costly Architecture A. For instance, we can add a new software component TMCHandler, which reduces TMCHandling task latency, or re-dimension one of the processing node. Another optimization technique would be to reduce the cost of the Architecture E, by sacrificing (within acceptable range) its performance and robustness.

5 Conclusion

The proposed DSE process includes the steps of designing, predicting quality attributes and evaluating the architectural alternatives. The accuracy of performance attribute prediction has been previously validated by a case study on a Linux-based MPEG-4 player [14]. The prediction accuracy on the general performance proved to be higher than 90%. In all case studies, the modelling effort required from application designer was fairly small - in the order of hours. The most of the modelling work goes to the component developer, because he should provide the component models. Thereby, the application developer may relatively easily model a system out of 100 components (scalability), because necessary models are already supplied within these components. The process enables early identification of the bottlenecks of individual alternatives and leads to selection of optimal solutions. In this paper we address strictly performance attributes, however the proposed DSE process enables targeting other important QAs, like reliability and availability. This extensibility is realized by open component model structure, in which new model types can be easily added.

Limitations. There are certain limitations of the process. Firstly, the component behaviour model represents an abstraction of the component source code, leaving out implementation details. That eases the assessment of the component and system behaviour, but limits the specification of all aspects of the source code, like complex parameter-dependent loops and condition forks implemented inside a component operation. Secondly, to explore the design space of a system, a designer can *only* select the components that already contains required cost, resource and behaviour models. Moreover, the QAs that are system-wide, like safety and security, cannot be easily localized and modeled at the component level. Thirdly, introduction of scenarios requires that the designer has a good understanding of the system-environment interaction aspects, and has some analytical skills in identifying the scenarios. The scenario identification criteria is our ongoing work. Finally, the RTIE tool does not facilitate generation of complete design space. Instead, the designer is responsible for identification of the architecture alternatives.

In our future plans, we focus on development of automated optimization algorithms as a back-end for this exploration process. Genetic algorithms can be used to generate better alternatives by varying the topology, mapping and scheduling-policy of an architecture.

References

1. I. Crnkovic and M. Larsson. *Building Reliable Component-based Software Systems*, Artech House, 2002
2. K.C. Wallnau, "Volume III: A Technology for Predictable Assembly from Certifiable Components", *CMU/ESI-2003-TR-009 report*, April 2003.
3. S.A. Hissam, *et al.*, "Packaging Predictable Assembly with Prediction-Enabled Component Technology", *CMU/ESI-2001-TR-024 report*, November 2001.
4. A. Bertolino, R. Mirandola, "CB-SPE Tool: Putting Component-Based Performance Engineering into Practice", *Proc. 7th Symp. on CBSE*, Edinburgh, UK. Vol. 3054 of LNCS, Springer (2004) 233-248.
5. S. Zschaler, "Towards a Semantic Framework for Non-functional Specifications of Component-Based Systems", *Proc. 30th EUROMICRO Conf.*, France, Sep. 2004.
6. E. Bondarev, *et al*, "Predicting Real-Time Properties of Component Assemblies: a Scenario-Simulation Approach", *Proc. 30th Euromicro Conf.*, Sep. 2004.
7. C.A. Mattson and A.Messac, "A Non-Deterministic Approach to Concept Selection Using s-Pareto Frontiers", *Proc. ASME DETC 2002*, Canada, Sep. 2002.
8. "Robocop: Robust Open Component Based Software Architecture", http://www.hitech-projects.com/euprojects/robocop/deliverables.htm
9. Schmidt, H.W. *et al*, "Modelling Predictable Component-based Distributed Control Architectures", *Proc OORTDS workshop*, 2003, 339-346
10. L. Thiele *et al*, Design Space Exploration of Network Processor Architectures, *Network Processor Design: Volume 1*, Morgan Kaufmann Publishers, 2002.
11. A. D. Pimentel *et al*, "A Systematic Approach to Exploring Embedded System Architectures at Multiple Abstraction Levels", *IEEE Trans. on Computers*, Vol. 55), Feb. 2006.
12. M. Zitzler *et al*, "SPEA2: Improving the performance of the strength pareto evolutionary algorithm", *Technical Report TIK-Report 103*, ETH, Zurich, May 2001.
13. E. Wandeler, L. Thiele, M. Verhoef, "System Architecture Evaluation Using Modular Performance Analysis - A Case Study", *Proc. 1th ISOLA Symposium*, 2004.
14. E. Bondarev *et al* "On Predictable Software Design of Real-Time MPEG-4 Video Applications", *SPIE Proc. VCIP 2005*. China. July, 2005.
15. E. Bondarev *et al.*, "Modelling of Input-Parameter Dependency for Performance Predictions of Component-Based Embedded Systems", *In Proc. of 31th Euromicro Conference; CBSE Track*, Porto, September 2005.
16. J. Fredriksson *et al*, "Optimizing Resource Usage in Component-Based Real-Time Systems", *Proc 8th CBSE Symposium*, May, 2005.

A Model Transformation Approach for the Early Performance and Reliability Analysis of Component-Based Systems

Vincenzo Grassi[1], Raffaela Mirandola[2], and Antonino Sabetta[1]

[1] Dipartimento di Informatica, Sistemi e Produzione
Università di Roma "Tor Vergata", Italy
vgrassi@info.uniroma2.it, sabetta@info.uniroma2.it
[2] Dipartimento di Elettronica e Informazione
Politecnico di Milano, Italy
mirandola@elet.polimi.it

Abstract. The adoption of a "high level" perspective in the design of a component-based application, without considering the specific features of some underlying supporting platform, has the advantage of focusing on the relevant architectural aspects and reasoning about them in a platform independent way, omitting unnecessary details that could even not be known at the earliest development stages. On the other hand, many of the details that are typically neglected in this high-level perspective must necessarily be taken into account to obtain a meaningful evaluation of different architectural choices in terms of extra-functional quality attributes, like performance or reliability. Toward the reconciliation of these two contrasting needs, we propose a model-based approach whose goal is to support the derivation of sufficiently detailed prediction models from high level models of component-based systems, focusing on the prediction of performance and reliability. We exploit for this purpose a refinement mechanism based on the use of model transformation techniques.

1 Introduction

Component-based development is one of the major current trends in software development. Other recently emerged trends are: the central role played by the *software architecture* concept in the software development; the *model driven paradigm* of development; and the attention given to the analysis of *extra-functional properties* during software development. Our work aims at leveraging concepts and methodologies developed within all these fields, to support the early analysis of extra-functional properties (such as performance and reliability) of component-based architectures.

The software architecture approach focuses on the high level modeling of an application in terms of coarse-grained components and interaction patterns among them (connectors), abstracting away low level details [2]. Also the model driven paradigm, even if from a somehow different perspective, calls for a focus on the high-level modeling of an application in the early development phases, neglecting low level platform-dependent details [21]. The underlying idea is that better software systems can result from modeling and analyzing their relevant architectural aspects in the early phases of the development lifecycle. The goal of this early analysis is to predict the

I. Gorton et al. (Eds.): CBSE 2006, LNCS 4063, pp. 270 – 284, 2006.

quality of the system before it has been built, to understand the main effects of an architectural choice with respect to quality requirements. In the case of component-based architectures, this prediction can be exploited to drive decisions about which components should be used and how they should be connected (connector selection) so as to meet the quality requirements imposed on the design. It can also be used for "what-if" experiments to predict the impact of architectural changes needed to adapt the system to new or changing requirements.

On the other hand, the prediction of extra-functional quality properties like performance and reliability generally requires the knowledge of low level details, like the characteristics and the patterns of use of some underlying interconnection infrastructure used to support component interactions. The absence of such details in an architectural model may actually hinder the possibility of carrying out a meaningful analysis at early development stages.

To reconcile these two contrasting aspects, our proposal is aimed at introducing details useful to support performance and reliability analysis into a high-level model of a component-based architecture. In particular, we focus on details concerning the underlying platform that provides the interconnection infrastructure among components, since different ways of connecting the same set of high level components can have a different impact on the overall extra functional characteristics of the system [15].

To achieve this goal, we exploit model transformation methodologies and tools mainly developed within the model driven development (MDD) paradigm [3, 12,14,16,17, 26]. In the MDD framework, the focus of model transformations is on a transformation path from high level to platform specific models (up to the executable code) of a software application. Besides, MDD based concepts and tools have proved useful also in supporting the early analysis of extra-functional quality attributes of the application being developed. Indeed, carrying out such an analysis can be seen as a transformation process that takes as input some "design-oriented" model of the software system (plus some additional information related to the extra-functional attribute of interest) and generates an "analysis-oriented" model, that lends itself to the application of some analysis methodology [1,10]. However, defining such a transformation could be quite cumbersome, for several reasons: the large "semantic gap" between the source and target model of the transformation, the heterogeneous design notations that could be used by different component providers, and the different target analysis notations one could be interested in to support different kind of analysis (e.g. queueing networks, Markov processes). To alleviate these problems, some "intermediate languages" have been recently proposed that capture the relevant information for the analysis of extra-functional attributes, to be used as a bridge between design-oriented and analysis-oriented notations [7,8,26].

In our approach to the performance/reliability oriented refinement of high level component-based models, we take advantage of the existence of these intermediate languages. Hence, we implement our refinement as a model transformation whose input and output models are both expressed in one of such languages. We assume that the input model has been directly obtained by means of suitable transformations from a high-level architectural model of the application, so lacking details about the performance and reliability "costs" of the adopted connectors. Then, the output model is obtained by enriching the input model with static and dynamic features concerning these connectors, which may be useful for performance and reliability prediction.

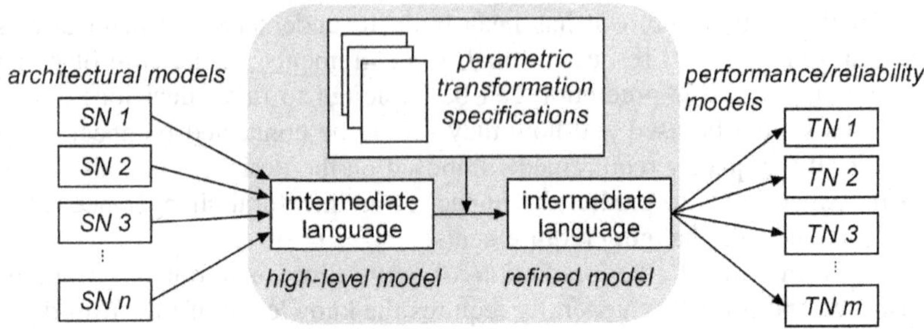

Fig. 1. Our contribution (shaded area) within a transformation path from architectural models of component-based applications (possibly expressed using heterogeneous notations *SN1, ..,SNn*) to different types of performance/reliability models (expressed by different notations *TN1, .., TNm*)

Working at the intermediate language level, we make our approach independent of both the specific notation(s) used to describe the high level architecture, and the target analysis-oriented model that will be finally generated. Fig. 1 provides a graphical representation of our approach.

The rest of the paper is organized as follows. In section 2 we briefly present the intermediate language we have selected. In section 3 we outline our general approach, based on the idea of using model transformations to support the refinement of models expressed in the intermediate language. In section 4 we present the implementation of this approach in terms of a specific model transformation methodology, using the QVT (Query/View/Transformation) language proposed by the OMG within its MDA framework [16]. For this purpose, we present two examples of parametric transformations referring to two different connector types, that can be used to refine a source "high-level" model, adding to it information about the actual connector resource usage. Section 5 reviews related work, while section 6 concludes the paper.

2 An Intermediate Language to Support Transformations from Design to Performance/Reliability Analysis Models

The intermediate language we have selected to implement our architectural refinement is KLAPER (Kernel LAnguage for PErformance and Reliability analysis). To make the paper self-contained we summarize here the relevant features of KLAPER, referring the reader to [7] for further details. The purpose of KLAPER is to capture in a lightweight and compact model only the relevant information for the performance and reliability analysis of component-based systems, while abstracting away irrelevant details. KLAPER is neither an architecture description language (ADL) nor an analysis language: it has been designed as an intermediate "distilled" language to help define transformations between design-oriented and analysis-oriented notations, filling the large semantic gap that usually divides them. Using KLAPER (or other similar languages) we may split the complex task of deriving an analysis model (e.g. a queueing network) from a high level design model (expressed using UML or other component oriented notations) into two separate and presumably simpler tasks:

- extracting from the design model only the information that may be relevant for performance/reliability analysis, and expressing it in KLAPER;
- generating an analysis model based on the information expressed in KLAPER.

We point out that this two tasks may be solved independently of each other. Moreover, as a positive side effect of this two steps approach built around a single intermediate language, we may mitigate the "*n-by-m*" problem of translating *n* heterogeneous design notation types into *m* performance/reliability model types, reducing it to a less complex task of defining *n+m* transformations: *n* from different design notations to KLAPER, and *m* from it to different analysis models.

To take advantage of the current state of the art in the field of model transformation methodologies, KLAPER has been defined as a MOF (Meta-Object Facility) compliant metamodel [14], where MOF is the metamodeling framework proposed by the Object Management Group (OMG) for the management of models and their transformations within the MDD approach to software development [12,21]. Fig. 2 shows the structure of the KLAPER MOF metamodel, while Fig. 3 summarizes the list of attributes and associations for the relevant KLAPER metaclasses[1]. We refer to [7] for details about this MOF specification.

To support the first task outlined above, KLAPER helps to distill from a design model the following basic information: the operation of a software system consists of

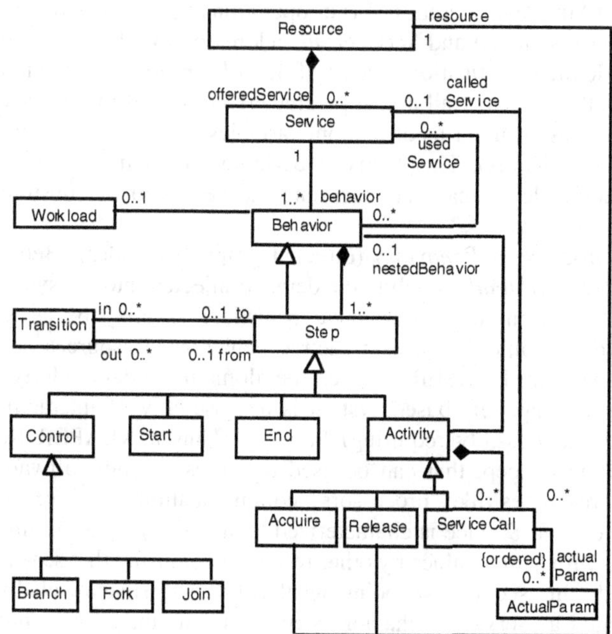

Fig. 2. Structure of the KLAPER MOF metamodel

1 This metamodel is a slight modification of the metamodel presented in [8], that fixes some minor problems.

Resource: *attributes*: name, type, capacity, schedulingPolicy, description; *associations*: offeredService.
Service: *attributes*:name, formalParams, speedAttr, failAttr, description; *associations*: behavior, resource.
Behavior : *associations*: usedService, step, workload.
Step : *attributes*: name; *associations*: in, out.
Activity : *attributes*: name, repetition, /internalExecTime, /internalFailProb, /internalFailTime,completionModel; *associations*: nestedBehavior, serviceCall.
Branch : *attributes*: branchProbs.
Acquire : *attributes* : resourceUnits; *associations*: resource
Release : *attributes*: resourceUnits; *associations*: resource
ServiceCall: *attributes*: resourceType, serviceName, isSynch; *associations*: step, actualParam, calledService;
ActualParam : *attributes*: value.
Transition : *associations*: to, from.
Workload : *attributes*: workloadType, arrivalProcess, population, initialResource; *associations*: behavior.

Fig. 3. Attributes and associations of the main KLAPER metaclasses

a set of *Steps*, where each step may take time to be completed, and/or may fail before its completion. For this purpose, the *internalExecTime*, *internalFailTime* and *internalFailProb* attributes of each step specify (according to a stochastic setting) the execution time or failure characteristics of that single step. A step may be a *Control* node (Branch, Fork, Join) that usually neither takes time nor fails, or an *Activity* node that consists of "internal operations" (i.e. operations that do not require any service offered by other resources) and *ServiceCalls* addressed to other Resources. A service call may include the specification of a set of *ActualParameters*. An interesting feature of KLAPER is that ServiceCall actual parameters are meant to represent abstractions (for example expressed in terms of random variables) of the "real" service parameters (see [7] for more details). This helps in defining parametric service requests at a suitable abstraction level that may facilitate the next step of constructing a representative analysis model.

Steps are grouped in *Behaviors* (directed graphs of nodes). Behaviors may be associated with a *Workload* modeling the demand injected into the system by external entities like the system users (proactive behavior), or may be associated with a *Service* offered by some *Resource* (reactive behavior). Resources are the topmost modeling element in KLAPER: hence, the domain model underlying KLAPER considers that a component-based system is an assembly of interacting Resources, each offering (and possibly requiring) Services. Thus a KLAPER Resource is an abstract modeling concept that can be used to represent both software components and physical resources like processors, communication links or other physical devices. Each offered Service is characterized by a list of *formal parameters* that can be instantiated with actual values by other resources requiring that service.

To conclude this section, we point out that the performance/reliability attributes associated with a service behavior step concern only the *internal* service characteristics; they do not take into account possible delays or failures caused by the use of other required services, needed to complete that step. In this respect, we remark that when we build a KLAPER model (first task outlined above) our goal is mainly "descriptive". The *calledService* association specified in a step helps in identifying which are the external services that may cause additional delays or failure possibilities, but how to properly mix this "external" information with the internal information to get an overall picture of the service performance or reliability is out of the KLAPER scope. It is a problem that must be solved during the generation and solution of an analysis model derived from a KLAPER model (second task outlined above).

3 Refinement of KLAPER High-Level Models

As already pointed out in the introduction, we assume that the starting point for our refinement is a KLAPER model directly obtained from a high-level model of a component-based application. Rules to generate this model from two different notations for component-based systems are presented in [7]. At this high level we may generally expect to only have information about the provided and required services of each component, and the type of connectors used to enable component interactions. As a consequence, the corresponding KLAPER model built using suitable transformation rules cannot contain more information than that already available in the original model.

Fig. 4 gives an example of this, in the case of a model representing two components connected through a "synchronous client/server" connector. In this example we use a UML 2.0 notation for the architectural model, that consists of a "structural view" expressed through a component diagram, and a "dynamic view" expressed through an activity diagram, where the latter provides some information about the two component dynamics. We also assume the existence of a *C/Ssynch* stereotype to label the connector between the two components. Without further specifications of the semantics of such annotation (from a performance or reliability viewpoint), we are only able to derive the KLAPER model in the lower part of fig. 4 (without the "dashed part"), where the interaction between the two components is simply modeled by a direct association between a *ServiceCall* step in the *Client* behavior and the *offeredService* of the *Server* (to avoid cluttering the figure, we have omitted some details of the KLAPER model). This model does not include any information about the use of resources of the underlying interaction infrastructure caused by the adoption of that particular type of connector (the "dashed part" of the figure partially outlines this lacking information, expressed in the KLAPER syntax).

Our idea to facilitate the inclusion into KLAPER models also of these lower level details, which are relevant from a performance/reliability viewpoint, is to build a library of KLAPER "parametric transformations", each corresponding to a specific connector type. Given a connector type specified in an architectural model, the goal of the corresponding transformation is to enrich the high-level KLAPER model directly obtained from the source architectural model with information concerning the resource consumption caused by the use of that connector.

Each transformation refers to "abstract" resources (e.g. cpu or communication link type resources), specified as parameters of the transformation. In a concrete application of the transformation, these parameters are mapped to concrete instances of KLAPER resources, which model the resources of some platform where the application will be deployed. We point out that, besides specifying the used resources, the goal of the transformation is also to specify a suitable pattern of use of these

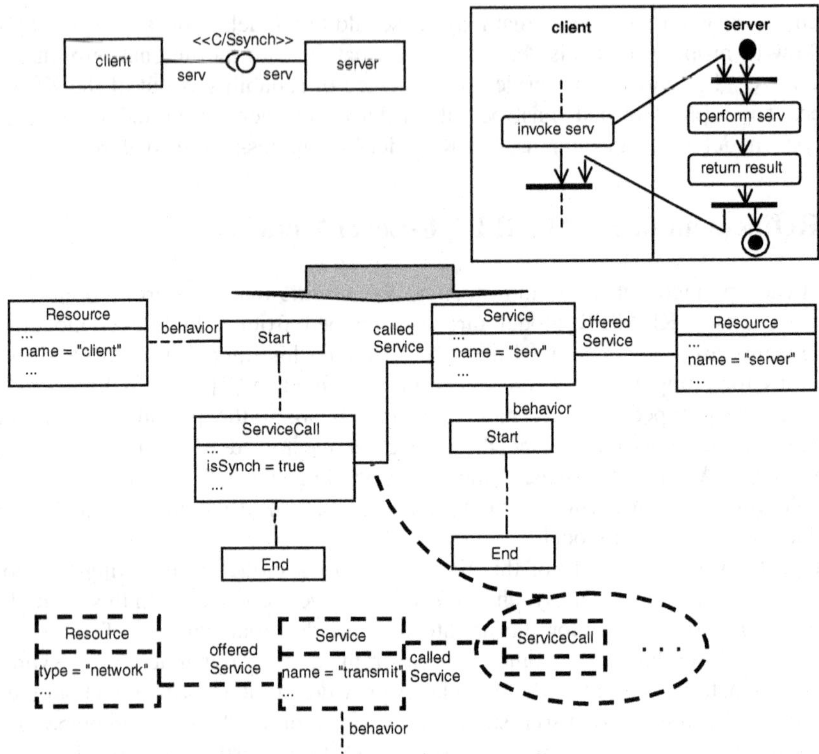

Fig. 4. From a (UML 2) architectural model to a corresponding "high-level" KLAPER model: the dashed part partially depicts the missing "low-level" details

resources. In particular, this means that it must also specify how to "weave" the resource usage pattern caused by a connector with the behaviors of the KLAPER resources that model the high level application components, to get a more refined description of the overall resource usage of that application.

4 Specifying Refinement Transformations of KLAPER Models

In this section we present two example transformations that manipulate high-level KLAPER models to represent the resource usage of two different types of connectors. To this end, we use two variants of the synchronous client/server connector (presented in the previous section): static synchronous client/server and dynamic synchronous client/server.

We express such transformations using the QVT (Query/View/Transformation) language, whose purpose is to enable the transformation of MOF-based models.

The QVT specification allows the definition of both *declarative* and *imperative* transformation rules. As in this paper we adopt the declarative style, we give some details only about it. The declarative specification is supported by a two-level

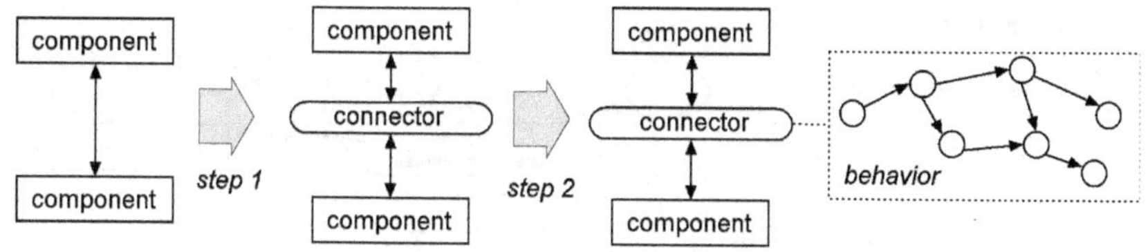

Fig. 5. Conceptual overview of the stepwise refinement approach

architecture, where the topmost level consists of a user-friendly language and metamodel, called *Relations*, which allows the definition of complex transformations by means of object pattern matching and object template creation. The semantics of this higher-level language is defined in terms of the lower-level *Core* language and metamodel, which is a more basic language defined as a minimal extension of the EMOF (Essential MOF) and OCL metamodels [18].

A QVT Transformation (expressed in the *Relations* language) is composed of *relations*. Each relation defines a bi-directional mapping between two (or more) domains for which the relation is defined. Each domain has a pattern, i.e. a configuration of object instances together with their mutual links and attributes that define the applicability conditions of a rule. A relation can have a *when* clause and a *where* clause, containing a set of OCL statements, that are used to further constrain the applicability of the mapping rule (when clause), or to enforce the deletion (or creation) of certain elements that are (or are not) found in the target model and that do not conform to the rule target pattern (where clause). We refer to [16] for further details.

For the purpose of this work, we express the refinement transformations on KLAPER models as relations, not as operational mappings, because an intuitive graphical syntax is defined in the standard specification for the former while only a textual syntax is available for the latter.

Technically speaking, the model refinements we are going to present here are "in-place" transformations, i.e. transformations where both the source and the target candidate models conform to the same metamodel and are bound to the same model at run-time [16].

When the general approach discussed in section 3 is rephrased in terms of QVT, the connector resource usage and the "weaving rules" are embedded in the QVT rule and encoded in the "right-hand side" of the rule. The conditions contained in the *when* clause constrain the application of the rule to the portion of the source model specified by the user. As shown in Fig. 5, the proposed approach is realized in two steps.

First the high-level KLAPER model is augmented with a resource modeling the connector. Such a connector model is minimal and is only meant to represent a structural change in the original model, ignoring the behavioral aspects related to the connector use. The second step is performed to attach a behavioral specification to the connector, modeling its dynamics and the service demand that in turn it addresses to other resources. Transformations that refer to connectors belonging to the same "family" (characterized by the same structure but different behaviors) share the first step and differ in the second step. In this paper, we give examples for the family of connectors that model a Client/Server interaction between two components.

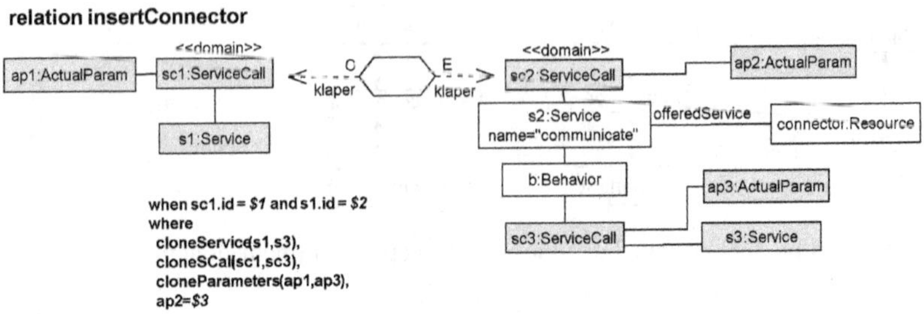

relation insertConnector

<<domain>> ap1:ActualParam sc1:ServiceCall s1:Service

C klaper E klaper

<<domain>> sc2:ServiceCall ap2:ActualParam s2:Service name="communicate" offeredService connector:Resource b:Behavior ap3:ActualParam sc3:ServiceCall s3:Service

```
when sc1.id = $1 and s1.id = $2
where
 cloneService(s1,s3),
 cloneSCall(sc1,sc3),
 cloneParameters(ap1,ap3),
 ap2=$3
```

Fig. 6. Insertion of a connector resource into a high-level KLAPER model

A QVT relation describing a "step one" refinement is shown in Fig. 6. The transformation, which in principle is bi-directional, is assumed to be executed from left to right. When a ServiceCall and a Service matching the pattern on the left-hand side are found in the model, the pattern on the right-hand side is enforced, creating (if not already existing) a connector resource (*connector*) offering a communication service (*s2*) whose behavior (*b*) is responsible for calling the service (*s*) that in the original model was called directly by *sc1*.

From the application of the first rule a structural enhanced model is obtained, which is still under-specified to be useful for analysis purposes. This problem is addressed using another refinement transformation that is applied to the model obtained after the execution of the first rule.

As a result, a behavioral specification is attached to the communication service offered by the connector resource. A complete implementation requires that a few more relations be enforced by the where clauses of both step-one and step-two rules, so that the resulting model remains consistent, but we prefer not to delve into details about these technicalities here. In fact we are not concerned by strict syntactic compliance with the QVT standard specification, but we rather prefer to convey the intuitive idea of using a stepwise refinement of a high-level model to yield an augmented model that is richer both from the structural and the behavioral standpoint. Such a refined model can give useful insights regarding performance or reliability problems that are not evident (or not captured at all) in the original model but that arise when the interaction dynamics between different components is taken into account. By the way, designing the transformation process in steps is a key feature of the proposed approach, as this eases the experimentation of different alternative behaviors (using different step-two transformations) that can be attached to a partial (i.e. only structural) model of a connector obtained through a step-one transformation applied to a high-level model.

The two examples presented in the remainder of the section illustrate the transformation of the generic structural model, obtained after the first step of the transformation process, into two different concrete connectors, each having a different dynamic behavior and resource requirement.

***Static synchronous client/server* connector.** In this first example we consider a Client-Server interaction with a static binding between the client that requires a service and the server that provides it. The left part of Fig. 7 defines the pattern that is looked for in the source model. When a match is found that satisfies the *when* clause,

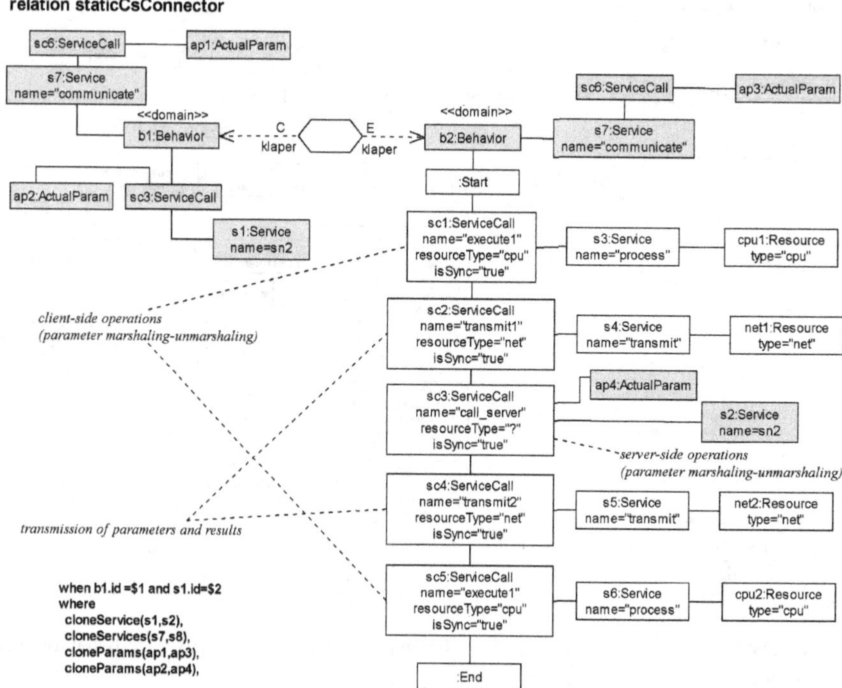

Fig. 7. QVT refinement rule to attach a *static synchronous client/server* behavior to the connector resource

the rule is enforced and new elements are introduced in the model, or are updated to conform to the right-hand side pattern if they already exist but their attributes are not appropriate. The behavior attached to the connector resource (in the right hand side) is meant to represent the fact that, to actually support an interaction, the connector itself must use some processing and network resources. The operations requested from those resources are modeled as KLAPER service calls addressed to them. For the sake of conciseness, we omit the specification of some KLAPER attributes. When the rule is applied, a new element is added to the model only if none is found matching the pattern in the right-hand side. The rule may cause the attributes of existing elements to be adjusted to match the enforced pattern. It is important to note that the formal parameters of the communication service provided by the connector are the same as those of the service provided by the server, thus representing the fact that in this example the connector works as a proxy through which the client communicates with the server.

***Dynamic synchronous client/server* connector.** This second example is similar to the first one but here the interaction between the client and the server goes through a preliminary discovery phase (Fig. 8). To retrieve a reference to the appropriate server, a discovery service is invoked and afterwards the binding between the two parties is established dynamically. It can be noted that in both transformations the user should supply the parameters for the service calls addressed by the connector to the services provided by the cpu and network resources that represent the supporting platform. Those (actual) parameters should represent the amount of the service demand

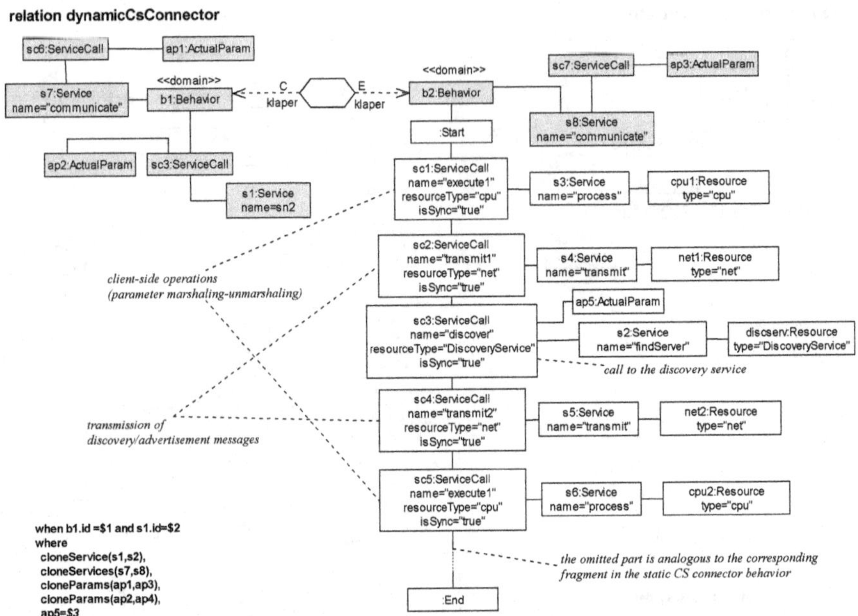

Fig. 8. QVT refinement rule to attach a *dynamic synchronous client/server* behavior to the connector resource

addressed to these resources, and typically depend on the size of the information transported through the connector. In the abstract it is difficult to give a general rule to model such dependency, so the modeler is required to define the where clauses of the transformations appropriately, evaluating different possible scenarios.

Even though the models presented in these examples are admittedly naïve, they show that the approach to the specification of connectors proposed in this work leads to parametric models that are sufficiently self-contained to allow switching from one interaction scheme to another with ease.

As a result of the stepwise application of a set of refinement transformations to a high level KLAPER model, more detailed models are produced where the information about the usage of resources of some underlying platform is explicitly captured and added incrementally to the model. Fig. 9 (partially) shows the result of the application of the *insertConnector* and the *staticCsConnector* transformations to the high level KLAPER model of Fig. 4. The elements in the dashed part of Fig. 9 have been added to the high-level model of Fig. 4 as a result of the transformation.

This refined model can be further transformed into another model expressed in some analysis-oriented notation that can be readily understood by experts or processed by an automatic analysis tool. As an example of the performance model that can be derived from a KLAPER model enriched with the connector templates we have defined, Fig. 10 depicts a fragment of a queueing network (QN) that models the resource usage of a request addressed by a client to a server mediated by a *static client-server connector*. Transformation rules to get this model from a KLAPER model are outlined in [7]. In the figure, the *CPU1*, *CPU2* and *Network* nodes model,

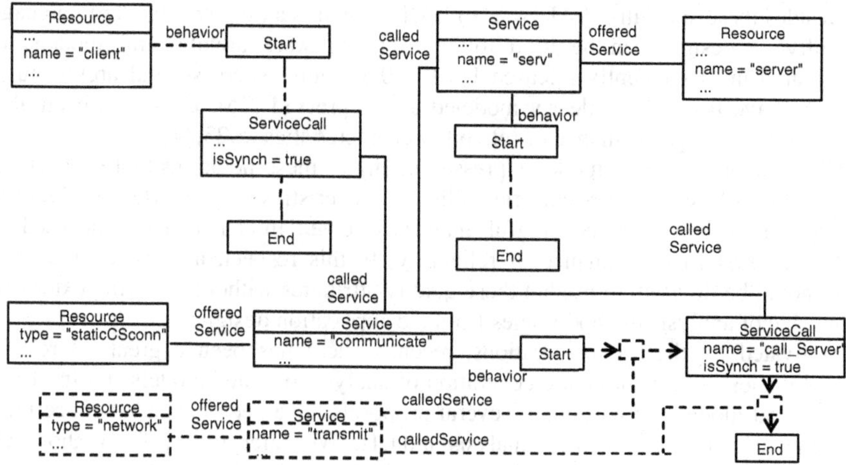

Fig. 9. Partial representation of the KLAPER model of fig. 4 refined through the *insertConnector* and *staticCsConnector* transformations

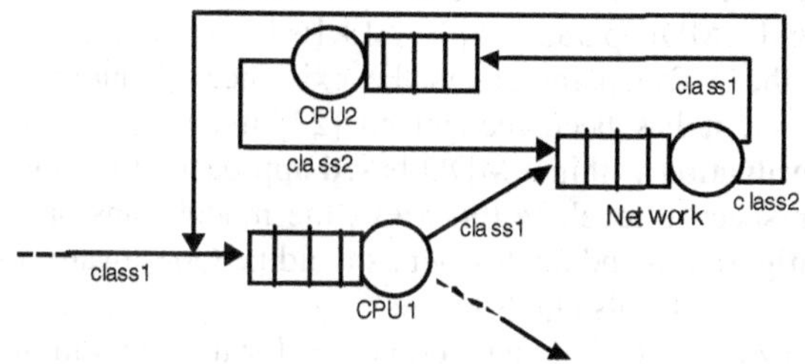

Fig. 10. Queueing model derived from the KLAPER model of figure 9

respectively, the processing resources where the Client and the Server are deployed and the communication resource that connects them. The service demand addressed to these resources by the Client/Server interaction (through a *static client-server connector*) is modeled, according to the QN notation, by jobs circulating among the QN nodes. Multiple jobs model concurrent requests to the same resources. In the figure, *class1* and *class2* are two job classes that model the client-to-server and the server-to-client paths of the Client/Server interaction, respectively. Existing solution techniques can be used to solve this model and to obtain standard figures of merit such as, for example, the application response time and/or the resource utilization [10].

5 Related Work

The rigorous modeling of software applications starting from the early development phases is strongly encouraged in the Software Architecture approach [2]. For this purpose, several architecture description languages (ADLs) have been proposed, that support the modeling of an application in terms of high-level components and connectors [13].

Besides these specialized ADLs, also UML, which is a *de facto* standard language for software design, can be used to represent software architectural models, in particular using its recently released UML 2.0 version, where several architectural concepts have been more clearly modeled and expressed [25]. UML has been also extended to model performance or reliability characteristics [5,23,24].

Given an architectural model expressed in any of these notations that support the specification of performance and reliability characteristics, an important problem is how to derive from it a meaningful analysis oriented model, that can be used to predict the system performance or reliability. In this respect, automatic prediction tools should be devised, to predict these quality attributes without requiring extensive knowledge of analysis methodologies from the application designer.

Motivated by these considerations, recently there has been a great interest in methodologies for the automatic generation of analysis-oriented models starting from architectural models. In particular, several proposals have been presented concerning the generation of performance analysis models. We refer to [1] for a thorough overview of these proposals. Some proposals have also been presented for the generation of reliability models [4,11,20].

The development of these methodologies has received a great impulse by the almost contemporary development of model transformation methodologies and tools aimed at supporting the MDD paradigm [3,12,14,16,17,26]. Indeed, a crucial issue for the application of the MDD paradigm is the existence of automatic model transformations. Moreover, it has been recognized [22] the need of incorporating QoS specification and evaluation within a MDD-based approach at the more abstract level and at the platform-specific level. In this view, the model transformations, the code generation, the configuration and deployment should be QoS-aware. Ideally the target execution platform should be also QoS-aware.

Examples of utilization of MDD methodologies for the generation of performance or reliability models can be found in [7,8,28]. The work in [28] describes an intermediate model called Core Scenario Model (CSM) expressed in a MOF-based notation, which is extracted from a UML design model, and a tool architecture called PUMA, which provides a unified interface between different kinds of UML diagrams and different kinds of performance models, for example Markov models, stochastic Petri nets and process algebras, queues and layered queues. The work in [8] proposes a transformation method of an annotated UML model into a performance model, based on graph transformation concepts and an intermediate language similar to the one used in [28]; the implementation of the transformation rules and algorithm uses lower-level XML trees manipulations techniques, such as XML algebra. The target performance model used as an example in this paper is a Layered Queueing Network (LQN). Similarly to [28] and [8], the work in [7] presents a MOF-based language to build intermediate models for a transformation from design to analysis models. Differently from [28,8], this intermediate language is intended to support the generation of both performance and reliability models.

As already outlined in the introduction, our work builds on the existence of such intermediate languages. The proposals in [6, 27] are close to our approach to the refinement of architectural models, as they address the problem of providing a performance-oriented refinement of high-level architectural connectors. With respect to these works, we leverage the existence of an intermediate language to remain independent of source and target notations used to express respectively the design and the analysis model. Moreover we explicitly exploit model transformation methodologies to integrate our approach within a model transformation path, aimed at generating performance/reliability analysis models from architectural models.

6 Conclusions

The definition of automatic tools for transformations from design models to analysis models is a crucial issue for the effective introduction of performance or reliability analysis at the early stage of component-based software development. Toward this end, we have presented an approach for the refinement of architectural models that exploits currently available model transformation methodologies and tools. Our refinement focuses on the introduction of information concerning the performance or reliability related features of the adopted connectors into an architectural model of a component-based application, since connectors play a key role in determining the overall quality of a software architecture. To remain independent of the design and analysis oriented notations that could be used, we have defined our refinement within the framework of a MOF-based language, proposed as an intermediate notation between design and analysis oriented notations. We are working on the automation of the proposed approach since this represents a key point for its successful application. Future works also include the development of other transformations to make available blueprints for various plausible interconnection infrastructures; and the validation of our approach by its application to industrial case studies.

Acknowledgements

Work partially supported by the MIUR-FIRB project "PERF: Performance evaluation of complex systems: techniques, methodologies and tools".

References

1. S. Balsamo, A. di Marco, P. Inverardi, M. Simeoni "Model-based performance prediction in software development: a survey" *IEEE Trans. on Software Engineering*, Vol. 30/5, May 2004, pp. 295-310.
2. L. Bass, P. Clements, R. Kazman, *Software Architectures in Practice*, Addison-Wesley, New York, NY, 1998.
3. J. Bezivin, E. Breton, G. Dupé, P. Valduriez "The ATL transformation-based model management framework" *Res. Report no. 03.08*, IRIN, Univ. de Nantes, Sept. 2003.
4. V. Cortellessa, H. Singh, B. Cukic, E. Gunel, V. Bharadwaj "Early reliability assessment of UML based software models" in Proc. *3rd Int.Workshop on Software and Performance (WOSP'02)*, July 24-26, 2002, Rome (Italy).
5. V. Cortellessa, A. Pompei "Towards a UML profile for QoS: a contribution in the reliability domain" in Proc. *4th Int. Workshop on Software and Performance (WOSP'04)*, Jan. 2004, pp. 197-206.
6. H. Gomaa, D.A. Menascé "Performance engineering of component-based distributed software systems" in *Performance Engineering* (R. Dumke et al. Eds.), LNCS 2047, Springer-Verlag, 2001.

7. V. Grassi, R. Mirandola, A. Sabetta "From Design to Analysis Models: a Kernel Language for Performance and Reliability Analysis of Component-based Systems" in Proc. *WOSP 2005: 5th ACM International Workshop on Software and Performance*, Palma de Mallorca, Spain, July 11-14, 2005, pp. 25-36.
8. G. Gu, D.C. Petriu "From UML to LQN by XML Algebra-Based Graph Transformations" in: Proc. *Fifth International Workshop on Software and Performance (WOSP 2005)*, Palma, Illes Balears, Spain, July 11-15, 2005, pp. 99-110.
9. Hissam, S.A., et al. "Packaging Predictable Assembly" in Proc. *Component Deployment (CD 2002)*, LNCS 2370, Springer Verlag (2002), pp. 108-124.
10. Lazowska E.D. et al., *Quantitative System Performance: Computer System Analysis using Queueing Network Models*, on line at: http://www.cs.washington.edu/homes/lazowska/qsp/
11. C. Leangsuksun, H. Song, L. Shen "Reliability Modeling Using UML" in Proc. *2003 Int. Conf. on Software Engineering Research and Practice*, June 23-26, 2003, Las Vegas, Nevada, USA.
12. "MDA Guide Version 1.0.1" OMG Document omg/03-06-01, on line at: www.omg.org/docs/omg/03-06-01.pdf.
13. N. Medvidovic, R.N. Taylor "A classification and comparison framework for software architecture description languages" *IEEE Trans. on Software Engineering*, vol. 26, no. 1, Jan. 2000, pp. 70-93.
14. "Meta Object Facility (MOF) 2.0 Core Specification", OMG Adopted Specification ptc/03-10-04, on line at: www.omg.org/docs/ptc/03-10-04.pdf.
15. N.R. Mehta, N. Medvidovic, S. Phadke "Toward a taxonomy of software connectors" in Proc. *22nd Int. Conference on Software Engineering (ICSE 2000)*, May 2000.
16. "MOF 2.0 Query/Views/Transformations RFP", OMG Document ad/2002-04-10, on line at: www.omg.org/docs/ad/02-04-10.pdf.
17. J. Oldevik "UMT UML model transformation tool" on line at: http://umt-qvt.sourceforge.net/ docs/UMTdocumentationv08.pdf.
18. "UML 2.0 OCL Specification", OMG Final Adopted Specification online at: www.omg.org/docs/ptc/03-10-14.pdf
19. "OWL-S: Semantic Markup for Web Services" White Paper, The OWL Services Coalition, Nov. 2003, on line at: www.daml.org/services/owl-s/1.0/owl-s.pdf.
20. R.H. Reussner, H.W. Schmidt, I. Poernomo "Reliability Prediction for Component-Based Software Architectures" *Journal of Systems and Software*, pp. 241-252, vol. 66, No. 3, 2003.
21. Bran Selic, "The Pragmatics of Model-Driven Development", IEEE Software, vol. 20, no. 5, pp. 19-25, Sep.-Oct. 2003
22. A. Solberg, K.E. Husa, J. Aagedal, E. Abrahamsen "QoS-Aware MDA" in Proc. *Workshop Model-Driven Architecture in the Specification, Implementation and Validation of Object-Oriented Embedded Systems (SIVOES-MDA '03)* (in conjunction with UML03) (2003).
23. "UML Profile for Modeling Quality of Service and Fault Tolerance Characteristics and Mechanisms", OMG Adopted Specification ptc/04-09-012, www.omg.org/docs/ptc/04-09-01.pdf.
24. "UML Profile for Schedulability, Performance, and Time Specification", OMG Adopted Specification ptc/02-03-02, on line at: www.omg.org/docs/ptc/02-03-02.pdf.
25. "UML 2.0 Superstructure Specification" OMG Adopted Specification ptc/03-08-02, on line at: www.omg.org/docs/ptc/03-08-02.pdf.
26. D. Varrò, G. Varrò, A. Pataricza "Designing the automatic transformation of visual languages" *Science of Computer Programming*, vol. 44(2), 2002, pp. 205-227.
27. T. Verdikt, B. Dhoedt, F. Gielen, P. Demesteer "Automatic Inclusion of Middleware Performance Attributes into Architectural UML Software Models" in *IEEE Trans. of Software Engineering*, Vol. 31, No. 8, Aug. 2005, pp. 695-711
28. M. Woodside et al. "Performance by Unified Model Analysis (PUMA)" in Proc. *WOSP 2005: 5th ACM International Workshop on Software and Performance*, Palma de Mallorca, Spain, July 11-14, 2005, pp. 1-12.

Impact of Virtual Memory Managers on Performance of J2EE Applications

Alexander Ufimtsev, Alena Kucharenka, and Liam Murphy

Performance Engineering Laboratory,
School of Computer Science and Informatics
University College Dublin, Belfield, D4, Ireland
alexu@ucd.ie, alena_kucharenka@tut.by, Liam.Murphy@ucd.ie
http://www.perfenglab.com

Abstract. We investigate the impact of Operating System's Virtual Memory Managers (VMMs) on performance of enterprise applications. By taking various popular branches of the Linux kernel and modifying their VMM settings, one can see the effects it introduces on ECPerf J2EE Benchmark. JBoss application server is used to run ECPerf. Our tests show that even the change of one parameter in VMM can have significant performance impacts. Performance of various kernel branches is compared. Parameter sensitivity and influence of specific settings are presented.

1 Introduction

Component systems nowadays run in a layers of software and hardware. A typical J2EE system runs inside the application servers (AS), which in their turn run inside Java Virtual Machines (JVM), which run on an Operating System (OS). And OSes either run on a hardware or within another host OS. Despite its great advantages, this layered model introduces a lot of complexities. For example, the effects of changes introduced at lower layers can be non-obvious, especially if layers are not directly connected. It is hard to anticipate the performance change of J2EE application if a certain parameter in the OS is modified.

This paper studies the effects of modifying kernel's Virtual Memory Manager (VMM) settings and implementation on performance of J2EE applications. Various Linux kernel branches were examined and tested. Changes of VMM parameters were reflected in performance of ECPerf, J2EE industry-standard benchmark. Parameters that affect performance the most were identified. Influence of specific VMM settings on performance was analysed. It must be noted that no attempt was made to understand the cause of performance differences. To determine the cause of the differences, one must examine the source code of VMM patches, as well as other changes introduced to specific kernel trees. The motivation for this work is not to find out what caused the differences in performance, but rather prove that they actually happen and they should not be ignored.

I. Gorton et al. (Eds.): CBSE 2006, LNCS 4063, pp. 285–293, 2006.

The rest of the paper is organized as follows: Section 2 contains detailed description of kernel branches and VMM parameters, Section 3 describes the experimental settings, including test scenarios, hardware and software used, Section 4 contains results and analysis, Section 5 describes related work, and Section 6 concludes the paper and discusses future work.

2 Kernel Branches and VMM Parameters

2.1 Kernel Branches

Linux kernel development process is not a centralized or unified process - anyone is free to fork the code and maintain his or her own repository. Though main development happens within the official 'vanilla' version with releases available from a central repository[1], many Linux distributions and kernel developers maintain their own branches of it, with changed or augmented functionality. The reasons for keeping a separate branch include, but are not limited to expanding the set of supported hardware, tightening security, improving stability and performance, maintaining compatibility with older versions, and quick bugfixing. Some kernel branches serve as a playground for new experimental features, which when proved stable and useful are merged into the main kernel branch.

A few kernel repositories have been examined. The main selection criteria was the presense of VMM patches. The following branches were selected:

- Debian 2.4;
- Debian 2.6;
- SUSE;
- Fedora Core;
- Alan Cox (-ac);
- Andrew Morton (-mm);
- Con Kolivas (-ck).

Debian 2.4 kernel was selected for comparison of speeds between 2.4 and 2.6 kernel branches. It was decided to produce two kernel versions for SUSE - one with its original configuration file and the other with the file common for all other kernel images. All kernels, except for Debian 2.4.26 and 2.6.8 have been compiled locally with *gcc-3.3.5*.

2.2 VMM Parameters

This study concentrates on the VMM implementation of the current stable Linux branch, 2.6. VMM parameters, typically configurable at runtime via manipulation with */proc/sys/vm* interface, have been examined. A list of parameters that could possibly affect performance has been created. Based on the description of parameters, they have been split into two groups - *red* and *blue*. During the

[1] ftp://ftp.kernel.org

experiments we test the hypothesis that *Red* group is more likely to affect VMM performance while the *blue* one less likely to do so.

Red:

- *dirty_background_ratio* - the percentage of memory that is allowed to contain 'dirty' or unsaved data;
- *dirty_expire_centisecs* - The longest # of centiseconds for which data is allowed to remain dirty;
- *dirty_ratio* - contains as a percentage of total system memory, the # of pages at which a process that is generating disk writes will itself start writing out dirty data;
- *dirty_writeback_centisecs* - interval between periodical wakeups of the pdflush writeback daemons;
- *page-cluster* - tunes the readahead of pages during swap;
- *swappiness* - drives the swappiness decision.

Blue:

- *lower_zone_protection* - determines how aggressive the kernel is in defending the lowmem zones;
- *min_free_kbytes* - used to force the Linux VM to keep a minimum number of memory free;
- *vfs_cache_pressure* - controls the tendency of the kernel to reclaim the memory which is used for caching of directory and inode objects;
- *overcommit_memory* - value which sets the general kernel policy towards granting memory allocations.

3 Experimental Environment

3.1 Hardware Platform

The testing environment includes three x86 machines:

- *app server* Pentium III-866 Mhz with 512 Mb RAM;
- *database* Pentium III-800 Mhz with 512 Mb RAM;
- *client* Pentium IV-2.2 Ghz, 1024 Mb RAM.

The client machine is more or as powerful as servers to ensure it does not become a bottleneck when generating the test load.

3.2 The Software Environment

The following software was used for testing purposes:

- *operating system*: Debian GNU/Linux 3.1 'sarge';
- *database server*: MySQL v. 5.0.7beta-1;
- *application server*: JBoss v. 4.01sp1 running on Java2SDK 1.4.2_08;
- *client*: ECPerf suit 1.1 on Java2SDK 1.4.2_08;

Debian 'sarge' was used for all the machines. The initial Java heap size of the app. server was set to $384MB$;

3.3 ECPerf and Its Tuning

ECperf is an Enterprise JavaBeans (EJB) benchmark meant to measure the scalability and performance of J2EE servers and containers. It stresses the ability of EJB containers to handle the complexities of memory management, connection pooling, passivation/activation, and caching. Originally developed by Sun Microsystems, ECPerf is now being developed and maintained by SPEC Corporation[2]. It is currently available from SPEC under the name of *SPECjAppServer2004*.

ECPerf Configuration: During initial experiments the following workload was identified as the one delivering the best performance: $txRate = 5, runOrderEntry = 1, runMfg = 1$, which is an equivalent of 40 threads: 25 for order entry, and 15 planned line.

The following parameters set the steady state for 10 minutes, with 8 minute warmup and 3 minute cooldown periods, respectively: $rampUp = 480, stdyState = 600, rampDown = 180$

3.4 Testing Algorithm

The following pseudocode describes the testing algorithm used in this study: every kernel is installed and booted into. Then for every parameter in the red and blue list one of them is set to a specific value, the following happens three times. First, the memory is cleaned then database is wiped out and recreated, swap is turned off, and application server is restarted. Logs and traces are saved for every individual run for later analysis.

```
for (all kernels) {
        boot();
        for(new vmm parameter) {
                set vmm parameter to a new value;
                new average;
                for(int i = 0; i++; i < 3) {
                        clean_memory();
                        clean_db();
                        turn_off_swap();
                        average += avg(run_ecperf());
                }
                save_tuple(kernel,parameter,value,average);
        }
}
```

Values of VMM parameters were changed two, three, or four times, depending on the type of the parameter. Tests with the default values were carried out as well. Swap partitions were turned off for the duration of the test due to significant improvement in performance.

[2] http://www.spec.org

4 Results and Analysis

Figure 1 shows the overall results obtained during the measurements. The results show averaged performance metric of ECPerf, in business operations per minute (Bops/min). Peak and lowest performance measurements were taken three times, while the default settings were tested ten times. An average performance improvement over standard settings was 5,19%, while average performance decline due to unintentional misconfiguration was -8,73%. The decline does not take into account *min_free_kbytes* VMM parameter, which if set to particularly high number effectively stops OS from working.

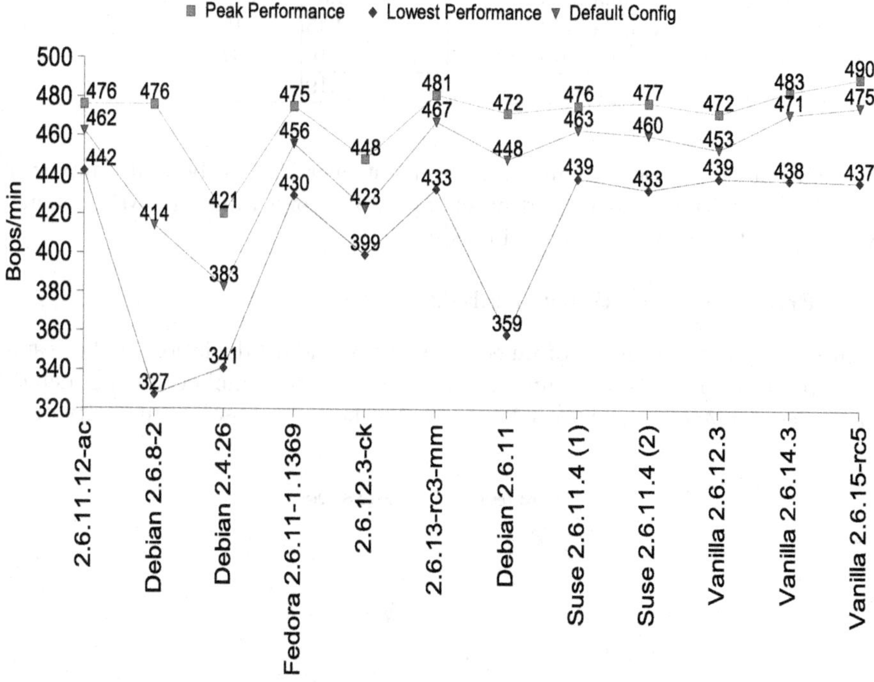

Fig. 1. Overall Results

It can also be noted that Debian kernels seem to be more sensitive to misconfiguration. SUSE kernel branch was performing similarly with both custom and original configuration from SUSE. Also, kernel branch maintained by Con Kolivas (-ck) demonstrated a similar drop in performance at all levels - the price one pays for improved user interactivity and context switching. Reference test subject - kernel 2.4 performed noticably slower than its 2.6 counterparts. Andrew Morton's branch, which is an experimental playground for new kernel features demonstrated performance improvement over 2.6.11 series. This was subsequently reflected in the mainline 2.6.14 and improved even more in 2.6.15. These three kernels seem to behave much better with default settings as well.

Table 1. Maximum Performance Improvement and Decline for Various Kernels, %

Kernel	Improvement	Decline
2.6.11.12-ac	2.95	-4.43
Debian 2.6.8-2	14.96	-20.93
Debian 2.4.26	9.89	-10.88
Fedora 2.6.11-1.1369	4.25	-5.77
2.6.12.3-ck	6.02	-5.59
2.6.13-rc3-mm	3.00	-7.34
Debian 2.6.11	5.29	-20.00
Suse 2.6.11.4 (1)	2.70	-5.32
Suse 2.6.11.4 (2)	3.61	-6.03
Vanilla 2.6.12.3	4.04	-3.27
Vanilla 2.6.14.3	2.45	-7.15
Vanilla 2.6.15-rc5	3.16	-8.04
Average	5.19	-8.73

We argue that a performance improvement over 5% can be quite important considering the fact it is caused by changing just one value in VMM settings. Kernel-specific results are shown in Table 1.

4.1 Error and Sensitivity Analysis

Figure 2 shows the number of failed tests and standard deviation of the results for appropriate kernels. It is quite low since the overall number of tests includes *11 kernel parameters * 3 values * 3 ECperf tests = 99.* Absolute majority of the

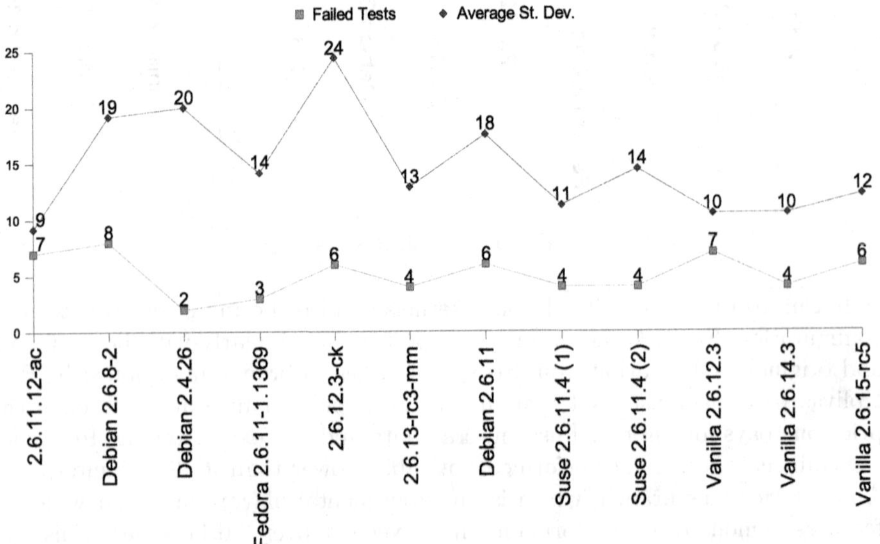

Fig. 2. Number of failed tests and Standard Deviation of results for tested kernels

failed tests happened due to setting VMM parameter *min_free_kbytes* to 256Mb which effectively cut half of the memory off the application server. Since half of the memory suddenly became not available, JVM failed to start thus failing the test. The hypothesis with preliminary separation of kernel VMM parameters into 'red' and 'blue' groups proved partially true, though the 'worst offender' was still *min_free_kbytes*.

The upper line in Figure 2 shows the averaged standard deviation for the tests. It can be noted that Debian kernels seem to have a higher deviation, while the worst is Con Kolivas's kernel.

The results of overall sensitivity analysis are shown in Figure 3. It shows the kernel parameters, which have the strongest, but not necessarily the best influence on performance of our J2EE system. This piechart was obtained by adding performance deltas across different kernels to the kernel parameters that caused it, depicted in Equation 1:

$$sensitivity = \sum(stdev(parameter, kernel)) \tag{1}$$

It can be seen that *dirty_expire_centisecs* and *min_free_kbytes* have the strongest influence on performance. Changes in the other parameters affect kernel performance on a smaller scale. More details are available in Figure 4.

An attempt to determine what VMM settings actually result in better performance is shown in Figure 5. The task was non-trivial since there was no clear winner - each kernel seemed to have its own 'winning' setting. To overcome this difficulty, the results for each kernel have been sorted by the ECPerf Bops/min number and each of the 33 parameters has been assigned a value from 1 (for showing the worst performance) to 33 (for showing the best performance). Then the appropriate parameters and their values have been aggregated across

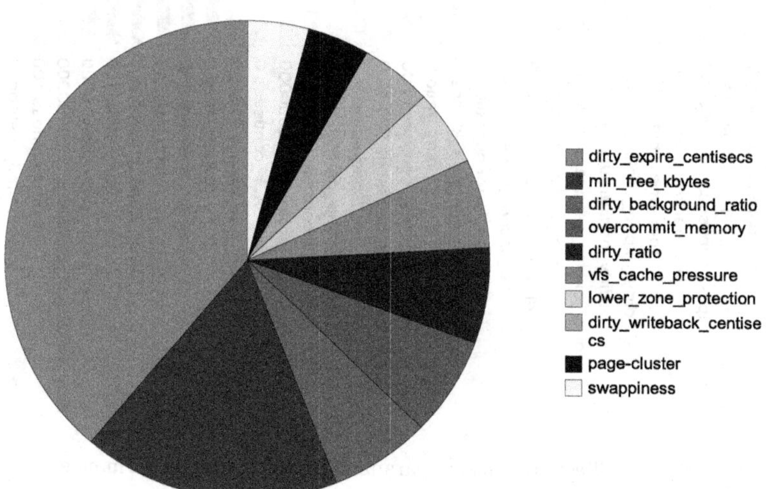

Fig. 3. Overall sensitivity of various VMM settings

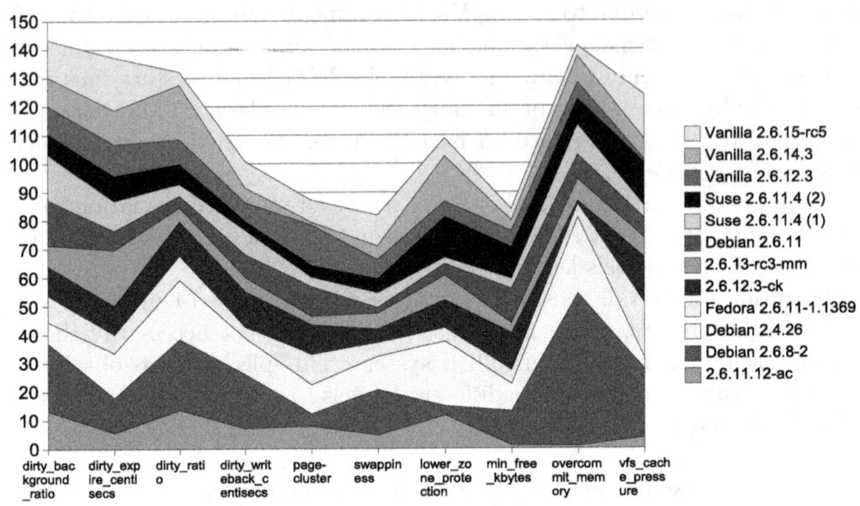

Fig. 4. Sensitivity of various VMM settings and kernels

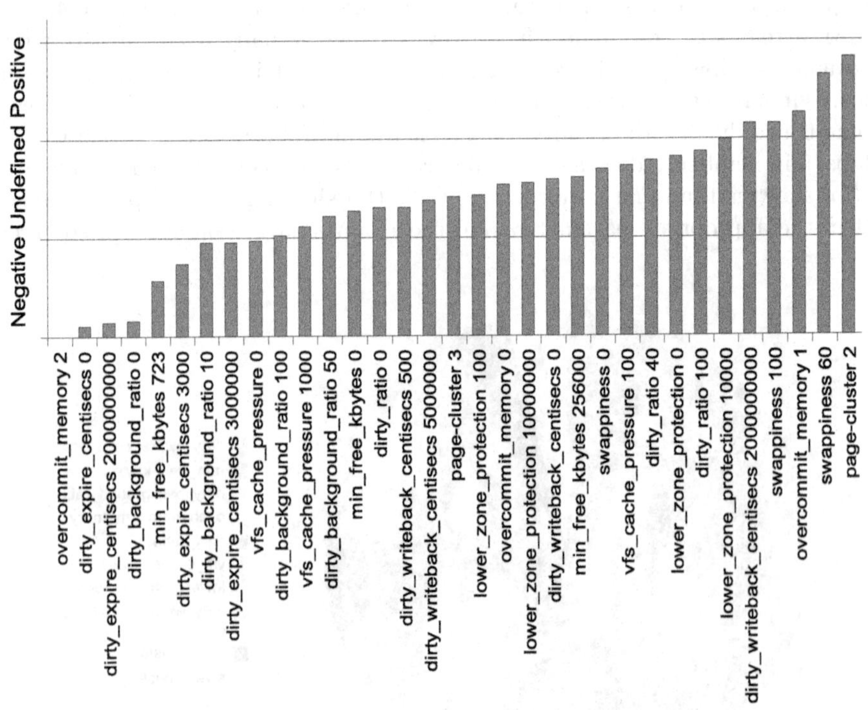

Fig. 5. Effects of various parameters settings on performance

different kernel branches. The results have been split into three categories 'likely positive', 'undefined', and 'negative'. Settings in 'likely positive' group are likely to increase the performance, while the settings in 'negative' group are very likely going to degrade your performance significantly. The rest of the settings are too close to call - they have to be tried individually on each kernel to determine what works best for that specific one.

5 Related Work

J2EE performance-related research generally deals with the software layer just beneath the application itself, *e.g.* the application server. Two most known studies have been done by Gorton *et al* [1] and Cecchet [2]. A lot of work is currently undertaken in JVM research, though it is mainly concerned with common runtime optimization and garbage collection. Also, an earlier study by the authors deals with the impact of method input parameters on the performance of EJB applications [3].

6 Conclusions and Future Work

Multiple branches of Linux kernel were tested to determine whether changes in Virtual Memory Manager (VMM) settings affect performance of J2EE applications using ECPerf benchmark. Parameters that affect performance the most were identified. Influence of specific VMM settings on performance was analysed.

We argue that performance change of above 5% by changing just one setting inside of the Virtual Memory Manager is important and cannot be overlooked, especially when dealing with performance-critical systems.

There are plans for more tests including multiple parameter optimization, more application servers: WebSphere Community Edition, WebSphere Enterprise Edition. We also plan to evaluate the influence of different process and I/O schedulers on J2EE performance as well.

Acknowledgment

The support of the Informatics Research Initiative of Enterprise Ireland is gratefully acknowledged.

References

1. Gorton, I., Liu, A., Brebner, P.: Rigorous Evaluation of COTS Middleware Technology IEEE Computer Mar (2003) 50-55
2. Cecchet, E., Marguerite, J., Zwaenepoel, W.: Performance and Scalability of EJB Applications Proc of 17th ACM Conference on Object-Oriented Programming, Seattle, Washington, (2002).
3. Oufimtsev, A. and Murphy, L.: Method Input Parameters and performance of EJB Applications. In Proc. of the OOPSLA Middleware and Component Performance workshop, ACM (2004).

On-Demand Quality-Oriented Assistance in Component-Based Software Evolution

Chouki Tibermacine, Régis Fleurquin, and Salah Sadou

VALORIA, University of South Brittany, France
{Chouki.Tibermacine, Regis.Fleurquin, Salah.Sadou}@univ-ubs.fr

Abstract. During an architectural evolution of a component-based software, certain quality attributes may be weakened. This is due to the lack of an explicit definition of the links between these non-functional characteristics and the architectural decisions implementing them. In this paper, we present a solution that aims at assisting the software maintainer during an evolution activity on his demand. It requires the definition of a documentation during development, organized in the form of bindings between formal descriptions of architectural decisions and their targeted quality attributes. Through an assistance algorithm, the approach uses this documentation in order to notify the maintainer of the possible effects of architectural changes on quality requirements. We also present a prototype tool which automates our proposals. This tool and the overall approach has been experienced on a real-world software in order to validate them.

1 Introduction

An intrinsic characteristic of software, addressing a real world activity, is the need to evolve in order to satisfy new requirements. Maintenance is now, more than ever, an inescapable activity, the cost of which is ever increasing (between 80 % and 90 % of the software total cost [5, 19]). Among the maintenance activities, the checking of functional and non-functional non regression of a software, after its evolution, is one of the most expensive. It consists in checking the existence of the newly required service or property after modification, on the one hand, and in verifying that the other properties and/or services have not been altered on the other hand. This checking is done during the regression testing stage. When problems are found, a rework on the software architecture is required. This involves a sequence of iterations of the maintenance activities, which make undoubtedly its cost grow more and more.

In this paper, we present an approach which helps to reduce the number of these necessary iterations, in the context of component-based software. It consists of warning the software developer of the possible loss of some quality attributes during an architectural evolution, well before starting regression tests. Under the assumption that the architecture of an application is determined by quality requirements such as, maintainability, portability or availability [1], we propose to formally document links between quality attributes and their

I. Gorton et al. (Eds.): CBSE 2006, LNCS 4063, pp. 294–309, 2006.

realizing architectural decisions. Thus, we automate the checking of these quality properties after an architectural change has been made.

In the next section, we show, through a system architecture, how some quality requirements can be mapped into architectural decisions and how problems can rise when evolving this architecture. We present, in section 3, the principles of our approach which helps to resolve the problem pointed in the section before. The proposed solution is based on a documentation, which is introduced in section 4. An algorithm which uses this documentation and assists the maintenance activity is discussed and illustrated by an example in section 5. A prototype tool for evolution assistance, and the validation of the approach are then presented in section 6. Before concluding and presenting the perspectives, we discuss some related works in section 7.

2 Illustrative Example

Along this paper, we use a simple imaginary example which represents a Museum Access Control System (MACS)[1]. Figure 1 provides an overview of its architecture. The system receives as input the necessary data for user authentication (`Authentication` component). After identification, the data is sent to the access control component (`AccessCtl`). The latter consults an authorization database (the component `AuthDataStore`) to check if the user[2] is authorized to enter the museum or not. Then, it adds other data elements (entrance hour, the visited gallery in the museum, etc.) to the received data flow and sends it to the `Logging` component. The component `AdminService` allows the administration of the database abstracted by the component `AuthDataStore`. The `Logging` component provides an interface for persistent local logging. This interface is used by the archiving data store component (`ArchivDataStore`) which provides an interface to a data retrieval service component (`DataRetrievalService`). This component implements an interface which allows local supervision of the museum and querying of logs. The two components `AdminService` and `DataRetrievalService` export their interfaces via the same component `DataAdminRetrieval`. After local archival storage, the data is transmitted (by the component `ServerTrans`) via the network to the central server of the organization responsible for the museum security for central archival storage.

2.1 Some Architectural Decisions and Their Rationale

The architecture, described in Figure 1, was designed taking into account quality requirements defined in the NFRs (Non-Functional Requirements) specification. We present some of these requirements and their architectural mappings.

[1] This software system is not a real-world component-based one. We just defined a few years ago within a development project a formal specification of it. We think that it is simple to present and to use as an illustrative example.

[2] Users of the museum are visitors, exhibition organizing committee members, museum administrative and service employees.

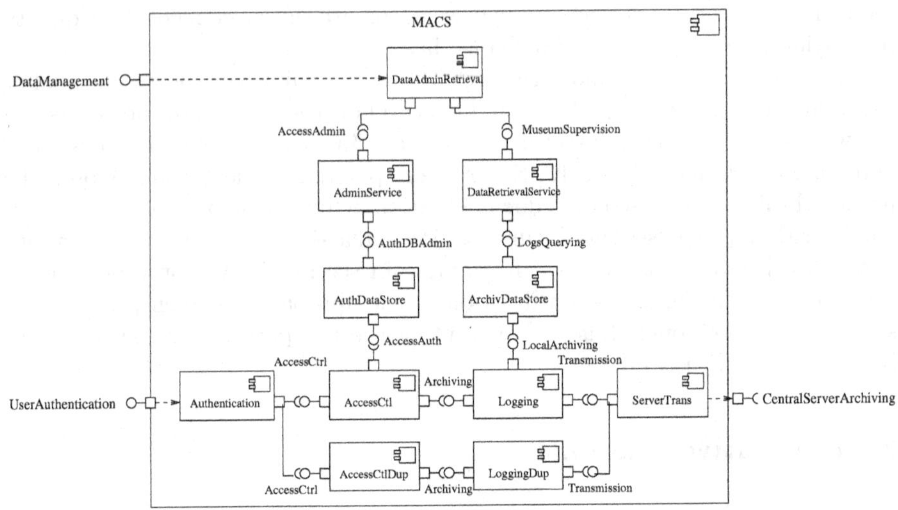

Fig. 1. A Simplified architecture of a Museum Access Control System

1. "*The system should be easily maintained.*" (We mark this maintainability quality attribute QA1.) This is ensured by the layered pattern [20], which can be seen if we decompose the system's architecture vertically. (We mark this architectural decision AD1.)
2. "*The software system should be portable over different environments. It can serve different applications for museum supervision or access control data administration.*" (This portability property is marked QA2.) To reach this *portability* level, a façade component -with analogy to façade objects [7]- was designed as front to MACS's internals. In Figure 1, this is performed by the component `DataAdminRetrieval`. All communications from client applications to access MACS's data management services transit by this component. (We mark this architectural decision AD2.)
3. "*The access control functionality should be more available for service employees.*" (We mark this availability property QA3) In the bottom of Figure 1, the sequence of components `AccessCtl` and `Logging` is duplicated. This redundancy scheme (marked AD3) is a mean to make the system fault tolerant and thus fulfills the availability requirement. If one of the two components (`AccessCtl` or `Logging`) fails, the sequence below (`AccessCtlDup` and `LoggingDup`) takes over the process. In this degraded mode of the system functioning, the component `AccessCtlDup` authorizes the access only to service employees. Logs remain in the state of the component `LoggingDup` and are not persistent in the `ArchivDataStore` component. Then, the data is transmitted to the central server.

   The sequence of these duplicates is organized as a pipeline [20]. (We mark this decision AD4.) In a pipeline each filter (component) has only one reference to the downstream component. This guarantees a certain level of maintainability (minimal coupling, QA1) required for such emergency solution. This pattern also guarantees a certain level of performance defined in the NFRs specification, but not detailed here. We mark this last quality attribute QA4.

The developers have introduced a data abstraction component (`DataRetrivalService`), which abstracts details of the underlying databases. This architectural decision is marked AD5. Indeed, this traditional practice fulfills the first attribute (QA1).

2.2 Some Evolution Scenarios and Their Consequences

Let us assume that the maintenance team receives two change requests that must be tackled urgently. As a consequence, changes are made without taking into account the associated design documentation. The first request imposes that henceforth some data should be directly transmitted to the central server. That is, a part of information about service employees should be directly sent to the `ServerTrans` component after identification. This gives the system more (time and space) performance. Thus, the system maintainers decide to create a link between `AccessCtl` component and `ServerTrans` component; and between `AccessCtlDup` and `ServerTrans` components. (We mark this change ACG1.) In the last case, the `AccessCtlDup` component finds itself with two links. The first one with the `LoggingDup` component for the data flow that is not affected by the modification and the second one with the `ServerTrans` component for the data that is directly transmitted to the central server. This modification makes the system lose the benefits of the pipeline structure (breaks AD4). Therefore, the initial level of maintainability (QA1) of the system is now weakened.

While the first change request has a non-functional goal, the second change is of functional nature. It asks to add a new component representing a notification service: `DB_UpdateNotification`. This component notifies the client applications, subscribed to its services, when updates are done on the archiving database. This new component exports a *publish/subscribe* interface via the port that provides the interface `DataManagement`. It implements a *publish on-demand* interaction pattern and uses directly the component `ArchivDataStore`. This change (marked ACG2) makes the system lose the benefits of the façade pattern guaranteed by the component `DataAdminRetrieval` (AD2) and consequently weakens the availability quality attribute QA2.

The lack of knowledge during evolution about the reasons which have led the initial architects to make such decisions, may easily lead to break some architectural decisions and consequently affect the corresponding quality attributes. The two simple examples above illustrate how can we lose such properties. This is often noticed during regression testing. Thus, it is necessary to perform changes on the architecture another time, and to iterate, frequently, for many times. Several similar remarks have been noticed by our industrial partner when evolving one of its complex system (a cartographic converter from different binary files and spatial databases to SVG (Scalable Vector Graphics) format, for using them in a Geographic Information System -GIS-). We didn't present this system as an illustrative example in this paper for reasons of brevity and simplicity.

3 Principles of the Approach

Our approach aims at solving the problems quoted in the previous section. It consists in making explicit and formal the reasons behind architectural decisions. The choice of a formal language to specify this documentation guarantees not only the unambiguity of descriptions but also allows the automation of some operations, like the preservation of architectural choices throughout the development process of a component-based software [23].

Based on the assumption that architectural decisions are determined by the quality information stated in the requirements specification, we propose to maintain the knowledge of the links binding quality attributes to architectural decisions. This knowledge is of great interest for maintainers on two accounts:

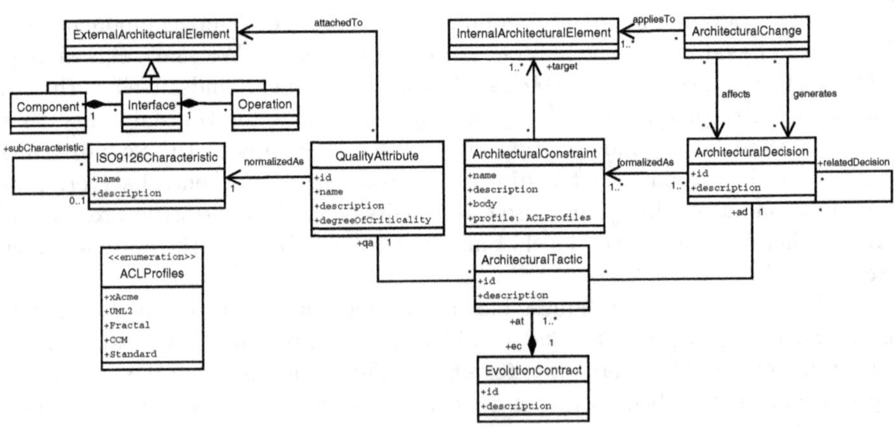

Fig. 2. Structure of Contracts

- **Preservation of Quality Attributes:** it will be possible to warn the developer, at each architectural maintenance stage, of the potential deterioration of some quality attributes;
- **Architecture Comprehension:** it is easier to understand a specific architecture when we already know its motivations. Starting from the specification of a targeted evolution, it becomes possible to identify the related architectural artifacts.

In the remaining of this paper, we use some terms which we define as following:

Quality Attribute (QA): a quality characteristic targeted by one of the statements in the non-functional requirements specification;

Architectural Decision (AD): a part of the software architecture that targets one or several QAs;
Architectural Tactic (AT): a couple composed of an AD and a QA defining the link between one architectural decision and one quality attribute;
Evolution Contract (EC): a set of ATs defined for a given software.

These definitions are illustrated in Figure 2. An architectural decision may have several related decisions, which are present in different ATs. For example, AD3 (replicated components) in section 2 has one related decision which is AD4 (pipeline). Indeed, if AD3 is removed from MACS architecture, AD4 will also disappear. As explained in section 4.2, an architectural decision is formalized as an architectural constraint. Each constraint is specified using an architectural predicate language, called ACL. This language has several profiles dedicated to existing architecture/component models, for example xAcme [26] or CORBA Component Model [14] (more details are given in section 4.2). A constraint targets an internal architectural element. Internal architectural elements are architectural abstractions present in the metamodel of the used architecture or component description language (e.g. a component, a connector or an interface). An architectural change is applied on one or many internal architectural elements. It can affect or generate one or several architectural decisions. A QA corresponds to an ISO/IEC 9126 [9] characteristic or sub-characteristic (e.g. maintainability, portability or usability). Each QA has a degree of criticality (inspired from Kazman's QA scores and Clements's QA priorities [3]). The value of this degree, specified by developers, stipulate the importance of this quality attribute in the architecture. It takes values between 1 and 100. The sum of values of all these degrees should be at most 100. Starting from non-functional requirements (NFRs), we may extract one or several QAs. Each one is attached to several external architectural elements. These elements represent the common **externally visible** architectural concepts present in existing component models (component, interface and operation). These external architectural elements are a subset of internal architectural elements.

4 Capturing Architecture Decisions and Their Rationale in Contracts

Based on the structure presented above, to document an architecture, we need a language for defining evolution contracts and a tool set to edit and interpret this documentation.

4.1 Evolution Contract Organization

In order to specify textually ECs, we use an XML representation which conforms to the structure presented in Figure 2. The following listing illustrates an example of such specification.

```
<evolution-contract id = "000001">
  <architecture-tactic id = "000100">
    <description>
      This tactic ensures the Portability quality requirement by
      using a Facade Design Pattern
    </description>
    <quality-attribute id = "001000" name = "Portability"
         characteristic = "Portability">
      <description>
        The software system should be portable
        over different environments. It can
        serve different applications for museum
        supervision or access control
        data administration
      </description>
    </quality-attribute>
    <architecture-decision id = "010000">
      <description>
        Facade design pattern
      </description>
      <formalization profile = "Fractal">
        <!--Here we edit the ACL constraint-->
      </formalization>
    </architecture-decision>
  </architecture-tactic>
</evolution-contract>
```

This simple example illustrates a simple EC composed of only one of the ATs presented in section 2. This AT concerns the façade design pattern AD associated to the portability QA. The `formalization` element of this EC contains the formal definition of the AD which is described in the next section.

4.2 AD Definition Language

In order to formalize architectural decisions, we proposed a predicate language called ACL (Architectural Constraint Language). This language is based on a slightly modified version of UML's Object Constraint Language [15], called CCL (Core Constraint Language), and on a set of MOF metamodels. Each metamodel represents the architectural abstractions used at a given stage in the component-based development process. A couple formed by CCL and a given metamodel represents an ACL profile. Each profile can be used at a stage in the development process. We defined ACL profiles for xAcme, UML 2 [16], CORBA components, Enterprise JavaBeans [21] and many others. CCL navigates in the architecture's metamodel in order to define constraints on its elements.

Instead of presenting the grammar of ACL, we preferred to illustrate it through the description of two AD examples from section 2.1. We describe this ADs using the standard profile of ACL, which is composed of CCL and of a generic architecture metamodel called ArchMM [23]. This metamodel is used as an intermediate representation when transforming ACL constraints from one profile to another.

The listing below describes the constraint enforcing the façade architectural pattern in the component MACS.

```
context MACS:CompositeComponent inv:
let boundToDataManagement:Bag=MACS.port.interface
->select(i:Interface|i.kind = 'Provided'
and i.name = 'DataManagement').port.binding
in
((boundToDataManagement->size() = 1)
and (boundToDataManagement.interface
->select(i:Interface|i.kind = 'Provided').port.component.name
->includes('DataAdminRetrieval')))
```

This constraint states that the `DataManagement` provided interface of MACS component must be bound internally to one and only one interface. The latter corresponds to the provided interface of `DataAdminRetrieval` component.

The following constraint concerns the replicated components stated by AD3.

```
context MACS:CompositeComponent inv:
let startingPort:Port=MACS.port->select(p:Port|
i.name='UserAuthentication') in
let startingComponent:Component=startingPort.getInternalComponent() in

let endingPort:Port=MACS.port->select(p:Port|
i.name='CentralServerArchiving') in
let endingComponent:Component=endingPort.getInternalComponent() in

let paths:OrderedSet=MACS.configuration
.getPaths(startingComponent,endingComponent) in

paths.size() = 2 and paths->first()->excludesAll(paths->last())
```

This constraint uses two operations from ArchMM. The first one (`getInternalComponent()`) returns the subcomponent attached to a given port of a composite component. The second operation (`getPaths(c1:Component,c2:Component)`) returns an ordered set of all the paths between the components given as parameters. The returned paths are also represented by ordered sets of components. A returned path excludes the parameter components. The constraint states that it must exist two distinct paths between the component attached to `UserAuthentication` port and the component attached to `CentralServerArchiving` port.

The two-level expression nature of ACL guarantees the homogeneity of constraints defined in different stages of the development process. Indeed, only metamodels change from one stage to another; the core constraint language remains the same. This has been of great interest when we performed transformations of constraints from one stage to another in order to automatically preserve architectural decisions [24].

5 Using Contracts in Evolution Assistance

In the proposed approach, an AT is perceived as a constraint which has to be checked for validity during each evolution. An evolution contract may be seen as a contract, because it documents the rights and the duties of two parties: the developer of the previous version of the architecture who guarantees the quality attributes and the developer of the new version who should respect the evolution contract established by the former. The evolution contract is elaborated during the development of the first version of the architecture. ATs appear in each development stage where a motivated AD is made. Thus, the evolution contract is built gradually and enriched as the project evolves. ATs can even be inherited from a Software Quality Plan and thus, can emerge even before starting the software development. Thereafter, this evolution contract can be modified in respect of the rules below:

- **Rule 1:** "*a consistent system is a system where each QA is involved in at least one AT*". This condition ensures that, at the end of the maintenance process, there is no dangling QA (i.e. with no associated ADs). The breach of this condition implies *de facto* the obligation to modify the non-functional specification;
- **Rule 2:** "*we should not prohibit an evolution stage. We simply notify, at the demand by the developer of a change validation, the attempt of breaking one or more ADs and we specify the affected QAs stated in the evolution contract*". It is of the developer's responsibility, fully aware of the consequences, to maintain or not the modification. If this modification is maintained, the corresponding ATs are discarded. Indeed, The substitution of an architectural decision by another may be done without affecting the targeted quality attributes. Moreover, we can be brought to invalidate, temporally, a decision to perform a specific modification;
- **Rule 3:** "*we can add new ATs to the evolution contract*". Thus, during an evolution, new architectural decisions can complete, improve or replace old ones.

The previous rules are illustrated by the simple architectural maintenance scenario in Figure 3. Consider the previous example presented in section 2. The evolution contract associated to the MACS component, which contain 6 ATs, is illustrated in the bottom part of the figure. Note that for reasons of simplicity we organized the evolution contract by factorizing QAs. Architectural changes are represented at the top of the figure. The minus symbol stipulates that the corresponding AD has been affected, and the plus symbol shows that the AD is preserved or enhanced. Forward arrows mean that the architectural maintainer decides to validate her/his change, however backward arrows mean she/he does not maintain her/his decision. At the middle of the figure, we illustrate the evolution of the assistance system, the different warnings that it triggers and the validation or not of the different intermediate evolution contracts.

Let us suppose that a software maintainer applies ACG1, which was presented in section 2, to MACS architecture (second column of figure 3). As stated

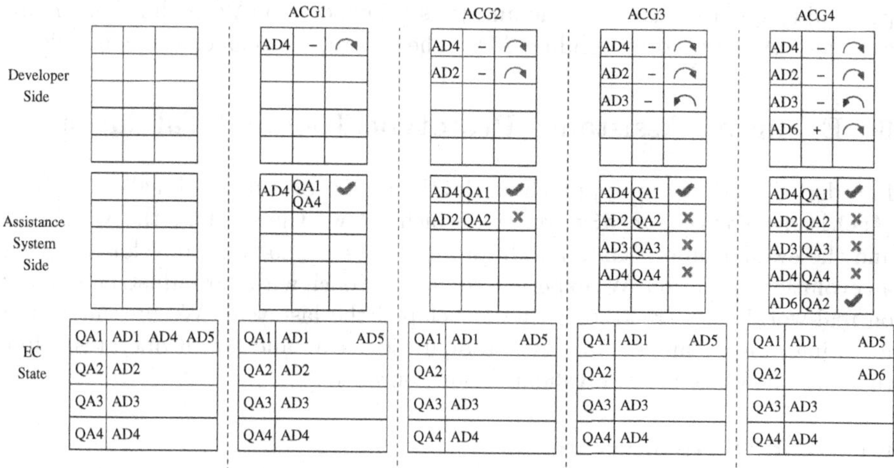

Fig. 3. Assisting the evolution activity with evolution contract

in that section, this change affects AD4. The assistance algorithm checks the ACL constraint present in MACS's EC which is associated to this decision, and consequently warn the maintainer that AD4 is altered and that QA1 and QA4 are also possibly affected. Knowing that ACG1 enhances QA4 -AT6(QA4,AD4) not affected-, the maintainer decides to validate his change. The EC is considered valid, while there is no QA without associated ADs (see the second table in the bottom of the figure).After that, the maintainer decides to apply ACG2, which was also presented in section 2. He is thus notified that AD2 and its associated QA, namely QA2, are potentially affected. He decides to continue, but the EC is in this case not valid, as soon as there is one QA (QA2) without associated AD (see the third table in the bottom of the figure). Later, the maintainer tries to apply ACG3. This change consists in removing the `LoggingDup` component. Concretely, the system maintainer discovered that data in this component is not consistent with data in the `ArchivDataStore` component. He is immediately notified that ACG3 alter AD3 (replicated components) and consequently QA3 (availability property) will be eventually affected. In addition, this AD has one related decision, namely AD4 which represents the pipeline pattern. The assistance system, by scanning the EC, warns the maintainer that AD4 and QA1 (Maintainability) and QA4 (Performance) are also affected. This time, the maintainer does not keep his changes and undoes the changes made on the architecture. Note that, the EC is still invalid. Finally, the maintainer decides to make a new architectural change (ACG4). It consists in removing the hierarchical connector between the newly added notification sub-component (`DB_UpdateNotification`) and MACS's `DataManagement` port, and adding a new connector between the former and the component `DataAdminRetrieval`. The motivation behind adding this new AD, marked **AD6**, is to re-ensure the portability quality characteristic and thus reintroduce QA2 in the EC. In this case, all QAs have corresponding ADs. The contract is thus considered valid.

6 Evolution Assistance Prototype Tool and Validation

In order to validate our approach we developed a prototype tool, called AURES (`ArchitURe Evolution aSsistant`), which allows the edition, the validation and the evaluation of ECs. In addition, it assists the software developer during an evolution operation. We experienced our approach with our industrial partner on real-world software system they developed the last year. We present in the following subsections the prototype tool, its structure and how it operates. After that, we introduce how we validated our approach.

6.1 AURES Architecture

This tool is organized as in Figure 4 and is composed of the following elements:

EC Editor: This component allows the edition of evolution contracts. It uses the XMI format of metamodels of the different ACL profiles to guide the developer in editing her/his architectural constraints. It asks the developer to introduce the necessary information discussed previously in order to complete and generate the EC.

EC Validator: This component validates an EC with an introduced architecture description. If the EC evaluation returns false, the developer is requested to correct either the EC or the architecture description; else this component produces an archive file composed of the architecture description and the EC files, saved by the `Version Handler` component.

Evolution Assistant: When a new version of the architecture is submitted, the EC of the latest version is then checked out from the `Version Handler` component. This EC is then reevaluated on the new architecture description. If the evaluation returns true, the new architecture description is associated to the EC and then it is saved in the `Version Handler` component; else the architecture evolver is warned that some ADs are altered and that consequently the associated QAs are affected.

EC Evaluator: To evaluate an EC, this component uses a temporary pivot model and the ArchMM metamodel. The pivot model is a direct instance of ArchMM, produced by the `Description Transformer` subcomponent, from a given architecture description. This subcomponent executes a set of XSL scripts to make XML transformations of architecture descriptions. For the moment, the prototype presented in this paper supports architectures described in the Fractal ADL [2] and in xAcme. However, the pivot model makes the tool easily extensible. The `EC Evaluator` is composed of an `ACL Compiler` which extends the OCL Compiler[11] and which requires the AD part of the EC. It also contains an `ACL Interpreter`, which evaluates ACL boolean expressions. Note that, this component is used by two other components: the `EC Validator` and the `Evolution Assistant`. When it is invoked

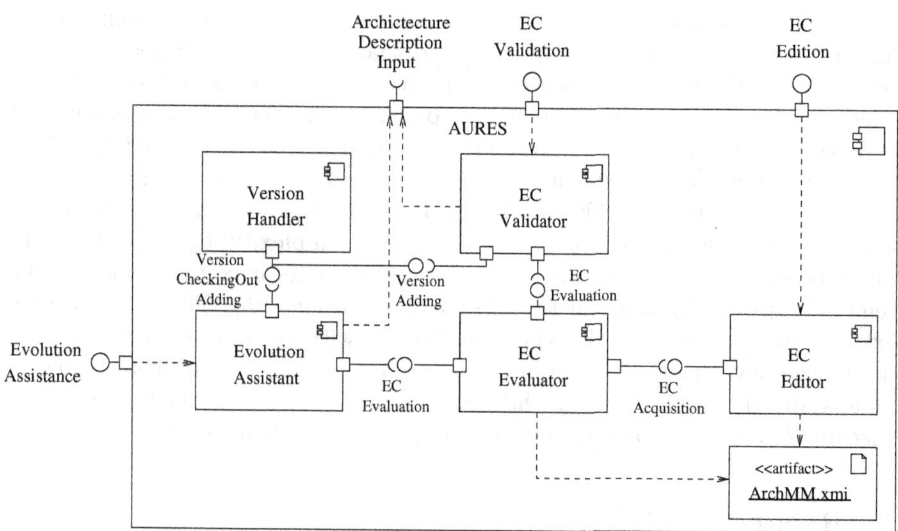

Fig. 4. A prototype tool for ECs edition and interpretation, and for evolution assistance

by the first one, only constraints involving one version of the architecture are evaluated. However, if it is requested by the second one, all constraints are evaluated. The latest architecture description is checked out with the EC and transformed to the pivot model to be evaluated.

6.2 Example of Use

Let us consider one of the evolution scenarios presented in section 2.2. This concerns the addition of a component representing a notification service. Once this new architecture description introduced to the `Evolution Assistant` component, the latter checks out the EC corresponding to `MACS` from the component `Version Handler` and then displays a warning report. This report notifies the architecture evolver that the Façade pattern does not hold anymore and that the portability property has been affected. The architecture evolver should either modify his new architecture description, or the EC and consequently the NFRs specification.

6.3 Validation of the Approach

We experienced our approach on Alkanet, a GIS developed by our industrial partner. The project cost has been estimated at 2500 men-hours and its maintenance cost at 1400 men-hours. Starting from maintenance logs, we took the software components that have been the most affected by the maintenance. These components perform the conversion of different types of data format to SVG. A team composed of developers, who know the initial NFRs specification, has documented these components (their initial version) by the necessary evolution contracts. After that, starting from this documented version of the components, another group of developers, equivalent to that who has performed the maintenance initially, has performed the same set of evolution scenarios as in logs. They use AURES for validating changes on the components after applying each scenario. We noticed that the maintenance cost has been reduced by 35 %. Indeed, we passed from 600 men-hours estimated for the maintenance of the converter components to 390 men-hours. It is true that the chosen components are the most complex. For components of less complexity, the gain would be undoubtedly less. But, the most complex components have the highest maintenance costs (Lehman's 2nd law of system evolution [10]). This allowed us to extrapolate this result on the whole application without a lot of errors. According to the developers' declarations, evolution contracts helped them to better understand the architecture of the software to evolve. Furthermore, automatic checking of architectural constraints has been of great benefit.

7 Related Work

Capturing and documenting design rationale is a research challenge, with an increased interest in the software engineering community [22]. Within the context of software architecture, Tyree and Akerman in [25] discussed the importance of documenting architecture decisions and making them first-class entities in architecture description. They present a template to describe them at a high-level of abstraction during development. Their paper focuses on the methodological aspect of describing these templates and not on how they can be used when evolving an architecture as in our approach. In the architecture evolution field, Lindvall et al. presented a survey on techniques employed in diagnosing or researching degeneration in software architectures and treating it [8]. Architecture degeneration is seen as the deviation of the actual architecture from the planned one. Many of the technologies presented in this paper focus on recognition of architecture styles and design patterns, and their extraction from code. This helps to identify deviations by comparing architectures and their properties before and after an evolution. The authors also discuss visualization techniques of architectural changes to understand software evolution and thus deduce degenerated portions in the evolved architecture. For treating this degeneration, the authors present a survey of existing refactoring techniques. Our approach allows the degeneration identification by checking formal documents (evolution contracts) on architecture descriptions before and after evolution. It alerts software evolvers about degenerated components in the architecture and the consequences of this degeneration on quality requirements. It then assists them by using quality information to treat this degeneration.

As in software architecture evaluation methods like ATAM or SAAM [3], our approach forces the architect to create architecture documentation. However, while these evaluation methods are applied during design to detect if a given architectural decision is risky or not according to quality requirements; in our approach, we assume that a posteriori all decisions are non-risky and we care about their preservation during evolution. Our approach can be seen as a complementary technique to these methods and is used downstream. In this manner, we may use an evaluation method only during analysis/design stage and avoid its use after each evolution.

In the literature, non-functional properties (which include quality attributes) has been supported on the software development through two approaches. The first one is process-oriented, while the second is product-centric. In the first approach, methods for software development driven by NFRs are proposed. They support NFR refinement to obtain a software product which complies to the initial NFRs [13, 4]. In the second approach, the non-functional information is embedded within the software product. It is the case in our approach, where evolution contracts, which embed statements of NFRs, are associated to architectural descriptions. In [6], Franch and Botella propose to formalize non-functional requirement specifications. The statements of these specifications are encapsulated in modules, which are associated to a component definition and to its implementations. They propose also an algorithm, which allows the selection of the best implementation for a given component definition. This selection method can be used when a new implementation is proposed to ensure that the best one is used. The authors mean by "best", the implementation that better fits to its non-functional requirements. In our work, we focus on the architectural (structural) aspect of components, while they consider the abstract data type view of components. In addition, in our case, the maintenance is performed on architectural descriptions or component configurations while changes in their approach are made at a fine-grained implementation level.

8 Conclusion and Future Work

In early 1990's, Perry and Wolf presented a model for software architectures. This model represents software architectures in the form of three basic abstractions: *Elements*, *Form* and *Rationale* [17]. *Elements* are architectural entities responsible for processing and storing data or encapsulating interactions. *Form* consists of properties -constraints on the choice of elements- and relationships -constraints on the topology of the elements-. The *Rationale* captures the motivation for the choice of an architectural style, the choice of elements and the form. While the description of the two first aspects have received a lot of attention by the software architecture community [12], there has been a little effort devoted to the last aspect. In this paper, we presented evolution contracts, as a contribution to the description of the last element in Perry's model. This evolution contract leads to make explicit and checkable architectural decisions (Elements and Form in Perry's model). Thus, it is possible to assist architectural evolution activity and prevent the loss of quality attributes (Rationale in Perry's model). It is, as we think best, a good practice for documenting software architectures and design rationale, and thus facilitating software comprehension in maintenance activities.

On the conceptual level, we plan studying: i) reusability, substitution and extension of ECs, and ii) quality quantification by associating metrics to QAs. This helps to better assist the maintenance activity. On the tool level, we project to stabilize the prototype before integrating it in a CASE tool. This would guide, in a continuous way, the system maintainer. We are also studying the feasibility of integrating the tool in a Configuration Management System. We limit our study to CMS dedicated to software architectures, like Mae [18]. Thus we take advantage from the enhanced control version capabilities of these systems.

References

1. L. Bass, P. Clements, and R. Kazman. *Software Architecture in Practice, 2nd Edition.* Addison-Wesley, 2003.
2. E. Bruneton, C. Thierry, M. Leclercq, V. Quéma, and S. Jean-Bernard. An open component model and its support in java. In *Proceedings of CBSE'04. Held in conjunction with ICSE'04*, Edinburgh, Scotland, may 2004.
3. P. Clements, R. Kazman, and M. Klein. *Evaluating Software Architectures, Methods and Case Studies.* Addison-Wesley, 2002.
4. L. M. Cysneiros and J. C. Sampaio do Prado Leite. Nonfunctional requirements: From elicitation to conceptual models. *IEEE TSE*, 30(5):328–350, 2004.
5. L. Erlikh. Leveraging legacy system dollars for e-business. *IEEE IT Professional*, 2(3), 2000.
6. X. Franch and P. Botella. Supporting software maintenance with non-functional information. In *Proceedings of the First IEEE Euromicro Conference on Software Maintenance and Reengineering (CSMR'97)*, pages 10–16, Berlin, Germany, March 1997. IEEE Computer Society.
7. E. Gamma, R. Helm, R. Johnson, and J. Vlissides. *Design Patterns: Elements of Reusable Object-Oriented Sofware.* Addison-Wesley Professional Computing Series. Addison Wesley Longman, Inc., 1995.
8. L. Hochstein and M. Lindvall. Combating architectural degenration: A survey. *Information and Software Technology*, 47(10):693–707, July 2005.
9. ISO. Software engineering - product quality - part 1: Quality model. International Organization for Standardization web site. ISO/IEC 9126-1. http://www.iso.org, 2001.
10. M. M. Lehman and J. F. Ramil. Software evolution in the age of component-based software engineering. *IEE Proceedings - Software*, 147(6):249–255, 2000.
11. S. Loecher and S. Ocke. A Metamodel-Based OCL-Compiler for UML and MOF. In *Proceedings of the workshop on OCL 2.0 - Industry standard or scientific playground?, 6th International Conference on the Unified Modelling Language and its Applications*, volume 154 of ENTCS, October 2003. Elsevier
12. N. Medvidovic and N. R. Taylor. A classification and comparison framework for software architecture description languages. *IEEE TSE*, 26(1):70–93, 2000.
13. J. Mylopoulos, L. Chung, and B. Nixon. Representing and using nonfunctional requirements: A process-oriented approach. *IEEE TSE*, 18(6):483–497, June 1992.
14. OMG. Corba components, v3.0, adpoted specification, document formal/2002-06-65. Object Management Group Web Site: http://www.omg.org/docs/formal/02-06-65.pdf, June 2002.
15. OMG. Uml 2.0 ocl final adopted specification, document ptc/03-10-14. Object Management Group Web Site: http://www.omg.org/docs/ptc/03-10-14.pdf, 2003.

16. OMG. Uml 2.0 superstructure final adopted specification, document ptc/03-08-02. Object Management Group Web Site: http://www.omg.org/docs/ptc/03-08-02.pdf, 2003.
17. D. E. Perry and A. L. Wolf. Foundations for the study of software architecture. *ACM SIGSOFT Software Engineering Notes*, 17(4):40–52, 1992.
18. R. Roshandel, A. van der Hoek, M. Mikic-Rakic, and N. Medvidovic. Mae - a system model and environment for managing architectural evolution. *ACM TOSEM*, 11(2):240–276, April 2004.
19. R. C. Seacord, D. Plakosh, and G. A. Lewis. *Modernizing Legacy Systems: Software Technologies, Engineering Processes, and Business Practices.* SEI Series in Software Engineering. Pearson Education, 2003.
20. M. Shaw and D. Garlan. *Software Architecture: Perspectives on an Emerging Discipline.* Prentice Hall, 1996.
21. Sun-Microsystems. Enterprise javabeans(tm) specification, version 2.1. http://java.sun.com/products/ejb, November 2003.
22. A. Tang, M. A. Babar, I. Gorton, and J. Han. A survey of the use and documentation of architecture design rationale. In *Proceedings of the 5th IEEE/IFIP Working Conference on Software Architecture (WICSA'05)*, pages 89–98, Pittsburgh, Pennsylvania, USA, November 2005, IEEE CS.
23. C. Tibermacine, R. Fleurquin, and S. Sadou. Preserving architectural choices throughout the component-based software development process. In *Proceedings of the 5th IEEE/IFIP Working Conference on Software Architecture (WICSA'05)*, pages 121–130, Pittsburgh, Pennsylvania, USA, November 2005. IEEE CS.
24. C. Tibermacine, R. Fleurquin, and S. Sadou. Simplifying transformations of architectural constraints. In *Proceedings of ACM SAC (SAC'06), Track on Model Transformation*, Dijon, France, April 2006. ACM Press.
25. J. Tyree and A. Akerman. Architecture decisions: Demystifying architecture. *IEEE Software*, 22(2):19–27, March/April 2005.
26. xAcme: Acme Extensions to xArch. School of Computer Science Web Site: http://www-2.cs.cmu.edu/ acme/pub/xAcme/, 2001.

Components Have Test Buddies

Pankaj Jalote[*], Rajesh Munshi, and Todd Probsting

Microsoft Corporation
One Microsoft Way
Redmond, WA 98052
jalote@iitk.ac.in, {rajeshm, toddpro}@microsoft.com

Abstract. Most large software systems are architected as component-based systems. In such systems, components are developed and tested separately. As components cooperate for providing services, testing of a component also reveals defects in other components. In this paper we study the role testing of other components plays in finding defects in a component by analyzing defect data of an earlier version of Windows. Our analysis shows that testing of other components often is the largest source of finding defects in a component. The analysis also shows that though many components reveal defects in a component, often a small set of components – the Test Buddies – exists whose testing reveals the vast majority of the defects found by testing other components. The Test Buddies of a component are those with a heavy interaction with the component and represent the high priority customers for testing. The Test Buddy information for a system can be determined by the test data of an earlier release, and then can be used in different ways to improve the testing.

1 Introduction

There are many large software systems today that have a few million Lines of Code in them. Almost all such systems now use a component-based architecture to organize their code and to manage the development. In a component-based software system, a software product is viewed as a set of components, each component providing a well defined functionality through a well defined interface. Components interact with each other through the interfaces. Generally, a component will use services of some other component to provide its own services, and this causes the dependency between components.

Testing a component-based software system throws up new challenges as a comprehensive testing should include testing of components, integration testing to test how components interact, and system testing [12]. Some approaches for testing component-based systems have been proposed (e.g. [1, 6, 13, 14]), mostly focusing on the situation where the software system being built uses some third party components, which introduces new issues like lack of source code availability, independent evolution, etc.

Though using commercial components for building new applications is indeed a major use of component-based software engineering, most large software products, which may not use any third party components, are engineered as component-based

[*] P. Jalote was a visiting researcher at Microsoft when the work was done. His current address is Department of Computer Science and Engineering; Indian Institute of Technology; Kanpur – 208016; India.

I. Gorton et al. (Eds.): CBSE 2006, LNCS 4063, pp. 310–319, 2006.

systems. Reasons for using component-based approach when all the components are developed within the organization include ease of work distribution, management and code ownership, modularity, separation of concerns, architectural considerations, etc. When building these large software products, a component is often developed independently by a dedicated team. A component is tested independently (often by a dedicated team) in different usage scenarios before it is made available for integration with other components through some source code control repository. Testing of the whole product often comprises of testing scripts of components enhanced by some system level testing scripts.

When testing a component, test cases are generally written from the perspective of that component. That is, the testers for a component write the test cases to drive the component under various scenarios it is can be used in. These scenarios are typically determined from the usage scenarios for the overall product. As there are dependencies between components, since they collaborate to provide the functionality of the larger system, the testing of a component inevitably exercises and tests some other components as well. That is, though the focus is to detect defects in a particular component, the test cases developed for that component inevitably detect defects in other components as well. Little work has been done to understand the defect finding relationship between components and the impact of testing a component on finding defects in other components. In this paper, we focus on this issue and study the defect finding relationship between components, based on the analysis of defect data of many components of an earlier release of Windows.

Our analysis shows that for a large system like Windows where there are complex interactions between components, testing of other components plays a critical role in revealing defects in a component. We found that the largest fraction of defects of a component is detected through testing of other components. On analyzing this further, we found that a component often has Test Buddies, which are the small set of components whose testing reveals most of the externally found bugs. In other words, though many defects in a component were being found through testing of other components, of these defects, a vast majority were actually being found by testing of only a few components – the Test Buddies.

Test Buddies of a component essentially represent the components which have a high bandwidth interaction with it, that is, those that depend most on it and interact most heavily with it. They can be viewed as the highest priority customers of a component. Though Test Buddies cannot be determined by static analysis, they can be determined easily from the defect data of a product.

The information about Test Buddies can be used in various ways to improve the testing and development process. It can be of particular help when a component changes and test cases have to be selected for regression testing.

2 Components and Testing

Let us first briefly describe how components are organized and tested. In Windows, there is a defined component hierarchy, which groups the components in some areas like networking, file system, process management, etc. [9]. The component hierarchy is centrally defined and all development occurs within this context. If a new component is needed, it has to be defined in this hierarchy, as all other support and tracking systems assume that only the components defined in this hierarchy exist.

Each component has a team which consists of a development team as well as a test team. The test team for the component develops the test cases based on system usage scenarios and develops the test scripts for them. The test team is responsible for executing these test cases and recording the defects they find in their component or in some other component. Defects found though means other than testing (e.g. using static analysis tool like PreFix[4]) are also logged.

Each test case has a unique test identifier. There is a testing framework that logs the execution of each of the test cases. Coverage and other data for each test case are recorded in a centralized database. When changes are made to some component, in-house tools are used to prioritize the test cases, based on which decisions are made on which test cases to execute [10].

As defects are found by many different groups, but are usually fixed by the owner of the code in which the defect exists, generally when the defect is recorded, a considerable amount of information is logged to facilitate debugging and fixing of defects. Often, a record for a defect will contain:

- Component where the defect is
- The person who found the defect
- The method of finding the defect
- Symptoms and how they can be recreated
- Date and time of logging (automatically recorded)
- Severity, criticality, priority, nature, etc (for prioritization purposes)

The life cycle of a defect is something like the following. During some quality control (QC) task performed to identify defects, some erroneous behavior is observed. This is logged, along with other information, by the person who finds the defect. Once a defect is entered, it is in "open" state. The defect is attributed to a component. For identifying the component to which a defect belongs, if needed, the defect triaging process, where people from different component groups meet to discuss the defects found, is employed. The open defects are typically assigned to some developer (often the owner of the code) for fixing. The developer fixes the bug; the fix is verified to ensure that the scenario that caused the defect now is successful, and then the defect is marked as "closed".

Defect logging is an industry best practice [3] and is widely followed. It is this recorded defect data that is the main data source of our analysis. Though there are over a thousand components and a large number of defects recorded, we focused only on those components that had contributed the most defects. These generally are the largest components, and each had over a thousand defects logged against it. There were over 50 such components for our analysis.

3 Finding Bugs in a Component – Role of Testing of Other Components

The first part of our analysis is to study the role testing of other components plays in testing a component. As testing of each component is being done separately and by separate test teams, and as the complete system testing is essentially testing of components, understanding this relationship will help.

This analysis is part of a wider analysis, the when-who-how analysis, which was done of the logged defects. In this three dimensional analysis, for a defect we focus on the data about when it was detected, who detected it, and how it was detected. For the when analysis, the development timeline is divided with milestones, each milestone representing some intermediate delivery. For the how analysis, the method for finding the defect was categorized into a few categories like testing, stress testing, application of code analysis tools, code review, etc. For the who analysis, the groups involved in finding defects were categorized into a few categories. This three dimensional analysis of defects was done to find areas of improvement in the overall quality control process being followed. Analysis along each of these dimensions offered a different perspective and new insights into the defect finding process.

For this work, it is the analysis along the "who" dimension that is pertinent. For this analysis, we consider each team that is independently detecting defects as a unit. This method can result in a large number of teams, most of them being test teams of components. As our analysis takes a component perspective, for a component, we can partition the test teams of components into two groups – "Internal" and "OtherTestTeams". For a component, the internal test team is its own test team while OtherTestTeams comprise of test teams of other components. Besides these two groups, there are other categories also, depending on the nature of the quality control process. For example, a category that we used for analyzing windows defects is the following (for OtherTestTeams we use OtherWinTeams):

- **AppGroup:** Teams focused on compatibility testing
- **Customer:** External customers
- **Internal:** The test team of the component
- **InternalCustomer:** Internal customers within the organization
- **OtherTestTeams (OtherWinTeams):** Test teams for other components
- **Ignored:** The rest

In this analysis, for each component we grouped the defects in these categories, and then found the percentage of defects in each category. The averages for the different categories are shown in Figure 1. (The actual percentages have been omitted to protect the confidentiality of data.)

As the result showed, the largest percentage of defects found for a component were actually by OtherTestTeams (OtherWinTeams for Windows) – that is through testing being done for other components by their test teams. This rather counter intuitive outcome that the defects in a component are found more through testing of other components reveals the key role testing of other components play in improving the reliability of a component. It should, however, be pointed out that defect logging is often not taken very seriously during the early unit testing stages, and defects found by the developers themselves during their private testing are often not logged. That is, this analysis reflects the situation for defects found in more formal testing that is done after the component is released internally for integration. This means that generally the internal defects are under represented as defects found by developers and in early

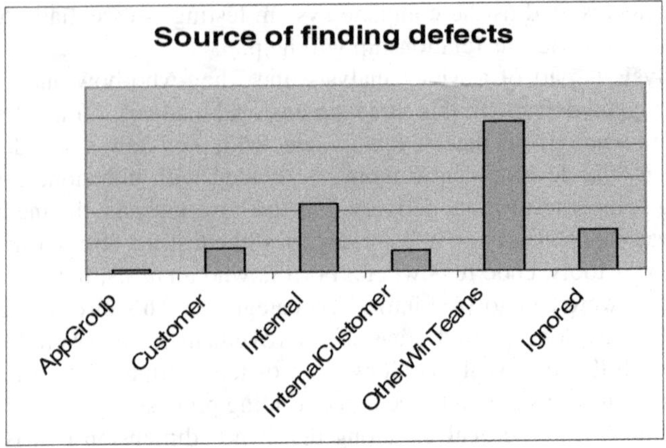

Fig. 1. Fraction of total defects found by different groups

stages of self testing are not included. However, our test buddy analysis is a further analysis of the defects found in a component by other components (i.e. OtherTest-Teams defects) – for that analysis, the number of defects found by Internal team is not important.

Another reason for the large contribution of OtherTestTeams in finding defects that was mentioned by many developers and testers who reviewed the analysis was that there are a lot more testers outside the component than in a component, and so the number of defects found by others is larger. Indeed it is true that the test team of a component is only a small fraction of the total number of test teams. In a product with 50 major components and each having a test team, for every component there is one Internal team while the OtherTestTeams consist of actually 49 test teams.

4 Test Buddies

If other components are finding most of the defects in a component, the next natural questions to ask is are there any special components that are finding these defects? That is, are there any critical components in the system which might be finding most of these defects for most of the components?

To identify the actual test team that found a defect and the component to which the test team belongs turns out to be tricky from the data we had. We started with the id of the person who logged the defect. Through corporate databases, we identified the cost center he or she belongs to, and then through there identified the project assigned to him. Using this information, we then identified the component team to which the person belongs. As this analysis is complex and has to be done separately for each component, we randomly selected some (about 15) components for this analysis. For each component, we attributed the defects found by OtherTestTeams to different components whose test teams found the defect. Then we ranked the test teams in order of their defect finding contribution. For these components, we then determined the average percentage of OtherTestTeams defects that are found by the highest ranking team, the 2nd highest ranking team, etc. The average percentages for all the components are shown in Figure 2.

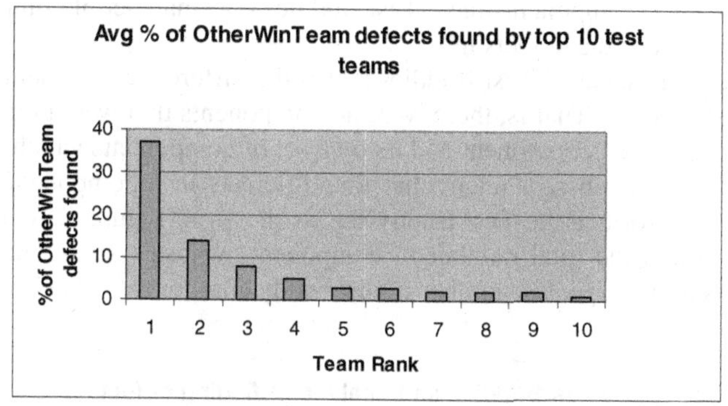

Fig. 2. Average percentage of defects found by top 10 other components

As we can see, on an average, the top ranked component finds more than a third of the defects, the second ranker finds about 12%, and the sixth rank onwards components find less than 5% of the defects. That is, the top 5 components find over 90% of the defects in a component that are being found by test teams of other components. This analysis clearly shows that for a component, only a few test teams contributed most of the defects. We also noted that for most components the total no of test teams finding defects in a component is quite large.

This led us to hypothesize that the 80-20 rule may hold – that 80% of the defects in a component are being found by 20% of the components. We define Test Buddies of a component as the set of other components whose test teams found 80% of the OtherTestTeam defects for this component. Of the components analyzed, we found that all expect one had a small number of Test Buddies. This analysis is shown in Figure 3.

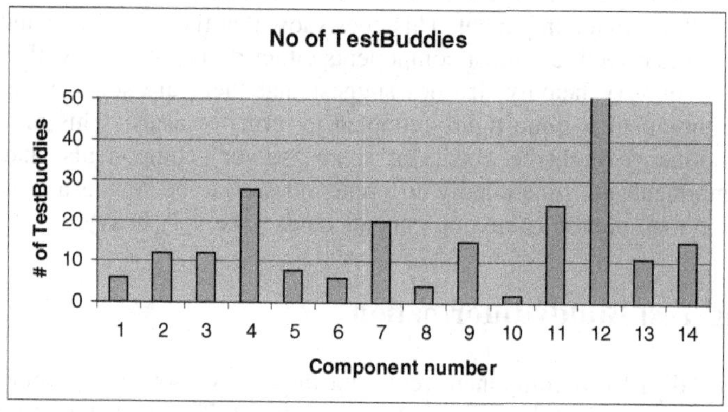

Fig. 3. No of Test Buddies for the different components

As we can see, the number of Test Buddies for many components is less than 5, for some it is around 10. There is only one component which really does not have Test Buddies – defects for this were found by a large number of components. This analysis suggests that most components have Test Buddies – a small set of components whose testing finds most of the defects in it.

An interesting aspect of Test Buddies is that the different components had a different set of test buddies. That is, there were no components that were globally critical in finding defects – each component had its own set of components which found defects. And, of the total number of teams that found defects in a component, only a small fraction of those formed the Test Buddy set, as shown in Figure 4. As can be seen in the figure, though the total number of components whose testing finds defects in a component is quite large, the number of test buddy components is rather small.

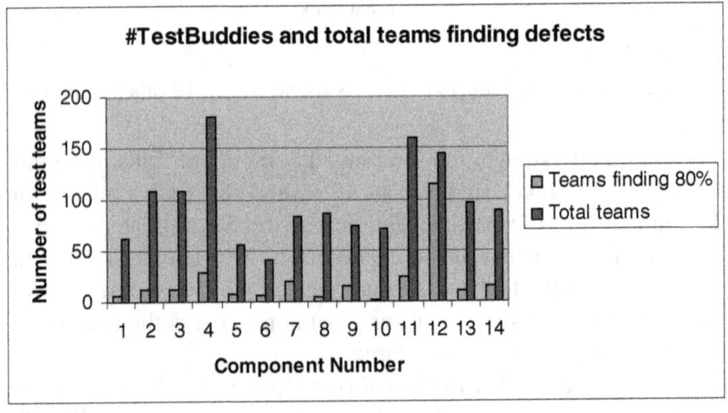

Fig. 4. No of test buddies as a fraction of total teams

Besides the components that find defects in a component, there are many other components which find no defects in this component. In fact, in this product there are well over a thousand components. As we can see from the data, only about a hundred or so find defects in a component. This does show that the modularity and componentization is quite effective – most components either do not interact with each other or do not interact very heavily. It does suggest that there are some components with which a component is quite tightly coupled in terms of usage. This may be because some components might be clients of some "server" components, and though the server components are functionally different and need to be kept as a separate component, the interaction with client components tends to be very heavy.

5 Using Test Buddy Information

The test buddies for a component represent the heavy users of a component, or the components that depend the most on this component. This is different from identifying dependency between components (using techniques like testing dependency graph [11], component interaction graph [13], or UML behavior models [14]) which focus only on identifying which component depends on which others, but not on the strength of dependency. Test buddies essentially identify the components that have the strongest dependency on this component. They can also be viewed as the highest priority clients of this component for the purpose of finding defects. That is, these are the defect finders on which the testing of this component heavily depends.

For a product under development, whose complete defect data is not available, test buddies can be determined either from the data from an earlier release, or defect data at an earlier milestone of this release. Often the component hierarchy and the nature of components is preserved through different releases, though new components do get added. Hence the data from an earlier release should give a close approximation of the test buddies. Same will hold for the test buddies determined from defect data at a milestone, as the relationship between components is unlikely to change substantially from milestone to milestone. As the test buddy information is to be used for improving the quality control and development processes, accurate information is not essential and approximate information is quite sufficient.

The information about Test Buddies of components can be used in different ways to improve the development. When there are many components interacting with each other, coordination between different component teams for testing or any other activity becomes extremely hard. Consequently, component teams start working independently with very lose cooperation with other components. With test buddies, the interaction can be limited to test buddies, limiting the scope strongly and making cooperation feasible.

For example, the test plan of a component can be reviewed by the teams of its test buddies – something that is eminently feasible even though it is not feasible to get it reviewed by all its client components. The review by test buddies can bring up the scenarios that are getting missed in the test plan. This feedback, if obtained early, can have a favorable impact on development also, besides improving the testing.

Other types of cooperation are also possible. A component can start paying closer attention to the bugs being reported by its test buddies – any prevention based on this feedback can have strong benefits. A virtual test script for a component can be formed by combing its test script with those of the test buddies. If this can be automated, then a components testing can become more rigorous, catching defects early.

Cooperation can be extended in other areas as well. Clearly, if specifications of a module are inspected by its test buddies, since these components have the maximum linkages, shortcomings are likely to be identified early in the development cycle. Once again, due to the set of reviewers becoming manageable, this is feasible.

Similarly, when changes occur, test buddy information can be leveraged. It is known that upgrading a component often has side effects on other components, and techniques like regression testing are used to evaluate the impact of a change. With test buddy information, when changes are to be made to a component, two specific measures can be taken. First, the change specifications and the approach for change can be reviewed by test buddies. This review can identify any undesirable side effects that might occur on the test buddies. Though a review by all dependent components is not feasible, review by a small set of components that form the test buddies is eminently feasible and can help identify and mitigate impact on the commonly used customer components.

Secondly, the test buddy information can be used for test prioritization of test cases in regression testing. A brute force method of handling changes is to run all the test cases every time some changes are committed. This is, unfortunately, not always feasible as regression tests for a large product may take many days to complete, and hence test cases are often prioritized and then highest priority test cases are executed to check that there are no undesirable side effects of a change. (There is a body of work in prioritizing test cases in regression testing, e.g. [5, 7, 8, 10]). The test buddy information can also be used for test case prioritization – the test cases of the test buddies are given a higher priority than test cases for other components.

6 Summary

There is a considerable interest in component-based software development and most large software systems that are getting developed use this approach now. For developing a component-based system (but without using third party components), components are often developed by separate teams who perform their testing independently. However, as components have dependencies, testing of a component can reveal defects in other components.

In this work we study the role testing of other component plays in finding defects in a component. Our study is based on the defect data of an earlier release of the Windows operating system. We used the rich data that is logged to analyze the defects of more than fifty components which have the largest number of defects. For each component we separated the defects into different categories; in particular defects found by test teams were separated into those found be the internal test team of the component and those found by test teams of other components. Our first analysis of classifying the defects by who is finding them showed that for a component the largest percentage of defects being found in formal testing runs is through testing of other components. That is, when test scripts of different components are executed in formal test runs (which does not include non-formal testing like the unit testing being done by programmers themselves), test scripts of other components find maximum defects in a component.

Though for a component there is one test team while there are a large number of test teams and test scripts of other components, this established that testing of other components plays a strong role in finding defects in a component.

We then analyzed this data further and found that of the defects being found by other components, the vast majority were being found by only a few components. We define test buddies of a component as those components whose testing finds 80% of the defects being found by other components. We found that most components have a very small set of test buddies. There were a much larger set of components that found the remaining 20% of the defects, and a yet larger set that found no defects. That is, the componentization did result in a structure in which most components had very little interaction with a component. But, there are a few "client" components which interact very heavily with a component and they end up finding most of the defects.

Test buddies of a component represent those components that use this component the most, and have a strong interconnection with it. For a product under development, test buddies can be identified from the defect data of an earlier release, or defect data at a milestone. This knowledge about test buddies can be used in many ways to improve coordination between components for improving quality. Without test buddies, this coordination for a large product is so complex that it is practically impossible. With test buddy information, coordination can be limited to test buddies. This opens up possibilities of joint testing, test case reviews, review of specifications, etc to improve the quality of a component – techniques that are not feasible without this data.

We feel that during evolution of large systems defect data should be mined to identify the test buddies of different components. And strategies should be evolved to leverage this information for improving the quality of the system built from components. This can go a long way in improving the reliability of the overall system. Of course, this analysis is only from data of one product and whether this phenomenon will hold in general needs to be validated further by doing this analysis on data from other products as well. We hope that the potential benefits of this information will encourage others to do this analysis and share the results.

References

1. S. Beydeda, V. Gruhn, An integrated testing technique for component-based software, International Conference on Computer Systems and Applications, IEEE Press, 2001
2. Rex Black Managing the Testing Process, Microsoft Press 1999
3. N. Brown. Industrial-strength management strategies, *IEEE Software,* July 1996.
4. W.R. Bush, J.D. Pincus, and D.J. Sielaff. A static analyzer for finding dynamic programming errors. Software Practice and Experience, 30(7):775--802, 2000
5. S Elbaum, AG Malishevsky, G Rothermel "Test case prioritization: A family of empirical studies", IEEE Transactions on Software Engineering, 2002
6. MJ Harrold, D Liang, S Sinha - An approach to analyzing and testing component-based systems, ICSE Workshop Testing Distributed Component-Based Systems, 1999
7. G Rothermel, RH Untch, C Chu, MJ Harrold "Prioritizing test cases for regression testing", IEEE Transactions on Software Engineering, 2001
8. AK Onoma, WT Tsai, MH Poonawala, H Suganuma "Regression testing in an industrial environment", Communications of the ACM, 1998
9. Salomon, David and Mark E. Russinovich *Inside Microsoft Windows 2000,* Third Edition, Microsoft Press
10. A Srivastava, J Thiagarajan "Effectively prioritizing tests in development environment", ACM SIGSOFT Software Engineering Notes, 2002
11. Y L Traon, T Jeron, J M Jezequel, and P Morel, "Efficient Object-Oriented Integration and Regression Testing", IEEE Transaction on Reliability, vol 49, no 1, pp 12-25, March 2000
12. EJ Weyuker "Testing Component-Based Software: A cautionary Tale", IEEE Software (5) pp 54-59 1998
13. Y. Wu, D Pan, and M H Chen, "Techniques for Testing Component-Based Software", proc. of ICECCS, pp 222-232, 2001
14. Y Wu, M H Chen, and J Offutt, "UML-based Integration Testing for Component-based Software", proc. of ICCBSS pp 251-260, 2003

Defining "Predictable Assembly"

Dick Hamlet*

Portland State University
Portland, OR, USA
hamlet@cs.pdx.edu

Abstract. *Predictable assembly* in component-based software development intuitively means the ability to predict effectively properties of a system, making essential use of properties of its components. A formal definition is difficult to give, because the idea is a large, vague one. As an outgrowth of an informal workshop, this paper frames a mathematical definition. A somewhat surprising consequence of the formal definition is that assembly is usually predictable, but each particular case requires engineering effort to establish.

1 Introduction

In September 2005, K-K. Lau organized an informal workshop at the University of Manchester whose goal was to define "predictable assembly of software components." The attendees spent two days in informal talks and discussion, and (predictably, for an assembly!) did not arrive at a satisfactory definition. This paper is an outgrowth of Lau's workshop.

The workshop subject of predictable assembly recognized that little could be gained by attempting a general definition of 'component'. Everyone seems to know what a software component is, and few are willing to reconsider their beliefs. The existing definitions range from broad generalities (e.g., Szyperski's much cited [1], "Anything executable") to the narrowly specific (e.g., an Eiffel class [2], or a Java Bean [3]). It is hard for those holding different ideas of 'component' to understand and use each other's work, just because it is difficult to shake off one's own intuitive baggage. The workshop took a different tack: Whatever 'components' are, it is desirable that properties of systems using them can be predicted from knowledge of the components. Defining an entity in terms of what is done with it is accepted mathematical practice, particularly in algebra. In Section 3 it will appear that predicable assembly as defined is almost always a possibility.

If we avoid using the "C-word" and thereby keep out the freight of different intuitive meanings, we still need to refer to parts of software systems that have an independent existence. 'Software elements' (or 'elements' for short) is a suitably vague term, conveying no more than the idea of being a part.

* Supported by NSF ITR grant CCR-0112654 and by an E.T.S. Walton grant from Science Foundation Ireland. Neither institution is in any way responsible for the statements made in this paper.

I. Gorton et al. (Eds.): CBSE 2006, LNCS 4063, pp. 320–327, 2006.

2 Semantic Background of Elements and Assemblies

Two underlying ideas are not in dispute[1]: *properties* and *assembly.*

2.1 Properties and Behaviors of Software

In mathematical logic, 'property' is another word for a logical predicate defined on a set comprising values of variables of the logic. The property 'holds' when its variables take on values that make it true. The intuitive sense of a predicate is often 'relational' in that some variables are identified as 'independent' (or 'input') and others as 'dependent' ('output') and truth of the predicate defines a relationship between the two. For example, a conventional Hoare-logic postcondition predicate Q may involve input x and output y for a program P, and $\{P\}\ Q(x, y)$ expresses correctness (without any precondition). Furthermore, such relational predicates may happen to be single-valued in that they are true for (x, y) of at most one output y for each input x. Such a single-valued predicate defines a (partial) function from inputs to outputs. When there is no output y such that the defining predicate holds for (x, y), the function is undefined at x.

One set over which predicates range is observable quantities for the software system to be assembled. In physical science it has been very useful to distinguish between quantities that can be detected by apparatus and others that are more tenuous. A corresponding distinction for programs could single out 'observable' values by the existence of engineering devices ('converters') and programming-language constructions that take a representation of an observable value back and forth between software and the physical world. For example, force is observable because a strain gauge 'reads' force; a stepping motor 'writes' it. Converters for text and graphical input/output observables are built into most programming languages. The observable quantities of interest differ from system to system; however, there is always an input domain that the system reads and an output domain that it writes. Programs are mappings that relate the input set of observables to the output set of observables; this is is their 'functional' behavior. Along the way, many internal quantities may arise in a program. It can be important to define and analyze predicates involving internal values, but in the end it is the observable input-output behavior that counts. Software engineering makes the distinction by stating requirements in observables and relegating internals to design.

Other, 'non-functional' software properties are often of interest, but these necessarily depend on functional behavior. The reason is that when one element invokes another the complete behavior—functional and non-functional—of the second element depends on the input it receives, which is influenced by the behavior of the first. Thus any contribution to system properties from the second element arises not from the system input, but rather from a functional transformation of system input. An archetype non-functional property is run time

[1] There is some truth in the aphorism that a group of experts seeking a definition will dispute *anything*.

(wall-clock elapsed time[2]), which is evidently observable. The example illustrates a confusion that runs through any discussion using the word 'functional'. On one hand, a program's functional behavior is by definition its input-output relationship, excluding things like run time. This makes run time 'non-functional'. But on the other hand, run time could be mathematically treated just as output is. Given an input, the run time can be measured and thus a run-time function can be defined, making run time 'functional'. Furthermore, in real cases where there is concurrency the run time may not be a single-valued relation, that is, non-functional. Finally, the input-output relation may also fail to be single-valued, making the defined 'functional' behavior technically non-functional.

In this paper, 'functional/non-functional' will be reserved for distinguishing input-output behavior from other less fundamental behaviors. The input-output behavior will also be called 'black-box' behavior. We will use 'relation' for the mathematical idea of ordered pairs. A single-valued relation will sometimes be called a 'mapping'. For example, we might say that in the absence of concurrency the functional behavior of a program is a mapping, and so is the non-functional run-time behavior.

It captures the black-box nature of software to stipulate that any program, system, or software element is described by a relation between sequences of input values and sequences of output values. In the simplest case there is a single input space X and a single output space Y. Let $X^\star$ be the set of finite, non-zero-length sequences drawn from X. Program P's semantics is defined by a relation $S \subseteq X^\star \times Y$ as follows:

Definition 1. *There exists a $y \in Y$ such that P has output y for some input sequence $x \in X^\star$ if and only if $S(x, y)$ holds.*

Termination is covered in Definition 1 as follows: If S contains a pair (x, y) then P must terminate on input x to meet the definition; if there is no y such that $(x, y) \in S$, then P does not terminate on input x. Non-deterministic program behavior is captured in Definition 1 by a relation that is not single-valued in its independent variables. The use of sequences in Definition 1 captures a program's use of persistent state, without making state explicit. Intuitively, programs begin every input sequence with state 'reset' to an initial value. Each member of an input sequence sends the program to a next state, but state is entirely under program control so it need not be described in the definition.

Definition 1 covers functional behavior. Non-functional behavior can sometimes be captured by additional relations on the cross product of input sequences and another value space. For example, program run time[3] might be defined by a mapping $T : X^\star \to \mathbb{R}$, where $\mathbb{R}$ is the non-negative reals. Program reliability might be a mapping from input sequences to a probability, $r : X^\star \to [0, 1] \subset \mathbb{R}$. A surprising number of non-functional properties can be defined using mappings.

---

[2] Things are more complicated for an internal quantity like 'processor time'.

[3] Intuitive run time is the time for just one, not a sequence, of executions. The single-input run time depends on the state, which is only implicitly known by position in the input sequence. The run time for part of an input sequence could be obtained by subtracting the defined values for two sequences, one a prefix of the other.

The intuitive character of the simplest relational Definition 1 of software semantics is that a program receives input sequences and produces outputs in response. What happens along the way is not modeled, so the definition does not capture temporal properties. An example of this deficiency is a program that receives an 'arming' input, sets an internal timer, and responds differently if a second input arrives before or after the timer expires. The example exposes 'elapsed time' as a fundamental parameter in computation, a kind of cross between input and state. Like input and state a time interval can influence program behavior. Unlike input, time cannot be arbitrarily set by the environment; unlike state, the program does not completely control its value.

A more complex definition better covers temporal variations:

Definition 2. *Program behavior is described by a relation between timed input sequences of pairs* $T = <(x_1, t_1), (x_2, t_2), ..., (x_n, t_n)>$ *and an output pair* (y, t').

Intuitively the ith input value x_i arrives at time t_i and the program output response to the input sequence is y at time t'. The inclusion of t' is necessary to model the possibility that a program can act differently depending on how long one waits after input arrives. The wall-clock run time(s) of the program on input sequence T therefore comprise the set of all $t' > t_n$ that (each with some output) stand in the program relation to T. (A "timed frame in the relational style" of Broy and Stølen [4] can express the same intuitive semantics as Definition 2. The Broy and Stølen notion of "timed stream", by modeling time only as tick marks separating message values, makes it easier to express synchronization. In their notation more of the semantic content is carried by the structured stream and less by the relation.)

If a software system is assembled from software elements, there must be an overlap in domains between some elements and the system. Some elements must read the same kind of values as the system reads; some elements must write the same kind of values the system does. These elements are the system interfaces to the physical world. Other input and output domains of elements making up a system are not visible in system behavior.

2.2 Series Assembly

How elements connect to each other in assembly poses a difficult definitional problem: Shall the connection be taken to be a property of the elements, or of the system? The extreme views are:

(System). Elements are combined using rules ('connectors') defined only at the system level. These connectors mediate between outputs produced by one element and inputs accepted by another. The elements themselves need not match in any way. This view has the virtue that it allows maximum reuse of the simplest elements, but at the expense of defining a whole new system entity, the connector.

(Element). Elements are combined using fixed interface rules that define a well-formed assembly. At the interface agreement is required for a system to be well-formed, but not so much that deciding well-formedness becomes intractable. Here the drawbacks are that the interface rules constrain the component developer and the choice of rules may limit system design possibilities.

Perhaps the idea of a 'component model' [5] is a compromise between these extremes. The model and its 'containers' define the allowed connections, and in turn restrict what elements placed in the containers must do.

This paper takes the 'element' view[4]. Section 2.1 has defined the semantics of programs. Assemblies are defined not by semantic 'composition' operators, but by syntactic connections, each with its own intuitive semantics. The simplest and most revealing connection of elements is 'series'. In a series connection, a first element invokes a second element, which receives as input the output of the first. A discussion of other connections, e.g., one element calling another, is beyond the scope of this short paper.

3 Predictable Assembly

Precise semantic definitions are the basis for a definition of the notion of 'predictable assembly'. Definitions 1 and 2 use relational semantics, but their details do not play an important role here. A different background formalism could be substituted without changing the character of this section.

Predictable assembly is intuitively the ability to effectively predict properties of the assembly from element properties. Inclusion of the adverb 'effectively'—that is, by algorithmic means—raises an old, old issue in program analysis. If element properties are obtained by testing methods, they are at best approximations to the actual properties. (For example, test run times necessarily fail to take account of some input values, which may conceal significant times.) Calculations concerning the assembly made from inaccurate element data may be effective, but are also inaccurate (likely even more inaccurate than the data). On the other hand, if element properties are expressed in formal mathematics, they can be perfectly accurate, but there are still two problems of effective prediction: (1) The accuracy of a formal description cannot be effectively checked in general, hence the formal expression may not in fact be true of the element. (2) There may be no effective way to obtain formal descriptions of the assembly. For example, to find the description may require an iterative procedure not known to terminate in general.

We are left with the familiar dichotomy that testing can be carried out but with dubious results; formal analysis has the potential for ideal results, but cannot always be carried out. An intuitively satisfying definition of predictable assembly must allow for the deficiencies of both methods. Such a definition is called 'relative' (to the underlying method). It will not do to give an absolute definition, then discover that in particular examples the prediction cannot be made, but the fault lies with the underlying testing or formalism, not with intuitive 'predictability'.

[4] On the other side, Arbab's work [6] is an elegant example of the 'system' view.

The statement[5] that non-functional software properties cannot be formalized most often reflects only confusion of terms. Sometimes it means that the formal properties are difficult to effectively manipulate. Sometimes it confuses the two kinds of 'functional' as mentioned in Section 2. Sometimes it refers to emergent properties like 'security' as discussed in Section 3 below. And sometimes the confusion is not easy to categorize. For example, the reliability property $r : X^\star \to [0, 1]$ is identically 1 whenever a program is correct on X, so no one bothers to mention it in a formal correctness theory.

Here are two relative definitions:

Definition 3 (relative to formal logic). *An assembly is predictable for its property Q when Q can be deduced for the assembly from formal descriptions of its elements.*

Definition 3 does not fail because of the failings of formalism in general. Assembly is predictable using a formal method if working from formal element descriptions (which may be wrong), there is a procedure (which may not be tractable) for predicting the assembly behavior. In cases where the element descriptions are shown to be right and the procedure can be carried out, the prediction will be effective.

Definition 4 (relative to testing). *An assembly is predictable for its property Q when calculations using element test results can be carried out to predict values of Q along with an error bound for the prediction.*

Element tests carry an inaccuracy and this will be give rise to a prediction inaccuracy. It is not unfair to insist that testing-based predictable assembly provide an effective error calculation relating the accuracy of the assembly predictions to the accuracy of the element tests. Definition 4 allows testing its intrinsic weakness. If the accuracy bound is not tight enough the prediction is not useful.

In both cases, the arbiter of prediction accuracy is system testing. A prediction is accurate if it agrees with system test results. The validation of any particular prediction procedure, formal or test-based, is therefore well defined. Ideally, validation can be theoretical—one can prove that system tests will go as predicted. Without a proof, experiments can provide support.

Relative definitions that allow methods to exhibit their intrinsic imperfections may seem to be useless—what good is a prediction that in a particular case can't be made (formalism), or can't be trusted (testing and formalism)? It is our intent to capture the sense of predictable assembly as an engineering practice. Engineers always use imperfect design- and analysis methods. A relative definition allows researchers and practitioners to add to the stock of such methods so that a body of experience can develop around predicting assembly properties. In the end, some assembly-prediction methods may be found to be a waste of time; or, a particular method may work only in special cases. Engineers will abandon the former and try to force the special cases of the latter to occur. If there are

[5] Usually made by those who don't like formalism.

methods to try, however imperfect, engineers may try them; without defined methods, they are out of work.

To illustrate Definitions 3 and 4, consider a series assembly with the simplest kind of program semantics, where program defining relations (Definition 1) are single-valued and non-temporal. For a non-functional property take run time.

Illustration 1. *The functional behavior of the series assembly of element 1 with program mapping F_1 and element 2 with program mapping F_2 is obtained by mathematical composition. The run time of the assembly is obtained by addition. Let an input sequence $X = <x_1, x_2, ..., x_n>$ be given. Element 1 has output sequence $Y = <y_1, y_2, ..., y_n>$, where:*

$$y_1 = F_1(<x_1>),\ y_2 = F_1(<x_1, x_2>),\ ...,\ y_n = F_1(<x_1, x_2, ..., x_n>).$$

The system output is $F_2(Y)$.

If T_1 and T_2 are the respective element run-time mappings, the system run time on input sequence X is $T_1(X) + T_2(Y)$.

In the formal view of Illustration 1, mappings F_1, T_1, F_2, T_2 would be given for the elements by logical predicates, and the formulas are derived to predict the functional and run-time mappings of the series assembly. The assembly is predictable according to Definition 3 and the proof is immediate from the definitions.

In the testing view, finite-support mappings to approximate F_1, T_1, F_2, T_2 can be obtained by testing the elements. The formulas in Illustration 1 can combine these finite-support approximations into an approximation for the assembly, subject to a technical difficulty in matching input test points for element 2 with output values from element 1. Subdomain testing is one way to solve this matching problem [7]. The hard part of proving that the assembly of Illustration 1 is predictable according to Definition 4 is bounding the error in a subdomain-based calculation. Empirical evidence indicates that properties of a series assembly can be predicted with less relative error than roughly the sum of the element relative errors, but no theoretical analysis has been attempted [7].

It is revealing to consider so-called 'emergent' properties of systems. An emergent property may not be present at the element level, but arises in the assembly. Intuitively, the relative definitions allow emergent properties to be predicable. One device that often works is to use in the proof an 'intermediate property,' something other than the property to be predicted, whose element values permit the prediction. For example, a system's memory-leak-free behavior does not always arise from elements that are leak-free. Using lists of allocated addresses as an intermediary, the system (leak-free) property can be predicted from the elements (address-list) properties [8].

Using Definitions 3 and 4, no system property fails to be predictable *a priori*. If a clever formal derivation or testing procedure can be found, the property is established as predictable; if not found today, more cleverness may be available tomorrow. It is the business of engineering to seek out such clever methods. A special case occurs when a system property is itself uncomputable in the Turing sense, for example the property of being deadlock-free. The relative definitions can push the unsolvable problem to the element level so that the deadlock-free property becomes technically predictable. For example, the proof might use as intermediate element property an undecidable restriction on resource allocation. Except as a means to demonstrate the unsolvability of the element property—a form of reducibility proof—such an exercise is not useful. However, a slight twist in the argument brings in an acknowledged strength of component-based development—restrictions on the general case are easier to devise and verify at the element level. In the deadlock-free example, simple restrictions might be placed on elements and their assembly connections that guarantee the absence of deadlock in the assembly. It should be easier to prove that elements observe a safe pattern of resource allocation that implies system safety than to analyze an assembly. The proof of predictable assembly then becomes a template for devising element properties that make prediction effective.

Examples of intrinsically non-predictable properties probably exist, but to construct one might require a contrived self-referential property.

4 Summary

A definition of predictable assembly was given relative to an underlying analysis method (formal logical description or testing). According to the definition, assembly properties are usually predictable, but to demonstrate this requires validating engineering procedures within a formal- or testing-analysis framework. The primary model that underlies the definition is a functional and non-functional relational semantics assigned to assemblies and their elements.

References

1. Szyperski, C.: Component Software. 2nd edn. Addison-Wesley (2002)
2. Meyer, B.: Object-oriented Software Construction. Prentice Hall (2000)
3. Roman, E., Ambler, S., Jewell, T.: Mastering Enterprise JavaBeans, 2nd Ed. John Wiley and Sons (2001)
4. Broy, M., Stølen, K.: Specification and development of interactive systems: FOCUS on streams, interfaces, and refinement. Springer (2001)
5. Heineman, G.T., Councill, W.T.: Component-Based Software Engineering: Putting the Pieces Together. Addison-Wesley (2001)
6. Arbab, F.: Abstract behavior types: a foundation model for components and their composition. Science of Computer Programming (2005) 3–52
7. Hamlet, D., Andric, M., Tu, Z.: Experiments with composing component properties. In: Proc. 6th ICSE Workshop on Component-based Software Engineering, Portland, OR (2003)
8. Hamlet, D., Mason, D., Woit, D.: Properties of software systems synthesized from components. In Lau, K.K., ed.: Case Studies in Computer-based Software Engineering. World Scientific (2004)

A Tool to Generate an Adapter for the Integration of Web Services Interface*

Kwangyong Lee[1], Juil Kim[2], Woojin Lee[2], and Kiwon Chong[2]

[1] Ubiquitous Computing Middleware Team, ETRI, Daejeon, Korea
kylee@etri.re.kr
[2] Department of Computing, Soongsil University, Seoul, Korea
{sespop, bluewj}@empal.com, chong@ssu.ac.kr

Abstract. As the number of available web services is steadily increasing, many applications are being developed by reusing web services. Accordingly, a tool to generate an adapter which integrates interfaces of several web services is proposed in this paper. The concept of the adapter for the integration of web services interface is described. The purpose of the adapter is to help developers use several web services with little effort for their application development. Then, implementation of the tool to generate an adapter is presented. The architecture of the tool, the process, and the algorithm to generate an adapter are described. The tool will help developers integrate several web services when they develop applications.

1 Introduction

The business process automation has been motivated by opportunities in terms of cost savings, higher quality and more reliable executions. This automation has generated the need for integrating different applications involved in the processes. Accordingly, application integration has been one of the main factors in the software market [1].

Web services were born as a solution to the integration problem [2]. To create applications using several web services, developers use service integration. Developers and users can then solve complex problems by combining available basic services and ordering them to best suit their problem requirements [3].

We propose the programming-level integration technique for improving the productivity and the maintainability of applications based on web services. We propose a tool to generate an adapter which integrates interfaces of several web services in this paper. The concept of the adapter for the integration of web services interface is described. Then, implementation of the tool to generate an adapter is presented. The architecture of the tool, the process, the templates and the algorithm to generate an adapter are described. The adapter will help developers to rapidly develop applicatons with high quality. Developers can use several web services like a single web service through the adapter of this paper because the adapter integrates interfaces of several web services. The productivity of application development will be improved because the adapter can be generated automatically. The maintainability of applications also

* This work was supported by the Soongsil University Research Fund.

I. Gorton et al. (Eds.): CBSE 2006, LNCS 4063, pp. 328–335, 2006.

will be improved because developers can reflect modification of web services and add new web services through the adapter. We hope the proposed tool will help developers generate the adapter when they develop applications.

2 An Adapter for the Integration of Web Services Interface

Developers search web services when they want to use web services as a part of their application. They should use several web services when they develop the application if there is not a single web service which satisfies their requirements. An application using several web services has a structure of figure 1-(a). However, controlling several web services costs a lot of effort, so developers make efforts to control several web services when they develop the application. Developers also modify source codes of every class which use the web service if a web service has been changed. To solve these problems, this paper proposes the adapter of figure 1-(b). The adapter performs the role of a middleware between a client application and web services. The adapter uses the façade and the proxy patterns [4]. The adapter is composed of two kinds of classes – the *WebServicesFacade* and the *WebServicesProxy*. The *WebServices Facade* provides interfaces of several web services and interfaces which compose several interfaces of the web services. The *WebServicesProxy* provides a local representative for a web service in a different address space and the same interfaces as a web service.

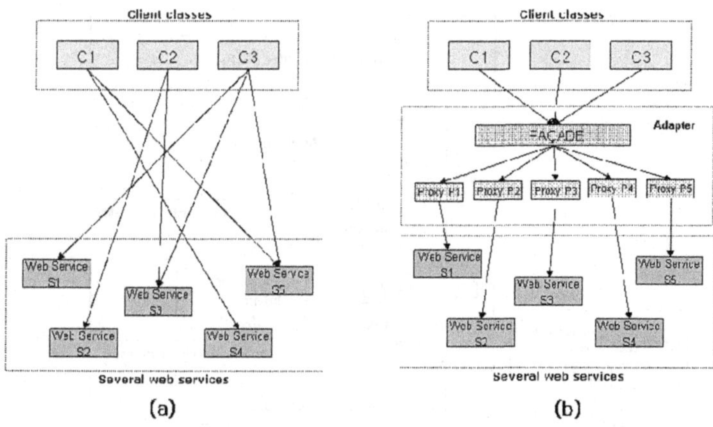

Fig. 1. The structure of an application using several web services

The adapter minimizes the complexity of connection and the dependency between a client application and web services. Therefore, developers can manage and control several web services with little effort for their application development through the adapter. Furthermore, the maintainability of applications increases through the adapter because developers modify only the source code of the adapter when web services are changed.

Users can access only the service specification of a web service through WSDL. Accordingly, the adapter integrates interfaces which are defined in the WSDL of web services. Developers can use several web services like a single web service through the adapter because the adapter integrates interfaces of several web services. They control only the adapter in order to use the web services. Developers can easily use the interfaces of several web services through the adapter in their application development. Users can call operations of web services and use the return values of the operations through the adapter even if they don't know the information of web services such as URL of WSDL document, web service name and port, and operation name. Users can use operations of web services just as methods of local object through the adapter.

3 A Tool to Generate an Adapter for Web Services Integration

3.1 The Architecture of the Tool

A tool to generate an adapter for the integration of web services interface consists of the Web Service Finder, the WSDL Analyzer, the Web Service Tester, the Adapter Information Generator, the Templates Storage, and the Adapter Generator. Figure 2 shows the architecture of the tool.

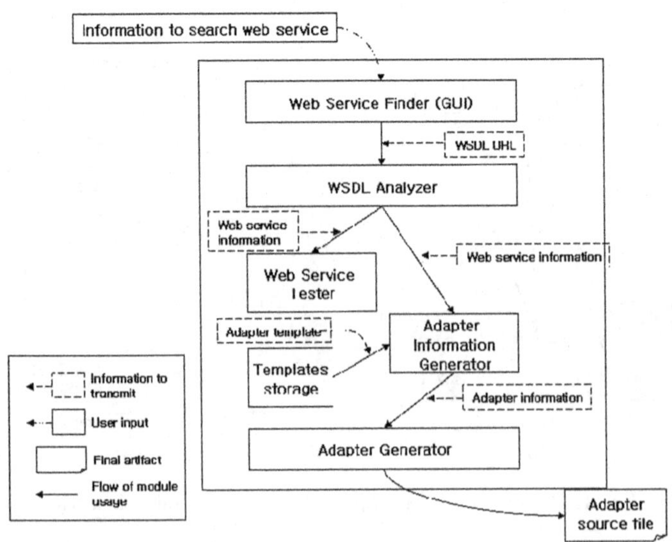

Fig. 2. The architecture of a tool to generate an adapter

Followings are detailed descriptions of modules of the tool.

* *Web Service Finder*: This is a GUI to search web services that are necessay for an application. This module stores the URLs of WSDL documents for web services to find.

* *WSDL Analyzer*: This module extracts web service information from WSDL document using the URL of the document. Web service information contains the access point URL, name of operations, parameters of operations, type of parameters, and return value type of operations.
* *Web Service Tester*: This module confirms the suitability of a web service. Because there are a lot of web services that perform similar service, users should find out the most appropriate web service. Users choose an operation to test, set parameter values, and check the test result of the operation for verifying the web service using this module.
* *Adapter Information Generator*: This module generates the adapter information using predefined templates and web service information.
* *Templates Storage*: This module stores predefined templates to generate an adapter. Templates for *WebServicesFacade* and *WebServicesProxy* class which consist of an adapter are stored in this module.
* *Adapter Generator*: This module creates java source files of an adapter using the adapter information generated by the *Adapter Information Generator.*

3.2 The Generation Process of an Adapter

The adapter is generated by following process.

① Search web services from UDDI. The web services should provide proper operations in requirement of application.
② Select several web services among the searched web services in order to use in the development of application.
③ Input the WSDL URL of selected web services to the *WSDL Analyzer.*
④ The *WSDL Analyzer* parses the information of the web services through the WSDL URL and stores the parsed information. The *Web Service Tester* calls the operations of the web services and confirms return values. The process is performed again from ② if the return values are not satisfied.
⑤ Adapter information is generated using the parsed information and the template of adapter.
⑥ The *Adapter Generator* creates java source files with the adapter information. Users can use several web services using the class files of an adapter by compiling the java source files of the adapter and customize the adapter by modifying the java files of the adapter.

3.3 The Algorithm for the Generation of an Adapter

Developers can use several web services using the class files of an adapter by compiling the automatically generated java source files of the adapter and customize the adapter by modifying the java files of the adapter.

Figure 3 presents the algorithm for the generation of the *WebServicesProxy* and the *WebServicesFacade* class. The proxy of each web service and the façade of an adapter are generated through these algorithms.

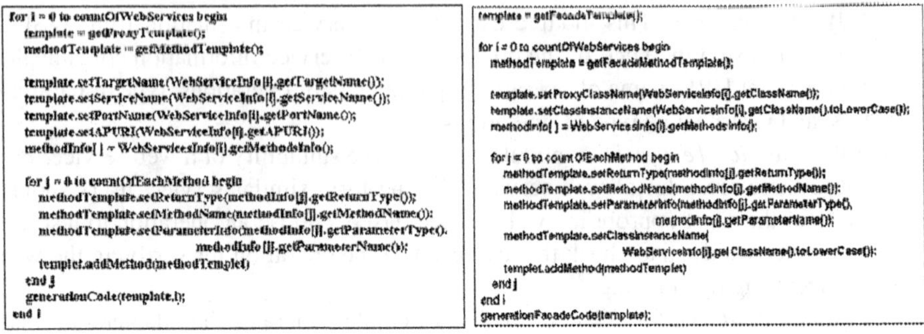

```
for i = 0 to countOfWebServices begin
  template = getProxyTemplate();
  methodTemplate = getMethodTemplate();

  template.setTargetName(WebServiceInfo[i].getTargetName());
  template.setServiceName(WebServiceInfo[i].getServiceName());
  template.setPortName(WebServiceInfo[i].getPortName());
  template.setAPURI(WebServiceInfo[i].getAPURI());
  methodInfo[ ] = WebServicesInfo[i].getMethodsInfo();

  for j = 0 to countOfEachMethod begin
    methodTemplate.setReturnType(methodInfo[j].getReturnType());
    methodTemplate.setMethodName(methodInfo[j].getMethodName());
    methodTemplate.setParameterInfo(methodInfo[j].getParameterType(),
                                  methodInfo[j].getParameterName());
    templet.addMethod(methodTemplet)
  end j
  generationCode(template,i);
end i
```

(a) WebServicesProxy generation algorithm

```
template = getFacadeTemplate();

for i = 0 to countOfWebServices begin
  methodTemplate = getFacadeMethodTemplate();

  template.setProxyClassName(WebServiceInfo[i].getClassName());
  template.setClassInstanceName(WebServiceInfo[i].getClassName().toLowerCase());
  methodInfo[ ] = WebServicesInfo[i].getMethodsInfo();

  for j = 0 to countOfEachMethod begin
    methodTemplate.setReturnType(methodInfo[j].getReturnType());
    methodTemplate.setMethodName(methodInfo[j].getMethodName());
    methodTemplate.setParameterInfo(methodInfo[j].getParameterType(),
                                 methodInfo[j].getParameterName());
    methodTemplate.setClassInstanceName(
                          WebServiceInfo[i].getClassName().toLowerCase());
    templet.addMethod(methodTemplet)
  end j
end i
generationFacadeCode(template);
```

(b) WebServicesFacade generation algorithm

Fig. 3. The algorithm for the generation of the WebServicesProxy and the WebServicesFacade class of the adapter

4 Case Study with Internet Library System

We generated an adapter for the Internet Libarary Sytem as a case study. The Internet Library System provides useful functions for searching, ordering and reserving domestic or international books. We developed the functions for searching domestic or international books as a part of the Internet Libarary System. We needed to use two web services for searching domestic books and international books, so we generated an adapter using the tool proposed in this paper in order to integrate a web service for domestic books search and a web service for international books search.

Figure 4 shows the GUI for web service search of the tool. When several proper web services are selected, they are analyzed through WSDLs and tested for identifying the most suitable web service.

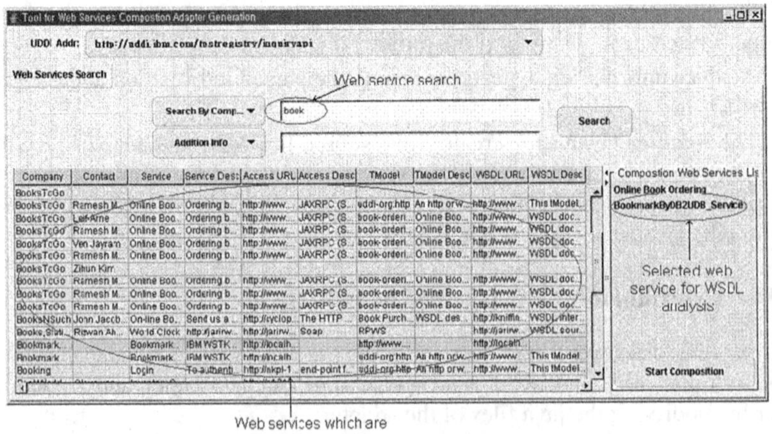

Fig. 4. The GUI for web service search of the tool

Figure 5 shows the GUI for web service test of the tool. For testing of a web service, a method of the web service is selected and invoked with testing values. The result of the invocation is displayed on the right of the GUI. If the result is acceptable, the user selects the web sevice. When all web sevices for implementation are selected, the tool generates an adapter for interface integration of the web services.

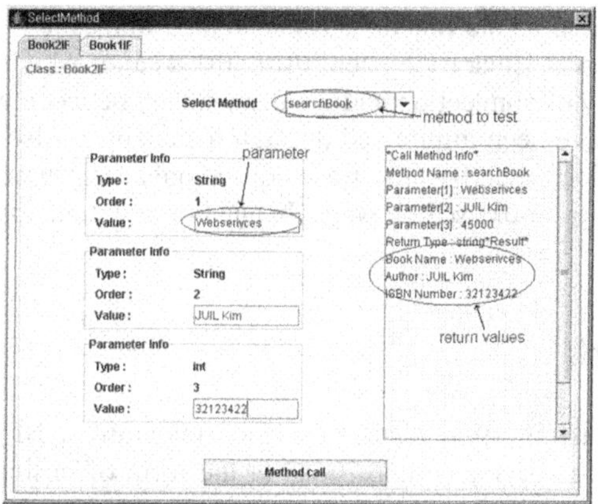

Fig. 5. The GUI for web service test of the tool

The WSDLs of web services for searching dosmetic books and international books are presented in the left side of figure 6.

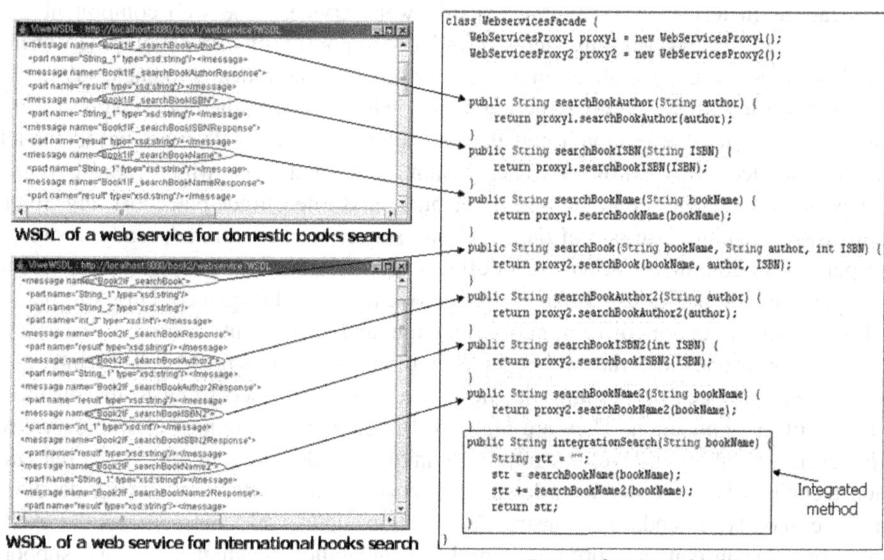

Fig. 6. The WSDLs of web services for searching dosmetic books and international books, and the source code of *WebServicesFacade* class generated by the tool

The source code of *WebServicesFacade* class which is a component of an adapter to integrate the web services is presented in the right side of figure 6. The code is generated by the tool proposed in this paper. The integrated mehod of the *WebServicesFacade* class can be used for integrated searching of books which are inside and outside of the country. Users can easily generate integrated methods using the methods of the *WebServicesProxy* classes.

We easily implemented the functions for searching domestic or international books as a part of the Internet Libarary System using the adapter which is generated by the tool. The complexity of connection and the dependency between web services and the client application have been minimized through the adapter. Also, the maintainability of applications has increased because we modified only the source code of the adapter when web services for books search were changed or new functions were added to the web services.

5 Related Work

There are many existing approaches to service integration. BPEL [5, 6] defines a language for creating service compositions in the form of business processes and is currently being standardized by the Organization for the Advancement of Structured Information Standards (OASIS). BPEL allows a set of existing web services to be composed into a new web service using well-defined process modeling constructs. OWL-S (previously DAML-S) [7] is a services ontology that enables automatic service discovery, invocation, composition, interoperation, and execution monitoring. Web component [8] is a packaging mechanism for developing web-based distributed applications in terms of combining existing web services. The web component approach treats services as components in order to support software development principles such as reuse, specialization and extension. The main idea is to encapsulate the composition logic and the construction scripts which oversee the combination of existing web services. R. Hamadi and B. Benatallah proposed a Petri net-based model for web service composition [9]. They assume that a Petri net, which represents the behavior of a service, contains one input place and one output place. At any given time, a service can be in one of the following states: not instantiated, ready, running, suspended, or completed. After users define a net for each service, composition operators perform composition: sequence, alternative, unordered sequence, iteration, parallel with communication, discriminator, selection, and refinement.

These approaches integrate web services in terms of business process. They integrate several web services by defining the flow of a service call according to the business process of an application. They are high-level integration techniques of web services. However, not only high-level integration technique but also programming-level integration technique is necessary in order to save cost and time when developers develop, manage, modify, extend, or reconstruct applications. Our work complements the existing works because it is a programming-level integration technique, and we support automatic generation of an adapter for the integration.

6 Conclusion

As the number of available web services is steadily increasing, many applications are being developed by reusing web services. Accordingly, web service integration has been issued. Users can access only the service specification of a web service through WSDL. Accordingly, web service integration is integration of interfaces which are defined in the WSDL of web services.

We described the adapter in order to integrate the interfaces of several web services. Developers search web services when they want to use web services as a part of their application. They should use several web services when they develop an application if there is not a single web service which satisfies their requirements. Controlling several web services costs a lot of effort, so developers make efforts to control several web services when they develop applications.

Accordingly, we proposed a tool to generate an adapter which integrates interfaces of several web services. We described the concept of the adapter for the integration of web services interface. Developers can use several web services with little effort for their application development if they use the adapter. Developers can use several web services like a single web service through the adapter because the adapter integrates several web services. They control only the adapter in order to use the web services. The adapter will help developers to rapidly develop applicatons with high quality. The time and the cost for development and maintenance of applications will also be saved through the adapter. Then, we presented the architecture of the tool, the process, and the algorithm to generate an adapter. The proposed tool will help developers generate the adapter when they develop applications.

References

[1] Boualem Benatallah et al., Developing Adapters for Web Services Integration, LNCS 3520, pp. 415-429, Springer-Verlag, 2005.

[2] Alonso, G., Casati, F., Kuno, H., Machiraju, V., Web Services: Concepts, Architectures, and Applications, Springer Verlag, 2004.

[3] Nikola Milanovic and Miroslaw Malek, Current Solutions for Web Service Composition, IEEE Internet Computing, vol. 8, no. 6, pp. 51-59, 2004.

[4] Erich Gamma, et al., Design Patterns, Addison Wesley, 1995.

[5] F.Curbera et al., The Next Step in Web Services, Comm. ACM, vol. 46, no. 10, pp. 29-34, 2003.

[6] BPEL Specification, http://www.ibm.com/developerworks/library//ws-bpel/

[7] A. Ankolekar et al., DAML-S: Web Service Description for the Semantic Web, Proc. Int'l Semantic Web Conf.(ISWC), LNCS 2342, pp. 348-363, Springer-Verlag, 2002.

[8] J. Yang and M.P. Papazoglou, Web Component: A Substrate for Web Service Reuse and Composition, Proc. 14th Conf. Advanced Information Systems Eng. (CAiSE 02), LNCS 2348, pp. 21-36, Springer-Verlag, 2002.

[9] R. Hamadi and B. Benatallah, A Petri-Net-Based Model for Web Service Composition, Proc. 14th Australasian Database Conf. Database Technologies, pp.191–200, ACM Press, 2003.

A QoS Driven Development Process Model for Component-Based Software Systems

Heiko Koziolek and Jens Happe

Graduate School Trustsoft *, University of Oldenburg, Germany
{heiko.koziolek, jens.happe}@informatik.uni-oldenburg.de

Abstract. Non-functional specifications of software components are considered an important asset in constructing dependable systems, since they enable early Quality of Service (QoS) evaluations. Several approaches for the QoS analysis of component-based software architectures have been introduced. However, most of these approaches do not consider the integration into the development process sufficiently. For example, they envision a pure bottom-up development or neglect that system architects do not have complete information for QoS analyses at their disposal. We extent an existing component-based development process model by Cheesman and Daniels to explicitly include early, model-based QoS analyses. Besides the system architect, we describe further involved roles. Exemplary for the performance domain, we analyse what information these roles can provide to construct a performance model of a software architecture.

1 Introduction

Quality of Service (QoS) analysis and prediction during early development stages of a software system is widely considered as an important factor for the construction of dependable and trustworthy systems. For component-based systems [10], the overall aim is to analyse QoS properties such as performance, reliability, availability, and safety based on specification documents of components and the architecture. For this purpose, compositional, analytical models can be constructed to allow predictions, even if the system only exists on paper. Using specifications of existing components, QoS predictions may be more precise than predictions for systems built from scratch.

To make early QoS analyses feasible in the IT industry, they have to become an integral part of the component-based development process. Cheesman and Daniels [2] describe a component-based development process model based on the Rational Unified Process (RUP). However, this approach does not contain any hint on how to include QoS analyses into the process.

On the other hand, several component-based QoS predictions approaches have been proposed. Most of these approaches focus on the analysis part and only contain very brief descriptions on how they are going to be integrated into the development process. For example, the component-based reliability [8, 9], performance [5, 1, 4], and safety [3] prediction approaches consider a pure bottom-up development where already existing components are assembled. This is a strong restriction, since combined top-down (starting from requirements) and bottom-up (starting from existing components) approaches as described in the following are more realistic.

* This work is supported by the German Research Foundation (DFG), grant GRK 1076/1.

I. Gorton et al. (Eds.): CBSE 2006, LNCS 4063, pp. 336–343, 2006.

All these approaches require a lot of additional information. QoS attributes of a component are not only determined by the component itself, but are influenced by the usage model, the deployment environment, its internal structure, and the services used by the component. In most cases, it is unclear how the information about all these factors is obtained and integrated. This is due to a lack of distinction concerning the roles and responsibilities during the development process.

The contribution of this position statement is an extension to the component-based development approach described by Cheesman and Daniels [2] to include QoS analyses. Augmenting the process model of the CB-SPE approach [1], we describe the responsibilities of the roles of component developer, system architect, system deployer, and domain experts. We discuss which information has to be provided by each role to construct a QoS prediction model. Our approach is not limited to performance analyses, but applicable to any QoS property.

This position statement is organised as follows. Section 2 introduces the roles in component-based development and discusses their responsibilities. Section 3 describes our QoS driven, component-based development process model and details on the specification and QoS analysis phases. In Section 4, we exemplary describe for a QoS property, which input values are needed for the construction of a performance model and associate these values with the roles discussed in Section 2. Conclusions follow in Section 5.

2 Roles in Component-Based Development

Since we want to evaluate QoS attributes at an early development stage, we need additional information about the internal component structure, the usage model, and the deployment environment. Not all of this information can be given by system architects themselves. Therefore, support of domain experts, component developers, and system deployers is required.

In our model, the *system architects* drive the development process. They design the software architecture and delegate work to other involved parties. Furthermore, they collect and integrate all information to perform QoS analyses and assemble the complete system from its parts. One of their information sources are the *domain experts*, who are involved in the requirements analysis, since they have special knowledge of the business domain. They are also familiar with the users' work habits and, thus, are responsible for analysing and describing the user behaviour.

On a more technical side, the *component developers* are responsible for the specification and implementation of components. They develop components for a market as well as on request. System architects may design architectures that are reusable in different deployment contexts. Sometimes, the actual deployment context is determined not until late development stages, especially if the software is developed for general markets. *System deployers* are responsible for specifying concrete execution environments with resources and connections. They also allocate components to resources. During the deployment stage of the development process, they are responsible for the installation, configuration, and start up of the application.

3 Integrating QoS Prediction into the Component-Based Development Process

In the following, the roles described in the former section are integrated into the component-based development process model featuring QoS analysis. We focus on the *development process* that is concerned with creating a working system from requirements and neglect the concurrent *management process* that is concerned with scheduling human resources and defining milestones. We base our model on the UML-centric development process model described by [2], which is itself based on the Rational Unified Process (RUP).

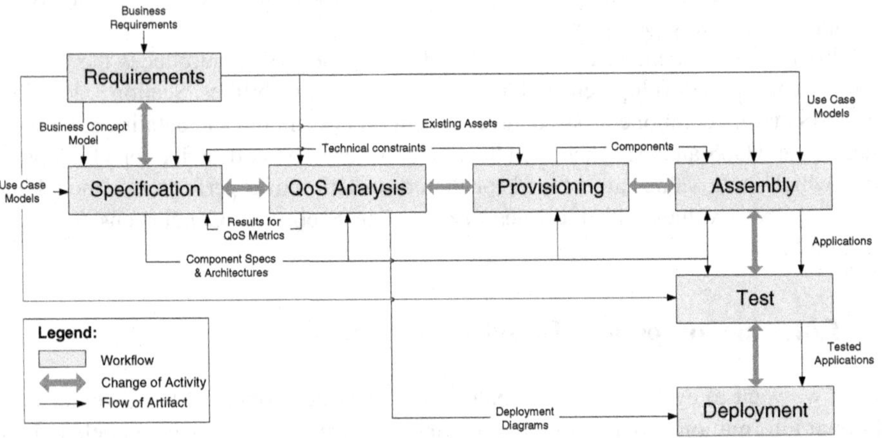

Fig. 1. Component-based Development Process Model with QoS Analysis

The main process is illustrated in Figure 1. Each box represents a workflow. The thick arrows between boxes represent a change of activity, while the thin arrows characterise the flow of artifacts between the workflows. The workflows do not have to be traversed linearly (i.e., no waterfall model). Backward steps into former workflows are allowed. The model also allows an incremental or iterative development based on prototypes. We have inherited the requirements, specification, provisioning, assembly, test, and deployment workflows from the original model and added the QoS analysis workflow. Component specifications, the architecture, and use case models are input to the QoS analysis workflow. Outputs of the QoS analysis are results for QoS metrics, which can be used during specification to adjust the architecture, and deployment diagrams that can be used during deployment.

In the following, we will only describe our extensions to the specification workflow and the new QoS analysis workflow. However, most of the other workflows are also influenced by QoS driven development. For example, a detailed description of the QoS requirements has to be compiled within requirements workflow. Furthermore, testing has not only to check functional properties, but also QoS attributes. For the other workflows and artifacts exchanged among them, we refer the interested reader to [2].

3.1 Specification Workflow

The specification workflow (see Figure 2, right column) is carried out by the system architect. The workflows of the system architect and the component developers influence each other. Existing components (e.g., from a repository) may have an impact on the component identification and specification workflow, as the system architect can reuse existing interfaces and specifications. Vice versa, newly specified components by the system architect can be input for the component requirements analysis of component developers, who design and implement new components.

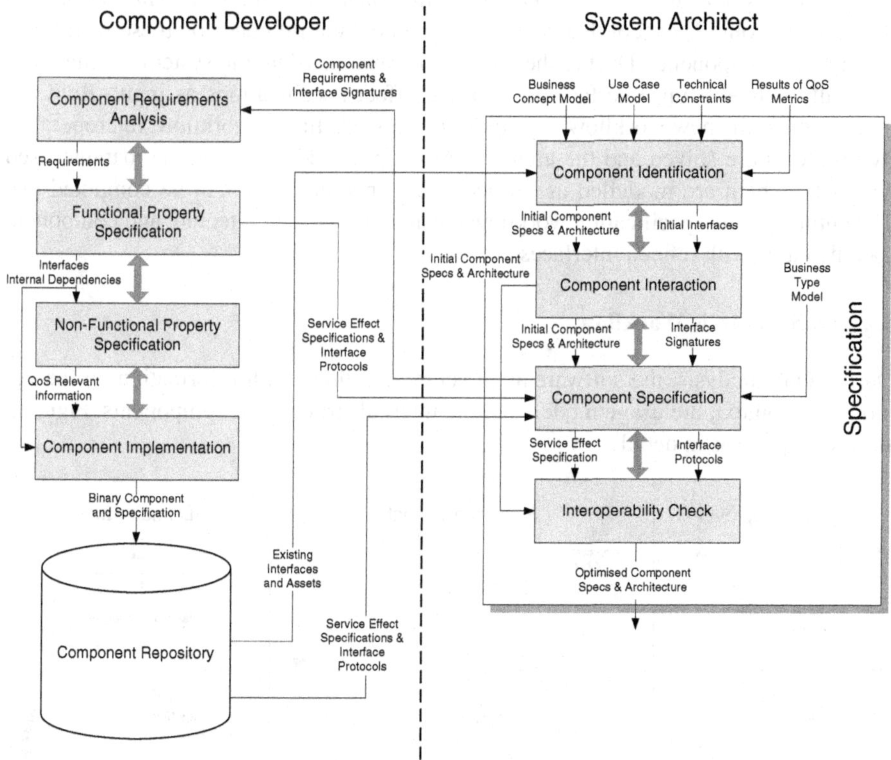

Fig. 2. Detailed View on the Specification Workflow

The workflows of the component developers are only sketched here, since they are performed separately from the system architect's workflows. If a new component needs to be developed, the workflow of the component developer (see Figure 2) can be assumed to be part of the provisioning workflow according to Cheesman and Daniels. Any development process model can be used to construct new components as long as functional and non-functional properties are specified properly. After the *component requirement analysis*, the *functional property specification* and then the *non-functional property specification* of the components follow. The functional properties consist of interface specifications (i.e., signatures and protocols) and descriptions of internal dependencies between provided and required interfaces. We use service effect specifications from [7] to describe such dependencies. They model how a provided services calls its required services and can be specified by state machines. Non-functional, QoS relevant information includes resource demands, reliability values, data flow, and transition probabilities for service effect specifications. After *component implementation* according to the specifications, component developers may put the binary implementations and the specifications into repositories, where they can be retrieved and assessed by third party system architects.

The specification workflow of the system architect consists of four inner workflows. The first two workflows (*component identification* and *component interaction*) are adapted from [2] except that we explicitly model the influence on these workflows by existing components. During the *component specification*, the system architect additionally gets existing interface and service effect specifications as input. Both are transferred to the new workflow *interoperability check*. In this workflow, interoperability problems are solved and the architecture is optimised. For example, parametrised contracts, which are modelled as service effect specifications, can be computed [7]. The outputs of the specification workflow are an optimised architecture and component specifications with refined interfaces.

3.2 QoS Analysis Workflow

During QoS analysis, the software architecture is refined with information on the deployment context, the usage model, and the internal structure of components. Figure 3 shows the process in detail.

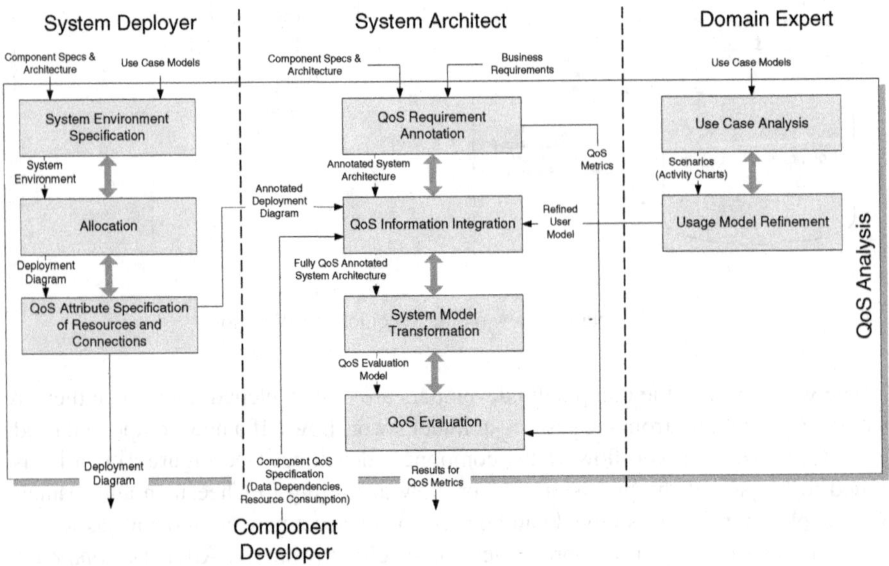

Fig. 3. Detailed View of the QoS Analysis Workflow

The system deployer starts with the *system environment specification* based on the software architecture and use case models. Given this information, the required hardware and software resources and their interconnections are derived. As a result, this workflow yields a deployment diagram that describes only the system environment without allocated components. The system deployer can also create a description of existing hardware and software resources. Moreover, a set of representative system environments can be designed if the deployment context is still unknown. During the *allocation*, the system deployer specifies the mapping of components to resources. The resulting deployment diagram is annotated with a detailed *QoS attribute specification* of the deployment environment. These specifications provide input parameters for the QoS analysis models used later. The resulting fully annotated deployment diagram is passed to the system architect.

The domain expert refines the use case models from the requirements during the *use case analysis*. A description of the scenarios for the users is created based on an external view of the current software architecture. The scenarios describe how users interact with the system and what dependencies exists in the process. For example, activity charts can be used to describe such scenarios. The scenario descriptions are input to the *usage model refinement*. The domain expert annotates the descriptions with, for example, branching probabilities, expected size of different user groups, expected workload, and user think times.

As the central role in QoS analysis, the system architect integrates the QoS relevant information, performs the evaluation, and delivers the feedback to all involved parties. In the *QoS requirement annotation* workflow, the system architect maps QoS requirements to the software architecture. For example, the maximum waiting time of a user becomes the upper limit of the response time of a component service. While doing so, the system architect specifies QoS metrics, like response time or probability of failure on demand, that are evaluated during later workflows.

During *QoS information integration*, the system architect collects the QoS specifications provided by the component developers, system deployers, and domain experts and integrates them into an overall QoS model of the system. This information is sufficient to transform the system and its behaviour into a stochastic process or simulation model as done in the *system model transformation*.

The *QoS evaluation* workflow either yields an analytical solution or the results of a simulation. QoS evaluation aims, for example, at testing the scalability of the architecture and at identifying bottlenecks. If the results show that the QoS requirements cannot be fulfilled with the current architecture, the system architect has to modify the specifications or renegotiate the requirements.

4 Information Required and Mapping to Roles

To construct a QoS prediction model, additional, extra-functional information besides the pure functional UML model is required. We will focus on information required for performance modelling as an example. The additional information needed to construct a performance model (e.g., a queueing network or stochastic Petri net) can be specified directly in UML with the SPT profile [6]. In this extension to UML, the performance analysis domain model describes the information needed to create a performance model. It allows the inclusion of workload, component-behaviour, and resources into UML expressed as stereotypes and tagged values.

Domain experts are responsible for specifying all information closely related to the users of the system. This includes specifying workloads with user arrival rates or user populations and think times. In some cases, these values are already part of the requirement documents. If method parameter values have an influence on the QoS of the system, the domain experts may assist the system architect in characterising these values.

The *system deployer* provides information about the resources of the system (e.g., hardware-related like processing devices or software-related like thread pools). In the UML SPT profile, resources in deployment diagrams can be characterised as active or passive. Further attributes are scheduling policies, processing rates, or context switch times and must be specified by the system deployer. The system deployer is also responsible for adapting the platform independent resource demand specifications of the component developer to the properties of the system under analysis.

The *system architect* is responsible for extracting information from the requirements (e.g., maximal response times for use cases) and including them into the model. All information provided by the other roles are integrated by the system architect, who also has to estimate missing values. For example, the system architect might have to specify a parameter distribution for certain services if it influences the performance or he has to estimate the resource demand of components that have been provided without extra-functional specifications.

Component developers specify the performance of their components without knowledge where the components will be deployed, thus enabling independent third party performance analysis. First, they need to characterise the execution demands on the resources of the system in a platform independent way, for example, by specifying the number of processor or byte code instructions their services execute. The system deployer will use these values and parametrise them for the environment under analysis. Second, component developers have to specify how provided services call required services. This is necessary, so that the system architect can describe the control flow through the architecture. External calls to required services will be mapped to performance model steps in the UML SPT profile. The component developer can obtain these by code analysis or by evaluating design documents of the components.

For a performance analysis, transition probabilities and the number of loop iterations are required for calls from provided to required services. These values cannot be fully determined by the component developer, in case they are not fixed in the source code. Influences on these values may come from external sources, for example from the parameter values the service is called with or the results of external services. If such an influence exists, the component developer has to state this dependency in the component specification explicitly, so that the system architect can specify probability distributions for parameter values or exploit the postconditions of required services for this service.

5 Conclusions and Future Work

In this position statement, we have described how QoS analyses can be integrated into the early stages of a component-based development process. Several developer roles participate in QoS analyses, as the system architects do not have all necessary information by themselves. We have demonstrated how component developers, system deployers, domain experts, and system architects interact during early QoS analyses. Additionally, we have described in detail, which information is necessary to conduct a performance analysis (exemplified by the UML SPT profile) and which of the roles can provide it.

A component-based development process model integrating QoS analysis is relevant for practitioners and researchers. Practitioners receive a recipe on how to tackle QoS problems during early development stages. Researchers are supported by showing a method on how to integrate their QoS analysis models into a practical development process.

Stating the specification responsibilities for the different values as in Section 4 is just a first step to an engineering approach to component-based performance prediction. Currently, we are looking for possibilities to retrieve some of the values from existing code (semi-) automatically. In this position statement, we have omitted an experimental evaluation of our development process model, which is planned for the future.

References

1. A. Bertolino and R. Mirandola. CB-SPE Tool: Putting Component-Based Performance Engineering into Practice. In *Component-Based Software Engineering*, volume 3054 of *Lecture Notes in Computer Science*, pages 233–248. Springer, 2004.
2. J. Cheesman and J. Daniels. *UML Components: A Simple Process for Specifying Component-based Software Systems*. Addison-Wesley, 2001.
3. L. Grunske, B. Kaiser, and Y. Papadopoulos. Model-Driven Safety Evaluation with State-Event-Based Component Failure annotations. In *Component-Based Software Engineering, 8th International Symposium, CBSE 2005, Proceedings*, volume 3489 of *Lecture Notes in Computer Science*, pages 33–48. Springer Verlag, 2005.
4. D. Hamlet, D. Mason, and D. Woit. *Properties of Software Systems Synthesized from Components*, volume 1, chapter Case Studies, pages 129–159. World Scientific Publishing Company, 2004.
5. S. A. Hissam, G. A. Moreno, J. A. Stafford, and K. C. Wallnau. Packaging Predictable Assembly. In *Proceedings of the IFIP/ACM Working Conference on Component Deployment (CD2002)*, pages 108–124, London, UK, 2002. Springer-Verlag.
6. Object Management Group OMG. UML Profile for Schedulability, Performance and Time. `http://www.omg.org/cgi-bin/doc?formal/2005-01-02`, 2005.
7. R. H. Reussner, I. H. Poernomo, and H. W. Schmidt. Reasoning on Software Architectures with Contractually Specified Components. In A. Cechich, M. Piattini, and A. Vallecillo, editors, *Component-Based Software Quality: Methods and Techniques*, number 2693 in Lecture Notes in Computer Science, pages 287–325. 2003.
8. R. H. Reussner, H. W. Schmidt, and I. H. Poernomo. Reliability Prediction for Component-Based Software Architectures. *Journal of Systems and Software*, 66(3):241–252, 2003.
9. R. Y. Shukla, P.A. Strooper, and D.A. Carrington. A Framework for Reliability Assessment of Software Components. In *Proceedings of the 7th International Symposium on Component-based Software Engineering (CBSE7), Edinburgh, UK*, volume 3054 of *Lecture Notes in Computer Science*, pages 272–279, 2004.
10. C. Szyperski, D. Gruntz, and S. Murer. *Component Software: Beyond Object-Oriented Programming*. Addison-Wesley, 2002.

An Enhanced Composition Model for Conversational *Enterprise JavaBeans*

Franck Barbier

PauWare Research Group – Université de Pau
Av. de l'université, BP 1155, 64013 Pau CEDEX – France
Franck.Barbier@FranckBarbier.com

Abstract. When designing applications with *Enterprise JavaBeans* (EJBs) and more specifically with *Stateful Session Beans*, a major difficulty (or even an impossibility) is being able to properly transform business models and more precisely UML 2 models, into such component types, while including the expression of their mutual compositions. This contradicts with the spirit of the emerging *Model-Driven Architecture* (MDA) software engineering paradigm based on the definition of seamless model transformations. In this scope, this paper proposes and describes an appropriate Java library in order to increase the composition power of EJBs. The proposition includes a support for a broadcast communication mode (assimilated to "horizontal composition" in the paper) which is, *a priori*, incompatible with non reentrance, a key characteristic of EJBs. Besides, "vertical composition" is the counterpart of "horizontal composition". "Vertical composition" enables the consistent hierarchical combination of composite behaviors and compound behaviors, both being specified and implemented by means of UML 2 *State Machine Diagrams*.

1 Introduction

Szyperski *et al.* have claimed for a long time that: "Components are for composition." [1]. In other words, all software components are software parts, although not all software parts are necessarily software components. Furthermore, if components are not specifically designed to have composition potentialities (*i.e.*, composability or compositionality attributes) at assembly time, the risk is high that components will fail to interoperate properly. That is the reason why technological component models exist: *Enterprise JavaBeans* (EJBs), CORBA Component Model (CCM), COM+ or Fractal. In providing a well-bounded accurate development and deployment framework, such component models support composition templates. A resulting advantage is that, by complying to the imposed format[1] of components, composition is easy and straightforward. A disadvantage is the difficulty of transforming business models like UML models for instance (which in essence are free of technical constraints) into technical components. In other words, stereotyped components (*e.g.*,

[1] The term "format" is here preferred to that of "model" since technological components obey to code construction and deployment rules rather than to formal/mathematical specifications.

I. Gorton et al. (Eds.): CBSE 2006, LNCS, pp. 344 – 351, 2006.

Entity Beans, *Session Beans* and *Message-Driven Beans*) of a given technological component model (*e.g.*, EJBs) may be considered as moulds. Melting business models down in order to fill these moulds is a strong expectation in the software industry.

In the spirit of MDA [2], model transformation rules have to formalize how a platform-independent model (PIM) is transformed into a platform-specific model (PSM). This theoretical principle may however stumble over incompatible model properties. We have carried out experimentations on this problem with UML 2 *State Machines Diagrams* and *Sequence Diagrams*, and more generally with the global "UML 2 Composition Model" [3]. Software components and compositions modeled by means of UML possess recognized features coming from the intrinsic "semantics" of UML itself. The most well-known characteristics are for instance the "coincident lifetime" of composites and compounds in, what we call below, "vertical composition". For "horizontal composition", which is closely related to component communication, broadcast is the underlying communication mode (a heritage of Harel's Statecharts [4]). In EJBs, the predefined composition mechanisms do not conform to these idealistic properties.

This paper proposes a solution for fitting conversational EJBs, which are *Stateful Session Beans*, to the most important conceptual composition mechanisms of UML 2. This occurs through the construction of a dedicated Java library named *PauWare* which is illustrated in this paper.

That is why Section 2 gives a brief overview of EJBs. Section 3 insists on the problem of non reentrance, which is particular to EJBs and which, *a priori*, precludes the implementation of broadcast in EJBs. Broadcast indeed comes from the executability facilities of UML 2 *State Machines Diagrams* and *Sequence Diagrams* and thus, cannot be ignored. Section 4 shows how this has been solved with *PauWare*: code samples are provided. Section 5 is about "vertical composition": how to compose conversational EJBs, hierarchically, starting from the hypothesis that they own and are governed by a statechart that exists inside themselves. A major challenge amounts to synchronizing the two statecharts of a composite and a compound. To conclude in Section 6, we evoke the link of this work with autonomic computing.

2 *Enterprise JavaBeans*

EJBs [5] constitute a technological component standard. They also represent a highly coercive computing framework as far as the format of an EJB is predefined and strict (Fig. 1). From the code viewpoint, an EJB must have a Java implementation class and appropriate interfaces for its clients. From the deployment viewpoint now, an EJB must also have values assigned to mandatory deployment parameters.

Since EJBs' shapes cannot be ordinary and have to satisfy many constraints, EJBs are by their very nature composable. Components that do not comply to standards can indeed be composable with much difficulty. However, in practice, the EJBs' composition model may demonstrate numerous limitations. This is especially the case for conversational EJBs. This specific EJB type offers interesting facilities to programmers. For instance, programmers can control creation decisions; and conversational EJBs remain unshared between clients. Unfortunately, even though it is possible to scrupulously control states within the inside of *Stateful Session Beans*, sophisticated combination of such conversational EJBs is poor. In UML, models such as different state machines[2] may be assigned to distinct business components. Composing these components amounts to taking into account scenarios embodying the communication between them. State machines and scenarios however rely on a composition semantics that has no direct mapping in EJBs. As a result, the benefits from having a formal semantics for statechart composition (see for instance [6] or [7]) cannot really be exploited at the implementation level.

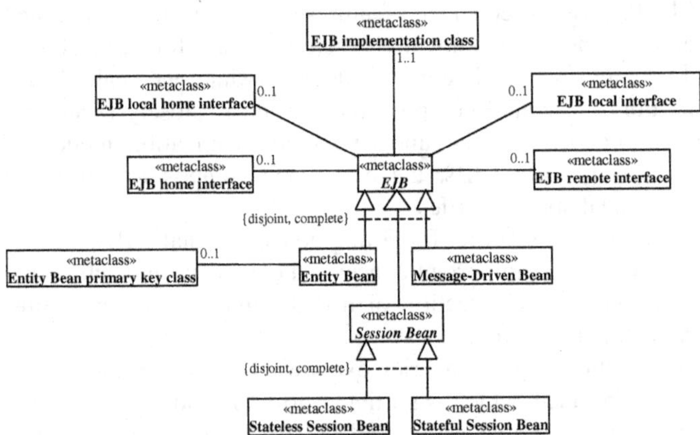

Fig. 1. UML metamodel expressing the contractual format of an EJB and the possible types of EJBs

3 Non Reentrance

In attempting to construct the inside of a *Stateful Session Bean* by means of a state machine, one problem is caused by the broadcast communication mode, which is the basis of Harel's Statecharts [4, p. 269]: "The statechart communication mechanism, on the other hand, is based on broadcast, whereby the sender proceeds even if nobody is listening." EJBs do not accept requests while transactions are in progress (this phenomenon is known as non reentrance) while broadcast supposes that requests may arrive at any time.

As an illustration, we reuse the *Railcar control system* case study presented in [8]. In Fig. 2, a railcar that is less than 80 meters far from a terminal, sends *crossing request* which is part of the remote interface of the *Terminal* component type (see the right hand side of Fig. 2). In Fig. 3, the sending of *crossing request* may be observed within the statechart of the *Railcar* component type by means of this expression: ^*my next possible stop.crossing request(self)*. The reception of and response to *crossing request* appears within the statechart of the *Terminal* component type (Fig. 3).

[2] UML 2 state machines are closely related to Harel's Statecharts. We comment on some key differences in the rest of the paper but we do not formally distinguish the expression "state machine" from the word "statechart" all along the paper.

In EJBs, the call of *crossing request* occurs within a transaction that started when *alert80* arrived. The receiver terminal may reply to the sender railcar (by using *self* which is a parameter of *crossing request*) that some passengers standing at the said terminal want to get onto the approaching railcar. How then may one guarantee that *candidate passengers* (the possible reply) is not received at an unsuitable moment, *i.e.*, if the transaction associated with *alert80* is not yet finished?

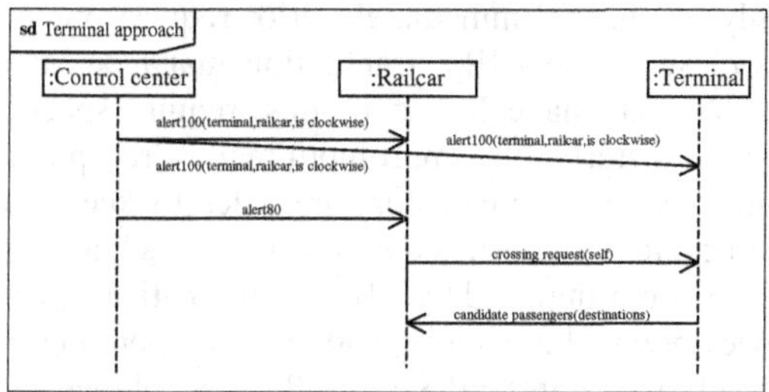

Fig. 2. Scenario of communication between three respective instances of a Control center, a Railcar and a Terminal components

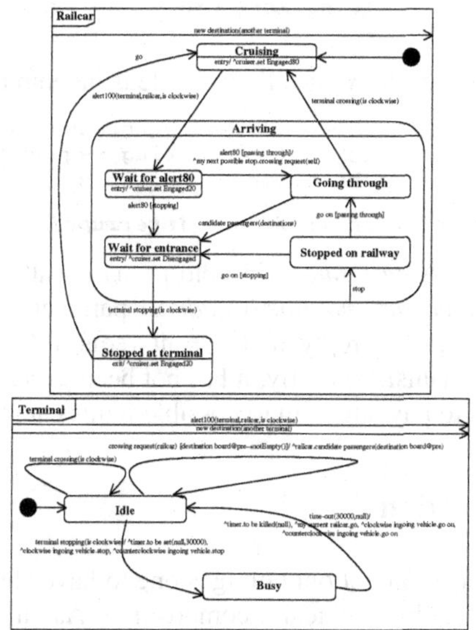

Fig. 3. Two communicating statecharts of a Railcar and Terminal components

4 Horizontal Composition of Conversational EJBS

So, the coercive composition model of EJBs precludes intertwined communication, but a consequence of broadcast is that a request receiver may immediately reply to the sender even though the latter is not, from the EJBs' composition model's viewpoint, in an "appropriate" state (while the transaction is in progress).

To solve this problem, we propose a MDA-based Java statechart execution engine that automates the complete and coherent management of statecharts at runtime. The chosen executability semantics is obviously that of UML 2 which is slightly different (even if broadcast remains) from that of the original Statecharts and of some Harel's variants [8]. In [9], two key subtle semantic differences are formally specified: UML 2 advocates a run-to-completion execution model (a first characteristic[3]) which ensures that, within a given state machine instance, the processing of a new request starts when, and only when, the immediately prior request processing is terminated. This mechanism is close to the EJBs' transaction management mechanism. In our approach, requests that may have linked replies, require special treatment so that statechart cycles are not disturbed by impromptu request receptions. Independently of EJBs, this mechanism is for us mandatory in order to keep statecharts consistent throughout execution cycles. A consubstantial result of such an implementation is that the non reentrance constraint imposed by EJBs is automatically satisfied.

From a design viewpoint, this simply leads to incorporating a statechart into the Java implementation class of a *Stateful Session Bean* as follows (code is incomplete):

```
protected Statechart _Arriving = new Statechart("Arriving"); // + the
other states

protected Statechart_monitor _Railcar = new
Statechart_monitor((_Arriving.xor(_Cruising)).xor(_Stopped_at_termina
l),"Railcar");
```

Next, coding *alert80* leads to what follows (code is incomplete):

```
_Railcar.fires(_Wait_for_alert80,_Going_through,passing_through,_my_n
ext_possible_stop.getEJBObject(),"crossing_request",args,Statechart_m
onitor.Broadcast); // + the other transitions

_Railcar.run_to_completion(); // non interruptible statechart cycle
```

In the code above, *crossing request* (in bold print) is called by means of the Java reflection API. The *Statechart_monitor.Broadcast* parameter value must be used if the specification shows that a reply to the sent request (*i.e.*, *crossing request*) is probable. Since this mechanism is costly, it has not been generalized within *PauWare*. Programmers have thus to pay attention to possible faults caused by reentrance.

5 Vertical Composition

The need for rich composition not only obliges one to have "horizontal" composition, but also "vertical" (a.k.a. "hierarchical") composition. As an illustration, the *Fractal* composition model [10] supports hierarchical composition. The notion of "vertical composition" consists in having a sub-component encapsulated in a composite component (irreflexivity applies in order to avoid any cycle). The latter hides the sub-component from clients and, more precisely, from the clients' service requests.

The implementation of vertical composition within *PauWare* relies on the theoretical research results exposed in [11-13]. In these three papers, a formal

[3] The second specificity of the UML 2 executability semantics is a special strategy for coping with conflicting transitions in statecharts. We do not address these issues in this paper. In short, nested transitions linked to inner states override upper transitions linked to outer states.

semantics for the *Aggregation* and *Composition* UML relationships is provided. A key feature of the UML *Composition* is coincident lifetime (a.k.a. "the fifth case of lifetime dependency" in [11]) between attached composites and compounds. This property of coincident lifetime makes the possibility realistic (and even relevant) that a component instance strongly refers to the states of another component instance. In comparison, the states of two different component instances do not have to be interrelated if these two components have unrelated lifecycles[4].

Going back to the *Railcar system* case study, one may thus consider that in terms of states, a single *Control center* component instance is a composition of all existing *Railcar* and *Terminal* component instances that participate in the system. In other words, following the logics of coincident lifetime assigned to *Composition* in UML, *Railcar* and *Terminal* component instances do not have to exist out of the life span of the *Control center* component instance. In terms of behaviors, a control center propagates or delegates environment data coming from sensors (*e.g.*, *alert100*, *alert80*) to railcars and terminals.

The proposed solution is based on the metamodel in Fig. 4. The *Whole-Part*, *Aggregation* and *Composition* types come from [11]. The right hand side of Fig. 4 is new and shows that the *Statechart monitor* type (embodying a global state machine) inherits from the *Statechart* type. In other words, a state machine is a kind of macroscopic state. However, the *Statechart monitor* type has interpretation capabilities as well: it possesses the *run_to_completion* Java method which is not owned by the *Statechart* type.

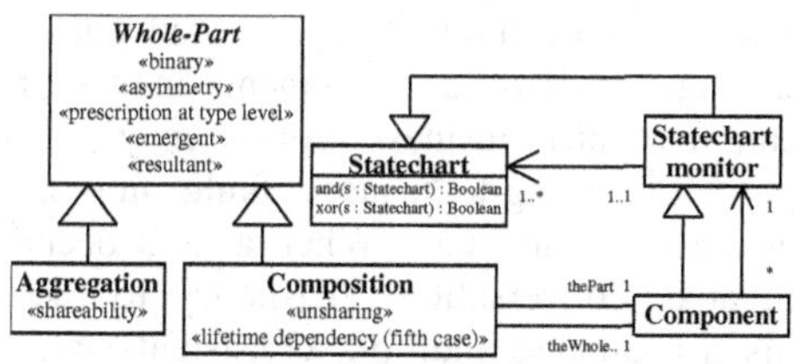

Fig. 4. UML metamodel for vertical composition

This leads to adding a specific service for the *Railcar* component type whose implementation is as follows:

```
public Statechart_monitor state_machine() {return _Railcar;}
```

Vertical composition is then instrumented as follows:

```
Statechart _Control = new Statechart("Control");

_Control_center = new
Statechart_monitor(_Control.and(railcar_remote.state_machine()),"Cont
rol center");
```

The code above illustrates the linking of a *Railcar* component instance state machine as a sub-state of the *Control center* component instance and as an orthogonal state of the *Control* sub-state: use of the *and* operator.

[4] In the worst case, two component instances may be connected together through their states but, in our opinion, with great care, since it is an error-prone situation.

Such a solution creates an automatic propagation/delegation mechanism. So, requests are forwarded from composites to compounds in a transparent way. In the code below, a multicast mode for sending the *alert80* request is used. All attached railcars, like the *railcar_remote* J2EE object in the code above, are concerned with the reception and the possible processing (depending upon their current state) of *alert80*:

```
public void alert80() throws Statechart_exception
{_Control_center.run_to_completion();}
```

In this code, no other processing except propagation/delegation occurs.

6 Conclusion: Perspectives and Benefits from an Enhanced Composition Model for Conversational EJBS

A side effect of having state machines inside components is the possibility for instrumenting dynamical re-configuration. For varied reasons, one may decide to force the state of a component. Externally, this leads to offering and to implementing a management service such as for instance *reset*:

```
public void reset() throws Statechart_exception
{_Terminal.to_state("Idle");}
```

Decisions may be taken by the components themselves. In this case, they become self-configuring and self-managing software entities, a concept of autonomic computing [14]. In this line of thought, a more advanced feature of autonomic computing is self-healing. *PauWare*'s components may support self-healing in the sense that the execution of any business request may generate faults. Fault self-management consists then in trying to "cancel" faults automatically. At this time, the implemented mechanism is rudimentary. When a fault occurs and if the autonomic mode has been activated, conversational EJBs try to recover their immediately previous "state": this amounts to multiple consistent states, since statecharts are composed of nested and parallel modeled/implemented states. Within the cycle of moving a statechart from one step to another, internal operations in components may change business data (just before the arrival of the "incriminated" fault). Going back to the immediately previous state may therefore lead to inconsistencies. For example, a requirement may be that a port must be closed in a given state. Returning to this state without having the port closed is inconsistent.

To improve such a situation, state invariants that may be attached to states, have the responsibility to check if the current values of business data are compliant with the reached states. Within the process of fault recovery, this leads to proving that returning to the immediately previous global state of a component is "correct". To sum up, self healing really succeeds if and only if all state invariants are true after rolling back to such an immediately previous state.

We have presented in this paper a concrete implementation of an enhanced composition model for conversational EJBs. A main motivation relating to such a research work, is the look for a better integration of the EJBs' technology within MDA. One especially tries to fill the gap between two execution semantics. Model executability in UML is somehow idealistic but it benefits from being abstract, *i.e.*, independent of technological platforms. Instead, execution constraints of EJBs may be considered as numerous. Nevertheless, this is the source of a robust, but limited, composition model. A tradeoff is thus required, a goal of this paper.

The proposed implementation also favors the creation of a support for autonomic computing. Short-term perspectives are the adaptation of *PauWare* for J2ME components, *i.e.*, components that are deployed and run in mobile and wireless devices. This implementation, currently in its testing phase, aims at being in better convergence with the demands of autonomic computing.

References

1. Szyperski, C., Gruntz, D., Murer, S.: Component Software – Beyond Object-Oriented Programming – Second Edition, Addison-Wesley (2002)
2. Mellor, S., Scott, K., Uhl, A., Weise, D.: MDA Distilled – Principles of Model-Driven Architecture, Addison-Wesley (2004)
3. Bock, C.: UML 2 Composition Model, Journal of Object Technology, Vol. 3, 10 (2004) 47-73
4. Harel, D.: Statecharts: A Visual Formalism for Complex Systems, Science of Computer Programming, Vol. 8 (1987) 231-274
5. Sun Microsystems: Enterprise JavaBeans™ Specification, Version 2.1 (2003)
6. Simons, A.: On the Compositional Properties of UML Statechart Diagrams, Proc. 3rd Conf. Rigorous Object-Oriented Methods (2000) 4.1-4.19
7. Prehofer, C.: Plug-and-play composition of features and feature interactions with statechart diagrams, Software and Systems Modeling, Vol. 3, 3 (2004) 221-234
8. Harel, D., Gery, E.: Executable Object Modeling with Statecharts, IEEE Computer, Vol. 30, 7 (1997) 31-42
9. von der Beck, M.: A structured operational semantics for UML-statecharts, Software and Systems Modeling, Vol. 1, 2 (2002) 130-141
10. Bruneton, E., Coupaye, T., Leclercq, M., Quéma, V., Stefani, J.-B.: An Open Component Model and Its Support in Java, Proc. 7th International Symposium on Component-Based Software Engineering, LNCS #3054, (2004) 7-22
11. Barbier, F., Henderson-Sellers, B., Le Parc-Lacayrelle, A., Bruel, J.-M.: Formalization of the Whole-Part Relationship in the Unified Modeling Language, IEEE Transactions on Software Engineering, Vol. 29, 5 (2003) 459-470
12. Tan, H. B. K., Hao, L., Yang, Y.: On Formalization of the Composition Relationship in the Unified Modeling Language, IEEE Transactions on Software Engineering, Vol. 29, 11 (2003) 1054-1055
13. Barbier, F., Henderson-Sellers, B.: Controversies about the Black and White Diamonds, IEEE Transactions on Software Engineering, Vol. 29, 11 (2003) 1056
14. Kephart, J., Chess, D.: The Vision of Autonomic Computing, IEEE Computer, Vol. 36, 1 (2003) 41-50

Dynamic Reconfiguration and Access to Services in Hierarchical Component Models

Petr Hnětynka[1] and František Plášil[1,2]

[1] Department of Software Engineering
Faculty of Mathematics and Physics, Charles University
Malostranské náměstí 25, Prague 1, 11800, Czech Republic
{hnetynka, plasil}@nenya.ms.mff.cuni.cz
[2] Institute of Computer Science, Academy of Sciences of the Czech Republic
Pod Vodárenskou věží, Prague 8, 18000, CzechRepublic
plasil@cs.cas.cz

Abstract. This paper addresses the unavoidable problem of dynamic reconfiguration in component-based system with a hierarchical component model. The presented solution is based on (1) allowing several well defined patterns of dynamic reconfiguration and on (2) introducing a *utility interface* concept, which allows using a service provided under the SOA paradigm from a component-based system. The paper is based on our experience with non-trivial case studies written for component-based systems SOFA and Fractal.

1 Introduction

Component-based development (CBD) [19] has become a commonly used technique for building software systems. There are many opinions as to what a component is. One typically agrees that it is a black-box entity with well defined interfaces and behavior, which can be reused in different contexts and without knowledge of its internal structure (i.e., without modifying its internals). However, from a design view, components – especially hierarchical ones – can be viewed as glass-box entities with the internal structure visible as a set of communicating subcomponents. Typically, the collection of the related abstractions, their semantics and the rules for component composition (creation of component architecture) are referred to as a *component model* and an implementation of it as a *component system/platform*. In our view, the concept of "component" has always to be interpreted in the semantics of a particular component model.

Many component systems currently exist and are used both in industry and academia. Typically, the industrial component systems, such as EJB [6] and CCM [15], are based on a flat component model. On the contrary, the academic component systems and models usually provide advanced features like hierarchical architectures, behavior description, coexistence of components from different platforms, dynamically updatable components, support for complex communication styles, etc.

However, it is hard to properly balance the semantics of advanced features – in our view, this fact hinders a widespread, industrial usage of hierarchical component

I. Gorton et al. (Eds.): CBSE 2006, LNCS 4063, pp. 352–359, 2006.

models. Based on our experience with the SOFA [17] and Fractal [4] component models, we claim that this issue is primarily related to dynamic reconfiguration of an architecture, i.e., adding and removing components at runtime, passing references to components, etc. A simple prohibition of dynamic reconfiguration (even though adopted by some systems [2]) would be very limiting, since dynamic changes of architecture are inherent to many component-based applications [14]. On the other hand, particularly in hierarchical component models, an arbitrary sequence of dynamic reconfiguration can lead to "uncontrolled" architectural modification, which is inherently error-prone (we call this *evolution gap problem*, also *architecture erosion* [3]). Moreover, for description of component architectures, most of the component models provide an architecture description language (ADL) [2,4,13,14], which typically captures just the initial components' configuration. (The idea of software architectures and ADL specification came from hardware design, which is static by nature). Thus a challenge is to somehow capture reconfiguration in an ADL.

Another currently emerging paradigm is the service-oriented architecture (SOA) [21]. SOA-based systems (WebServices, etc.) are commonly used in industry. In a high-level view, there is no difference between the SOA and CBD paradigms [10] – both a service and component have a well defined interface, their internal structure is not visible to their environment, and they can be reused in different contexts without modification. However, in SOA, services are not nested and their composition is typically done with the granularity of each request call, frequently being data driven. Thus, because of lack of any continuity in the architecture, there is no problem with dynamic reconfiguration similar to component models.

In this paper, we employ experience with our hierarchical component model SOFA [17] which supports many advanced features like dynamic update, behavior description via behavior protocols, software connectors, and an open-source prototype of which is available [18]. However, based on case studies, we identified deep-going SOFA limits, including dynamic reconfiguration restricted to a dynamic update of a component and the lack of any cooperation with external services, which lead us to the design of the SOFA 2.0.

The goal of the paper is to show how we propose to address the dynamic reconfiguration in SOFA 2.0 with the aim to avoid the evolution gap problem and allow for accessing external services provided through the SOA paradigm. To address the goal, the paper is structured as follows. Section 2 introduces the key contribution – the nested factory pattern and utility interface pattern. Section 3 contains evaluation and related work, while the concluding Section 4 summarizes the presented ideas.

2 Dynamic Reconfiguration and Its Patterns

By *dynamic reconfiguration* we mean a run time modification of an application's architecture. As a special case this includes dynamic update of a component supported by the original SOFA (and also in SOFA 2.0); here the principle is that a particular component is dynamically replaced with another one having compatible interfaces. This kind of dynamic reconfiguration is easy to handle, because all the changes are located in the updated component and are transparent to the rest of the application. Since the new component can have a completely different internal structure, such a component update in principle means replacing a whole subtree in the component hierarchy, being thus a "real" architecture reconfiguration. Also, as an aside, dynamic update is not usually initiated by the application itself but by an external entity (the user, provider, etc.); on the contrary though, a general dynamic reconfiguration is an arbitrary modification of an application architecture typically initiated by the application itself. We have identified the following five elementary operations such a dynamic reconfiguration is based upon: (1) removing a component, (2) adding a component, (3) removing a connection, (4) adding a connection, (5) adding/removing a component's interface.

As mentioned in Sect.1, in hierarchical component models an arbitrary sequence of these operations can lead to "uncontrolled" architectural modification (the evolution gap problem). To avoid it in SOFA 2.0, we limit dynamic reconfigurations to those compliant with specific *reconfiguration patterns*. At present, we allow the following three reconfiguration patterns: (i) nested factory, (ii) component removal, and (iii) utility interface. In principle the operations (1) – (4) are to be employed in these patterns only, and the operation (5) is limited to the use of collection interfaces (an unlimited array of interfaces of a specific type in principle [8]). The choice of these patterns is based on our experience gained out of non-trivial case studies. Due to space constrains, we below discuss and analyze only (i) and (iii) which we consider the key ones.

2.1 Nested Factory Pattern

The nested factory pattern covers *adding a new component* and *a new connection* to an architecture. The new component is created by a *factory* component as result of a method invocation on this factory. The key related issues are (i) where in the hierarchy the new component should be placed, and (ii) how the connections of/to the new component should be lead.

Consider the situation on Fig. 1a) capturing a fragment of an application featuring the DAccess component, which logs all method calls to a set of loggers connected via a required collection interface. The DAccess is a data access component, which is bound to LFactory (the logger factory) featuring a collection required interface for accessing the loggers. As a result of a call to its provided interface, the logger factory creates a new logger component and returns a reference pointing to it. Such a call is issued by the DAccess component, which in response receives a reference to a new logger and binds to it via the collection interface (dashed line on Fig. 1a).

Provided the DAccess and LFactory components are siblings in the flat architecture, such a dynamic reconfiguration is easy. However, a problem arises when this assumption does not hold as on Fig. 1b). The issue is, where the newly created component (Logger) should be placed in the architecture and how the connection to it should be established.

A straightforward answer to the question where to put the dynamically created Logger components might be into the FactoryManager. However a decision how to manage their connections to DAccess is not that intuitively obvious. If we allow a direct connection between the DAccess and Logger, then the connection will go through the FactoryManager component boundaries and violate the requirement of encapsulation. The second option, to add a copy of the Logger provided interface to the FactoryManager component and lead the connection through it is also not ideal, because it would mean that FactoryManager had to mediate traffic of all connections. In general, if a component A asking creation of another component B (and also assuming A is to be connected to B) is located in a different part of the hierarchical architecture than B is, the problem of mediating connections becomes pressing.

In SOFA 2.0, we have adopted the following rule: The newly created component B becomes a sibling of the component A that initiated the creation (and A's call to the factory also determines the A's collection interface the connection is to be established to). In the example above, the Logger component becomes a sibling of the DAccess component – see Fig. 1c).

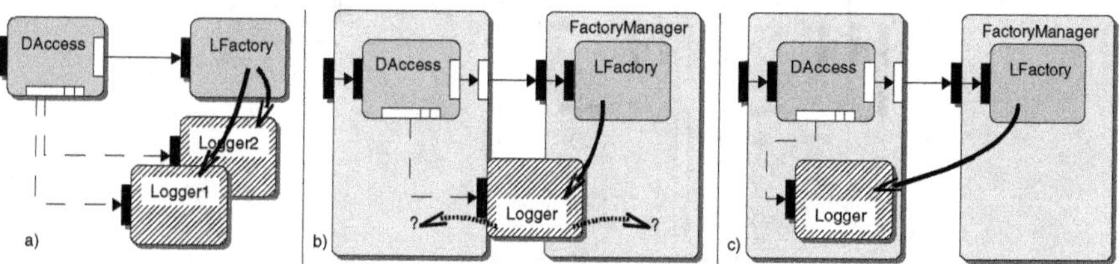

Fig. 1. Dynamic application example

The main reason, why the newly created component B does not become a sibling of the factory component (as this can seem to be also an obvious simple solution) is that the component A which initiated the creation typically needs to intensively collaborate with B which is obviously easier to manage when B is a sibling of A. The next positive outcome of the rule is better performance, because it is not necessary to create complicated connections going up and again down through the hierarchy.

Technically, to identify a factory component, *factory* annotation can be syntactically attached to the factory methods of an interface.

The newly created component B is not limited to having just a provided interface (as it is shown in Fig.1) but it can have also required interfaces. However, these are restricted just to the types featured by the component A initiating the creation. At the moment the provided interface of B is bound, the required interfaces are also bound to the same provisions as the required interfaces of A are. As an aside, this pattern works also in the case when B is a composite component.

2.2 Utility Interface Pattern

While working on case studies, we frequently faced the situation when a component provides a functionality, which is to be used by multiple components in the application at different levels of nesting (i.e. the need of use is orthogonal to the components' hierarchy). The functionality is typically some kind of a broadly-needed service such as printing. A solution can be to place such a component on the top level of the architecture hierarchy and arrange "tunnel" for connections through all the higher-level composite components to those nested ones where the functionality is actually needed. But this solution leads to an escalation of connections and makes the whole component architecture blurred (by making the utility features visible to the components where they are not actually needed) and consequently error-prone. Another typical situation we faced is that a reference to such a service is to be passed among components (e.g., returning reference to a service from a call of a registry/ naming/trading component).

For these reasons, we have introduced *utility* interfaces (the complete meta-model is in [8]). The reference to a *utility* interface can be freely passed among components and the connection made using this reference is established orthogonally to the architecture hierarchy (Fig. 2).

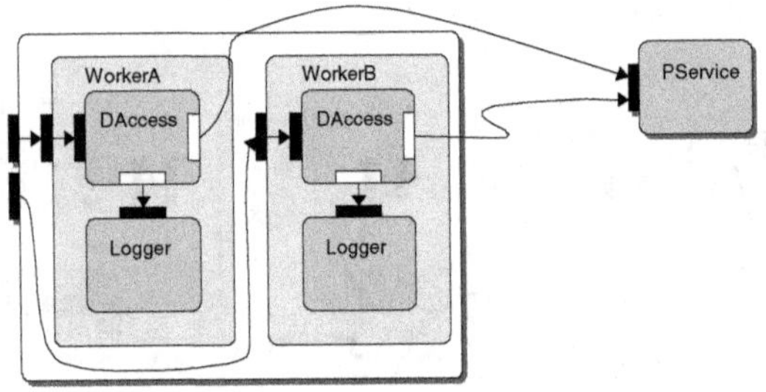

Fig. 2. Utility interface example

From a high-level view, the introduction of utility interfaces brings into component-based models a feature of service-oriented architectures (since Pservice can be seen as an external service). Such feature fusing allows to take advantages of both these paradigms (e.g., encapsulation and hierarchical components of component models and simple dynamic reconfiguration of SOA).

As a side effect, the introduction of utility interfaces this way consequently means that – in a limiting case – the whole application can be built only of components with utility interfaces and therefore the component-based application becomes an ordinary service-oriented application (inherently dynamically reconfigurable). Thus, service oriented architecture becomes a specific case of a component model.

3 Evaluation and Related Work

Evaluation: The approach to dynamic reconfiguration in a hierarchical component model presented in this paper is based on our experience with not-trivial case studies crafted for the SOFA and Fractal component models.

In principle, our approach to handling dynamic reconfiguration is based on combining the features of hierarchical component models and service-oriented architecture. From the component models point of the view, we allow just several types of dynamic reconfiguration compliant with well-defined patterns. Such a prohibition of an arbitrary reconfiguration and allowance of several well-defined modifications only is used in the most of component models (as discussed below), however none of them tackles the issue of how the component factory concept should be integrated into a hierarchical component model. Nevertheless, in addition to addressing this factory issue, the novel contribution of this paper is the introduction of utility interfaces which brings into a component-based system a feature of SOA and allows simplified dynamic reconfiguration without losing some advantages of component models such as focus on reusability and support for integration. Overall, in our view, the utility interface concept sophisticatedly integrates paradigms of the hierarchical component model and service-oriented architecture.

The authors of [12] define a taxonomy of component-based models using the criterion of component composition at different stages of component lifecycle (design and deployment). Using this taxonomy, they classify the existing component systems, including SOFA (the original version), which with Koala and KobrA fits into the most advanced category characterized by (i) composing components at design time, (ii) storing composed components in a repository and (iii) reusing already stored components (including composite ones) in further composition. The only missing feature of these three systems is no composition at deployment time and runtime. With incorporating the proposed dynamic reconfiguration patterns, SOFA 2.0 meets all the criteria imposed in [12] (assuming the authors under "deployment" understand also runtime).

As mentioned in Sect. 2, our choice of reconfiguration patterns is based on our experience with non-trivial case studies of component-based applications. In most of them, we faced a situation where dynamic reconfiguration was necessary. Since the original SOFA has dynamic reconfiguration limited to updates only, we usually had to overcome this lack by restricting the desired dynamic architecture modification via employing "dynamic parts" of a predefined static architecture (e.g., in the example application from Sect. 2.1, a maximum number of concurrent loggers was predefined and the corresponding number of the Logger components was instantiated at launch time). But this approach led to non-generic applications with rather big performance penalties (creating all necessary instances during launching). Also, several of our case studies have been based on the Fractal component model. Fractal provides support for dynamic reconfiguration but as we discuss below it suffers the evolution gap problem.

Related work: Component systems with a flat component model (CCM [15], C2 [20]) do not consider dynamic reconfiguration as an issue, since there is no problem where to place a newly created component and a service can be seen as another component in the flat component space. However, the evolution gap problem is inherently present.

In the area of hierarchical component models, there are several approaches as to how to deal with dynamic reconfiguration.

(1) *Forbidding*. A very simple and straightforward approach used in several component systems (e.g., [2]) is not to allow dynamic reconfiguration at all. But this is very limiting, revealing in essence all the flaws of the static nature of an ADL.
(2) *Flattening*. Another solution is to use hierarchical architecture and composite components only at the design time and/or deployment time. However, at run time the application architecture is flattened and the composite components disappear – this way the evolution gap problem becomes even more pressing, since the missing composite components make it very hard to trace the dynamic changes with respect to the initial configuration. This approach is used, e.g., in the OMG Deployment & Configuration specification [16], which defines deployment models and processes for component-based systems (including CCM). The component model introduced in this

OMG specification is hierarchical, but finally, in the deployment plan, the application structure is flattened and the composite components are removed.
(3) *Restricted reconfiguration.* Several systems forbid an arbitrary reconfiguration but allow special and well-defined types of dynamic reconfiguration:

(a) *Patterns.* Being an extension of Java, ArchJava [1] is a component system employing a hierarchical component model. Components in ArchJava can be dynamically added (using the *new* operator), but an addition of new connections is restricted by *connection patterns.* These patterns define through which interfaces and to which types of components the new component can be connected. Moreover, only the direct parent component can establish these connections (among direct subcomponents).

(b) *Shared components.* Fractal introduces shared components (at the ADL level); a shared component is a subcomponent of more than one other components. This way, component hierarchy becomes a DAG in general (not a tree). Appling this idea to the Fig. 1 would mean that the Logger component would be used by LFactory and DAccess. This solution works nicely, however, an architecture with shared components can be confusing, since it is not easy to determine who is responsible for lifecycle of a shared component, reasoning about architecture (e.g., checking behavior compliance) is very complicated, and several advanced features of component models (e.g., dynamic update of a component subtree) cannot be applied.

(c) *Formal rules.* Several systems (e.g., CHAM [9], "graph rewriting" [23]) define a formal system for describing the permitted dynamic reconfigurations. These systems allow complex definition of all architecture states during an application's lifecycle. But they are very complicated, even for simple architectures.

(4) *Unlimited.* Darwin [13] uses direct dynamic instantiation, which allows defining architecture configurations that can dynamically evolve in an arbitrary way (but the new connections among components are not captured). Julia [11], an implementation to Fractal, allows a general component reference passing (so that any time a reference is passed, it mimics establishing a new connection – this works orthogonally to specifying a shared component in ADL). Obviously, the evolution gap problem is ubiquitous in these cases.

However, let's emphasize that SOA is typically based on dynamic reconfiguration, since the composition of services is done with the granularity of individual calls captured in coordination languages like Linda [22] or by routing of messages [5].

4 Conclusion

We have shown a way of addressing dynamic reconfiguration in a hierarchical component model. With the aim to avoid uncontrolled architecture modification, the presented solution is based on the proposition of three reconfiguration patterns, which include the introduction of the utility interface concept that allows to use a service provided under the SOA paradigm from a component-based system. The paper is based on our experience with non-trivial case studies written for component-based systems SOFA and Fractal. Currently, we have specified the whole meta-model of SOFA 2.0, all necessary interfaces for the development time, deployment and runtime. A working prototype is expected within several months.

Acknowledgements

The authors would like to thank Tomáš Bureš, Vladimír Mencl and Lucia Kapová for valuable comments, Jan Klesnil, Ondřej Kmoch, Tomáš Kohan and Pavel Kotrč for contributing to meta-model design, and Pavel Ježek and Jan Kofroň for sharing experience with a Fractal case study. This work was partially supported by the Grant Agency of the Czech Republic project 201/06/0770.

References

1. Aldrich, J., Chambers, C., Notkin, D.: ArchJava: Connecting Software Architecture to Implementation, Proceedings of ICSE 2002, Orlando, USA, May 2002
2. Allen, R.: A Formal Approach to Software Architecture, PhD thesis, CMU, 1997
3. Baumeister, H., Hacklinger, F., Hennicker, R., Knapp, A., Wirsing, M.: A Component Model for Architectural Programming, Proceedings of FACS'05, Macao, Oct 2005
4. Bruneton, E., Coupaye, T., Leclercq, M., Quema, V., Stefani, J. B.: An Open Component Model and Its Support in Java, Proceedings of CBSE 2004, Edinburgh, UK, May 2004
5. Chappell, D. A., Enterprise Service Bus, O'Reilly Media, Jun 2004
6. Enterprise Java Beans specification, version 2.1, Sun Microsystems, Nov 2003
7. Hnětynka, P., Píše, M.: Hand-written vs. MOF-based Metadata Repositories: The SOFA Experience, Proceedings of ECBS 2004, Brno, Czech Republic, IEEE CS, May 2004
8. Hnětynka, P., Plášil, F., Bureš, T., Mencl, V., Kapová, L.: SOFA 2.0 metamodel, Tech. Rep. 11/2005, Dept. of SW Engineering, Charles University, Prague, Dec 2005
9. Inverardi, P., Wolf, A. L.: Formal Specification and Analysis of Software Architectures Using the Chemical Abstract Machine Model, IEEE Trans. on Soft. Eng., v. 21, n. 4, 1995
10. Iribarne, L.: Web Components: A Comparison between Web Services and Software Components, Colombian Journal of Computation, Vol. 5, No. 1, Jun 2004
11. Julia, http://forge.objectweb.org/projects/fractal/
12. Lau, K.-K., Wang, Z.: A Taxonomy of Software Component Models, Proceedings of EUROMICRO-SEAA'05, Porto, Portugal, Sep 2005
13. Magee, J., Kramer, J.: Dynamic Structure in Software Architectures, Proceedings of FSE'4, San Francisco, USA, Oct 1996
14. Medvidovic, N.: ADLs and dynamic architecture changes, Joint Proceedings SIGSOFT'1996 Workshops, ACM Press, New York, USA, Oct 1996
15. OMG: CORBA Components, v 3.0, OMG document formal/02-06-65, Jun 2002
16. OMG: Deployment and Configuration of Component-based Distributed Applications Specification, OMG document ptc/05-01-07, Jan 2005
17. Plášil, F., Bálek, D., Janeček, R.: SOFA/DCUP: Architecture for Component Trading and Dynamic Updating, Proceedings of ICCDS'98, Annapolis, USA, IEEE CS, May 1998
18. SOFA prototype, http://sofa.objectweb.org/
19. Szyperski, C.: Component Software: Beyond Object-Oriented Programming, 2nd edition, Addison-Wesley, Jan 2002
20. Taylor, R. N., et al: A Component- and Message-Based Architectural Style for GUI Software, IEEE Transactions on Software Engineering, Vol. 22, No. 6, Jun 1996
21. WebServices, http://www.w3.org/2002/ws/
22. Wells, G.: Coordination Languages: Back to the Future with Linda, Proceedings of WCAT'05, Glasgow, UK, Jul 2005
23. Wermelingera, M., Fiadeiro, J. L.: A graph transformation approach to software architecture reconfiguration, Science of Computer Programming, Vol. 44, Iss. 2, Aug 2002

MaDcAr: An Abstract Model for Dynamic and Automatic (Re-)Assembling of Component-Based Applications

Guillaume Grondin[1,2], Noury Bouraqadi[1], and Laurent Vercouter[2]

[1] Dépt. GIP, École des Mines de Douai,
841, rue Charles Bourseul, 59500 Douai, France
{grondin, bouraqadi}@ensm-douai.fr
[2] Dépt. G2I, École des Mines de Saint-Etienne,
158, cours Fauriel, 42023 Saint-Étienne, France
vercouter@emse.fr

Abstract. Dynamicity is an important requirement for critical software adaptation where a stop can be dangerous (e.g. for humans or environment) or costly (e.g. power plants or production lines). Adaptation at run-time is also required in context-aware applications where execution conditions often change. In this paper, we introduce MaDcAr, an abstract model of dynamic automatic adaptation engines for (re-)assembling component-based software. MaDcAr aims at being a conceptual framework for developing customizable engines reusable in multiple applications and execution contexts. Besides, MaDcAr provides a uniform solution for automating both the construction of application from scratch and the adaptation of existing component assemblies.

Keywords: Automatic Assembling ; Dynamic Adaptation ; Context-Awareness.

1 Introduction

In many application domains (medical, financial, telecoms, etc), there is a requirement for applications to be *dynamically* adaptable[1], i.e. without stopping or disturbing their execution. Indeed, some applications have to run continuously during adaptations (e.g. to install a security patch). The need for dynamic adaptation can be accentuated by the cost of an application stop (e.g. a production chain). In this paper, we consider applications that should never stop even if they are subject to unpredictable and frequent (environment) changes, like in Ubiquitous Computing [Wei93].

In the context of component-based applications, the need for dynamic adaptation can be fulfilled by dynamic reconfiguration of applications [WLF01] [OT98] [KM90]. In this paper, a component-based application is symbolized by an *assembly*, i.e. a set of connected software components. Hence, a reconfiguration

[1] Adaptation is the process of conforming a software to new or different conditions [KBC02].

I. Gorton et al. (Eds.): CBSE 2006, LNCS 4063, pp. 360–367, 2006.

of such an application is called a *re-assembling*. Dynamic re-assembling allows not only to modify locally a part of an application (by dynamic component replacement), but also to adapt the whole application architecture. Indeed, the architecture of an application can evolve thanks to *dynamic assembling* operations like the addition or the removal of components.

During this process of assembly reconfiguration, the application components must be initialized and linked to each other. Initialization refers to assigning some values to component attributes. Linking refers to connecting interfaces of different components.

In the case of applications that need to be frequently adapted, the adaptation process needs to be automated to help humans to use or configure such applications. This requirement translates into an *automatic (re-)assembling process* in component-based applications. Automation can be partial and covers for example only the triggering or the realization of adaptations. Automation can be total and covers the full adaptation process without requiring human intervention.

In this paper, we present MADCAR, an abstract Model for Automatic and Dynamic Component Assembly Reconfiguration. MADCAR models engines able to build and to reconfigure component-based applications at run-time on behalf of humans. By reconfiguration, we mean all kind of adaptations ranging from a simple change of some component attribute value to a complete replacement of the application architecture or components.

The reminder of this article is organized as following. In section 2, we describe MADCAR, our abstract model for assembling engines. In section 3, we discuss other works on automatic and dynamic assembling. In section 4, we sum up the main characteristics of MADCAR and sketch some future works.

2 MADCAR: A Model for Automatic and Dynamic Component Assembly Reconfiguration

The automation of the assembling task requires an *assembling engine* which can behave on behalf of humans. This engine has to automatically build applications by assembling components. Moreover, dynamic adaptation requires the assembling of an application to be performed at runtime. MADCAR[2] is an abstract model for dynamic and automatic assembling engines. As illustrated by figure 1, a MADCAR assembling engine requires four inputs: a set of *components* to assemble, an *application description* that refers to a specification of the application's functionalities and its non functional properties, an *assembling policy* that directs the assembling decisions and a *context* that refers to a set of data (e.g. state of the application, CPU availability, bandwidth, etc) measured by some sensors. The application description and the assembling policy are specified in terms of constraints. In other words, an application re-assembling consists in a Constraint Satisfaction Problem [Kum92, RLP00]. Therefore, MADCAR assembling engines include a constraint solver to compute automatically appropriate

[2] Model for Automatic and Dynamic Component Assembly Reconfiguration.

assembling decisions. The proposed model aims at providing a totally automated solution to component-based applications assemblings, i.e. where assemblings can be triggered and performed without any human intervention.

MADCAR is abstract in that it makes only few assumptions on the assembling engines' inputs. Those assumptions are:

1. We restrict our study to the case of *homogeneous components*, i.e. where components to assemble comply with the same component model,
2. The components must have customizable attributes and contractually specified interfaces that are either required or provided,
3. Also, we do not make distinction between components and connectors. We view connectors just as components dedicated to interaction. So, the assembling engine deals with connectors in the same way it deals with components.

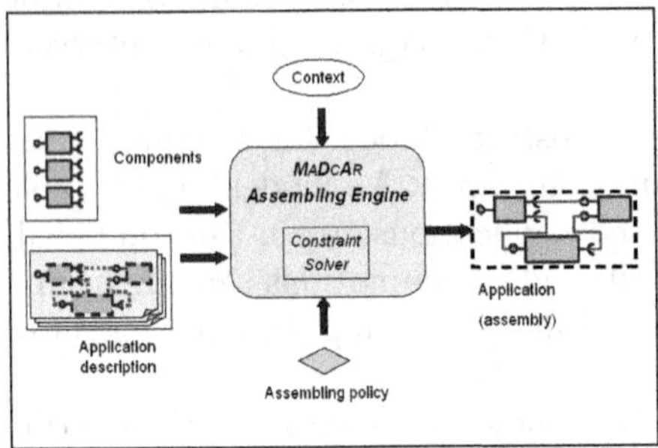

Fig. 1. A MADCAR assembling engine

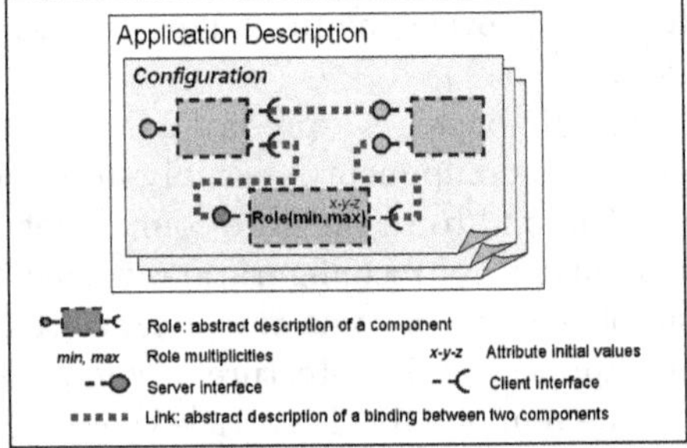

Fig. 2. A MADCAR application description

2.1 Application Description

An *application description* consists of a set of alternative configurations, as shown in figure 2. **Configurations** are "blueprints" for component assemblies, they consists in a graph of roles. A **role** is an abstract component description specified as a set of *contracts* [Mey92, BJPW99]. Those contracts which describe the roles and the configurations are expressed as **constraints**. Moreover, the contracts of a role must at least specify[3] (1) a set of interfaces (provided or required) which symbolize the role's possible interactions with other roles, (2) a set of attributes which values allow to initialize components and (3) two multiplicities. The *multiplicities* of a role permit to define the minimal (min) and the maximal number (max) of components which can fulfill this role simultaneously (i.e. within the same assembly). When necessary, we note a role $R(min, max)$, where $0 \leq min$, $min \leq max$ and $max \leq \infty$.

At a point in time only one configuration is used as a blueprint to assemble application components. When adaptation is triggered, the assembling engine chooses a configuration among available ones and re-assembles components accordingly.

[3] But are not restricted to.

MADCAR's configurations differ from the homonymous concept in Architecture Description Languages (ADLs) [Fux00, MT97]. In MADCAR, each configuration aims at describing a set of component assemblies abstractly and concisely. The degree of reconfigurability of an application's architecture is clearly symbolized in MADCAR by the use of a set of fixed configurations instead of a single adaptable configuration. Moreover, our configurations are characterized by two degrees of freedom/flexibility. First, they do not refer directly to component instances nor component types, but rather refer to component's abstract descriptions, namely roles. As a consequence, MADCAR's roles allow to minimize the coupling between a configuration and the components which can be used for this configuration. Second, a single MADCAR configuration allows to describe multiple assemblies even if they must contain different numbers of components, thanks to role multiplicities.

2.2 Assembling Process

MADCAR assembling engines can be used both to automatically build assemblies from unconnected components, and to dynamically adapt existing component assemblies. The assembling process of a MADCAR engine is composed of five successive steps :

1. *Triggering:* the engine may trigger (re-)assembling only once some changes occur in one of the four engine's inputs (execution context, set of available components, application description, assembling policy).
2. *Identification of eligible configurations:* the engine must build a *compatibility matrix* which maps the roles of each configuration to the corresponding compatible[4] components. A configuration is eligible if it can be minimally fulfilled[5] by a subset of available components.
3. *Selection of a configuration:* the engine selects a configuration based on the assembling policy and the compatibilities obtained in the previous step.
4. *Selection of a subset of components:* the engine selects components that are to be assembled according to the selected configuration and the assembling policy.
5. *(Re-)assembling:* the engine performs the assembling of the selected components according to the selected configuration.

2.3 Context and Assembling Policy

In MADCAR, the definition of a **context** just consists in specifying a set of sensors (software/hardware) which can provide some "interesting values", i.e. values which are to be used in an assembling process. Assembling policies permit to direct (re-)assembling. Directing MADCAR's assembling process consists in specifying when (i.e. for which context) and how (cf. configuration/component

[4] A component is said to be compatible with a role when it satisfies all the role's contracts.

[5] That is, given the set of available components, each configuration's role can be fulfilled by a number of components equal to the role's minimal multiplicity.

selection) assembling must be done. In MADCAR, the **assembling policy** is decomposed into two different parts:

1. the detection of the contextual situations that may concern (re-)assembling, and
2. the decisions that the assembling engine has to take for each contextual situation.

Detection. We model the context as a set of contextual elements, where each element can be obtained using some **sensors**. Sensors can be used for both *automatic triggering of re-assembling* (during particular contextual changes) and *collection of data required by the engine to make assembling decisions.* Those data may concern both external (e.g. CPU, memory,...) and internal (e.g. component attribute values of the current assembly) aspects of the application.

Decision. In MADCAR, decisions are expressed by **sets of rules** which produce constraints that can be injected to the constraint solver included in the assembling engine. These decisions allow the engine to select a configuration and to plan the assembling. However, several **default choices** are used in MADCAR in order to ensure that the decision process results in a single configuration:

- When several configurations satisfy the assembling policy, one of them is arbitrary selected by the assembling engine (unless the current configuration is also satisfying).
- When none of the configurations satisfies the assembling policy, then the assembling engine automatically selects one of the eligible configurations (unless the current configuration is also eligible).

Once a single configuration is selected, the engine selects the components to assemble in two successive steps:

1. the selection of the minimum number (min) components for each role $R(min, max)$ of the new configuration, and
2. the selection of extra components[6] for the roles which are not maximally fulfilled[7], according to the assembling policy.

This component selection process is performed by the constraint solver included in the assembling engine. The eligible components are those which satisfy the functional contracts of the chosen configuration's role. Extra-functional properties on a part of the application[8] or on the whole application[9] (like constraints on memory consumption or performance) may influence the number of selected

[6] However, some assembling policies (e.g. resource-saving oriented ones) may lead to a zero component selection in this second step.

[7] That is, the roles for which the number of selected components are less than their maximal multiplicity.

[8] In MADCAR, local extra-functional properties can be expressed as role contracts.

[9] In MADCAR, global extra-functional properties can be expressed in the assembling policy.

components during the second step. However, the **default component selection policy** consists in selecting the maximum number of components for each role.

3 Related Work

Many works on automatic and dynamic assembling can be found in literature. The importance of automation and dynamicity is not the same in all approaches and often depends on the kinds of applications which are targeted.

C2 [MORT96, Med96, OT98] allows dynamic modifications of compositions while the system is executing. But, in C2, it is not possible to generally define when or under what condition (for instance due to an exception) configurations are to be carried out. The degree of automation of a re-assembling in C2 is low, because any reconfiguration needs to be triggered manually. However, the flexibility of C2 connectors facilitates the binding/unbinding of components. Indeed, they mediate and coordinate the communication among components using generic filtering policies (e.g. priority-based or publish/subscribe-based). These policies permits to automatically adapt the interactions between the components each time a component is binded/unbinded to a connector. In other words, the connectors of C2 contain the assembling logic of the architecture. Hence, C2 provide an acceptable degree of uncoupling between the components functioning and the assembling logic. But, this dispersion of the assembling logic of the architecture makes the dynamic evolution of an architecture very hard to manage globally, as a separated concern.

David and Ledoux [DL03] present an approach for runtime adaptation of applications in response to changes in the execution context. Starting from the Fractal component model [BCS02], they introduce a reflective extension in order to transparently modify the behavior of components. The adaptation process is based on an adaptation policy for each component. Each adaptation policy is a set of *Event Condition Action* rules. For openness, the adaptation policies can be added or deleted dynamically. The re-assembling process consists in a sequence of components reconfigurations: firstly, structural reconfigurations of composite components, and secondly, parameterization and addition or removal of a service for both primitive and composite components. This extension of Fractal allows to re-assemble an application while running. However, the degrees of availability and performance of the services of this application is not considered in the re-assembling process. Moreover, global re-assembling seems hard to be automated because the adaptation policies are defined locally for each component.

SPARTACAS [Mor04] is a framework for automating retrieval and adaptation of contract-based components. This framework has been successfully applied to synthesis of software for embedded and digital signal processing systems. This solution is based on the first order logic. When SPARTACAS cannot retrieve a component that is a complete match to a problem, it retrieves a component that partially satisfies the requirements of a problem. Such components have to be adapted. SPARTACAS proposes three possibilities when a component cannot be retrieved. Indeed, the missing component can be replaced by a composite formed by (1) two sequential components, (2) two alternative components or (3) two parallel components, depending on the required behavior. A major advantage of this framework is that it offers the possibility to build the applications by assembling components hierarchically and progressively. However, dynamic re-assembling is not addressed.

4 Conclusion and Future Work

In this paper have presented MADCAR, an abstract model for engines that dynamically and automatically (re-)assemble component-based applications. In MADCAR, an assembling engine has four inputs: a set of components to assemble, an application description (set of alternative configurations), an assembling policy to drive application building and adaptation and a context. Based on these inputs, a MADCAR compliant engine computes a configuration ("assembly blueprint") and builds the application. And, when the execution context changes, MADCAR chooses a more appropriate configuration and re-assembles the components accordingly. Thus, the same mechanism apply both for building applications and adapting them. Moreover, MADCAR does support unplanned adaptations since application descriptions and components can be changed at run-time, i.e. without stopping the whole application. Another interesting property of MADCAR is that it models customizable engines. The assembling policy is not fixed, but it can be replaced, even at run-time. Besides, this policy is separated from the application description. Hence MADCAR encourages a clear separation of concerns.

Currently, we are working on an implementation of MADCAR for Fractal [BCS02], a hierarchical component model. This projection is a first step toward identifying specificities related to the re-assembling of composite components. Another direction for future work is to explore how to lower developers' overhead. We envision providing them with a high-level formalism to express MADCAR configurations.

References

[BCS02] E. Bruneton, T. Coupaye, and J. Stefani. Recursive and dynamic software composition with sharing. In *WCOP'02–Proceedings of the 7th ECOOP International Workshop on Component-Oriented Programming*, Malaga, Spain, Jun 2002.

[BJPW99] Antoine Beugnard, Jean-Marc Jezequel, Noel Plouzeau, and Damien Watkins. Making components contract aware. *Computer*, 32(7):38–45, 1999.

[DL03] Pierre-Charles David and Thomas Ledoux. Towards a framework for self-adaptive component-based applications. In *DAIS*, pages 1–14, 2003.

[Fux00] A. D. Fuxman. A survey of architecture description languages. Technical Report CSRG-407, Department of Computer Science, University of Toronto, Canada, 2000.

[KBC02] Abdelmadjid Ketfi, Noureddine Belkhatir, and Pierre-Yves Cunin. Adapting applications on the fly. In *ASE '02: Proceedings of the 17 th IEEE International Conference on Automated Software Engineering (ASE'02)*, page 313, Washington, DC, USA, 2002. IEEE Computer Society.

[KM90] Jeff Kramer and Jeff Magee. The evolving philosophers problem: Dynamic change management. *IEEE Trans. Softw. Eng.*, 16(11):1293–1306, 1990.

[Kum92] V. Kumar. Algorithms for constraint satisfaction problems: A survey. *AI Magazine*, 13(1):32–44, 1992.

[Med96] Nenad Medvidovic. Adls and dynamic architecture changes. In *Joint proceedings of the second international software architecture workshop (ISAW-2) and international workshop on multiple perspectives in software development (Viewpoints '96) on SIGSOFT '96 workshops*, pages 24–27, 1996.

[Mey92] Bertrand Meyer. Applying "design by contract". *Computer*, 25(10):40–51, 1992.

[Mor04] Brandon Morel. Spartacas automating component reuse and adaptation. *IEEE Trans. Softw. Eng.*, 30(9):587–600, 2004. Senior Member-Perry Alexander.

[MORT96] Nenad Medvidovic, Peyman Oreizy, Jason E. Robbins, and Richard N. Taylor. Using object-oriented typing to support architectural design in the c2 style. In *SIGSOFT '96: Proceedings of the 4th ACM SIGSOFT symposium on Foundations of software engineering*, pages 24–32, New York, NY, USA, 1996. ACM Press.

[MT97] Nenad Medvidovic and Richard N. Taylor. A framework for classifying and comparing architecture description languages. In *ESEC '97/FSE-5: Proceedings of the 6th European conference held jointly with the 5th ACM SIGSOFT international symposium on Foundations of software engineering*, pages 60–76, New York, NY, USA, 1997. Springer-Verlag New York, Inc.

[OT98] P. Oreizy and R. Taylor. On the role of software architectures in runtime system reconfiguration. In *CDS '98: Proceedings of the International Conference on Configurable Distributed Systems*, page 61, Washington, DC, USA, 1998. IEEE Computer Society.

[RLP00] P. Roy, A. Liret, and F. Pachet. The framework approach for constraint satisfaction. *ACM Computing Surveys*, 32(1es), 2000.

[Wei93] M. Weiser. Ubiquitous computing. *Computer*, 26(10):71–72, 1993.

[WLF01] Michel Wermelinger, Antonia Lopes, and Jose Luiz Fiadeiro. A graph based architectural (re)configuration language. In *ESEC/FSE-9: Proceedings of the 8th European software engineering conference held jointly with 9th ACM SIGSOFT international symposium on Foundations of software engineering*, pages 21–32, 2001.

Adaptation of Monolithic Software Components by Their Transformation into Composite Configurations Based on Refactoring

Gautier Bastide[1], Abdelhak Seriai[1], and Mourad Oussalah[2]

[1] Ecole des Mines de Douai, 941 rue Charles Bourseul, 59508 Douai, France
{seriai, bastide}@ensm-douai.fr
[2] LINA, université de Nantes, 2 rue de la Houssinière, 44322 Nantes, France
oussalah@lina.univ-nantes.fr

Abstract. We present in this paper an approach aiming at adapting component structures instead of adapting component services. It focuses on transforming a software component from a monolithic configuration to a composite one. Among the motivations of this kind of adaptation, we note its possible application to permit flexible deployment of software components and flexible loading of component service-code according to the available resources (CPU, memory). This adaptation is based on the analysis and the instrumentation of component codes.

Keywords: Software component, adaptation, restructuration, composite-component, refactoring.

1 Introduction

Component-based software engineering (CBSE) [6] [10] focuses on reducing application development costs by assembling reusable components like COTS [11] (Commercial-Off-The-Shelf). However, experiments show that direct component reuse is extremely hard and this one usually has to be adapted in order to be integrated into an application. This difficulty is due to the available large variety of infrastructures and software environments, going from the simple mobile phone equipped with minimal capacities to the cluster of several multi-processor computers. The solution may consist in the development of software components which can adapt themselves to these constraints. To deal with this issue, many approaches were proposed to adapt component-based applications. They differ according to several criteria. Among these last, we can quote: the adaptation target, the adaptation moment, the adaptation actor, the adaptation goal, etc.

Nevertheless, we can note that, in spite of this diversity of proposed approaches, all ones which are interested to adapt components, focus on adapting their services and only some works are interested to adapt the component structures. Moreover, to our knowledge, all these last approaches are interested in the adaptation of the component implementation by the replacement of an algorithm by another (i.e. code replacement). The result is that, no approach

I. Gorton et al. (Eds.): CBSE 2006, LNCS 4063, pp. 368–375, 2006.

proposes techniques for restructuring software components (i.e. adapting their structures).

While being based on the above considerations, our objective in this paper is to propose a software component restructuring approach. In fact, our approach permits us to restructure component implementation while preserving its behaviour and its services. First, following the component use needs, this one is fragmented into new generated components. Next, these new components are recomposed to create a new configurable composite-component. This transformation process is based on the analysis and the instrumentation of component codes.

Among the motivations of this kind of adaptation, we note its possible application to allow flexible component deployment and flexible component-code loading according to the available resources (e.g. CPU). For example, the component structure adaptation by its fragmentation in some generated components can be used to define a flexible deployment strategy. Indeed, this adaptation allows us to organize component services in separate sub-sets. Each sub-set is defined in a new component generated by fragmenting the original one. Then, the generated components can be deployed on one or more machines (Fig. 1)[1].

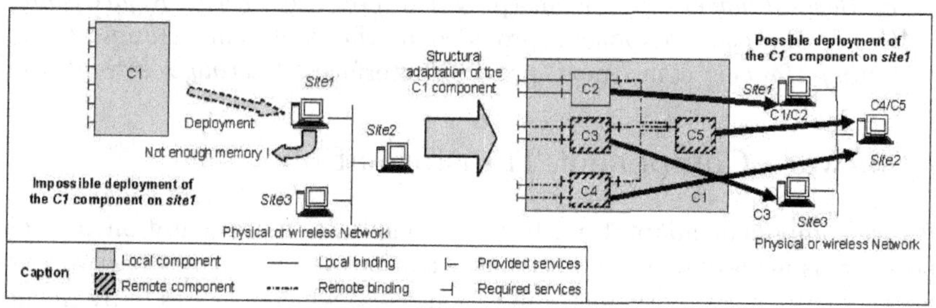

Fig. 1. Structural adaptation for flexible deployment

We discuss the proposed approach in the rest of this paper as follows. Section 2 presents an example of experimentation that we use to illustrate our approach. Section 3 details the transformation process allowing us to fragment a component into new generated components and next, to recompose them to form a configurable composite-component. Section 4 reviews related work. Conclusion and future works are presented in section 5.

2 Example of Experimentation: A Shared-Diary System

In order to illustrate our purpose, we use throughout this paper an example of a monolithic software component providing services of a shared-diary system which can be accessible to multiple users. It defines the following provided services:

[1] In [1], we presented different types of structural adaptation possibilities and discussed their possible applications.

1. Managing personal diary. This includes authentication, consulting events, etc. These services are provided through the *Diary* interface.
2. Organizing a meeting. This includes services permitting users to confirm the possibility to organize a meeting, etc. (*Meeting* interface)
3. Managing absence. This includes services permitting users to verify the possibility to add an absence event, to consult absences, etc. (*Absence* interface)
4. Right management. This includes services concerning absence right attribution, service related to diaries initialization, etc. (*Right* interface)
5. Updating diary, meeting dates, absence dates and absence rights of a person (*DiaryUpdate*, *MeetingUpdate*, *AbsenceUpdate* and *RightUpdate* interfaces).

We assume that, due to the load balancing policy adopted for the used deployment infrastructure, the *Shared-Diary* component cannot be deployed on only one host. Then, our goal is to adapt it in order to be deployed on a distributed infrastructure. This result can be obtained by transforming this component into a composite-component, where sub-components are deployed on distributed hosts. To achieve this goal, this composite-component is decomposed to/recomposed from four sub-components which are:

1. *Diary-Manager* component (provided interfaces: *Diary*, *DiaryUpdate*),
2. *DataBase-Manager* component (provided interfaces: *Right*, *RightUpdate*),
3. *Absence-Manager* component (provided interfaces: *Absence*, *AbsenceUpdate*),
4. *Meeting-Manager* component (provided interfaces: *Meeting*, *MeetingUpdate*).

3 Software Component Transformation

Software component adaptation, from a monolithic implementation to a composite one, is achieved through a transformation which is based on two phases (Fig. 2). The first one is the decomposition phase which consists in fragmenting component code according to a given specification, where each generated code-part matches with a new generated component implementation. The second phase is the recomposition which consists in assembling components generated during the first phase and integrating them into a new generated composite-component.

We consider here, an oriented-object implementation of components. Thus, the internal structure of a component consists of some class hierarchies representing the implementation code of its services and its interfaces. Our approach deals with the Fractal component model [3] and its Java implementation called Julia [4]. To create a Fractal component, it is necessary to specify an unique class which implements all methods specified by the corresponding component interfaces.

3.1 Software Component Decomposition

During the decomposition phase, the adaptation administrator specifies the new structure which must be created by indicating new components to be generated. Then, the component implementation is fragmented.

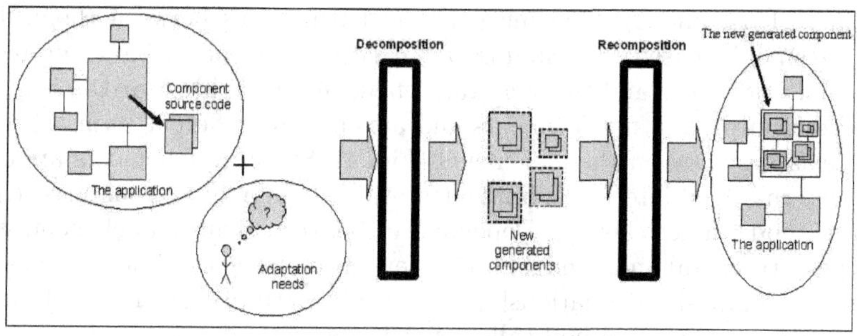

Fig. 2. Component transformation process

Specification of the New Component Structure. This first step of the decomposition stage consists in specifying the external structures of the components to be generated. This is realized by specifying, using an ADL script, these components, and for each components, its provided interfaces. We defined control operations allowing us to check the specification validity: each new sub-component must provide a set of interfaces which must be included in the interface set of the component to be adapted. Moreover, the union of these subsets must be equal to the set of interfaces provided by the initial component. In addition, no element specified in this ADL must be in contradiction with the initial ADL. To illustrate this, let us reconsider our example of the *shared-diary* component. The goal of the structural adaptation of this component is to reorganize services provided by this one in four new generated sub-components (Fig. 3).

```
<component name="Shared-Diary">
     <component name="Diary-Manager">
               <service signature="Diary">
               <service signature="DiaryUpdate">     </component>
     <component name="DataBase-Manager">
               <service signature="Right">
               <service signature="RightUpdate">     </component>
     <component name="Meeting-Manager">
               <service signature="Meeting">
               <service signature="MeetingUpdate">     </component>
     <component name="Absence-Manager">
               <service signature="Absence">
               <service signature="AbsenceUpdate">     </component>
</component>
```

Fig. 3. The ADL specification script of the *shared-diary* component

Component Fragmentation. Once the fragmentation specification is given, component structure is refactored. This sub-stage consists in fragmenting this component into a set of new generated components, while guaranteeing the component integrity and coherence. In fact, the fragmentation is realized by analysing the monolithic component code-source, determining for each new component to be generated its corresponding code, separating these codes, one from the others, and determining existing dependences between them. These steps are mainly based on building, for each component to be generated, its SBDG (i.e. Structural and Behavioural Dependence Graph). A SBDG is a graph where nodes are structural elements and arcs are the different forms of dependences existing between these elements (Fig. 4). Structural elements are of two types: external (e.g. interfaces, implementation class) and internal ones (e.g. internal methods, inner classes). Dependences between structural elements are of two types: structural and behavioural dependences. Structural dependences correspond to composition relationship between structural elements. Behavioural dependences represent method-calls defined in a method code.

Once, the SBDG corresponding to a component to be generated is built, code of each one of its structural elements is generated. These codes are connected between them in order to reflect the existing structural links between their corresponding structural elements. All the generated code represents the first version of a new component source-code. The next version of the generated component source-code transforms behavioural links, existing between methods defined respectively by two different SBDG, on composition links defined between the corresponding components (see Sect. 3.2).

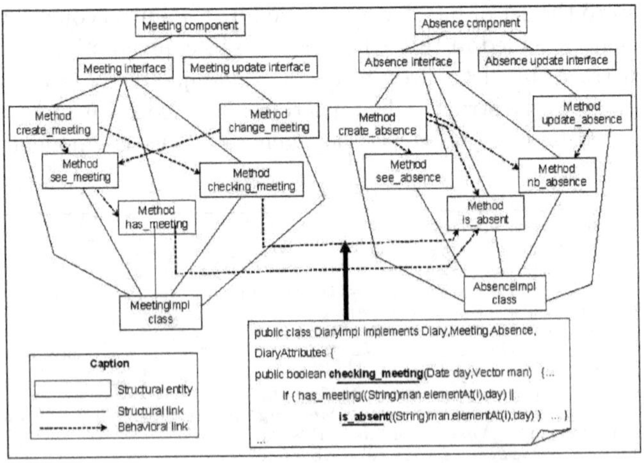

Fig. 4. A part of the *Shared-diary* SBDG

3.2 Software Component Composition

Once the component to be adapted is fragmented and the new components are generated, the initial component must be recomposed. This operation requires two steps. First, we have to assemble generated components together (i.e. horizontal composition) while taking into account their dependences. Then, the result of this operation is encapsulated into a composite-component (i.e. vertical composition) which can be configured according to the adaptation needs.

Horizontal Composition: Generated Component Assembly. The decomposition stage generates unconnected components providing each one a sub-set of services among the initial component services. However, these services are not independent of each other. In fact, they are linked through behavioural or resource sharing dependences.

Connecting components via behavioural-dependence interfaces: Components generated by fragmentation are connected using behavioural-dependence interfaces. These interfaces are used to materialize behavioural-dependences between generated components according to the SBDG graph. These are:

1. Interfaces defining required behavioural-dependence services.
2. Interfaces defining provided behavioural-dependence services.

Connecting components via resource-sharing interfaces: Components are also connected via interfaces used to manage resource sharing. We consider as resource every structural entity defined in the component code with an associate state. For example, instance and class attributes are considered as resources. Shared-resources are those defined and used in two or more component implementations. So, we need to preserve a coherent state of these resources in all components sharing them. Coherence is ensured through two types of interfaces: communication interfaces and synchronisation-access interfaces. Communications interfaces aim at permitting components to communicate, between components, updates occurred on shared-resources. These are:

1. An interface defining required services permitting components to notify shared-resource state updates.
2. An interface defining provided services allowing components to update shared-resource states every time when this resource is updated.

The second type of interfaces (i.e. synchronisation-access interfaces) allows components to synchronise access to a shared-resource. These are:

1. An interface defining required services permitting components to acquire, from components sharing a resource, an authorisation to update this one.
2. An interface defining provided services allowing components to release rights to update a shared-resource.

Vertical Composition: Composite-Component Generation. The last step of our transformation process aims to guarantee:

- Transparency property. The component adaptation must be achieved in a transparent way compared to the application components.
- Autonomy property: New generated component may be accessible and handled as separate entities, ones from the others.

This goal is achieved by the integration of the horizontal composition result into a composite-component. In fact, the composite-component allows us to replace the adapted component without any modification of the other application components. It permits us to ensure that application components should not be able to access, after the component transformation, to other services than those provided by the adapted component before its transformation. Furthermore, composite-component provides interfaces allowing it to handle sub-components in independent manner. For example, we define a deployment interface as provided by generated composite-component. This interface allows the administrator to specify and realize deployment of each composite sub-component. Furthermore, we define a composite-component as providing facilities for possible functional adaptations. This is done via a second non-functional interface integrated to the composite-component interface set. This interface allows the administrator to set a collection of configurable properties. These properties are:

- Sub-component encapsulation: This property refers to the visibility and the accessibility of sub-components considering other application components. A generated composite-component can be specified as (1) “white-box”, which means that composite structure is visible and sub-components are directly accessible, (2) "black-box", which imposes sub-components to be neither visibles nor accessibles by other application components or (3) “mix-box”, which means that some sub-components, not all, can be accessibles directly by the other application components.
- Internal access: This property permits us to specify how a sub-component can be accessed by other sub-components. This can be configured either via the composite-component or via a direct reference to a sub-component. Access through the composite allows us to prepare a future functional adaptation. In fact, as all service-invokes exchanged between sub-components are analysed by the composite, post or pre-conditions may be set up easily.

4 Related Work

Many approaches have been proposed in the literature in order to adapt software component-based applications. These ones can be classified according to different criteria. Software component-based application can be adapted in order to improve performances [8], design or implementation [5]. Also, these applications can be adapted to a better taking into account of the deployment environment (i.e. adaptive adaptation). Another adaptation need is the evolution of the application functionalities [7]. Concerning our approach, it can be classified as adaptive adaptation. In fact, it aims, for example, at taking into account component deployment environment and consequently to adapt this one by restructuring it.

Adaptation techniques can be categorized as either “white-box” or “black-box”. “White-box” techniques typically require understanding of the internal implementation of the component to be adapted, whereas “black-box” techniques [2] only require knowledge about the component's interfaces. Our adaptation approach can be considered as “black-box” considering adaptation administrator which does not need to manipulate component source-code. But, it can be considered as "white-box" when considering the adaptation process which needs component source-code.

5 Conclusion

We presented in this article an approach allowing us to create customisable composite-components from monolithic ones. Our proposal is based on a new adaptation technique allowing the administrator to reorganize a software component basing on code refactoring. First, component code is decomposed according to a specification given by an adaptation administrator and then, new components are generated. Next, the generated components are recomposed to form a composite-component whose properties can be configured following adaptation needs. The transformation process is based on component source-code analysis and instrumentation.

The proposed approach has been implemented and a prototype, developed using the Java implementation of the Fractal component model [4], is available. Our approach does not consider run-time adaptation issues. Structural dynamic adaptation constitutes one of our future focuses.

References

1. G. Bastide, A-D. Seriai, M. Oussalah: Adapting Software Components by Structure Fragmentation. ACM Symposium on Applied Computing, Dijon, France, April 2006.
2. J. Bosch: Superimposition: A Component Adaptation Technique. Information and Software Technology, 1999.
3. E. Bruneton, T. Coupaye, M. Leclercq, V. Quema, J.-B. Stefani: An Open Component Model and Its Support in Java. CBSE, 7-22, 2004.
4. E. Bruneton: Julia Tutorial. http://fractal.objectweb.org/tutorials/julia/
5. E. Gamma, R. Helm, R. Johnson, J. Vlissides: Design Patterns: Elements of Reusable Object-Oriented Software, Addison-Wesley Professional, 1995.
6. G. Heineman, W. Councill: Component Based Software Engineering: Putting the Pieces Together, ISBN 0-201-70485-4, Addison Wesley Professional, 2001.
7. R. Keller, U. Holzle: Binary Component Adaptation. ECOOP, 307-329, 1998.
8. K. U. Mtzel and P. Schnorf: Dynamic Component Adaptation. Ubilab Technical Report 97.6.1, Union Bank of Switzerland, Zrich, Switzerland, 1997.
9. M.E. Segal, O. Frieder: On-the-Fly Program Modification: Systems for Dynamic Updating,IEEE Softw., 10(2):53-65, 1993.
10. C. Szyperski, Component software: beyond object-oriented programming,ISBN 0-201-17888-5,ACM Press/Addison-Wesley Publishing Co., 1999.
11. K. Wallnau, S. Hissam, R. Seacord: Building Systems from Commercial Components, ISBN 0-201-70064-6, Addison Wesley, 2002.

Towards Encapsulating Data in Component-Based Software Systems

Kung-Kiu Lau and Faris M. Taweel

School of Computer Science,
The University of Manchester,
Manchester, M13 9PL, UK
{kung-kiu, faris.taweel}@cs.manchester.ac.uk

Abstract. A component-based system consists of components linked by connectors. Data can reside in components and/or in external data stores. Operations on data, such as access, update and transfer are carried out during computations performed by components. Typically, in current component models, control, computation and data are mixed up in the components, while control and data are both communicated by the connectors. As a result, such systems are tightly coupled, making reasoning difficult. In this paper we propose an approach for encapsulating data by separating it from control and computation.

1 Introduction

A software system consists of three elements: *control*, *computation*, and *data*. The system's behaviour is the result of the interaction between these elements. Therefore, the latter determines whether the system has desirable properties such as loose coupling and ease of analysis and reasoning. It is reasonable to expect that it is advantageous to encapsulate these elements, and separate them from one another, since this should make reasoning more tractable. For example, some recent research in stimulus reactive systems has focused on separating control flow from data flow [9, 5].

Paradoxically perhaps, for component-based software systems, it is not any easier to achieve such separation of concerns. A component-based system consists of components linked by connectors, as exemplified by software architectures [17]. In such a system, data can reside either in components or in external databases (which are often also regarded as components). Operations on data, such as access, update and transfer are carried out during computations performed by components. Typically, in current component models, control, computation and data are mixed up in the components, while control and data are both communicated by the connectors. As a result, such systems are tightly coupled, making reasoning difficult. More seriously, this impedes component reuse, which is a key objective for component-based development.

In this paper we introduce an approach for encapsulating data by separating it from control and computation, in component-based systems. Our approach is based on our earlier work on encapsulating control and computation in component-based systems [10].

I. Gorton et al. (Eds.): CBSE 2006, LNCS 4063, pp. 376–384, 2006.

2 Data in Current Component Models

In current component models, computation, control and data are intermixed (Fig. 1). Components initiate control and perform computation (Fig. 1(b)). Connectors provide communication between components for both control and data (Fig. 1(c)). Some

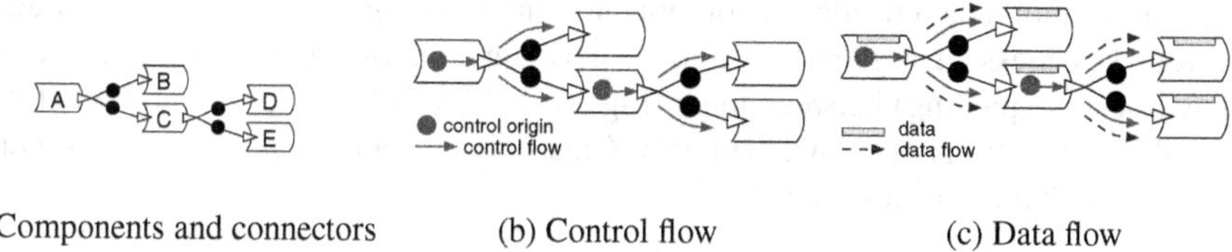

(a) Components and connectors (b) Control flow (c) Data flow

Fig. 1. Current component models

components may act as (external) databases, but for simplicity we will treat them all as components.

In these models, data exists in components, and during the computation performed by a component, data can be accessed from other components, updated, and transferred to other components. Component models with external data stores provide special abstractions modelling these sources. For example, EJB [4, 15] provides the *entity bean* that connects to an external database; .NET [14] provides the *Dataset component*, and CCM [16] provides *persistent components*. .NET takes an extra step by providing a database connector called the .NET Data Adaptor Framework [14]. However, in these models, data is not separated from computation or control.

In general, connection schemes in current component models use message passing, and fall into two main categories:[1]. (*i*) connection by direct message passing; and (*ii*)

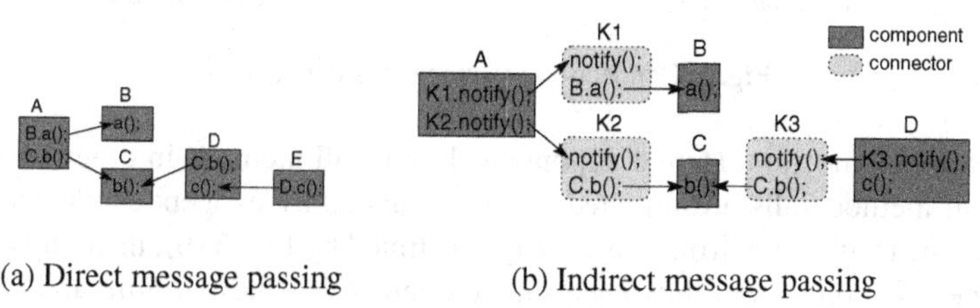

(a) Direct message passing (b) Indirect message passing

Fig. 2. Connection by message passing

connection by indirect message passing. Direct message passing corresponds to direct method calls, as exemplified by objects calling methods in other objects (Fig. 2 (a)), using method or event delegation, or remote procedure call (RPC). Component models that adopt direct message passing schemes as composition operators are EJB, CCM, COM [2] etc.

Indirect message passing corresponds to coordination (e.g. RPC) via connectors, as exemplified by ADLs. Here, connectors are typically glue code or scripts that pass

[1] For a survey, see [11].

messages between components indirectly. A connector, when notified by a component invokes a method in another component (Fig. 2 (b)). Besides ADLs, other component models that adopt indirect message passing schemes are JavaBeans [8], Koala [19], SOFA [1] etc.

In connection schemes by message passing, direct or indirect, control originates in and flows from components (Fig. 1(b)). This is clearly the case in both Fig. 2(a) and (b). Furthermore, data resides in components, and as components perform computation (invoked by message passing), data flows between components in tandem with control flow (message passing) between them (Fig. 1(c)). This is the case in both Fig. 2(a) and (b), although data is not shown explicitly. Clearly in current component models, neither control nor data is encapsulated.

3 Encapsulating Computation and Control

We are developing a component model [10] in which components encapsulate *computation* (unlike objects or port-connector type components, Fig. 2), and connectors encapsulate *control* (unlike current component models, Fig. 1). In our model, components do not call methods in other components, and control originates in and flows from connectors, leaving components to encapsulate only computation. This is illustrated by Fig. 3. We call our connectors *exogenous connectors*. Fig. 3 (a) shows an example

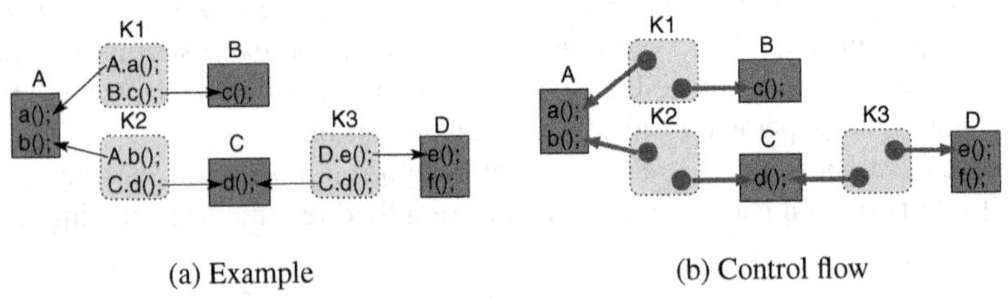

(a) Example (b) Control flow

Fig. 3. Connection by exogenous connectors

of exogenous connection. Here components do not call methods in other components. Instead, all method calls are initiated and coordinated by exogenous connectors. The latter thus encapsulate control, as is clearly illustrated by Fig. 3 (b), in contrast to Fig. 1 (b). Exogenous connectors thus encapsulate control, i.e. they *initiate* and *coordinate* control.

Exogenous connectors are hierarchical in nature, with a type hierarchy [10]. At the bottom of the hierarchy, because components are not allowed to call methods in other components, we have an exogenous *method invocation connector*. This is a *unary* operator that takes a component, invokes one of its methods, and receives the result of the invocation. To structure the control flow in a set of components or a system, at the next level of the type hierarchy, we have other connectors for sequencing exogenous method calls to different components. So we have n-*ary* connectors for connecting invocation connectors, and n-*ary* connectors for connecting these connectors, and so on. As well as invocation connectors, we have defined and implemented *pipe* connectors, for sequencing, and *selector* connectors, for branching.

Example 1. Consider a system whose architecture can be described in the Acme [6] and C2 [18] ADLs by the architectures in Fig. 4 (a) and (b) respectively. Using exogenous connectors in our component model, the corresponding architecture is that shown in Fig. 4 (c). In the latter, the lowest level of connectors are unary invocation connectors

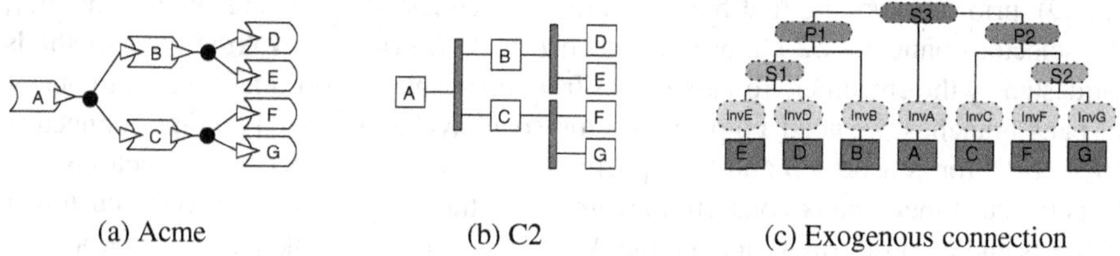

(a) Acme (b) C2 (c) Exogenous connection

Fig. 4. Corresponding architectures

that connect to single components, viz., *InvA*, *InvB*, ...; the second-level connectors are binary selector connectors *S1* and *S2* and connect pairs of invocation connectors; and the connectors at levels 3 and 4 are of variable arities and types: *P1* and *P2* are pipes, while *S3* is a selector.

4 Encapsulating Data

In our component model, a system consists of a hierarchy of exogenous connectors sitting atop a flat layer of components, as illustrated in Fig. 4(c). The components encapsulate computation while the connectors encapsulate control (Fig. 5). Since it is the

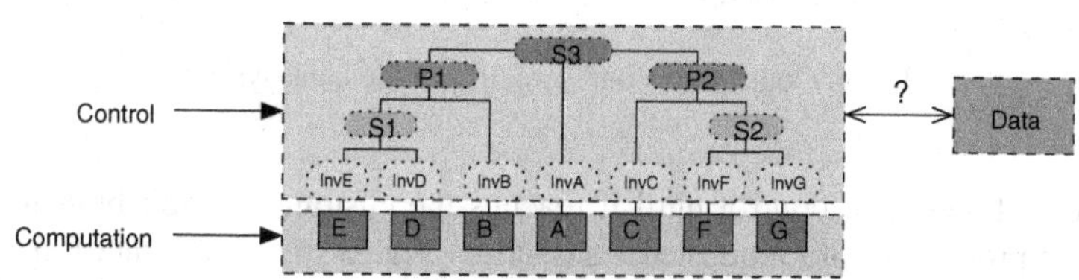

Fig. 5. Encapsulating data

only model we know of that has these two kinds of encapsulation, we believe our component model is a good basis for attempting to encapsulate data as well. So the question we want to address in this paper is how we can encapsulate data in our component model (Fig. 5).

In our component model, components already encapsulate *local data*, like objects in object-oriented languages. However, for *system* or *global state* we have not provided any encapsulation. To clearly illustrate the challenge we face, consider what happens if data flow follows control flow, as in current component models (Fig. 1).

Example 2. The architecture in Fig. 4(c) can be used to represent a bank system, with A being an *ATM*, B and C two bank consortia, each containing two bank branches,

E and D, and F and G respectively. At level 1, each component has its own invocation connector. The ATM (A) can display a menu, accept a customer card, read its information, accept customer requests such as choice of operations (deposit, withdrawal, check balance, etc.).

At level 2, the selector connector $S1$ selects the customer's bank branch (from E and D), prior to invoking that branch's methods requested by the customer. Similarly, the selector connector *S2* chooses between F and G, prior to invoking their methods requested by the customer. To pass values from one bank consortium (B or C) to one of its bank branches, we need a pipe connector; so at level 3, we have two pipe connectors *P1* and *P2*, for consortia *B* and *C* respectively. At level 4, the selector connector *S3* selects the customer's bank consortium from consortia *B* and *C*, after receiving customer requests and card information from the ATM (A). Thus, the bank system's operational cycle is initiated by passing the customer requests and card information from the ATM (A) to the connector *S3*.[2]

We will show what happens if data flow follows control flow. Initially, data comes with a customer request to the ATM. This data comprises customer details on his card (customer identification, account number, bank consortium identification code, etc.), the customer's choice of transaction (say withdrawal), and the amount involved.

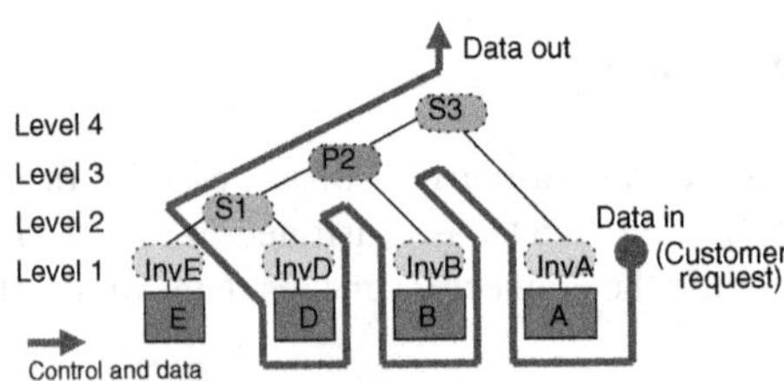

Fig. 6. Control flow and data flow of the bank system

This data flows with control until it reaches the customer's bank branch where it is used for processing the requested transaction. Fig. 6 traces the data (and control) flow for an example where the customer bank branch is D, belonging to consortium B. At *S3*, the bank consortium code is used to determine the next connector, in this case *P2*. All the data, except the bank consortium code, is then passed on to *P2*. Using the customer account number, *P2* invokes *B* to identify the customer bank branch, which is D in this case. So the bank branch code together with the rest of data is passed to $S1$. Here, the bank branch D is selected and the customer's request, account number and amount are passed to D, and the customer's request is processed.

The main observation here is that, apart from the bank consortium identification code, customer data traverses a long route, with the control flow, to its final destination. This property is not unique to exogenous connectors, but also pertains to any component model with explicit connectors where data flow follows control flow, e.g. Fig. 4(a) and (b). It clearly raises performance and space concerns.

[2] A pipe selector should be used to connect A and *S3*, but for simplicity, we omit it here.

As clearly illustrated by Example 2, rather than leaving global data to flow with control, it is desirable to separate the two. To this end, it is necessary to store data in a shared *data space* (a repository), and to allow access to such data via *data connectors* (Fig. 5) at suitable points in the control flow. Furthermore, for data access operations to be generic against the data space, the type of data stored in data spaces must be *generic* with respect to the programming environment. A generic data type for a programming environment is a type that subsumes all its other data types. We call this type the type *Universal* to be independent from different names provided by different programming languages.

The data space is a transient data store that every system must have to maintain its global state. In a data space, data is created and accessed indirectly via data connectors. A data element stored in a data space has many properties including a unique string *reference*; a *state* indicating whether it is transient or persistent; and a set of *access permissions* specifying which exogenous connector in the system can read (r), write (w), persist (p) and execute (x) this data element. Any data element is a collection element that can contain executable string code such as SQL data manipulation statements. To execute these elements, they must have the execute (x) permission.

Data connectors link data elements stored in (global) data spaces to exogenous connectors as well as to other data connectors. In effect, they *set*, *get* and *execute* data elements in the data space; and encapsulate data access coordination and data flow in a system. They are hierarchical in nature. At the bottom of the hierarchy, because exogenous connectors only encapsulate control they cannot access (global) data directly, we need a *data accessor connector*. This is a unary data connector that can link to only one data element in the data space; and store, return and execute that specific data element. In order to structure flow and access coordination for a set of data elements, at the next level of the hierarchy, we have other connectors for sequencing access and execution of data elements. Accordingly, we have n-*ary* data connectors for connecting accessor data connectors, and n-*ary* data connectors for connecting these connectors, and so on.

Data connectors and exogenous connectors are both connectors However, they form two separate kinds of hierarchies that can be connected at design time at specific points, where data values are required by exogenous connectors.

Example 3. To explain our approach for encapsulating data, we consider Example 2 again. In particular, we consider the case in (Fig. 6). Here the data flow can be partitioned into three paths: (i) customer's request and card information passing through *InvA, S3, P2* and *InvB*; (ii) data passing through *InvB, P2, S1* and *InvD*; and (iii) data passing information back to the ATM (*A*), where the returned data can be, for example, a bank statement.

To prevent data from flowing along these paths in the hierarchy of exogenous connectors, we store the customer's request and card information in the system's data space, as three data elements (bank consortium code, bank branch code and transaction data), and use data connectors to link these data elements to exogenous connectors in which they are needed (Fig 7). As a result, data flows separately from control. At the start of the system's operation, data is exported to the data space by *InvA*, then at *S3* only the first element (consortium code) is retrieved to evaluate the next pipe connector. At the connector *P2*, control is passed to *InvB* which in turn uses the second element (branch

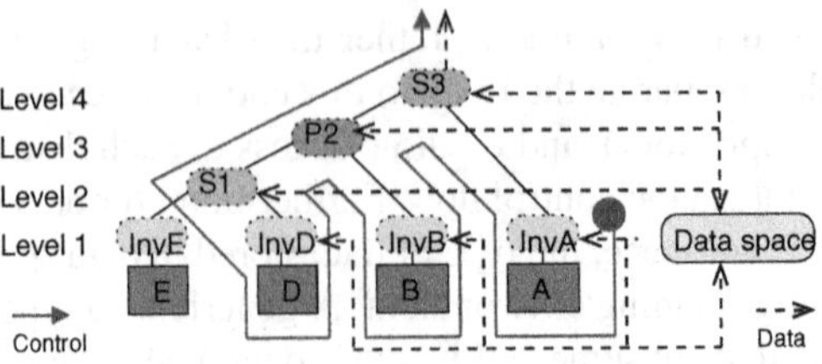

Fig. 7. Data connectors for the bank system

code) to determine the customer's bank branch. When control reaches $S1$, the bank branch identity is used to direct control to *InvD*. *InvD* retrieves from the data space the third data element (transaction data), and passes it by value to *D*, to process the requested service. *InvD* stores a report in the data space that is ultimately accessed by *S3* and displayed to the customer. Thus, instead of data following control, we have separated data from control.

This example shows only the basic idea of data connectors, but not their hierarchies, i.e. data connectors that compose other data connectors. So, while this example may give the impression that data connectors are just a means of handling global data, the whole picture about our data connectors will only become complete when composition operations among them are addressed.

Nevertheless, Example 3 does illustrate how in our approach data no longer flows with control. In fact, what flows in exogenous connectors is just a unique signal identifying the required service. Data is encapsulated in data spaces; and its flow and access coordination in data connectors. This results in not only reduced coupling between components (and even connectors), but also enables data structuring as well as compositional operations on data.

5 Evaluation

In present approaches to software connectors, control and data are mixed up in connectors [13]. Some approaches even allow for the parameterisation of computation for connectors [12]. Current component models are no exceptions. Either they provide no explicit connectors (EJB, CCM, COM, etc), or have connectors that mix data and control (Koala, SOFA, ADLs, etc). Furthermore, an example of a basic set of connectors that can be composed systematically is yet to be seen. As connectors encapsulate interactions among components, data and control flowing together does not make the analysis of a system any easier. It has been demonstrated that separation of data and control makes the analysis of systems' properties easier [9, 5]. Compared to these approaches, the novelty in our work lies in the total separation and hence encapsulation of control, computation, and data. Our motivation is to make component-based development more amenable to analysis, reasoning, and above all reuse. Our data connectors lead to loose coupling between components, and therefore contribute to our objective.

Compared to other component models, our data connectors are unique in that they encapsulate data completely. Compared to data processing languages, the hierarchy of our data connectors is also unique in that they provide a structured way of accessing and processing data (by composition). As a result, our work should provide a useful basis for developing data-intensive applications which can benefit from component-based solutions.

Using our data connectors, we can distinguish between global data, i.e. data shared by all the components in the whole system, and data that is shared by a specific subset of components in the system. This is not just a distinction between global data and local data as in current programming languages, e.g. object-oriented languages, but it is a distinction between local data for individual components and shared data between a composite component, or a sub-system, made up of sub-components. It is thus a finer distinction, and more importantly, it allows us to encapsulate data at different levels of granularity, i.e. at the level of individual components, at the level of composite components, or at the level of the whole system. For database applications, we believe such encapsulation provides a new dimension.

Our data space is similar to tuple spaces in generative communication and coordination languages [7, 3]. But we are different in using explicit connectors to data spaces.

6 Conclusion

In this paper we have proposed a way to encapsulate data in a component model that already encapsulated control and computation. The resulting model is, to the best of our knowledge, the first model with encapsulation of control computation *data*. However, the work is preliminary, and serves to demonstrate the feasibility of our idea. More practical evaluation will be needed, and in future work, we intend to do such evaluation.

Nevertheless, compared to related work, viz. component models with explicit connectors, our work seems unique in that global data is really separated from control and computation. In fact, using our connectors we can differentiate between global data, i.e. data global to the whole system, and data shared by specific components.

We also have operations for structuring and composing data, making our approach potentially very useful for data-intensive applications, which also benefit from component-based solutions.

References

1. Dusan Balek. Connectors in software architectures, 2002.
2. Don Box. *Essential COM*. Addison-Wesley, Harlow, 1998.
3. Nicholas Carriero and David Gelernter. Linda in context. *Commun. ACM*, 32(4):444–458, 1989.
4. Linda G. DeMichiel, editor. *Enterprise JavaBeans Specification, Version 2.1*. Sun Microsystems, Inc., 4150 Network Circle, Santa Clara, California 95054, U.S.A, November 12 2003.
5. Berndt Farwer and Mauricio Varea. Object-based control/data-flow analysis. Technical Report DSSE-TR-2005-1, University of Southampton, Department of Electronics and Computer Science, Highfield, Southampton SO17 1BJ, United Kingdom, March 2005.
6. David Garlan, Robert T. Monroe, and David Wile. Acme: Architectural description of component-based systems. In Gary T. Leavens and Murali Sitaraman, editors, *Foundations of Component-Based Systems*, pages 47–68. Cambridge University Press, 2000.

7. David Gelernter. Generative communication in linda. *ACM Trans. Program. Lang. Syst.*, 7(1):80–112, 1985.
8. Graham Hamilton, editor. *JavaBeans*. Sun Microsystems, Inc., 4150 Network Circle, Santa Clara, California 95054, U.S.A, August 8 1997.
9. Ouassila Labbani1, Jean-Luc Dekeyser1, and Pierre Boulet1. Mode-automata based methodology for scade. In Manfred Morari and Lothar Thiele, editors, *Hybrid Systems: Computation and Control, 8th International Workshop, HSCC 2005*, volume LNCS 3414, pages 386–401, Berlin Heidelberg, March 9-11 2005. Springer-Verlag GmbH.
10. K.-K. Lau, Perla I. Velasco, and Zheng Wang. Exogenous connectors for components. In *Eighth International SIGSOFT Symposium on Component-based Software Engineering (CBSE'05)*, May 2005.
11. Kung-Kiu Lau and Zheng Wang. A survey of software component models. Survey CSPP-30, The University of Manchester, Manchester, UK, April 2005.
12. Antnia Lopes, Michel Wermelinger, and Jos Luiz Fiadeiro. Higher-order architectural connectors. *ACM Trans. Softw. Eng. Methodol.*, 12(1):64–104, 2003.
13. Nikunj R. Mehta, Nenad Medvidovic, and Sandeep Phadke. Towards a taxonomy of software connectors. In *ICSE*, pages 178–187, 2000.
14. Microsoft. *Data access development overview: within the Microsoft Enterprise Development Platform*. Microsoft Enterprise Development Strategy Series. Microsoft, http://msdn.microsoft.com/netframework/technologyinfo/entstrategy/default.aspx, March 2005.
15. Richard Monson-Haefel. *Enterprise JavaBeans*. O'Reilly, Farnham ; Sebastopol, Calif., 4th ed. edition, 2004.
16. OMG. *CORBA Component Model, V3.0*. Object Management Group, http://www.omg.org/docs/formal/02-06-69.pdf, 2002.
17. Mary Shaw and David Garlan. *Software Architecture: Perspectives on an Emerging Discipline*. Prentice Hall, 1996.
18. Richard N. Taylor, Nenad Medvidovic, Kenneth M. Anderson, E. James Whitehead Jr., Jason E. Robbins, Kari A. Nies, Peyman Oreizy, and Deborah L. Dubrow. A component- and message-based architectural style for GUI software. *Software Engineering*, 22(6):390–406, 1996.
19. Rob C. van Ommering, Frank van der Linden, Jeff Kramer, and Jeff Magee. The koala component model for consumer electronics software. *IEEE Computer*, 33(3):78–85, 2000.

Virtualization of Service Gateways in Multi-provider Environments

Yvan Royon, Stéphane Frénot, and Frédéric Le Mouël

INRIA Ares - CITI Lab - INSA Lyon
Bat. Leonard de Vinci, 69621 Villeurbanne cedex, France
{yvan.royon, stephane.frenot, frederic.le-mouel}@insa-lyon.fr

Abstract. Today we see more and more services, such as entertainment or home automation, being brought to connected homes. These services are published and operated by a variety of service providers. Currently, each provider sells his own box, providing both connectivity and a closed service environment. The open service paradigm aims at mixing all services within the same box, thus opening the service delivery chain for home users. However, open service gateways still lack important mechanisms. Multiple service providers can access and use the same gateway concurrently. We must define what this use is, *i.e.* we must define a notion of *user*. Also, service providers should not interfere with each other on the gateway, except if explicitly required. In other words, we must isolate services from different providers, while still permitting on-demand collaboration. By combining all these mechanisms, we are defining a multi-user, multi-service execution environment, which we call a virtualized service gateway. We implement part of these features using OSGi technology.[1]

Keywords: Virtual gateway, multi-user, service-oriented programming.

1 Introduction

During the last years, high speed connectivity to the home has evolved at a very fast pace. Yesterday, home network access consisted in bringing IP connectivity to the home. The services made available were common application-level programs, such as web or e-mail clients. Today, the operators are moving to integrating value-added services in their offer, mainly multicast TV and Voice over IP. These network-enabled services are provided by the same connectivity box, or by a dedicated set-top box. It is foreseen that in the next few years, both the number and the quality of available services will increase drastically: home appliances, entertainment, health care... However, these services would be developed, maintained and supervised by other parties, for instance respectively whitegoods manufacturers, the gaming industry, and hospitals. Until today, the entire service chain and the delivery infrastructure, including the home gateway, are under the control of a single operator. Emerging standards push towards open solutions that enable both integration and segmentation of various markets such as connectivity, entertainment, security, or home automation. This

[1] This work was partially supported by the IST-6thFP-507295 MUSE Project.

I. Gorton et al. (Eds.): CBSE 2006, LNCS 4063, pp. 385–392, 2006.

approach implies that, on the single access point that connects the home network to the internet (*i.e.* the home gateway), many service vendors are each able to deploy and manage several services.
Current and ongoing service platform efforts enable multi-party service provisioning, but they still lack strong concepts and mechanisms to completely support it. In particular, no isolation of services that belong to different parties has been defined.

We propose an isolation of services, depending upon which party, or *user*, deploys, manages and owns them. Consequently, we also define the notion of user in this context. By isolation, we mean that a service provider should only be able to "see" her own services on the common service platform. We represent this as a *virtual service gateway*. Each service provider owns and manages his own virtual gateway and the services it runs. All virtual gateways are run and managed by a unique *core service gateway*, typically hosted inside the home gateway (physical box), and operated by the home gateway provider.

The paper is structured as follows. Section 2 describes ongoing works on multi-application Java environments. Section 3 defines the notion of virtual service gateway in this context. Section 4 explains how we implement these concepts on top of OSGi. Finally, section 5 discusses and concludes the article.

2 Multi-application Java Environments

This paper focuses on Java-based environments. Java applications are architecture- and OS-agnostic, which is an interesting feature when using very diverse hardware platforms (*e.g.* home gateways). Also, Java Virtual Machines are available and already deployed on lots of architectures, which range from enterprise servers through PCs to mobile phones. Reusing the existing software base is a key to technology acceptance. The main alternative to Java is Microsoft's .NET. Our main concern with .NET is the lack of unloading facilities for assemblies. This would cause the environment to grow huge if applications were often updated. Therefore, in this section, we examine solutions to make the JVM a multi-application environment, which is essential for an open service gateway.

2.1 Current Java Environments

A standard Java Virtual Machine is a multi-thread but mono-application environment (figure 1). In order to run two applications, two JVMs are launched. In this case, the applications run independently, *i.e.* if they need to collaborate, they must access the operating system's communication facilities (*e.g.* TCP/IP network stack, file system...). We can see that the problems with this solution are both the overhead from running two JVMs, and the inefficiency of communications, even though there are proposals to limit these [1].

There are two kinds of responses to these insufficiencies: bringing multi-application capabilities to the JVM, or using an overlay on top of the JVM, *e.g.* a J2EE or similar application server.

2.2 Multi-application Java Environments

• Sun's Multi-tasking Virtual Machine [2] (figure 2), for instance, runs several Java applications, called *isolates*, in the same Java environment. Isolates share class representation, so that only static fields are duplicated. Applications are instrumented using a resource management interface, for heap memory management in particular.

• Rival proposals are Java operating systems [3] [4]. These mix the JVM with the operating system layer, and often come with multi-process capabilities.

• A last option is to add multi-application-like functionalities using an overlay on top of the JVM (figure 3). The overlay is the single application that runs in the JVM, but it allows several pseudo-applications to run concurrently on top of it.

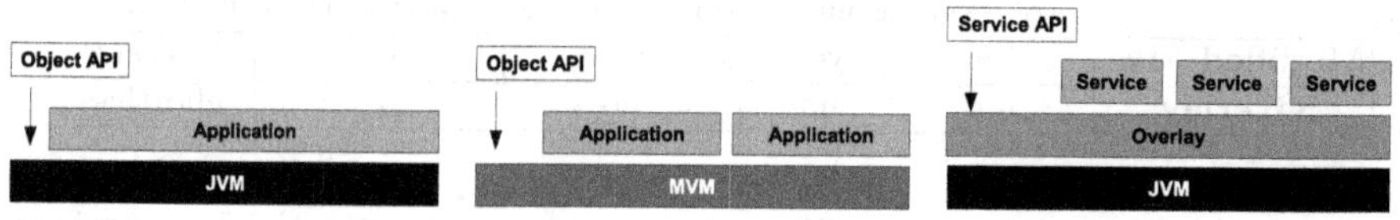

Fig. 1. Mono-application **Fig. 2.** Multi-task **Fig. 3.** Multi-service

2.3 Isolation Terminology

The term "isolation" may imply several kinds of mechanisms. We attempt here to basically classify them.

• The first family of mechanisms is namespace isolation. A namespace is a context for identifiers, and, in our case, for applications or services. Applications in different namespaces cannot "see" each other: this is an access right enforcement. With Java technology, this namespace isolation may be achieved through the use of classloaders, or more advanced loading facilities such as the Module Loader [5] or MJ [6].

• The second family of isolation mechanisms concerns low-level resources. In a resource-isolated environment, applications are supposed to be protected from one another. For instance, schedulers provided by operating systems allocate CPU slots for applications according to their priority. Recent Linux kernels also endorse out-of-memory kills, *i.e.* if a process endangers the whole system using too much memory, it gets killed. Such memory protection can be qualified as a reactive mechanism, versus proactive mechanisms. An example of a proactive mechanism would be Xen's hypervisor [7].

There are two ways to combine namespace isolation and resource isolation. The first one is to complete namespace isolation with reactive resource isolation, for instance by checking specific constraints such as CPU usage [8]. The second one is to build a combination of proactive, strong resource isolation and namespace isolation through the use of different virtualization techniques. Proposals such as Xen [7] or Denali [9] run multiple lightweight or full-featured operating systems on the same machine. Other attempts, such as Java *isolates*, provide an isolation API for Java applications.

2.4 Our Goals

The advantages of a modified runtime are performance (communications, memory sharing) and resource isolation (see below). Inversely, the advantages of overlays are their usability on any standard JVM, and their ease of development through their level of abstraction. Table 1 summarizes this comparison.

Table 1. Summary of Multi-application Java Environments

	Namespace isolation	Resource isolation	Performance optimizations	Uses a standard JVM	Easiness of integration[2]
Modified JRE	yes	yes	yes	no	intrusive
Overlay	no	no	no	yes	effortless

Our goal in this paper is to define a multi-user, service-oriented Java environment, without modifying the standard Java Runtime Environment. This implies that we use an overlay. Our contribution is divided in two steps: first we add namespace isolation to the overlay solution, then, we add a definition of users.

3 Towards a Multi-user, Service-Oriented Environment

In this section, we evoke the notion of service-orientation and its benefits. We then detail the terms multi-user, through the definition of *core* and *virtual* service gateways. We explain on one hand how they should be isolated, and on the other hand when and how they should be able to cooperate.

3.1 Service-Oriented Programming

For clarification, the term "service" in this paper refers to Service-Oriented Programming (SOP). SOP is based on Object-Oriented Programming, which relies on ideas such as encapsulation, inheritance and polymorphism. SOP additionally states that elements (*e.g.* components) collaborate through behaviors. These behaviors, also called services or interfaces, allow to separate what must be done (the contract) from how it is done (its implementation) [10].

Some service-oriented solutions, such as Web Services, deal with the interoperability in communications, and are referred to as Service-Oriented Architectures. By contrast, SOP environments such as the OSGi Service Platform [11] and Openwings are centered on the execution environment, which is the focus of this paper.

[2] Easiness of integration means the easiness of developing the environment itself, using it, and developing applications for it.

3.2 Namespace Isolation

Core and Virtual Gateways. A core service gateway is a software element, managed by an operator. It makes resources available in order to run services. Such resources, physically supplied by the underlying hardware (*i.e.* the home gateway), include CPU cycles, memory, hard disk storage, network bandwidth, and optionally standard services (*e.g.* logging, HTTP connectivity). The gateway operator grants service providers access to these resources. This access is symbolized by a virtual service gateway, and provides a namespace isolation. Figure 4 illustrates this architecture.

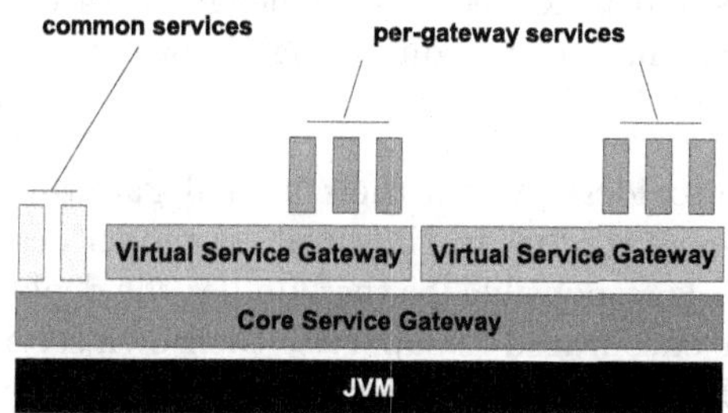

Fig. 4. Multi-service, namespace-isolated environment

Service cooperation. In an isolated, multi-application environment, applications are cloistered by default. However, they still should be able to cooperate on demand. In resource isolated environments, they cooperate through data communications. They either use standard OS facilities (*e.g.* sockets, IPCs, filesystem), or dedicated facilities (*e.g.* Links in the Java *isolates* API). By contrast, in open, non-isolated service environments, applications pass references on services (or interfaces). In an open, multi-service, multi-user, namespace-isolated environment, this still must be possible if explicitly permitted. The framework is then responsible for passing these references.

3.3 Multi-user Java Environment

The gateway operator, through the core service gateway, acts much like a Unix root user. He allows users (service providers) to launch their shell or execution environment (their virtual service gateway). The core gateway also runs services accessible to all users. However, contrary to Unix root users, the core gateway does not have access to service gateways' data, files, *etc*, since these would belong to different, potentially competing companies. Figure 5 represents the architecture with participating users.

The root user, *i.e.* the gateway operator, is responsible for the management of the virtual gateways it runs. This management layer is structured around 4 activities. Lifecycle management provides a mean to start and stop virtual gateways. Performance management provides information about the current status of a gateway (a virtual gateway or the core gateway itself). Security management

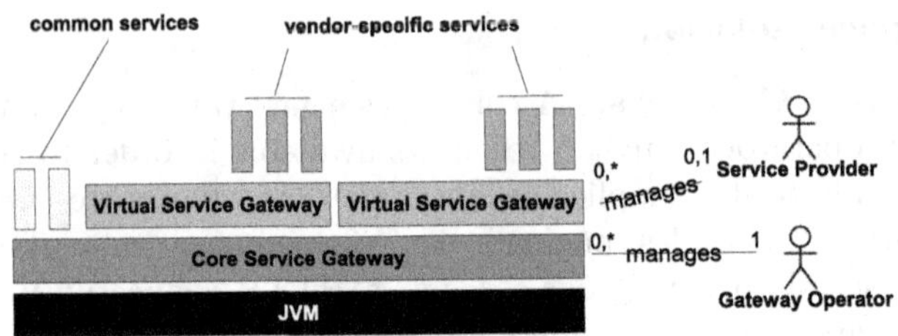

Fig. 5. Multi-service, multi-user residential gateway

positions credentials and make security challenges with core and virtual gateways. Finally, Accounting and Logging brings information about service usage for each gateway.

Users, or service providers, access their virtual gateways through a remote monitoring interface. According to the business model described in section 1, each service provider is responsible for the bundles she deploys. This means that service providers are encouraged to supervise their own services on their clients' service gateways. Also, some business services may inherently need remote monitoring: health care, home automation.

4 Implementation

4.1 OSGi and Virtualized OSGi

The service-oriented overlay we use for our prototype implementation is the OSGi Service Platform [11]. The OSGi specification defines a service-oriented API (figure 3), deployment units (components called bundles), and a container (the service platform) which guarantees dependencies resolution for hosted components.

In order to create virtual gateways, we launch several OSGi gateway instances from within a core OSGi instance (figure 4). The core gateway also instruments and manages virtual gateways. This solution allows us to create a straightforward matching with the concepts of root user and users detailed above.

4.2 Service Isolation

The advantages of running several service gateway instances inside a single core gateway instance are quite immediate. Each service gateway can only access OSGi bundles and services it directly hosts. The core gateway itself does not see the hosted virtual gateways, but only a management agent that allows their life cycle management. This is a straightforward way to enforce namespace isolation.

Each service provider sees his own virtual gateway as if it was a standard OSGi service platform. Therefore, at deployment time, standard OSGi deployment schemes come in action. At runtime, namespace isolation is provided through a hierarchy of classloaders. Each deployed component (*i.e.* OSGi bundle) comes with its own classloader, which delegates to its service gateway's classloader [12]. This way, by default, services from different providers (*i.e.* running in different virtual service gateways) are in different namespaces.

4.3 Service Cooperation

The core service gateway can provide services to its virtual service gateways. Currently, a static list of shared services and implementations is passed from the core gateway to virtual gateways. Each virtual gateway then needs to internally publish these shared services, so that its own services may access them. A more dynamic solution is planned, but not yet implemented.

4.4 Performance

We chose to run several OSGi Framework instances inside a core Framework instance. The main drawback to this approach is that it induces a resource consumption overhead. We ran a first set of performance tests on a standard Pentium IV PC, using a Gentoo Linux operating system, and Sun's JDK 1.5 with standard parameters (*e.g.* initial memory allocation pool). Our measures compare a vanilla Oscar 1.0.5 gateway with a core gateway that runs six virtual gateways, each launching a standard set of bundles. After 24 hours, we observe an overall 33% increase in memory use within the JVM's pre-allocated memory pool. This corresponds to a 2.9 MB consumption overhead. More thorough benchmarks are planned and under progress.

4.5 Available Code

We provide an OSGi bundle[2] that allows to start and stop virtual OSGi instances. The project, called `vosgi` for Virtual OSGi, has been tested on patched versions of both ObjectWeb's Oscar[3] and Apache's Felix[4] open source implementations of the OSGi Service Platform specifications. The management activities expressed in section 3 are enabled through a JMX architecture [13] called `mosgi` (for Managed OSGi).

5 Discussion and Conclusion

In this paper, we have proposed a first step toward a multi-user, service-oriented execution environment. It can target the same markets as OSGi service platforms (mobile phones, vehicles, home gateways...), while improving isolation and management.

Since we use a standard Java virtual machine as the lower layer, our best option for service provider separation is to provide a namespace isolation. If we want to go further into resource isolation, we need a JVM and an operating

[2] Available at `http://ares.inria.fr/~sfrenot/devel/` under the CeCILL open source licence.

[3] `http://oscar.objectweb.org/`

[4] `http://incubator.apache.org/felix/`

system that provides such a functionality. For instance, we could provide a multi-user environment on top of real-time virtual machines. But these are not available on a large scale yet, and they are not aimed at this "in-the-middle" market (neither embedded nor high-end PCs).

The proposed multi-user environment currently has two main alternatives. The first one is the multi-tasking virtual machine, and the second one is the use of "standard" operating systems (*e.g.* Linux, Windows).

From the MVM point of view, Sun's team works on mapping OS-level users rights within the JVM [14]. This project is aimed at big server systems that host many users and applications (SPARC/Solaris). Inversely, our approach is focused on embedded systems, using standard JREs. Also, we believe that cooperation through service sharing, or interface sharing, is a better abstraction for developers than data sharing (`Link` objects between isolates).

Compared to standard operating systems, we assume that a service-oriented approach is a real improvement over "classical" C programming. We argue that both layers (Java and service orientation) are beneficial to service development for the targeted market. It enables many advantages (code structure, code hot-plugging...) with only few drawbacks (mainly startup time).

References

1. Czajkowski, G., Daynès, L., Nystrom, N.: Code sharing among virtual machines. ECOOP (2002)
2. Czajkowski, G., Daynès, L.: Multitasking without comprimise: a virtual machine evolution. In: OOPSLA, New York, NY, USA, ACM Press (2001) 125–138
3. Golm, M., Felser, M., Wawersich, C., Kleinoeder, J.: The JX operating system. In: USENIX. (2002) 45–58
4. Prangsma, E.: JNode. (http://jnode.sourceforge.net)
5. Hall, R.S.: A Policy-Driven Class Loader to Support Deployment in Extensible Frameworks. In: Component Deployment, Edinburgh, UK. (2004) LNCS 3083, pp. 81 - 96.
6. J. Corwin, D.F. Bacon, D.G., Murthy, C.: MJ: a Rational Module System for Java and its Applications. In: (OOPLSA. (2003) pp. 241-254.
7. Barham, P., Dragovic, B., Fraser, K., Hand, S., Harris, T., Ho, A., Neugebauer, R., Pratt, I., Warfield, A.: Xen and the art of virtualization. In: SOSP. (2003)
8. Yamasaki, I.: Increasing robustness by code instrumenting: Monitoring and managing computer resource usage on OSGi frameworks. OSGi World Congress (2005)
9. Whitaker, A., Shaw, M., Gribble, S.: Denali: Lightweight virtual machines for distributed and networked applications (2002)
10. Bieber, G., Carpenter, J.: Introduction to service oriented programming. http://www.openwings.org (2001)
11. The OSGi Alliance: OSGi Service Platform. 4th edn. IOS Press (2005)
12. Liang, S., Bracha, G.: Dynamic class loading in the Java virtual machine. In: OOPSLA. (1998) pp. 36–44
13. Fleury, E., Frénot, S.: Building a JMX management interface inside OSGi. Technical report, Inria RR-5025 (2003)
14. Czajkowski, G., Daynès, L., Titzer, B.: A Multi-User Virtual Machine. In: Usenix. (2003) pp. 85–98

Author Index

Lecture Notes in Computer Science

For information about Vols. 1–3960

please contact your bookseller or Springer

Vol. 4063: I. Gorton, G.T. Heineman, I. Crnkovic, H.W. Schmidt, J.A. Stafford, C.A. Szyperski, K. Wallnau (Eds.), Component-Based Software Engineering. XI, 394 pages. 2006.

Vol. 4060: K. Futatsugi, J.-P. Jouannaud, J. Meseguer (Eds.), Algebra, Meaning and Computation. XXXVIII, 643 pages. 2006.

Vol. 4058: L.M. Batten, R. Safavi-Naini (Eds.), Information Security and Privacy. XII, 446 pages. 2006.

Vol. 4056: P. Flocchini, L. Gąsieniec (Eds.), Structural Information and Communication Complexity. X, 357 pages. 2006.

Vol. 4055: J. Lee, J. Shim, S.-g. Lee, C. Bussler, S. Shim (Eds.), Data Engineering Issues in E-Commerce and Services. IX, 290 pages. 2006.

Vol. 4054: A. Horváth, M. Telek (Eds.), Formal Methods and Stochastic Models for Performance Evaluation. VIII, 239 pages. 2006.

Vol. 4053: M. Ikeda, K.D. Ashley, T.-W. Chan (Eds.), Intelligent Tutoring Systems. XXVI, 821 pages. 2006.

Vol. 4045: D. Barker-Plummer, R. Cox, N. Swoboda (Eds.), Diagrammatic Representation and Inference. XII, 301 pages. 2006. (Sublibrary LNAI).

Vol. 4044: P. Abrahamsson, M. Marchesi, G. Succi (Eds.), Extreme Programming and Agile Processes in Software Engineering. XII, 230 pages. 2006.

Vol. 4043: A.S. Atzeni, A. Lioy (Eds.), Public Key Infrastructure. XI, 261 pages. 2006.

Vol. 4041: S.-W. Cheng, C.K. Poon (Eds.), Algorithmic Aspects in Information and Management. XI, 395 pages. 2006.

Vol. 4040: R. Reulke, U. Eckardt, B. Flach, U. Knauer, K. Polthier (Eds.), Combinatorial Image Analysis. XII, 482 pages. 2006.

Vol. 4039: M. Morisio (Ed.), Reuse of Off-the-Shelf Components. XIII, 444 pages. 2006.

Vol. 4038: P. Ciancarini, H. Wiklicky (Eds.), Coordination Models and Languages. VIII, 299 pages. 2006.

Vol. 4037: R. Gorrieri, H. Wehrheim (Eds.), Formal Methods for Open Object-Based Distributed Systems. XVII, 474 pages. 2006.

Vol. 4036: O. H. Ibarra, Z. Dang (Eds.), Developments in Language Theory. XII, 456 pages. 2006.

Vol. 4034: J. Münch, M. Vierimaa (Eds.), Product-Focused Software Process Improvement. XVII, 474 pages. 2006.

Vol. 4033: B. Stiller, P. Reichl, B. Tuffin (Eds.), Performability Has its Price. X, 103 pages. 2006.

Vol. 4031: M. Ali, R. Dapoigny (Eds.), Innovations in Applied Artificial Intelligence. XXIII, 1353 pages. 2006. (Sublibrary LNAI).

Vol. 4027: H.L. Larsen, G. Pasi, D. Ortiz-Arroyo, T. Andreasen, H. Christiansen (Eds.), Flexible Query Answering Systems. XVIII, 714 pages. 2006. (Sublibrary LNAI).

Vol. 4026: P. Gibbons, T. Abdelzaher, J. Aspnes, R. Rao (Eds.), Distributed Computing in Sensor Systems. XIV, 566 pages. 2006.

Vol. 4025: F. Eliassen, A. Montresor (Eds.), Distributed Applications and Interoperable Systems. XI, 355 pages. 2006.

Vol. 4024: S. Donatelli, P. S. Thiagarajan (Eds.), Petri Nets and Other Models of Concurrency - ICATPN 2006. XI, 441 pages. 2006.

Vol. 4021: E. André, L. Dybkjær, W. Minker, H. Neumann, M. Weber (Eds.), Perception and Interactive Technologies. XI, 217 pages. 2006. (Sublibrary LNAI).

Vol. 4020: A. Bredenfeld, A. Jacoff, I. Noda, Y. Takahashi, RoboCup 2005: Robot Soccer World Cup IX. XVII, 727 pages. 2006. (Sublibrary LNAI).

Vol. 4018: V. Wade, H. Ashman, B. Smyth (Eds.), Adaptive Hypermedia and Adaptive Web-Based Systems. XVI, 474 pages. 2006.

Vol. 4016: J.X. Yu, M. Kitsuregawa, H.V. Leong (Eds.), Advances in Web-Age Information Management. XVII, 606 pages. 2006.

Vol. 4013: L. Lamontagne, M. Marchand (Eds.), Advances in Artificial Intelligence. XIII, 564 pages. 2006. (Sublibrary LNAI).

Vol. 4012: T. Washio, A. Sakurai, K. Nakashima, H. Takeda, S. Tojo, M. Yokoo (Eds.), New Frontiers in Artificial Intelligence. XIII, 484 pages. 2006. (Sublibrary LNAI).

Vol. 4011: Y. Sure, J. Domingue (Eds.), The Semantic Web: Research and Applications. XIX, 726 pages. 2006.

Vol. 4010: S. Dunne, B. Stoddart (Eds.), Unifying Theories of Programming. VIII, 257 pages. 2006.

Vol. 4009: M. Lewenstein, G. Valiente (Eds.), Combinatorial Pattern Matching. XII, 414 pages. 2006.

Vol. 4007: C. Àlvarez, M. Serna (Eds.), Experimental Algorithms. XI, 329 pages. 2006.

Vol. 4006: L.M. Pinho, M. González Harbour (Eds.), Reliable Software Technologies – Ada-Europe 2006. XII, 241 pages. 2006.

Vol. 4005: G. Lugosi, H.U. Simon (Eds.), Learning Theory. XI, 656 pages. 2006. (Sublibrary LNAI).

Vol. 4004: S. Vaudenay (Ed.), Advances in Cryptology - EUROCRYPT 2006. XIV, 613 pages. 2006.

Vol. 4003: Y. Koucheryavy, J. Harju, V.B. Iversen (Eds.), Next Generation Teletraffic and Wired/Wireless Advanced Networking. XVI, 582 pages. 2006.

Vol. 4001: E. Dubois, K. Pohl (Eds.), Advanced Information Systems Engineering. XVI, 560 pages. 2006.

Vol. 3999: C. Kop, G. Fliedl, H.C. Mayr, E. Métais (Eds.), Natural Language Processing and Information Systems. XIII, 227 pages. 2006.

Vol. 3998: T. Calamoneri, I. Finocchi, G.F. Italiano (Eds.), Algorithms and Complexity. XII, 394 pages. 2006.

Vol. 3997: W. Grieskamp, C. Weise (Eds.), Formal Approaches to Software Testing. XII, 219 pages. 2006.

Vol. 3996: A. Keller, J.-P. Martin-Flatin (Eds.), Self-Managed Networks, Systems, and Services. X, 185 pages. 2006.

Vol. 3995: G. Müller (Ed.), Emerging Trends in Information and Communication Security. XX, 524 pages. 2006.

Vol. 3994: V.N. Alexandrov, G.D. van Albada, P.M.A. Sloot, J. Dongarra (Eds.), Computational Science – ICCS 2006, Part IV. XXXV, 1096 pages. 2006.

Vol. 3993: V.N. Alexandrov, G.D. van Albada, P.M.A. Sloot, J. Dongarra (Eds.), Computational Science – ICCS 2006, Part III. XXXVI, 1136 pages. 2006.

Vol. 3992: V.N. Alexandrov, G.D. van Albada, P.M.A. Sloot, J. Dongarra (Eds.), Computational Science – ICCS 2006, Part II. XXXV, 1122 pages. 2006.

Vol. 3991: V.N. Alexandrov, G.D. van Albada, P.M.A. Sloot, J. Dongarra (Eds.), Computational Science – ICCS 2006, Part I. LXXXI, 1096 pages. 2006.

Vol. 3990: J. C. Beck, B.M. Smith (Eds.), Integration of AI and OR Techniques in Constraint Programming for Combinatorial Optimization Problems. X, 301 pages. 2006.

Vol. 3989: J. Zhou, M. Yung, F. Bao, Applied Cryptography and Network Security. XIV, 488 pages. 2006.

Vol. 3987: M. Hazas, J. Krumm, T. Strang (Eds.), Location- and Context-Awareness. X, 289 pages. 2006.

Vol. 3986: K. Stølen, W.H. Winsborough, F. Martinelli, F. Massacci (Eds.), Trust Management. XIV, 474 pages. 2006.

Vol. 3984: M. Gavrilova, O. Gervasi, V. Kumar, C.J. K. Tan, D. Taniar, A. Laganà, Y. Mun, H. Choo (Eds.), Computational Science and Its Applications - ICCSA 2006, Part V. XXV, 1045 pages. 2006.

Vol. 3983: M. Gavrilova, O. Gervasi, V. Kumar, C.J. K. Tan, D. Taniar, A. Laganà, Y. Mun, H. Choo (Eds.), Computational Science and Its Applications - ICCSA 2006, Part IV. XXVI, 1191 pages. 2006.

Vol. 3982: M. Gavrilova, O. Gervasi, V. Kumar, C.J. K. Tan, D. Taniar, A. Laganà, Y. Mun, H. Choo (Eds.), Computational Science and Its Applications - ICCSA 2006, Part III. XXV, 1243 pages. 2006.

Vol. 3981: M. Gavrilova, O. Gervasi, V. Kumar, C.J. K. Tan, D. Taniar, A. Laganà, Y. Mun, H. Choo (Eds.), Computational Science and Its Applications - ICCSA 2006, Part II. XXVI, 1255 pages. 2006.

Vol. 3980: M. Gavrilova, O. Gervasi, V. Kumar, C.J. K. Tan, D. Taniar, A. Laganà, Y. Mun, H. Choo (Eds.), Computational Science and Its Applications - ICCSA 2006, Part I. LXXV, 1199 pages. 2006.

Vol. 3979: T.S. Huang, N. Sebe, M.S. Lew, V. Pavlović, M. Kölsch, A. Galata, B. Kisačanin (Eds.), Computer Vision in Human-Computer Interaction. XII, 121 pages. 2006.

Vol. 3978: B. Hnich, M. Carlsson, F. Fages, F. Rossi (Eds.), Recent Advances in Constraints. VIII, 179 pages. 2006. (Sublibrary LNAI).

Vol. 3977: N. Fuhr, M. Lalmas, S. Malik, G. Kazai (Eds.), Advances in XML Information Retrieval and Evaluation. XII, 556 pages. 2006.

Vol. 3976: F. Boavida, T. Plagemann, B. Stiller, C. Westphal, E. Monteiro (Eds.), Networking 2006. Networking Technologies, Services, and Protocols; Performance of Computer and Communication Networks; Mobile and Wireless Communications Systems. XXVI, 1276 pages. 2006.

Vol. 3975: S. Mehrotra, D.D. Zeng, H. Chen, B. Thuraisingham, F.-Y. Wang (Eds.), Intelligence and Security Informatics. XXII, 772 pages. 2006.

Vol. 3973: J. Wang, Z. Yi, J.M. Zurada, B.-L. Lu, H. Yin (Eds.), Advances in Neural Networks - ISNN 2006, Part III. XXIX, 1402 pages. 2006.

Vol. 3972: J. Wang, Z. Yi, J.M. Zurada, B.-L. Lu, H. Yin (Eds.), Advances in Neural Networks - ISNN 2006, Part II. XXVII, 1444 pages. 2006.

Vol. 3971: J. Wang, Z. Yi, J.M. Zurada, B.-L. Lu, H. Yin (Eds.), Advances in Neural Networks - ISNN 2006, Part I. LXVII, 1442 pages. 2006.

Vol. 3970: T. Braun, G. Carle, S. Fahmy, Y. Koucheryavy (Eds.), Wired/Wireless Internet Communications. XIV, 350 pages. 2006.

Vol. 3969: Ø. Ytrehus (Ed.), Coding and Cryptography. XI, 443 pages. 2006.

Vol. 3968: K.P. Fishkin, B. Schiele, P. Nixon, A. Quigley (Eds.), Pervasive Computing. XV, 402 pages. 2006.

Vol. 3967: D. Grigoriev, J. Harrison, E.A. Hirsch (Eds.), Computer Science – Theory and Applications. XVI, 684 pages. 2006.

Vol. 3966: Q. Wang, D. Pfahl, D.M. Raffo, P. Wernick (Eds.), Software Process Change. XIV, 356 pages. 2006.

Vol. 3965: M. Bernardo, A. Cimatti (Eds.), Formal Methods for Hardware Verification. VII, 243 pages. 2006.

Vol. 3964: M. Ü. Uyar, A.Y. Duale, M.A. Fecko (Eds.), Testing of Communicating Systems. XI, 373 pages. 2006.

Vol. 3963: O. Dikenelli, M.-P. Gleizes, A. Ricci (Eds.), Engineering Societies in the Agents World VI. XII, 303 pages. 2006. (Sublibrary LNAI).

Vol. 3962: W. IJsselsteijn, Y. de Kort, C. Midden, B. Eggen, E. van den Hoven (Eds.), Persuasive Technology. XII, 216 pages. 2006.